Teacher's Edition

Career Planning
AGS PUBLISHING

by
Thomas F. Harrington
and
Spencer G. Niles

with Garbette A. M. Garraway

AGS Publishing
Circle Pines, Minnesota 55014-1796
800-328-2560
www.agsnet.com

About the Authors

Thomas F. Harrington, Ph.D.

Thomas F. Harrington holds a Ph.D. in counseling from Purdue University and teaches vocational psychology and career counseling courses in the Department of Counseling and Applied Educational Psychology at Northeastern University in Boston. In 2004 he received the National Career Development Association's highest honor, The Eminent Career Award. He has edited or co-edited several books and is the co-author of the award winning *Harrington-O'Shea Career Decision-Making System*. He has served as President of the Association for Assessment in Counseling, a division of the American Counseling Association, and the Massachusetts Personnel and Guidance Association. He is a frequent speaker at regional, national, and international career development conferences.

Spencer G. Niles, Ed.D., LPC, NCC

Spencer G. Niles holds a Doctor of Education in Counselor Education from Penn State University and is currently Professor-in-Charge of the Counselor Education Program there. He has served as President of the National Career Development Association, President of the Pennsylvania Association of Counselor Education and Supervision, President of the Virginia Career Development Association, and editor of *The Career Development Quarterly*. In 2003, he received the American Counseling Association (ACA) David Brooks Distinguished Mentor Award and in 2004 he received the ACA Extended Research Award. He has been a visiting scholar at several international universities and is the author or co-author of over 75 publications. He has delivered over 75 presentations at international, national and regional conferences.

Garbette A. M. Garraway

Garbette A. M. Garraway holds master's degrees in English Education from Simon Fraser University, and Counseling Psychology from the University of British Columbia. He is currently a doctoral student in Counselor Education at Penn State University. He has worked as a teacher and a counselor in the public school system for 14 years. He has been a co-presenter at the National Career Development Association conference.

Photo credits for this textbook can be found on page 324.

The publisher wishes to thank the following educators for their helpful comments during the review process for *Career Planning*. Their assistance has been invaluable.

Kathy Bedre, Counselor, Flour Bluff High School, Corpus Christi, TX; **Larry Greer,** Special Day Class Teacher, Loara High School, Anaheim, CA; **Mary Hartfield,** Special Education Instructor in MIMS program, Marion Park Alternative School, Meridian, MS; **Debora J. Hartzell,** Lead Teacher for Special Education, Columbia and Lakeside High Schools, Atlanta, GA; **Karen Larimer,** Transition Coordinator, Keystone Area Education Agency, Elkader, IA; **Susan Loving,** Transition Specialist, Utah State Office of Education, Salt Lake City, UT; **Carole Mottar,** Coordinator, Renaissance Academy, River Falls, WI; **Ann C. Moore,** Transition Specialist, Spartanburg County School District Number 7, Spartanburg, SC; **Cindi A. Nixon,** Director, Special Services, Richland School District Two, Columbia, SC; **Karen M. Owens,** Special Education Teacher, Bruce High School, Bruce, MS; **Richard D. Scott,** Guidance Specialist, Maryland State Department of Education, Baltimore, MD; **Cecilia E. Williams,** ESE Teacher, Gaither High School, Tampa, FL; **Judy S. Wright,** Language Arts Instructor/Curriculum Director, Carlisle Community School, Carlisle, IA.

Publisher's Project Staff

Vice President of Curriculum and Publisher: Sari Follansbee; Director, Curriculum Development: Teri Mathews; Managing Editor: Julie Maas; Senior Editor: Jody Peterson; Development Assistant: Bev Johnson; Director, Creative Services: Nancy Condon; Production Coordinator/Designer: Katie Sonmor; Project Coordinator/Designer: Carol Bowling; Purchasing Agent: Mary Kaye Kuzma; Curriculum Product Manager: Brian Holl

© 2006 AGS Publishing
4201 Woodland Road
Circle Pines, MN 55014-1796
800-328-2560 • www.agsnet.com

AGS Publishing is a trademark and trade name of American Guidance Service, Inc.

Printed in the United States of America

ISBN 0-7854-4032-1

Product Number 94212

3 4 5 V088 13 12 11

Contents

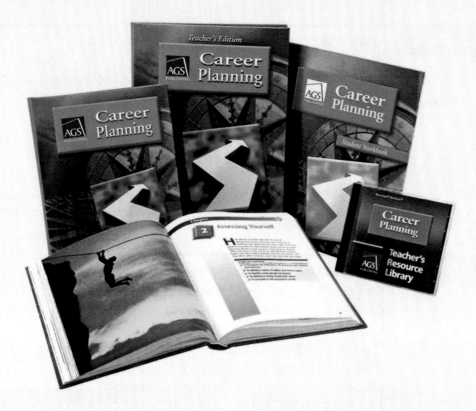

Career Planning is designed to help students develop a language which "decodes" the complexities of educational planning and entering the workplace based on their personal strengths. It gives them power to see how their interests, abilities, and values are used to solve problems in the major industrial areas of a changing workplace. Through exploration of work and learning options, students will better set goals and plan for options found within most communities. By learning to "honor differences" in others, and exploring their unique assets tied to accomplishments, students will gain insights and skills about education and career options. Students learn about themselves, gather and use feedback, and develop personal networking skills. Students complete the book by developing an action plan to enhance their career-building skills.

The textbook has a developmental focus and also satisfies the career standards and competencies for school counselors. The lessons in the text are meant to foster new student knowledge and to integrate personal goals with labor market information. Thus, the lessons are knowledge based, while also reflecting the reality of student maturation. In addition, this book provides a vehicle to fit with standards-based learning and satisfy all of the career standards and student competencies promulgated by the American School Counselors Association.

The text is student centered. The issues and examples are selected to maximize student interest, understanding, and relevance. In brief, this text is designed to inform and guide students as they plan and prepare for further education and careers after high school.

Enhance your program with AGS Publishing textbooks

These exciting, full-color books use student-friendly text and real-world examples. The short, concise lessons will motivate even your most reluctant students. With readabilities below fourth-grade reading level, your students can concentrate on learning content. AGS Publishing is committed to making learning accessible to all students.

Everyday Life Skills offers an easy, effective way to teach students the practical skills they need to transition to life after high school. This skills-based program helps build a foundation for independent living. Some topics covered are nutrition and fitness, self-advocacy, financial responsibilities, computer technology, social awareness, the employment setting, and the educational setting.

Math for the World of Work and *English for the World of Work* help students acquire the skills needed to find and keep a job. Students practice math and English skills related to job searches, résumés, applications, interviews, business and travel expenses, wages, and benefits.

For more information on AGS Publishing worktexts and textbooks:
call 800-328-2560, visit our Web site at www.agsnet.com, or e-mail AGS Publishing at agsmail@agsnet.com

CDM: The Harrington-O'Shea Career Decision-Making® System

Exploring careers is fast and easy with CDM

Authors: Thomas F. Harrington & Arthur J. O'Shea

CDM paves the path to future success

Successfully used by millions of people, the *Harrington-O'Shea Career Decision-Making® System* (CDM) is still your best interest inventory choice. Its 400+ jobs cover about 95% of current occupations.

Use CDM to help people in their career search

Students and adults self-assess their abilities, work values, school subject preferences, and interests. Users are able to:

- Match abilities, interests, and values to possible career options
- Identify occupational interests
- Acquire specifics about education and training requirements

CDM then suggests career clusters that feature action steps and career exploration resources.

Level 1

Level 1 is ideal for middle and junior high school students, and individuals with limited reading ability. It features:

- 96 Interest Survey items that are easy to read and score in less than 30 minutes (fourth-grade reading level)
  - Easy hand-scoring with all item responses on one large page
  - A self-contained Survey Booklet that includes an Interpretive Folder
  - Updated Job Charts for six CDM Career Interest Areas linked to eighteen job groups

Benefits

- Level 2 is now available on-screen
- Self-assesses abilities, interests, and work values all in one instrument
- Easy and fast to administer, with quick results in less than 45 minutes
- Ideal individual or group career exploration tool
- Profiles the current United States job market
- CDM software offers four separate administrated and scoring methods for quick, efficient results
- www.cdmcareerzone.com gives you up-to-the-minute information on the jobs you are most interested in

Level 2

For high school and college students and adults with average or better reading ability, Level 2 offers:

- A comprehensive inventory of 120 updated and gender-neutral items that yield results in fewer than 45 minutes
- Survey Booklet and separate Interpretive Folder
- Easy administration and hand-scoring

Level 1 and Level 2 Interpretive Charts

Multiple advantages are offered on a single page:

- Occupational outlooks
- Education and training requirements
- School subjects, job values, abilities, and career clusters
- Relevant college major and training programs
- RIASEC Crosswalk classifications
- A self-contained Survey Booklet that includes an Interpretive Folder

Visit CareerZone™—your cyberlink to popular CDM materials

CareerZone, developed by the New York Department of Labor, is an occupational information system available on the Internet at **www.cdmcareerzone.com**. It provides up-to-date information about all the jobs listed in the O*NET—the U.S. Department of Labor's replacement for the *Dictionary of Occupational Titles*. *CareerZone* has been customized for use with CDM at no additional cost to CDM users.

CareerZone allows users to:

- Find brief on-screen videos of real people on the job

- Download detailed career descriptions for all occupations

- Use tools like Resume Maker, Cover Letter Maker, and Reference List Maker to develop complete, professional job-seeking materials

- Find job opportunities for careers in your state

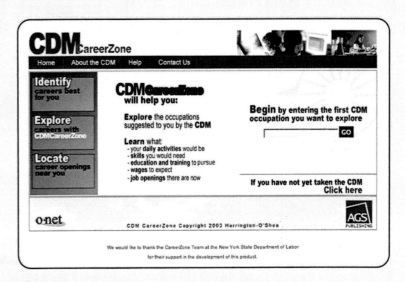

CDM Software gets quick results!

Now job seekers can use the computer to find occupations they can excel in. Best of all, they get immediate information. Job seekers can complete the CDM Level 2 entirely on the computer. They receive an interpretive report about career choices matching their personal interests, values, abilities, and favorite school subjects. Or, you may simply enter the individual's choices and interest scores, or use scannable forms to process large groups.

System Requirements

Windows: Requires Microsoft Windows 95 or newer, a 400 Mhz processor, at least 10 MB of available hard drive space, and 64 MB of available RAM (96 is recommended). If you would like to utilize the scanning feature, go to **www.agsnet.com/tech** for scanner requirements.

Macintosh: Requires a Power Macintosh or newer, 10 MB of hard drive space, 64 MB of available RAM, (96 is recommended), and Macintosh OS 8.1 or newer.

◆ Each lesson is clearly labeled to help students focus on the skill or concept to be learned.

◆ Vocabulary terms are bold-faced and then defined in the margin at the top of the page and in the glossary.

Ability

A talent; something a person is able to do well

Self-confidence

Feeling good about oneself

◆ Goals for Learning at the beginning of each chapter identify learner outcomes.

Goals for Learning

◆ To recognize the importance of assessing one's abilities and interests

◆ To identify a variety of ability and interest areas

◆ To identify career groups of interest

◆ To identify a variety of personal values

◆ To complete a self-assessment profile

◆ Lesson Review questions allow students to check their understanding of key concepts presented in the text.

Lesson 1 Review Write your answers to these questions on a sheet of paper.

1. What is the difference between a job and an occupation? Give an example of each.

2. What are some reasons people have for choosing a particular occupation?

3. What is an example of a work stereotype that you know of? Why should you be careful about using work stereotypes?

Communication Connection

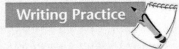
Writing Practice

◆ Many features reinforce and extend student learning beyond the lesson content.

Technology Note

On the Job

The Economy

Get Involved

Portfolio Activity

Self-Assessment Profile

1. Choose the two school subjects you enjoy most. Write the names of the two subjects on your Self-Assessment Profile.

School Subjects
- Agriculture
- Art
- Business/Management
- Clerical Studies
- English
- Family/Consumer Science
- Finance
- Health
- Languages
- Math
- Music
- Science
- Shop/Industrial Arts
- Social Studies
- Technology/Computers

2. What skills do you have in the two subjects you wrote for number 1? Write these skills on your Self-Assessment Profile.

3. What are some of your achievements that relate to your skills? Write them on your Self-Assessment Profile.

4. What four abilities are your strongest? Write them on your Self-Assessment Profile.

Abilities
- Artistic
- Clerical
- Interpersonal
- Language
- Leadership
- Manual
- Mathematical/Numerical
- Musical/Dramatic
- Organizational
- Persuasive
- Scientific
- Social
- Technical/Mechanical
- Visual (Spatial)

5. What are two areas in which you have interest? Write them on your Self-Assessment Profile.

Interests
- The Arts
- Business
- Crafts
- Office Operations
- Scientific
- Social

6. Which two career groups are you the most interested in? Write them on your Self-Assessment Profile.

Career Groups
- Art
- Clerical
- Customer Service
- Data Analysis
- Education
- Entertainment
- Legal
- Literary
- Management
- Manual
- Math and Science
- Medical/Dental
- Music
- Personal Service
- Sales
- Skilled Crafts
- Social Service
- Technical

7. What are four of your work values? Write them on your Self-Assessment Profile.

Work Values
- Creativity
- Good Salary
- High Achievement
- Independence
- Job Security
- Leadership
- Outdoor Work
- Physical Activity
- Prestige
- Risk
- Variety
- Work with Your Hands
- Work with Your Mind
- Work with People

8. Include your Self-Assessment Profile in your career portfolio.

50 Chapter 2 Assessing Yourself

Assessing Yourself Chapter 2 51

◆ Portfolio Activities at the end of each chapter allow students to put the skills they learn to practical use. Students add these activities to their personal career portfolios.

Chapter 1 REVIEW

Word Bank
business cycle
career
economy
job
job security
occupation
prestige
stereotype
unemployed
work
workplace

Vocabulary Review

Choose the word or phrase from the Word Bank that best completes each sentence. Write the answer on your paper.

1. A general belief held by many people about a certain activity or group of people is a(n) _____.

2. The state of business and use of resources in an area is the _____.

3. A group of similar or related jobs or job skills is known as a(n) _____.

4. Some people choose a type of work based on how important most people think it is, or its _____.

5. The pattern of ups and downs in supply and demand in the economy is known as the _____.

6. To be out of work is to be _____.

7. The way people spend their time earning a living is known as _____.

8. A formal or informal area where work is done is the _____.

9. The job path a person follows throughout a lifetime is a(n) _____.

10. The work you choose to do for pay is called a(n) _____.

11. An understanding that workers will not lose their jobs is _____.

Concept Review

Choose the word or phrase that best completes each sentence. Write the letter of the answer on your paper.

12. A week of work for full-time workers in the United States consists of _____.

 A 25 to 30 hours
 B 30 to 40 hours
 C 40 to 50 hours
 D 50 or more hours

13. The most important reason to work is _____.

 A money
 B prestige
 C helping others
 D different for each person

14. Being a ski instructor is an example of a job which _____.

 A does not require special clothing
 B affects where a person lives
 C involves a formal workplace
 D has great job security

15. An example of a work stereotype is that _____.

 A news reporters are very nosy
 B accountants work with numbers
 C lawyers went to law school
 D veterinarians treat animals

16. A bank where workers follow a strict schedule is an example of _____.

 A an informal workplace
 B an unstructured workplace
 C a casual workplace
 D a formal workplace

17. An example of a job affected most by the business cycle is that of _____.

 A an emergency-room nurse
 B a carpenter working on new homes
 C an elementary school teacher
 D a dentist

Critical Thinking

Write the answer to each question on your paper.

18. Why is it important for a person to carefully choose an occupation?

19. What advantages do American workers have over workers in many other countries?

20. Suppose you are interested in working in a casual, flexible workplace. What are three jobs you might like?

Test-Taking Tip

When studying for a test, work with a partner to write your own test questions. Then answer each other's questions. Check your answers.

16 Chapter 1 What Is a Career?

What Is a Career? Chapter 1 17

◆ Chapter Review questions allow students and teachers to check skill mastery. These cover the objectives in the Goals for Learning at the beginning of each chapter.

◆ Test-Taking Tips at the end of each Chapter Review help reduce test anxiety and improve test scores.

The comprehensive, wraparound Teacher's Edition provides instructional strategies at point of use. Everything from preparation guidelines to teaching tips and strategies are included in an easy-to-use format. Activities are featured at point of use for teacher convenience.

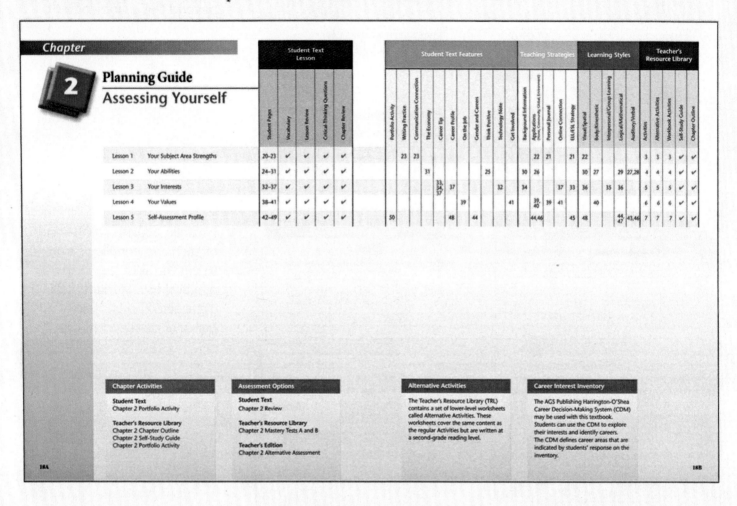

Chapter Planning Guides

- The Planning Guide saves valuable preparation time by organizing all materials for each chapter.

- A complete listing of lessons allows you to preview each chapter quickly.

- Assessment options are highlighted for easy reference. Options include:

    Chapter Reviews
    Chapter Mastery Tests, Forms A and B
    Alternative Assessment
    Midterm and Final Tests

- Page numbers of Student Text and Teacher's Edition features help customize lesson plans to your students.

- Many teaching strategies and learning styles are listed to support students with diverse needs.

- Activities for the Teacher's Resource Library (TRL) are listed.

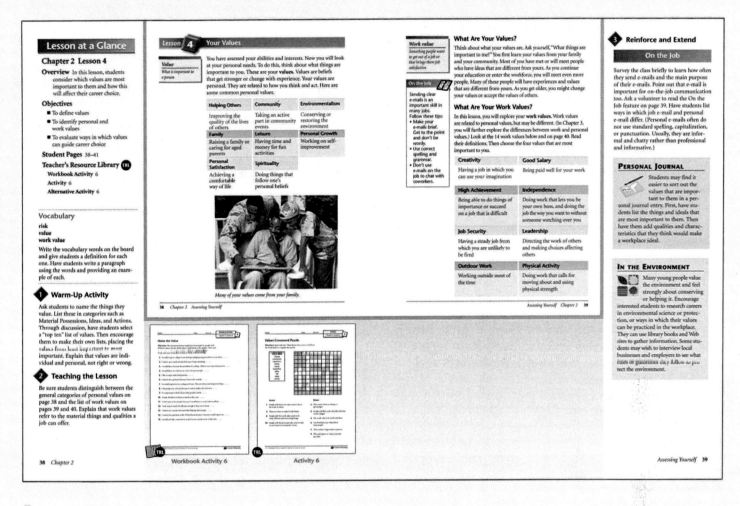

Lessons

- Quick overviews of chapters and lessons save planning time.

- Lesson objectives are listed for easy reference.

- Page references are provided for convenience.

- Easy-to-follow lesson plans in three steps save time: Warm-Up Activity, Teaching the Lesson, and Reinforce and Extend.

- Background Information provides interesting details that extend the lesson content.

- Applications: Four areas of application—Home, Community, Global, and Environment—help students relate lesson content to the world outside the classroom. Applications motivate students and make learning relevant.

- Personal Journal features give students the opportunity to write in response to lesson content.

- Relevant Web sites are listed in Online Connections.

- ELL/ESL Strategy features include teaching strategies to meet the specific needs of students learning English.

- Learning Styles provide teaching strategies to help meet the needs of students with diverse ways of learning. Modalities include Auditory/Verbal, Visual/Spatial, Body/Kinesthetic, Logical/Mathematical, and Interpersonal/Group Learning.

- Answers are provided in the Teacher's Edition for all reviews in the Student Text. Answers to the Teacher's Resource Library and Student Workbook are provided at the back of this Teacher's Edition and on the TRL CD-ROM.

- Worksheet and Activity pages from the Teacher's Resource Library are shown at point of use in reduced form.

Support for Students Learning English

Increasing numbers of students learning English are among the students in most schools and classrooms. The purpose of the ELL/ESL Strategy feature in this Teacher's Edition is to incorporate the language and content needs of English Language Learners in a regular and explicit manner.

ELL/ESL Strategy activities promote English language acquisition in the context of content area learning. Students should not be separated or isolated for these activities and interaction with English-speaking peers is always encouraged.

The ELL/ESL Strategy helps the teacher scaffold the content and presentation in relation to students' language and skill proficiency. Each activity suggests to the teacher some ideas about how to adjust the presentation of content to meet the varying needs of diverse learners, including students learning English. *Scaffolding* refers to structuring the introduction of vocabulary, concepts, and skills by providing additional supports or modifications based on students' needs. Ideally, these supports become less necessary as students' language proficiency increases and their knowledge and skill level becomes more developed.

ELL/ESL STRATEGY

Language Objective:

To explain the meaning of vocabulary terms using a graphic

To help students understand the concepts *economy, job security, interest rate,* and *business cycle,* ask them to tell what they understand about each term. If necessary, stimulate discussion with sentences like this: *If business is good, then the economy is _____. If I am not likely to lose my job, then I have _____. If ___ are low, I am more likely to borrow money and make my business larger.* Then have them trace the graphic on page 12 and explain how each curve is related to the terms. For example, ask: *As the line moves upward, is the economy stronger or weaker?* (stronger) *Is job security better or worse?* (better) *Do interest rates go up or down?* (down)

Each activity includes a language objective and strategy related to *listening, speaking, reading,* or *writing*. The language objective and activity relate to one or more content objectives listed in the Teacher's Edition under Lesson at a Glance. Some examples of language objectives include: reading for meaning, understanding different styles or purposes of writing, identifying and practicing common grammar structures, learning vocabulary specific to the content area, preparing and giving a group presentation, speaking in front of a group, or discussing an assigned topic as a small group.

Strategies That Support English Learners

- Identify and build on prior knowledge or experience; start with what's familiar and elaborate to include new content and new connections, personal associations, cultural context
- Use visuals and graphic organizers—illustrations, photos, charts, posters, graphs, maps, tables, webs, flow charts, timelines, diagrams
- Use hands-on artifacts (realia) or manipulatives
- Provide *comprehensible input*—paraphrase content, give additional examples, elaborate on student background knowledge and responses; be aware of rate of speech, syntax, and language structure and adjust accordingly
- Begin with lower-level, fact recall questions and move to questions that require higher-order critical-thinking skills (application, hypothesis, prediction, analysis, synthesis, evaluation)
- Teach vocabulary—pronunciations, key words or phrases, multiple meanings, idioms/expressions, academic or content language

- Have students create word banks or word walls for content (academic) vocabulary
- Teach and model specific reading and writing strategies—advance organizers, main idea, meaning from context, preview, predict, make inferences, summarize, guided reading
- Support communication with gestures and body language
- Teach and practice functional language skills— negotiate meaning, ask for clarification, confirm information, argue persuasively
- Teach and practice study skills—structured note-taking, outlining, use of reference materials
- Use cooperative learning, peer tutoring, or other small group learning strategies
- Plan opportunities for student interaction—create a skit and act it out, drama, role play, storytelling
- Practice self-monitoring and self-evaluation—students reflect on their own comprehension or activity with self-checks

How Do AGS Publishing Textbooks Support Students Learning English?

AGS Publishing is committed to helping all students succeed. For this reason, AGS Publishing textbooks and teaching materials incorporate research-based design elements and instructional methodologies configured to allow diverse students greater access to subject area content. Content access is facilitated by controlled reading level, coherent text, and vocabulary development. Effective instructional design is accomplished by applying research to lesson construction, learning activities, and assessments.

AGS Publishing materials feature key elements that support the needs of students learning English in sheltered and immersion settings.

Key Elements	AGS Publishing Features
Lesson Preparation	◆ Content- and language-specific objectives
Building Background	◆ Warm-Up Activity ◆ Explicit vocabulary instruction and practice with multiple exposures to new words ◆ Background information; building on prior knowledge and experience
Comprehensible Input	◆ Controlled reading level in student text (Grades 3–4) ◆ Highlighted vocabulary terms with definitions ◆ Student glossary with pronunciations ◆ Clean graphic and visual support ◆ Content links to examples ◆ Sidebar notes to highlight and clarify content ◆ Audio text recordings (selected titles) ◆ Alternative Activity pages (Grade 2 reading level)
Lesson Delivery	◆ Teaching the Lesson/3-Step Teaching Plan ◆ Short, skill- or content-specific lessons ◆ Orderly presentation of content with structural cues
Strategies	◆ ELL/ESL Strategy activities ◆ Learning Styles activities ◆ Writing prompts in student text ◆ Teaching Strategies Transparencies provide additional graphic organizers ◆ Study skills: Self-Study Guides, Chapter Outlines
Interaction	◆ Vocabulary-building activities ◆ Language-based ELL/ESL Strategy activities ◆ Learning Styles activities ◆ Reinforce and Extend activities
Practice/Application	◆ Skill practice or concept application in student text ◆ Reinforce and Extend activities ◆ Career, home, and community applications ◆ Student Workbook ◆ Multiple TRL activity pages
Review and Assessment	◆ Lesson reviews, chapter reviews, unit reviews ◆ Skill Track monitors student progress ◆ Chapter, Unit, Midterm, and Final Mastery Tests

For more information on these key elements, see Echevarria, J., Vogt, M., & Short, D. (2004). *Making content comprehensible for English language learners: The SIOP model* (2nd ed.). Boston, MA: Allyn & Bacon.

Learning Styles

Differentiated instruction allows teachers to address the needs of diverse learners and the variety of ways students process and learn information. The Learning Styles activities in this Teacher's Edition provide additional teaching strategies to help students understand lesson content by teaching or expanding upon the content in a different way. The activities are designed to help teachers capitalize on students' individual strengths and learning styles.

The Learning Styles activities highlight individual learning styles and are classified based on Howard Gardner's theory of multiple intelligences: Auditory/Verbal, Body/Kinesthetic, Interpersonal/Group Learning, Logical/Mathematical, and Visual/Spatial. In addition, the various writing activities suggested in the Student Text are appropriate for students who fit Gardner's description of Verbal/Linguistic intelligence.

Following are examples of activities featured in the *Career Planning* Teacher's Edition:

Logical/Mathematical

Students learn by using logical/mathematical thinking and problem solving in relation to the lesson content.

LEARNING STYLES

Logical/Mathematical
Discuss with students the importance of research and logic in developing both scientific and persuasive abilities. Explain that these abilities can be learned through practice. Present a problem your community or school is facing. (Examples might include whether to eliminate extracurricular sports, music, and art because of lack of funds, or whether to allow a large subdivision to be built on farmland.) Group students by their position on a chosen issue. Have them work together to find evidence to support or prove their position, and then explain their conclusion and list evidence they have found that supports it.

Visual/Spatial

Students learn by viewing or creating illustrations, graphics, patterns, or additional visual demonstrations beyond what is in the text.

LEARNING STYLES

Visual/Spatial
Invite interested students to create a collage or original artwork to illustrate what a specific workplace is like, including surroundings, appropriate dress, and so on. Suggest that students reflect the feeling of the workplace (formal vs. informal, calm vs. energetic, and so on) using color, line, symbols, and organizational plan.

Interpersonal/Group Learning

Students learn from working with at least one other person or in a cooperative learning group on activities that involve a process and an end product.

LEARNING STYLES

Interpersonal/Group Learning
Establish pairs or small groups of students based on their common interest in a career group. Students are to prepare a multimedia presentation profiling two or more of the occupations listed under their career group heading. Instruct partners and groups to cooperate to determine what research, writing, and organization tasks need to be completed, then to carry out the work. Allow time for groups to give their presentations in class.

Body/Kinesthetic

Students learn from activities that include physical movement, manipulatives, or other tactile experiences.

LEARNING STYLES

Body/Kinesthetic
Help students understand the concept of prestige. List things that students believe have a high prestige, such as starting on a championship team, making the honor roll, or having a nice car. Invite volunteers to role-play scenes illustrating each of these accomplishments. Students can show by their words, gestures, and body language how having prestige makes them feel.

Auditory/Verbal

Students learn by listening to text read aloud or from an audiorecording, and from other listening or speaking activities. Musical activities related to the content may help auditory learners.

LEARNING STYLES

Auditory/Verbal
Many students will benefit from reading the two paragraphs on page 11 aloud to each other in pairs, or listening to a recorded version of it. Instruct partners or listeners to pause after each paragraph or two to summarize main ideas. Ask them to write down any questions they have about the material and listen for answers. Discuss any questions that are not answered in the reading and suggest sources where students can find answers.

TRL All of the activities you'll need to reinforce and extend the text are conveniently located on the AGS Publishing Teacher's Resource Library (TRL) CD-ROM. All of the reproducible activities pictured in the Teacher's Edition are ready to select, view, and print. Additionally, you can preview other materials by directly linking to the AGS Publishing Web site.

Workbook Activities

Workbook Activities are available to reinforce and extend skills from each lesson of the textbook. These activities are also available in a bound workbook format.

Activities

Activities for each lesson of the textbook give students additional skill practice.

Alternative Activities

These activities cover the same content as the regular Activities but are written at a second-grade reading level.

Portfolio Activities

Portfolio Activities for each chapter allow students to put the skills they learn to practical use. These activities directly relate to the Portfolio Activities in the Student Text and can be added to students' personal career portfolios.

Self-Study Guides/Chapter Outlines

An assignment guide provides teachers with the flexibility for individualized instruction or independent study. Fill-in-the-blank outlines highlight the most important chapter concepts and are a valuable study tool for students.

Mastery Tests

Chapter, Midterm, and Final Mastery Tests are convenient assessment options.

Answer Key

All answers to reproducible activities are included in the TRL and in the Teacher's Edition.

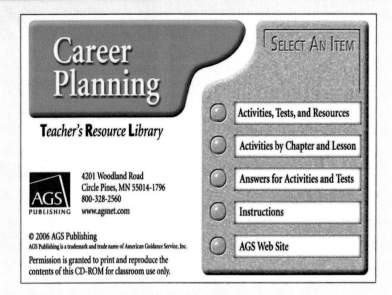

Workbook Activities

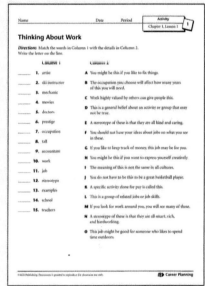

Activities

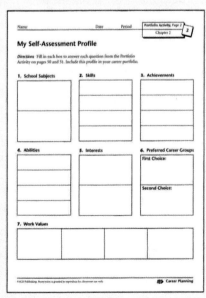

Portfolio Activities

Mastery Tests

Synopsis of the Scientific Research Base

Research-Based Principles	AGS Publishing Textbooks	References
Standards Alignment		
Subject area instruction needs to be based on skills, concepts, and processes represented by common standards for that subject area.	◆ Textbook content and skills aligned with national standards and state grade-level or course-specific content standards, where available	Matlock, L., Fielder, K., & Walsh, D. (2001). Building the foundation for standards-based instruction for all students. *Teaching Exceptional Children, 33*(5), 68–72. Miller, S. P., & Mercer, C. D. (1997). Educational aspects of mathematics disabilities. *Journal of Learning Disabilities, 30*(1), 47–56. Reys, R., Reys, B., Lapan, R., Holliday, G. & Wasman, D. (2003). Assessing the impact of standards-based middle grades mathematics curriculum materials on student achievement. *Journal of Research in Mathematics Education, 34*(1), 74–95.
Readability		
Many students struggle to learn from core content-area textbooks that are written too high above their reading level. Students need access to textbooks written at a level they can read and understand, where the reading level is within the students' range of comprehension.	◆ Grade 4.0 or lower readability using the Spache formula ◆ Controlled vocabulary matched to student reading ability and use of synonyms to replace non-essential difficult words above grade 4 ◆ Simple sentence structures ◆ Limited sentence length	Allington, R. L. (2002). You can't learn much from books you can't read. *Educational Leadership, 60*(3), 16–19. Chall, J. S., & Conard, S. S. (1991). *Should textbooks challenge students? The case for easier or harder textbooks.* New York: Teachers College Press. *Readability calculations.* (2000). Dallas: Micro Power & Light Company.
Language Complexity and Sequence		
Students struggling with vocabulary and text comprehension need textbooks with accessible language.	◆ Simple, direct language using an active voice ◆ Clear organization to facilitate understanding ◆ Explicit language signals to show sequence of and links between concepts and ideas	Anderson, T. H., & Armbruster, B. B. (1984). Readable texts, or selecting a textbook is not like buying a pair of shoes. In R. C. Anderson, J. Osborne, & R. J. Tierney (Eds.), *Learning to read in American schools* (pp. 151–162). Hillsdale, NJ: Lawrence Erlbaum Associates, Inc. Curtis, M. E. (2002, May 20). *Adolescent reading: A synthesis of research.* Paper presented at the Practice Models for Adolescent Literacy Success Conference, U.S. Department of Education. Washington, DC: National Institute of Child Health and Human Development. Retrieved September 15, 2003, from http://216.26.160.105/conf/nichd/synthesis.asp McAlpine, L., & Weston, C. (1994). The attributes of instructional materials. *Performance Improvement Quarterly, 7*(1), 19–30. Seidenberg, P. L. (1989). Relating text-processing research to reading and writing instruction for learning disabled students. *Learning Disabilities Focus, 5*(1), 4–12.
Vocabulary Use and Development		
Students need content-related vocabulary instruction in the context of readable and meaningful text.	◆ New vocabulary boldfaced on first occurrence, used in context, and defined in a sidebar ◆ Glossary with pronunciation, definition, and relevant graphic illustrations for all vocabulary words ◆ Direct vocabulary instruction introduced in the Teacher's Edition and reinforced in context throughout ◆ Multiple exposures to new vocabulary in text and practice exercises	Ciborowski, J. (1992). *Textbooks and the students who can't read them: A guide to teaching content.* Cambridge, MA: Brookline. Kameenui, E. J., & Simmons, D. C. (1990). *Designing instructional strategies.* Columbus, OH: Merrill Publishing Company. Marzano, R. J. (1998). *A theory-based meta-analysis of research on instruction.* Aurora, CO: Mid-Continent Research for Education and Learning. Retrieved October 1, 2003, from http://www.mcrel.org/topics/productDetail/asp?productID=83 McAlpine, L., & Weston, C. (1994). The attributes of instructional materials. *Performance Improvement Quarterly, 7*(1), 19–30. National Reading Panel. (2000). *Teaching children to read: An evidence-based assessment of the scientific research literature on reading and its implications for reading instruction.* Reports of the subgroups. Washington, DC: National Institute of Child Health and Human Development. Taylor, S. E., Frackenpohl, H., White, C. E., Nieroroda, B. W., Browning, C. L., & Birsner, E. P. (1989). *EDL core vocabularies in reading, mathematics, science, and social studies.* Austin, TX: Steck-Vaughn.

Research-Based Principles	AGS Publishing Textbooks	References

Text Organization: Presentation and Structure

Students need an uncluttered page layout, with easy-to-read print, that clearly directs the reader to main ideas, important information, examples, and comprehensive practice and review.

Reading comprehension is improved by structural features in the text that make it easier for learners to access the content.

Print characteristics and page layout:
◆ Serif font for body copy; sans serif font for boxed features, examples
◆ Maximum line length of 5" for ease of reading
◆ Unjustified (ragged) right margins
◆ Major/minor column page design presents primary instructional information in the major column and support content in the sidebar or in a box

Presentation characteristics:
◆ Lesson introductions, summaries
◆ Explicit lesson titles, headings, and subheadings label and organize main ideas
◆ Signals alert readers to important information, content connections, illustrations, graphics
◆ Cues (e.g., boldface type) highlight important information

Text structure:
◆ Lesson heads in question or statement format guide comprehension
◆ Text written to explicitly link facts and concepts within and across lessons; text cohesiveness
◆ Each skill or concept linked to direct practice and review

Armbruster, B. B., & Anderson, T. H. (1988). On selecting "considerate" content area textbooks. *Remedial and Special Education, 9*(1), 47–52.

Beck, I. L., McKeown, M. G., & Grommoll, E. W. (1989). Learning from social studies texts. *Cognition and Instruction, 6*(2), 99–158.

Chambliss, M. J. (1994). Evaluating the quality of textbooks for diverse learners. *Remedial and Special Education, 15*(5), 348–362.

Ciborowski, J. (1992). *Textbooks and the students who can't read them: A guide to teaching content.* Cambridge, MA: Brookline.

Dickson, S. V., Simmons, D. C., & Kameenui, E. J. (1995). *Text organization and its relation to reading comprehension: A synthesis of the research* (Technical Report No. 17) and *Text organization: Curricular and instructional implications for diverse learners* (Technical Report No. 18). National Center to Improve the Tools of Educators. Eugene, OR: University of Oregon. Retrieved January 26, 2000, from http://idea.uoregon.edu/~ncite/documents/techrep/tech17.html and http://idea.uoregon.edu/~ncite/documents/techrep/tech18.html

Dickson, S. V., Simmons, D. C., & Kameenui, E. J. (1998). Text organization: Research bases *and* Text organization: Instructional and curricular basics and implications. In D. C. Simmons & E. J. Kameenui (Eds.), *What reading research tells us about children with diverse learning needs: Bases and basics* (pp. 239–278; 279–294). Mahwah, NJ: Lawrence Erlbaum Associates, Inc.

Mansfield, J. S., Legge, G. E., & Bane, M. C. (1996). Psychophysics of reading. XV: Font effects in normal and low vision. *Investigative Ophthalmology and Vision Science, 37*, 1492–1501.

McAlpine, L., & Weston, C. (1994). The attributes of instructional materials. *Performance Improvement Quarterly, 7*(1), 19–30.

McNamara, D. S., Kintsche, E., Songer, N. B., & Kintsche, W. (1996). Are good texts always better? Interactions of text coherence, background knowledge, and levels of understanding in learning from text. *Cognition and Instruction, 14*(1), 1–43.

Tyree, R. B., Fiore, T. A., & Cook, R. A. (1994). Instructional materials for diverse learners: Features and considerations for textbook design. *Remedial and Special Education, 15*(6), 363–377.

Differentiated Instruction and Learning Styles

Student learning is more successful when tasks are aligned with academic skill levels and developmental stage, and adjustments are made to allow students multiple means to engage and express their learning strengths and styles at appropriate levels of challenge and support.

Differentiated instruction allows teachers to organize instruction to adjust for diverse learning needs within a classroom.

Learning activities that capitalize on students' learning styles can structure planning for individual differences based on multiple intelligences theory.

◆ Multiple features, including Learning Styles activities, help teachers match assignments to students' abilities and interests
◆ Variety of media to select from—print, audio, visual, software
◆ Step-by-step, part-by-part basic content and skill-level lessons in the Student and Teacher's Editions
◆ Alternative Activities written at a Grade 2 (Spache) readability in the Teacher's Resource Library
◆ Variety of review materials, activities, sidebars, and alternative readings
◆ Multiple assessments—lesson or chapter reviews, end-of-chapter tests, cumulative midterm/final mastery tests, alternative assessment items

Learning Styles activities include:
◆ Auditory/Verbal
◆ Body/Kinesthetic
◆ Interpersonal/Group Learning
◆ Logical/Mathematical
◆ Visual/Spatial

ELL/ESL Strategies provide support for students who are learning English and lesson content concurrently

Allington, R. L. (2002). You can't learn much from books you can't read. *Educational Leadership, 60*(3), 16–19.

Carnine, D. (1994). Introduction to the mini-series: Diverse learners and prevailing, emerging, and research-based educational approaches and their tools. *School Psychology Review, 23*(3), 341–350.

Forsten, C., Grant, J., & Hollas, B. (2003). *Differentiating textbooks: Strategies to improve student comprehension and motivation.* Peterborough, NH: Crystal Springs Books.

Gardner, H. (1983). *Frames of mind: The theory of multiple intelligences.* New York: Harper and Row.

Gersten, R., & Baker, S. (2000). The professional knowledge base on instructional practices that support cognitive growth for English-language learners. In R. Gersten, E. P. Schiller, & S. Vaughn (Eds.), *Contemporary special education research: Syntheses of the knowledge base on critical instructional issues* (pp. 31–80). Mahwah, NJ: Lawrence Erlbaum Associates, Inc.

Hall, T. (2002, June). *Effective classroom practices report: Differentiated instruction.* Wakefield, NJ: National Center on Accessing the General Curriculum. Retrieved September 29, 2003, from http://www.cast.org/cac/index.cfm?i=2876

Lazear, D. (1999). *Eight ways of knowing: Teaching for multiple intelligences* (3rd ed.). Arlington Heights, IL: Skylight Training and Publishing.

Orlich, D. C., Harder, R. J., Callahan, R. C., & Gibson, H. W. (2001). *Teaching strategies: A guide to better instruction* (6th ed.). Boston: Houghton Mifflin Company.

Roderick, M. & Camburn, E. (1999). Risk and recovery from course failure in the early years of high school. *American Educational Research Journal, 36*(2), 303–343.

Tomlinson, C. A. (1999). *The differentiated classroom: Responding to the needs of all learners.* Alexandria, VA: Association for Supervision and Curriculum Development.

Synopsis of the Scientific Research Base, *continued*

Research-Based Principles	AGS Publishing Textbooks	References

Instructional Design: Lesson Structure and Learner Support Strategies

Instruction that includes the components of effective instruction, utilizes effective strategies and interventions to facilitate student learning, and aligns with standards improves learning for all students, especially diverse learners and students who are struggling.

Elements of effective instruction:

Step 1: Introduce the lesson and prepare students to learn
Step 2: Provide instruction and guided practice
Step 3: Provide opportunities for applied practice and generalization

Organizational tools:
Advance organizers
Graphic organizers

Instructional process techniques:
Cooperative learning
Student self-monitoring and questioning
Real-life examples
Mnemonics

Step 1: Introduce the lesson and prepare students to learn
In the Student Edition:
- "How to Use This Book" feature explicitly teaches text organization
- Chapter and lesson previews with graphic and visual organizers
- Goals for Learning
- Sidebar notes review skills and important facts and information

In the Teacher's Edition:
- Lesson objectives
- Explicit *3-Step Teaching Plan* begins with "Warm-Up Activity" to inform students of objectives, connect to previous learning and background knowledge, review skills, and motivate students to engage in learning

Step 2: Provide instruction and guided practice
In the Student Edition:
- Short, manageable lessons break content and skills into smaller, step-by-step, part-by-part pieces
- Systematic presentation of lesson concepts and skills
- Chapter and lesson headings presented as questions or statements
- Graphic organizers arrange content visually—charts, graphs, tables, diagrams, bulleted lists, arrows, graphics, mnemonics, illustrations, and captions
- Models or examples link directly to the explanation of the concept
- Multiple opportunities for direct practice throughout

In the Teacher's Edition:
- *3-Step Teaching Plan* for each lesson includes "Teaching the Lesson" with direct instruction, and helps teachers present and clarify lesson skills and concepts through guided practice and modeling of important ideas
- Supplemental strategies and activities, including hands-on modeling, transparencies, graphic organizers, visual aids, learning styles

Step 3: Provide opportunities for applied practice and generalization
In the Student Edition:
- Each skill or concept lesson is followed by direct practice or review questions
- Multiple exercises throughout
- Generalization and application activities in sidebars and lessons link content to real-life applications
- Chapter reviews and summaries highlight major points

Allsopp, D. H. (1990). Using modeling, manipulatives, and mnemonics with eighth-grade math students. *Teaching Exceptional Children, 31*(2), 74–81.

Chambliss, M. J. (1994). Evaluating the quality of textbooks for diverse learners. *Remedial and Special Education, 15*(5), 348–362.

Ciborowski, J. (1992). *Textbooks and the students who can't read them: A guide to teaching content.* Cambridge, MA: Brookline.

Cole, R. W. (Ed.). (1995). *Educating everybody's children: Diverse teaching strategies for diverse learners.* Alexandria, VA: Association for Supervision and Curriculum Development.

Curtis, M. E. (2002, May 20). *Adolescent reading: A synthesis of research.* Paper presented at the Practice Models for Adolescent Literacy Success Conference, U.S. Department of Education. Washington, DC: National Institute of Child Health and Human Development. Retrieved September 15, 2003, from http://216.26.160.105/conf/nichd/synthesis.asp

Dickson, S. V., Simmons, D. C., & Kameenui, E. J. (1995). *Text organization: Curricular and instructional implications for diverse learners* (Technical Report No. 18). National Center to Improve the Tools of Educators. Eugene, OR: University of Oregon. Retrieved January 26, 2000, from http://idea.uoregon.edu/~ncite/documents/techrep/tech18.html

Dixon, R. C., Carnine, D. W., Lee, D., Wallin, J., & Chard, D. (1998). *Review of high quality experimental mathematics research: Report to the California State Board of Education.* Sacramento, CA: California State Board of Education.

Jarrett, D. (1999). *The inclusive classroom: Mathematics and science instruction for students with learning disabilities—It's just good teaching.* Portland, OR: Northwest Regional Educational Laboratory.

Johnson, D. W., Johnson, R. T., & Stanne, M. B. (2000, May). *Cooperative learning methods: A meta-analysis.* Minneapolis: The Cooperative Learning Center, University of Minnesota. Retrieved October 29, 2003, from http://www.cooplearn.org/pages/cl-methods.html

Kameenui, E. J., & Simmons, D. C. (1990). *Designing instructional strategies.* Columbus, OH: Merrill Publishing Company.

Lovitt, T. C., & Horton, S. V. (1994). Strategies for adapting science textbooks for youth with learning disabilities. *Remedial and Special Education, 15*(2), 105–116.

Marzano, R. J. (1998). *A theory-based meta-analysis of research on instruction.* Aurora, CO: Mid-Continent Research for Education and Learning. Retrieved October 1, 2003, from http://www.mcrel.org/topics/productDetail/asp?productID=83

Marzano, R. J., Pickering, D. J., & Pollock, J. E. (2001). *Classroom instruction that works: Research-based strategies for increasing student achievement.* Alexandria, VA: Association for Supervision and Curriculum Development.

Miller, S. P., & Mercer, C. D. (1993). Mnemonics: Enhancing the math performance of students with learning difficulties. *Intervention in School and Clinic, 29*(2), 78–82.

Montague, M. (1997). Cognitive strategy instruction in mathematics for students with learning disabilities. *Journal of Learning Disabilities, 30*(2), 164–177.

Reiser, R. A., & Dick, W. (1996). *Instructional planning: A guide for teachers* (2nd ed.). Boston: Allyn and Bacon.

Roderick, M., & Camburn, E. (1999). Risk and recovery from course failure in the early years of high school. *American Educational Research Journal, 36*(2), 303–343.

Steele, M. (2002). Strategies for helping students who have learning disabilities in mathematics. *Mathematics Teaching in the Middle School, 8*(3), 140–143.

Swanson, H. L. (2000). What instruction works for students with learning disabilities? Summarizing the results from a meta-analysis of intervention studies. In R. Gersten, E. P. Schiller, & S. Vaughn (Eds.), *Contemporary special education research: Syntheses of the knowledge base on critical instructional issues* (pp. 1–30). Mahwah, NJ: Lawrence Erlbaum Associates, Inc.

Tyree, R. B., Fiore, T. A., & Cook, R. A. (1994). Instructional materials for diverse learners: Features and considerations for textbook design. *Remedial and Special Education, 15*(6), 363–377.

Vaughn, S., Gersten, R., & Chard, D. J. (2000). The underlying message in LD intervention research: Findings from research syntheses. *Exceptional Children, 67*(1), 99–114.

In the Teacher's Edition:
◆ *3-Step Teaching Lesson Plan* concludes with "Reinforce and Extend" to reinforce, reteach, and extend lesson skills and concepts
◆ Unit or chapter projects link and apply unit or chapter concepts
◆ Multiple supplemental/alternative activities for individual and group learning and problem solving
◆ Career, home, and community application exercises

In the Teacher's Resource Library:
◆ Multiple exercises in Student Workbook and reproducibles offer applications, content extensions, additional practice, and alternative activities at a lower (Grade 2 Spache) readability

Skill Track Online:
◆ Monitors student learning and guides teacher feedback to student

Ongoing Assessment and Tracking Student Progress

Textbooks can incorporate features to facilitate and support assessment of learning, allowing teachers to monitor student progress and provide information on mastery level and the need for instructional changes.

Assessment should measure student progress on learning goals over the course of a lesson, chapter, or content-area textbook.

Students and teachers need timely and ongoing feedback so instruction can focus on specific skill development.

◆ Test-taking tips and strategies for students who benefit from explicit strategy instruction
◆ Lesson and chapter reviews check student understanding of content
◆ Workbook and reproducible lesson activities (Teacher's Resource Library) offer additional monitoring of student progress
◆ Discussion questions allow teachers to monitor student progress toward lesson objectives
◆ Self-Study Guides (Teacher's Resource Library) allow teacher and student to track individual assignments and progress
◆ Chapter assessment activities and curriculum-based assessment items correlate to chapter Goals for Learning:
  • Chapter reviews
  • End-of-chapter tests
  • Cumulative Midterm and final mastery tests
  • Alternative chapter assessments
  • Skill Track Online assesses and tracks individual student performance by lesson and chapter

Deshler, D. D., Ellis, E. S., & Lenz, B. K. (1996). *Teaching adolescents with learning disabilities: Strategies and methods* (2nd ed.). Denver, CO: Love Publishing Company.

Jarrett, D. (1999). *The inclusive classroom: Mathematics and science instruction for students with learning disabilities—It's just good teaching.* Portland, OR: Northwest Regional Educational Laboratory.

Reiser, R. A., & Dick, W. (1996). *Instructional planning: A guide for teachers* (2nd ed.). Boston: Allyn and Bacon.

Tyree, R. B., Fiore, T. A., & Cook, R. A. (1994). Instructional materials for diverse learners: Features and considerations for textbook design. *Remedial and Special Education, 15*(6), 363–377.

For more information on the scientific research base for AGS Publishing Textbooks, please go to www.agsnet.com or call Customer Service at 800-328-2560 to request a research report.

Standard A

Standard A sets forth two major goals: the development of career awareness and the development of employment readiness. In order to achieve career awareness, the standard lists 10 student competencies:

	Career Planning
Develop skills to locate, evaluate and interpret career information	Pages 1, 4, 7–10, 13, 16, 32, 54–64, 74–141, 144–147, 155, 162, 166–173, 182–183, 188–190, 198, 233, 250, 278–279
Learn about the variety of traditional and non-traditional occupations	Pages 3, 4, 7–9, 16, 19, 32, 35–37, 43–48, 51–52, 59, 63, 67, 75–81, 83, 86, 88–89, 93, 94–96, 98–141, 147, 162, 178, 205, 251, 278, 279, 282
Develop an awareness of personal abilities, skills, interest and motivations	Pages 18–53, 68–72, 77, 144–146, 156, 171, 194–199, 221–227, 234–236, 245
Learn how to interact and work cooperatively in teams	Pages 176–181, 191, 223–224
Learn to make decisions	Pages 55, 64–65, 69, 145, 269–271
Learn how to set goals	Pages 14–15, 63–64, 69, 70, 72, 194–199, 226, 281–282
Understand the importance of planning	Pages 28, 64–65, 69, 71, 143–149, 278–279, 284–287
Pursue and develop competency in areas of interest	The opportunity to explore this concept can be found on pages 11, 19–20, 23, 30–37, 41, 52, 62, 63, 78–79, 135, 143, 150–155, 170, 197–199, 223–225, 237, 245, 265, and 286.
Develop hobbies and vocational interests	Pages 3, 19, 30–35, 37, 42–53, 65, 171, 197, 223–227, 243–251, 254, 272–275
Balance between work and leisure time	Pages 3, 245–257, 274

The second major goal in Standard A refers to the development of employment readiness, which is to be achieved through nine student competencies:

Acquire employability skills such as working on a team, problem-solving and organizational skills	Pages 27–29, 33, 95–96, 98–100, 102–104, 110–116, 119–121, 123–124, 126–128, 130–132, 161, 176–181, 185, 228, 236–237
Apply job readiness skills to seek employment opportunities	The opportunity to explore this concept can be found on pages 152–155, 187–217, and 224–227.
Demonstrate knowledge about the changing workplace	Pages 1, 8–10, 76–78, 84, 87, 90, 94, 101, 105, 109, 111, 115, 117, 122, 125, 129, 133, 136
Learn about the rights and responsibilities of employers and employees	Pages 178–181, 266–271, 274–275
Learn to respect individual uniqueness in the workplace	Pages 153, 178–181, 185, 231
Learn how to write a resume	Pages 190–191, 200–211, 234
Develop a positive attitude toward work and learning	Pages 7, 25, 67, 120, 149, 177–181, 184, 191, 223–225, 227, 236, 252, 255, 285
Understand the importance of responsibility, dependability, punctuality, integrity and effort in the workplace	Pages 178, 197, 223–225, 227, 229, 236, 243, 252–257, 266–271, 274–275
Utilize time-management skills	Pages 153, 170, 231, 236, 243, 252–257, 274

Standard B

Standard B concerning students employing strategies to ensure career success and satisfaction expresses two major goals, the first acquiring career information, the second identifying career goals. According to this standard, students will need to achieve eight competencies in acquiring career information:

	Career Planning
Apply decision-making skills to career planning, course selection and career transition	Pages 54–73, 78–79, 143, 146–155, 161, 171–175, 191, 197, 227, 230, 249–251, 279, 284–290
Identify personal skills, interests, and abilities and relate them to current career choice	Pages 18–53, 68–72, 77, 144–146, 156, 171, 194–199, 221–227, 234–236, 245
Demonstrate knowledge of the career planning process	Pages 18–53, 64–65, 69, 71, 74–141, 143–149, 186–217, 218–241, 278–279, 284–287; Portfolio Activities: pages 14–15, 50–51, 70–71, 138–139, 156–157, 182–183, 214–215, 238–239, 272–273, 288–289
Know the various ways in which occupations can be classified	Pages 74–141
Use research and information resources to obtain career information	Pages 1, 4, 7–10, 13, 16, 32, 54–64, 74–141, 144–147, 155, 162, 166–173, 182–183, 188–190, 198, 233, 250, 278–279
Learn to use the Internet to access career planning information	Pages 7, 32, 57, 61, 155, 166, 173, 189, 287
Describe traditional and non-traditional career choices and how they relate to career choice	Pages 3, 4, 7–9, 16, 19, 32, 35–37, 43–48, 51–52, 59, 63, 67, 75–81, 83, 86, 88–89, 93, 94–96, 98–141, 147, 162, 178, 205, 251, 278, 279, 282
Understand how changing economic and societal needs influence employment trends and future training	Pages 1, 5, 7–15, 31, 59, 76–78, 84, 87, 90, 91, 94, 101, 105, 109, 111, 115, 117, 122, 125, 129, 133, 136, 162–166, 233, 284

The second major goal of Standard B is identifying career goals, and calls for the following competencies:

Demonstrate awareness of the education and training needed to achieve career goals	Pages 37, 48, 67, 78–79, 118, 143, 146–155, 178, 205, 221, 251, 282
Assess and modify their educational plan to support career goals	The opportunity to explore this concept can be found on pages 37, 48, 67, 78–79, 118, 143, 145–155, 178, 195–199, 202–203, 205, 221, 251, 277, 282, 288–289, and 291.
Use employability and job readiness skills in internship, mentoring, shadowing and/or other work experience	Pages 11, 31, 41, 62, 63, 78, 135, 153, 160–185, 186–217, 218–241, 265, 286
Select coursework that is related to career interests	The opportunity to explore this concept can be found on pages 37, 48, 67, 78–79, 118, 143, 145–155, 178, 195–199, 202–203, 205, 221, 251, 277, 282, 288–289, and 291.
Maintain a career-planning portfolio	Portfolio Activities: pages 14–15, 49–53, 70–71, 138–139, 156–157, 182–183, 214–215, 238–239, 272–273, 288–289

Standard C

Standard C looks at students as they are about to take their first actual career step, that is, go beyond the planning stage, for example, by selecting a major, entering an apprenticeship, or taking a full-time job. It clearly looks to the future and proposes two major goals: (a) the acquisition of knowledge and (b) the application of skills in achieving career goals. The first of these two goals has seven competencies:

	Career Planning
Understand the relationship between educational achievement and career success	Pages 1, 78–79, 84, 87, 90, 94, 97, 191, 105, 109, 111, 115, 117, 122, 125, 129, 133, 136, 148, 150–152, 154–157
Explain how work can help to achieve personal success and satisfaction	Pages 4–5, 38–48
Identify personal preferences and interests influencing career choice and success	Pages 18–53, 68–72, 75–141, 144–146, 156, 171, 194–199, 221–227, 234–236, 245
Understand that the changing workplace requires lifelong learning and acquiring new skills	Pages 191, 197, 227, 230, 249–251, 288–289
Describe the effect of work on lifestyle	Pages 1–5, 8–10, 196–197, 199, 258
Understand the importance of equity and access in career choice	Pages 6, 44, 69, 127, 151, 181, 208, 235, 270, 285
Understand that work is an important and satisfying means of personal expression	Pages 2, 4–5, 18–53, 68–72, 75–141, 144–146, 156, 171, 194–199, 221–227, 234–236, 245

Standard C's second goal is skills application, with the following four competencies:

Demonstrate how interests, abilities and achievement relate to achieving personal, social, educational and career goals	The opportunity to explore this concept can be found on pages 14–15, 18–53, 63–64, 68–72, 77, 144–146, 156, 171, 194–199, 221–227, 234–236, 245, and 281–282.
Learn how to use conflict management skills with peers and adults	Pages 161, 176–181, 185
Learn to work cooperatively with others as a team member	Pages 176–181, 191, 223–224
Apply academic and employment readiness skills in work-based learning situations such as internships, shadowing and/or mentoring experiences	The opportunity to explore this concept can be found on pages 18–53, 54–73, 142–159, 160–185, 186–217, 218–241, and 276–290.

by
Thomas F. Harrington
and
Spencer G. Niles
with Garbette A. M. Garraway

AGS Publishing
Circle Pines, Minnesota 55014-1796
800-328-2560

About the Authors

Thomas F. Harrington, Ph.D.

Thomas F. Harrington holds a Ph.D. in counseling from Purdue University and teaches vocational psychology and career counseling courses in the Department of Counseling and Applied Educational Psychology at Northeastern University in Boston. In 2004 he received the National Career Development Association's highest honor, The Eminent Career Award. He has edited or co-edited several books and is the co-author of the award winning *Harrington-O'Shea Career Decision-Making System*. He has served as President of the Association for Assessment in Counseling, a division of the American Counseling Association, and the Massachusetts Personnel and Guidance Association. He is a frequent speaker at regional, national, and international career development conferences.

Spencer G. Niles, Ed.D., LPC, NCC

Spencer G. Niles holds a Doctor of Education in Counselor Education from Penn State University and is currently Professor-in-Charge of the Counselor Education Program there. He has served as President of the National Career Development Association, President of the Pennsylvania Association of Counselor Education and Supervision, President of the Virginia Career Development Association, and editor of *The Career Development Quarterly*. In 2003, he received the American Counseling Association (ACA) David Brooks Distinguished Mentor Award and in 2004 he received the ACA Extended Research Award. He has been a visiting scholar at several international universities and is the author or co-author of over 75 publications. He has delivered over 75 presentations at international, national and regional conferences.

Garbette A. M. Garraway

Garbette A. M. Garraway holds master's degrees in English Education from Simon Fraser University, and Counseling Psychology from the University of British Columbia. He is currently a doctoral student in Counselor Education at Penn State University. He has worked as a teacher and a counselor in the public school system for 14 years. He has been a co-presenter at the National Career Development Association conference.

Photo credits for this textbook can be found on page 324.

The publisher wishes to thank the following educators for their helpful comments during the review process for *Career Planning*. Their assistance has been invaluable.

Kathy Bedre, Counselor, Flour Bluff High School, Corpus Christi, TX; **Larry Greer,** Special Day Class Teacher, Loara High School, Anaheim, CA; **Mary Hartfield,** Special Education Instructor in MIMS program, Marion Park Alternative School, Meridian, MS; **Debora J. Hartzell,** Lead Teacher for Special Education, Columbia and Lakeside High Schools, Atlanta, GA; **Karen Larimer,** Transition Coordinator, Keystone Area Education Agency, Elkader, IA; **Susan Loving,** Transition Specialist, Utah State Office of Education, Salt Lake City, UT; **Carole Mottar,** Coordinator, Renaissance Academy, River Falls, WI; **Ann C. Moore,** Transition Specialist, Spartanburg County School District Number 7, Spartanburg, SC; **Cindi A. Nixon,** Director, Special Services, Richland School District Two, Columbia, SC; **Karen M. Owens,** Special Education Teacher, Bruce High School, Bruce, MS; **Richard D. Scott,** Guidance Specialist, Maryland State Department of Education, Baltimore, MD; **Cecilia E. Williams,** ESE Teacher, Gaither High School, Tampa, FL; **Judy S. Wright,** Language Arts Instructor/Curriculum Director, Carlisle Community School, Carlisle, IA.

Publisher's Project Staff

Vice President of Curriculum and Publisher: Sari Follansbee; Director, Curriculum Development: Teri Mathews; Managing Editor: Julie Maas; Senior Editor: Jody Peterson; Development Assistant: Bev Johnson; Director, Creative Services: Nancy Condon; Production Coordinator/Designer: Katie Sonmor; Project Coordinator/Designer: Carol Bowling; Senior Project Coordinator: Barb Drewlo; Purchasing Agent: Mary Kaye Kuzma; Curriculum Product Manager: Brian Holl

© 2006 AGS Publishing
4201 Woodland Road
Circle Pines, MN 55014-1796
800-328-2560 • www.agsnet.com

Printed in the United States of America

ISBN 0-7854-4031-3

Product Number 94210

3 4 5 V088 13 12 11

Contents

Chapter 4 **Career Clusters and the Major Industries** **74**

Career Profiles

Communication Connections

Gender and Careers

The Economy

On the Job

Get Involved

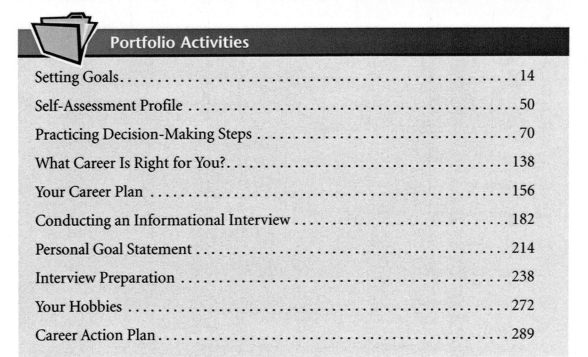

Portfolio Activities

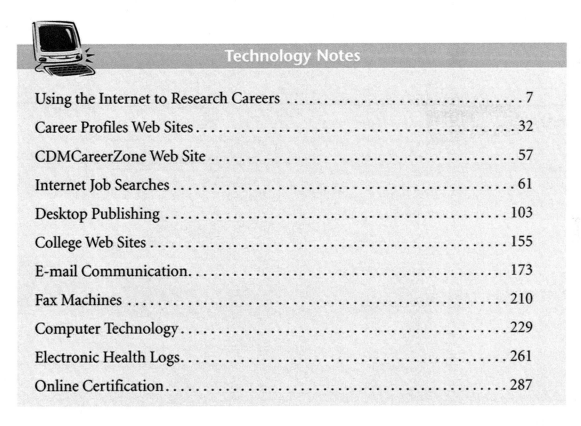

Technology Notes

Writing Practice

Figures

Tables

How to Use This Book: A Study Guide

Overview This section may be used to introduce the textbook, to preview the book's features, and to review effective study skills.

Objectives

- To introduce the textbook
- To preview the student textbook features
- To review study skills

Student Pages xiv–xxi

Teacher's Resource Library
How to Use This Book pages 1–4

Introduction to the Book

Have students read aloud the two paragraphs of the introduction. Discuss with students why career planning is important and what kinds of activities it involves.

How to Study

Read aloud each bulleted statement, pausing to discuss with students why the suggestion is a part of good study habits. Distribute copies of How to Use This Book 1: Study Habits Survey. Read the directions together and then have students complete the survey. After they have scored their surveys, ask them to make a list of the study habits they plan to work on improving. After three or four weeks, have students complete the survey again to see if they have improved their study habits. Suggest that they keep the survey and review it every month or so to see whether they are maintaining and improving their study habits.

How to Use This Book: A Study Guide

Welcome to *Career Planning*. Everyone needs to develop skills that will help them choose and plan for a career. Whether you are going on to a job or to a postsecondary school after high school, career planning skills will help you prepare for your future.

As you read the chapters and lessons in this book, you will learn skills that will help you assess yourself, make career decisions, and plan for your future. You will learn about many career opportunities in different industries. You will practice writing a résumé, preparing for interviews, and gathering references. You will also learn conflict resolution, self-advocacy, and time-management skills. In addition to making a career plan, you will learn about living a productive life outside of work.

How to Study

These tips can help you study more effectively:

◆ Plan a regular time to study.

◆ Choose a quiet place where you will not be distracted. Find a desk or table in a spot that has good lighting.

◆ Gather all the books, pencils, and paper you need to complete your assignments.

◆ Decide on a goal. For example, "I will finish reading and take notes on Chapter 1, Lesson 1, by 8:00."

◆ Take a five- or ten-minute break every hour to stay alert.

◆ If you start to feel sleepy, take a break and get some fresh air.

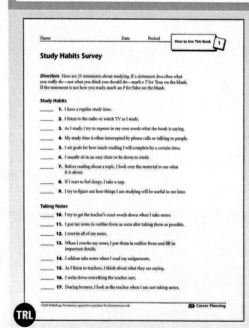

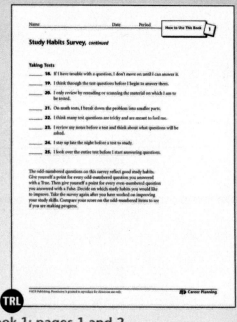

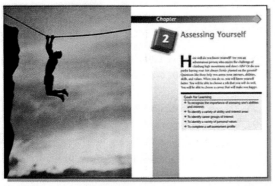

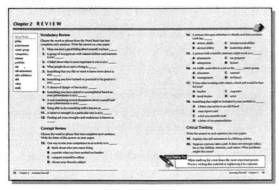

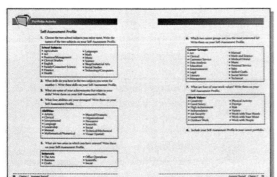

Before Beginning Each Chapter

◆ Read the chapter title and study the photograph. What does the photo say to you about the chapter title?

◆ Read the opening paragraphs.

◆ Study the Goals for Learning. The chapter review and tests will ask questions related to these goals.

◆ Look at the Chapter Review. The questions cover the most important information in the chapter.

◆ Look at the Portfolio Activity. Each chapter has an activity that will give you a chance to practice an important career planning skill.

Before Beginning Each Chapter

When students begin their study of Chapter 1, have them turn to page 1. Read aloud the first bulleted statement under "Before Beginning Each Chapter." Have a volunteer read the Chapter 1 title. Ask students what the photograph tells them about the title. Read aloud the second bulleted statement and have volunteers read the opening paragraphs. After reading the third bulleted statement, volunteers can read the Goals for Learning. Discuss why knowing these goals can help them when they are studying the chapter. Read aloud the fourth bulleted statement. Direct students to the Chapter Review on pages 16–17. Point out how the questions can help them identify important information in a chapter.

Chapter Openers organize information in easy-to-read formats. To help students organize their time, have them fill out How to Use This Book 2: Weekly Schedule. Encourage them to keep the schedule in a notebook or folder where they can refer to it easily. Suggest that they review the schedule periodically and update it as necessary.

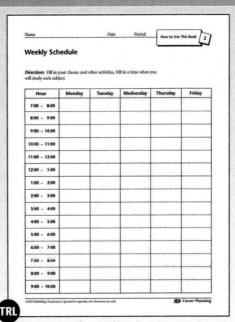

How to Use This Book 2

Note These Features

Read through the descriptions of each feature listed on page xvi. Then assign each of the two lessons of Chapter 1 to a small group of students. Have them list the features in their lesson and be prepared to report to the class on their findings. Encourage them to speculate on the content of the features based on their titles. Now that students are familiar with the chapter structure and features of the textbook, help them become familiar with other features and parts of the book. Write the following list on the board:

• Chapter Opener
• Figures
• Photographs
• Appendix
• Glossary
• Index

Direct students to skim their textbooks and find one of each of the listed features. You may wish to remind students of a book feature that can help them with this activity—the Table of Contents. Ask volunteers to tell the page numbers on which they found the features and have the other students check to see that the features do appear on these pages.

Note the Features

Career Tips—Short, easy-to-use tips about career-related topics

Career Profiles—Up-close, high-interest looks at specific careers or jobs.

Communication Connection—Communication skills related to chapter or lesson content

 The Economy—Aspects of the U.S. or the global economy that relate to careers

 Gender and Careers—Aspects related to gender roles, gender stereotyping, and gender equality in the workplace

 Get Involved—Civics, Community, or Volunteer activities that provide an opportunity to learn interpersonal and job skills

 On the Job—Skills used in the workplace that are important for any career

 Technology Notes—Uses of current technology related to the chapter or lesson topic

 Think Positive—Examples of how a positive attitude can affect career success

 Writing Practice—Writing tasks related to chapter or lesson content

Before Beginning Each Lesson

Read the lesson title and restate it in the form of a question. For example, write: *What is the importance of work?*

Look over the entire lesson, noting…

- ◆ photographs
- ◆ charts
- ◆ tables
- ◆ bold words
- ◆ vocabulary words
- ◆ headings
- ◆ lesson review questions

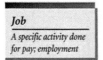

As You Read the Lesson

- ◆ Read the major headings.
- ◆ Read the paragraphs that follow the headings.
- ◆ Before moving on to the next heading, make sure you understand what you read. If you do not, reread the section or ask for help.

Using the Bold Words

Job
A specific activity done for pay; employment

Knowing the meaning of all the boxed words in the narrow column will help you understand what you read.

These words appear in **bold type** the first time they appear in the text and are often defined in the paragraph.

The **job,** or work you choose to do for pay, will affect how you spend most of your time as an adult.

All of the words in the narrow column are also defined in the **glossary.**

Job (job) A specific activity done for pay; employment (p. 3)

Definitions of Occupational Titles

The titles of specific occupations are used throughout this textbook. They appear in tables and charts as well as in the text. All the occupational titles that appear in the book are defined in the **appendix.**

computer systems analyst studies and solves problems related to computer systems and software; finds ways to use computer systems better (Ch. 2, 4)

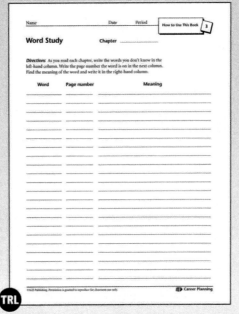

Before Beginning Each Lesson

Read the first statement on page xvii. Direct students' attention to the lesson pictured on page xvii. Ask a volunteer to restate the lesson title as a question. Then read aloud the bulleted elements. Tell students that before beginning each lesson, they should preview the lesson by locating these elements.

As You Read the Lesson

Read aloud the first bulleted statement in this section on page xvii. Have students turn to page 2 and read the major heading, or lesson title, for Lesson 1 of Chapter 1. Then read the second bulleted statement and have students locate the first subhead. Ask for other volunteers to read the paragraphs that follow. Direct students to answer the question in the subhead in their own words. You may wish to repeat this procedure using the other subheads in the lesson. Read the last bullet statement. Return to Lesson 1 and encourage students to identify and discuss the concepts they do not understand. Have students look at the Lesson 1 Review on page 7. Discuss how the questions in the subheads relate to the questions in the Lesson Review.

Using the Bold Words

Read aloud the third section on page xxvi. Make sure students understand *bold type* and *glossary*. Ask students to find the boxed word on page 2 and to compare the definition of the word in the box, in the text, and in the glossary at the back of the textbook. Explain that this word appears in the box on page 2 because it is first used on this page.

Explain to students that occupational titles may not be bold, but they all appear in the appendix at the back of the book. Distribute copies of How to Use This Book 3: Word Study. Suggest that as they read, students write unfamiliar words, their page numbers, and definitions on the sheet. Point out that this list will be useful when reviewing vocabulary.

Word Study Tips

Have a volunteer read aloud Word Study Tips on page xviii. You may wish to demonstrate how to make a vocabulary card. Fill out an index card for the word *occupation* and its definition (page 4 in the student text). Encourage students to create a vocabulary card file from the words listed on their copy of How to Use This Book 3: Word Study.

Word Study Tips

◆ Start a vocabulary file with index cards to use for review.

◆ Write one term on the front of each card. Write the chapter number, lesson number, and definition on the back.

◆ You can use these cards as flash cards by yourself or with a study partner to test your knowledge.

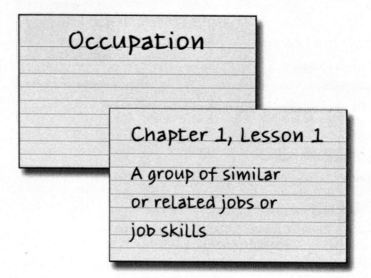

What to Do with a Word You Do Not Know

When you come to a word you do not know, ask yourself:

◆ Is the word a compound word?

◆ Can you find two words within the word? This could help you understand the meaning. For example: *salesperson.*

◆ Does the word have a prefix at the beginning?

◆ For example: *improper.* The prefix *im-* means "not," so this word refers to something that is not proper.

◆ Does the word have a suffix at the end?
For example: *variable, -able.* This means "able to vary."

◆ Can you identify the root word? Can you sound it out in parts? For example: *un known*

◆ Are there any clues in the sentence that will help you understand the word?

Look for the word in the margin box, glossary, appendix, or dictionary. If you are still having trouble with a word, ask for help.

Learning New Words

Ask students what they do when they come to a word they do not know. Read aloud the bulleted tips on page xix and discuss them as a class. Encourage students to use these tips as they read this textbook.

Taking Notes in Class

Ask students why note taking is an important study skill. Encourage them to describe the method they use to take notes during class discussions or when reading.

Ask for volunteers to read the bulleted statements on taking notes in class. Discuss each statement to ensure that students understand the suggestion fully.

Taking Notes in Class

As you read, you will be learning many new facts and ideas. Your notes will be useful and will help you remember when preparing for class discussions and studying for tests.

◆ Write the main ideas and supporting details.

◆ Use your own words.

◆ Keep your notes brief. You many want to set up some abbreviations to speed up your note-taking. For example: with = w/, United States = US, dollars = $, etc.

◆ Make notes on your worksheets or in your Student Workbook. Use them to study.

◆ Use the same method all the time. Then when you study for a test, you will know where to find the information you need to review.

Some Students prefer taking notes on index cards.

Some Students write down key ideas in a notebook

Using the Lesson Reviews

◆ Answer the questions for each lesson.

◆ Review the lesson content before moving on.

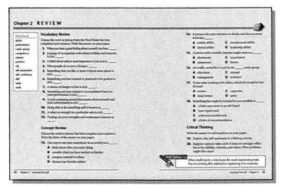

Using the Chapter Reviews

◆ Answer the questions under Vocabulary Review.

◆ Study the words and definitions. Say them aloud to help you remember them.

◆ Answer the questions under Concept Review.

◆ Use complete sentences to answer the questions under Critical Thinking.

Preparing for Tests

◆ Complete the Lesson Reviews and Chapter Reviews. Make up similar questions to practice what you have learned. You may want to do this with a classmate and share your questions.

◆ Review your answers to Lesson Reviews and Chapter Reviews.

◆ Test yourself on vocabulary words and key ideas.

◆ Read the Test-Taking Tips at the end of each chapter.

Using the Reviews

Point out the Lesson 1 Review on page 7. Then instruct students to turn to pages 52–53. Point out that a Chapter Review is intended to help them focus on and review the key facts and main ideas of a chapter before they are tested on the material. Suggest that they might want to complete the review after they have studied their notes, vocabulary lists, and worksheets.

Preparing for Tests

Remind students to read the tips about preparing for tests on page xix after they complete their study of each chapter and before they are tested on the chapter.

Read aloud the bulleted statements and discuss how each contributes to doing well on a test. Have students share successful techniques they use when studying for a test. Point out that that at the end of each Chapter Review is a Test-Taking Tip. Lead students to recognize that these suggestions, along with those on page xxi, can help them improve their test-taking skills.

Encourage students to refer back to the pages in How to Use This Book: A Study Guide throughout their study of *Career Planning*. Depending on your students' abilities, you might remind them about the section when beginning or finishing a chapter. You might also review the appropriate page each time students begin a new chapter or prepare for a test.

Chapter 1

Planning Guide
What Is a Career?

		Student Text Lesson				
		Student Pages	Vocabulary	Lesson Review	Critical-Thinking Questions	Chapter Review
Lesson 1	The Importance of Work	2–7	✔	✔	✔	✔
Lesson 2	The Workplace and the Economy	8–13	✔	✔	✔	✔

Chapter Activities

Student Text
Chapter 1 Portfolio Activity

Teacher's Resource Library
Chapter 1 Chapter Outline
Chapter 1 Self-Study Guide
Chapter 1 Portfolio Activity

Assessment Options

Student Text
Chapter 1 Review

Teacher's Resource Library
Chapter 1 Mastery Tests A and B

Teacher's Edition
Chapter 1 Alternative Assessment

| | Student Text Features | | | | | | | | | | | Teaching Strategies | | | | | Learning Styles | | | | | Teacher's Resource Library | | | | |
Portfolio Activity	Writing Practice	Communication Connection	The Economy	Career Tip	Career Profile	On the Job	Gender and Careers	Think Positive	Technology Note	Get Involved	Background Information	Applications (Home, Community, Global, Environment)	Personal Journal	Online Connection	ELL/ESL Strategy	Visual/Spatial	Body/Kinesthetic	Interpersonal/Group Learning	Logical/Mathematical	Auditory/Verbal	Activities	Alternative Activities	Workbook Activities	Self-Study Guide	Chapter Outline
				4, 5	4		6	7	7			3, 5	4		4		5		6	3	1	1	1	✔	✔
14	9	8	13	13		10				11	12	10		11	12	10		12	11	11	2	2	2	✔	✔

Alternative Activities

The Teacher's Resource Library (TRL) contains a set of lower-level worksheets called Alternative Activities. These worksheets cover the same content as the regular Activities but are written at a second-grade reading level.

Career Interest Inventory

The AGS Publishing Harrington-O'Shea Career Decision-Making System (CDM) may be used with this textbook. Students can use the CDM to explore their interests and identify careers. The CDM defines career areas that are indicated by students' response on the inventory.

Chapter at a Glance

Chapter 1:
What Is a Career?
pages 1–17

Lessons

Audio CD

Teacher's Resource Library TRL

Workbook Activities 1–2

Activities 1–2

Alternative Activities 1–2

Portfolio Activity 1

Chapter 1 Chapter Outline

Chapter 1 Self-Study Guide

Chapter 1 Mastery Tests A and B
(Answer Keys for the Teacher's
Resource Library begin on page 328
of this Teacher's Edition.)

| Name | | Date | Period | **SELF-STUDY GUIDE** |

Chapter 1: What Is a Career?

| Goal 1.1 | To define work, to describe how the work you do affects many parts of your life, and to recognize work stereotypes. |

Date	Assignment		Score
	1. Read pages 1–7.		
	2. Complete the Lesson 1 Review on page 7.		
	3. Complete Workbook Activity 1.		

Comments:

| Goal 1.2 | To identify formal and informal workplaces, and to explain how the business cycle influences the job market. |

Date	Assignment		Score
	4. Read pages 8–13.		
	5. Complete the Lesson 2 Review on page 13.		
	6. Complete Workbook Activity 2.		
	7. Read the Portfolio Activity and answer the Portfolio Questions on pages 14–15.		
	8. Complete the Chapter Review on pages 16–17.		

Comments:

©AGS Publishing. Permission is granted to reproduce for classroom use only.   Career Planning

Chapter 1 Self-Study Guide

1 What Is a Career?

People work for a lot of reasons. Most people need to earn money to live. People also choose to work to use skills they enjoy, to express themselves creatively, and to help people. How you choose to make your living as an adult will have a great impact on the kind of life you will lead. It will affect how much money you make and how you spend most of your time. Your job will affect how much freedom you have to be creative. It will also affect what kind of training or education you will need. It could also determine where you will live. Choosing and preparing for a career that you will enjoy may not be a piece of cake. However, the rewards of doing work that suits your interests, talents, and goals will be great. In this chapter, we will look at what work is, why it is important, and how it is impacted by the economy.

Goals for Learning

◆ To define work

◆ To describe how the work you do affects many parts of your life

◆ To recognize work stereotypes

◆ To identify formal and informal workplaces

◆ To explain how the business cycle influences the job market

1

Introducing the Chapter

Have students look at the photo on page xxii in the student edition and describe what is happening in the picture. Discuss it using these questions: *What career is associated with this skill? How might the person have learned this skill? What other skills does such a worker have? How do you think the person chose this career?* Have students read the introductory paragraph to consider the importance of one's choice of work.

Have students read the Goals for Learning. Explain that as they read the chapter, they will encounter these ideas. Students might rephrase the statements as questions and read to answer the questions.

Career Tips

Ask volunteers to read the career tips that appear in the margins throughout the chapter. Then discuss them with the class.

Alternative Assessment

The Alternative Assessment box on page 17 of the Chapter Review includes activities using various learning styles to assess students' understanding of the Goals for Learning.

Chapter 1 Chapter Outline

Lesson at a Glance

Chapter 1 Lesson 1

Overview In this lesson students consider how their choice of work will affect their lives, why people choose the work they do, and why work stereotypes are misleading.

Objectives
- To define work
- To list ways work affects a person's life
- To explain motives for one's choice of career
- To understand that work stereotypes are often wrong

Student Pages 2–7

Teacher's Resource Library

Workbook Activity 1

Activity 1

Alternative Activity 1

Vocabulary

career
job
occupation
prestige
stereotype
work

Write each vocabulary word on the board, divided into syllables. Have students read the words and group them by number of syllables. Discuss the words' meanings. Write a sentence for each word, leaving a blank where the word belongs. Have students read the sentences aloud and fill in the blanks with the correct vocabulary words.

1 Warm-Up Activity

Display magazine pictures of people doing different kinds of work. Discuss what each person is doing, what skills the task involves, and what the person is wearing and why. Explain that students will read about people's reasons for choosing a certain kind of work.

Work
What people do or how they spend their time to earn a living

The word *work* seems like a simple word, but what does it mean? If you look it up in a dictionary, you can see it has many different meanings. Work could mean the effort needed to get something done: "It takes a lot of *work* to build a bridge." It could mean something that someone has created: "That painting is one of the artist's greatest pieces of *work*." Work could also mean that something performs or operates as it should: "I changed the batteries, but I could not get my flashlight to *work*." In this lesson, the word *work* refers to how people spend their time to earn a living.

Why Is Work Important?

If work refers to how people spend their time to earn a living, what is the importance of work in your life? You might not know how to answer that question yet. First, think about examples of work you might see in your day-to-day life. You might see adults going to work or hear them talking about work. You see people at work whenever you turn on the television. On your way to school, you might see workers repairing roads or bus drivers driving to school.

A janitor is one example of a worker you might see at school.

Workbook Activity 1

Name _____ Date _____ Period _____ Workbook Activity **1**
Chapter 1, Lesson 1

The Work You Choose

Directions Write the correct word from the Word Bank to complete each sentence.

Word Bank				
all	career	enjoy	fun	money
occupation	paid	reasons	stereotypes	work

1. The work you do will affect how much time and money you have for _____.
2. A(n) _____ is a group of similar or related jobs or job skills.
3. People want and need to be _____ for their work.
4. A stereotype may be true for many people in an occupation, but not for _____.
5. A(n) _____ is a job path one prepares for and follows.
6. In choosing a career, _____ may not be most important to everyone.
7. Movie and TV characters may act in ways that are based on work _____.
8. People have many _____ for working.
9. What people do to earn a living is called _____.
10. If you enjoy the work you do, you are more likely to _____ your life.

 Career Planning

Activity 1

Name _____ Date _____ Period _____ Activity **1**
Chapter 1, Lesson 1

Thinking About Work

Directions Match the words in Column 1 with the details in Column 2. Write the letter on the line.

	Column 1		Column 2
___ 1.	artist	**A**	You might be this if you like to fix things.
___ 2.	ski instructor	**B**	The occupation you choose will affect how many years of this you will need.
___ 3.	mechanic		
___ 4.	movies	**C**	Work highly valued by others can give people this.
___ 5.	doctors	**D**	This is a general belief about an activity or group that may not be true.
___ 6.	prestige	**E**	A stereotype of these is that they are all kind and caring.
___ 7.	occupation	**F**	You should not base your ideas about jobs on what you see in these.
___ 8.	tall		
___ 9.	accountant	**G**	If you like to keep track of money, this job may be for you.
___ 10.	work	**H**	You might be this if you want to express yourself creatively.
___ 11.	job	**I**	The meaning of this is not the same in all cultures.
___ 12.	stereotype	**J**	You do not have to be this to be a great basketball player.
___ 13.	examples	**K**	A specific activity done for pay is called this.
___ 14.	school	**L**	This is a group of related jobs or job skills.
___ 15.	teachers	**M**	If you look for work around you, you will see many of these.
		N	A stereotype of these is that they are all smart, rich, and hardworking.
		O	This job might be good for someone who likes to spend time outdoors.

Career Planning

Workbook Activity 1

Activity 1

Job
A specific activity done for pay; employment

At school, you see teachers, janitors, cafeteria workers, and office workers. There are also many workers you don't see. Workers build the school buses you ride, grow the food you eat, and repair the computers you use. Work is all around us! When you think about the many examples of work in your daily life, you can see that work is very important.

So why is work important to you? Well, the **job,** or work you choose to do for pay, will affect how you spend most of your time as an adult. Full-time workers in the United States spend between 40 and 50 hours per week at work. The type of work you choose to do will affect many parts of your life:

- How many years of school you will need to prepare for a job
- Who you spend your time with each week
- How much money and time you will have available for fun activities
- Where you will live
- How you will have to dress each work day

Look at these examples to see how different jobs compare.

Oceanographer
- Studies oceans and things in oceans
- Lives near the ocean
- Spends a lot of time on a boat
- Dresses in casual clothing

Accountant
- Keeps track of money and spending for a business
- Can work/live anywhere
- Spends a lot of time in an office
- Dresses in more formal clothing

Ski Instructor
- Teaches people to ski
- Lives where there is cold weather and snow or mountains
- Spends a lot of time outdoors
- Dresses for the weather, in outdoor clothing
- May need to find other work during the summer months

What Is a Career? Chapter 1 **3**

 ## Teaching the Lesson

Have students rephrase the lesson objectives as questions. Allow time for students to write a sentence answering each question as they complete the lesson.

Brainstorm a list of different occupations. Together decide how the occupations should be ranked to show income and prestige. Note any misconceptions students have about the wages or "glamour" of certain jobs.

Discuss with students the concept of work stereotypes and gender stereotyping in careers. You may wish to point out that women work in almost every field today, whereas a hundred years ago, few were allowed to work outside the home. On the other hand, more men have entered fields such as nursing, which was once almost exclusively female.

 ## Reinforce and Extend

LEARNING STYLES

 Auditory/Verbal
Have students explain how the terms *work, job, occupation,* and *career* differ in meaning. You might ask them to select several occupations from the list brainstormed earlier and explore how the four terms relate to each occupation. Volunteers might use a script such as the following, and speak as though they were the workers: "I am a(n) _____. My job is to _____. Some of the tasks or work I perform in a day include _____. In my career, I will probably take these steps: _____."

AT HOME

Ask students to interview an adult at home about his or her work. Students' objectives should be to learn about the job, the reasons for choosing it, and the person's plans for future work. Encourage students to find out what work stereotypes, if any, the adult has encountered in his or her occupation. Remind students they should write out their questions first, and avoid questions that have yes or no answers.

Ask students to write a journal entry on their own paper. Have them explore a career that interests them. Encourage students who are having difficulty to list their strengths and interests first. This should suggest a direction that is suitable for them. Students can list what they know about the career, questions they have about it, why it appeals to them, and why they feel it suits them.

ELL/ESL STRATEGY

Language Objective: *To read for meaning*

If necessary, rephrase content about people's reasons for working: *Why do people want a job?* Focus on the concept of *meaningful work.* Explain that something is meaningful if you think it is important or useful or it brings you enjoyment. Invite students to name a kind of project they like to do and tell why. Explain that this is what makes it meaningful to them.

Career Profile

Park Ranger

Read the Career Profile feature aloud together. Have students make a word web showing facts and details about a park ranger's job. Encourage them to include information they know from experience, too. Then ask them to highlight duties or aspects of the job that appeal to them. You may wish to display a list of national parks and have students locate several on a map of the United States. Discuss what each park is like and how a park ranger's job might differ from park to park.

Occupation
A group of similar or related jobs or job skills

Career Tip

Looking for a career that interests you?

Read the business section of a newspaper. Look for special career sections in newspapers and magazines.

Because adults spend a lot of their time working, they arrange their lives according to the work they do. So, it makes sense that you should choose to work in an **occupation** that you enjoy. An occupation is a group of similar or related jobs or job skills. When you choose to work in an occupation you enjoy, you will likely be happier with your life. However, if you work in an occupation that you do not like, then your life might be less enjoyable. The occupation you choose is important if you want to live a more enjoyable life.

What Are the Reasons People Work?

Most people will say that work is important to them. However, they give different reasons for working. At first, you might think that everyone works for money. People want and need to be paid for the work they do. Money may not be the most important reason people work, however. For example, people who want to help others might work for less money if they can help other people in their job. Teachers, counselors, and ministers often view helping others as the most important part of their work. People who like to work with their hands might be mechanics or construction workers.

Career Profile

Park Ranger

Would you like to spend your days looking out over the Grand Canyon? Or watching storks in the swamps of the Florida Everglades? Or looking at the huge carvings of Washington, Lincoln, Jefferson, and Roosevelt at Mount Rushmore? Some lucky employees of the National Park Service have national parks as their workplaces. Park rangers do a variety of jobs. Some help visitors and make sure they care for our national parks. Others help care for forests or wildlife. Many states also employ park rangers. For example, Dan is a ranger at Governor Nelson State Park near Madison, Wisconsin. He spends his days observing and helping visitors to the park. One day he may issue a ticket to campers who disobey rules. Another day, he may give first aid to an injured lake swimmer. Not all park rangers have the great outdoors as their workplace. Some work in historic buildings. Still others do research or office work. The job market for park rangers is competitive, but it offers a wide variety of jobs and job locations.

Prestige

How important or valuable people believe something is

Career Tip

To learn about careers, talk to people with interesting jobs. Ask about their training, typical day, and workplace.

These people enjoy fixing or building things. This makes their work meaningful to them. Artists, musicians, and actors express themselves creatively. They feel this is the most important part of the work they do. It is important to understand what makes work meaningful to you.

You have seen how work is important to people for different reasons. People who live in countries other than the United States also have different reasons for working. In some countries, people work to survive. They spend time hunting for food, growing crops, preparing meals, and caring for children. In other countries, people may be expected to do the same work as their parents. In some countries, parents choose the work that their children will do when they grow up. In many countries, including the United States, people choose a type of work because of its **prestige.** Prestige is how important people think something is. The meaning of work is different for different people.

These workers in China are harvesting rice.

Body/Kinesthetic

Help students understand the concept of prestige. List things that students believe have a high prestige, such as starting on a championship team, making the honor roll, or having a nice car. Invite volunteers to role-play scenes illustrating each of these accomplishments. Students can show by their words, gestures, and body language how having prestige makes them feel.

GLOBAL CONNECTION

Ask students to research differences in the work of farmers in the United States and in another country, such as India, China, or South Africa. They might use the Internet or an encyclopedia to gather information. Students could compare the equipment used, the jobs usually performed by a farmer, and the time it takes to run a typical farm in each place.

IN THE COMMUNITY

Using the business sections of local newspapers, have students highlight ads for jobs that sound appealing. Have students point out information in the ads that would make them want to apply for the job. Help students formulate statements about characteristics they think make a job desirable.

Logical/Mathematical

Ask students to name occupations that are modeled on TV shows and explain how the work is characterized: glamorous, important, exciting, fast-paced, and so on. Have students analyze one of the occupations as depicted on TV, then use logic and experience to suggest ways the job may differ in reality. For example, police work calls for lots of paperwork and may seldom involve the use of weapons. Summarize the information in a chart comparing the TV version of a job with real characteristics of the job.

Gender and Careers

Ask students to list jobs they think are intended for men and those intended for women. Write these in two columns on the blackboard. Invite discussion of specific jobs to show that men and women now do many jobs once reserved for the opposite sex. Have students read the feature, then cross off any jobs they think no longer belong on the lists they made.

Stereotype
General belief about a person or group of people that is not necessarily true

What Are Work Stereotypes?

You may have noticed that when adults first meet each other, they often ask "What do you do?" People want to know what type of work others do. Then, they expect to know what kind of person someone is. For example, you meet a doctor. You might think that he or she is smart, rich, and hard working. You probably think he or she cares about the health of others. Maybe you meet a grade-school teacher. You might think he or she is kind, caring, and interested in helping others learn. Your ideas in both cases are based on work **stereotypes**. A stereotype is a general belief that many people have about an activity or group of people. For example, a general belief that many people have about basketball players is that "all basketball players are tall." This may be a true statement for many basketball players, but it is not true for all basketball players. In fact, some basketball players who were not very tall were great players. You must be very careful when using stereotypes because they are not always true.

Gender and Careers

One kind of work stereotype is gender stereotyping. For example, "Construction is a male field" or "Nursing is a job for women." At one time, there was some truth to gender stereotypes like these. Few women worked as carpenters or road builders. Few men went to nursing school. But today, almost every career is open to both men and women. Men have jobs in fields based on caring for others, such as child care and senior care. Women have jobs in fields where only men used to work, such as engineering and the military. Avoid thinking of an occupation as a "man's job" or a "woman's job." Also, avoid gender stereotypes when you observe jobs and the people who do them.

Think Positive

Keep a positive attitude as you consider career choices. Suppose you want to be an architect, a job requiring much skill and training. If you doubt your ability, you might choose a less challenging career path. Think positively about your strengths and abilities. Then find out the steps needed to make your dream come true.

It is also important to be careful about drawing conclusions about jobs based on what you see on TV. Characters might act in ways that are based on work stereotypes. You might think you would like certain jobs based on what you see on TV and in the movies. However, these TV and movie images of what a job is like are not usually correct.

As you plan for your future, you need to understand the things you enjoy doing. You should know what things are important to you. This will help you to choose jobs and find the occupation that is right for you. This book will help you choose and plan for a **career.** Your career is the job path that you prepare for and follow throughout your lifetime.

Lesson 1 Review Write your answers to these questions on a sheet of paper.

1. What is the difference between a job and an occupation? Give an example of each.

2. What are some reasons people have for choosing a particular occupation?

3. What is an example of a work stereotype that you know of? Why should you be careful about using work stereotypes?

Technology Note

The Internet is an excellent resource for finding out more about specific careers. Suppose you are interested in the field of marine biology. You would like to know about some careers in this field. You can use a search engine to look up Web sites on marine biology careers. Start with the key words "marine biology careers." The search engine will lead you to a variety of articles about careers in the field. You can find out about several different careers. Some might be familiar to you, like "oceanographer." Others might be unfamiliar, such as "marine mammal trainer" and "whale biologist." Researching careers on the Internet is a good way to learn about different career paths. Your research will also help you avoid work stereotypes.

Think Positive

Together read the Think Positive feature on page 7. Explain that negative thinking undermines confidence and can lead to failure, while keeping a positive attitude can help one stay upbeat and energetic—qualities that help a person keep working toward a goal. Help students brainstorm a list of positive, encouraging statements. Ask them to find or draw pictures that will remind them of their goal and inspire them. Students can make posters combining encouraging words and images to place in a location where they will see them often—such as a locker or bedroom door.

Lesson 1 Review Answers

1. A job is work done for pay, such as nurse or financial planner; an occupation involves a group of related jobs and job skills, such as health care or finance.

2. People may choose work for the money, prestige, or the aspects that make it meaningful for them: creative freedom, working with one's hands, satisfaction of helping others, and so on.

3. Possible answer: Many people feel that women make better nurses than men because they are better at taking care of sick people. Like other stereotypes, this one does not allow for individual differences and is not always true.

Technology Note

Ask volunteers to read the Technology Note feature on page 7 about using the Internet to research careers. If possible, have students use the Internet to research an interesting career. Point out that their search may result in a long listing of Web sites with information about the career.

Explain that it is helpful to read the short description and look at the Web address listed for each item in the first page of entries to see which sites are most likely to offer the kind of information they seek. Remind them that Web addresses that end in *.org, .gov,* and *.edu* are most likely to have reliable information.

Chapter 1 Lesson 2

Overview In this lesson, students consider how the nature of the workplace, the business cycle, and the economy affect the work experience.

Objectives

- To compare differences in workplaces for differing jobs
- To explain the effect of the economy on jobs
- To understand the business cycle and its relationship to unemployment

Student Pages 8–13

Teacher's Resource Library **TRL**

Workbook Activity 2

Activity 2

Alternative Activity 2

Vocabulary

business cycle
economy
interest rate
job security
unemployed
workplace

Have students form pairs. Give one partner a list of the vocabulary words and the other a list of definitions. Have students read the words, tell what they already know about them, then match each word with its definition. If students have difficulty, suggest that they analyze word parts of compound words and think about their meanings, then predict what the compound means.

Communication Connection

Ask students to describe different ways to communicate with others. If students do not mention it, ask them how their clothing sends messages to others. Read the Communication Connection feature aloud. Ask students to describe clothing worn by different workers they have observed and describe what message it sends.

Lesson 2 The Workplace and the Economy

Workplace
Where work is done

You have learned ways in which work is important. You know that work is a major part of your life. It is also important to understand the **workplace**. A workplace is where work is done. Each job has a specific workplace. A construction worker has a different workplace than a schoolteacher. An accountant has a different workplace than a mechanic.

How Are Workplaces Different?

Workplaces have their own "cultures," or ways of dressing, behaving, and interacting. They can be formal or informal. In a formal workplace, you would have to wear a suit or a dress. You would not be able to joke and laugh with your coworkers. Your boss would expect you to be at your job on time. You would have to follow rules as you do your work. The military is an example of a formal workplace. Workers must be in uniform and salute officers. They have to follow a set schedule each day. The rules are strongly enforced.

A park ranger works outdoors and wears a uniform.

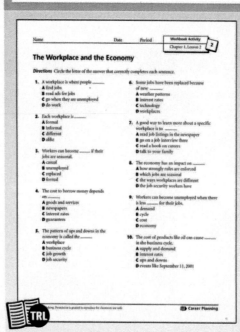

Workbook Activity 2

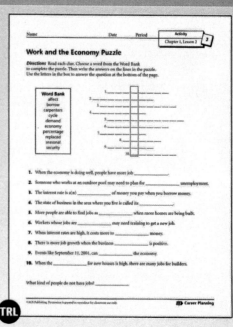

Activity 2

Communication Connection

Did you know that the way you dress is a form of communication? The clothes you wear send a message to people. A t-shirt and shorts say "time to relax." Wearing neat, tailored clothes shows respect for a job and for coworkers. Dressing properly for your job is key in any workplace.

In an informal workplace, you can wear more casual clothing. You can be more relaxed when dealing with your boss and coworkers. Work hours are often more flexible in an informal workplace. For example, college professors work in an informal workplace. They often can dress casually. They can usually schedule their own hours. For the most part, they are in charge of their own work. Look at the workplaces of these four jobs to see how they compare.

Job	Workplace
Zookeeper	outdoors, working with animals
Architect	indoors, working with computers and drawing equipment
Park Ranger	outdoors, taking care of land or animals
Teacher	indoors, working in a classroom with others

Each workplace is different. The workplace depends on the work being done. It also depends on what the workers in a job are like.

Writing Practice

What would your ideal workplace be like? Would it be an office with formally dressed workers? Would it be outdoors where the dress code is to be comfortable? Write a description of the kind of workplace you would like. Describe the surroundings, dress code, time flexibility, and interaction with coworkers.

What Is a Career? Chapter 1 **9**

---

1 Warm-Up Activity

Ask students to compare the way they dress, behave, and interact in these different environments: at home, in class, at a mall, or at a part-time job. Explain that surroundings and the expectations of the people around you determine what each place is like and what you are like in that place. Ask students to describe two very different workplaces, such as a bank and a veterinary clinic. Invite students to contrast the way workers dress and act in each place.

2 Teaching the Lesson

Remind students that text that explains processes often uses a cause and effect organization. Create a graphic organizer like the following on the board and have students copy it:

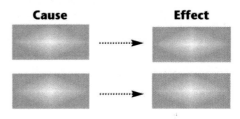

Model recording one cause and effect.

Cause
Need money for college

Effects
Get a job and save
Study hard to get good grades
Apply for a scholarship

As they read, have students use the organizer to record causes and effects they find.

To help students understand the concept of the economy, discuss statistics the government and economists analyze to measure its strength:

- *gross national product*—total value of goods and services produced by workers of a nation during a year
- *balance of trade*—a nation's exports compared to imports
- *rate of inflation*—rise in price level of goods and services
- *unemployment rate*—percentage of people eligible for work who cannot find work

Writing Practice

Read aloud the Writing Practice feature on page 9. Discuss the questions with students. Then have students answer the questions on their own paper.

What Is a Career? **9**

3 Reinforce and Extend

On the Job

Have a volunteer read the On the Job feature on page 10. Model appropriate and inappropriate styles of answering the phone in a business. Then have students form pairs and have them take turns being receptionist and client on the phone. Give students different types of businesses to role-play.

IN THE ENVIRONMENT

Students who enjoy working outdoors might wish to explore careers that give an opportunity to help protect or improve the environment. Encourage them to esearch Web sites that discuss a part of the environment that interests them, such as wildlife, wetlands, or air pollution.

LEARNING STYLES

Visual/Spatial
Invite interested students to create a collage or original artwork to illustrate what a specific workplace is like, including surroundings, appropriate dress, and so on. Suggest that students reflect the feeling of the workplace (formal vs. informal, calm vs. energetic, and so on) using color, line, symbols, and organizational plan.

IN THE COMMUNITY

Have students select a local place of employment that is public, such as a department store, municipal building, or park, and observe the workplace to note what kind of atmosphere and surroundings it has and how employees dress and act. If appropriate, students might ask a supervisor at the workplace what rules employees are asked to follow. Have students report their findings and compare local workplaces.

On the Job

Answering the phone is an important part of many jobs. Your voice may be the first impression a person gets of your company. How you answer the phone depends on the kinds of calls your company deals with. Also, formal workplaces have different phone styles than informal workplaces. Answering the phone in a clear, pleasant voice is appropriate for any workplace.

The military has a formal workplace.

Think about what jobs you might want. It is helpful to know what kind of a workplace you would like. Keep in mind that workplaces can be different even within the same job. For example, one university may be an informal workplace while another may be more formal. You need to understand the workplaces for the different jobs in which you may be interested. You need to find a job that fits who you are. This will help you to feel comfortable in your workplace.

Learning facts about workplaces in general is relatively easy. For example, it is easy to see that most park rangers work outdoors and wear uniforms. Learning about a specific workplace, however, takes more work. When you go on a job interview or talk to workers, you can get more detailed information about a workplace. You will learn more about interviews in Chapter 8.

How Does the Economy Affect Work?

Economy

State of business of an area or country, including how resources are used for goods and services

Job security

An understanding that workers will not lose their jobs

Interest rate

A percentage of money charged for borrowing money

Business cycle

The pattern of ups and downs in production and need, supply and demand, in the economy

In addition to understanding the workplace, you need to know how the **economy** affects work. The economy is the state of business of an area or country, including how resources are used for goods and services. Perhaps the most important thing to know is how the economy can impact **job security.** Job security is an understanding that workers will not lose their jobs. For example, one part of the economy deals with **interest rates.** These rates reflect the cost of borrowing money. If interest rates are low, it costs less to borrow money. If interest rates are high, it costs more to borrow money.

With high interest rates, people may not be able to buy certain things. When interest rates are low, more people can afford to buy a home. When more people are buying homes, the need to build more homes increases. So, more homes are built. Then, more people are able to find work as carpenters, plumbers, and painters. There are also more jobs in banks, where people borrow money to build homes. When more people are finding jobs, then more people are able to buy things. Then, more people are needed to work in places like department stores, grocery stores, and car dealerships. This pattern is called the **business cycle.**

Get Involved

Young people looking for jobs have a challenge. Most do not have much work experience. One excellent way to get work experience is to volunteer. High school students can volunteer in their communities after school and on weekends. In the summer, they can volunteer full time. For example, many young people volunteer at Boys and Girls Harbor each summer. This is a summer camp on Long Island, New York. It is for children from Harlem in New York City. Teens from all over the country volunteer their services. They work and play with children. They help maintain the camp with painting and repair projects. Volunteer service says a lot about a potential employee. One volunteer said, "I not only helped out others but I also learned about myself."

Unemployed
To be without a job

The Business Cycle

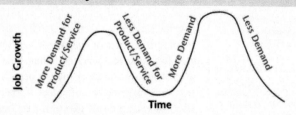

What Affects the Business Cycle?

Many things can affect the business cycle. Events like September 11, 2001, can have a big impact on the economy. The cost of oil and other products we buy from other countries can affect the economy. The cost of products we sell can also cause ups and downs in the business cycle.

Certain jobs are more by influenced by changes in the business cycle than others. Jobs related to homebuilding are good examples of jobs that are influenced by the business cycle. When the business cycle is positive (interest rates are low and it costs less to borrow money), there are more work opportunities. When the business cycle is not as positive (interest rates are high and it costs more to borrow money), more people are out of work. When people are out of work or do not have a job, they are **unemployed**.

It is important for workers to know if their jobs are influenced by the business cycle. Workers will need to plan for the times when they are unemployed. Ways to plan for this include saving money and identifying other jobs that can be done when regular employment is not available.

What Are Other Causes of Unemployment?

There are other reasons besides changes in the business cycle that people experience unemployment. For example, the demand for some jobs can decrease because of new inventions and technology. Today, jobs related to designing, building, and repairing typewriters are not in demand. They have been replaced with jobs related to the computer. In these situations, people who are unemployed often need to identify new jobs. They often need more education or training to get the new job they want.

12 Chapter 1 *What Is a Career?*

People can also be unemployed when their jobs are influenced by the change in season or the weather. For example, people who work as ski instructors must find other work to do in the summer months. Lifeguards in cold climates must find other work to do in the winter months. Some teachers need to find work to do in the summer to earn more money. It is usually easy to know if you are interested in a job that is affected by seasonal unemployment. Workers can plan for seasonal unemployment. They can save money. They can also find other jobs to do when they are not working their main jobs.

There are many things that are important to know about how the economy affects work. When workers know whether a job they are interested in is likely to be influenced by unemployment, they can plan for it when it happens.

Lesson 2 Review Write your answers to these questions on a sheet of paper.

1. What are some differences between a formal workplace and an informal workplace?
2. What are three ways to get more detailed information about a workplace?
3. What effect does the economy have on job security?
4. What effects do low interest rates have on the economy?
5. Jobs related to typewriters are not in demand today because of new technology. Describe another job with little demand today because of new inventions or technology.

The Economy

Unemployment is often related to a certain industry or region. For example, most Americans were working and making money during the 1920s. But many shoe and clothing factories in New England closed down. So unemployment was high in that region. In the 1970s, the steel industry faced challenges. There was less demand for steel, so many plants closed. Workers in steel factories in Indiana, Ohio, and Pennsylvania became unemployed. In the late 1980s, the oil industry in Texas and Louisiana had economic problems. Many oil industry employees in these states became unemployed. In the late 1990s, many Internet companies went out of business. Many of these companies were based in the "Silicon Valley" region of Northern California. This became an area of high unemployment.

What Is a Career? Chapter 1 **13**

Lesson 2 Review Answers

1. In a formal workplace, employees dress in suits or dresses, act serious, and usually have more rules to follow. In an informal workplace, employees wear casual clothing and are relaxed in dealing with coworkers and bosses.
2. Observe the workplace, ask workers, or inquire when you interview for a job.
3. There is less job security when the economy is poor and more job security when it is thriving.
4. Low interest rates encourage borrowing, which encourages home buying and building. These results lead to more jobs and more hiring, which makes the economy healthier.
5. Answers will vary. Possible answer: Jobs related to VCRs and 35 mm cameras are less in demand today because of the popularity of DVD players and digital cameras.

The Economy

Ask volunteers to read the feature at the bottom of page 13 aloud. With students, brainstorm a list of local or regional businesses, offices, and factories that have closed or laid off employees in recent years. Choose one of these entities and have students make a diagram showing the effects of its closing or cutting back. Remind students that an effect (such as people losing jobs) can also be a cause leading to other effects (local grocery stores and restaurants getting less business, laying off workers, and so on). This kind of cause-and-effect relationship can be diagrammed as a chain.

Invite interested students to research the national level of unemployment at this time and see how it compares to the level of unemployment in your state and region.

Ask students to define the term *goal* in their own words and give an example of a goal they have set. Encourage volunteers to describe the steps they took to attain a goal. Explain that in this activity, students will learn about the importance of goals in choosing a career.

Have students look at the picture and read the caption on page 14. Ask them to describe what they see and tell how it might be related to setting goals. Then have volunteers read the text on page 14 aloud.

Ask students to visualize themselves as they will be in 5 years, in 10 years, and in 15 years.

Setting Goals

As you know, choosing a job affects many parts of your life. To choose a career path, you need to decide what you hope to achieve. You need to think about achievements in different aspects of your life.

Most people have both short-term goals and long-term goals. A short-term goal is one that you can reach in the near future. A long-term goal is one that can be reached in the more distant future.

For example, your short-term goal related to money may be to save enough money for a car. Your long-term goal related to money may be to buy a house in the next 15 years.

You may be unsure about the career path you will follow. Still, you can set job-related goals. Perhaps you know that you would like to be a manager by the time you are 25. Maybe you would like to own your own shop or business by the time you are 30.

Write one or more sentences to answer each question on page 15. Add the activity to your career portfolio.

One of your goals might be to travel to a different country.

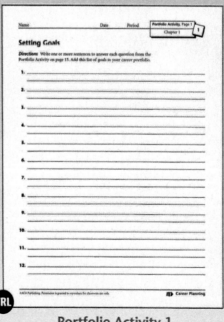

1. What short-term goal have you achieved recently?

2. What long-term goal have you achieved in the past?

3. What are your short-term educational goals?

4. What are your long-term educational goals?

5. What are your short-term goals related to money?

6. What are your long-term goals related to money?

7. What short-term goals do you have for sports, travel, and other fun activities?

8. What long-term goals do you have for sports, travel, and other fun activities?

9. Where would you like to live in 5 years?

10. Where would you like to live in 15 years?

11. What kind of job would you like to have in 5 years?

12. What kind of job would you like to have in 15 years?

Read through questions with students and clarify them as necessary. If necessary, model how to answer one set of questions. Explain what amount of time you will consider as short term and long term. Then have students write their answers to each question on the TRL page for Portfolio Activity 1 or on their own paper and add this to their career portfolio.

Portfolio Activity Answers

1.–12. Answers will vary.

Chapter 1 Review

Use the Chapter Review to prepare students for tests and to reteach content from the chapter.

Chapter 1 Mastery Test TRL

The Teacher's Resource Library includes two forms of the Chapter 1 Mastery Test. Each test addresses the chapter Goals for Learning. An optional third page of additional critical-thinking items is included for each test. The difficulty level of the two forms is equivalent.

Review Answers

Vocabulary Review

1. stereotype 2. economy 3. occupation
4. prestige 5. business cycle 6. unemployed
7. work 8. workplace 9. career 10. job
11. job security

Concept Review

12. C 13. D 14. B 15. A 16. D 17. B

Critical Thinking

18. The work you do will determine how you spend your time, whom you spend your time with, how you dress, how much money you make, where you live, and so on. By choosing an occupation, you are directly affecting all these aspects of life. Also, choice of occupation should take into account individual interests and strengths. A hasty or poor choice could make a person very unhappy. 19. Most people in the United States can choose work that fulfills needs that are important to them. They are able to get an education that will allow them to pursue their dreams. There are many different kinds of jobs available. Industry and technology are state-of-the-art, so new types of jobs are always becoming available. Many countries are so poor that people work just to survive, or so traditional that people do not choose their careers themselves. 20. Possible answer: landscape architect, horse trainer, toy research and development

---

Chapter 1 REVIEW

Word Bank

business cycle
career
economy
job
job security
occupation
prestige
stereotype
unemployed
work
workplace

Vocabulary Review

Choose the word or phrase from the Word Bank that best completes each sentence. Write the answer on your paper.

1. A general belief held by many people about a certain activity or group of people is a(n) _____.

2. The state of business and use of resources in an area is the _____.

3. A group of similar or related jobs or job skills is known as a(n) _____.

4. Some people choose a type of work based on how important most people think it is, or its _____.

5. The pattern of ups and downs in supply and demand in the economy is known as the _____.

6. To be out of work is to be _____.

7. The way people spend their time earning a living is known as _____.

8. A formal or informal area where work is done is the _____.

9. The job path a person follows throughout a lifetime is a(n) _____.

10. The work you choose to do for pay is called a(n) _____.

11. An understanding that workers will not lose their jobs is _____.

Concept Review

Choose the word or phrase that best completes each sentence. Write the letter of the answer on your paper.

12. A week of work for full-time workers in the United States consists of _____.

   A 25 to 30 hours   C 40 to 50 hours
   B 30 to 40 hours   D 50 or more hours

13. The most important reason to work is _____.

   A money   C helping others
   B prestige   D different for each person

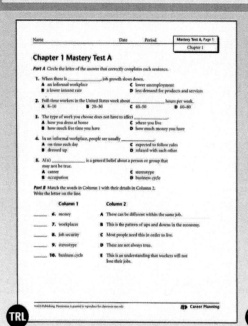

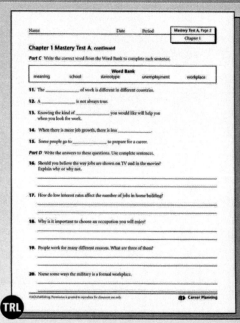

14. Being a ski instructor is an example of a job which _____.

    A does not require special clothing
    C involves a formal workplace

    B affects where a person lives
    D has great job security

15. An example of a work stereotype is that _____.

    A news reporters are very nosy
    C lawyers went to law school

    B accountants work with numbers
    D veterinarians treat animals

16. A bank where workers follow a strict schedule is an example of _____.

    A an informal workplace
    C a casual workplace

    B an unstructured workplace
    D a formal workplace

17. An example of a job affected most by the business cycle is that of _____.

    A an emergency-room nurse
    C an elementary school teacher

    B a carpenter working on new homes
    D a dentist

Critical Thinking

Write the answer to each question on your paper.

18. Why is it important for a person to carefully choose an occupation?

19. What advantages do American workers have over workers in many other countries?

20. Suppose you are interested in working in a casual, flexible workplace. What are three jobs you might like?

Test-Taking Tip

When studying for a test, work with a partner to write your own test questions. Then answer each other's questions. Check your answers.

Chapter 1 Mastery Test B, Pages 1–3

Chapter

2

Planning Guide

Assessing Yourself

		Student Text Lesson				
		Student Pages	Vocabulary	Lesson Review	Critical-Thinking Questions	Chapter Review
Lesson 1	Your Subject Area Strengths	20–23	✔	✔	✔	✔
Lesson 2	Your Abilities	24–31	✔	✔	✔	✔
Lesson 3	Your Interests	32–37	✔	✔	✔	✔
Lesson 4	Your Values	38–41	✔	✔	✔	✔
Lesson 5	Self-Assessment Profile	42–49	✔	✔	✔	✔

Chapter Activities

Student Text
Chapter 2 Portfolio Activity

Teacher's Resource Library
Chapter 2 Chapter Outline
Chapter 2 Self-Study Guide
Chapter 2 Portfolio Activity

Assessment Options

Student Text
Chapter 2 Review

Teacher's Resource Library
Chapter 2 Mastery Tests A and B

Teacher's Edition
Chapter 2 Alternative Assessment

	Student Text Features											Teaching Strategies					Learning Styles					Teacher's Resource Library				
Portfolio Activity	Writing Practice	Communication Connection	The Economy	Career Tip	Career Profile	On the Job	Gender and Careers	Think Positive	Technology Note	Get Involved	Background Information	Applications (Home, Community, Global, Environment)	Personal Journal	Online Connection	ELL/ESL Strategy	Visual/Spatial	Body/Kinesthetic	Interpersonal/Group Learning	Logical/Mathematical	Auditory/Verbal	Activities	Alternative Activities	Workbook Activities	Self-Study Guide	Chapter Outline
	23	23										22	21		21	22					3	3	3	✔	✔
			31					25			30	26				30	27		29	27,28	4	4	4	✔	✔
				33, 34, 37	37				32		34			37	33	36		35	36		5	5	5	✔	✔
						39				41		39, 40	39	41				40			6	6	6	✔	✔
50					48		44					44,46			45	48			44, 47	43,46	7	7	7	✔	✔

Alternative Activities

The Teacher's Resource Library (TRL) contains a set of lower-level worksheets called Alternative Activities. These worksheets cover the same content as the regular Activities but are written at a second-grade reading level.

Career Interest Inventory

The AGS Publishing Harrington-O'Shea Career Decision-Making System (CDM) may be used with this textbook. Students can use the CDM to explore their interests and identify careers. The CDM defines career areas that are indicated by students' response on the inventory.

Chapter 2: Assessing Yourself

pages 18–53

Audio CD 🎧

Teacher's Resource Library (TRL)

Workbook Activities 3–7

Activities 3–7

Alternative Activities 3–7

Portfolio Activity 2

Chapter 2 Chapter Outline

Chapter 2 Self-Study Guide

Chapter 2 Mastery Tests A and B
(Answer Keys for the Teacher's Resource Library begin on page 328 of this Teacher's Edition.)

Chapter 2 Self-Study Guide

Chapter 2

Assessing Yourself

How well do you know yourself? Are you an adventurous person who enjoys the challenge of climbing high mountains and sheer cliffs? Or do you prefer having your feet always firmly planted on the ground? Questions like these help you assess your interests, abilities, skills, and values. When you do so, you will know yourself better. You will be able to choose a job that you will do well. You will be able to choose a career that will make you happy.

Goals for Learning

◆ To recognize the importance of assessing one's abilities and interests

◆ To identify a variety of ability and interest areas

◆ To identify career groups of interest

◆ To identify a variety of personal values

◆ To complete a self-assessment profile

Introducing the Chapter

Have students look at the photo on page 18 in the student edition and describe what is happening in the picture. Invite students to tell what impression the man hanging from the rope makes. Discuss how the man might have decided to do this activity. What did he have to know about himself? Have a volunteer read the introductory paragraph aloud. Explain that when you assess something, you make up your mind how important or valuable it is. Ask students to tell what they think is involved in assessing themselves.

Have students read the Goals for Learning. Ask them to tell what they think will be involved in each one by rephrasing each goal in their own words.

Career Tips

Ask volunteers to read the career tips that appear in the margins throughout the chapter. Then discuss them with the class.

Alternative Assessment

The Alternative Assessment box on page 53 of the Chapter Review includes activities using various learning styles to assess students' understanding of the Goals for Learning.

19

Chapter Outline, Page 1
Chapter 2

Name _____ Date _____ Period _____

Assessing Yourself

Directions Fill in the outline below. Filling in the blanks will help you as you read and study Chapter 2.

I. Lesson 1: Your Subject Area Strengths (pp. 20–23)

  A. Subject Area Strengths

    1. Things you can do that come from training or practice are _____.

    2. Competency is the ability _____.

  B. Favorite Subjects and Skills

    1. Think about the specific _____ you learned in your favorite _____ subjects.

  C. Achievements

    1. An _____ is something you earned based on performance.

    2. You can rate your competence by looking at your _____ over time.

    3. You can also rate your competence by _____ yourself with others.

II. Lesson 2: Your Abilities (pp. 24–31)

  A. Abilities

    1. The things you do well are your _____.

    2. Self-confidence is _____.

  B. Developing Abilities

    1. Find out what abilities a school subject or job _____.

    2. Areas outside of school can also give you _____ about your abilities.

III. Lesson 3: Your Interests (pp. 32–37)

  A. Interests

    1. Things that you like, or want to know more about, are your _____.

    2. Choose which _____ group is most important to you.

©AGS Publishing. Permission is granted to reproduce for classroom use only.

Career Planning

Chapter Outline, Page 2
Chapter 2

Name _____ Date _____ Period _____

Assessing Yourself, continued

  B. Interest Areas and Careers

    1. See what _____ are listed under each interest area.

  C. Career Groups

    1. Occupations in a career group are related by _____, _____, and _____.

    2. Try to find out what workers in an _____ do.

IV. Lesson 4: Your Values (pp. 38–41)

  A. Values

    1. A value is what is _____.

    2. Values get stronger or change with _____.

  B. Work Values

    1. A _____ is something people want to get out of a job.

  C. Values Affect Careers

    1. Your work values can affect your _____ choices.

    2. Look at your values to get an idea of the _____ you might make.

V. Lesson 5: Self-Assessment Profile (pp. 42–49)

  A. Self-Assessment Profile

    1. See how your school experience, abilities, values, and interests may match a _____.

    2. Use the information in the Self-Assessment Profile as a _____.

  B. A Portfolio

    1. A portfolio is a tool you can use as you explore _____ choices and develop a career _____.

©AGS Publishing. Permission is granted to reproduce for classroom use only.

Career Planning

Chapter 2 Chapter Outline

TRL

Lesson at a Glance

Chapter 2 Lesson 1

Overview Students identify their favorite school subjects and some of their skills and achievements.

Objectives

- To identify academic interests and skills
- To list achievements and areas of competence

Student Pages 20–23

Teacher's Resource Library

Workbook Activity 3

Activity 3

Alternative Activity 3

Vocabulary

achievement	self-assessment
competency	skill

Write the vocabulary words on the board. Read the words aloud and discuss their meanings. Then ask students to write a sentence about themselves for each word. The sentence should suggest the meaning of the word.

 Warm-Up Activity

Ask students to list the classes they are taking now and rate them in order of preference. Then have them rate the classes according to how well they do in them. Compare the rankings. Are they the same? Discuss reasons why students like some classes more than others.

2 Teaching the Lesson

Explain to students that assessing their school performance is one step in creating a realistic "picture" of themselves. They can use this picture to help guide them in choosing a career path that is right for them.

Discuss with students how student understanding in a subject area is determined. In most classes, teachers use a combination of written work, test scores, class discussion, and project completion to evaluate how well a student has mastered core concepts of a subject.

Self-assessment
Finding out your strengths and weaknesses
Skill
Something you can do that comes from training or practice
Competency
Being able to do something well

In this lesson, you will use **self-assessment** to find out what you have liked learning in school. You can use this knowledge in many ways. You may be required to tell an admissions counselor or an employer what you are good at. Or, you may need to write a personal essay for an application. You should be able to describe your school experience and what your plans are for the future. To do this, you need to know what **skills** you have. A skill is something you can do because you have practiced or trained. You also need to know in which skills you have developed **competency**. When you have competency in something, you are able to do it well.

What Are Your Favorite School Subjects?

To investigate your skills and competencies, start by choosing what school subjects you like the most. Look at the school subjects listed here. Choose the two you like the best. For help, look at the list of possible class titles under each school subject.

Agriculture	**Business and Management**
animal science	accounting
farming	business administration
forestry	management
horticulture	marketing
landscaping	sales
Art	**Clerical Studies**
drawing	office practices
fashion design	spreadsheets and databases
graphic design	typing
interior decorating	word processing
painting	
sculpture	

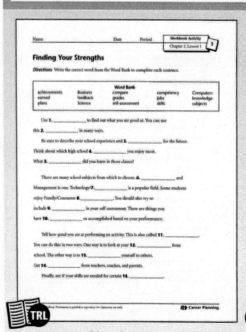

Workbook Activity 3

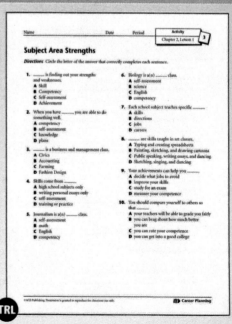

Activity 3

English
communications
creative writing
essay writing
journalism
literature
public speaking

Family/Consumer Science
child care
cooking and food service
cosmetology (beauty care)
sewing

Finance
accounting
business law
economics

Health
health
physical education
recreational studies

Languages
Chinese
French
German
Italian
Japanese
Russian
Spanish

Math
algebra
basic math
calculus
geometry
pre-algebra
statistics

Music
band
choir
dance
drama
orchestra

Science
biology
chemistry
computer science
earth science
environmental science
geology
physical science
physics

Shop/Industrial Arts
automotive
carpentry
machine shop
metal working
plumbing
printing
woodworking

Social Studies
civics
government
history
political science
psychology
social work
sociology

Technology/Computers
computer-aided design (CAD)
computer programming
computer technology
drafting
engineering
electronics

As students read the subjects and possible class titles, be ready to offer a brief description of those with which students may not be familiar. You might have on hand a student handbook or a list of course offerings for your school. Assist students in placing classes they have taken under the correct subject area.

When students assess achievements, have them consider clubs, sports, part-time work, and other extra-curricular activities as well as classes.

3 Reinforce and Extend

PERSONAL JOURNAL

 As students choose their favorite subjects, ask them to write these on their own paper, leaving space after each. Then have them write several sentences listing specific activities and ideas they enjoy or find satisfying about each subject. As they progress through the lesson, students can add to their journals the skills they have developed as well as their achievements in school.

ELL/ESL STRATEGY

 Language Objective: *To understand vocabulary for different subject areas*

Students who are learning English may be unfamiliar with some of the terms used in class titles, such as *animal science, horticulture, machine shop,* and *cosmetology*. Pair students with an English-proficient partner to read the lists on pages 20–21. Any words that are unfamiliar to both partners can be marked with sticky notes and addressed in a whole-class discussion.

Visual/Spatial

Before having students brainstorm skills they have gained from a class, model making a word web to show skills associated with a common class, such as basic math. (Skills might include using logic, being able to add and subtract mentally, estimating total purchases in a store, comparing cost per unit of two products, budgeting, and so on.) Ask students to create their own word webs for the subjects they have chosen. Then provide guidance as they analyze the skills they have listed. This analysis can help students to understand how school learning carries over into the "real world."

AT HOME

As students think of skills they have learned in previous classes, they may find it helpful to review any materials they have saved from those classes. Since students probably only saved items that they were proud of or found especially interesting, the review should also enable them to evaluate further why they liked this class and how much progress they made in it.

What Skills Do You Have?

Now that you have chosen your favorite subjects, you need to choose some specific skills you learned in a course. This step may be more difficult than the first step. Think about why you chose the subjects you did. What skills do you have in those areas? For example, if you chose art as a favorite subject, you might have the following skills:

- sketching
- drawing portraits
- drawing cartoons
- etching on glass
- editing music or film
- painting
- making pottery

This student shows her skill of using a pottery wheel.

What Are Some of Your Achievements?

You could also think about some of your **achievements**. An achievement is something you have earned or done successfully based on your performance. For example, an achievement might be that a photograph you took won a prize at an art show. Knowing your achievements can show your competence—how good you are at performing an activity. You can rate your competence two ways. One way is to look at your grades over time. Let's say your grades show that you are better in math than in English. You would rate yourself as good in math. Another way is to compare yourself with others. You can use grades or feedback from teachers, coaches, and parents to do this. If you feel that others are better than you at a certain activity, you might rate yourself as average.

Lesson 1 Review Write your answers to these questions on a sheet of paper.

1. Why is self-assessment important?

2. List the two school subjects you like the most.

3. What is the difference between skill and competency?

4. List two skills you have and an achievement in each.

5. How would you rate yourself in the area you chose as your favorite subject? Why did you rate yourself the way you did?

Writing Practice

What was your most enjoyable learning experience? Recall a class or an after-school activity you especially liked. For example, you might remember a speech class in which you did well. Or you might recall a cooking or tennis class. Write a journal entry. Describe the experience. Explain why you enjoyed it.

Communication Connection

Ask students what each person involved in an interview communicates. (Questions communicate what one person wants to find out, and responses communicate the answers as well as how the interviewee feels about the subject.) Have students read the Communication Connection feature on page 23. Invite them to suggest thoughtful questions they might ask a prospective employer. (*What skills are needed for this job? What does it contribute toward the big picture of your ___ [company, office, school, etc.]?*)

Lesson 1 Review Answers

1. Self-assessment is important to enable a person to choose a career path based on his or her skills, competency, interests, and achievements. **2.** Answers will vary. **3.** A skill is something you have trained or practiced to be good at while a competency is the ability to do something well. **4.** Answers will vary. **5.** Answers will vary.

Writing Practice

Read the Writing Practice assignment to students. Remind them that descriptive writing calls for exact and vivid details to recreate the experience. Sensory details such as colors, sounds, smells, and sights help focus a description. If students wish to re-create a scene from a class, you may want to suggest that they include dialogue. Invite interested students to share their recollections by reading aloud their journal entries.

Lesson at a Glance

Chapter 2 Lesson 2

Overview In this lesson, students assess their talents and abilities and consider ways to develop them further.

Objectives

- To identify work-related abilities
- To associate abilities with specific occupations
- To assess ways of developing abilities

Student Pages 24–31

Teacher's Resource Library

Workbook Activity 4

Activity 4

Alternative Activity 4

....

Vocabulary

ability
self-confidence

Have students give their own definitions for each vocabulary term and think of how each applies to them. Then ask them to tell how their experiences show how ability and self-confidence are related.

....

 Warm-Up Activity

Ask students to name a physical ability, a mental ability, a social ability, and a perceptual ability that is important to them. (Examples might include being strong or fast, being able to memorize things fast, being able to make friends easily, and being observant.) Explain that every person has a different set of abilities. In the section they will read now, they will consider 14 different categories of ability. As they read, they should decide which abilities describe them best and note the types of careers for which these abilities are essential.

Ability
A talent; something a person is able to do well

Self-confidence
Feeling good about oneself

An **ability** is something a person can do well. You know best what things you are good at. These are your abilities. People have different abilities. Some people do certain things better than others. Things you do well are your strengths. Things you have a hard time doing are your weaknesses. Everyone has strengths and weaknesses. In this lesson, you will learn about the 14 major work-related abilities.

How you feel about your ability to do an activity affects how you perform that activity. For example, if you feel you talk differently than others, you might not think you are a good communicator. You might not feel comfortable talking to people. So, you may not want to work in a job that requires you to talk to a lot of people. Or, you might be good at fixing computers. Knowing and believing that you are skilled with computers can help your **self-confidence**. Feeling good about yourself can help you to succeed. It can also help you find an occupation.

Now read about the 14 abilities on the next few pages. See what occupations are listed for each ability area. Think about what three or four abilities you believe are your strongest. These abilities are your strengths.

A photographer has artistic ability.

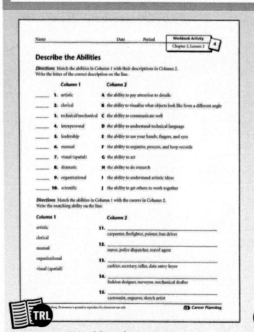

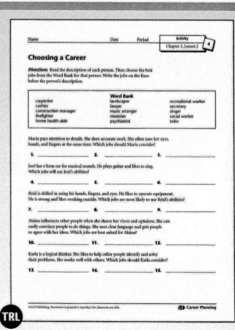

Artistic

People who have this ability understand artistic ideas. They may use their skills to draw, paint, sculpt, or take photographs. They may also use their artistic ability to decorate, design, or create products. Artistic ability is important in these careers:

- art director
- cartoonist
- commercial designer
- engraver
- fashion designer
- industrial designer
- interior designer
- photographic developer
- professional photographer
- sketch artist

Clerical

People who have clerical ability pay attention to details. They do accurate work. They often use their eyes, hands, and fingers at the same time. They might enter figures in books and forms, or operate calculators, computers, and other office machines. Here are some clerical careers:

- bookkeeping clerk
- cashier
- data entry keyer
- medical records technician
- secretary
- teller
- police dispatcher
- postal service clerk

Interpersonal

People with this ability can communicate well. They are understanding, friendly, adaptable, and polite in many different situations. Most employers would agree that this is an important ability in any career. Careers that require interpersonal ability include the following:

- bank manager
- customer service representative
- elementary school teacher
- flight attendant
- home health aide
- human resources assistant
- police officer
- retail salesperson

2 Teaching the Lesson

Be sure students understand that abilities are not just things one is born knowing how to do well. Most people must develop abilities through learning, effort, and practice. Ask volunteers to suggest specific ways a person might develop an ability to pay attention to details, to treat people in a friendly and understanding manner, and so on.

Have students scan the subheadings in the lesson and identify any whose meanings they do not know. *Interpersonal* skills, for example, involve the ways people relate to one another. Most jobs calling for strong interpersonal skills are those in which workers meet the public, or deal with many people every day.

3 Reinforce and Extend

Think Positive

After students have read the Think Positive feature on page 25, ask them to list one or two of their abilities. They might talk with family members, friends, and teachers and add more abilities that others see in them. Remind students that some of their abilities are latent—that is, they must be developed through activities and classes. As they try new things and take new courses, students can add to their list of abilities.

LEARNING STYLES

Interpersonal/Group Learning

Ask students to write one note card to each person in the class to describe admirable qualities or abilities they have observed in that person. Stress that the notes are intended to reflect a realistic but positive image of the individual through classmates' eyes. After students have read their notes from classmates, ask them what effect the notes had on them. **Note:** You should read through the notes before giving them to the students to read. Remove any notes that are not positive.

Language

People who have this ability can use spelling, grammar, and punctuation correctly. They are skilled at writing letters, manuals, reports, proposals, or stories. They can speak clearly. They can also understand and respond to feedback. They know what questions to ask and when to ask them. Being able to communicate well through speaking and writing is a basic skill needed in any career. Language ability is very important in these careers:

- editor
- paralegal
- receptionist
- reporter
- sales manager
- secretary
- social worker
- special education teacher
- translator

A leader sets good examples for others.

Leadership

People who have leadership ability are able to get others to work together. They also have the ability to share thoughts, feelings, and ideas in order to explain a position. Leaders must be able to react quickly in emergencies. They may make choices that involve money or the safety of other people. The ability to lead is important in these careers:

- administrative assistant
- executive secretary
- educational administrator
- food service manager
- lawyer
- property or real estate manager
- surgeon

Manual

People with manual ability are skilled in the use of their hands, fingers, and eyes. They use these skills to operate equipment, adjust controls, use hand tools, or to build products. They can read and follow directions well. Careers in which manual ability is important may involve outdoor work. The jobs often require physical strength. Examples of these careers include the following:

- animal caretaker
- bus driver
- carpenter
- firefighter
- forest and conservation worker
- highway maintenance worker
- landscaper
- machine operator
- painter
- product assembler

Mathematical/Numerical

People who have mathematical and numerical ability are very good at solving problems in business, technology, or science. They use math skills to solve these problems. They are also able to express mathematical ideas aloud and in writing. Today's employers value mathematical and numerical ability in many careers. Here are some examples:

- accountant
- bookkeeping clerk
- cashier
- computer programmer
- computer software engineer
- financial analyst
- information systems manager
- mathematician
- medical assistant
- optometrist
- pharmacist
- teller

LEARNING STYLES

Auditory/Verbal
To help students learn the 14 abilities discussed in this lesson, assign one or more of them to pairs or small groups. Partners or groups are responsible for a presentation to explain an ability, model one or more aspects of it, and role-play a scene in which a worker uses the ability in an everyday situation.

LEARNING STYLES

Body/Kinesthetic
You might suggest that students select one of the 14 abilities and create an activity that would show an individual's level of skill in that area. For example, a language activity might call for a job applicant to give a short talk on a subject or to correct language mistakes in a document. A test for manual ability might ask the individual to assemble loose parts into a simple machine or demonstrate how to use an appliance. You may want to encourage students who choose the same ability to join efforts and ideas to make one creative activity.

Auditory/Verbal

Ask students to write several sentences praising a classmate's abilities. (Names should be omitted.) Challenge students to incorporate the written contributions into a song about the things classmates can do well. They will need to adapt the sentences as lyrics. They might use the melody and rhythms of an existing song or create an original composition. Allow time for the song to be presented to the class.

Musical/Dramatic

People who have musical ability have a keen ear for musical sounds. They might play instruments, sing or teach, or direct instrumental or vocal music. People with dramatic ability are skilled at acting. They interpret roles and express ideas and emotions through gestures and facial expressions. They may also produce, direct, or perform in plays. Careers that use musical and/or dramatic ability include the following:

- choral director
- dancer
- drama teacher
- music arranger
- musician
- radio/TV/movie producer
- singer

Organizational

Individuals with organizational ability know how to plan. They make sure the most important task is done first and on time. They can organize, process, and maintain records and information in a orderly way. Most employers expect employees to be well organized. Careers in which organizational ability is important include these:

- air traffic controller
- computer systems analyst
- medical and health services manager
- nurse
- operations research analyst
- police dispatcher
- tax preparer
- travel agent

A police dispatcher must be organized.

Persuasive

Persuasive people can influence others by sharing their own views and opinions. They can convince people to do things. They can get people to agree with certain ideas. Persuasive people are able to talk to others using clear language. They are good at selling things. These are some careers in which the ability to be persuasive is important for success:

- construction manager
- lawyer
- marketing manager
- psychiatrist
- retail salesperson
- secondary school teacher

Scientific

Individuals who have this ability are good at research, logic, or scientific thinking. They use their skills to solve problems. They might apply their skills in the medical sciences, life sciences, or natural sciences. They may diagnose or treat human and animal injuries and illnesses. Often they base their conclusions on information that can be measured or proven. Scientific ability is important for success in many careers. Here are some examples:

- agricultural inspector
- athletic trainer
- biologist
- dental assistant
- dietician
- electrical engineer
- licensed nurse practitioner
- physical therapist
- veterinarian

Social

People with social ability use logical thinking and special skills to counsel others. These people may help others identify and solve personal problems. People with social ability work well with others. Individuals who have this ability may gather and study information about other people. They may also work one-on-one or with groups of people. Careers requiring good social skills include the following:

- educational, vocational, or school counselor
- home health aide
- nurse
- psychiatric aide
- recreational worker
- social worker
- sociologist

Logical/Mathematical
Discuss with students the importance of research and logic in developing both scientific and persuasive abilities. Explain that these abilities can be learned through practice. Present a problem your community or school is facing. (Examples might include whether to eliminate extracurricular sports, music, and art because of lack of funds, or whether to allow a large subdivision to be built on farmland.) Group students by their position on a chosen issue. Have them work together to find evidence to support or prove their position, and then explain their conclusion and list evidence they have found that supports it.

Visual (Spatial)

People with visual or spatial ability can visualize what objects would look like from a different angle or point of view. They can see differences in size and shape. They understand how things fit together or come apart. Visual or spatial ability is important for success in many careers. Some of these careers include the following:

- carpenter
- dentist
- fashion designer
- graphic designer
- interior designer
- landscaping and groundskeeping worker
- mechanical drafter
- surveyor

Technical/Mechanical

Individuals with this ability understand technical and mechanical language. They understand how to set up and operate machines such as vending machines. They can also determine how to use or fix various machines. Many careers require technical/mechanical ability, including these:

- airplane pilot
- automotive master mechanic
- computer service technician
- electrician
- electronic equipment installer and repairer
- heating and air-conditioning mechanic

How Can You Develop Your Abilities?

To develop your abilities, you need to get involved in activities. You need to get experience. If you have never had a chance to play an instrument or to sing, how would you know your musical ability? Self-assessment can help you see what abilities you have. It can also show you in which areas you want to get more experience. It is helpful to know what abilities a job requires. You can then find out more about how you can develop that ability. For example, if you want to become an engineer, you might be more willing to learn about math and physics.

A landscaper has visual ability.

Activities outside of school can also give you information about your abilities. For example, if you play a sport, you might learn whether you are a good leader. Do you want to be the captain of the team? Do you enjoy leading or being in charge of others? Feedback from others can be helpful. They can give you specific information on how well you are performing a task. You can also find out if you need to work on certain skills in order to get better at them.

Lesson 2 Review Write your answers to these questions on a sheet of paper.

1. What is an ability?

2. What are your four strongest abilities?

3. How can your self-confidence affect your abilities?

4. What school subjects, out-of-school activities, part-time work, or volunteer activities can help you improve in an ability area? Have you done any of these yet?

The Economy

A current issue related to the U.S. economy is offshore outsourcing. In offshore outsourcing, American companies give work to employees in other countries. They hire the employees to do some specific jobs. For example, a computer company may hire workers in India. They pay the employees to help customers who call the company. The American companies save money because employees in India will work for less. But the American companies lay off the American workers who had done the job. Some people feel that this type of outsourcing leads to more unemployment for Americans. Others believe that it helps American companies make more money. They say that strong companies help the American economy. Lawmakers are currently debating the issue of offshore outsourcing.

Lesson 2 Review Answers

1. An ability is a talent or something a person does well. **2.** Answers will vary. **3.** Having self-confidence can help you be successful and develop your abilities. **4.** Answers will vary.

The Economy

Ask volunteers to read The Economy on page 31 aloud. Write *offshore outsourcing* on the board. Above it write component words *off* and *shore*, and *out* and *source*. Ask students to define each word, then tell how the meanings combine to give the meaning of *offshore outsourcing*. Point out that this technique involves sending jobs outside the boundaries of a country in order to save money. Have volunteers find and summarize articles on the subject of offshore outsourcing. On the basis of this information, encourage students to debate both sides of the issue.

Chapter 2 Lesson 3

Overview In this lesson, students analyze six interest areas and explore career groups to decide which careers their personal interests suit them for.

Objectives

- To assess personal interests
- To explore career groups
- To select career groups based on interests

Student Pages 32–37

Teacher's Resource Library

Workbook Activity 5

Activity 5

Alternative Activity 5

Vocabulary

career group
interest

Write the vocabulary terms on the board and have students look them up in the Glossary. After discussing their meanings, have students write a sentence using each term.

 Warm-Up Activity

Invite volunteers to name some of their interests, then some of their abilities. Ask how they think these two concepts are different. Before they read the section, have students consider whether it is better to choose a career based on an interest or on an ability.

Technology Note

After students read the Technology Note on page 32, point out that their Web search will turn up a more manageable number of sites if they enter an additional term in the search engine, for example, they might type in "Career Profiles, Business."

Interest
Something you like, want to know more about, or want to see or do

Career group
Occupations with related abilities, interests, and education requirements

Interests are things that you like or want to know more about. If you know your interests, you can more easily plan a career. For many people, interests are things that they can do well. But you might have an interest in something that you cannot do well. In this way, interests are different from abilities. It can be easier to assess your abilities in an area you like or have interest in.

By exploring your interests, you can discover what school or work plans might be the best for you. This lesson will show you two ways to find out your interests. One way is to choose which of the six interest areas are the most important to you. Another way is to use **career groups**. A career group includes several related occupations.

What Are Your Interests?

Look at the six interest areas on pages 33 and 34. Interests can show you details about yourself. See what occupations are listed under each interest area. You will probably have interests in several areas. Think about two interest areas that best describe you and your interests.

Technology Note

You can find career profiles on the Internet. Type key words such as "Career Profiles" on a search engine. You will find many Web sites about careers. In fact, you will probably be surprised at how many different careers exist. The sites provide some or all of the following facts:
- Pay
- Education and training needed
- Job descriptions
- Future demand
- Related careers

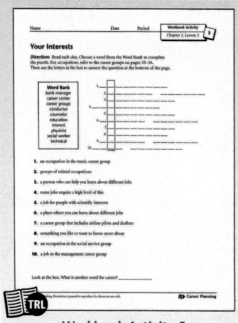

Workbook Activity 5

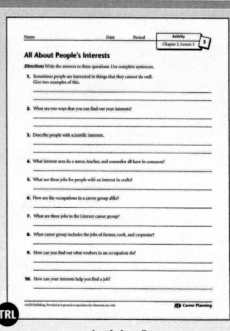

Activity 5

Talking to others is a good way to find a job. Ask people for job tips. Do their companies have job openings? Do they have friends who work in your field?

The Arts

People interested in the arts enjoy music, painting, writing, and entertaining others. They are creative and independent. They enjoy visiting museums, going to the theater, and reading books. Here are some jobs related to the arts:

- actor/actress
- artist
- editor
- fashion designer
- musician
- photographer
- radio/TV announcer
- reporter

Business

People with business interests are leaders. They are good at selling things. They can also easily get people to think the way they do. They enjoy coming up with new ideas. People interested in business might work at these jobs:

- bank manager
- business executive
- lawyer
- salesperson

Crafts

People with interests in crafts like to work with tools and build things. They enjoy seeing the results of their work. They are interested in mechanical activities. They like work that requires physical strength. Jobs related to crafts include the following:

- animal caretaker
- auto mechanic
- construction equipment operator
- cook
- electrician
- farmer
- truck driver

Office Operations

These people work with words and numbers. They like jobs in which they know exactly what to do. They are well organized. Here are some jobs in the office operations area:

- accountant
- bank teller
- computer operator
- medical records technician
- secretary
- tax preparer

Assessing Yourself Chapter 2 **33**

2 Teaching the Lesson

Be sure students understand that the jobs listed under each interest area are those in which the worker gets to carry out some duties or tasks that fit in with that interest area. Many of the jobs combine two or more interest areas. For example, a social worker deals with people but also must have office operation skills and a scientific mind.

Point out the special meaning of *crafts* as used on page 33. Rather than artistic ability, the term refers to an occupation or trade requiring manual dexterity. You may wish to point out that as a verb *craft* refers to the making of an object with care, skill, and ingenuity.

3 Reinforce and Extend

ELL/ESL STRATEGY

Language Objective: *To learn job title vocabulary*

ELL students will need strategies for understanding and remembering the lengthy lists of job titles, especially since they appear without context. Be sure students are familiar with the endings *-er, -or, -ist,* and *-ian,* which indicate "one who." When they see one of these endings, students should analyze the root word that appears before the ending: a banker works in a bank, an editor edits or corrects the writing of others, an electrician works with electricity, a psychologist knows psychology, or the reasons for the behavior of others. Students can also work with English proficient readers to create cards for job titles. They can place the job name and a definition as well as simple symbols and illustrations, including tools the worker might use, on a card. Then students can use the cards to learn the titles.

Social Interests/ Abilities

People with social interests and abilities are able to understand other people. They notice others' goals, motivations, and intentions. They are able to work effectively with people. In part, this ability to communicate with—and sometimes to manipulate—others stems from the capacity to empathize with others, to work cooperatively with others, and to be sensitive to the feelings of others.

Career Tip
When talking to others about finding a job, share your career goals with them.

Scientific

People with scientific interests believe math and science are important. They are curious and creative. They study a lot and often work by themselves. They enjoy thinking about ideas. Scientific jobs include the following:

- architect
- biologist
- computer scientist
- economist
- forester

- mechanical engineer
- medical lab technician
- pharmacist
- physician
- veterinarian

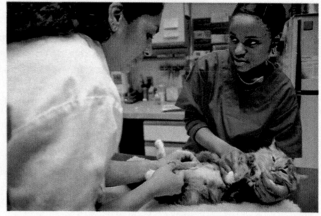

A veterinarian may have scientific and social interests.

Social

Social people enjoy helping others. They like to provide services for others. Social people get along well with others. They have good communication skills. People with social interests might have one of these jobs:

- clinical psychologist
- counselor
- nurse
- police officer/sheriff

- recreation worker
- school administrator
- social worker
- teacher

It is important to know what your interests are. Counselors, college admissions officers, and employers will ask what you are interested in. You can use the words from the six interest areas to answer their questions.

What Career Groups Interest You?

You are now ready to explore the career groups. A career group includes related occupations. The occupations in each group are related by abilities, interests, and educational requirements. Read the occupations under all 18 groups listed on the next two pages.

Art	Clerical	Customer Service
• art teacher	• cashier	• hair stylist
• artist	• court reporter	• flight attendant
• fashion designer	• hotel/motel clerk	• park ranger
• floral designer	• medical records technician	• police officer
• graphic designer	• police dispatcher	• security guard
• interior designer	• receptionist	• taxi driver
• photographer	• secretary	• waiter/waitress
	• word processor	

Data Analysis	Education	Entertainment
• accountant	• college administrator	• actor/actress
• auditor	• college professor	• advertising manager
• bookkeeping clerk	• elementary school teacher	• comedian
• computer operator	• preschool teacher	• model
• financial analyst	• school administrator	• producer
• payroll clerk	• secondary school teacher	• radio/TV announcer
• real estate appraiser		• radio/TV program assistant
		• stage director

Legal	Literary	Management
• customs inspector	• editor	• bank manager
• FBI agent	• novelist	• business executive
• insurance claims adjuster	• playwright	• farm manager
• judge	• poet	• hotel/motel manager
• lawyer	• reporter	• office manager
• legal assistant	• technical writer	• restaurant manager
• police detective	• translator	• store manager
• private investigator		

Logical/Mathematical

List the 18 career group headings on the board leaving space under each. Ask students to name skills that would be appropriate for each kind of career. Then call out occupations randomly from pages 35 and 36 and ask students to deduce where each should be placed. If students are unfamiliar with an occupation, discuss what it involves or have students look it up in a reference book. Students should be able to give reasons for their placement of jobs.

LEARNING STYLES

Visual/Spatial

Students who learn best through visual information can become familiar with the career groups by drawing a symbol, illustration, or cartoon for each to show what the occupations in that group have in common. Display the names of the groups on a poster or bulletin board. Invite students to place their visuals next to the heads and explain why they are appropriate.

Manual
- animal caretaker
- construction laborer
- food preparation worker
- landscaper
- machine operator
- product assembler
- truck driver

Math and Science
- architect
- biologist
- chemist
- computer programmer
- database administrator
- engineer
- physicist
- Web site developer

Medical/Dental
- chiropractor
- dental hygienist
- dentist
- family practitioner
- optometrist
- pharmacist
- physical therapist
- veterinarian

Music
- choreographer
- composer
- conductor
- dancer
- music teacher
- musician
- producer
- singer

Personal Service
- child care worker
- coach
- emergency medical technician
- home health aide
- recreation leader
- vocational teacher

Skilled Crafts
- auto technician/ mechanic
- carpenter
- cook
- desktop publishing specialist
- electrician
- farmer
- electronics repairer
- military service

Social Service
- clergy
- clinical psychologist
- counselor
- dental hygienist
- nurse
- social worker
- sociologist

Sales
- auto salesperson
- buyer
- financial planner
- insurance agent
- real estate agent
- retail sales worker
- travel agent

Technical
- air traffic controller
- airline pilot
- computer support specialist
- diagnostic medical sonographer
- drafter
- medical technician
- surveyor
- technical illustrator

Now choose the two career groups you like the most. What occupations appeal to you from those two groups? If you do not know what workers in an occupation do, ask your teacher or counselor or look it up in your school's career center. Here is an example of how your interests can help you learn what jobs you might like:

> Marcos likes people. He always likes to meet new people. He enjoys talking to them and finding out about them. Marcos also has an after-school job. He takes care of two children who live next door to him. He really likes helping them play and learn.

Marcos sees that he has social interest. He might want to think about a career as a teacher or child-care provider. He would probably be most happy in an occupation where he works with people every day. You will find out how you can get more information about an occupation in Chapter 3.

Lesson 3 Review Write your answers to these questions on a sheet of paper.

1. What is an interest?
2. List the two interest areas you like the most.
3. What is the difference between an interest and an ability?
4. What is a career group?
5. List the two career groups you like the most.

Career Profile

Nurse Practitioner

Nursing is a career for which there continues to be great demand. One nursing job that is growing in popularity is nurse practitioner. A nurse practitioner is a Registered Nurse who has two to three years additional training. This training allows the nurse practitioner to take on added responsibilities. A nurse practitioner is supervised by a doctor. Doctors often have nurse practitioners take medical histories and treat routine problems. A nurse practitioner may order lab tests and prescribe some medicines. Nurse practitioners work for hospitals and private medical practices. They also work in nursing homes, women's clinics, and even the Peace Corps. Students in Nurse Practitioner programs usually must be Registered Nurses. The programs award a master's degree or a certificate.

Lesson 3 Review Answers

1. An interest is something you like. **2.** Answers will vary. **3.** An interest is something you enjoy doing while an ability is something you can do well. **4.** A career group is several occupations with related abilities, interests, and education requirements. **5.** Answers will vary.

Career Profile

Nurse Practitioner

Read the feature subheading aloud and have students predict what a nurse practitioner is. Then have students read the feature on page 37 silently and list features of the job that make it different from the traditional nursing job. (More school is required; do more medical jobs than nurses, such as treating conditions, ordering lab tests, and prescribing medicines.) Ask interested students to find out about any local nurse practitioners and where they work.

ONLINE CONNECTION

The Career Services Web site for the University of Wisconsin at Eau Claire offers a thorough and easy-to-read career profile for nurse practitioner at www. uwec.edu/Career/Students/explore/ Profiles/nurse%20practitioner.htm. At www.jobprofiles.org/heapediatric. htm a pediatric nurse practitioner tells about her work experience and career choice in a personal response.

Lesson at a Glance

Chapter 2 Lesson 4

Overview In this lesson, students consider which values are most important to them and how this will affect their career choice.

Objectives

- To define values
- To identify personal and work values
- To evaluate ways in which values can guide career choice

Student Pages 38–41

Teacher's Resource Library

Workbook Activity 6

Activity 6

Alternative Activity 6

Vocabulary

risk
value
work value

Write the vocabulary words on the board and give students a definition for each one. Have students write a paragraph using the words and providing an example of each.

 Warm-Up Activity

Ask students to name the things they value. List these in categories such as Material Possessions, Ideas, and Actions. Through discussion, have students select a "top ten" list of values. Then encourage them to make their own lists, placing the values from least important to most important. Explain that values are individual and personal, not right or wrong.

 Teaching the Lesson

Be sure students distinguish between the general categories of personal values on page 38 and the list of work values on pages 39 and 40. Explain that work values refer to the material things and qualities a job can offer.

> **Value**
> *What is important to a person*

You have assessed your abilities and interests. Now you will look at your personal needs. To do this, think about what things are important to you. These are your **values.** Values are beliefs that get stronger or change with experience. Your values are personal. They are related to how you think and act. Here are some common personal values.

Helping Others	Community	Environmentalism
Improving the quality of the lives of others	Taking an active part in community events	Conserving or restoring the environment
Family	**Leisure**	**Personal Growth**
Raising a family or caring for aged parents	Having time and money for fun activities	Working on self-improvement
Personal Satisfaction	**Spirituality**	
Achieving a comfortable way of life	Doing things that follow one's personal beliefs	

Many of your values come from your family.

38 Chapter 2 *Assessing Yourself*

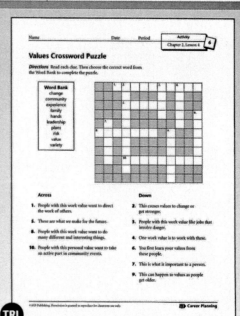

Workbook Activity 6

Name the Value

Directions The statements below might have been made by people with different values. Decide which value is important to the speaker. After each statement write **H** for Helping Others, **S** for Good Salary, **M** for Work with Your Mind, **O** for Outdoor Work, or **P** for Prestige.

1. It is silly to go to college if you don't get a high paying job when you are done. _____
2. I want to go to medical school because I enjoy studying. _____
3. I would like to become the president of a college. That's a very important person. _____
4. I would like to be a doctor at a clinic for poor people. _____
5. I like trying to solve hard puzzles. _____
6. I want to be a gardener because I love to be outside. _____
7. It would be great to be a college professor. They are always learning new things. _____
8. I am going to be a doctor because I want to make a lot of money. _____
9. It is important to think about other people's needs. _____
10. People should try to learn as much as they can. _____
11. I don't want to be a banker because I would have to work indoors all day. _____
12. I only want to teach if I will earn enough money to buy a nice home. _____
13. I want to be a teacher because I like helping other people. _____
14. I want to be a gardener at the White House because everyone would respect me. _____
15. I would only like construction work if I were outside most of the time. _____

Activity 6

Values Crossword Puzzle

Directions Read each clue. Then choose the correct word from the Word Bank to complete the puzzle.

Word Bank
change
community
experience
family
hands
leadership
plans
risk
value
variety

Across

1. People with this work value want to direct the work of others.
5. These are what we make for the future.
6. People with this work value want to do many different and interesting things.
10. People with this personal value want to take an active part in community events.

Down

2. This causes values to change or get stronger.
3. People with this work value like jobs that involve danger.
4. One work value is to work with these.
6. You first learn your values from these people.
7. This is what is important to a person.
9. This can happen to values as people get older.

What Are Your Values?

Think about what your values are. Ask yourself, "What things are important to me?" You first learn your values from your family and your community. Most of you have met or will meet people who have ideas that are different from yours. As you continue your education or enter the workforce, you will meet even more people. Many of these people will have experiences and values that are different from yours. As you get older, you might change your values or accept the values of others.

What Are Your Work Values?

In this lesson, you will explore your **work values.** Work values are related to personal values, but may be different. (In Chapter 3, you will further explore the differences between work and personal values.) Look at the 14 work values below and on page 40. Read their definitions. Then choose the four values that are most important to you.

Creativity	Good Salary
Having a job in which you can use your imagination	Being paid well for your work

High Achievement	Independence
Being able to do things of importance or succeed on a job that is difficult	Doing work that lets you be your own boss, and doing the job the way you want to without someone watching over you

Job Security	Leadership
Having a steady job from which you are unlikely to be fired	Directing the work of others and making choices affecting others

Outdoor Work	Physical Activity
Working outside most of the time	Doing work that calls for moving about and using physical strength

❸ Reinforce and Extend

On the Job

Survey the class briefly to learn how often they send e-mails and the main purpose of their e-mails. Point out that e-mail is important for on-the-job communication too. Ask a volunteer to read the On the Job feature on page 39. Have students list ways in which job e-mail and personal e-mail differ. (Personal e-mails often do not use standard spelling, capitalization, or punctuation. Usually, they are informal and chatty rather than professional and informative.)

PERSONAL JOURNAL

Students may find it easier to sort out the values that are important to them in a personal journal entry. First, have students list the things and ideals that are most important to them. Then have them add qualities and characteristics that they think would make a workplace ideal.

IN THE ENVIRONMENT

Many young people value the environment and feel strongly about conserving or helping it. Encourage interested students to research careers in environmental science or protection, or ways in which their values can be practiced in the workplace. They can use library books and Web sites to gather information. Some students may wish to interview local businesses and employers to see what rules or guidelines they follow to protect the environment.

Encourage students to talk with family members or close family friends who work. They can ask which of the work values listed on pages 39 and 40 are most important to the adults and why. Have students compare the responses they got from adults with the choices they made after reading the lesson. How were they different? Was this surprising to students?

LEARNING STYLES

Body/Kinesthetic

Write short paragraphs that set up a scene in which students have an opportunity to model personal values. For example, one scene might call for one person to confront another about littering (environmentalism). Another could focus on feelings about family or helping others. Still another might involve friends who try improve themselves (personal growth). Have partners or small groups make up impromptu skits. Ask the audience to identify the personal value illustrated in each skit. Then discuss how it fits into their lives.

Risk	
A chance of danger or loss	

Prestige	Risk
Having a job in which you are respected and feel important	Working in a job that involves danger or requires you to take risks

Variety	Work with Your Hands
Doing many different and interesting things	Having a job in which you can use your hands, machines, or tools to make or repair things

Work with Your Mind	Work with People
Doing work that requires a high level of thinking and mental ability	Working in close contact with people and being able to comfort and help others

How Do Your Values Affect Your Career?

Now that you have chosen your four strongest work values, think about how these values can affect your career choices. For example, if you value taking **risks**, you might get a job as a stock broker, one who invests money in order to make more money. Or you might choose a job that involves adventure or requires you to work outdoors, such as a river rafting guide. You would feel successful in these jobs because you are achieving something you value—taking risks. By looking at your values, you can get an idea of what plans you might make for your future.

Lesson 4 Review Write your answers to these questions on a sheet of paper.

1. What are three of your personal values?

2. What are three of your work values?

3. How do your personal values differ from your work values?

4. How can your values change?

5. How can your values affect your career choice?

Get Involved

Have you ever thought about working in a zoo? Zookeepers, veterinarians, and zoo administrators all spend their workdays among animals. Many zoos have volunteer programs for young people. For example, the National Zoo in Washington, D.C. has a summer program for teens. Volunteers do several different jobs. Some work in the kids' zoo or the kids' farm. They greet kids who come to see the animals. They help them enjoy the activities. Other volunteers welcome visitors at the doors to special exhibits. Still other volunteers help the zoo's gardeners. They learn about the zoo's plants and help keep the zoo beautiful. Zoos in other areas of the country also offer volunteer opportunities. Zoo volunteers get to help their community. They also get to learn more about some exciting occupations.

Lesson 4 Review Answers

1. Answers will vary. **2.** Answers will vary. **3.** Answers will vary. **4.** Values can change and strengthen with experience. **5.** If you choose a career based on your values, you will feel successful.

Get Involved

Ask students to share their experiences and observations in zoos. Have them predict what jobs are available in a zoo. Then have several volunteers read the Get Involved feature on page 41. Review the jobs teens can have as volunteers at a zoo. Discuss the skills they can gain doing such work. Finally, have students apply what they learned in this lesson by naming the personal values and work values relevant to someone who works in a zoo. If there is a zoo in or near your community, ask interested students to find out what opportunities it offers for volunteers and report their findings to the class.

ONLINE CONNECTION

Interested students may want to visit the American Zoo and Aquarium Association Web site at www.aza.org/. The home page has links to articles and summaries explaining what zoos offer to everyone, including careers, special projects, and ways to get involved. It also offers information about the importance of conservation education to save wildlife.

Chapter 2 Lesson 5

Overview This lesson presents two example Self-Assessment Profiles and discusses how they illustrate appropriate and inappropriate choices in filling out the form.

Objectives

- To analyze example Self-Assessment Profiles featuring high school students
- To determine how a Self-Assessment Profile can help prepare for a career
- To identify materials to include in a portfolio

Student Pages 42–49

Teacher's Resource Library TRL

Workbook Activity 7

Activity 7

Alternative Activity 7

....

Vocabulary

portfolio

Have students analyze the structure of the vocabulary terms using questions such as *What two words are used to make* portfolio? (port, folio) *What do they mean?* (carry, page or sheet) *How do these words help you determine the meaning of* portfolio? (A portfolio probably refers to papers you carry with you.)

....

1 Warm-Up Activity

Review with students what they have learned so far in the chapter about assessing their best subjects, interests, abilities, and values. Have them predict a way they could combine this knowledge to help them plan the future.

Lesson 5 — Self-Assessment Profile

You have now identified several things about yourself. You have named the things that you can do best and the things you like most. You have identified what you have learned and enjoyed in school. You have also determined what values are most important to you. Now you will see how your school experience, abilities, values, and interests may match possible career areas. If you know what careers would be a good fit for you, you can increase your chances of enjoying your work.

The following examples of Self-Assessment Profiles will show you two ways to use this information. One way is to search for connections between abilities and interest areas and school subjects you like. Another way is to examine the connections between your abilities, interests, values, and education to find a possible career path. These connections can point to ways that encourage you to succeed. After reading each profile, you can complete and study your own profile.

Jamie is a junior in high school. She plays on the soccer team. She works part-time as a helper for her father who is an electrician. Her father owns his business. He says Jamie will get the business after he retires. Jamie is not sure if she wants to be an electrician. She has also thought about a career as a police officer. However, she cannot apply to be a police officer until she is 21 years old. Jamie has also thought about going to college. She would like to study criminal justice. This would help prepare her to be a police officer. When she graduates from college, she would be old enough to apply for a job as a police officer.

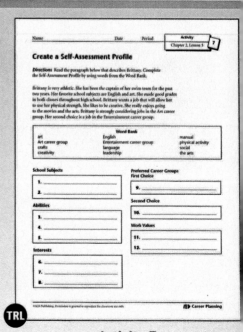

Workbook Activity 7   **Activity 7**

Jamie's Self-Assessment Profile

1. School Subjects

Math
Science

2. Skills

good at algebra
good with numbers
able to solve problems
good reasoning ability

3. Achievements

highest score on math test
math league team trophy
science fair award
As and Bs in science classes

4. Abilities

Manual
Technical/ Mechanical
Interpersonal
Social

5. Interests

Social
Crafts

6. Preferred Career Groups

First Choice: Customer Service
Second Choice: Skilled Crafts

7. Work Values

Work with Your Mind	Work with Your Hands	Outdoor Work	Variety

Draw a simple profile on the board. Explain that a profile of this kind is an outline representing the face or head of a subject from the side. Point out that the features are clear in the profile. Have students read the lesson title. Ask them to predict what the word *profile* means in this context. (a set of data showing the significant features of something or someone)

Tell students the lesson they will read now will show them how to develop and analyze a profile of themselves.

Have students study the Self-Assessment Profile on page 43. Ask them where Jamie got the words and phrases that she placed in each box. (*Lessons 1 through 4 listed subjects, abilities, values, and interests.*) Point out to students that they may need to refer to the lists in these lessons as they study the profile and the text that discusses it.

Explain that in number 6, the First and Second Choices refer to career groups Jamie has chosen after considering her best subjects, abilities, values, and interests. These were chosen from a list that appears on pages 35 and 36 of the chapter.

3 ▶ **Reinforce and Extend**

LEARNING STYLES

Auditory/Verbal

Have students form pairs and have them read the lesson aloud together, alternating paragraphs. Suggest that they pause frequently and summarize the ideas expressed in what they have read. They will need to refer to the example Self-Assessment Profiles on pages 43 and 47 as they read about Jamie and Derrick's profiles. This will help them to follow the text explanation.

Logical/Mathematical
Review with students the first four lessons they have read. Create a graphic organizer on the board to show how subject area interests, abilities, general and career interests, and values intersect and interact to give a person direction in planning a career. Have students plug into the diagrams specific interests, abilities, and so on, discussed in the previous lessons. Students should use the diagram to explain how the information suggests a logical career choice.

Gender and Careers

Have students predict what career Jamie will choose based on her profile information. Invite them to voice their opinions about whether she would have difficulty in a career as an electrician. Then have volunteers read the Gender and Careers feature on page 44 aloud. Ask students to give two reasons why women make less money than men. (*They tend to take jobs that earn less, and they may receive less pay for the same job than a man receives.*)

GLOBAL CONNECTION

Explain to students that in many countries, attitudes toward women are not like those in the United States. In some countries, females may not be educated and are expected to work only in the home. Invite interested students to research gender roles and how they affect women in other countries. Ask students to report their findings.

Use the information in the Self-Assessment Profile as a map. A map can help you get where you want to go. For example, you can start by looking at the area in which Jamie has some work experience—Skilled Crafts—her second Preferred Career Group. Jamie likes the school subjects of Math and Science. These subjects would help prepare her for one of her career choices—to be an electrician. What skills do electricians need? They need math for measuring, and scientific knowledge to understand theories. School, then, is a good place for Jamie to begin to prepare for a career as an electrician.

Jamie rated herself as strong in the manual and technical/mechanical abilities. These abilities also match her best-liked school subjects. Her technical/mechanical abilities show that she can figure out or fix a problem. Solving problems is useful in math or science classes.

Gender and Careers

Many jobs have traditionally been held by mostly men or mostly women. But, there are no occupations that are for men only or for women only. As long as a person has the knowledge, skills, and physical characteristics required for a job, either a male or female can do it. You can enter any field of study or job you wish.

Before the 1960s, many businesses paid men higher salaries than they paid women. This was because men had traditionally provided the main source of income for their families. As more and more women entered the workforce, people found this salary gap unfair. In 1963, Congress passed the Equal Pay Act. It said women must receive the same pay as men for the same job. Over the years, the gap between men's pay and women's pay has narrowed. However, in 2002, women were paid only 77 cents for every dollar men earned. One problem is deciding when two jobs are equivalent. Also, some jobs, such as clerical jobs, still pay less than other jobs. These are often jobs that women have traditionally held. Today men and women are both working to close the gender pay gap.

Jamie can satisfy all her work values by doing the work of an electrician. This career would require her to use her mind and her hands on the job. No matter where she lives, in a large city or a small town, her skills would always be needed. She could work outdoors or indoors. She could do different tasks for variety.

Jamie had a hard time deciding what her best interests were. She wrote down both Crafts and Social interests. She was not sure about the Crafts area because not many females are working there. But, she knows that she gets along well with men in other trades during her summer job. She enjoys the good pay she receives for her work. She makes more money than some of her friends who have other summer jobs. But Jamie finally picked Social interest over Crafts.

Jamie sees two sides to her personality. She gets along well with people. She would like to help others. But she does not see herself as a teacher, nurse, or social worker. Instead, she knows that she likes to see results from her work right away. She likes that she can use tools and fix things. It makes her feel independent.

What does Jamie's Self-Assessment Profile show that relates to police work? The values of Work with Your Mind, Outdoor Work, and Variety match with police work. Social and Interpersonal abilities and Social interest also fit with police work.

When Jamie chose her two Preferred Career Groups, she picked Customer Service and Skilled Crafts. Customer Service includes police officer. Skilled Crafts includes electrician. Jamie knows she needs more information about law enforcement. She wants to talk with police officers. She wants to know how to get experience in the field. She also understands that choosing a career takes time, information, and careful choices.

ELL/ESL STRATEGY

Language Objective:
Understand how to scan for specific information

As they read Lesson 5, students will need to refer back to previous lessons to locate specific areas of interest, abilities, values, and so on, and relate them to occupations. Students who are learning English may need help finding information efficiently in a text. Have them practice the skill by determining key words and searching for them in an earlier lesson. For example, Social and Interpersonal abilities (paragraph 4, page 45) are described as being suitable for a police officer. Have students recall which lesson discussed abilities (Lesson 2) and turn to the lesson. Students can then run a finger down the lines on each page searching for those words. *Social* and *Interpersonal* appear as headings on pages 25 and 29. Students can review the text under these heads to see why these abilities are suitable for a career in police work.

AT HOME

Encourage students to share their Self-Assessment Profile with an adult at home. The adult can share favorite subjects, abilities, interests, and values and help the student assess how these factors played a role in the adult's current occupation.

LEARNING STYLES

Auditory/Verbal
You might have students choose the factor (subject strengths, abilities, interests, values) they think is most important to consider in selecting a career, and then have them debate the issue. When all volunteers have finished giving their arguments, the class can vote to see which factor most people agree is key.

Now let's look at another example. You will read about Derrick. His interests, abilities, and values are different from Jamie's. It is helpful for you to see how different students fill out a Self-Assessment Profile. Think about yourself and how you would fill out your own profile as you read about Derrick.

Derrick is in ninth grade. He is a good student and an athlete. His mom always talks to Derrick about going to college when he graduates from high school.

Look at Derrick's Self-Assessment Profile. There are no clear-cut connections between his best-liked subjects, abilities, and interests. This will make it hard for him to choose what he should study in his sophomore year. He wants to study computers.

Derrick's first Preferred Career Group is Math and Science because he likes computers. This matches one of his best-liked school subjects, Technology. It also matches his Scientific ability. But these choices do not match the things he says he is interested in—Business or Social. He did not pick values consistent with careers in math, science, and law. For example, he did not select High Achievement, which is needed to succeed in a job that is difficult. He also did not choose Work with Your Mind.

If Derrick wants to combine his interest in business with his interest in computers, he could explore the career opportunities in information technologies, management information systems, and database administration. However, Derrick must research what these careers involve. He should find out the courses and skills he needs to fulfill his plans.

Derrick's Self-Assessment Profile

1. School Subjects

Technology
English

2. Skills

creating Web pages
programming computers
good at persuading people
good leader

3. Achievements

designed Web page for high school
spelling bee award
accepted into Honors English class
short stories printed in school paper

4. Abilities

Persuasive
Language
Scientific
Social

5. Interests

Business
Social

6. Preferred Career Groups

First Choice: Math and Science
Second Choice: Legal

7. Work Values

Good Salary	Job Security	Independence	Physical Activity

Logical/Mathematical
Have students study the Self-Assessment Profile for Derrick and explain the qualities suggested by his choices. Compare his profile with Jamie's. In what way do Derrick's choices seem less conclusive than Jamie's? Point out that Derrick is at least two years younger, a fact which may help account for his much more general profile.

Visual/Spatial
Provide each student with a folder or binder that is to be their portfolio for the class. Have them read the section titled "What Is a Portfolio?" on page 49. Then ask them to design and create a cover for their portfolio that represents its importance to them and suggests its contents.

Career Profile

Electrician

Read aloud the Career Profile on page 48. Ask students if they know anyone who is an electrician. Find out what that person does and compare that information with the information in the profile. Ask if any students might be interested in becoming an electrician.

Derrick's second choice of Career Group is Legal. One of his best-liked school subjects, English, is a very important skill for law. He has to have a strong reading ability. Management courses are also important. In these courses, Derrick could study contracts and labor relations. Derrick could use his Language, Social, and Persuasive abilities in the practice of law. Attorneys, or lawyers, can earn a good income. Business is an interest that includes legal studies.

Derrick described himself as a leader. He said he is a good communicator. He can persuade people to his point of view. Law appears to be a good career direction for Derrick. But he needs to find more information about the legal field. He will learn that he must finish four years of college before he can apply to law school. He will be in law school for at least three more years. Derrick will also need to think about how he will be able to pay for his education. Getting accepted into law school is competitive and difficult. Finding legal jobs is also very competitive. Knowing what steps he needs to take to start a law career can make it easier for Derrick to plan.

Career Profile

Electrician

Electricians work with electrical wiring and equipment. Some electricians work on wiring inside homes or buildings. Others might repair street lights or outside electric wires. Electricians are good at working with their hands. They are able to find out what the problem is and then decide how to repair it. They may have to climb ladders to work on equipment. They often have to build or fix electronic parts. Sometimes, electricians need to do special tasks during a power failure like drive vehicles, operate flood lights, or set up emergency flares. Electricians need to have a license. They must do their work according to government rules and regulations. Most electricians go to vocational schools and earn either two-year or four-year degrees. They also need to get on-the-job experience or training. Jobs for electricians are expected to grow at an average rate.

Portfolio

A collection of evidence of planning, skills, competencies, achievements, letters of recommendation, résumés, references, jobs held, activities performed, and writing samples

Career Tip

A *résumé* is a summary of knowledge, abilities, and experience that shows how a person is qualified for a particular occupation.

References are someone who can share skills, personal qualities, and job qualifications with an employer.

You will learn more about these in Chapter 7.

What Is a Portfolio?

A **portfolio** is a tool you can use as you explore career choices and develop a career plan. Your portfolio can be a folder or electronic device that contains these things:

- evidence of planning
- skills
- competencies
- achievements
- letters of recommendation
- a résumé
- references
- jobs held
- activities performed
- writing samples

A portfolio shows your school and career progress. It also shows that you have done self-assessment. An early step for you to begin your portfolio is to include your Self-Assessment Profile. You will complete this in the Portfolio Activity on pages 50 and 51. You will update and continue to add to your portfolio as you work through this book.

Lesson 5 Review Write your answers to these questions on a sheet of paper.

1. How can a portfolio help you choose a career?

2. What are three things you might include in your portfolio?

Lesson 5 Review Answers

1. A portfolio can show you evidence of planning, your skills and competencies, and activities you have done that relate to certain careers. **2.** Answers will vary. Items include skills, competencies, achievements, letters of recommendation, a resume, references, jobs held, activities performed, and writing samples.

Portfolio Activity

Self-Assessment Profile

Explain to students that they will create a profile like the examples they just studied. Pass out copies of the TRL Portfolio Activity 2 or have students set up a form for organizing their self-assessment answers like the one displayed on pages 43 and 47.

Students who have completed the journaling activities in earlier lessons (see pages 21 and 39) may refer to their journals to help them complete items 1, 2, 3, and 7 of the profile.

Remind students that each list in the profile also appears in a lesson in the chapter, where its terms are explained or described. If they cannot remember what qualities were assigned to various abilities, interests, career groups, or values, they can refer to these pages in the text:

School Subjects: 20–21

Abilities: 25–30

Interests: 33–34

Career Groups: 35–36

Work Values: 39–40

Portfolio Activity

Self-Assessment Profile

1. Choose the two school subjects you enjoy most. Write the names of the two subjects on your Self-Assessment Profile.

> **School Subjects**
> - Agriculture
> - Art
> - Business/Management
> - Clerical Studies
> - English
> - Family/Consumer Science
> - Finance
> - Health
> - Languages
> - Math
> - Music
> - Science
> - Shop/Industrial Arts
> - Social Studies
> - Technology/Computers

2. What skills do you have in the two subjects you wrote for number 1? Write these skills on your Self-Assessment Profile.

3. What are some of your achievements that relate to your skills? Write them on your Self-Assessment Profile.

4. What four abilities are your strongest? Write them on your Self-Assessment Profile.

> **Abilities**
> - Artistic
> - Clerical
> - Interpersonal
> - Language
> - Leadership
> - Manual
> - Mathematical/Numerical
> - Musical/Dramatic
> - Organizational
> - Persuasive
> - Scientific
> - Social
> - Technical/Mechanical
> - Visual (Spatial)

5. What are two areas in which you have interest? Write them on your Self-Assessment Profile.

> **Interests**
> - The Arts
> - Business
> - Crafts
> - Office Operations
> - Scientific
> - Social

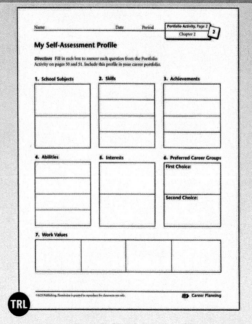

Portfolio Activity 2

6. Which two career groups are you the most interested in? Write them on your Self-Assessment Profile.

Career Groups
- Art
- Clerical
- Customer Service
- Data Analysis
- Education
- Entertainment
- Legal
- Literary
- Management
- Manual
- Math and Science
- Medical/Dental
- Music
- Personal Service
- Sales
- Skilled Crafts
- Social Service
- Technical

7. What are four of your work values? Write them on your Self-Assessment Profile.

Work Values
- Creativity
- Good Salary
- High Achievement
- Independence
- Job Security
- Leadership
- Outdoor Work
- Physical Activity
- Prestige
- Risk
- Variety
- Work with Your Hands
- Work with Your Mind
- Work with People

8. Include your Self-Assessment Profile in your career portfolio.

Remind students as they complete item 7 that work values are not the same as personal ethics or morals, although there is some overlap. Instead, work values indicate the things, ideas, and actions in a job that give a worker satisfaction.

When students have completed their profiles, have them place them in their career portfolios. After a few days, have students look over their profiles and look for any patterns or connections that give a strong suggestion of a good career path.

Portfolio Activity Answers

1.–7. Answers will vary.

Chapter 2 Review

Use the Chapter Review to prepare students for tests and to reteach content from the chapter.

Chapter 2 Mastery Test

The Teacher's Resource Library includes two forms of the Chapter 2 Mastery Test. Each test addresses the chapter Goals for Learning. An optional third page of additional critical-thinking items is included for each test. The difficulty level of the two forms is equivalent.

Review Answers

Vocabulary Review

1. self-confidence 2. career cluster 3. value 4. equity 5. interest 6. skill 7. risk 8. achievement 9. portfolio 10. competency 11. ability 12. self-assessment

Concept Review

13. C 14. B 15. A 16. D 17. A 18. D

Critical Thinking

19. Answers will vary. Possible answer: Self-assessment is a lifelong activity because as you grow older you change. Your abilities, interests, and even values might be different than when you were younger. Continual self-assessment helps you adjust your job and your life.

20. Answers will vary. Possible answer: The person might be unhappy with his or her job. He or she might not perform well. Also, other aspects of the person's life would suffer as a result.

Chapter 2   R E V I E W

<table>
<tr><th colspan="2">Word Bank</th></tr>
<tr><td colspan="2">ability</td></tr>
<tr><td colspan="2">achievement</td></tr>
<tr><td colspan="2">career group</td></tr>
<tr><td colspan="2">competency</td></tr>
<tr><td colspan="2">interest</td></tr>
<tr><td colspan="2">portfolio</td></tr>
<tr><td colspan="2">risk</td></tr>
<tr><td colspan="2">self-assessment</td></tr>
<tr><td colspan="2">self-confidence</td></tr>
<tr><td colspan="2">skill</td></tr>
<tr><td colspan="2">value</td></tr>
<tr><td colspan="2">work</td></tr>
</table>

Vocabulary Review

Choose the word or phrase from the Word Bank that best completes each sentence. Write the answer on your paper.

1. When you have a good feeling about yourself, you have _____.

2. A group of occupations with related abilities and interests is a(n) _____.

3. A belief about what is most important to you is a(n) _____.

4. What people do to earn a living is _____.

5. Something that you like or want to know more about is a(n) _____.

6. Something you have trained or practiced to be good at is a(n) _____.

7. A chance of danger or loss is a(n) _____.

8. Something you have earned or accomplished based on your performance is a(n) _____.

9. A tool containing several documents about yourself and your achievements is a(n) _____.

10. Being able to do something well is known as _____.

11. A talent or strength in a particular area is a(n) _____.

12. Finding out your strengths and weaknesses is known as _____.

Concept Review

Choose the word or phrase that best completes each sentence. Write the letter of the answer on your paper.

13. One way to rate your competence in an activity is to _____.

    A think about what you enjoy doing

    B consider what you have worked on hardest

    C compare yourself to others

    D choose your favorite subject

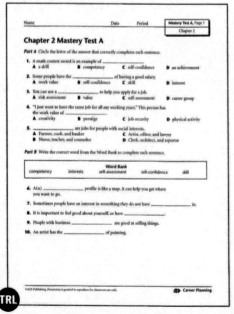

14. A person who pays attention to details and does accurate work has _____.

   A artistic ability   **C** interpersonal ability

   B clerical ability   **D** leadership ability

15. A person with scientific interests might work as a _____.

   A pharmacist   **C** tax preparer

   B salesperson   **D** farmer

16. Air traffic controller is a job in the _____ career group.

   A education   **C** manual

   B management   **D** technical

17. If you value working with others, which job would be best for you?

   A teacher   **C** carpenter

   B stock broker   **D** artist

18. Something that might be included in your portfolio is _____.

   A a letter you wrote to an old friend

   B your report card

   C a test you recently took

   D a letter of recommendation

Critical Thinking

Write the answer to each question on your paper.

19. Explain why self-assessment is a lifelong activity.

20. Suppose a person takes a job. It does not strongly reflect his or her abilities, interests, and values. What problems might this cause?

Test-Taking Tip

When studying for a test, learn the most important points. Practice writing this material or explaining it to someone.

ALTERNATIVE ASSESSMENT

- Have students list as many reasons as they can why it is helpful to assess their personal abilities and interests. Then ask students to number the reasons from least important to most important and explain their ranking.

- Ask each student to identify their strongest abilities and interests from the lists on pages 25–30 and 33–34. Students should be able to explain why they chose each ability or interest area.

- Have students tell which career groups they identified as most interesting to them. Have students select one group and picture themselves working in this career. Ask students to write a page describing how they got there and how they feel about the work they are doing.

- After students identify personal values that are important to them, have them make a logo or crest that symbolizes those values and explain what each part represents.

- Ask students to write a paragraph explaining what they learned about themselves by completing a Self-Assessment Profile.

Chapter 2 Mastery Test B

Part A Circle the letter of the answer that correctly completes each sentence.

1. A _____ might include letters of recommendation.
   A competency list B self-assessment C portfolio D career group

2. The education career group includes _____.
   A every job in a high school C all jobs for students
   B jobs for people interested in education D only elementary school jobs

3. What people do to earn a living is called _____.
   A competency B value C work D risk

4. A model, producer, and actress are all part of the _____ career group.
   A Entertainment B Legal C Art D Music

5. Look at your favorite school subjects. This will help you _____.
   A find out what subjects you want to teach
   B know what to tell your friends to take next year
   C decide whether or not to go away for college
   D figure out your interests and competencies

Part B Write the correct word from the Word Bank to complete each sentence.

Word Bank
| ability | experience | prestige | risk | values |

6. People who have clerical _____ pay attention to details.

7. A river rafting guide might value _____.

8. You first learn your _____ from your family.

9. A person's values may get stronger or change with _____.

10. People who value _____ want to feel important.

Chapter 2 Mastery Test B, continued

Part C Match the words in Column 1 with their meanings in Column 2. Write the letter on the line.

Column 1	Column 2
____ 11. self-assessment	A being able to do something well
____ 12. skill	B something you like or want to know more about
____ 13. competency	C something you can do that comes from training or practice
____ 14. achievement	D something people want to get out of a job
____ 15. interest	E finding out your strengths and weaknesses
____ 16. self-confidence	F feeling good about oneself
____ 17. work value	G something you earn based on performance

Part D Write the answers to these questions. Use complete sentences.

18. How can you use self-assessment?

19. Describe a person who has the work value of job security.

20. Name two of your interest areas and tell some jobs for people with those interests.

Chapter 2 Mastery Test B, continued

Part E Write your answer to each question. Use complete sentences. Support each answer with facts and examples from the textbook.

21. What are educational requirements? How do they affect people's career choices? (2 points)

22. Describe how a person's abilities can help him or her decide on a career. (2 points)

Part F Write a paragraph for each topic. Include a topic sentence, body, and conclusion. Support each answer with facts and examples from the textbook.

23. Compare and contrast the ways that two people with different values go about choosing a job. Give specific examples of different values. (3 points)

24. Write a paragraph to convince other students to complete a self-assessment. Include an explanation of a self-assessment. Also tell how this activity will be helpful to them. (3 points)

Chapter 2 Mastery Test B, Pages 1–3

3

Planning Guide

Careers and Decision Making

	Student Pages	Vocabulary	Lesson Review	Critical-Thinking Questions	Chapter Review
Student Text Lesson					
Lesson 1 Researching Careers	56–63	✔	✔	✔	✔
Lesson 2 Making Career Decisions	64–69	✔	✔	✔	✔

Chapter Activities

Student Text
Chapter 3 Portfolio Activity

Teacher's Resource Library
Chapter 3 Chapter Outline
Chapter 3 Self-Study Guide
Chapter 3 Portfolio Activity

Assessment Options

Student Text
Chapter 3 Review

Teacher's Resource Library
Chapter 3 Mastery Tests A and B

Teacher's Edition
Chapter 3 Alternative Assessment

Portfolio Activity	Writing Practice	Communication Connection	The Economy	Career Tip	Career Profile	On the Job	Gender and Careers	Think Positive	Technology Note	Get Involved	Background Information	Applications (Home, Community, Global, Environment)	Personal Journal	Online Connection	ELL/ESL Strategy	Visual/Spatial	Body/Kinesthetic	Interpersonal/Group Learning	Logical/Mathematical	Auditory/Verbal	Activities	Alternative Activities	Workbook Activities	Self-Study Guide	Chapter Outline
			59	56, 62, 63		57			57, 61	63	58	58, 59		63	57	59		61	60	58	8	8	8	✔	✔
70	66	64			67		69	67				65	69		68	68	66		66		9	9	9	✔	✔

Alternative Activities

The Teacher's Resource Library (TRL) contains a set of lower-level worksheets called Alternative Activities. These worksheets cover the same content as the regular Activities but are written at a second-grade reading level.

Career Interest Inventory

The AGS Publishing Harrington-O'Shea Career Decision-Making System (CDM) may be used with this textbook. Students can use the CDM to explore their interests and identify careers. The CDM defines career areas that are indicated by students' response on the inventory.

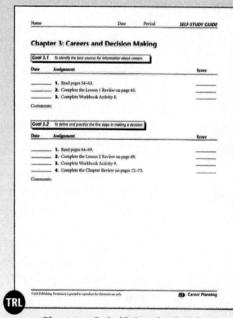

Chapter 3 Self-Study Guide

3 Careers and Decision Making

Would you choose a dentist or buy a car without first researching your options? Then why would you choose a career without doing just as much research? The Internet, libraries, books, and newspapers are some sources of career information. This chapter will help you use these resources wisely. It will help you make decisions and set goals related to your career.

Goals for Learning

◆ To identify the best sources for information about careers

◆ To define and practice the five steps in making a decision

Introducing the Chapter

Have students look at the photo on page 54 in the Student Edition and describe what the girl in the picture is doing. Discuss why she is studying the newspaper and why she needs a pen and paper. Invite students to share their ideas about how she decided which of the job opportunities in the paper to pursue.

Have students read the introductory paragraph and think about steps that are important in choosing and working toward a career goal.

Have students read the Goals for Learning, and then predict what sources are most useful for gathering career information. Ask volunteers to summarize the steps they have used in the past to make important decisions.

Career Tips

Ask volunteers to read the career tips that appear in the margins throughout the chapter. Then discuss them with the class.

Alternative Assessment

The Alternative Assessment box on page 73 of the Chapter Review includes activities using various learning styles to assess students' understanding of the Goals for Learning.

55

Chapter 3 Lesson 1

Overview In this lesson students learn about CDMCareerZone and the *Occupational Outlook Handbook* (OOH), two information-rich resources for learning about careers. Students also consider other resources their school and community may offer.

Objectives

■ To understand the importance of researching career choices

■ To learn what information is offered at the CDMCareerZone Web site and how to access it

■ To understand what information OOH offers and how it is organized

■ To identify school and community career resources

Student Pages 56–63

Teacher's Resource Library TRL

Workbook Activity 8

Activity 8

Alternative Activity 8

Vocabulary

wage
wage equity

Use the vocabulary words in context-rich sentences. (*Jim agreed to work for a wage of $40 a day* or *The factory pays starting wages of $12.50 per hour.*) Ask students to read the sentence(s), substituting a synonym for wage. (Possible synonyms: *pay, earnings, salary, compensation*) Point out that *wage* is often used in its plural form and that it usually refers to a specific amount per hour, per day, or per job, paid by contract to a worker. Follow a similar method for *wage equity*.

1 Warm-Up Activity

Remind students of the career groups they chose in their Self-Assessment Profile at the end of Chapter 2. Ask them how they would find information about the careers they listed. Explain that in this lesson they will read about two very useful resources for researching careers.

Wage
A set amount of money earned per hour of work

This lesson will show you how to find and use information about occupations. Remember that an occupation is a group of similar or related jobs or job skills. The job market is always changing. How do you find the most current information about an occupation? What occupations are growing? What knowledge and skills do jobs in these fields require? What is the **wage** for a job? To answer these questions, you need to do research. There are many good reasons to research occupational information:

1. Before a job interview, you will know what an employer might want you to be able to do on the job.

2. You will know what skills and knowledge you need for an occupation.

3. When you plan for college you will know what programs or classes you need for your career.

How Can I Find Career Information?

Career Tip

The U.S. Department of Labor is a part of the government. It provides services for American workers and sets safety standards for workplaces. The Department of Labor oversees laws that set working conditions, uphold workers' rights, set wages, and relate to other job issues.

Two resources you can use to find career information are CDMCareerZone and the *Occupational Outlook Handbook* (OOH). Both are based on information from the U.S. Department of Labor. CDMCareerZone is a Web site that describes nearly 1,000 occupations. The OOH is a book. It is available in most libraries. You might also find it in guidance offices and career centers. Both

of these resources include the knowledge, skills, and personal characteristics needed for specific jobs.

You can use a computer to research careers.

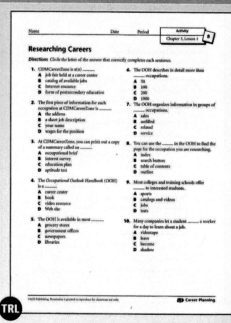

Workbook Activity 8

Activity 8

As you explore these resources, you will notice that the information you will study does not say whether a job is for men or women. Remember that there is no occupation that is for only men or only women. CDMCareerZone and the OOH both follow **wage equity**—men and women doing the same job earn the same amount of money.

What Information Can I Find on CDMCareerZone?

At the CDMCareerZone Web site, you can enter the name of an occupation you want to explore. When you enter an occupation, the first piece of information you will see is a short job description. After the description, you can read about the following:

- Interests
- Tasks/Job Duties
- Skills
- Knowledge
- Education/Training Needed
- School Programs
- Wages
- Job Outlook
- Similar Jobs
- Locations of Job Openings

On CDMCareerZone, you can print out a copy of a summary called an occupational brief. Figure 3.1 on page 58 is an example of this summary for cashiers. At the end of the brief, you can choose to see all of the occupations within the CareerZone system. By looking at the list, you can choose another job to explore. You can also view videos for more than 300 occupations.

Technology Note

Go to the CDMCareerZone Web site (www.cdmcareerzone.com). Enter one of the occupations you identified in Chapter 2. If you do not know the name of an occupation or how to spell it, click on the Go button. This will give you a list of all the CareerZone occupations. Read the information about the occupation you chose. Now, use the information to answer these questions: Do I think I would like doing this kind of work? How much money do these workers earn? Do I want to spend that much money and time preparing to enter this career? Are there similar occupations that require less investment of time and money?

Technology Note

Have students read the Technology Note on page 57. Then have them write their career choice from Chapter 2 at the top of a sheet of paper. Below this, they can write the four questions found in the feature, leaving space for answers. If possible, schedule class time for students to use school computers to visit the CDMCareerZone site. As an alternative, students may be able to access the Internet using computers at a local library. Ask students to report on their experience with the site and whether it changed their career goals.

2 Teaching the Lesson

Have students make a chart to compare the CDMCareerZone Web site and the OOH. As they read the lesson, students can list the kinds of information each provides and highlight features that distinguish the two. After students have finished reading, discuss when each resource would be most useful.

Point out to students that Figure 3.1 (page 58) displays only the first page of the occupational brief for cashier. This page lists information for the first two bullets in the list on page 57. The other categories are explored on the second and third pages of the brief.

On the Job

Ask students to list different ways computers are used on the job. How would they rate the importance of computers to most workplaces? Have students read the On the Job feature on page 57. Ask a volunteer to explain the meaning of *word processing*. Survey the class informally to find out how many students have keyboarding skills. As a group, research opportunities in your school and community for students to take a class to acquire or sharpen this skill.

3 Reinforce and Extend

Figure 3.1

> Cashiers, page 1 of 3
>
> A CDMCareerZone Occupational Brief for:
> **Cashiers**
>
> Job Description
>
> Receive and disburse money in establishments other than financial institutions. Usually involves use of electronic scanners, cash registers, or related equipment. Often involved in processing credit or debit card transactions and validating checks.
>
> Interests
>
> **Office Operations** - High Scorers on the Office Operations scale usually:
>
> - prefer jobs with clearly defined duties
> - like to work with words and numbers
> - are orderly and systematic
> - value financial success and status
>
> *Typical jobs: bank teller, secretary, accountant, insurance clerk, computer operator, budget analyst*
>
> Tasks
>
> 1. Answers questions and provides information to customers.
> 2. Bags, boxes, or wraps merchandise.
> 3. Cashes checks.
> 4. Compiles and maintains non-monetary reports and records.
> 5. Computes and records totals of transactions.
> 6. Keeps periodic balance sheet of amount and number of transactions.
> 7. Learns prices, stocks shelves, marks prices, weighs items, issues trading stamps, and redeems food stamps and coupons.
> 8. Monitors checkout stations, issues and removes cash as needed, and assigns workers to reduce customer delay.
> 9. Operates cash register or electronic scanner.
> 10. Receives sales slip, cash, check, voucher, or charge payments and issues receipts, refunds, credits, or change due to customer.

CDM CareerZone ©2003 Harrington-O'Shea

Figure 3.1. *Occupational Brief for Cashiers*

You can find job openings for the occupation you have researched. Use the drop-down menu to find job openings by state. The job openings listed are from America's Job Bank. You will find the job title, company or organization name, and city or town. Sometimes you may read that there are no jobs available. This may not be true. It may mean only that the jobs are not listed with America's Job Bank.

What Information Is in the Occupational Outlook Handbook?

The *Occupational Outlook Handbook* (OOH) describes in detail more than 200 occupations in which about 128 million people work. That is 88 percent of all jobs in the United States! The handbook also explains other jobs in less detail. In the OOH, you can learn in what jobs 95 percent of the people in the United States work. The handbook is reprinted every two years to keep the information up-to-date.

In the OOH, information is usually organized in groups of related occupations. These groups allow you to see similar or related jobs you may not have known about. These are the groups in the OOH:

- Management, business, and financial occupations
- Professional occupations
- Service occupations
- Sales occupations
- Office and administrative support occupations
- Farming, fishing, and forestry occupations
- Construction trades
- Installation, maintenance, and repair occupations
- Production occupations
- Transportation and material moving occupations
- Armed Forces

The Economy

You are probably familiar with the minimum wage. This is an hourly wage set by the government. It is the smallest amount that a company can legally pay its employees. Many young people earn the minimum wage for part-time jobs in stores and restaurants. However, it is difficult for parents to support a family on minimum wages. The living wage enables a worker to support a family. Many American cities have enacted living wage regulations. The amount of a living wage is different in each place. In Milwaukee, Wisconsin, it is considered to be about one dollar more per hour than the minimum wage. In Santa Cruz, California, it is about ten dollars per hour above the minimum wage.

Logical/Mathematical
Have students compare the headings for the OOH found on page 60 with those for CDMCareerZone (see page 57). They should note that the OOH lists fewer categories and makes them more general. Ask students to match the categories where possible (both lists have Outlook as a category), then decide which have the same meaning (Earnings and Wages, Similar Jobs and Related Occupations). Finally, ask students to group remaining CDMCareerZone categories of information under parallel OOH categories:

OOH	CDMCareerZone
Nature of the Work	Tasks/Job Duties
Training and Advancement	Skills, Knowledge, Education/Training Needed, School Programs

Occupations are described under different headings. First go to the heading you are most interested in. Then, you can choose to research other information. Here are the different heading topics:

1. Nature of the Work
2. Working Conditions
3. Employment
4. Related Occupations
5. Training and Advancement
6. Earnings
7. Outlook
8. Sources of Additional Information

Figure 3.2

OUTLOOK   [About this section]   ▲ Back to Top

Employment of hotel, motel, and resort desk clerks is expected to **grow faster than the average** for all occupations through 2012, as more hotels, motels, and other lodging establishments are built and occupancy rates rise. Job opportunities for hotel and motel desk clerks also will result from a need to replace workers, because many of these clerks either transfer to other occupations that offer better pay and advancement opportunities or simply leave the workforce altogether. Opportunities for part-time work should continue to be plentiful, with front desks often staffed 24 hours a day, 7 days a week.

Employment of hotel and motel desk clerks should benefit from an increase in business and leisure travel. Shifts in preferences away from long vacations and toward long weekends and other, more frequent, shorter trips also should boost demand for these workers, because such stays increase the number of nights spent in hotels. The expansion of budget and extended-stay hotels relative to larger, luxury establishments reflects a change in the composition of the hotel and motel industry. As employment shifts from luxury hotels to those extended-stay establishments offering larger rooms with kitchenettes and laundry services, the proportion of hotel desk clerks should increase in relation to staff such as waiters and waitresses and recreation workers. Desk clerks are able to handle more of the guest's needs in these establishments, answering the main switchboard, providing business services, and coordinating services such as dry cleaning or grocery shopping.

New technologies automating check-in and checkout procedures now allow some guests to bypass the front desk in many larger establishments, reducing staffing needs. As some of the more traditional duties are automated, however, many desk clerks are assuming a wider range of responsibilities.

Employment of desk clerks is sensitive to cyclical swings in the economy. During recessions, vacation and business travel declines, and hotels and motels need fewer clerks. Similarly, employment is affected by seasonal fluctuations in tourism and travel.

Bureau of Labor Statistics

Figure 3.2. *Job Outlook for Hospitality Careers*

The OOH presents information differently than the CDMCareerZone Web site. The OOH provides complete career information in one book. You can use the book's index to find the page for an occupation you are researching. Look at the example in Figure 3.2 on page 60. Under Outlook, you can see that there are many opportunities for part-time work for Hotel/Motel Desk Clerks. Hotels and motels usually have someone working at the front desk 24 hours a day, seven days a week. These clerks might work late evening or early morning shifts or weekends. Employment can be seasonal. This is important information to have if you are considering this job.

Jobs as hotel desk clerks are growing faster than the average for all occupations.

Technology Note

The Internet is an excellent resource for job hunting. But job listings found online may not always be up-to-date. Before applying for a specific job, send an e-mail or make a phone call to the company. Make sure the job is still available.

IN THE ENVIRONMENT

One's environment includes indoor as well as outdoor surroundings. As they read about careers using the OOH, have them take notes on any working conditions that they think might be unhealthy. For example, prolonged exposure to a high level of noise is harmful to hearing. Spending very long hours in front of a computer screen can strain eyesight and cause other problems. As students make their decisions, they should factor in the kind of work environment that they would like.

Technology Note

Ask students if they have applied for jobs. Invite students with prior knowledge to describe their experiences. Have students read the Technology Note on page 61. If no one has searched the Internet for job listings, model such a search, or display a printout of the results of a search you have made. Explain that many newspapers post jobs on the Internet as well as in their pages. In addition, many companies list their open positions independently on the Web. Discuss reasons why an Internet listing might include jobs that have already been filled.

LEARNING STYLES

♦ Interpersonal/Group Learning

Have groups of students research resources for career exploration in your community. First, brainstorm a list of businesses and organizations that might have career resources. Have several phone books with business listings on hand. Students can look under key words such as *employment, job,* or *career* for organizations that might provide information about local sources of jobs. Ask each group to investigate opportunities at two different places. Have students find out whether these businesses permit students to shadow workers. Students should also find out if the businesses will offer tours, give out information, or provide speakers. Devise a form for groups to fill out about each entity they investigated. Staple the forms together in alphabetical order to create a reference booklet of local career resources.

Career Tip

Many schools have Career Resources Centers. Does your school have one? Do you know where it is? Find out and make use of this resource!

What Are Some School and Community Resources?

Most schools have many other career information resources. Books, computer programs, and videos may be available for career planning. Many colleges and postsecondary schools have catalogs and videos for students who are interested in those schools.

Community groups and businesses may also offer career resources. A business might send a guest speaker to a school. Or, a business or group might give tours. Many companies have opportunities to "shadow" or join a worker for a day. The Armed Forces also have programs to explore military careers.

These students learn about jobs on a tour of a television show set.

Career Tip

Where is the first place you look when job hunting? About 85 percent of job hunters use the newspaper's classified ads. However, only 20 percent of jobs are actually found through these ads. The Internet and networking are more effective.

You have now learned several ways to find career information. Remember that gathering this information will help you set a goal and make good choices as you plan for your future.

Lesson 1 Review Write your answers to these questions on a sheet of paper.

1. Why is it important to research information about occupations?

2. What are some resources in your school or community you can use to find career information?

3. Research an occupation using CDMCareerZone or the OOH. Write a brief description of the occupation.

4. What is wage equity? What are your feelings about wage equity?

Get Involved

Have you ever considered working in a medical field? One way to learn more about health-related careers is by volunteering in a hospital. Many community hospitals have volunteer programs for teens. Teen volunteers do a variety of jobs. They may help organize charts or answer telephones. They may help customers in gift shops. They may entertain children. Some volunteers may interact with patients. They may make beds, deliver food trays, or transport patients. Volunteering at a hospital gives you a close-up look at medical professionals. It also helps your community and adds to the work experience on your résumé.

Lesson 1 Review Answers

1. To know what an employer might expect of you, to know the skills and knowledge you need, and to plan for college or postsecondary school.

2. The school's Career Center, the library, the Internet, the OOH, and the CDMCareerZone Web site.

3. Answers will vary. Students should write a short description of an occupation they choose.

4. Wage equity is men and women earning the same amount of money for doing the same job; Answers will vary.

Get Involved

Have students read the Get Involved feature on page 63. Poll students to see if any have worked or are working as volunteers at a local hospital or clinic. Invite these students to explain how they decided to get involved and what steps were necessary to become a volunteer. Ask them to describe what work they do and how they feel about their volunteer work. If possible, display brochures describing volunteer openings at a local hospital. Encourage students to read this literature.

ONLINE CONNECTION

At www.dmoz.org/ Kids_and_Teens/ Teen_Life/ Volunteering _and_ Service, students can find an open directory with many links to sites describing volunteer opportunities. From here, they can click on Volunteer Match to reach a database that finds volunteering opportunities with nonprofit organizations in their area. They will enter the local zip code to search the database.

Lesson at a Glance

Chapter 3 Lesson 2

Overview In this lesson, students learn the steps in making a decision. They apply these steps to making career decisions.

Objectives

- To learn the steps in the decision-making process
- To understand how to prioritize goals
- To analyze the probable risk of a choice

Student Pages 64–69

Teacher's Resource Library **TRL**

Workbook Activity 9

Activity 9

Alternative Activity 9

Vocabulary

decision	option
goal	priority
motivation	probability

Give pairs of students a vocabulary word to look up. Have them learn the word's history, pronunciation, and meaning(s). Partners can develop a lesson to teach classmates the word, showing how its original and current meanings are related. For example, *decision* is based on the Latin root word *decidere*, meaning "to cut off." A decision cuts off, or eliminates, all options but the one chosen. Other histories are as follows: *goal*, from Middle English *gol*, "boundary, limit" *motivation/motive*, from Latin *motus*, past participle of the verb "to move" *option*, from Latin optare, "to choose" *priority/prior* from Latin prae, "before" *probability/probable*, from Latin *probare*, "to test, approve, prove"

Communication Connection

After students have read the Communication Connection feature on page 64, ask them to make a list of people who might give them good advice about career goals. Encourage students to talk to one of these people, making notes about the advice they received and how they feel about it. Students can place these notes in their portfolios along with the self-assessment profile they completed for Chapter 2.

64 *Chapter 3*

Lesson 2 Making Career Decisions

Decision
A choice to take action

Goal
A plan, an intention, or aim; something that a person wants to get or reach

Decisions are choices people make. You can show that you are independent and responsible by the choices you make. Adults and employers value people who are able to make responsible decisions. This lesson will focus only on making career decisions. Career decision making is about planning for your future. It will help you know exactly what you need to do in order to get what you want. Here are the five decision-making steps:

1. Set Goals
2. Make Priorities
3. Explore the Options
4. Assess the Risks
5. Make a Plan

Decision making takes time. Give yourself enough time to make good choices. Do not rush any of the steps. If you feel pressured or worried about your decisions, talk to a teacher, parent, or career counselor. It is important to make good decisions and these people can help you to do that.

Communication Connection

Talking to others about your career goals can be helpful. You may have a close friend who can help you see how well a specific career might suit you. Parents, guardians, and teachers, however, often know much about careers from personal experience. Try talking to them about your career goals.

Step 1: Set Goals

Setting **goals** is the first step in decision-making. A goal is something you want to get or reach. To plan your career, you need to state your career goals. By setting goals, you are starting a plan of action. Think about what you want to get, do, or be in the future.

Try to set realistic goals. A goal might not be right for you if it does not match up with your grades, test scores, or personality. Sometimes, other people can see that a goal is not right for you more easily than you can. Ask parents, guardians, friends, teachers, or people you work with if they think your goals are appropriate. These people know you well. They might tell you that they believe you cannot reach a goal you have chosen. They might be able to help you set other goals. A teacher or counselor might ask you to talk with them about your decision-making process.

64 *Chapter 3 Careers and Decision Making*

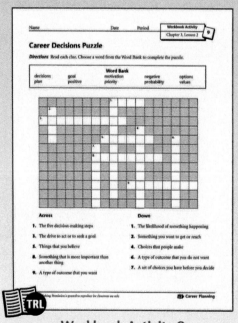

Workbook Activity 9

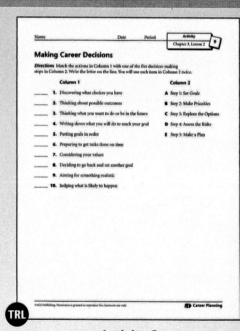

Activity 9

Step 2: Make Priorities

Priority
Something that is more important than something else

Next, you need to make **priorities**. A priority is something that you feel is more important than something else. When you make priorities, you choose what goals you will try to achieve first. Often, the first things you will do are those that are the easiest. When it is easy to get a successful result, you are more likely to continue. More difficult goals may take more time, more learning, or more experience.

Courage and determination are values that can help you reach your goals.

You can also put your goals in order of priority by looking at your values. Remember that values are things that bring you satisfaction. Recall the work values you identified in Chapter 2. These values reflect what is important to you—your priorities. For example, you might value outdoor work. You might decide that looking for a summer job at a camp or park will be your first priority. You may find that your work values do not always match your personal values. When that happens, think about how the conflict between these two will affect your work and non-work life.

Values can change as you get older or form relationships with people who have backgrounds different from yours. Values are important, but interests influence you more when you are younger. As you grow older, values play a larger role in your life. You might change your priorities as your values change. No matter how you decide to make priorities, you are setting up a plan to follow. As you do this, share your ideas and plans with others. They can often help you find ways to achieve a goal.

 Warm-Up Activity

Ask students to describe some decisions they make every day. Then have students describe decisions they have made that have affected their lives. Write a decision on the board as a statement, for example: *I decided I will not smoke.* Then ask students what goals and important values they think went into making this decision.

 Teaching the Lesson

Discuss the five steps listed on page 64 before students read about the steps in detail. Clarify the meanings of key words such as *priorities* and *risks* by asking students to make statements relating the words to actions that affect their lives. For example, they might complete the statements _____(name an action) is one of my highest priorities because _____. I will/will not _____ (name an action) if it seems risky.

Encourage students to think of a school-related decision they have to make, such as joining a club, taking a class, or trying out for a team. As they read, have them apply each step to their situation. Students can write out their goals and priorities, list options, assess the risks of each option, and then make a plan to carry out the option they choose. This approach should help students comprehend what they read and form questions about steps they do not understand.

 Reinforce and Extend

AT HOME

Students may want to talk with family members at home to see how the steps in the decision-making process can be applied to a decision the family needs to make, such as where to go on vacation or how to plan a budget. Students should be prepared to explain each step to family members and partici-pate in the decision-making process.

Body/Kinesthetic

Write a set of circumstances and a goal on an index card, for example: *Two students want to improve their strength and general health. Their goal is to get regular exercise.* Have volunteers role-play this situation and make a decision about how to get exercise. Other pairs could repeat the skit, illustrating differences in priorities, values, and motivation. Add more situational cards, or have students write their own, and use the decision-making model in the lesson to role-play decision making.

LEARNING STYLES

Logical/Mathematical

Present students with hypothetical situations and have them list the choices a participant has. For each choice, ask students to assess whether it has no risk, a measurable risk, or an unknown risk. Explain to students that measurable risk can be expressed numerically: There are x possible outcomes and there are y chances the desired outcome will occur. (The probability is y/x.) Then pair students and have them determine the chances of the following outcomes:

1. A student will choose a red marble if she gets one try to choose from a bag with 50 blue marbles, 45 green marbles, 4 white marbles, and 1 red marble. ($P = 1/100$)

2. You will not have to wash the dishes if you and your brother flip a coin to decide. ($P = 1/2$)

3. You will get a number greater than four if you roll a 1–6 number cube. ($P = 2/6 = 1/3$)

Option
A choice

Probability
The likelihood that an event will happen

Step 3: Explore the Options

Once you have decided what goals you will try to achieve first, you need to explore the **options** related to each goal. Options are choices you have. You need to have at least two choices to make a decision. In this step, you move closer to one of your goals by selecting one of the options.

By looking at the options in detail, you may find that you have not chosen a good goal. You can always change a goal or choose a new one. For example, you may have chosen a goal based on some advice from your brother or sister. Maybe your friends have influenced you to choose a certain job because it is a job that they like. After assessing your abilities, you should come to your own conclusion about what you like to do and how well you do it. To set a new goal, simply go back to Step 1. The process should move more quickly the second time because you have already done a lot of the work. You may even need to return to Step 1 more than once. It is very important that you set goals that are right for you. Exploring your options can help you choose good goals.

Step 4: Assess the Risks

When you make decisions and explore your options, you need to think about the possible outcomes of your choices. A decision may have a positive or a negative outcome. A positive outcome is one that you would like to happen. A negative outcome is one you do not want to happen. When you make a decision, think about the risk—the chance of a negative outcome. The likelihood of either a positive or a negative outcome is called **probability**.

Writing Practice

Do you think you are a risk taker when it comes to facing challenges? Think about risks you have taken in the following areas: learning, athletics, and friendships. Write a journal entry about a risk you have taken. Explain why you took it and how it turned out. Then discuss whether you are willing to take risks that come with choosing a career.

Writing Practice

Read the Writing Practice feature on page 66 aloud to students. You may want to model the prewriting process that is involved in this activity:

1. List risks taken.
2. Choose one to write about.
3. Write an outline giving reasons for taking the risk and outcomes of the choice.

Then have students follow these steps and write their responses.

Think Positive

Keep a positive, open mind in considering careers. Children sometimes make remarks like "I don't like broccoli." They have probably never tried it! Don't make negative generalizations like "I would not like to be an engineer." Instead, research many different careers, including engineering, with an open mind. Like a child who finally tries broccoli, you might find you like it!

Probability has the following ranges:

No risk: The outcome is known and certain. For example, if you flip a coin, it will land on either heads or tails. This outcome is certain. There can be no other outcomes.

Risky: The outcome has a specified probability. For example, you spin a spinner with 4 different colors: blue, red, yellow, and green. There is a 1 in 4 probability that the color will be red.

Uncertain: The chances of the outcome happening are unknown. For example, you are going to choose one marble out of a bag of marbles. If you choose a red marble, you win a prize. However, you do not know how many marbles are in the bag. You also do not know what colors the marbles are. You have no way of knowing if you will choose a red marble. The outcome is uncertain and you cannot tell how likely it is to happen.

Career Profile

Interior Designer

Do you love creating a wonderful room out of gleaming woods, beautiful fabrics, and unique accessories? Then you have probably considered an interior designing career. Interior designers do many tasks that are less glamorous than putting pretty rooms together. They must often deal with building codes and technical features such as lighting and plumbing. Interior designers need more than just artistic talent. They must communicate well with many different types of people, including clients, architects, and contractors. They need good management skills in order to complete projects on schedule.

The two main fields for interior designers are residential design and commercial design. A residential designer works with homeowners. Some specialize in kitchen or bathroom design. A commercial designer may design offices, restaurants, health-care facilities, or other businesses. Some interior designers have associates degrees from two-year colleges. Some colleges offer four- or five-year interior design degrees. Today many employers look for designers with these degrees. Interior design is a growing field, but it is also a competitive one.

Careers and Decision Making Chapter 3 **67**

Think Positive

Ask students to think of a food or activity they avoided because they didn't think they would like it, only to find later that they enjoyed it. Have volunteers explain the meaning of the phrase "Keep an open mind." Then have a student read the Think Positive feature on page 67 aloud. Remind students that many careers have been stereotyped in the media. They may have a negative or a positive impression of a career based on misleading or false information.

Career Profile

Interior Designer

Ask students if they enjoy "fixing up" a room at home—a bedroom, kitchen, or living room—to see what look is most exciting, useful, or inviting. This can be as simple as moving furniture or as involved as painting walls, changing floor covering, and putting in new doors and windows. Have volunteers read aloud the Career Profile for an interior designer on page 67. Encourage students who are interested in this career to visit the Web site of the American Society of Interior Designers at www.asid.org. It presents information on education and careers in interior design and much more.

Motivation
An inner drive or encouragement from others for a person to act on or seek a goal

You cannot totally control probabilities, but you can assess risks. To do this, you determine the probability (high, medium, or low) that the outcome you want will happen.

Read these examples of how Marinda and Tyler assessed the risks involved in their decisions.

Developing your abilities involves taking risks.

Marinda is deciding whether to try out for the varsity soccer team this year. She played on the junior varsity soccer team last year. She was voted the most valuable player. She scored the most goals of anyone on the team. She knows that more people will try out for the varsity team than there are spots available. She considers the probability of making the team high based on her abilities and past performance. She considers her risk to be low. Marinda decides to try out for the team.

Tyler wants to apply to an internship program at a large company. Each year, thousands of students apply, but only one is chosen. The competition for the internship is very high. Tyler considers the probability that he will be the one chosen to be low. However, he really wants the internship so he takes the risk and applies for it.

Some people will take many chances. Other people simply are not risk takers. Developing your talents always involves some kind of risk. Taking a risk depends on the situation and personal **motivation**. Motivation is what drives a person to act or to seek a goal. Motivation can be an inner desire. It can also be encouragement from others. In Tyler's case, he was motivated to apply for the internship because he had a strong inner desire to get it.

Step 5: Make a Plan

The final step is to write down what you need to do and when you need to do it. This sounds simple. However, it is very important to have a plan in place. This helps you put the earlier steps into action and achieve your goals.

Some of the steps on the way to your goals may be simple. Perhaps all that you need to do to sign up for a class you want is to check off a box on a class registration form. Great!

However, you might need to include a personal essay as part of an application. You will need to make a plan so you can accomplish this step on time. Then, you have to wait for a decision on whether you were accepted. What other things can you accomplish while you are waiting? You need to have a plan in place so you can keep moving toward your goal. If you wait too long to achieve a goal, you will be less motivated. Having a plan will keep you on track.

Gender and Careers

Some careers, such as law and medicine, were once considered "men's" careers. In the last 25 years, many more women have entered these careers. One career which has had a striking change in gender is veterinary medicine. In the 1960s, only five percent of veterinary students were women. By 2005, the majority of students in veterinary schools will be women. In 2002, there were 24,356 women veterinarians. There were 33,461 men veterinarians. One reason for the change is that being a veterinarian has become less difficult physically. In the past, most vets worked on farm animals. So physical strength was required. Today, many vets work only with pets. Veterinarians must take demanding courses in college plus about four additional years of study.

Lesson 2 Review Write your answers to these questions on a sheet of paper.

1. Why is decision making important?

2. What are the five decision-making steps?

3. What is one big decision you have made in the last few months? How did you make that decision?

4. Why is making decisions often difficult?

Ask students to write their thoughts about themselves as risk takers. How much risk are they willing to take to reach a goal? What goals or values motivate them enough to overcome their fear of risk? Students may not want to share their thoughts with others but can add their journal entries to their career portfolios.

Gender and Careers

Ask students to name qualities they think a person needs to become a veterinarian. Then have students read the Gender and Careers feature on page 69. Ask them to summarize the change that has occurred in veterinary medicine as a career over 45 years. Ask interested students to read more about the work a veterinarian does and report to the class on it.

Lesson 2 Review Answers

1. It is important so that you can put your earlier plans in action in order to meet your goals.

2. Set goals; make priorities; explore the options; assess the risks; make a plan.

3. Answers will vary. Students should identify a recent decision and explain how they made it.

4. Making decisions can be difficult because it can involve risk.

Practicing Decision-Making Steps

Have students review the profiles they completed for their portfolios in Chapter 2. Then have them read the Portfolio Activity on pages 70 and 71 and complete the steps using information from their self-assessment profiles. Students can write responses on their own paper or on Portfolio Activity 3 in the TRL.

You may want to model an appropriate format for students' answers on the board. See the example below.

	Occupation Choice 1	Occupation Choice 2
1. abilities match		
2. interests match		
3. values match		
4. personality fit		
5. salary okay		
6. willing to get more education		
7. willing to move		
8. job outlook		
9. qualified when finish education		
10. liking for the field		

[E-excellent, G-good, P-poor; Y-yes, N-no]

Practicing Decision-Making Steps

In this activity, you will practice the five decision-making steps you learned in Lesson 2. Your responses will become part of your portfolio.

Step 1: Set Goals

What are your career goals? Ask yourself, "What would I really want to do or be in five years?" Use the information that you discovered in Chapter 2 about your abilities, interests, and personal characteristics. Consider the occupation you researched in Lesson 1 of this chapter. What fields of study do you like? What career areas require a college education? On a separate sheet of paper, or on Portfolio Activity 3, write at least two of your career goals.

Step 2: Make Priorities

In Chapter 2 you identified the work values that are most important to you. Review the values you selected. Below each goal you wrote in Step 1, write how that goal will help you fulfill any of your highest values. Remember to keep your personal values separate from your work values. If you cannot connect your goals and values, you may need to modify your goals or re-assess your values.

Step 3: Explore the Options

Once you have prioritized your goals, you should examine the choices you will need to make. To do this, write down any two areas of study or jobs you are considering. Use the information you studied in previous lessons to rate each of your two choices with the ratings below. For each choice, answer these questions. Write your answer under the choice.

1. How well do your abilities match those required by the major, field of study, or job? Excellent match, good match, or poor match?

2. How well do your interests match those activities that the major, field of study, or job will involve? Excellent match, good match, or poor match?

3. How well do your values match the values of people in the occupations in this major, field of study, or job? Excellent match, good match, or no match?

Name ____ Date ____ Period ____ Portfolio Activity, Page 1 — Chapter 3

Practicing Decision-Making Steps

Step 1: Set Goals
Write at least three career goals.

Step 2: Make Priorities
For each goal you wrote in Step 1, write how that goal will help you fulfill your work values.

Step 3: Explore the Options
Write down any two postsecondary areas of study or jobs you are considering. Rate each of those options by using the questions on pages 70 and 71. Write your ratings in the space provided.

Option 1   Option 2

©AGS Publishing. Permission is granted to reproduce for classroom use only.   Career Planning

---

Name ____ Date ____ Period ____ Portfolio Activity, Page 2 — Chapter 3

Practicing Decision-Making Steps, continued

Step 4: Assess the Risks
Based on your answers to Step 3, which of the two options involves more risk than the other? Write down the risk.

Step 5: Make a Plan
Use this table to help you make a career plan.

Career Action Plan

Goal

Action Step (what needs to be done)	Resources or People to Contact	Date to Be Completed

©AGS Publishing. Permission is granted to reproduce for classroom use only.   Career Planning

4. How do your personal characteristics fit with people who enter occupations from this major, field of study, or job? Excellent fit, good fit, or poor fit?

5. Is the salary acceptable to you? Yes or no?

6 Would you be willing to get additional schooling or more education? Yes, no, or not sure?

7. Would you be willing to move to find employment? Yes, no, or not sure? Would you be willing to move to go to school in this major, field of study, or job? Yes, no, or not sure?

8. What is the job outlook for careers in this major, field of study, or job? Excellent, good, or poor?

9. Will you be qualified for the employment you want when you finish your education? Yes or no?

10. How much do you like the field in which the occupation is? Very much, somewhat, or not at all?

Now that you have answered these questions, you can identify the areas that are keeping you from making a decision. By exploring your options, you can weigh the positives and negatives of possible decisions.

Step 4: Assess the Risks

Which of the options you listed in Step 3 involves more risk than the other(s)? Write down the risk.

Step 5: Make a Plan

Look at the table below. You can use this table as a guide to plan your future.

Career Action Plan

Goal	Action Step (what needs to be done)	Resources or People to Contact	Date to Be Completed
	_____	_____	_____
	_____	_____	_____
	_____	_____	_____
_____			

Before students complete Step 4, review with them the levels of risk in any given choice:

1. The outcome may be certain, so there is no risk.
2. The outcome may be highly probable, with a low risk, or highly improbable with a high risk. You can determine how much risk is involved.
3. The outcome may be impossible to predict. You have no way of assessing the risk you are taking.

Once students choose the option they prefer, help them make their plan. For example, have them consult a reference such as the OOH to find out what kinds of classes they should take and whether they need to plan on going to college. They may need to talk with a guidance counselor to learn more about what steps to take and people to contact, and when each step should be completed.

Portfolio Activity Answers

Answers will vary.

Chapter 3 Review

Use the Chapter Review to prepare students for tests and to reteach content from the chapter.

Chapter 3 Mastery Test TRL

The Teacher's Resource Library includes two forms of the Chapter 3 Mastery Test. Each test addresses the chapter Goals for Learning. An optional third page of additional critical-thinking items is included for each test. The difficulty level of the two forms is equivalent.

Review Answers
Vocabulary Review

1. option 2. wage 3. decision 4. probability 5. goal 6. motivation 7. priority

Concept Review

8. C 9. D 10. A 11. D 12. C

Chapter 3 REVIEW

Word Bank

Word Bank
decision
goal
motivation
option
priority
probability
wage

Vocabulary Review

Choose the word or phrase from the Word Bank that best completes each sentence. Write the answer on your paper.

1. A choice is a(n) _____.

2. The set amount of money a person makes per hour of work is a(n) _____.

3. A choice that helps people take control of their lives is a(n) _____.

4. The likelihood that an event will happen is called _____.

5. An intention or something a person wants to reach is a(n) _____.

6. When a person has an inner drive or encouragement from others to act on a goal, the person has _____.

7. Something that a person feels is most important is a(n) _____.

Concept Review

Choose the word or phrase that best completes each sentence. Write the letter of the answer on your paper.

8. A source that describes in detail 88 percent of all the jobs in the United States is the _____.

   A CDMCareerZone
   B Career Resource Center
   C OOH
   D newspaper classified ads

9. When you determine the probability that a certain outcome will occur, you are _____.

   A making a decision
   B taking a risk
   C making a plan
   D assessing risks

Name _____ Date _____ Period _____ | Mastery Test A, Page 1 | Chapter 3

Chapter 3 Mastery Test A

Part A Circle the letter of the answer that correctly completes each sentence.

1. An occupation is a _____.
   A place to get training for a career
   B job market
   C group of similar or related jobs or skills
   D plan to find the right career

2. CDMCareerZone is a _____.
   A Web site on the Internet
   B postsecondary school
   C catalog of jobs that are available
   D resource center in some school libraries

3. The *Occupational Outlook Handbook* is a _____.
   A Web site on the Internet
   B book published by the U.S. Department of Labor
   C video resource
   D newspaper section published in Sunday papers

4. The first step in making career decisions is to _____.
   A set goals
   B make priorities
   C explore the options
   D make a plan

5. One of the most important things about making a plan is to _____.
   A wait until you know everything you need to know
   B never change it
   C keep it to yourself
   D write it down

Part B Match the words in Column 1 with their definitions in Column 2. Write the letter on the line.

Column 1	Column 2
6. priority	A something a person wants to get or reach
7. options	B choices that a person has about a decision
8. probability	C the drive to act or to seek a goal
9. motivation	D something that is more important than something else
10. goal	E the likelihood that an event will happen

Career Planning

Name _____ Date _____ Period _____ | Mastery Test A, Page 2 | Chapter 3

Chapter 3 Mastery Test A, *continued*

Part C Write the correct word or phrase from the Word Bank to complete each sentence.

Word Bank				
risks	decisions	plan	positive outcome	values

11. Your _____ reflect what is important to you.

12. Something that you want to happen is called a _____.

13. The third step in making career decisions is to assess the _____.

14. You can show that you are independent and responsible by the _____ you make.

15. Writing a _____ can help you move toward your goal.

Part D Write the answers to these questions. Use complete sentences.

16. What is wage equity?

17. What is the easiest way to find the page for an occupation you are researching in the *Occupational Outlook Handbook*?

18. Why is the "Education Needed" section for a CDMCareerZone summary useful in making a plan?

19. Why is it important to set realistic goals when you are considering an occupation?

20. What could "shadowing," or joining a worker for a day teach you about an occupation?

Career Planning

Name _____ Date _____ Period _____ | Mastery Test A, Page 3 | Chapter 3

Chapter 3 Mastery Test A, *continued*

Part E Write your answer to each question. Use complete sentences. Support your answers with facts and examples from the book.

21. How does researching information about occupations lead to making better decisions about careers? (2 points)

22. How might discovering a negative outcome help you in choosing a career? (2 points)

Part F Write a paragraph for each topic. Include a topic sentence, body, and conclusion. Support each answer with facts and examples from the textbook.

23. Why are values important to the decision-making process? (3 points)

24. Why do you think people sometimes make poor decisions? Explain your ideas in terms of decision-making steps. (3 points)

Career Planning

10. Men and women earning the same amount for doing the same job is called _____.

   A wage equity   **C** a job description

   B an occupational brief **D** probability

11. One thing about careers found in CDMCareerZone but not in the OOH is _____.

   A earnings   **C** job outlook

   B training required   **D** current job openings

12. The first step in making a decision is _____.

   A setting priorities   **C** setting goals

   B assessing risks   **D** making a plan

Critical Thinking

Write the answer to each question on your paper.

13. Suppose a friend says he does not need to use a resource such as CDMCareerZone. His reason is that he has already chosen a career. What might you tell him about other reasons to use the resources?

14. Is it a good idea to talk to others about your career goals? Explain why or why not.

15. Suppose a person decides to pursue acting. She knows there is a risk she will not get acting jobs or make much money. Do you think taking the risk is a good idea or not? Explain.

Test-Taking Tip

It is easier to learn new vocabulary words if you use them often. Make them part of your speaking and writing in other discussions and subject areas.

Review Answers
Critical Thinking

13. Answers will vary. Students may say that using CDMCareeerZone might provide more information and the friend might learn about other careers. **14.** Answers will vary. Students should explain that talking to others about their career goals can be helpful. **15.** Answers will vary. Students should explain whether they think taking a risk is a good idea.

ALTERNATIVE ASSESSMENT

- Have students name the two best ways to learn about a specific career and model how to use these resources to get information about the career. They should include a summary of the kinds of information each resource gives.

- Have each student write down a decision he or she must make and develop a plan for making it by using the decision-making steps.

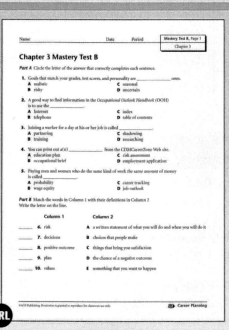

Chapter

Planning Guide

Career Clusters and the Major Industries

	Student Pages	Vocabulary	Lesson Review	Critical-Thinking Questions	Chapter Review
Lesson 1 What Are the Career Clusters?	76–79	✔	✔	✔	✔
Lesson 2 Agriculture, Food, and Natural Resources	80–84	✔	✔	✔	✔
Lesson 3 Manufacturing	85–87	✔	✔	✔	✔
Lesson 4 Transportation, Distribution, and Logistics	88–91	✔	✔	✔	✔
Lesson 5 Architecture and Construction	92–94	✔	✔	✔	✔
Lesson 6 Health Science	95–97		✔	✔	✔
Lesson 7 Science, Technology, Engineering, and Mathematics	98–101	✔	✔	✔	✔
Lesson 8 Information Technology	102–105	✔	✔	✔	✔
Lesson 9 Arts, Audio-Video Technology, and Communication	106–109		✔	✔	✔
Lesson 10 Education and Training	110–111		✔	✔	✔
Lesson 11 Human Services	112–115	✔	✔	✔	✔
Lesson 12 Hospitality and Tourism	116–118	✔	✔	✔	✔
Lesson 13 Law, Public Safety, and Security	119–122	✔	✔	✔	✔
Lesson 14 Finance	123–125	✔	✔	✔	✔
Lesson 15 Marketing, Sales, and Services	126–129		✔	✔	✔
Lesson 16 Business Management and Administration	130–133		✔	✔	✔
Lesson 17 Government and Public Administration	134–137		✔	✔	✔

Chapter Activities

Student Text
Chapter 4 Portfolio Activity

Teacher's Resource Library
Chapter 4 Chapter Outline
Chapter 4 Self-Study Guide
Chapter 4 Portfolio Activity

Assessment Options

Student Text
Chapter 4 Review

Teacher's Resource Library
Chapter 4 Mastery Tests A and B

Teacher's Edition
Chapter 4 Alternative Assessment

Student Text Features											Teaching Strategies					Learning Styles					Teacher's Resource Library				
Portfolio Activity	Writing Practice	Communication Connection	The Economy	Career Tip	Career Profile	On the Job	Gender and Careers	Think Positive	Technology Note	Get Involved	Background Information	Applications (Home, Community, Global, Environment)	Personal Journal	Online Connection	ELL/ESL Strategy	Visual/Spatial	Body/Kinesthetic	Interpersonal/Group Learning	Logical/Mathematical	Auditory/Verbal	Activities	Alternative Activities	Workbook Activities	Self-Study Guide	Chapter Outline
				78								78, 79		78	77				77, 78		10	10	10	✔	✔
				81								82	84		83	81	82		84	81	11	11	11	✔	✔
											87				86			86	87		12	12	12	✔	✔
			91	89, 90							90	89									13	13	13	✔	✔
												93	94			93			94		14	14	14	✔	✔
	96											96			97		96		97		15	15	15	✔	✔
101																99		100	100	99	16	16	16	✔	✔
				103						103		104, 105			103	104					17	17	17	✔	✔
												108			109			107	107		18	18	18	✔	✔
														111				111			19	19	19	✔	✔
												114			114			113	114	115	20	20	20	✔	✔
		118										118		118		117	117				21	21	21	✔	✔
									120		121	121, 122	120						122	121	22	22	22	✔	✔
															124	125		125		124	23	23	23	✔	✔
					127							128	128			127	127		128		24	24	24	✔	✔
						131						131			133			132	131		25	25	25	✔	✔
138										135		136		135	136				136		26	26	26	✔	✔

Alternative Activities

The Teacher's Resource Library (TRL) contains a set of lower-level worksheets called Alternative Activities. These worksheets cover the same content as the regular Activities but are written at a second-grade reading level.

Career Interest Inventory

The AGS Publishing Harrington-O'Shea Career Decision-Making System (CDM) may be used with this textbook. Students can use the CDM to explore their interests and identify careers. The CDM defines career areas that are indicated by students' response on the inventory.

Chapter at a Glance

Chapter 4: Careers and Decision Making
pages 74–141

Lessons

1. **What Are the Career Clusters?**
   pages 76–79

2. **Agriculture, Food, and Natural Resources**
   pages 80–84

3. **Manufacturing**
   pages 85–87

4. **Transportation, Distribution, and Logistics**
   pages 88–91

5. **Architecture and Construction**
   pages 92–94

6. **Health Science**
   pages 95–97

7. **Science, Technology, Engineering, and Mathematics**
   pages 98–101

8. **Information Technology**
   pages 102–105

9. **Arts, Audio-Video Technology, and Communication**
   pages 106–109

10. **Education and Training**
    pages 110–111

11. **Human Services**
    pages 112–115

12. **Hospitality and Tourism**
    pages 116–118

13. **Law, Public Safety, and Security**
    pages 119–122

14. **Finance**
    pages 123–125

15. **Marketing, Sales, and Service**
    pages 126–129

16. **Business Management and Administration**
    pages 130–133

17. **Government and Public Administration**
    pages 134–137

Portfolio Activity

What Career is Right for You?
pages 138–139

4 Career Clusters and the Major Industries

How are the cars of the future designed? People who design cars have computer knowledge. They are also familiar with the automotive industry. Car designers are creative. They think about what the customer will want in the next generation of cars. In their jobs, they use all of these skills. No matter what job you are interested in, you should know how your skills and interests match a particular career field. Every field includes a range of people with a variety of strengths and skills. In this chapter, you will begin to look more closely at specific career clusters. You will learn the types of work that are done in each field. You will learn about the workers and the workplaces for each field. You will learn what skill areas are the best fit for certain occupations. As you read about the wide range of career paths available today, you may just find one that matches your talents, skills, and interests.

Goals for Learning

- ◆ To identify the major career clusters
- ◆ To examine the jobs, wages, and outlooks in the major career clusters
- ◆ To understand the jobs of workers in major industries
- ◆ To identify occupations to explore in more detail

75

Chapter Review
pages 140–141
Audio CD 🎧
Teacher's Resource Library **TRL**
  Workbook Activities 10–26
  Activities 10–26
  Alternative Activities 10–26
  Portfolio Activity 4
  Chapter 4 Chapter Outline
  Chapter 4 Self-Study Guide
  Chapter 4 Mastery Tests A and B
  (Answer Keys for the Teacher's Resource Library begin on page 328 of this Teacher's Edition.)

Introducing the Chapter

Have students look at the photo on page 74 and describe what is happening in the picture. Discuss the photo using these questions: *What skills do you think this person had to learn to do this career? How would you describe this workplace? How well do you think this kind of job pays? Do you think there are a lot of jobs in this field? How could you find out?* Have students read the introductory paragraph and consider how the "personality" of a career field could aaffect how well they would perform at and enjoy a career.

Have students read the Goals for Learning. Explain that as they read the chapter they will learn about occupations in different career clusters.

Career Tips

Ask volunteers to read the career tips that appear in the margins throughout the chapter. Then discuss them with the class.

Alternative Assessment

The Alternative Assessment box on page 141 of the Chapter Review includes activities using various learning styles to assess students' understanding of the Goals for Learning.

Name   **Date**   **Period**   Chapter Outline, Page 1 — Chapter 4

Career Clusters and the Major Industries

Directions Fill in the outline below. Filling in the blanks will help you as you read and study Chapter 4.

I. **Lesson 1: What Are the Career Clusters? (pp. 76–79)**
   A. **Learning about Occupations and Industries**
      1. Occupations with similar qualities are career _____
   B. **Industry Growth and Preparation for Employment**
      1. As the economy changes, be aware of which career areas will _____
      2. Knowing about different jobs helps you plan your _____

II. **Lesson 2: Agriculture, Food, and Natural Resources (pp. 80–84)**
   A. **Agriculture Workers and Workplaces**
      1. Agriculture deals with plants, animals, and _____
   B. **Natural Resources Workers and Workplaces**
      1. Natural resources occupations include jobs related to _____ and _____
   C. **Agriculture, Food Production, and Natural Resources Outlook**
      1. Employment in these areas will grow _____ than in other occupations.

III. **Lesson 3: Manufacturing (pp. 85–87)**
   A. **The Manufacturing Workplace**
      1. In a manufacturing plant, parts may be _____, or put together in one of several buildings.
   B. **Manufacturing Workers**
      1. Most manufacturing workers operate _____
      2. Workers in the manufacturing cluster enjoy _____

RL

Chapter 4 Chapter Outline

Name   **Date**   **Period**   Chapter Outline, Page 2 — Chapter 4

Career Clusters and the Major Industries, continued

   C. **Manufacturing Outlook**
      1. By 2012, manufacturing workers will make up _____ percent of all employed workers.

IV. **Lesson 4: Transportation, Distribution, and Logistics (pp. 88–91)**
   A. **The Transportation Workplace**
      1. Freight is taken from _____ or _____ and delivered to the customer.
   B. **Transportation Workers**
      1. Transportation workers often have a main interest in the _____ area.
   C. **Transportation Outlook**
      1. Employment of drivers in this cluster is expected to _____

V. **Lesson 5: Architecture and Construction (pp. 92–94)**
   A. **The Architecture and Construction Workplace**
      1. The workplace for an actual construction job is the _____
   B. **Architecture and Construction Workers**
      1. Most construction workers learn their craft _____
   C. **Architecture and Construction Outlook**
      1. Employment in this cluster will increase by about _____ percent by 2012.

VI. **Lesson 6: Health Science (pp. 95–97)**
   A. **The Health Science Workplace**
      1. _____, and other healthcare workers may work in hospitals, private clinics, or home health agencies.

©AGS Publishing. Permission is granted to reproduce for classroom use only.   **TRL** Career Planning

Lesson at a Glance

Chapter 4 Lesson 1

Overview In this lesson, students look at the size and outlook for various industries. They consider how to learn about occupations in the industries and how to prepare for them.

Objectives

- To understand what career clusters are
- To compare job outlooks for major industries
- To survey average income for various levels of education

Student Pages 76–79

Teacher's Resource Library

Workbook Activity 10

Activity 10

Alternative Activity 10

....

Vocabulary

apprenticeship
industry

Have students analyze the word *apprenticeship*. Ask students what the suffix *-ship* might mean by thinking about the meanings of the words *friendship* and *sportsmanship*. ("*condition or quality*") Then explain that *apprentice* comes to us from a Latin word meaning "to learn." Explain that *industry* combines two Latin words meaning "in" and "to build." Have students predict the meanings of the words, and then check their predictions in the glossary.

....

 Warm-Up Activity

Have students name the occupations they think will be most in demand and will pay the best wages ten years from now. Require students to give reasons for their predictions. Explain that for most occupations, workers with more education and training earn more. Ask students to tell whether they think this is fair and explain why or why not.

Lesson 1 What Are the Career Clusters?

Industry
A large-scale business or service area that provides a product or service

The U.S. government collects detailed information on about 1,100 occupations. In order to look at an occupation more easily, these occupations are grouped into similar career areas. These groups are called clusters. The clusters show related occupations. The occupations in each cluster require similar preparation, draw upon similar worker skills, and have similar workplaces. Occupations in a cluster can range from entry-level opportunities to professional, technical, and management positions. The 16 lessons that follow are the U.S. Department of Education career clusters. These clusters include the occupations where 97 percent of the workers are expected to be employed in 2012.

How Can I Learn About Occupations?

By exploring each career cluster, you can learn about occupations that you may like. You can discover, examine, and research the activities that a worker in a certain **industry** does. An industry is a large-scale business or service area that provides a product or service. You can learn the knowledge and skills that workers need in order to be employed in industries you are interested in.

How Many People Work in Each Industry?

As you read about different industries, you will learn that not all industries are the same size. Some industries will have more employment opportunities than others. Some industries have occupations that are not located in every region of the country. These things may affect your career choice. You may need to move in order to work in a certain occupation. Table 4.1 on page 77 shows the amount of people by percent expected to be employed in each of the major industries in 2012.

You can see from Table 4.1 that 6.4 percent of the workers in 2012 will be self-employed. These workers are not employed by someone else. They work for themselves. The greatest opportunities for self-employment will be in arts, design media, entertainment, sports, mathematical, and computer occupations.

---

76 *Chapter 4   Career Clusters and the Major Industries*

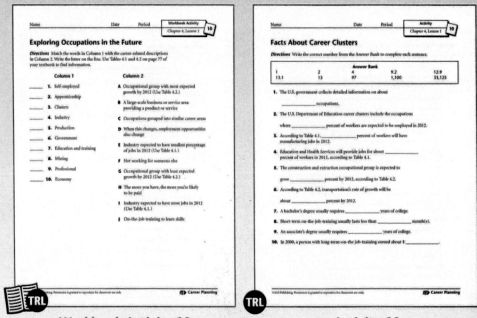

Workbook Activity 10   **Activity 10**

Table 4.1

Industry	Percent
Agriculture, Forestry, and Fishing	1.2
Construction	4.7
Education and Health Services	12.9
Finance, Insurance, and Real Estate	5.3
Government	14.5
Information	2.5
Leisure and Hospitality	8.5
Manufacturing	9.2
Mining	0.3
Other Services	4.3
Professional and Business Services	12.6
Self-Employed	6.4
Transportation, Communication, and Utilities	3.4
Wholesale and Retail Trade	14.2
Total	**100.0**

Source: Bureau of Labor Statistics

Table 4.1 *Projected Number of Employed Persons by 2012 by Major Industry Area in the United States in Percents*

Table 4.2

Occupational Group	Percent Growth
Construction and extraction	15.0
Farming, fishing, and forestry	3.3
Installation, maintenance, and repair	13.6
Management, business, and financial	15.4
Office and administrative support	6.8
Production	3.2
Professional	23.3
Sales	12.9
Service	20.1
Transportation and material moving	13.1

Source: Bureau of Labor Statistics

Table 4.2 *Growth in Percent of the Major Occupational Groups from 2002 to 2012*

2 Teaching the Lesson

Be sure students understand that *industry*, as used in this lesson, applies to any large grouping of occupations that are similar. Whereas it is natural to think of mining and manufacturing as industries, students may be unfamiliar with thinking of education and finance as industries.

Point out that the groupings listed in Tables 4.1 and 4.2 are not the same as the career cluster names used in the 16 lessons that follow. The table information is taken from the U.S. Department of Labor, whereas the career clusters were devised for educational purposes.

Point out to students that the numbers in the tables represent different quantities. Table 4.1 takes all employees in the United States and places them into industries, then divides to find the percentage of the total workforce in each industry. In Table 4.2, the percent growth shows how many more employees an occupational group will have in 2012 than it had in 2002. These numbers are not related to each other, that is, they cannot be added together to get 100 percent.

3 Reinforce and Extend

LEARNING STYLES

Logical/Mathematical
Have students study Table 4.1 to rank the top five major industries from 1 to 5, according to number of employees. (*1. Government—14.5 percent; 2. Wholesale and Retail Trade—14.2 percent; 3. Education and Health Services—12.9 percent; 4. Professional and Business Services—12.6 percent; 5. Manufacturing—9.2 percent*) Then have them use Table 4.2 to identify the two occupational groups that will be hiring the largest percentage of new employees for the near term. (*Professional—23.3 percent increase; Service—20.1 percent increase*) Discuss in general terms what kind of work is dominating our economy.

ELL/ESL STRATEGY

Language Objective: *To identify lists separated by commas in series and to read them for sense*

Students who are learning English may not be familiar with punctuation conventions of English grammar. Explain that commas have several uses. One of them is to set off three or more items in a series or list. The items may be single words, phrases, or whole clauses. Lists help writers combine ideas and make sentences more interesting and efficient. Have students underline each item listed. Identify the kind of grammatical structure in each list. (Example, page 76, paragraph 1: *The occupations in each cluster require similar preparation, draw upon similar worker skills, and have similar workplaces.* List combines three complete predicates.)

What Occupational Group Will Grow the Most?

As you learned in Chapter 1, another thing that may affect your career choice is the economy. When the economy changes, different employment opportunities arise. For example, by the year 2012 the government predicts that employment in mining will decrease. The largest growth in employment will occur in educational and health, and professional and business services.

As the economy changes, workers need to be aware of which career areas will grow and be in demand. It is also good information to have when you are planning your career. Look at Table 4.2 on page 77. It shows the predicted growth in percent of the major occupational groups from 2002 to 2012.

You can see in Table 4.2 that some occupations will increase faster than others. For example, the professional and service areas will have the most new jobs. Occupational groups in farming, fishing, and forestry and those in production will experience the fewest number of new jobs.

How Do I Prepare for the Job I Want?

The different jobs in the occupational groups in Table 4.2 require different kinds of educational preparation and training. In the rest of this chapter you will learn the education and training level required for several occupations. This information will help you decide what school subjects to take and what your plans for the future will be. You will need to decide whether to attend college or vocational school, start military training, or start on-the-job training. On-the-job training is also often called an **apprenticeship.** In an apprenticeship program, you learn from an experienced worker. Eventually, you do the job yourself.

Some jobs require little or no training and education. Other jobs require four years of college or more. You might begin in a job that does not require a lot of training. Then, if you learn more skills or get more education, you can advance to a higher-level job. Jobs that are related in this way are called **career ladders.** The more new skills, job duties, and education you get, the higher you can move on the ladder.

Look at the chart below of the average weekly earnings for full-time workers with different education and training levels for the year 2002. You can see that getting more education and training results in higher pay.

Education/Training	Average Weekly Earnings
Less than high school	$409
High school	$562
Some college, no degree	$644
Associate's degree (2 years of college), educational	$673
Associate's degree (2 years of college), vocational	$711
Bachelor's degree (4 years of college)	$996
Master's degree or higher (more than 4 years of college)	$1,273

Source: Horrigon, Michael. (February 2004). Employment projections to 2012: Concepts and context. *The Monthly Labor Review*. p. 21.

More than 20 percent of the workers referenced in Tables 4.1 and 4.2 have attended and graduated from a college. Another 8 percent went to a community college or postsecondary school. The information in this chapter will help you plan to meet your career goal.

In Chapters 2 and 3, you stated activities in which you have an interest. You identified the school subjects you like and the skills in which you have competence. You also identified your abilities and strengths and determined what work values are important to you. School subjects, abilities, and values that relate to each cluster are given in the next lesson. As you read about each cluster, you can refer to this information.

Lesson 1 Review Write your answers to these questions on a sheet of paper.

1. What is an industry?
2. How many workers in 2012 are expected to be self-employed?
3. Which fields will have the most new jobs from 2002 to 2012? Which fields will have the fewest?
4. People with a bachelor's degree or more education earn more money than other workers. Why do you think this is so?

GLOBAL CONNECTION

For comparison to U.S. data, have students research average yearly earnings in a number of other nations of the world. Some poor countries have few skilled and educated workers. For countries where students find that average income is very low, ask students to find information that might explain this difference—such as that most people live by subsistence farming or that unemployment is very high. If students are able to find extensive data, students can compare income averages for workers with varying amounts of training and education.

Lesson 1 Review Answers

1. An industry is a large-scale business or service area that provides a product or service.
2. 6.4 percent
3. The professional and service areas will have the most new jobs. Farming, fishing, forestry, and production will have the least.
4. Answers will vary. Students may say that college graduates have more prestige, a wider variety of interests, and more opportunities for advancement.

Chapter 4 Lesson 2

Overview This lesson describes workers, workplaces, and outlook in the occupations of agriculture, food, and natural resources.

Objectives

- To identify agricultural regions
- To compare agricultural occupations and the level of training or education they require
- To describe the typical natural resources workplace
- To compare workers in fields of mining and extraction and their training or education
- To understand the outlook for workers in agriculture and natural resources

Student Pages 80–84

Teacher's Resource Library

Workbook Activity 11

Activity 11

Alternative Activity 11

Vocabulary

agriculture
extraction
mining
natural resources

Write the vocabulary terms on the board. After students have read them, read aloud one definition from the text. Have students identify the matching term and provide an example or instance of the concept. (For example, raising soybeans is one kind of agriculture.) Repeat the process for each vocabulary term. Then ask students to write a sentence for each term.

1 Warm-Up Activity

Have students read the lesson title and list some occupations they can think of that fall into this cluster. Then ask them to suggest what the agriculture, food, and natural resources occupations have in common that caused them to be grouped together.

Lesson 2 Agriculture, Food, and Natural Resources

Agriculture
Farming; producing crops and raising livestock

Natural resources
Minerals and other things found in nature

Key to Education and Training Needed

1—Entry Level training a few days up to 2 months with an experienced worker

2—On-the-Job Training 2 to 6 months of training with an experienced worker

3—Apprenticeship training 6 months up to 5 years with an experienced worker

4—Technical/Vocational Program completion of program lasting usually 1 to 4 years

5—College 4-year degree or advanced degree completed

This cluster includes two main areas: **agriculture** and **natural resources.** Agriculture deals with plants, animals, and food production. Natural resources involves the mining of resources beneath the earth. These industries are the oldest in the world. They help us meet our basic needs for food, shelter, and heat.

The Agriculture Workplace

The workplaces for most agricultural jobs are where conditions are best. For example, oranges are grown in Florida and California. The weather, soil conditions, and length of the growing season are good for growing oranges there. Different parts of the country are known for the agricultural products they provide. For example, the Midwest is known for corn, wheat, and soybeans. The South is known for cotton and rice.

Agriculture Workers

Farmers are agricultural workers. They till the soil, plant seed, and care for and harvest their produce. Landscapers and gardeners may water and trim trees. Some workers pick fruits and nuts and pack them for shipping. Ranchers breed and care for animals. Inspectors and graders make sure food is safe to eat before it is sold.

Sample Agriculture Occupations	
Animal Scientist	5
Farm and Ranch Manager	3, 4, or 5
Farmworkers, Farm and Ranch Animals	1
Landscaping and Groundskeeping Worker	1
Plant Scientist	5
Veterinarian Technologist and Technician	4

The number after each occupation shows the minimum education and training needed for that occupation. See the key on the left.

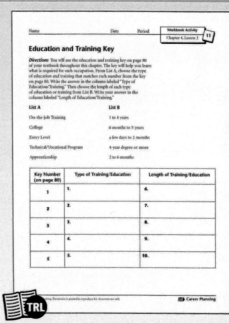

Workbook Activity 11

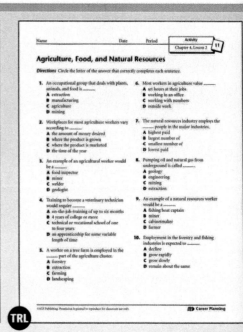

Activity 11

Career Tip

Pay attention to stories about businesses or companies in local newspapers and TV news programs. Consider contacting interesting companies with a letter or résumé.

Related School Subjects
Agriculture
Math
Science
Shop

Related Abilities
Manual
Mathematical
Technical/Mechanical
Visual (Spatial)

Related Values
Outdoor Work
Risk
Work with Hands

Forestry

Another part of the agricultural cluster is forestry. Wood from trees is used to make products like furniture and paper. Forestry workers include machine and tractor operators who drag the logs from the forests. Sorters separate logs to grade them for type of wood and quality. Loggers load the logs onto trucks for sawmills or papermaking plants. Some forest workers raise trees on tree farms to use for special events, or to plant around the outside of homes.

Sample Forestry Occupations	
Faller	1
Forest and Conservation Worker	2
Forester	5
Log Grader and Scaler	3
Logger	1

(See the key on page 80.)

Fishing

Workers in the fishing industry harvest fish and shellfish. A large amount of fish, such as catfish and salmon, is raised on fish farms. Workers usually fish for only one kind of fish, such as lobsters, oysters, shrimp, or tuna. Fishing is hard work. Nets and other equipment need to be repaired often. Boats can be very expensive to buy and operate.

Sample Fishing Occupations	
Fisher	1
Ship and Boat Captain	3 or 4

(See the key on page 80.)

LEARNING STYLES

Auditory/Verbal

Students may be better able to comprehend this fact-loaded lesson if they read it in pairs. Have students take turns reading aloud sections and quizzing their partners about the main ideas. When reading tables, students should describe in their own words what each table represents and summarize what they learned about the occupations listed.

2 Teaching the Lesson

Explain to students that Lessons 2 through 17 all have the same organizational plan:

1. The career cluster is defined.
2. Its workplaces are described.
3. The types of workers and their traits are summarized.
4. The outlook for occupations in this cluster is explained.

This chapter contains many facts and statistics. As a result, students will need to read slowly and think about what they are reading to infer its significance. Point out that they may need to read each section more than once to comprehend all it offers.

Have students mark the key on page 80 with a sticky note, or create a poster of it and hang it in a location that is easy to see. It applies to tables that appear in each of the next 16 lessons and students will need to refer to it often.

Also point out to students that on the first page of each lesson there is a chart that lists the school subjects, abilities, and values that are related to the cluster.

3 Reinforce and Extend

LEARNING STYLES

Visual/Spatial

Have students view a resources map of the United States in a social studies text or other reference resource. Ask them to identify types of agriculture that dominate in each region of the country and locate places where forestry and fishing are important industries. Display a blank map of the United States and have students work together to make a key and draw symbols for each type of agriculture, forestry, and fishing where they belong on the map.

Body/Kinesthetic

After they have read the lesson, have students choose an agricultural, natural resources, or food-related occupation described in the lesson and think of a person with that job. Ask them to write what this person could say to describe his or her job and tell what he or she enjoys about it. Have each student role-play the worker by reading the script.

IN THE ENVIRONMENT

Have students read and discuss the highlighted paragraph titled "Agriculture and the Environment" on page 82. Then have students search periodical indexes and newspaper files for articles describing ways the agricultural, forestry, or fishing industry works to avoid harming the environment. If possible, students can report on whether pollution and erosion are increasing or decreasing in your region.

GLOBAL CONNECTION

The worldwide demand for oil has grown so much that finding new sources of oil for extraction is of vital interest to many nations. Have several students find information about the world's richest oil reserves using reference books. Ask students to locate these deposits on a world map outline, using color-coding to show comparative amounts of oil available. Then have them note where any untapped oil reserves have been found, add them to the map, and predict why they have not been tapped.

Mining
Removing minerals from the earth

Extraction
The pumping of oil and natural gas from underground

Workers in agriculture value working on their own. They do not have to work in office jobs for a set amount of hours. People in this cluster like to do things and see results. They are skilled at working with their hands. They enjoy a variety of tasks in their jobs. They also value status within their community, outside work, and the opportunity for high achievement. They have crafts interests. This is one of the interest areas you learned about in Chapter 2.

Agriculture and the Environment

Farming, forestry, and fishing can affect the land, water, and air. The government has laws to protect the environment. The agriculture industry must follow these laws. Workers make sure chemicals do not pollute lakes and rivers. They replant seedlings to create new forests. They are careful not to overfish the oceans. The government teaches farmers and other agricultural workers how to protect the environment.

The Natural Resources Workplace

The natural resources industry employs the smallest number of people of the major industries. Natural resources occupations include jobs related to **mining** and **extraction.** Mining is the removal of minerals from the ground, including coal and iron. Coal provides heat. Iron is used to make steel. Steel is used to make buildings, bridges, and automobiles. Extraction is the pumping of oil and natural gas from underground. People use oil or gas to power their cars, light and heat their homes, and operate factories.

Mining is done where there are mineral deposits. Geologists find out where the deposits are by using scientific equipment. Before mining begins, geologists and petroleum engineers estimate the cost of mining and extracting these minerals or fuels. Then the actual removal can begin. The removal may include drilling or blasting. The minerals are then moved to storage areas. Extracted oil and gas is collected, pumped, and transported in pipes.

Natural Resources Workers

Workers in this career cluster work outside almost all the time. The weather can be very hot, cold, wet, or windy. Workers are still expected do their jobs no matter what the weather. The main interest of people in this cluster is crafts. Workers should be strong. They should be able to work well with their hands. Well and core drill operators run the drills. Petroleum engineers design oil pipes. Surveyors and civil engineers draw the maps of the mineral deposits. Mining engineers need management skills. They need to monitor airflow, drainage, water, communications, power supplies, and transportation systems. Like agriculture workers, natural resources workers value independent work, a variety of job tasks, status, and high achievement. People in this industry observe what is happening. They have good memory for detail. They seek facts in order to make judgments.

Sample Natural Resources Occupations

Civil Drafter	4
Construction Equipment Operator	3
Continuous Mining Machine Operator	2
Derrick Operator, oil and gas	2
Explosive Worker and Blaster	2
Geologist	5
Metal-Refining Furnace Operator	2
Mining and Geological Engineer	5
Mobile Heavy Equipment Mechanic	3
Petroleum Engineer	5
Pump Operator	2
Rotary Drill Operator, small oil and gas	3
Roustabout, oil and gas	2
Well and Core Drill Operator	3

(See the key on page 80.)

ELL/ESL Strategy

Language Objective: *To identify and understand verb phrases in sentences*

Students whose first language is not English may have difficulty with syntax in English sentences. Establish the subject-verb order and components of the sentence, then explain the concept of a verb phrase (one word expresses the action or state of being and one or more words help express action or state of being), modeling examples:

subject	verb	verb phrase
people	use	have used
workers	harvest	will harvest
weather	is	can be

Select several sentences from pages 82 and 83 that contain verb phrases. Write them on the board and have students underline the subject and verb phrase. Possible sentences: Iron is used to make steel. Farming, forestry, and fishing can affect the land, water, and air. Workers are still expected to do their jobs.

Lesson 2 Review Answers

1. The oldest industries are agriculture and natural resources because they help people meet basic needs for food, shelter, and heat.

2. Workplaces are where conditions are best for growing a specific crop.

3. The natural resources industry employs the least number of people.

4. Answers will vary. Students may say that working outdoors and having the satisfaction of producing foods and other products make the hardships worthwhile.

Agriculture, Food, and Natural Resources Outlook

Most workers in this industry are farm workers and laborers. Employment in these areas will grow more slowly than other occupations. Employment in the forestry and fishing industries is expected to decline. The parts of the agricultural industry that will expand are farm labor contractors, agricultural managers, and horticultural service workers. Landscapers and nursery workers will also see more job opportunities.

Jobs in mining are expected to decrease by almost 12 percent by 2012. There will be fewer jobs available as mining machine operators and petroleum engineers. Natural resources jobs that are expected to grow include environmental scientists, gas plant operators, and explosives workers. By 2012, jobs in water and waste treatment plants are expected to increase by 16 percent.

Of all workers employed in 2012, only 3.2 percent will have jobs in the Agriculture, Food, and Natural Resources cluster. Average national wages for occupations in this cluster depend on the amount of training and education required.

Entry Level	$20,500–$21,000
On-the-Job Training/Apprenticeship	$31,000–$33,300
Technical/Vocational Program	$35,500–$37,000
College Degree	$47,500–$67,300

Lesson 2 Review Write your answers to these questions on a sheet of paper.

1. What are the oldest industries in the world? Why are they the oldest?

2. What determines the workplaces for agricultural jobs?

3. Which industry employs the smallest number of people of the major industries?

4. Workers in agriculture and natural resources fields often do hard physical work in uncomfortable weather. Do you think there are positive features that make up for this hard work? Explain.

Lesson 3 — Manufacturing

Manufacturing
Turning raw material into products people use every day

Production worker
Person who manufactures products

Manufacturing plant
A group of buildings where manufacturing happens

Assemble
To put together

Related School Subjects
General Science
Math
Shop
Technology

Related Abilities
Manual
Mathematical
Scientific
Visual (Spatial)

Related Values
Good Salary
Independence
Outdoor Work
Work with Hands

Manufacturing involves making products. It can also be called production. Manufacturing begins with raw material. That material is made into something else. Look at the example below.

Raw Material → **Final Product**

The people who manufacture products are called **production workers.** They make many of the things we use every day, such as toothbrushes and soap. One of the largest manufacturing industries is the automobile industry. Many manufacturing workers have jobs related to making cars and trucks. Other manufacturing industries include electronics, printing, and paper products.

The manufacturing cluster also includes the utilities and telecommunication industries. The utilities industry includes power plants and nuclear reactor plants. Telecommunications includes telephones, wireless or cellular phones, the Internet, and cable.

The Workplace

A group of buildings where manufacturing happens is called a **manufacturing plant.** Different buildings are used for different things. One building may be for storage of raw materials or parts. Parts might be put together, or **assembled,** in another building.

Other buildings may be for painting, storage, or shipping. Some plants may be very large, have noisy machines, or be very hot or cold inside. Other plants may be small, quiet, or air-conditioned. Utilities and telecommunications work can take place in an office or a plant. It can also take place outdoors on power or telephone lines.

Chapter 4 Lesson 3

Overview This lesson looks at occupations involved in production, or manufacturing, by analyzing the workers, the workplaces, and the outlook for these occupations.

Objectives

- To describe the types of work involved in manufacturing
- To explain what happens at a manufacturing plant
- To tell about different kinds of manufacturing workers
- To analyze what will happen to jobs available in this sector in the future

Student Pages 85–87

Teacher's Resource Library

Workbook Activity 12

Activity 12

Alternative Activity 12

Vocabulary

assemble
automation
manufacturing

manufacturing plant
offshore outsourcing
production worker

Pair students and have them find the definitions for the vocabulary terms. Ask partners to make a crossword puzzle using the terms, with definitions as clues. Pairs can exchange puzzles and complete them.

 Warm-Up Activity

Have students choose a product they are wearing, carrying, or using today and write it at the top of a sheet of paper. Below this, have them list all the steps they think it took to make this product. Beside each step, have them name the workers needed to complete the step. Invite students to share their information.

2 Teaching the Lesson

Have students scan the headings in the lesson to see that it has the sections The Workplace, The Workers, and Outlook. As they read, they should watch for key phrases and topic sentences that inform them about the type of work, the workers and workplace, and the outlook of this cluster.

LEARNING STYLES

**Interpersonal/
Group Learning**
Have the class brainstorm
a list of products that are
produced in your city, county, or
state. Assign one product each to
small groups of students. Ask members of each group to research the
raw materials and the processes used
to produce the product. Have them
cooperate to create a graphic organizer, such as a sequence chart, to
explain the steps in the process.

ELL/ESL STRATEGY

**Language
Objective:** *To identify
suffixes that show
occupations*

Students who are learning English
will strengthen their word analysis
skills as they learn to recognize
common suffixes. Explain that *-er*
and *-or* are suffixes that mean "one
who." They are usually added to a
verb. The suffix *-ist* means "one who
produces, operates, or specializes in."
It is usually added to a noun. Write
on the board:

act + *-or* = *actor*—"one who acts"
bake + *-er* = *baker*—"one who bakes"
novel + *-ist* = *novelist*—"one who
    produces novels"

Pair students and have them locate
words in the lesson that use these
suffixes to name occupations. Hint:
Most of them are located in the table
on page 86. (*assembler, baker, operator,
fabricator, installer, welder, jeweler,
machinist, installer*)

Have partners write definitions for
each of the words. They can take turns
reading definitions to each other so
the listener can name the occupations.

The Workers

Most manufacturing workers operate machines, such as drills,
grinders, furnaces, or forklifts. Machine repairers make sure the
equipment is in working order. Assembly workers put things
together. They might repeat the same task over and over again.
Manufacturing work often requires strength and lifting. Some
workers put raw materials into machines. Other workers move
materials around the plant. Workers might also package
and label products. Manufacturing managers make sure
their products are of high quality.

Power plant operators and dispatchers work throughout the
country. Power plant operators monitor and control the working
parts and machinery of the plant. Dispatchers control the flow of
electricity through power lines.

Sample Manufacturing Occupations	
Aircraft Structure Assembler	3
Baker, Manufacturing	3
Cabinetmaker and Bench Carpenter	3
Electronic Assembler	2
Engine and Other Machine Assembler	3
Jeweler	3
Machinist	3
Manufacturing Optician	2
Mechanical Inspector	2 or 3
Molding and Casting Worker	2
Painting, Coating, and Decorating Worker	1
Photographic Processing Machine Operator	2
Printing Press Machine Operator	3
Stationary Engineer	3
Structural Metal Fabricator	4
Telecommunications Line Installer	3
Tool and Die Maker	3
Welders, Production	2 or 3

(See the key on page 87.)

Workers in the manufacturing
cluster enjoy physical activities.
They like to work with their
hands. They enjoy seeing the
results of their work right away.
Manufacturing and production
workers have crafts interests
such as working with tools
and repairing things. Utility
workers usually have good
math and science skills.
They also have mechanical
and technical abilities.
Telecommunications workers
need skills in computers. They
also need to know how to relate
to customers. Many of these
workers must be physically
strong to do their jobs.

Outlook

Some manufacturing areas will grow slightly. There will be more jobs in computer, electronic, and plastic manufacturing. Clothing manufacturing jobs will decrease. Many assembly industries will see a decrease in jobs because of **automation.** Automation is the use of machines to do jobs that used to be done by people. Automation makes it easier for plants to do more work with fewer workers. Other manufacturing jobs are being given to workers in other countries. This is called **offshore outsourcing.** It is cheaper for companies to pay these workers than it is to pay workers in the United States. This will also lead to a decrease in some manufacturing occupations.

There will be more telecommunications jobs for workers in central offices. There will also be more jobs for workers who set up new telecommunications services. This is because of the growth of the Internet, more video options, and a growth in high-speed data transmission. In the utilities industry, job growth will be less for electrical power line installers and repairers than for all occupations.

By 2012, manufacturing workers will make up 8.5 percent of all employed workers. Here are the average wages for occupations in manufacturing, based on training and education:

Entry Level	$25,400
On-the-Job Training/Apprenticeship	$26,700–$30,200
Technical/Vocational Program	$30,700
College Degree	$57,600

Lesson 3 Review Write your answers to these questions on a sheet of paper.

1. Why is manufacturing an important industry?

2. Why must many workers in the manufacturing cluster be physically strong?

3. Why are many companies in the United States using offshore outsourcing? Explain why you think offshore outsourcing is a good idea or not.

Chapter 4 Lesson 4

Overview In this lesson, students read about the nature of the work, workplaces, and job outlook in the transportation, distribution, and logistics sector.

Objectives

■ To understand the purpose of the transportation, distribution, and logistics sector

■ To identify jobs carried out by workers in the sector and traits needed for the work

■ To compare the average income of workers with varying education and experience

Student Pages 88–91

Teacher's Resource Library **TRL**

Workbook Activity 13

Activity 13

Alternative Activity 13

Vocabulary

distribute
freight
logistics

Write the vocabulary words on the board and read them aloud. Ask students to use what they already know to predict the meaning of each word. (Point out that *logistics* uses the same base as *logic*, which has to do with well-ordered and reasonable thought.) Then have students look up the meaning of each word in the glossary and confirm or revise their predictions. Ask students to use all three words in a brief paragraph about transportation.

1 Warm-Up Activity

Challenge students to list all the ways they can think of that goods and services are delivered, or transported, to consumers. Capture students' suggestions on a word web on the board. Explain that the lesson they will read tells them about occupations relating to movement of materials and products, which requires both transportation and planning.

Distribute
To move or give out goods and products to buyers or customers

Logistics
Planning and operations involved in moving people and products

Freight
Goods or products transported by truck, train, boat, or airplane

Related School Subjects
Keyboarding
Math
Science
Shop
Technology

Related Abilities
Leadership
Manual
Mathematical
Scientific
Technical/Mechanical
Visual (Spatial)

Related Values
Good Salary
Independence
Physical Activity
Risk
Work with Hands
Work with Mind

This industry deals with the use of roads, waterways, and rail and air systems. The transportation industry connects the product with the customer. The purpose of transportation is to **distribute** materials and products. Transportation also involves helping people get to places they need to go. People use highways and airlines to travel across the United States. Businesses ship heavy materials by railroad or ship.

Transportation is more than driving a truck or flying a plane. Many sales and service occupations are related to the transportation industry. People prepare billing statements and sell tickets. Others collect payments for transportation services. These jobs deal with the planning and daily tasks needed to move people and products. This part of the industry is called **logistics.**

The Workplace

Truck drivers deliver **freight** from companies, warehouses, or distribution centers. Freight is goods or products that are transported. Local drivers might drive small trucks and work in only one city or town. Other truck drivers might own their own large trucks and travel from state to state. Railroad workers work on freight and passenger trains. They also work on subways. Water transportation is a relatively small industry. It takes place on coastlines, rivers, and lakes. Passenger ferries and tourist boats operate on the waterways. Barges tow freight and oil. The airline industry includes maintenance work on planes in addition to the pilots and flight crew who work on the airplane itself.

The Workers

Transportation workers include truck, taxi, and bus drivers. Some drivers might also sell products out of their trucks. These drivers may sell and deliver bread, bottled water, or laundry services. Freight truck drivers drive heavy trucks or tractor-trailers to deliver products. Drivers are paid by the number of miles they drive. In addition to drivers, dispatchers work for trucking companies. They keep track of where the company trucks are. They also let drivers know of bad weather or road conditions.

Name _____ Date _____ Period _____ | Workbook Activity **13** Chapter 4, Lesson 4

Describing Transportation

Directions Write the answers to these questions. Use complete sentences.

1. With what does the transportation industry deal?

2. What are two purposes of transportation?

3. How are freight truck drivers usually paid?

4. What does a dispatcher for a trucking company do?

5. What are three common railroad occupations?

6. How do many seamen or deckhands learn their jobs?

7. What agency grants licenses to airplane pilots?

8. Identify three skills that transportation workers usually have.

9. What is the employment outlook for drivers in the transportation industry?

10. In 2012, what percent of all workers will have jobs in transportation, distribution, and logistics operations?

TRL | **Career Planning**

Workbook Activity 13

Name _____ Date _____ Period _____ | Activity **13** Chapter 4, Lesson 4

Transportation, Distribution, and Logistics Occupations

Directions Circle the letter of the answer that correctly completes each sentence.

1. The transportation industry connects the product with the _____.
   A customer
   B manufacturer
   C materials
   D distributor

2. The part of transportation that plans how to move people and products is called _____.
   A distribution
   B logistics
   C controlling
   D conducting

3. Goods or products transported by truck, train, boat, or airplane are called _____.
   A supplies
   B property
   C commodities
   D freight

4. Most railroad workers begin as _____.
   A students
   B laborers
   C apprentices
   D brake operators

5. A special school that teaches about ships and business at sea is called a _____.
   A department of transportation
   B shipping school
   C maritime academy
   D logistics center

6. Many airlines require _____ experience for pilots.
   A military
   B freight
   C logistics
   D clerical

7. A transportation job that is not an airline job is _____.
   A baggage handler
   B flight attendant
   C airplane mechanic
   D sailor

8. Workers responsible for keeping air travel safe are known as _____.
   A flight attendants
   B co-pilots
   C air traffic controllers
   D schedule programmers

9. Railroad transportation occupations are expected to _____ by 2012.
   A disappear
   B remain steady
   C grow slightly
   D decrease

10. Employment in the logistics area of transportation is expected to _____ by 2012.
    A decrease
    B grow
    C drop sharply
    D remain steady

TRL | **Career Planning**

Activity 13

Key to Education and Training Needed

1—Entry Level

2—On-the-Job Training

3—Apprenticeship

4—Technical/ Vocational Program

5—College

Common railroad occupations are locomotive engineer (train driver), brake operator (joins and separates train cars), and conductor. Other railroad workers maintain the tracks. Most railroad workers begin as laborers. They may take a formal training program to advance to locomotive engineer or conductor later.

The water transportation industry employs captains, ship engineers, oilers, and sailors. Seamen or deckhands learn on the job. Deck and engineering officers typically are graduates of maritime academies. Maritime academies are special schools that teach about a ship's operation, travel, and business at sea.

Common airline occupations include pilots, airplane mechanics, and air traffic controllers. Flight attendants, baggage and cargo handlers, airport security personnel, and gate attendants also work in the airline industry. Pilots are usually college graduates. Most airlines require at least two years of college. Military experience is often a requirement for pilots as well. Pilots must be licensed by the Federal Aviation Administration. Air traffic controllers make sure air travel stays safe. They prepare for this job with a lot of training, testing, and schooling. Other airline jobs require less preparation and training, such as clerical occupations that involve office work.

Sample Transportation Occupations

Occupation	
Airline Pilot	4
Cargo and Freight Agent	1
Locomotive Engineer	3 or 4
Railroad Conductor	3
Sailor	1 or 2
Ship's Engineer	4 or 5
Shipping, Receiving, and Traffic Clerk	1
Tractor-Trailer Truck Driver	1 or 2
Transportation Attendant (Ticket Taker)	1
Truck Driver, Light or Delivery Services	1

The number after each occupation shows the minimum education and training needed for that occupation. See the key on the left.

Teaching the Lesson

By now, students should be familiar with the organization of the lessons in this chapter. Remind them to read the first section to learn the nature and purpose of transportation, distribution, and logistics work; the second section to remember details about where the work is done; and so on.

Also remind students that this content has many facts. They may need to read each section more than once to be sure they have comprehended all the information.

Reinforce and Extend

IN THE COMMUNITY

Using the business listings in a phone book for your community, have students find names and locations of local companies that specialize in transportation. (Examples might include moving and storage companies, bus companies, delivery services, freight lines, truck rental businesses, and truck repair and service companies.) Encourage students to contact one or more of the companies and find out the range of its distribution: local, regional, statewide, or interstate.

The U.S. Economy

When goods and services are produced at an increasing rate, the economy grows. A nation's gross domestic product (GDP) is the value of all goods and services produced in a year. Since the mid-1970s, the GDP of the United States (adjusted for inflation) has increased an average of 2 percent per year. Millions of workers produce trillions of dollars worth of goods and services each year. At times, the U.S. economy has grown rapidly. At other times, known as recessions, it has declined. When business activity drops drastically and stays down, a depression occurs. During recessions and depressions, production drops and many people lose their jobs. The Federal Reserve System of the government may lower interest rates to encourage borrowing and spending in an attempt to combat rising unemployment when the economy is weak.

Career Tip

Federal agencies monitor and certify the skills of most of the workers in the airline industry. Workers usually need to pass an exam after training to show competence. Work is also periodically inspected.

People who work in the transportation, distribution, and logistics career cluster have a main interest in the crafts area. Some occupations involve office operations interests and require clerical skills. Transportation workers have a range of skills. These include physical strength, the ability to handle emergencies, good eye-hand coordination, and the ability to make good judgments. Pilots and ship officers need to understand complicated equipment and the weather. People in this cluster enjoy traveling, working alone, and being paid well.

Outlook

In this cluster, the employment of drivers is expected to increase. By 2012, jobs as bus, truck, and taxi drivers will increase by 15 to 20 percent. Jobs in the airline industry are also expected to increase. There will be job growth for occupations in logistics such as laborers, truck operators, production clerks, shipping clerks, and record keepers. Railroad transportation occupations are expected to decrease by about 5 percent.

About 9.3 percent of all workers in 2012 will be employed in transportation, distribution, and logistics occupations. Average wages for these occupations depend on the amount of training and education a job requires.

Entry Level	$21,300
On-the-Job Training/Apprenticeship	$28,400–$46,900
Technical/Vocational Program	$66,000
College Degree	$50,000

Lesson 4 Review Write your answers to these questions on a sheet of paper.

1. Explain why the transportation industry is more than just driving a truck or flying a plane.

2. Name one occupation in each of the following fields: road transportation, railroads, water transportation, and airlines.

3. Experts forecast that more drivers will be employed in the future. How might this fact affect people in other industries?

The Economy

Employment is closely related to a healthy economy. Government economists use several kinds of statistics to measure how much our economy grows. A large percentage of unemployed people is a sign of a weak economy. On the other hand, adding many new jobs is a sign of a healthy, growing economy. Government economists collect facts on jobs regularly. For example, in July of 2004, 5.5 percent of the American workforce was unemployed. This figure had not changed much since December 2003. So it was not a sign of a rapidly growing economy. Thirty-two thousand new jobs were added in July of 2004. This sounds like a positive sign. However, economists hoped for even greater job growth. Job facts like these have a wide-ranging effect on the American economy.

Lesson 4 Review Answers

1. Many sales and service occupations are related to the transportation industry.

2. Road transportation—truck, taxi, bus, and freight truck drivers. Railroads—locomotive engineer, brakeman, conductor, track maintenance workers. Water transportation—captains, ship engineers, oilers, sailors. Airlines—pilots, mechanics, air traffic controllers, flight attendants, gate attendants.

3. Answers will vary. Possible answer: More drivers will result in the need to build new roads or maintain existing roads. So, the road construction industry may see an increase in jobs as well.

The Economy

Ask students what the phrase *a healthy economy* means to them. Then have volunteers read the Economy feature on page 91 aloud. Create a graphic organizer to represent the relationship between unemployment, job growth, and a healthy economy. (One possible graphic representation could show arms of a scale. When unemployment is low and job growth is high, the economy is growing and strong. When unemployment is high and job growth low, the economy is stagnant and weak.)

Chapter 4 Lesson 5

Overview In this lesson, students learn about the architecture and construction industries and jobs associated with them.

Objectives

- To compare architecture and construction as career fields
- To survey jobs, workplaces, and worker characteristics in each industry
- To identify job outlook for various occupations in the cluster

Student Pages 92–94

Teacher's Resource Library TRL

Workbook Activity 14

Activity 14

Alternative Activity 14

Vocabulary

architecture
construction
developer

Write *architect, construct,* and *develop* on the board in a column. Talk about the meaning of each word and use it in a sentence. Have students identify its part of speech. (*architect*—noun; *construct*—verb; *develop*—verb) Write *-ure, -ion,* and *-er* in another column. Ask students to match each base word with a suffix to make a new noun. Have students write a sentence using each vocabulary word.

1 Warm-Up Activity

Ask students what steps they think it takes to build a skyscraper. List these on the board. Brainstorm at least one occupation related to each step. (For example, planning and design—architect, urban planner, surveyor) As they read the lesson, have students add to the list.

Lesson 5 — Architecture and Construction

Architecture
Planning and designing buildings or other structures

Construction
The act of building

Related School Subjects
Art
Health
Math
Science
Shop
Technology

Related Abilities
Artistic
Interpersonal
Language
Manual
Mathematical
Mechanical
Scientific

Related Values
Creativity
Good Salary
Independence
Outdoor Work
Physical Activity
Risk
Work with Hands

This cluster involves **architecture** and **construction**. Think of some famous buildings—the Egyptian pyramids, the Eiffel Tower in France, or the Opera House in Australia. What does it take to build one of these structures? Building begins with an idea. It involves planning and design. People need to pay for the building and the land it will be built on. The building plan needs to be safe and meet building codes and laws. As you can see, a lot of work goes into building. There are many occupations related to building, from planning to construction. Construction can involve many projects besides buildings, such as roads, bridges, and tunnels.

The Eiffel tower in Paris, France, is famous for its design.

The Workplace

Architects and other people who design and plan building projects may work in offices. They may also visit the building site while they are planning the project. In order to get approval for the project, workers may need to visit city government buildings or offices to get permits.

The workplace for the actual construction of a project is the job site itself. Construction involves both indoor and outdoor work at the job site.

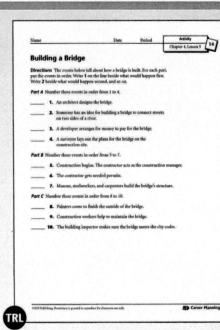

The Workers

The construction industry employs workers with a lot of different skills. Usually, construction workers learn their craft on the job. Most workers need to have special licenses. Building inspectors check that the workers have done everything correctly. The work must meet the codes and laws of a state or city. Once a project is complete, many workers help to maintain buildings, bridges, and tunnels. Other workers make sure the structures stay safe.

When planning a building project, **developers** arrange for money to pay for building costs. Architects design the structure itself. Surveyors lay out the plans for the building site. Other workers get the needed permits. Once the actual work begins, contractors act as construction managers. They oversee all the different workers on the job site. Masons, carpenters, steelworkers, and roofers build the general building structure. Then electricians, plumbers, and sheet metal workers work on the inside. Drywall workers, plasterers, and painters, and cabinetmakers come next to finish the inside. Building a bridge or other structure also involves many different workers.

Workers in this cluster usually have interests in the crafts area. They like hands-on activities. They enjoy seeing results of their work right away. They also enjoy the variety of working at different job sites. Planners and developers have business and office operations interests. Architects have scientific and artistic interests. Most construction workers have physical strength, good depth perception, and balance. They need good math skills for measuring. An important ability construction workers need is the ability to read and follow plans. Construction workers need to understand directions and safety warnings. Construction sites can be dangerous. The more skills required for a construction job, the longer the training period is.

 Teaching the Lesson

Review with students the types of information that have been provided for each career cluster so far. Ask them to predict what workplaces, workers, and outlook will be for the architecture and construction sector before they read.

As students read the table on page 94, ask them to notice which number appears most often. (*Three.*) Ask what general statement they can make about training or education requirements for this career cluster. (*Few of the jobs require a college education and some call for little education or training.*)

Have students compare data on average pay for all the clusters they have read about so far. Which cluster has the highest average for technical/vocational training? (*transportation, distribution, and logistics, $66,000*) Which offers the best income for entry-level work? (*manufacturing, $25,400*)

 Reinforce and Extend

LEARNING STYLES

 Visual/Spatial

Have students refer to the photo of the Eiffel Tower on page 92. Ask them to use this image and their imaginations to describe the nature of the work required to build this structure.

IN THE ENVIRONMENT

 Ask several students to do research to find out ways builders try to protect and preserve the environment as they plan and build. Each student might look for information on one of these areas: land use, water and air safety, light, ventilation and health of employees, or aesthetic concerns (how pleasing the structure is and how well it fits in with the surroundings). Students may gather information from the Internet, trade books, or interviews with professionals.

PERSONAL JOURNAL

Have students think of an interest or talent they have in crafts, science, or arts. Ask them to match it with a job mentioned in the lesson. (For example, artistic ability can be helpful to an architect.) Have students write a paragraph on their own paper explaining how their interests or talents would help them in this career.

LEARNING STYLES

Logical/Mathematical

Have students analyze the data in the table "Sample Architecture and Construction Occupations" and in the chart on average pay on page 94. They can refer to this data to answer questions such as the following:

How much more could an architect expect to make than a construction laborer? (up to $36,720) *If you began working as a trades helper, then become a cement mason, how much could you expect your income to go up?* (up to $12,700)

Lesson 5 Review Answers

1. Architects, building inspectors, developers, carpenters, steelworkers, electricians, plumbers, and painters are some of the workers involved. Each has a task that is essential to the final building, so they must work together closely.

2. They need to understand directions and safety warnings.

3. Jobs like designing a building and creating a structure from wood and other materials requires artistic talent and skilled craftsmanship. These same jobs require much technical knowledge.

Sample Architecture and Construction Occupations

Occupation	
Architect	5
Boilermaker	3
Brickmason and Blockmason	3
Carpenter	3
Cement Mason	3
Contractor	3, 4, or 5
Construction Equipment Operator	3
Construction Laborer	2
Drywall Installer	2
Electrician	3
Elevator Installer	3
Glazier (installs windows)	3
Helper, Construction and Trades	1 or 2
Insulation Worker	3
Painter, Construction and Maintenance	3
Paving, Surfacing, and Tamping Equipment Operator	2
Pipefitter	3
Plasterer	3
Plumber	3
Roofer	2
Sheet Metal Worker	3
Structural Iron and Steel Worker	3
Tile and Marble Setter	3

Key to Education and Training Needed

1—Entry Level

2—On-the-Job Training

3—Apprenticeship

4—Technical/Vocational Program

5—College

Outlook

Employment in this cluster is expected to increase by about 15 percent by 2012. Most of the growth will be in the construction of new houses, roads, bridges, and tunnels. The construction industry expects to have 1.1 million new workers by 2012.

Architecture and construction workers will make up 5.7 percent of all employed workers by 2012. Average pay for occupations in this cluster are listed below, based on training and education.

Entry Level	$22,650
On-the-Job Training/ Apprenticeship	$31,000–$35,350
Technical/Vocational Program	$50,500
College Degree	$41,060–$67,720

Lesson 5 Review Write your answers to these questions on a sheet of paper.

1. Name the different workers who contribute to the construction of a building. Why is it important for the different workers to work together?

2. Why is it important for construction workers to be good readers?

3. Describe ways in which the construction field is artistic. Describe ways in which it is based on technical knowledge.

94   *Chapter 4   Career Clusters and the Major Industries*

**Related School
Subjects**
Agriculture
Clerical Studies
English
Math
Science

Related Abilities
Clerical
Interpersonal
Language
Leadership
Manual
Mathematical
Mechanical
Organizational
Scientific
Social
Visual (Spatial)

Related Values
Creativity
Good Salary
High Achievement
Independence
Job Security
Leadership
Prestige
Variety
Work with Mind
Work with People

The Health Science career cluster includes occupations related to keeping people healthy. Workers in this field work to prevent and treat disease and illness. Common occupations in health science are doctors and nurses. Others you might not think of right away are biologists, dieticians, athletic trainers, and physical therapists.

The Workplace

Doctors, nurses, and many other health-care workers may work in hospitals, private clinics, home health agencies, schools, or public health settings. Other health-care jobs, like administrative support and clerical work, may take place in offices. Health scientists may work in laboratories or research centers. Athletic trainers might work at health clubs or gyms.

The Workers

Medicine is a major part of this career cluster. One-third of medical doctors provide primary care. A primary care doctor is your personal doctor. He or she coordinates all of your medical care, answers your questions, and works to make sure you get the kind of treatment you need. Other doctors may provide care for only certain parts of the body, like the heart or lungs. Surgeons operate to fix broken bones or remove sick parts of the body. In addition to medical doctors, other doctors focus on a variety of areas. Here are some examples.

Doctor	Specialty
Chiropractor	back
Dentist	teeth and gums
Podiatrist	feet
Optometrist	eyes
Veterinarian	animals

Career Clusters and the Major Industries Chapter 4 **95**

Lesson at a Glance

Chapter 4 Lesson 6

Overview In this lesson, students learn about conditions, occupations, workplaces, and outlook in the health care industry.

Objectives

- To identify a variety of occupations within the health science cluster
- To describe the kinds of work performed by health science workers
- To analyze education requirements, employment outlook, and average earnings for workers in health science

Student Pages 95–97

Teacher's Resource Library

Workbook Activity 15
Activity 15
Alternative Activity 15

1 Warm-Up Activity

Make a word web on the board with *health care* in the center circle. As students brainstorm kinds of workers in this industry, write them in the circles around the outside. Survey students about whether they are interested in a career in health care. As they read, students can assess whether their expectations of the field are realistic.

Workbook Activity 15

Activity 15

Career Clusters and the Major Industries **95**

2 Teaching the Lesson

Be sure students recall that the key for all the tables that list sample occupations in a cluster is found on page 80 (or on the poster if you have created one).

Point out the chart of doctors and specialties on page 95. Assist students in expanding this list. Students may name, among other specialists,

Oncologist: cancer
Obstetrician: pregnancy and childbirth
Cardiologist: heart
Dermatologist: skin
Ophthalmologist: eyes

You may wish to point out that an ophthalmologist is a medical doctor specializing in care of the eyes. An optometrist is a technician who checks eyesight.

When they finish reading, ask students to make a generalization about occupations in health sciences. (*Possible generalization: Many are professions that require education beyond a college degree.*)

3 Reinforce and Extend

Communication Connection

Read the Communication Connection on page 96 aloud to students. Ask them to name some forms of verbal and written communication that take place in the workplace. Then have them brainstorm a list of kinds of work-related communication necessary in a hospital. List these on the board under the headings *Verbal* and *Written*. (Examples might include: verbal—requests and commands of surgeon in the operating room, interview of a patient by a nurse or admitting person; written—instructions and notes on a hospital patient's chart, medical records)

Communication Connection

There are many kinds of communication among coworkers in the workplace. Most communication revolves around work, both in meetings and in one-to-one conferences. But most workplaces also include informal chats among workers. Getting to know your coworkers helps you do your job better. Just remember to save informal communication for appropriate times such as lunches and breaks.

Key to Education and Training Needed

1—Entry Level

2—On-the-Job Training

3—Apprenticeship

4—Technical/ Vocational Program

5—College

Other health-care occupations include pharmacists, physician assistants, nurses, and social workers. Jobs related to health science and research include x-ray and medical technologists, laboratory technicians, and clinical laboratory personnel.

Health care also has administrative requirements. Health care is a business. People work to make sure hospitals and doctors follow government rules. Other administrators work with insurance companies or the health insurance industry. Admitting clerks record patient information. Other workers keep medical records up to date.

Sample Health Science Occupations	
Athletic Trainer	5
Chiropractor	5
Dentist	5
Dietician	5
Licensed Practical Nurse	4
Medical and Clinical Laboratory Technician	4
Medical and Clinical Laboratory Technologist	5
Medical and Health Services Manager	5
Medical Assistant	3 or 4
Medical Records and Health Information Technician	4
Optometrist	5
Pharmacist	5
Pharmacy Technician	2
Physical Therapist	5
Physician	5
Registered Nurse	4 or 5
Social Worker	5
Speech-Language Pathologist	5
Veterinarian	5

The number after each occupation shows the minimum education and training needed for that occupation. See the key on the left.

Most of the careers in this cluster require an education beyond high school. The main interest area is science. People in this career field value high achievement, variety, prestige, and helping others. It is important for workers to have good communication skills when dealing with patients and families.

LEARNING STYLES

Body/Kinesthetic

Have students choose an occupation from the table on page 96 and do research to find out the sorts of tasks this worker does at work. (Students might explore online sources, check with a guidance counselor, or interview an adult health-care worker for information.) Ask students to model performing one or more of the tasks they learned about as they explain its purpose.

IN THE COMMUNITY

Provide several copies of the business listings of a phone book for your community. Have students look in them to find businesses that offer health-care services. Post a local map and ask students to label locations of health-care institutions and offices in your community. Students might color-code different types of health-care providers, such as hospitals and clinics, optometry offices, dentists' offices, and so on. When the map is complete, analyze it as a class to evaluate how well your community's health-care needs are being served.

Outlook

Health science occupations are expected to increase greatly by 2012. This is partly because more people are getting older in the United States. The aging population requires more health care. Jobs that will see the most growth include dental hygienists and dental assistants. There will also be more jobs for physician assistants, medical records technicians, and physical therapy aides. All of these jobs are expected to increase by more than 40 percent by 2012. No occupations in the Health Science cluster are expected to see a decrease in employment.

Workers in health science will account for 7 percent of all people employed by 2012. The average wages for health science occupations can vary greatly. Pay depends on the amount of education and training a job requires.

On-the-Job Training (Moderate-Term Preparation)	$29,100
Technical/Vocational Program	$31,300
College Degree (4 years)	$54,400
Advanced Degree (more than 4 years)	$73,600

Lesson 6 Review Write your answers to these questions on a sheet of paper.

1. Name five places where health-care workers may work.

2. Explain why health care is a business.

3. People who choose health-care fields value prestige. Explain why these fields provide prestige.

3 Reinforce and Extend

LEARNING STYLES

Logical/Mathematical
Refer students to the table on page 96 and have them compare the education and training required for a licensed practical nurse and for a registered nurse. (*An LPN receives vocational or technical training; an RN usually must have a college degree.*) Then ask students to compute the difference in average pay for this pair of occupations. (*An LPN earns $23,100 less each year, on average, than an RN.*)

ELL/ESL STRATEGY

Language Objective: *To recognize words with a common root*

Write the words *medicine* and *medical* on the board. Have a volunteer underline the parts that are identical. Ask students to look in a dictionary to learn the meaning of the root (*medicus* was the Latin word for *physician; mederi* means "to remedy or heal") and the meaning of each word. Repeat the procedure for the following pairs: *dentist/dental technician* (*dent* is the Latin word for *tooth*), *pharmacist/pharmacy* (The Greek word *pharmakon* meant *magic potion*) Tell students to be alert for root words and try to decode new words by comparing the new word to a familiar word with the same root.

Lesson 6 Review Answers

1. hospitals, private clinics, home health agencies, schools, offices laboratories, health clubs.

2. There are many administrative requirements related to government rules and insurance companies.

3. Many of the occupations require several years of special training, so people must be intelligent and hard-working in these professions. Helping people become healthy has always been respected. Also, many of the professions have traditionally been high-paying.

Chapter 4 Lesson 7

Overview In this lesson, students consider jobs, conditions, and outlook for the science, technology, engineering, and mathematics career cluster.

Objectives

- To compare work and workers in related fields of engineering, life and physical science, and mathematics
- To become familiar with some occupations in the career cluster
- To understand the job growth and pay opportunities in the cluster

Student Pages 98–101

Teacher's Resource Library TRL

Workbook Activity 16

Activity 16

Alternative Activity 16

Vocabulary

engineering
technology

Write the vocabulary words on the board. Have students find two shorter words in *engineering*. (*engineer, engine*) Explain that *engine* can refer to a machine for converting energy into motion or to a mechanical tool, and it has other meanings as well. The related Old French word *engignier* means "to contrive." An engineer is someone who skillfully contrives, or plans out, the design and manufacture of useful products or structures. Ask students to define *technology.* Then have students use the glossary or the lesson itself to provide definitions for *engineering* and *technology.*

1 Warm-Up Activity

Have students think about each noun in the lesson title and explain why these areas might be grouped in one cluster. (*Possible answer: Occupations related to each field call for a good understanding of math and science.*) Have students read the lesson to find out if they are right.

Engineering
The science of planning and building machines, tools, and transportation systems

Technology
The use of science to create new products or make old ones better

Related School Subjects
Agriculture
English
Math
Science
Technology

Related Abilities
Clerical
Language
Leadership
Manual
Mathematical
Mechanical
Organizational
Scientific
Visual (Spatial)

Related Values
Creativity
Good Salary
High Achievement
Independence
Job Security
Leadership
Prestige
Variety
Work with Hands
Work with Mind

Most of the occupations in this cluster require a basic knowledge of math and science. Some occupations directly put this knowledge to use, like **engineering**. The occupations in this cluster relate to **technology**. Technology is the use of science to create new products or make old ones better. In 2012, an estimated 50 percent of the people employed in this cluster will be in engineering and related occupations. Forty-six percent will work in life and physical science, and 4 percent in mathematical science.

Engineering

Engineering requires knowledge in science and math. Most engineers design, develop, and test products. The four major engineering fields are electrical, civil, mechanical, and industrial.

The Engineering Workplace

Engineers work in every state, including urban and rural areas. They may work for large research companies, universities, governments, or small businesses. They might work in labs, offices, or schools. Their work may require both indoor or outdoor locations.

Engineering Workers

Electrical and electronics engineers can be involved in getting power and light to homes, schools, and businesses. They may also work on telephones, computers, and electric motors—anything that is designed to use electricity.

Civil engineers design roads, buildings, airports, bridges, water treatment systems, and similar structures. As the population of the United States grows, more and larger buildings, roads, and other transportation systems are needed.

Mechanical engineers work on many different projects. They design tools and machines such as refrigerators, air conditioners, and car motors. They may prepare plans and drawings of the parts needed to create a product.

Name _____ Date _____ Period _____ | Workbook Activity 16 — Chapter 4, Lesson 7

Science, Technology, Engineering, and Mathematics

Directions Write the answers to these questions. Use complete sentences.

1. What is technology?
2. What are the four main engineering fields?
3. What do industrial engineers do?
4. What fields do life scientists work in?
5. What area of science includes nuclear energy and aerospace?
6. Why do scientists need good writing and computer skills?
7. What skills are important for mathematics workers?
8. Name a job in this career group that requires technical or vocational training.
9. What jobs are expected to decrease by 2012?
10. What is the average yearly salary for a worker in this field with an advanced degree?

TRL Career Planning **Workbook Activity 16**

Name _____ Date _____ Period _____ | Activity 16 — Chapter 4, Lesson 7

Identify the Field

Directions The statements below describe different fields in this career group. Decide which field the statement describes. Write **E** for Engineering, **S** for Physical and Life Science, or **M** for Mathematics.

____ 1. Chemists are part of this group.
____ 2. By 2012, about half of all workers in this career cluster will be in this field.
____ 3. This field includes workers in almost any other field.
____ 4. People in this field design, develop, and test products.
____ 5. People in this field teach mathematics.
____ 6. People in this field may study genetics or small living things.
____ 7. People in this field design airports.
____ 8. People in this field work in nuclear energy and medical technology.
____ 9. People in this field have jobs that deal with numbers, amounts, and symbols.
____ 10. People in this field design car motors.
____ 11. People in this field help make sure workers are safe.
____ 12. These jobs will decrease slightly by 2012.
____ 13. This field can involve the study of ideas.
____ 14. People in this field work in medical research.
____ 15. People in this field get power into people's homes.

TRL Career Planning **Activity 16**

Industrial engineers try to find the best way to make a product or provide a service. They help companies make the best use of their people, machines, and raw materials. They also make sure workers stay safe.

Other engineering specialties are computer, environmental, chemical, aerospace, petroleum, mining, and biomedical.

In general, engineers pay attention to details and are organized. They need to communicate well with others. They also need good writing skills to write reports. They value and enjoy being creative and working on their own. They may have scientific or business interests.

Life and Physical Science

Life scientists work in fields related to biology, food and agriculture, forestry, and the environment. Physical scientists work in the fields of physics, space exploration, chemistry, and weather.

The Life and Physical Science Workplace
Most chemists work in industrial areas. Most physicists work either for the federal government or colleges and universities. Four in ten biological scientists work for the government. Others are employed in labs, drug companies, or schools and colleges.

Life and Physical Science Workers
Life scientists may be biologists who study genetics or small living things. They may also be food scientists who help keep food safe and healthy. Other occupations in life science are animal scientists, medical researchers, chemists, and scientists who study our use of soil and water. Biologists and life scientists are interested in science and technology. They value prestige, variety, and getting a good salary.

Physical scientists work in occupations related to nuclear energy, electronics, optics, aerospace, and medical technology. They try to find out how and why things work by studying things like electricity, heat, gravity, and the particles that make up non-living things. Scientists are required to plan, record information, and write reports. They need good writing and computer skills.

2 Teaching the Lesson

Students should understand after reading the lesson that the occupations for this cluster do not fall into an industry. Rather, they are found in many different industries. They are grouped together largely because of their common requirement for higher education and emphasis on mathematics and science.

Point out to students that workers in occupations in this cluster also need strong abilities to communicate verbally and in writing.

3 Reinforce and Extend

LEARNING STYLES

Visual/Spatial

Students who learn best by graphic representations can make word webs for the engineering, life and physical science, and mathematics areas. Around each category, they can list various types of workers (for example, circles around science could include *biologist, chemist, physicist, meteorologist, medical researcher*).

LEARNING STYLES

Auditory/Verbal

Provide an audiocassette or CD recording of the lesson and have students read along as they listen to it. Pause the recording after each subsection and have students summarize the main points, and then discuss the ideas they found interesting.

Interpersonal/Group Learning

Ask small groups of students to cooperate to "invent" an innovative product that would improve life. After groups sketch or model their invention and write a description of its parts and purpose, ask them to brainstorm a list of the different workers or abilities needed to take their idea from the drawing board to a finished product. For example, a robot that will clean a house might call for the services of a computer engineer, applied mathematician, development engineer, industrial engineer, materials analyst, quality-control scientist, technical writer, and others. Allow groups to present their ideas to the class.

LEARNING STYLES

Logical/Mathematical

Have students review paragraph 1 on page 101 and summarize the changes in engineering and science jobs for the near future. (*Manufacturing jobs in engineering and science will decrease; government jobs in both will increase.*) Then ask students to review the next paragraph and summarize its main points. (*Workers in this cluster form a small portion of the nation's workforce and must have extensive training and education.*) Last, have students compare the wage data for this cluster to other clusters they have read about and make a generalization. (*A possible answer: Since workers in science, technology, engineering, and mathematics are highly trained and specialized, they tend to earn more in general than many other clusters, which have entry-level and on-the-job training jobs.*)

Mathematics

Mathematics deals with numbers, amounts, and symbols. Mathematics can involve the study of ideas. Or, it can involve using mathematical rules to solve problems or answer questions. Many other fields rely on mathematical knowledge.

The Mathematics Workplace

Mathematics workers may be employed in almost any field. They are often involved in scientific work in laboratories or computer-related businesses. They may also teach mathematics in schools or universities.

Mathematics Workers

Many workers use mathematical skills and knowledge. They may be engineers, computer scientists, physicists, or economists. Mathematicians have scientific interests. They may study and teach mathematics. They need to have reasoning and computer skills. Those working in this cluster value variety, prestige, and a good salary.

Key to Education and Training Needed

1—Entry Level

2—On-the-Job Training

3—Apprenticeship

4—Technical/ Vocational Program

5—College

Science, Technology, Engineering, and Mathematics Occupations	
Anthropologist	5
Architectural Drafter	4
Biologist	5
Chemical Engineer	5
Chemist	5
Civil Engineer	5
Computer Hardware Engineer	5
Economist	5
Electrical Engineer	5
Environmental Scientist	5
Geologist	5
Mathematician	5
Mechanical Engineer	5
Science Teacher	5
Statistician	5

(See the key on the left.)

100   *Chapter 4   Career Clusters and the Major Industries*

Science, Technology, Engineering, and Mathematics Outlook

The occupations in this cluster do not form their own industry. Workers with science, technology, engineering, and mathematics jobs can work in any industry. In 2002, about one out of every three engineers worked in manufacturing. By 2012, one out of every eight engineers will work for the government. Occupations that will see the most job growth in this cluster include environmental and biomedical engineers, biochemists, biological scientists, veterinary assistants, and laboratory animal caretakers. By 2012, jobs for mining, nuclear, and petroleum engineers are expected to decrease. Jobs for mathematicians are expected to decrease slightly.

Only 1.6 percent of all workers in 2012 will have occupations in the Science, Technology, Engineering, and Mathematics cluster. Most jobs in this cluster require a lot of training and education. Average wages depend on the amount of preparation needed for a job.

Technical/Vocational Program (Long-Term Preparation)	$37,300
College Degree (4 years)	$53,700
Advanced Degree (more than 4 years)	$65,500

Lesson 7 Review Write your answers to these questions on a sheet of paper.

1. Name the four engineering fields and explain what each involves.

2. Give an example of a job in the life and physical science field and one in the mathematics field.

Writing Practice

Did you have a career goal when you were a child? Maybe you wanted to work on a ranch or fight fires. Write a journal entry. Describe the career goals you had when you were a child and how they have changed.

Lesson 7 Review Answers

1. Electrical—getting power and light to buildings; civil—designing structures such as roads, buildings, and bridges; mechanical—designing tools and machines; industrial—finding the best way to make a product or provide a service.

2. Life scientists—biologist, food scientist, medical researcher, chemist; physical scientist—jobs related to nuclear energy, electronics, optics, aerospace, medical technology; mathematics—teacher, mathematician.

Writing Practice

Have a volunteer read the Writing Practice feature on page 101 to the class. Invite students to share their childhood career goals. Poll the class to see how many students still plan to pursue this career goal. If students' chosen careers have been covered in the text to this point, have them jot down what they have learned, and then write how these facts differ from their early ideas about the job. Review paragraph structure. (A strong topic sentence is followed by sentences that provide supporting details, examples, or reasons.) Then have students write a paragraph about their changing career goals.

Chapter 4 Lesson 8

Overview In this lesson, students learn about four areas of information technology (IT), the cluster including computer-related industries. They also identify traits of IT workers and the job outlook for this fast-growing cluster.

Objectives

- To understand the nature of network design and database administration, technical writing and support, interactive media, and programming and software development
- To identify qualities needed for IT work
- To understand the job growth and income opportunities in IT

Student Pages 102–105

Teacher's Resource Library **TRL**

Workbook Activity 17

Activity 17

Alternative Activity 17

Vocabulary

database
information technology
network
software

Write component words of each compound word in the vocabulary list on separate index cards. Tape them in random order on the board. Phrase a definition for one word as a question (for example, *What do we call a group of computers linked together?*) Have volunteers answer the question by choosing two cards from the board and placing them together to form the term. (*network*) Continue with questions until all the words have been formed. Have students write each word and its definition.

> **Information technology**
> *The way information is stored and used in a computer or computer system*
>
> **Database**
> *Stored information*
>
> **Network**
> *A group of computers linked together*

Related School Subjects
English
Math
Science
Technology

Related Abilities
Interpersonal
Language
Mathematical
Organizational
Scientific

Related Values
Good Salary
High Achievement
Independence
Leadership
Prestige
Variety
Work with Mind

The occupations in this cluster relate to computer jobs. Careers in the **information technology** field can be grouped into four areas. The areas are 1) network design and database administration, 2) technical writing and support, 3) interactive media, and 4) programming and software development.

The Information Technology Workplace

People who work in the Information Technology cluster may work in offices or in their own homes. Some workers might travel to different businesses. Most of the jobs in this area involve sitting at a computer for long periods of time. People who work in this cluster need to be aware of physical problems they could encounter. These problems include eyestrain, back and arm pain, and stiffness and soreness in the hands, wrists, and fingers.

Network Design and Database Administration

Businesses store a lot of information on computers. Stored information on a computer is called a **database.** In order for a business to best use, store, and share information, its computers need to connect and communicate with each other. A group of computers linked together is called a **network.** There are many occupations related to computer networks and databases.

Network Design and Database Administration Workers
Systems analysts help plan and develop these networks for businesses. They help businesses to share and store information. Because technology keeps changing, systems and network analysts need to be current with new products.

Name _____ Date _____ Period _____ | **Workbook Activity** Chapter 4, Lesson 8 **17**

Information Technology Jobs

Directions The jobs below belong to different areas in the Information Technology field. Decide which area the career belongs in. Write **N** for Network Design and Database Administration, **T** for Technical Writing and Support, **I** for Interactive Media, or **P** for Programming and Software Development.

_____ 1. Web page designer
_____ 2. Computer software engineer
_____ 3. Computer scientist
_____ 4. Systems analyst
_____ 5. Desktop publisher
_____ 6. Programmer
_____ 7. Art director
_____ 8. Layout artist
_____ 9. Database administrator
_____ 10. Help-desk technician
_____ 11. Software tester
_____ 12. Technical writer
_____ 13. Graphic designer
_____ 14. Web editor
_____ 15. Network analyst

Workbook Activity 17

Name _____ Date _____ Period _____ | **Activity** Chapter 4, Lesson 8 **17**

Careers in Information Technology

Directions Write the correct word or phrase from the Word Bank to complete each sentence.

		Word Bank		
computers	eyestrain	increase	programmer	systems analyst
database	help-desk technician	Internet	scientific	technical writer
education	home	network	software	Web editor

1. Information technology workers might work in an office or at _____.
2. Most information technology workers sit at _____ for long hours.
3. Sometimes this leads to _____ and sore hands and fingers.
4. A(n) _____ is stored information.
5. Computers use a(n) _____ to communicate with each other.
6. A(n) _____ writes and edits text.
7. People who have problems with their computers can call a(n) _____.
8. Web page designers put photos or videos on the _____.
9. A(n) _____ makes sure that Internet links take users to the right places.
10. Programs that tell a computer what to do are called _____.
11. Someone who writes and maintains software is a(n) _____.
12. Information technology workers have _____ interests.
13. A job that will see the most growth by 2012 is _____.
14. Jobs for desktop publishers are expected to _____ 20 to 30 percent by 2012.
15. Most information technology jobs require a high level of _____.

Activity 17

Telecommunication specialists work on connecting computers and related equipment. Computer scientists are inventors and use research in developing theory. They can work on creating computer hardware. They might also develop language used in programming. They can be involved in designing computer games.

Database administrators use software programs to save and organize data on computers. They also keep the information secure. Properly managing saved information is very important so that no records will be lost.

Technical Writing and Support

When you work with computers you see text on the screen. Technical writers and desktop publishers write and prepare what you see on the computer screen. As more people use computers, e-mail, and the Internet, more people need help solving computer-related problems.

Technical Writing and Support Workers

Technical writers write and edit text. Desktop publishers create graphics, place photographs, and separate colors on a page. They can also be called electronic publishers, layout artists, or image designers. Computer support specialists and help desk technicians handle calls from people who need help. Because many users are not computer experts, they need the help of these experts.

> **Technology Note**
>
> Desktop publishing is a way to create professional-looking documents. A desktop publishing system can print a variety of typefaces. It can incorporate graphics and illustrations. Many companies use desktop publishing to create newsletters and brochures. Knowing how to use desktop publishing software is an impressive skill for your résumé.

1 Warm-Up Activity

As a class, brainstorm a list of places where students have seen computers being used. Point out that they have become so important that they are necessary in almost every business, office, factory, and home. Have students read the lesson to learn about occupations that are related to these uses and to computer design and production.

2 Teaching the Lesson

As students read the lesson, have them name additional uses for computers when they read about them.

3 Reinforce and Extend

> ### ELL/ESL STRATEGY
>
>
> **Language Objective:** *To understand the different functions of four subdivisions of IT*
>
> Students who are learning English may be struggling with word identification and syntax differences. By rereading text to find important words and phrases, their level of comprehension can be improved. Assist ELL students in comprehending the purpose of each of the areas of IT discussed in the lesson by creating a four-column table on the board. Head each column with one of the four areas. Read through the section "Network Design and Database Administration" with students and model how to summarize its functions. Your column might look like this:
>
> **Network Design and Database Administration**
> - Store information on computer
> - Share information among linked computers

> **Technology Note**

Read aloud the Technology Note on page 103. Display brochures and other publications that local businesses produce using desktop publishing. If possible, model or have a student model the use of a desktop publishing program to format and illustrate text.

Software
Program that tells a computer what to do

Interactive Media

Interactive media occupations involve work on computers. Workers in this field help people and companies do business on the Internet. They might be Web page designers, Web editors, art directors, graphic designers, or media designers.

Interactive Media Workers

Web page designers put text, photos, videos, or sounds on the Internet. They create Web pages for individuals or businesses. Web editors make sure that the information on a Web page is correct. They also make sure that people who use the Web site get the information they need. They might make sure that Internet links take users where they need to go. Art directors, graphic designers, and media designers are in charge of the photos, illustrations, and art that go on a Web page. They choose the art that best helps a business get its message to users.

Programming and Software Development

To do work on a computer, you use **software,** or a program that tells the computer what to do. There are many jobs related to computer software. Computer software engineers design, build, test, and maintain computer software. They tell a computer how to perform a task.

Programming and Software Development Workers

Computer systems software engineers work for companies that design, build, and install complete computer systems. Programmers write, repair, update, and maintain programs or software packages. Programmers and software testers check their work to make sure programs work without any problems.

Information Technology Workers

People who work in the Information Technology cluster have scientific interests. They are able to think logically and make good decisions. They pay close attention to detail. They communicate well. They value high salary, mental challenge, and variety in their work.

Key to Education and Training Needed

1—Entry Level

2—On-the-Job Training

3—Apprenticeship

4—Technical/ Vocational Program

5—College

Sample Information Technology Occupations

Occupation	
Computer Programmer	4 or 5
Computer Software Engineer	5
Computer Support Specialist	4
Computer Systems Analyst	4 or 5
Database Administrator	4 or 5
Desktop Publisher	3 or 4
Network Systems and Data Communications Analyst	4 or 5

(See the key on the left.)

Information Technology Outlook

Information Technology is a fast-growing career cluster. All occupations in this field are expected to continue growing. Jobs that will see the most growth by 2012 are systems analysts (57 percent), database administrators (44.2 percent), and software engineers (45.5 percent). Jobs for Web designers, desktop publishers, and computer support specialists are all expected to increase from 20 to 30 percent by 2012.

Most occupations in information technology require a high level of education. Pay depends on how much education a job requires. Here are average wages based on education for information technology jobs:

College Degree (4 years)	$52,600
Advanced Degree (more than 4 years)	$62,900

Lesson 8 Review Write your answers to these questions on a sheet of paper.

1. Explain what a systems analyst, a database administrator, and a technical writer do.

2. Why is information technology a fast-growing field? Give specific examples.

3. People in the Information Technology cluster may work in their own homes. Explain why you think this is an advantage or not.

AT HOME

Have students search at home for products and appliances that use microchips to function. (*Handheld electronic games, PDAs, newer TVs, cars, digital watches, microwave ovens, and some kitchen appliances contain microchips.*) You may want to suggest that students read owner's manuals for information.

Lesson 8 Review Answers

1. Systems analyst—plans and develops computer networks; Database administrator—uses software programs to save and organize data on computers; Technical writer—writes and prepares content on computers or other products.

2. Uses for computers continue to increase. Workers such as technical writers must provide content and support specialists must help people with new applications.

3. Answers will vary. Advantages would be working in a comfortable environment, having a flexible schedule, and not having to commute. Disadvantages would be not having as much contact with co-workers.

Chapter 4 Lesson 9

Overview This lesson organizes arts, audio-video technology, and communications careers into four areas: literary, arts, music, and entertainment. It describes characteristics of workers in these sectors and explains the outlook for such work in the future.

Objectives

- To explain why arts and communications workers have a big impact on society
- To identify kinds of work in the literary, arts, music, and entertainment sectors
- To compare what workers in these sectors do and how much money they are likely to earn

Student Pages 106–109

Teacher's Resource Library

Workbook Activity 18

Activity 18

Alternative Activity 18

1 Warm-Up Activity

Ask students to name a favorite singer, actor, writer, or disc jockey. Encourage them to tell what they know about these people. Discuss their impressions of what it is like to work in the arts or entertainment industry. How many of them want to work in this sector? Tell students they will learn about the nature of these kinds of work in this lesson. Have them read to evaluate the difficulty of succeeding in one of these careers.

2 Teaching the Lesson

Explore the different kinds of literary occupations with students by displaying an assortment of magazines, newspapers, novels, technical manuals, and scripts. Invite students to read parts of different media and compare the kinds of writing in them. You may also want to suggest that students explore different forms of writing employed on the Internet.

Lesson 9 — Arts, Audio-Video Technology, and Communications

This career cluster includes only a few workers in a small number of occupations. However, the work they do impacts almost everyone. Workers in the area write what you read in newspapers and books. They create what you see and hear in the movies, on television, or at a theater. The cluster includes four areas: 1) literary, 2) the arts, 3) music, and 4) entertainment.

Related School Subjects
Art
English
Family/Consumer Science
Management
Music
Social Science

Related Abilities
Artistic
Interpersonal
Leadership
Manual
Musical
Persuasive
Visual (Spatial)

Related Values
Creativity
Good Salary
High Achievement
Independence
Leadership
Prestige
Variety
Work with Hands
Work with Mind
Work with People

Literary

Work in the literary field involves writing and communication. There are writers for newspapers, TV news, magazines, movies, radio, books, and the Internet. Another set of literary occupations is editors and copywriters. They review the writing for news, newspapers, magazines, and books.

The Literary Workplace

People with literary occupations may work in offices or newsrooms. They may also work from their own homes. Others may work at a variety of locations, interviewing people for stories. Meeting time deadlines is important in this line of work.

Literary Workers

Literary workers include news writers, authors, technical writers, script writers, editors, and copywriters, and translators. They write and edit a variety of material including news stories, books, and movie scripts. Translators help people who speak different languages to communicate.

Sample Literary Occupations	
Columnist	5
Copywriter	5
Film and Video Editor	5
Interpreter	5
Novelist	5
Reporter	5
Script Editor	5
Technical Writer	5
Translator	5

People with literary occupations must be able to express ideas clearly. They need to use correct grammar. They need to make sure they get the facts.

(See the key on page 107.)

---

106 Chapter 4 *Career Clusters and the Major Industries*

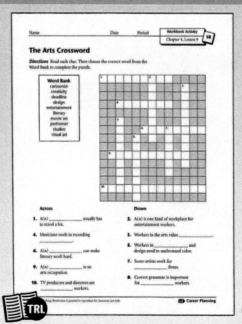

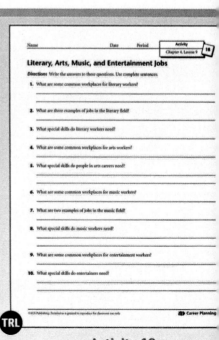

Sample Arts Occupations	
Camera Operator	3
Cartoonist	3
Commercial Designer	4
Floral Designer	2
Graphic Designer	4
Interior Designer	5
Painter (Artist)	3
Photographer	3 or 4

Sample Music Occupations	
Composer	5
Dancer	3 or 4
Musician	3 or 4
Singer	3

(See the key below.)

Key to Education and Training Needed

1—Entry Level

2—On-the-Job Training

3—Apprenticeship

4—Technical/ Vocational Program

5—College

The Arts

This area involves visual art and design. Arts occupations include painters, sculptors, photographers, cartoonists, designers, and illustrators. There are also technical behind-the-scenes jobs in the art field such as camera operators, multi media artists, editors, and photographers.

The Arts Workplace

Artists may work in studios. They may also work for design firms. Many artists work out of their own homes or in a variety of locations.

Arts Workers

Workers in the art field need to understand color. They pay attention to detail, size, and proportion. They need good eye-hand coordination. They often need computer knowledge. They view themselves as creative.

Music

There are three groups of performers in the music field: 1) dancers and choreographers, 2) singers, and 3) musicians. Dancers and choreographers perform and create dances. Singers sing all types of music. Musicians play instruments. Composers write and arrange music for these three groups to perform.

The Music Workplace

Performers usually work in theaters, recording studios, or concert halls. They often travel throughout the country to perform. Composers may work almost anywhere. Many work in their own homes or in studios.

Music Workers

In the music field, preparation and practice are important. Singers and musicians need to know different forms and styles of music. They must be able to read and understand music. Dancers need to be strong and move gracefully.

Point out the tables of sample occupations for each sector. If there are jobs students do not know about, describe them and explain their purpose to students. You might ask students to describe the kind of skills certain workers need.

Point out the average incomes for workers in this cluster at different levels of training and education (see page 109). Students may be surprised to see that they are lower than average income in other clusters they have studied. Explain that, while a few workers make huge incomes, most workers in this sector work for little. Only a small handful of aspiring actors become stars.

 Reinforce and Extend

LEARNING STYLES

Logical/Mathematical
Have students summarize lesson information using a graphic organizer. For example, they could make a table with the following column and row labels:

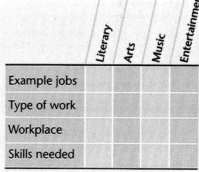

	Literary	Arts	Music	Entertainment
Example jobs				
Type of work				
Workplace				
Skills needed				

As they read, students can jot down information in their tables. Compare and contrast the information in each area.

LEARNING STYLES

Body/Kinesthetic
Some students will have training in arts, music, or entertainment. Invite them to share what they have learned about dancing, singing, cartooning, graphic designing, and so on. If possible, have students demonstrate a technique and explain how they learned it. These students may also be able to report on the training and backgrounds of their teachers.

Entertainment

The entertainment field includes announcers, performers, and directors. These people work in radio and TV, in the theater, and in movies.

The Entertainment Workplace

Entertainers can work almost anywhere. They work on TV and movie sets, in radio studios, and on stages. Many of them travel all over the world for their jobs.

Entertainment Workers

Radio and television workers include news announcers, sports announcers, talk show hosts, and disc jockeys. Announcers and disc jockeys must have nice-sounding voices. They need to pronounce words clearly. Sports announcers need a good knowledge of sports, their rules, and well-known athletes. Talk show hosts usually have a nice appearance and are good at making conversation with others.

Other performers include circus performers, comedians, and actors and actresses. Actors need to have good memories to learn their lines. They should be able to project their voices. Actors should appear comfortable in front of many people.

Directors put together the production of a show. They are managers who hire the cast, direct practices, and approve set designs, costumes, and music. Producers handle the business and financial decisions of a production. They are administrators who hire the director and rent the facilities where the show will occur.

Sample Entertainment Occupations	
Actor/Actress	3, 4, or 5
Announcer	3, 4, or 5
Radio/Movie/TV Producer	3, 4, or 5
Radio/TV Program Director	3, 4, or 5

(See the key on page 107.)

Arts, Audio-Video Technology, and Communications Workers

Most people working in this career cluster are interested in literary, musical, and artistic expression. They value creativity, imagination, and independent thought. Most jobs require a high level of education or training because there are many more people who want these jobs than there are opportunities. Job applicants must be very talented. Most people in this cluster are good communicators. They are friendly and enjoy being with others.

Arts, Audio-Video Technology, and Communications Outlook

There will be a very small amount of job growth in this cluster. It will be difficult to find a job in the entertainment field. There are very few popular singers or movie stars. The occupations that support these people are what make the entertainment industry large. These occupations include food service workers, event promoters, and security personnel. Jobs that will see the most growth in this cluster by 2012 include technical writers, translators, and film and video editors.

Only 1.6 percent of all employed workers in 2012 will have literary, arts, music, drama, or entertainment jobs. The average wages for occupations in this cluster depend on how much training and education a job requires.

On-the-Job Training	$25,100–$26,600
College Degree (4 years)	$36,500
Advanced Degree (more than 4 years)	$42,100

Lesson 9 Review Write your answers to these questions on a sheet of paper.

1. Give an example of a worker in each of these fields: literary, arts, music, and entertainment.

2. What are some behind-the-scenes jobs in the arts cluster?

3. The arts cluster employs a very small number of workers. Yet many people would like to work in these fields. Explain why.

Career Clusters and the Major Industries Chapter 4 **109**

Lesson 9 Review Answers

1. Literary—newspaper, magazine, book, radio, and Internet writers; Arts—painters, sculptors, photographers, cartoonists, designers, illustrators; Music—dancers, choreographers, singers, musicians; Entertainment—radio and TV announcers, performers, directors

2. Behind-the-scenes arts jobs include camera operators, multi media artists, editors, and photographers.

3. Answers will vary. Students may say artistic work is fun and satisfying. It can lead to travel, meeting interesting people, and making a lot of money. It gives people a chance to have an appreciative audience.

Chapter 4 Lesson 10

Overview This lesson summarizes facts about occupations devoted to learning, necessary traits for workers in this field, and the outlook for these careers.

Objectives

- To identify jobs related to education and training
- To describe traits of educators
- To summarize future opportunities in education and training

Student Pages 110–111

Teacher's Resource Library TRL

Workbook Activity 19

Activity 19

Alternative Activity 19

1 Warm-Up Activity

Invite students to describe a favorite teacher they have had. Encourage volunteers to name traits that they feel made this teacher effective. Have students read the lesson to learn about other types of jobs in education.

2 Teaching the Lesson

Create a word web on the board. Write *Teachers* in the center circle. Have students list different kinds of teachers as they read about them in the lesson. A second graphic organizer could illustrate other types of trained workers in schools, such as librarians, principals, and counselors.

You may want to hold a class discussion on reasons for strong growth in the number of jobs in education. (Jobs in manufacturing, which call for less education, are declining. More jobs are being created that require higher education. Many people need to be re-educated as their occupation changes or they must switch to a new field.)

Related School Subjects
Clerical Studies
English
Languages

Related Abilities
Clerical
Language
Leadership
Organizational
Persuasive
Social

Related Values
Creativity
Good Salary
High Achievement
Job Security
Leadership
Variety
Work with Mind
Work with People

This career cluster includes education, training, and library occupations. These occupations make up the largest group of professional workers—31 percent of all professional occupations.

The Workplace

Educators and librarians usually work in schools or colleges. They may work in public or private schools. Many preschool teachers work in places other than a school, such as child care centers, churches, or their own homes. Trainers may work in schools or businesses. They may travel to different places to do their jobs.

The Workers

Teachers help students to learn. They also need to make sure students follow the rules. Teachers work with every age group. Early childhood and preschool teachers work with young children. Elementary school teachers work with children between the ages of five and 11. Middle and high school teachers work with older students. Special education teachers, teacher assistants, physical education teachers, and coaches can work with any age group.

Besides teachers, there are many other occupations in the education and training fields. Some examples of these occupations are school counselors, principals, librarians, college professors, and corporate trainers. School counselors help students with their problems. They can help students adjust to school. Counselors help students choose classes. They help students plan for a future career. Principals oversee the work of teachers and school support staff. Librarians buy materials for and run the school library. College professors teach a variety of subjects at colleges and universities. Corporate trainers or training and development specialists work in business and industry. They provide programs for workers and managers to learn new information and skills.

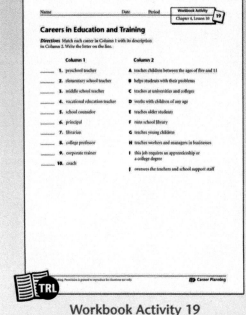

Workbook Activity 19

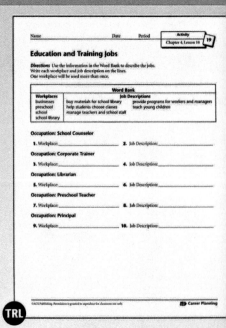

Activity 19

Education and Training Occupations	
Corporate Trainer	5
Elementary Teacher	5
Librarian	5
Postsecondary Teacher	5
Preschool Teacher	3 or 4
School Counselor	5
Secondary Teacher	5
Special Education Teacher	5
Teacher Assistant	3
Vocational Education Teacher	3 or 5

(See the key below.)

Key to Education and Training Needed

1—Entry Level

2—On-the-Job Training

3—Apprenticeship

4—Technical/ Vocational Program

5—College

In general, workers in this cluster have social interests. They are good at talking with and working with others. They value using their minds and working with people. They like to express their creativity. They enjoy variety in their work. Administrators and trainers are also good with people. Some might have business interests. Some teachers are well organized and serious. Others are friendly and outgoing.

Outlook

Education, training, and library occupations will see a large amount of growth by 2012. This field is one of the largest-growing career areas. By 2012, there will be a 38.1 percent increase in jobs for college or postsecondary teachers. Jobs as preschool and kindergarten teachers will increase by 33.6 percent. Child, family, and school social workers will see job growth of 23.2 percent.

By 2012, workers in the Education and Training cluster will make up 8.3 percent of all workers employed. Pay for jobs in this cluster can vary, depending on how much preparation a job requires. Here are the average wages for education and training jobs:

On-the-Job Training (Long-Term Preparation)	$19,000
College Degree, Teacher (4 years)	$42,600
Advanced Degree, Teacher (more than 4 years)	$57,000
Advanced Degree, Administrator (more than 4 years)	$71,500

Lesson 10 Review Write your answers to these questions on a sheet of paper.

1. What percent of all professional occupations is made up by the education and training occupations?

2. What are three different jobs included in the teaching profession?

3. Why do you think there are so many workers in education and training occupations?

Lesson 10 Review Answers

1. 31 percent

2. Any three: Special education teachers, teacher assistants, physical education teachers, coaches

3. Answers will vary. Possible answer: Our society respects education, and there are always many children to educate. Teaching is a satisfying career.

3 Reinforce and Extend

LEARNING STYLES

Interpersonal/ Group Learning

Explain that teachers employ methods to help students learn and remember new material, such as involving all the senses in the learning experience or having students apply what they learn in projects. Create small groups and have each member design and present a lesson to teach a specific subject or skill to the group. Ask students to plan their lesson to involve the group actively in some way. After each lesson is presented, students can write an evaluation telling which methods helped them learn best. Have each "teacher" write a summary, including what he or she found most difficult and what was most surprising about teaching others.

ONLINE CONNECTION

Recruiting New Teachers, a national teacher recruitment clearinghouse, produces a Web site that may be of interest to students considering a career in education. It offers first-hand accounts by teachers as well as a wide range of resources to help students consider what is involved in preparing for this field and finding a job. The Web site is located at www.rnt.org.

The National Education Association produces a magazine called *Tomorrow's Teachers* for members of its Student Program, which has chapters on college campuses across the country. This publication is available online at www.nea.org/tomorrowsteachers. Students will find interesting articles about training for and starting out in the teaching profession.

Lesson at a Glance

Chapter 4 Lesson 11

Overview In this lesson, students learn about the human services industries, their workers, and job outlooks for the industries.

Objectives

- To identify and define four service areas
- To describe the workplace and workers for preschool services, psychological and counseling services, community services, and personal care
- To identify job outlooks for various occupations in human services

Student Pages 112–115

Teacher's Resource Library (TRL)

Workbook Activity 20

Activity 20

Alternative Activity 20

Vocabulary

clergy
psychological
psychologist

Write *biologist* and *geologist* on the board. Ask students what the ending *-ologist* means. (*one who studies*) Add *psychologist* to the list and have students predict its meaning. Read the textbook definition and then write *psychological* below *psychologist* and have a volunteer circle the parts that are the same. After students predict the meaning of *psychological*, read its definition. Add *clergy* to the list and have students use prior knowledge to explain what it means to them. Read the definition aloud.

 Warm-Up Activity

List the following kinds of workers on the board: *child-care provider, hairdresser, home health aide, pastor, counselor.* Invite volunteers to tell why they think all these kinds of workers might be grouped together. (*Possible answer: They all help care for the needs of people on a one-on-one basis.*) Have students read the lesson to answer this question.

Psychological
Having to do with the mind or brain

Psychologist
Someone who studies the mind and human behavior

Related School Subjects
English
Languages
Science
Social Science

Related Abilities
Interpersonal
Language
Leadership
Organizational
Persuasive
Scientific
Social

Related Values
Creativity
Good Salary
High Achievement
Independence
Job Security
Leadership
Prestige
Variety
Work with Mind
Work with People

The Human Services cluster covers four main service areas: 1) preschool and early childhood, 2) **psychological** and counseling, 3) community, and 4) personal care. Workers in each area need different levels of education and skills. The occupations in this cluster are located in almost every community.

Preschool Services

Child care work employs a large number of people, about 1.3 million workers. Child care providers and preschool teachers work with young children. They help the children to learn, play, and get along with others.

The Preschool Services Workplace

Child care workers may be employed by child care centers or nursery schools. Many people provide child care services out of their own homes.

Preschool Services Workers

Child care workers involve children in games, art, and storytelling. They help children to create relationships. They teach children about rules for playing with others. Preschool teachers need to know how to judge what things a child is good at and what things need more work. Then, they help that child learn new skills.

Psychological and Counseling Services

Psychological workers, called **psychologists,** study the mind and human behavior. Some study memory, learning, and mental health. Most psychologists work directly with people. Counselors help people in non-medical ways. They talk with people about personal, family, education, mental health, or career problems.

The Psychological and Counseling Services Workplace

Counselors and psychologists can work in hospitals, colleges, or schools. Many of these workers have private practices, or offices they own themselves.

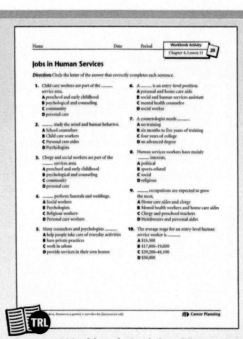

Workbook Activity 20

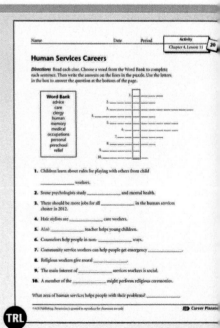

Activity 20

Psychological and Counseling Services Workers

Psychologists help people with their emotional or mental problems. They work with people who are depressed or have other mental health issues. Some psychologists help people deal with things like divorce, family arguments, or the death of a loved one. Other psychologists work with children.

Counselors help people with their problems as well. They use different skills for different things people need help with. For example, substance abuse counselors help people who have problems with alcohol, drugs, gambling, and eating disorders. School counselors help young people deal with crises they may experience at school, at home, or with classmates.

Community Services

The community services area includes religious occupations, social workers, and human services assistants. These workers provide help to people in different ways.

The Community Services Workplace

Clergy and religious workers usually work in churches, synagogues, mosques, temples, and other places of worship. They may also travel to visit community members. Social workers and human services assistants work in many different offices and settings. They might work in schools, medical centers, or places of business.

Community Services Workers

Clergy and religious workers might counsel people when they need religious or moral advice. They visit the sick. They help families deal with problems. They also perform funerals, weddings, and other religious ceremonies. Most clergy members do not work regular hours and many work longer than an average workday.

Social workers help people solve personal and family problems. Social and human service assistants usually help professionals such as psychologists, rehabilitation counselors, or social workers. They provide services or support for families. Some human service assistants provide emergency relief in disasters.

Teaching the Lesson

You may want to tell students that psychologists and psychiatrists both go to school after completing college and specialize in mental health. However, a psychiatrist is a medical doctor and can prescribe medications. A psychologist has advanced training in psychology but has not been to medical school.

To help students understand the dimensions of the personal care services area, you might list other occupations included in it: funeral directors, spa attendants, personal trainers, and massage therapists, for example.

When students have completed the lesson, have them analyze the education and training levels in the table on page 114 and the income data on page 115. Ask: *Which two areas are better paid?* (psychological and counseling services; community services) *Why do you think these workers receive higher pay?* (They get more education and training.)

Reinforce and Extend

LEARNING STYLES

Interpersonal/ Group Learning

Make four student groups and assign each group one of the human services areas. Provide each group with a local phone book that includes business listings. Ask each group to brainstorm key words under which to look for businesses that provide their service. (For example, preschool services might appear under *day care, child care, preschool,* or *school.*) Have students write down at least five of the listings in the phone book and cooperate to find out more about them. Each business might have a Web site, brochures, and other means of educating the public. Students might call one or two businesses that especially interest them and ask if it is possible to interview an employee.

Personal Care Services

Personal care services occupations include personal and home care aides. These people work with elderly, disabled, or sick people. This area also includes hairdressers, hair stylists, and barbers.

The Personal Care Services Workplace

Personal and home care aides work in private homes, residential care centers, or nursing homes. Hair stylists work in salons. Many hair stylists own their own businesses.

Personal Care Services Workers

Personal care aides might help parents who need help caring for their children. They might also help people after they return home from the hospital. They work with the person to do everyday activities like feed and dress themselves. Home care aides may clean a person's house, do laundry, or plan meals. Hairdressers, hair stylists, and barbers shampoo, cut, color, and style hair. They provide a personal appearance or beauty service.

The number following the occupations below represents the minimum education and training needed for each occupation.

Key to Education and Training Needed

1—Entry Level

2—On-the-Job Training

3—Apprenticeship

4—Technical/Vocational Program

5—College

Sample Human Services Occupations	
Child Care Worker	1 or 4
Clergy	5
Clinical Psychologist	5
Counseling Psychologist	5
Hairdresser, Hairstylist, and Cosmetologist	3
Mental Health Counselor	5
Personal and Home Care Aide	1
School Counselor	5
School Psychologist	5
Social and Human Services Assistant	2 or 4
Social Worker	5

(See key on the left.)

The main interest of human service workers is social. They need to be good communicators. In general, they are sensitive to people and their problems. Psychologists usually have scientific interests. Religious workers, counselors, and social workers are very good at teaching and leading others. Child care workers are energetic. They must be able to deal with children who misbehave.

Human Services Outlook

All occupations within the Human Services cluster are expected to increase by 2012. Jobs that will see the most growth include mental health and substance abuse social workers, mental health and rehabilitation counselors, social and human service assistants, personal aides, and home care aides. These occupations are expected to grow between 26.7 and 48.7 percent.

Human services workers will account for 3.3 percent of all employed workers by 2012. The average wages for occupations in this cluster varies. Here is a list of average wages based on training and education:

Entry Level	$16,300
On-the-Job Training/Apprenticeship	$17,800–$19,000
College Degree	$39,200–$44,100

Lesson 11 Review Write your answers to these questions on a sheet of paper.

1. Do you think child care jobs will increase or decrease in the next few years? Explain why.

2. What are two different jobs in the personal care services field?

3. Why do you think clergy and psychological workers are included in the same career cluster?

Chapter 4 Lesson 12

Overview In this lesson, students learn about conditions, occupations, workplaces, and outlook in the hospitality and tourism industry.

Objectives

- To identify a variety of occupations in hospitality and tourism
- To describe the tasks performed by hospitality and tourism workers
- To analyze education requirements, employment outlook, and average earnings for workers in hospitality and tourism

Student Pages 116–118

Teacher's Resource Library (TRL)

Workbook Activity 21

Activity 21

Alternative Activity 21

Vocabulary

hospitality
tourism

Ask students to tell in their own words what the statement *Thank you for your hospitality* means. (*Possible response: gratitude for the way people have made one feel welcome and comfortable*) Write the words *tourist* and *tourism* on the board and have students tell what they know about each word. Then have students read the text definitions for each vocabulary word and use them in oral sentences with the meanings they have in this context.

1 Warm-Up Activity

Based on the definitions of *hospitality* and *tourism*, have students predict what kinds of work will be included in this career cluster. If students have difficulty, write the following headings on the board: *restaurants and food service, lodging, travel, amusements and attractions.* Have students think of businesses in each category and name people needed to staff them.

Hospitality
Taking care of guests or customers

Tourism
Business of providing services to visitors and travelers

Related School Subjects
Family/Consumer Science
Health
Math
Social Science

Related Abilities
Clerical
Interpersonal
Language
Manual
Organizational
Persuasive
Social

Related Values
Outdoor Work
Physical Activity
Risk
Variety
Work with Hands
Work with People

This cluster includes occupations in **hospitality** and **tourism**. Tourism is the largest industry in some states, cities, and regions. For example, Las Vegas, Nevada, is a well-known attraction for visitors. Other tourist locations include beaches and national parks, as well as historical and cultural places. This cluster also includes the cruise ship industry.

The Workplace

People employed in hospitality and tourism can work in many different places. They may work in hotels, motels, at national parks, or on cruise ships. Others work at resorts, amusement parks, and restaurants. Some workers might drive buses or cabs. People who work for travel agencies usually work in an office.

The Workers

Tourism includes transportation workers such as bus and cab drivers. Travel agents are another transportation-related occupation in the tourism industry. Travel agents help people plan trips. Tourism workers have many interests.

Sample Hospitality and Tourism Occupations	
Chef	3, 4, or 5
Food Services Manager	3, 4, or 5
Hotel Desk Clerk	2
Lodging Manager	3, 4, or 5
Maid/Housekeeper	1
Meeting and Convention Planner	5
Recreation Worker	3 or 5
Reservation and Transportation Ticket Agent	2
Restaurant Host/Hostess	1
Short Order Cook	1
Travel Agent	2
Tour Guide	2
Waiter/Waitress	1

(See the key on page 117.)

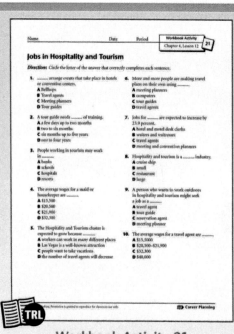

Workbook Activity 21

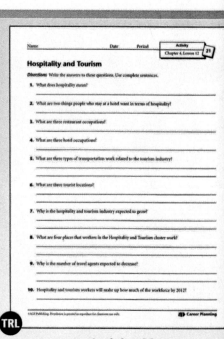

Activity 21

Hospitality means giving good service to visitors. People want to be treated nicely when they check into a hotel, motel, or resort. Hotels and motel clerks, reservation agents, housekeepers, groundskeepers, and bellhops all try to make the guests comfortable.

Other hospitality occupations are tour guides, food service workers, chefs, and meeting planners. Tour guides show visitors around an area. Waiters, waitresses, and food service workers prepare and serve food at restaurants. Chefs supervise cooks and food service workers. They plan menus and cook meals. Meeting planners make arrangements for events to take place at a hotel or convention center.

Outlook

The hospitality and tourism industry is expected to grow. People want to take vacations and be entertained. Food preparation and serving occupations will see a 20 percent increase in jobs by 2012. There will be 21.3 percent more jobs for meeting and convention planners. Job growth for hotel and motel desk clerks is expected to be 23.9 percent. The employment of travel agents is expected to decrease. This is because more people use the Internet to make travel plans on their own.

Hospitality and tourism is a large industry. By 2012, workers in this industry will make up 11.4 percent of all employed workers. The amount of training and education a job requires determines the wages.

Entry Level	$15,500
On-the-Job Training/Apprenticeship	$20,500–$21,900
Technical/Vocational Program	$32,300
College Degree (2 years)	$32,300

Key to Education and Training Needed

1—Entry Level

2—On-the-Job Training

3—Apprenticeship

4—Technical/ Vocational Program

5—College

LEARNING STYLES

Visual/Spatial
Interested students might enjoy clipping pictures from magazines or printing images from Web sites that show workplaces and workers in the hospitality and tourism industry. Have them combine their images and use them to create a bulletin board or poster. Suggest that they use headings such as *Food Service, Lodging,* and so on to group the pictures and write a caption for each picture, naming the occupation or workplace.

 Teaching the Lesson

Be sure that students recall that the key for all the tables that list sample occupations in a cluster is found on page 80 (or on the classroom poster if you made one).

As students read definitions and descriptions for the hospitality and tourism industries, you may want to have them list businesses in your community or region that supply these services.

Have students analyze the table on page 116 and the wage data on page 117. Ask a volunteer to make a generalization about these occupations relative to other clusters. (Possible response: Most hospitality and tourism jobs do not require advanced education but also do not pay very well compared to other careers.)

Discuss with students reasons why most occupation categories in this cluster are expected to grow rapidly. (Example reason: Today, an increasing number of people have more leisure and discretionary income, so they travel and eat out more.)

 Reinforce and Extend

LEARNING STYLES

Body/Kinesthetic
Discuss with students the concept of body language and what it communicates about a person. (*attitude, state of mind, emotional reaction to what someone is saying or doing*)

Ask volunteers who are familiar with one or more occupations in the hospitality and tourism industry to model the kind of posture, facial expressions, gestures, and movements that a worker in this field should adopt to convey a welcoming, friendly, or helpful attitude.

IN THE ENVIRONMENT

Workers in the tourism industry encourage travelers to visit sites of natural beauty, such as national parks. Large numbers of visitors to a natural site can stress or damage it. Ask students to learn about a place with many visitors each year (*Yellowstone National Park or the Grand Canyon, for example*). Have them imagine they are tourism experts and create a brochure to explain how visitors need to behave to prevent damage to the environment of the park.

Lesson 12 Review Answers

1. Answers will vary. Possible answer: Some places, like Las Vegas employ a huge number of these workers. Other places have little or no tourism.

2. Food preparation and serving are growing; the occupation of travel agents is not.

3. Answers will vary. Possible answer: Advantages would be working in a fun environment, helping others enjoy themselves, and possibly earning a lot of money from tips. A disadvantage might be having to work closely with many different kinds of people, so having to deal at times with unhappy customers.

Career Profile

Ask students who have heard the term *paralegal* to tell what they know about this occupation. Explain that most attorneys require the help of trained assistants. Then read the opening paragraph of the Career Profile on page 118 aloud. Have students read the rest of the feature silently and list any questions they have about paralegal work. Discuss ways that students can find answers to their questions. (They might search the Internet, look up the career in the *Occupational Outlook Handbook* or check with a guidance counselor for brochures and pamphlets.) If possible, ask a paralegal from the community to provide answers to questions, either in person or via e-mail. Explain that students will learn more about occupations in the legal system in Lesson 13.

Lesson 12 Review Write your answers to these questions on a sheet of paper.

1. Why do the hospitality and tourism fields differ from place to place?

2. Which jobs in tourism are growing? Which are not?

3. What are some positive features of working in the hospitality and tourism industries? What are some negative features?

Career Profile

Paralegal

Have you ever pictured yourself before a jury, arguing an important case? Perhaps you should become a lawyer. You might also consider other legal careers, such as a paralegal. Paralegal, or legal assistant, is a rapidly growing law career. A 28.7 percent growth in the paralegal field is expected between 2002 and 2012. Paralegals cannot argue cases before a jury. But they can do many varied tasks related to law.

Paralegals may conduct interviews with clients and witnesses. They may research cases for lawyers. They may attend hearings or trials with lawyers. Beginning paralegals may do many routine administrative tasks. Experienced paralegals do more difficult work such as drafting legal documents.

There are several different career paths for paralegals. Paralegals must pass the Certified Legal Assistant exam. Some paralegals get a four-year college degree. Then they get on-the-job training or take a 60-hour paralegal course. Others have a paralegal major or minor in college. Others get a two-year degree with a paralegal major. Paralegals are interested in business and law and have good writing and speaking skills.

ONLINE CONNECTION

Students can find information on a paralegal career at www.abanet.org/legalservices/legalassistants/career.html or www.paralegals.org. (Click on Career Center from this home page to view an explanation by career experts, read articles, and order a free booklet on income statistics.)

Corrections
Field that involves the treatment and rehabilitation of prisoners in jails

Related School Subjects
Clerical Studies
English
Science
Social Science

Related Abilities
Clerical
Interpersonal
Language
Leadership
Manual
Organizational
Persuasive
Scientific

Related Values
Creativity
Good Salary
High Achievement
Independence
Job Security
Leadership
Physical Activity
Prestige
Risk
Variety
Work with Mind
Work with People

This cluster covers occupations in the legal system as well as in law enforcement and **corrections.** It also includes emergency medical, fire, and security services.

The Legal System

The legal system deals with laws. Governments, courts, and elected officials are all part of the legal system.

The Legal System Workplace

Legal workers live within most communities. They work in courthouses, government buildings, and offices. Some legal workers own their own businesses.

Legal System Workers

Many different people are part of the legal system. Legal workers include judges, lawyers, and legal assistants. Judges oversee what goes on in court. They also make decisions about cases. Lawyers, also called attorneys, make arguments in court. They might work for the government or for the person they are defending. Law is a large field, so lawyers usually focus on one type of law such as family, business, or real estate. Legal assistants, or paralegals, research topics or prepare documents for lawyers or judges.

Legal workers have many interests. They usually like to be involved in business. Judges and lawyers have good language and persuasive skills. They like to be in leadership positions.

Law Enforcement

Law enforcement occupations include corrections officers, police officers, detectives, sheriffs and deputies, and dispatchers.

Career Clusters and the Major Industries **Chapter 4** **119**

Lesson at a Glance

Chapter 4 Lesson 13

Overview In this lesson, students consider jobs, conditions, and outlook for the law, public safety, and security career cluster.

Objectives

■ To understand the nature of work in the legal system, law enforcement, and emergency services

■ To identify and describe occupations in law, public safety, and security

■ To understand job growth and pay opportunities in law, public safety, and security jobs

Student Pages 119–122

Teacher's Resource Library

Workbook Activity 22
Activity 22
Alternative Activity 22

Vocabulary

corrections

Write the word *correct* on the board and ask students to list different meanings the word can have (*for example, "right," "proper," "to change in order to make right," "to punish so as to improve"*). Add *-ion* to the word and explain that this ending makes the verb into a noun. Then have students predict the meaning of *corrections* in a lesson about law, public safety, and security. (*Possible answer: punishments or systems that punish lawbreakers while trying to improve their outlook*) Then have students read the textbook definition to check their predictions.

1 Warm-Up Activity

Have students read the lesson title on page 119. Ask: *What kinds of jobs are related to these three areas?* (Students may suggest lawyer, paralegal, and judge for law; police officer, firefighter, and parole officer for public safety; and security guard for security.) Invite volunteers to describe what they know about these occupations.

---

2 Teaching the Lesson

Be sure that students understand the difference between police and detective work. Police officers try to prevent crime and accidents before they happen (through such activities as patrolling, enforcing speed limits, and directing traffic) or they respond to crimes while they are in progress. Detectives investigate crimes that have already occurred and gather evidence that can be used in court.

After students have read the lesson, ask them to point out similarities in requirements for law enforcement and emergency services workers. (Possible answer: Both types of work require quick thinking, physical conditioning, and willingness to be exposed to danger.)

3 Reinforce and Extend

Think Positive

Read the Think Positive feature on page 120 aloud. Explain that some young people who think they are interested in a career in law first train as paralegals. After they have experience and understand the field, they may decide to attend law school, often continuing with work as they attend classes on evenings and weekends.

PERSONAL JOURNAL

Review with students the physical and personality qualities needed by workers in law enforcement, public safety, and security. Ask students to write a paragraph on their own paper telling whether and why they would be good candidates for a job in law enforcement or emergency services.

Think Positive

Think positively about all the jobs included in a career cluster. Remember that they all have similar workplaces and interests. Maybe a law career interests you. Are you ready to commit to several years of college and law school? If not, consider another occupation such as a paralegal. It could lead to other law careers or be rewarding in itself.

The Law Enforcement Workplace

Corrections officers work in jails and prisons. Police officers, detectives, and sheriff's deputies might work on patrol in cars. They might also work in offices or police stations doing work related to solving cases. Dispatchers usually work at police stations.

Law Enforcement Workers

Corrections officers include jailers, guards, and wardens. They watch over the prisoners in a jail. They also help move prisoners throughout the jail or to other places. Wardens oversee everything that goes on at the jail. They make sure the jail operates safely.

Occupations related to corrections officers are probation and parole officers. These people work with people on probation or people who have been released from prison. Their job is to make sure these people follow the rules of their release from prison.

Police officers provide public safety. They do this by preventing crime. Police officers, sheriffs, and deputies enforce speed limits. They stop the destruction of property. They keep people from hurting others or themselves. Police officers might arrest criminals, resolve arguments, or help at traffic accidents. Detectives are police officers who investigate crimes. They try to figure out how and why a crime happened. They often try to find out who committed a crime.

Dispatchers use radios and other equipment to help police, firefighters, and emergency workers communicate with each other. Dispatchers answer 911 calls or other calls to the police or fire departments. They give the call information to police, fire, or emergency workers.

The United States government has its own law enforcement system. The Federal Bureau of Investigation (FBI) investigates all violations of federal laws. Other government agencies enforce different laws related to things such as money, taxes, the postal service, drugs, alcohol, and firearms. Other law enforcement occupations in the government include customs agents, federal marshals, immigration officers, and park rangers.

Law enforcement officers must be in good physical condition. They should be alert and be able to work well with others. They need to know how to investigate. They often have to make decisions quickly. They have social interests and enjoy working with people. They like to be in control of situations and are good problem solvers.

Emergency Services

Workers such as firefighters, emergency medical technicians (EMTs), and lifeguards deal with fire and medical emergencies. Security workers at airports or malls also handle emergencies. Emergency services workers often put themselves in personal danger on the job.

The Emergency Services Workplace

Firefighters and EMTs usually travel to the location where help is needed. They drive or ride in fire trucks and ambulances. Life guards and ski patrol workers usually work outdoors. Security guards can work almost anywhere, including airports, malls, and banks, and other businesses.

Emergency Services Workers

Firefighters and EMTs help people by putting out fires and providing medical care. They need to think and act quickly. They might not know what kind of emergency they are going to handle. Other protective workers like lifeguards and ski-patrol staff work to make sure people stay safe. They may need to rescue people who are hurt. Guards and security officers work to prevent fire, theft, vandalism, or other illegal activities. They protect airports, homes, businesses, and factories.

Emergency service workers need to have physical strength. They should be able to work as part of a team. These workers often deal with the public. They need to be able to communicate well.

BACKGROUND INFORMATION

Public Safety Jobs

In 2002, the approximate number of workers in each of the listed categories of public safety jobs was as follows:

corrections officers	300,000
EMTs	150,000
firefighters	300,000
law enforcement employees*	840,000

*Federal, state, and local combined; about 81 percent of these are employed by local governments, 11 percent by state agencies, and 6 percent by federal agencies.

Civil service regulations govern appointment of police officers and detectives. For example, in most communities, candidates must be U.S. citizens, be 21 to 37 years old at time of appointment, and have a high school or college degree. They must pass rigorous physical tests for skills such as strength, agility, hearing, and vision. They must do well on written exams.

LEARNING STYLES

Auditory/Verbal

Many young people admire law enforcement and emergency services workers such as police officers, paramedics, and firefighters because these workers risk danger to save lives. Invite students to write a song, musical composition, or story about one of these occupations, or an individual who works in one of them. Ask them to perform their works for the class.

AT HOME

After they have read and discussed the lesson, ask students to talk with an adult or adults at home about the services they rely on for help in the event of a medical emergency, fire, crime, or security issue. Suggest that students compile a list of local emergency numbers such as police, fire department, ambulance, and poison center. They should make copies and post the lists near home telephones.

Logical/Mathematical
Have students look at the pay information on page 122 and comment on the income averages for this cluster. Which number surprises them most? (*Students should note that the $90,300 average for advanced degree training is the highest for any career cluster so far. Other figures are comparable or low.*) Have students find the occupations in the Sample Law, Public Safety, and Security Occupations table on page 122 that require advanced study. (*lawyer, detective*) Have students make a generalization based on their comparison. (*Possible answer: Many lawyers and detectives have very great earning power.*)

IN THE COMMUNITY

Have students research how many lawyers, police officers, detectives, dispatchers, firefighters, and emergency medical technicians are employed in your town or county. Suggest that students contact the chamber of commerce or municipal office first to see if either has statistics on these jobs. Students might also contact local hospitals, fire departments, and police departments. Have students share their data and sources, and then summarize it in chart form on the board.

Lesson 13 Review Answers

1. Legal system jobs deal with laws in the government and courts. Law enforcement jobs deal more directly with the community to provide public safety.

2. Firefighters, EMTs, lifeguards

3. Answers will vary. Possible answer: The prisons are heavily populated and will continue to be.

4. Advantages would be helping people stay safe. Disadvantages would be personal danger.

Sample Law, Public Safety, and Security Occupations	
Corrections Officer	2
Detective	3, 4, or 5
Dispatcher	2
Emergency Medical Technician (EMT)	3 or 4
Immigration and Customs Inspector	3 or 4
Lawyer	5
Legal Secretary	4
Paralegal	4
Police Officer	2
Security Guard	1

(See the key below.)

Key to Education and Training Needed

1—Entry Level

2—On-the-Job Training

3—Apprenticeship

4—Technical/Vocational Program

5—College

Law, Public Safety, and Security Outlook

The job outlook until 2012 for this cluster is excellent. All occupations in this cluster are expected to see job growth. EMTs can expect to see 33.1 percent job growth. Jobs for security guards will increase by 31.9 percent. Police and sheriff patrol officer jobs will increase by 24.7 percent. Corrections officer occupations will grow 24.2 percent.

Law, public safety, and security workers will make up 4.3 percent of the workforce by 2012. There can be a big difference in wages for occupations in this cluster. Usually, pay depends on the amount of training and education a job requires.

Entry Level	$19,100
On-the-Job Training/Apprenticeship	$30,200
Technical/Vocational Program	$42,900
College Degree (4 years)	$38,000
Advanced Degree (more than 4 years)	$90,300

Lesson 13 Review Write your answers to these questions on a sheet of paper.

1. How do the jobs in the legal system and the law enforcement fields differ?

2. Name three jobs in the emergency services field.

3. Why do you think the job outlook for jobs in this cluster is excellent for the next few years?

4. What are some positive and negative features of jobs in the law enforcement field?

Finance
Management of money
Commodity
Something that is bought or sold

Related School Subjects
Clerical Studies
English
Finance
Management
Math

Related Abilities
Clerical
Interpersonal
Language
Leadership
Mathematical
Organizational
Persuasive

Related Values
Good Salary
High Achievement
Job Security
Leadership
Prestige
Work with Hands
Work with Mind
Work with People

This career cluster includes occupations in the **finance** industry. The finance industry involves the management of money.

The Workplace

Finance workers do their jobs at various financial institutions such as banks, insurance companies, and investment companies. Banks are located in most cities. Insurance agents visit clients' homes or businesses. Financial companies are usually located in large cities around the country.

The Workers

There are four groups of workers in this career cluster: 1) administrative support workers, 2) salespeople, 3) financial analysts, and 4) administration and professional staff. Each group of workers has different skills and interests.

Administrative support workers are involved in office operations. They gather information, fill out forms, and record data. They answer customer questions. They enter data into computer systems, calculate numbers, and prepare reports. One example of an administrative support worker is a bank teller.

Salespeople sell products. They learn about the products and services their company sells. They help customers decide what to buy and how to pay for it. **Commodity** sales agents are a type of salespeople. They buy and sell products. Commodity sales agents might buy eggs from farmers. Then, they sell the eggs to stores to sell to customers. Insurance agents are also salespeople. They sell customers protection against car, home, or fire damage. They also sell medical insurance to handle health problems. Real estate agents are also salespeople. Real estate involves buying and selling homes, hotels, factories, and buildings.

Career Clusters and the Major Industries Chapter 4 **123**

Lesson at a Glance

Chapter 4 Lesson 14

Overview In this lesson, students learn about occupations in the sector responsible for money management.

Objectives

■ To describe four kinds of finance workers: administrative support workers, salespeople, financial analysts, administration and professional staff

■ To summarize the outlook for jobs in the finance industry

Student Pages 123–125

Teacher's Resource Library
Workbook Activity 23
Activity 23
Alternative Activity 23

Vocabulary

commodity
finance

Write definitions for the two vocabulary words on the board. Then write a context-rich sentence for each word, leaving a blank where the word belongs. Ask students to read the sentences and suggest words that make sense to fill in the blanks. If students do not mention the vocabulary words, write the terms in the appropriate blanks. Have students identify the definition of each underlined word.

1 Warm-Up Activity

Ask students why it is necessary to have businesses and institutions for managing money. (*Possible response: Money is the basis for our economy. Because it is essential to our lives, it is important to manage, or handle it efficiently, in order to get the most out of it.*) Explain that early in our country's history, few people were employees or made a wage. Cash, if it existed within a family, was often kept at home. Fluid transfer of money is a hallmark of our society. Have students read about careers in money management to observe ways this industry helps individuals and the economy meet financial needs.

Career Clusters and the Major Industries **123**

2 Teaching the Lesson

Help students understand the scope of the administrative support workers in finance by listing others in addition to bank teller: loan officer, mortgage underwriter, bank and credit card customer service representative, data processor, credit report provider, debt counselor, and so on.

Explain that the insurance industry falls into a cluster involving money management because insurance policies help individuals, families, and businesses protect their assets. The products of commodities sales agents can be thought of as ways of investing money.

3 Reinforce and Extend

Financial analysts study trends related to money. They collect information by reading company reports, interviewing business executives, and studying related laws. Then they make decisions about how a company should use its money. They often give reports about investments to managers and decision-makers.

Administration and professional staff plan and manage banking, investments, and insurance. They are decision-makers and supervisors. They use information from financial analysts to make decisions about handling money. Financial managers fall into this group. These managers keep track of how much money a business has. They invest available money. They prepare required financial reports. Local bank branch managers are financial managers. Banks also offer services like investments and business, personal, and home loans. Bank managers oversee all of these services.

In addition to the four groups of workers you just read about, home builders and real estate developers are a part of the financial industry. Land developers buy land and plan for how it will be used. They plan to build shopping centers, houses, apartments, office buildings, or industrial parks.

Workers in the financial industry are excellent communicators. They are good at working with numbers. They also have good computer skills. People working in finance value making money. They enjoy being recognized for doing their jobs well. They have business and office operations interests.

Key to Education and Training Needed	Sample Finance Occupations	
1—Entry Level	Bill Collector	1
2—On-the-Job Training	Brokerage Clerk	3 or 4
3—Apprenticeship	Credit Analyst	5
4—Technical/ Vocational Program	Finance Manager	5
5—College	Financial Analyst	5
	Insurance Claim and Policy Processing Clerk	2
	Insurance Sales Agent	3 or 5
	Insurance Underwriter	5
	Loan Officer	5
	New Accounts Clerk	3
	Purchasing Agent	3
	Sales Agent: Securities and Commodities	5
	Tax Preparer	2

(See the key on the left.)

124   *Chapter 4   Career Clusters and the Major Industries*

Outlook

The finance industry is expected to grow by 12.3 percent from 2002 to 2012. There will be more jobs for accountants, tax preparers, and those in payroll services. The real estate area will add the most jobs. This is because the demand for housing will grow as the population grows.

By 2012, workers in finance occupations will make up 3.2 percent of all employed workers. Average wages for finance occupations vary. Here is a list of average pay, based on training and education:

On-the-Job Training (Moderate-Term Preparation)	$27,900
Technical/Vocational Program	$37,800
College Degree (4 years)	$50,300
Advanced Degree (more than 4 years)	$55,100

Lesson 14 Review Write your answers to these questions on a sheet of paper.

1. What are some places where finance workers do their jobs?

2. Why will the real estate field grow in the next few years?

3. Why must workers in the financial industry be excellent communicators?

Lesson 14 Review Answers

1. banks, insurance companies, investments companies

2. The demand for housing will grow as population grows.

3. They must work with many different kinds of people; they must be able to explain financial issues; they often must sell products to clients.

Chapter 4 Lesson 15

Overview This lesson describes jobs related to the marketing, sales, and servicing of products.

Objectives

- To identify the different functions of marketing, sales, and service jobs
- To identify the purposes, tasks, and characteristics of marketing, sales, and service workers
- To understand how jobs in marketing and sales will grow

Student Pages 126–129

Teacher's Resource Library (TRL)

Workbook Activity 24

Activity 24

Alternative Activity 24

Warm-Up Activity

Survey your students to see how many have or have had jobs in sales (including selling products for fund-raisers). Invite students with sales experience to describe or model how they conducted their business with customers. Ask them to brainstorm a list of skills and qualities that they think are helpful in sales.

Teaching the Lesson

You may want to have students outline the lesson as they read, using headings as major divisions (I, II), topic sentences of paragraphs as middle divisions (A, B), and details as minor divisions (1, 2).

The marketing, sales, and service cluster is one of the largest of the sixteen groups described in the chapter. You may want to have students compare the outlook for several sectors they have already read about for a perspective on how many people and jobs are involved in this cluster.

Lesson 15 Marketing, Sales, and Service

Related School Subjects
Art
Clerical Studies
English
Finance
Languages
Math
Management
Social Science

Related Abilities
Artistic
Clerical
Interpersonal
Language
Leadership
Mathematical
Organizational
Persuasive

Related Values
Creativity
Good Salary
High Achievement
Independence
Leadership
Variety
Work with Mind
Work with People

Occupations in the Marketing, Sales, and Service cluster deal with how businesses get their products to customers in order to make money. Marketing is creating an awareness and desire for products and services. The sales field involves getting customers to buy products or services. Service is providing customers with answers to their questions about a product or service.

The Marketing, Sales, and Service Workplace

Sales and marketing workers can work almost anywhere. They may work in offices or they may travel to cities all over the country. Many sales workers also use the Internet or telephone to do business. Most salespeople prefer to have personal contact with buyers.

Marketing Workers

Marketing workers get customers to buy a product. They do this by advertising. Marketing occupations include marketing managers, promotions workers, and advertising representatives.

Marketing managers oversee the creation of good advertisements or promotions. They use information to plan the best way to sell a product to customers. These people need good judgment. They often have to make decisions or solve problems quickly.

Promotion workers plan and set up displays of products. They try to make the product look good to the customer. These workers usually have art or photography experience. They must be good at communicating a message. They are creative people.

Advertising representatives sell businesses time or space to advertise their products. They may work for radio or TV stations, newspapers, magazines, or other industries that get messages to the public.

Marketing workers usually have business interests. They value challenges. They enjoy solving problems creatively. People in marketing occupations should be good at working with others.

126 Chapter 4 *Career Clusters and the Major Industries*

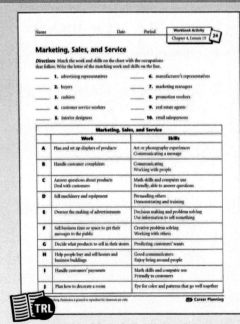

Workbook Activity 24

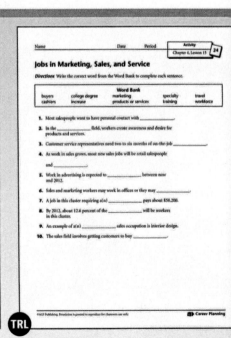

Activity 24

Sales Workers

Most of the workers in this cluster are sales workers. Other sales occupations include buyers, manufacturer's representatives, real estate agents, and customer service representatives.

Most sales workers are cashiers and retail salespeople. Cashiers and retail salespeople need good math skills. They should know how to use a computer and make change. They also need to be friendly when dealing with customers. Customers want salespeople to know about the product they are selling. Salespeople should be able to answer questions about the product.

Buyers or purchasing agents buy products directly from the manufacturers. They then resell the products to stores that will sell the products to customers. Buyers decide what products and services to sell in their stores. They need to predict what people will like and want to buy. Planning is an important skill for buyers. For example, swimsuits need to be in stores in early spring. The buyer needs to plan when to order them so the stores get them in time for the summer season.

Manufacturer's representatives can sell machinery and equipment. The manufacturer's representative tries to persuade the buyer that this is the best machinery available. If a business buys the machine, the manufacturer's representative may demonstrate how to use the machine and train workers to use it. These sales workers must be able to answer questions about the product. They may need to be able to read blueprints or engineering plans.

Gender and Careers

Some careers have traditionally been closed to women. For example, 50 years ago there were few female doctors and lawyers. The job of secretary, however, was almost exclusively filled by women. Today, both men and women work as secretaries, receptionists, and administrative assistants. Workers in all these jobs support managers. They schedule appointments and handle mail. They communicate with employees, customers, and clients. They often use photocopiers, word processors, and other office technology. All secretaries or administrative assistants must be organized and be excellent communicators.

Career Clusters and the Major Industries Chapter 4 **127**

LEARNING STYLES

Visual/Spatial
Students are constantly bombarded by advertising. Ask them to analyze one or more ads and a point-of-sale (display) for a product they would like to buy. What kinds of decisions do they think went into the advertising plans? Have students write an illustrated one-page report explaining how marketing and sales workers try to influence buyers with their ads and displays. As an alternative, students might invent a product and make an illustrated plan for marketing it.

LEARNING STYLES

Body/Kinesthetic
Have students brainstorm a list of qualities they think a retail salesperson should possess to do a good job. Invite students to describe their best and worst experiences in being assisted by a salesperson, for example, in buying clothing, shoes, or electronics. Then pair volunteers and have them create impromptu skits in which one is a customer and the other a salesperson. Have them demonstrate good and bad sales techniques.

Gender and Careers

Have volunteers read the Gender and Careers feature on page 127 aloud. Ask students to list people they know who serve as assistants to managers. Compare the ratio of males to females. You may wish to have an administrative assistant that works at your school speak to students about his or her work (or read and post a summary job description for such a position in your district).

Specialty sales occupations are also part of the sales cluster. Two examples of specialty sales are interior design and real estate. Interior designers plan how to decorate a room. They may work for large department stores or they may own their own businesses. Interior designers help a customer decide what to buy for a room. They decide where to place the furniture and what colors and patterns go together.

Real estate agents usually have their own businesses within a community. They find people who want to sell or rent their homes or business buildings. They also help buyers find homes to purchase. When a match is found between a buyer and seller, real estate agents help both sides decide on the final price of the property. Real estate agents can also help buyers with financing options for buying a house.

People in sales value mental challenges. They have business interests and they like to persuade and influence others. Salespeople usually are good communicators and enjoy being around people. They like competition and they value a good salary.

Service Workers

Customer service workers handle customer complaints. They might handle complaints such as billing errors or product repairs. They also deal with customers who are returning products and want their money back. They need to keep a written or computer record of the return. Customer service workers need excellent communication skills. They should be very good at working with people.

Key to Education and Training Needed

1—Entry Level

2—On-the-Job Training

3—Apprenticeship

4—Technical/ Vocational Program

5—College

Sample Marketing, Sales, and Service Occupations	
Advertising and Promotion Representative	3, 4, or 5
Buyer	3
Cashier	1
Customer Service Representative	2
Interior Designer	5
Manufacturer's Representative	3
Marketing Manager	3, 4, or 5
Real Estate Sales Agent	3
Retail Salesperson	1
Sales Manager	3, 4, or 5
Sales Worker Supervisor	3
Wholesale Sales Representative	3

(See the key on the left.)

Marketing, Sales, and Service Outlook

Work in sales is expected to grow. Most new sales jobs will be for retail salespeople and cashiers. There will be more than one million new workers in these two occupations by 2012. Jobs for sales managers will increase by 30.5 percent. Occupations in advertising and marketing are expected to increase between 25 and 30 percent.

The Marketing, Sales, and Service cluster employs many people. Workers in this cluster will account for 12.6 percent of the workforce by 2012. Pay for sales occupations depends on the amount of training and education a job requires.

Entry Level	$15,400
On-the-Job Training (Moderate-Term Preparation)	$38,500
Technical/Vocational Program	$35,250
College Degree (4 years)	$58,200

Lesson 15 Review Write your answers to these questions on a sheet of paper.

1. If you were a creative person and wanted a job in the Marketing, Sales, and Service cluster, what job or jobs would you seek?

2. Name five specific kinds of sales workers.

3. What are some positive features of being a sales worker? What are some negative features?

Lesson 15 Review Answers

1. Creative jobs include promotion workers and interior designers.

2. Cashiers, retail salespersons, buyers, manufacturer's representatives, real estate agents, customer service workers

3. Answers will vary. Possible answer: Positive features include working with the public and working with interesting merchandise; negative features might include dealing with unhappy customers or feeling pressured to make sales.

Lesson at a Glance

Chapter 4 Lesson 16

Overview This lesson summarizes the purposes, occupations, and outlook for careers in business management and administration

Objectives

- To define managerial and administrative leadership
- To describe the company workers who carry out plans and policies for a business
- To understand the nature of jobs that support business managers
- To summarize the opportunities and average pay for jobs in the cluster

Student Pages 130–133

Teacher's Resource Library

Workbook Activity 25

Activity 25

Alternative Activity 25

1 Warm-Up Activity

Ask students to think of a manager they know and have observed. They may suggest a team manager, a store manager, an office manager, a sales manager. Have them suggest a definition for a manager, based on what they know about the duties of the managers they listed. (*Possible response: A manager supervises or directs people or things according to a master plan in order to help them function most efficiently.*)

2 Teaching the Lesson

Emphasize to students the importance of organization, leadership, and communication skills to managers and administrators. You might have students choose a local manager with whom most are familiar (a principal of a school, a city manager, or a store manager, for example) and use him or her as an example. Have students name tasks the manager must perform. For each task, discuss the way organization, leadership, and communication play a part.

Related School Subjects
Clerical Studies
English
Finance
Languages
Management
Math
Social Science
Technology

Related Abilities
Clerical
Interpersonal
Language
Leadership
Manual
Mathematical
Mechanical
Organizational
Persuasive
Scientific

Related Values
Creativity
Good Salary
High Achievement
Independence
Job Security
Leadership
Prestige
Variety
Work with Hands
Work with Mind
Work with People

Business generally refers to the making, buying, or selling of products and services to make money. The Business Management and Administration cluster includes management and administrative support occupations. Every company, business, organization, and school needs leadership. The occupations in this cluster relate to two kinds of leadership: administrative leadership and managerial leadership. Administrators make the plans and policies for a business. Managers put those plans and policies into action. For example, in a school the administrators decide what classes and programs to offer to students. They decide what school rules will be. The managers, such as principals and teachers, teach the students and make sure students follow the rules.

The Business Management and Administration Workplace

People with occupations in the Business Management and Administration cluster can work for very large companies or for small companies. They often work in office buildings. Many of these workers travel as part of their jobs.

Management Workers

Management workers include accountants, human resources workers, computer and information systems managers, budget analysts, operations research analysts, and administrative services managers.

Accountants keep track of money for a business. They prepare financial reports. They give the business team advice on taxes. They study how a business uses its money and find ways to help the business spend its money wisely.

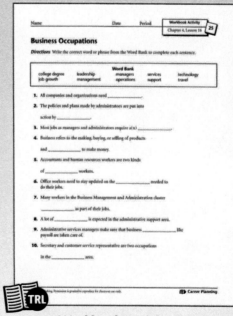

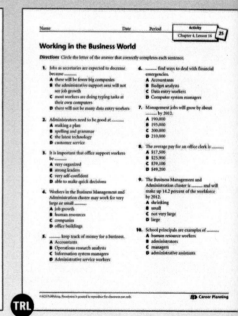

Human resources workers help businesses find people to hire. Some human resources workers visit colleges to recruit new hires. Human resources workers also make sure that businesses follow proper legal procedures. They help employees with benefits like insurance and retirement funds. They also help workers resolve work-related problems. Human resources workers also handle training of new employees.

Another part of management is overseeing information and computer systems. People in these jobs study what people want and need computers to do. They meet with workers to decide how to design new computer programs or change old ones. They also provide help when computers do not work. Sometimes, they provide training. They also make recommendations when new equipment or software packages are needed.

Budget analysts are in charge of monitoring the spending of money. They want to help the business make money. They talk with supervisors and accountants. They give advice on how to solve money-related problems. They find good ways to deal with financial emergencies.

Operations research analysts are mathematicians. They study a business and test out their ideas by using mathematical models. For example, they might develop airline schedules to make the best use of fuel, pilots, airplanes, and time. Or, they might plan delivery schedules to make sure the right parts arrive at a manufacturing plant on time. These analysts try to find creative ways to solve problems a business might have.

Administrative services managers can be vice presidents or mid-level managers. These people make sure that business operations like payroll, planning and travel, mail, security, parking, and scheduling happen. In a large business, an administrative service manager may handle just one or two of the tasks listed. In smaller companies, one person may handle all of the tasks.

Have students compare the sample occupations in the tables on pages 132 and 133 and make a generalization about business managers and administrators compared to support workers. (*Possible response: Managers and administrators must have more education and training than support workers.*)

3 Reinforce and Extend

On the Job

Ask students if they think it is important to be on time. Discuss problems that can arise when people are late for classes, meetings, dates, or jobs. Then have a volunteer read aloud the On the Job feature on page 131.

LEARNING STYLES

Auditory/Verbal
Pair students and have partners take turns reading paragraphs in the lesson aloud. Suggest that partners pause after each paragraph so that the listener can summarize its content. If the reader disagrees with the listener's summary, he or she can point out information in the paragraph to correct it.

GLOBAL CONNECTION

Many large companies are international in their scope; they sell products or services around the world. Assign several students the task of researching international operations of a corporation. Students should try to identify countries where the corporation has a presence and how management of those facilities differs from that in U.S. facilities. If possible, students can find information about the role of the international manager in the company.

Sample Business Management and Administration Occupations	
Accountant	5
Administration Services Manager	3, 4, or 5
Computer Systems Manager	5
Management Analyst	5
Office Manager	3
Operations Research Analyst	5
Personnel Recruiter	3, 4, or 5
Training and Development Specialist	5

(See the key on the left.)

Managers and administrators need leadership skills. They should be self-confident. They often need to work with a variety of people. They need to be able to communicate and to make quick decisions. Managers and administrators are good at gathering facts and making a plan. They have business interests.

Office and Administrative Support Workers

Office and administrative support workers provide support to business managers. Occupations in the support area include administrative assistants, receptionists, secretaries, office clerks, data entry workers, word processors, and customer service representatives.

Administrative assistants schedule, plan, and give important information to employees and the public. Receptionists answer phones. They connect customers to the right people in the company. Secretaries write reports, research and answer questions, take notes, and help managers with other tasks. Office clerks may run photocopiers and fax machines. They get mail ready to send. Data entry workers and word processors enter information into computers. Customer service representatives answer customer questions. They also handle customer complaints.

Administrative and office support workers need good listening skills. They also need to be good at spelling, punctuation, and grammar. They are expected to be excellent communicators and to be very organized. They have office operations interests.

These workers need to stay updated on the latest technology and computer programs needed to do their jobs. They should also be good at working under pressure when they need to meet deadlines.

Sample Office and Administrative Support Occupations	
Administrative Assistant	4
Customer Service Representative	2
Human Resource Assistant	2
Medical Transcriptionist	4
Office Clerk	1
Receptionist	1
Secretary	4
Word Processor/Typist	2

(See the key on page 132.)

Business Management and Administration Outlook

Management jobs in companies and organizations will increase by about 195,000 by 2012. Occupations in the administrative support area, such as customer service representatives, are expected to see a lot of growth. Jobs as secretaries and data entry workers are expected to decrease. This is because most workers have their own computers and do typing tasks themselves.

The Business Management and Administration cluster is large. By 2012, workers in business occupations will make up 14.2 percent of all employed workers. Average wages for occupations in this cluster depends on the amount of training and education a job requires.

Entry Level	$17,500
On-the-Job Training	$25,900
Vocational Program/College (2 years)	$39,100
College Degree (4 years)	$49,200

Lesson 16 Review Write your answers to these questions on a sheet of paper.

1. Name three business management jobs included in the Business Management and Administration cluster. Name three administrative support occupations.

2. Administrative support occupations will decrease while customer service representative occupations will increase. How do you think these two facts are related?

3. The business management and administration cluster covers many different kinds of jobs. Which one appeals to you most? Explain why.

Lesson 16 Review Answers

1. Business Management—accountants, human resources workers, computer managers, administrative services managers; Administrative Support—receptionists, office clerks, customer service representatives

2. Because people do their own work on computers, they do not need assistants to do it for them; however, they may often need help with technical problems.

3. Answers will vary.

Lesson at a Glance

Chapter 4 Lesson 17

Overview This lesson explains that government jobs encompass every cluster and focuses on describing those jobs unique to government and public administration.

Objectives

- To understand that governments supply jobs related to many industries
- To describe the workers and the work in the armed forces, government agencies, and public administration
- To survey education and training requirements and average wages for government and public administration jobs

Student Pages 134–137

Teacher's Resource Library

Workbook Activity 26

Activity 26

Alternative Activity 26

1   Warm-Up Activity

Invite volunteers to describe the structure of your local government and name offices and workers in it. Remind students that a similar structure exists at the state and federal level as well. Then have students tell what they know about the armed forces. List students' responses on the board. Suggest that they add to the list as they read the lesson.

Lesson 17   Government and Public Administration

Governments may be small or large. There are federal, state, county, and city governments. They collect taxes, pass and enforce laws, and provide for the safety and protection of their citizens. Several government occupations are not found in other career clusters, such as tax collectors and military personnel. Other government jobs, however, are similar to jobs in other clusters. For example, governments operate hospitals, airports, schools, and parks. They also run tourism agencies, power plants, highways, courthouses, and research laboratories.

The Workplace

Government workers may work anywhere. Governments operate in every city or town across the country. Government employees might work at a county courthouse, a military base, or at a national park. The workplace is different according to the job.

The Workers

Governments employ people in all six interest areas: business, office operations, social, the arts, scientific, and crafts. Many government jobs are similar to jobs in the other industries and clusters you have learned about. There are some jobs, however, that are specific to government. These include occupations in the armed forces and occupations in public administration.

Armed Forces

The military provides a country's national security. The United States Military, or the Armed Forces, includes the Army, Navy, Air Force, and Marine Corps. Members of the Armed Forces are not considered to be part of the work force. In 2003 more than 2.5 million people served in the Armed Forces. More than 1.4 million people were on active duty. In addition, more than 1.1 million people serve in the Reserves and the Air and Army National Guard. Fifteen percent are officers who are the leaders, managers, and supervisors. Eighty-five percent are called enlisted personnel.

134   *Chapter 4   Career Clusters and the Major Industries*

Name _____ Date _____ Period _____ **Workbook Activity 26**
Chapter 4, Lesson 17

Government and Public Administration Puzzle

Directions Read each clue. Choose a word from the Word Bank to complete the puzzle. Then write the answer from the box.

Word Bank
communicate
county
decisions
elderly
Homeland
housing
military
organized
postal
visit

1. Government administrators need to be _____ and pay attention to details.
2. There are federal, state, _____, and city governments.
3. Some government workers help people _____ the United States.
4. Administrators need to be able to make good _____.
5. In the _____, 15 percent of workers are officers.
6. Administrators need to _____ and write well.
7. The Coast Guard is now part of the U.S. Department of _____ Security.
8. Some government workers arrange for the care of children, families, and the _____.
9. Military personnel receive free _____.
10. Job growth is expected in this cluster, except in the _____ service.

What word do the letters in the box spell? _____

Workbook Activity 26

Name _____ Date _____ Period _____ **Activity 26**
Chapter 4, Lesson 17

Working in Government and Public Administration

Directions Write the answers to these questions. Use complete sentences.

1. Why do workplaces differ for different workers in the Government and Public Administration cluster?
2. List four places in which a government job is like a job in another industry.
3. What are the six interest areas in which governments employ people?
4. How many workers in the military are enlisted personnel?
5. Why is it possible for government workers to work anywhere?
6. What are three roles of military officers?
7. List four things military enlisted personnel are involved in.
8. How do wages in the Government and Public Administration cluster compare to wages for the same jobs in other clusters?
9. What do military personnel receive in addition to wages?
10. What is the outlook for new jobs in the Government and Public Administration cluster?

Activity 26

134   *Chapter 4*

Enlisted personnel are involved in combat, transportation, construction, healthcare, and more. Also, 38,000 people served in the Coast Guard, which is now part of the U.S. Department of Homeland Security.

Government Agencies and Public Administration

Government agencies such as the Central Intelligence Agency (CIA), Federal Bureau of Investigation (FBI), Customs, the Drug Enforcement Agency (DEA), and the Internal Revenue Service (IRS) provide several different employment opportunities. Workers in these agencies include police officers, detectives, accountants, and tax clerks. The federal government also employs workers in countries all over the world. These workers help American citizens who visit those countries. They also help citizens from other countries visit the United States. They help businesspeople trade or do business with one another. Other government jobs provide services to the public. For example, government workers might arrange for the care of children, families, or the elderly who are having troubles.

Most administrators have business interests. They need to communicate and write well. They should be able to work with all kinds of people. Government administrators should pay attention to details and be organized. They need to be able to make good decisions.

Get Involved

What is more basic than having a comfortable home? That is the philosophy of Habitat for Humanity. This organization helps families build new homes. All the work is contributed by volunteers. Many teens contribute their services. In one community in Michigan, 60 percent of the volunteers are teens. Josh, one volunteer there, said, "I've worked with Habitat at least 50 hours this year. I've learned new things, and I really felt like I helped people." For safety reasons, there are rules about the jobs teens can do. They can use hand tools but not power tools. They cannot climb ladders. However, they can help clean sites, clean up after workers, paint, and landscape. Teen volunteers for Habitat enjoy the comforts of their own homes. They help others share this pleasure.

---

2 Teaching the Lesson

To help students visualize the three levels of government structure, create a graphic organizer on the board. It should illustrate how all three levels serve the same functions but at a different level. For example, more taxes are collected at the state level than at the local level, and still more at the federal level. See below for one possible graphic aid.

	Local	State	Federal
laws	▶	▶▶	▶▶
safety	▶	▶▶	▶▶
protection	▶	▶▶	▶▶
taxes	▶	▶▶	▶▶
management	▶	▶▶	▶▶

Get Involved

Ask students what they already know about Habitat for Humanity. Read the Get Involved feature on page 135 together. Then invite students who have had experience with construction or home repair to describe the work they did. Discuss ways students feel the work of Habitat for Humanity benefits society. Interested students might locate information and report on opportunities for teen involvement in Habitat in your area.

ONLINE CONNECTION

The home page for Habitat for Humanity is found at www.habitat.org. From here, students can access information about specific opportunities in the United States and other countries. There is also a box in which they can enter their own community information and access a database of information about local Habitat organizations and their projects.

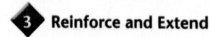

3 Reinforce and Extend

LEARNING STYLES

Auditory/Verbal
Assign interested students to research and report on career opportunities in a branch of the armed forces, the Reserves, the Air and Army National Guard, or the Coast Guard. Reports might include such information as term of service, educational opportunities, pay, types of work, and codes that enlistees must obey.

IN THE ENVIRONMENT

Explain that the Environmental Protection Agency (EPA) is a branch of the federal government that monitors the status of the environment and enforces laws protecting the environment. Have interested students research current events involving the EPA. Suggest that they refer to the *Readers' Guide to Periodical Literature,* an index of recent articles, or use the Internet to locate up-to-date information. In either source, the key words *Environmental Protection Agency* or *EPA* can be entered to generate possible sources of information.

The number after each occupation shows how much education and training is needed for that occupation. See the key on the left.

Key to Education and Training Needed
1—Entry Level
2—On-the-Job Training
3—Apprenticeship
4—Technical/Vocational Program
5—College

Sample Government and Public Administration Occupations	
Animal Caretaker	1
Building Inspector	3 or 4
Computer Programmer	4 or 5
FBI Agent	5
Firefighter	2
Government Administrator	5
Mail Carrier	1
Military Officer	5
Police Chief	3, 4, or 5
Police Officer	2
Post Office Clerk	2
Public Relations Specialist	5
School Administrator	5
Surveyor	4
Translator	5

Outlook

Government workers can work in any cluster. The outlook for new jobs depends on the cluster. Occupations in the postal service are expected to decrease slightly by 2012. Postal service occupations are found only in government. Most other government-related occupations are expected to grow.

The wages for most occupations in this cluster are the same as for those in other industries. The average wage for government supervisors and managers is $64,100 in 2003. Wages for government administrators can vary widely. For example, a small-town city council member may earn little or no pay. The president of the United States earns $400,000 per year. For people serving in the armed forces, starting pay in 2003 ranged from $12,780 to $26,208. Military personnel also receive free housing, food, healthcare, and clothing.

Lesson 17 Review Write your answers to these questions on a sheet of paper.

1. What are two government occupations not found in other career clusters?

2. Name two cities where you might find a larger than average number of government workers.

3. What are some positive features of working for a government?

ELL/ESL STRATEGY

Language Objective: *To learn acronyms for government agencies*

Students who are learning English may not be familiar with acronyms for government agencies commonly used in the United States, such as CIA, DEA, and IRS. Have students make flash cards for the agencies listed in this lesson and any others you think they should learn (for example, BLS/Bureau of Labor Statistics, NASA/National Aeronautics and Space Administration, EPA/-Environmental Protection Agency, USPS/United States Postal Service). You may want to suggest that students write the acronym and a symbol suggesting its purpose on one side. On the other side, they can write the agency name and a sentence summarizing its function. Pair students and have them practice identifying the agencies using their cards.

Lesson 17 Review Answers

1. tax collectors and military personnel

2. Answers will vary. Possible answer: Washington, D.C., and any state capital

3. Answers will vary. Possible answer: Advantages would be to help run our nation and to have a steady, well-defined job with a secure salary.

What Career Is Right for You?

List on the board the titles of the 16 career clusters students have studied in the chapter. Highlight the kinds of jobs each includes to review the clusters with students. Then have students read the Portfolio Activity introduction on page 138.

Ask a volunteer to read the caption under the photograph on page 138 aloud. Have students look at the photo and explain what the people are doing. Tell students that the young man is learning about the landscaping field by seeing what a landscape designer does on the job.

Suggest that students scan the lessons in Chapter 4 again and consider which careers appeal most to them before they answer the Portfolio Activity questions on page 139. Students can write their responses on their own paper or on Portfolio Activity 4 in the TRL.

What Career Is Right for You?

Each career cluster has a wide variety of occupations. As you learn about each cluster, you can decide whether the careers interest you. You may change the opinions you have had about a particular career. For example, you may find that the tourism industry offers more potential than you thought. You might find there are fewer administrative assistant jobs available than you realized. Think about your responses to the careers and career clusters described in the chapter. Then answer the questions on page 139. Put the answers in your portfolio.

You can learn about a career by going to work with an experienced worker.

138 *Chapter 4 Career Clusters and the Major Industries*

1. What is one career cluster in which you have had work or volunteer experience? Describe the experience. Describe its positive and negative features. Explain whether you would consider the cluster for a future career.

2. What is one career cluster in which someone you know is employed? Describe the person's job.

3. Learning more about a career can change a person's opinions about it. Choose one career cluster that you might reconsider after having learned more about it. Explain why your opinion has changed.

4. Which career cluster appeals to you most? Name two or three jobs in the cluster that especially interest you. Describe the features, such as good pay, prestige, or outlook, that are attractive.

5. Choose one of the jobs you named in question 4. Summarize what you have learned about the job's tasks, pay, workplace, and outlook. You can find additional information about jobs by using the CDMCareerZone Web site or the *Occupational Outlook Handbook*.

As students answer the questions on page 139, they may find a form like the following helpful for capturing their responses:

1. Work/Volunteer Experience:
Job I did: _____
Description of job: _____
_____
What I liked: _____
What I did not like: _____
I would/would not consider this job as a future career because _____
_____

2. Employed person: _____
Career cluster of his/her job: _____
_____
Job title: _____
Types of work the person does: _____
_____

3. Career cluster I would consider now:
_____
Why I changed my mind about it: _____
_____
_____

4. Top Jobs for Me	**Features That Attract Me**
_____	_____
	_____
_____	_____
	_____
_____	_____
	_____

5. My First Choice for a Career: _____
_____
Tasks Involved: _____
_____
Pay I would expect to earn: _____
Workplace: _____
Outlook for the future of this career: ____
_____
_____

Portfolio Activity Answers

1.–5. Answers will vary.

Chapter 4 Review

Use the Chapter Review to prepare students for tests and to reteach content from the chapter.

Chapter 4 Mastery Test TRL

The Teacher's Resource Library includes two forms of the Chapter 1 Mastery Test. Each test addresses the chapter Goals for Learning. An optional third page of additional critical-thinking items is included for each test. The difficulty level of the two forms is equivalent.

Review Answers
Vocabulary Review

1. engineering 2. offshore outsourcing
3. finance 4. information technology
5. industry 6. tourism 7. hospitality
8. career ladder 9. manufacturing
10. commodity 11. corrections

Concept Review

12. D 13. C 14. A 15. C 16. B 17. D

Word Bank

career ladder
commodity
corrections
engineering
finance
hospitality
information technology
industry
manufacturing
offshore outsourcing
tourism

Vocabulary Review

Choose the word or phrase from the Word Bank that best completes each sentence. Write the answer on your paper.

1. The science of planning and building machines, tools, and transportation systems is _____.

2. Giving jobs to workers in countries outside the United States is _____.

3. The management of money is _____.

4. The _____ field deals with the way information is stored and used in computers.

5. A large-scale business or service area that provides a product or service is a(n) _____.

6. The business of providing services to visitors and travelers is _____.

7. Taking care of guests or customers is _____.

8. You can move up a _____ by getting more training and education.

9. Turning material into products people use every day is _____.

10. Something that is bought or sold is a(n) _____.

11. The field that involves the treatment and rehabilitation of prisoners in jails is _____.

Concept Review

Choose the word or phrase that best completes each sentence. Write the letter of the answer on your paper.

12. On average, the highest yearly pay is earned by people with _____.

    A long-term on-the-job training

    B an Associate's degree

    C a postsecondary vocational award

    D a Bachelor's degree

Chapter 4 Mastery Test A

Part A Circle the letter of the answer that correctly completes each sentence.

1. The U.S. Department of Education groups related occupations into similar career areas called _____.
   A wages   B jobs   C occupations   D clusters

2. Long-term on-the-job training is often called an _____.
   A occupation   C internship
   B apprenticeship   D associate's degree

3. Workers in the natural resources area are involved in _____.
   A mining of resources from the earth   C forestry
   B plants, animals, and food production   D manufacturing

4. Using machines to do jobs that used to be done by people is called _____.
   A automation   C assembly
   B outsourcing   D distribution

5. Related jobs that allow movement to a higher-level job are _____.
   A internships   B apprenticeships   C career ladders   D career clusters

Part B Match the career clusters in Column 1 with their descriptions in Column 2. Write the letter on the line.

Column 1	Column 2
_____ 6. Architecture and Construction	A planning and building machines, tools, and transportation systems
_____ 7. Health Science	B planning, designing, and building structures
_____ 8. Science, Technology, Engineering, and Mathematics	C writing and entertainment are parts of this cluster
_____ 9. Information Technology	D a fast-growing computer-related field
_____ 10. Arts, Audio-Video Technology, and Communications	E occupations related to keeping people healthy

---

Chapter 4 Mastery Test A, continued

Part C Write the correct word or phrase from the Word Bank to complete each sentence.

Word Bank
corrections   education   finance   hospitality   human services

11. A school counselor is part of the _____ career cluster.

12. A social worker would be an example of a person working in _____.

13. The _____ industry is closely associated with travel and tourism.

14. An area of law enforcement that involves the treatment and rehabilitation of prisoners is _____.

15. The career area involved with the management of money is called _____.

Part D Write the answers to these questions. Use complete sentences.

16. What are the jobs of most people in the Marketing, Sales, and Service cluster?

17. What does an accountant do?

18. What are four types of government that may offer employment possibilities?

19. How does the U.S. Department of Education group occupations into clusters?

20. What is an industry?

Chapter 4 Mastery Test A, continued

Part E Write your answer to each question. Use complete sentences. Support your answers with facts and examples from the book.

21. How does knowing the job outlook help you make career plans? (3 points)

22. Why does the Arts, Audio-Visual Technology, and Communications cluster have such a big impact? (3 points)

Part F Write a paragraph for each topic. Include a topic sentence, body, and conclusion. Support each answer with facts and examples from the textbook.

23. What kind of personal qualities do you think would be important in performing any job, no matter what occupational cluster it is in? (3 points)

24. Why do some job areas grow and some job areas shrink? Use at least one job's growth or decline as an example. (3 points)

25. Why are there more jobs available now for people who provide technical and computer support than there were in the past? (3 points)

13. _____workers enjoy working with their hands.

    A Sales   **C** Manufacturing

    B Tourism   **D** Finance

14. An occupation in the education and training field is _____.

    A school counselor   **C** technical writer

    B customer service   **D** loan officer
       representative

15. A field in which workers get customers to buy a product is _____.

    A extraction   **C** marketing

    B logistics   **D** public administration

16. An industry that distributes materials and products is

    _____.

    A mining   **C** information technology

    B transportation   **D** hospitality

17. One job that is specific to government is _____.

    A truck driver   **C** hotel clerk

    B engineer   **D** military officer

Critical Thinking

Write the answer to each question on your paper.

18. Why is it a good idea to know which career areas will grow and be in demand in the future?

19. Do you need to decide on a particular career before planning further education? Or can you just decide on a career cluster? Explain.

20. Which career cluster interests you more after reading about it? Explain why you are interested in that cluster.

Test-Taking Tip

When studying for a chapter test, review the topics in the chapter. Then make up a practice test for yourself.

Review Answers
Critical Thinking

18. It is essential in planning a career, so that after several years of training there will be jobs available. **19.** If a person has not decided on a particular career, knowing the cluster is very helpful, because he or she can begin training that will be helpful for several of the careers in the cluster. **20.** Answers will vary.

ALTERNATIVE ASSESSMENT

- Have students name the two best ways to learn about a specific career and model how to use these resources to get information about the career. They should include a summary of the kinds of information each resource gives.

- Have each student write down a decision he or she must make and develop a plan for making it by using the decision-making steps.

Chapter 4 Mastery Test B

Part A Circle the letter of the answer that correctly completes each sentence.

1. Career clusters are grouped by the U.S. Department of Education according to _____.
  A level of education needed for all jobs
  B geographic regions
  C similarity of preparation, skills, and workplaces
  D salaries

2. A large-scale business or service area that provides a product or service is called an _____.
  A occupation   **C** apprenticeship
  B industry   **D** assembly plant

3. You can advance to a higher level on a(n) _____ by getting more experience and training.
  A career ladder   **C** workplace
  B internship   **D** career cluster

4. In business management, the person who keeps track of money is usually the _____.
  A president   **C** administrative assistant
  B human resources manager **D** accountant

5. Most people who work in the Marketing, Sales, and Service cluster are _____.
  A cashiers and retail salespersons **C** promotion workers
  B real estate agents   **D** advertising representatives

Part B Match the occupation in Column 1 with its career cluster in Column 2. Write the letter on the line.

Column 1	Column 2
_____ **6.** hotel clerk	**A** Education and Training
_____ **7.** insurance agent	**B** Finance
_____ **8.** librarian	**C** Hospitality and Tourism
_____ **9.** paralegal	**D** Human Services
_____ **10.** mental health counselor	**E** Law, Public Safety, and Security

---

Chapter 4 Mastery Test B, continued

Part C Write the correct word or phrase from the Word Bank to complete each sentence.

Word Bank

developers	engineering	health science	information technology	the arts

11. People who arrange money for the construction of buildings are _____.

12. Because more people are aging in the United States, the field of _____ is expected to grow a lot.

13. In the field of _____, some people work on computers in their own homes.

14. Electrical and civil are two of four major fields of _____.

15. People who work in _____ create what you read in newspapers, see on television, and watch in movies.

Part D Write the answers to these questions. Use complete sentences.

16. What are career clusters?

17. What is the difference between an associate's degree and a bachelor's degree?

18. How does agriculture differ from natural resources in the Agriculture, Food, and Natural Resources cluster?

19. What is offshore outsourcing and how does it affect the outlook for manufacturing?

20. What is the purpose of transportation?

Chapter 4 Mastery Test B, continued

Part E Write your answer to each question. Use complete sentences. Support your answers with facts and examples from the book.

21. Why does it help to know what interests people in each cluster usually have? (3 points)

22. What plans should you make if an area that interests you has a job outlook with little or no growth? (3 points)

Part F Write a paragraph for each topic. Include a topic sentence, body, and conclusion. Support each answer with facts and examples from the textbook.

23. Why is it important to know what education is required for a career area? (3 points)

24. Is honesty an important trait in the Arts, Audio-Video Technology, and Entertainment cluster? Explain. (3 points)

25. How have changes in technology affected jobs in the Information Technology cluster? (3 points)

Chapter

Planning Guide

Your Preferred Careers

Chapter Activities

Student Text
Chapter 5 Portfolio Activity

Teacher's Resource Library
Chapter 5 Chapter Outline
Chapter 5 Self-Study Guide
Chapter 5 Portfolio Activity

Assessment Options

Student Text
Chapter 5 Review

Teacher's Resource Library
Chapter 5 Mastery Tests A and B
Chapters 1–5 Midterm Mastery Test

Teacher's Edition
Chapter 5 Alternative Assessment

Student Text Features											Teaching Strategies					Learning Styles					Teacher's Resource Library				
Portfolio Activity	Writing Practice	Communication Connection	The Economy	Career Tip	Career Profile	On the Job	Gender and Careers	Think Positive	Technology Note	Get Involved	Background Information	Applications (Home, Community, Global, Environment)	Personal Journal	Online Connection	ELL/ESL Strategy	Visual/Spatial	Body/Kinesthetic	Interpersonal/Group Learning	Logical/Mathematical	Auditory/Verbal	Activities	Alternative Activities	Workbook Activities	Self-Study Guide	Chapter Outline
	148			145	147	146		149				147, 148	146	147	145	146			148	145	27	27	27	✔	✔
156		151	152				151		155	153	153	151, 153, 155		154	154		152	152			28	28	28	✔	✔

Alternative Activities

The Teacher's Resource Library (TRL) contains a set of lower-level worksheets called Alternative Activities. These worksheets cover the same content as the regular Activities but are written at a second-grade reading level.

Career Interest Inventory

The AGS Publishing Harrington-O'Shea Career Decision-Making System (CDM) may be used with this textbook. Students can use the CDM to explore their interests and identify careers. The CDM defines career areas that are indicated by students' response on the inventory.

Chapter at a Glance

Chapter 5:
Your Preferred Careers
pages 142–159

Lessons

Audio CD 🎧

Teacher's Resource Library TRL

(Answer Keys for the Teacher's
Resource Library begin on page 328
of this Teacher's Edition.)

Chapter 5 Self-Study Guide

Chapter

5 Your Preferred Careers

Do you ever wish you could look into the future? It would be great to see yourself in your chosen career in five or 10 years. Of course, no one can see the future. But you can prepare for it. You must actively make choices and take steps. These choices and actions will lead you to where you want to be five or 10 years down the road. This chapter will help you make specific career and education choices that will lead you to a bright future. It provides a plan to help you talk with your parents or guardians about your future.

Goals for Learning

◆ To make a career plan

◆ To explore the education and training needed for a chosen career

---

143

Introducing the Chapter

Have students look at the photo on page 142 in the Student Edition and describe what the boy in the picture is doing. Ask: *What do the binoculars allow him to do?* (see a great distance) *What function does the lighthouse serve?* (It guides ships at sea safely to their destination.) Invite volunteers to explain a way in which this scene represents their situation as they think about careers they might want to pursue.

Have students read the introductory paragraph on page 143, and then discuss ways they can prepare for the future. Ask them to suggest several types of career preparation this chapter may discuss.

Have students read the Goals for Learning. Ask students to explain what steps they have followed when they have made a plan, such as what classes to take in a school year. Then ask them to predict what steps a career plan might contain. Suggest that as they read the chapter, students write down a good working definition of a career plan and make notes about how to find out what education and training a specific career requires.

Career Tips

Ask volunteers to read the career tips that appear in the margins throughout the chapter. Then discuss them with the class.

Alternative Assessment

The Alternative Assessment box on page 159 of the Chapter Review includes activities using various learning styles to assess students' understanding of the Goals for Learning.

Name ___ Date ___ Period ___ | Chapter Outline, Page 1 — Chapter 5

Your Preferred Careers

Directions Fill in the outline below. Filling in the blanks will help you as you read and study Chapter 5.

I. Lesson 1: Exploring Careers (pp. 144–149)

A. The Seven Steps of a Career Plan

1. The first step in a career plan is choosing ___

2. The second step is finding out ___

3. The third step is to see what ___ you need for the career you want.

4. The fourth step is thinking about what work-related ___ you can fulfill in the career you choose.

5. The fifth step is researching the career's ___ to see if the occupation will grow.

6. The sixth step is deciding what your plans will be after you finish ___

7. The final step is ___ your plan with parents or guardians.

B. Career Plan

1. Choose two ___ in a career that you are interested in.

2. The CDM CareerZone Web site or the *Occupational Outlook Handbook* tells you what ___ you should take for a career.

3. With training and practice, you can develop ___ related to your abilities.

4. Fulfilling work-related ___ can bring you job satisfaction.

5. For each possible career, you should examine the ___ and ___

6. Use career information you've gathered to make a ___ for what you should do after high school.

7. Education after high school is called ___ education.

Name ___ Date ___ Period ___ | Chapter Outline, Page 2 — Chapter 5

Your Preferred Careers, continued

II. Lesson 2: Investing in Your Future (pp. 150–155)

A. The Importance of Finishing High School

1. About ___ of students who do not finish high school will not find work.

2. By deciding to continue your education, you make an ___ in your future.

B. Basic Math, Reading, and Writing Skills

1. Employers are very good at identifying those who have ___

2. People who have strong basic skills often earn ___

C. Work Experience

1. Working part time can help you build ___ and ___ that employers value.

2. Young adults who worked 20 hours a week in high school earn ___ percent more than young adults who did not work in high school.

D. Developing Job Skills

1. If you do not work in high school, you can develop job skills by ___ after high school.

E. Deciding How Much Education You Need

1. Students who graduate from two-year degree programs earn ___ percent more than high school graduates.

2. Students with ___ degrees earn 75 percent more each year than high school graduates.

F. Paying for a Postsecondary Education

1. For many people, ___ is the biggest investment they make.

2. Financial aid includes ___ ___ and ___

TRL | Career Planning

TRL | Career Planning

Chapter 5 Chapter Outline

Your Preferred Careers 143

Chapter 5 Lesson 1

Overview In this lesson students learn seven steps to building a career plan and consider how to use what they have learned from the first four chapters to make a plan.

Objectives

- To identify and understand the steps in a career plan
- To understand how knowledge gained in Chapters 1–4 will be used in creating a career plan

Student Pages 144–149

Teacher's Resource Library

Workbook Activity 27

Activity 27

Alternative Activity 27

Vocabulary

postsecondary

Write *secondary* on the board. Explain that this word is used to refer to education between elementary school and college. Add the prefix *post-* to the word. Ask students to list other words in which this prefix occurs (*postgame, postdate, postoperative*) and predict its meaning (*after, later*). Then have students predict the meaning of *postsecondary*. Read the textbook definition together and have students use the word in a sentence.

1 Warm-Up Activity

Have students look at the photograph on page 144 as a volunteer reads the caption. Ask students to describe what the students are doing in the picture. Invite them to list activities and abilities needed in a science lab. Discuss how this, and other classes, can help prepare them for the workplace.

You have learned about many different occupations. Now, you can decide what occupations interest you. You can begin to explore these occupations. You can learn more details about the jobs you want. As you explore, you are gathering information. This information will help you make decisions about your future. You are starting a career plan.

What Are the Steps of a Career Plan?

The first step in a career plan is choosing the careers you are interested in. The second step is identifying what you need to learn in school. It is important to take classes that will prepare you for the occupation you want.

Taking science classes is one way to prepare for a career in math, science, or technology.

144 *Chapter 5 Your Preferred Careers*

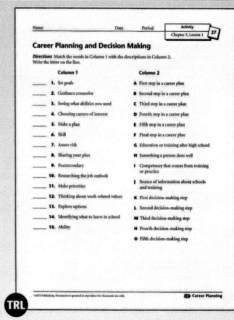

Workbook Activity 27   **Activity 27**

The third step is to see what abilities you need for the career you want. You may need to work on some abilities to get better at them. The fourth step is thinking about what work-related values you can fulfill in the career you choose. The fifth step is researching the job outlook for a career. See what occupations will have new job openings. Find out what certain jobs pay. The sixth step is deciding what your plans will be after you finish high school. The final step is sharing your plan with parents or guardians. You need to think about how you are going to reach your career goals. Reaching a career goal will cost money. How will you pay for training or a college education? You need a plan that shows your parents or guardians that you have given some thought to your future.

Before you start your career plan, let's first review what you have discovered so far. In Chapter 1, you learned what work is. You learned how work affects your life. Think about how the job you want will impact your life. It may seem too early to decide the exact job you want. However, it is never too early to begin thinking about and planning for your future career.

In Chapter 2, you practiced self-assessment. You stated what school subjects you like. You named the skills you are learning in each subject. You identified your work-related abilities. You also explored the values that are most important to you. You examined your interests. Finally, you thought about how much time and energy you want to invest in more education and training.

In Chapter 3, you learned the five decision-making steps.

1. Set Goals

2. Make Priorities

3. Explore the Options

4. Assess the Risks

5. Make a Plan

 Teaching the Lesson

As they read the first section of the lesson, encourage students to turn back to each chapter they have read and scan its headings to review its main points. Explain that these concepts will help them organize a career plan in this chapter.

 Reinforce and Extend

ELL/ESL STRATEGY

Language Objective: *To use listening and speaking to show comprehension*
Have ELL students partner with fluent English speakers to read the lesson. Partners can take turns reading paragraphs aloud. The listener should ask questions about any concept or language he or she did not understand. After the reader explains or rewords the concept, the listener can summarize the paragraph's main idea. As they review earlier chapters, partners can continue to summarize the main ideas and discuss how what they learned can help them create a career plan.

LEARNING STYLES

Auditory/Verbal
After students read the lesson, have them explain what they learned in Chapters 1, 2, 3, and 4. Encourage them to use examples to apply what they recall. For example, in explaining decision making, students might describe each step they took in deciding on a class to take, or sport or club to join.

On the Job

Write *On time* and *Late* on the board. Ask students to think of a time they were on time and a time they were late for a scheduled event. How did they feel about being late? What effects did their timeliness or their lateness have? Have students brainstorm a list of describing words for people who are usually on time, and then one for people who are usually late. Read the On the Job feature on page 146 together. Add any additional describing words students wish to the list.

PERSONAL JOURNAL

Have students write a journal entry listing their abilities and describing how they might use them in a career. Students may want to refer to their Self-Assessment Profile, created for Chapter 2, and then expand on an ability listed there or explore an ability that has been revealed or enhanced more recently. Students might use a format such as a letter to an employer or a narrative to elaborate on their abilities and how they can use them.

LEARNING STYLES

Visual/Spatial
A visual aid can help students plan what subjects to take and when to take them. Have students create a table for the subjects they need to take to prepare for their chosen careers. By referring to a school catalog, they can list classes that fit each category by name and create columns for each semester remaining in their high school tenure. Students can mark the column for the best time to take each course. Explain to students that they will have to find out about any prerequisites for classes to make sure those are scheduled first.

On the Job

You probably never thought about being on time as a job skill. However, it is a trait that employers expect from workers. Good employees arrive at work on time in the morning and after lunch. They are prompt for meetings and appointments. When you are on time, you show that you take your job seriously and that you respect the time of others.

You learned about the major industries in the United States in Chapter 4. You learned details about many occupations by reading about career clusters. Now, you will make a specific career plan based upon everything you have learned.

Career Plan

Preferred Careers
First you need to choose the careers that interest you. Select two occupations. Be specific. For example, you may know you like science, but what scientific occupation do you want to prepare for? Do you want to be a biologist, a pharmacist, or an engineer? Maybe you are interested in business and the tourism industry. Do you want to be a travel agent, a hotel manager, or a chef? Identify two occupations you want to look at more closely.

School Subjects
Use the resources such as the CDMCareerZone Web site or the *Occupational Outlook Handbook* (OOH) to find out what school subjects you need to take for the careers you chose. Have you completed the classes required for each of your chosen careers? Do you still need to take certain courses?

Abilities
Recall the abilities you wrote down on your Self-Assessment Profile in Chapter 2. Remember that an ability is something a person does well. Think about some skills you have developed that are related to your abilities. Recall that a skill is a competency that comes from training or practice. For example, a skill related to artistic ability would be the good use of colors in a painting. How do your skills relate to your two chosen careers? What skills must you develop in order to be prepared for these careers?

Values

Remember that work-related values are things people want to get from performing a job. Fulfilling certain work values can bring you job satisfaction. What values could you fulfill in both of your chosen careers? Think of work-related values for each career. If similar values appear in both careers, this means they are strong beliefs of yours. If different values appear in the two careers, this means you may have several strong values. Try to prioritize your values. Decide which ones are most important.

Employment Outlook and Wages

For each of your chosen careers, you should examine two pieces of information. First, will jobs be available in this field when you are ready to begin work? Second, how much money will you be paid for doing the work? You can find this information on CDMCareerZone, in the OOH, or in other materials available at libraries or in your school's career center.

Career Profile

Television News Producer

On a television news program, the anchor gets most of the attention. But have you ever thought about the people behind the scenes? Many reporters, camera operators, videotape editors, and producers combine their talents to create television news.

Many people in television news start their careers as news producers or production assistants. The job of a producer varies according to the size of the station. At a small station, a producer keeps a close eye on news from wire services, newspapers, and cable news networks. Then he or she might schedule the stories that will air. He or she might write the stories to be read by the news anchor. A producer or production assistant might edit video clips to show during the program. A producer must communicate with reporters, camera operators, and anchors.
He or she has responsibility for coordinating the news program.

A degree in broadcast journalism is the best background for the job of news producer. Many television stations offer unpaid internships for college journalism students. These help students learn about television news.

AT HOME

After they review the work-related values discussed in Chapter 2, have students list these values on a sheet of paper and share them with working adults at home or in their neighborhood. Students can ask these workers which values are most important to them and why. Students may gain a perspective from the exchange that will help them clarify their own work-related values.

ONLINE CONNECTION

Students are asked to find employment outlook and wage information using the CDMCareerZone Web site or the *OOH*. The home page for the CDMCareerZone Web site is found at this address: www.cdmcareerzone.com. Remind students that the *OOH* information is also available online, through the Bureau of Labor Statistics site at http://www.bls.gov/oco/home.htm.

Career Profile

Ask students with experience in theater productions to tell about work done behind the scenes that the audience does not see. Have students think about jobs in a television station that support the news and weather personalities they see on TV. Then have volunteers read the Career Profile on page 147 aloud. Ask students to list the tasks done by a TV news producer. Write these on the board in a column. Elicit from students the skills a producer needs to carry out each task. List these in a second column. Have interested students communicate with a local or regional TV station to find out whether it sponsors internships.

LEARNING STYLES

Logical/Mathematical

Help students brainstorm a list of postsecondary options in your community or region. List these on the board under heading categories such as:

Junior Colleges, Colleges and Universities, and *Technical/ Vocational Schools.*

As institutions are listed, offer information about their purpose and the length of their program of study. If possible, locate each on a local or regional map. Have students make their own tables, copying down the names of institutions they want to research.

IN THE COMMUNITY

Using their tables from the previous activity, students can call or go to one or more postsecondary schools in your area and request information about programs or training offered in the careers they have chosen. Suggest that students prepare a card with important questions to ask, in case they can speak with an official or employee in admissions. Among questions students may want to ask:

- Do you offer a program of study in _____? What classes does it include?

- What are your requirements for admission?

- When do you accept applications for admission?

- What are the costs of attending your school?

- About how long does it take to complete the course of study in _____?

Postsecondary
After high school

Plans After High School

What are your plans after you finish high school? Do you want to find a job right away? Do you see the military as an opportunity? Would you move to a different location to receive training for a specific job? Do you want to travel or stay at home? Think about the two careers you chose. How would deciding on one or the other change your plans after high school?

Postsecondary Education

Employers today expect job applicants to have better job skills than they once did. To learn these skills, more and more students are going on to **postsecondary** education. Postsecondary means after high school. Postsecondary education can include technical school or college. How do you decide which school to attend? You need to do some research. You have identified two occupations that interest you. Now you need to identify the schools and institutions that offer the program or programs you want to study. You can find this information in your school's guidance office or career center. Most schools have catalogs or videos about postsecondary schools. Your local library also is a good resource for information. You can search for schools using catalogs or the Internet.

As you find schools that offer a program that interests you, you will see that schools are different. Tuition, fees, and room and board charges vary. Some schools have more modern equipment than others. Other schools have more instructors and course offerings. Some schools are very proud of their graduates and will tell you the names of employers who hire their graduates.

Writing Practice

Spend a few minutes thinking about yourself in a specific career. Use your imagination to picture yourself and your workplace. Picture the people you are with and what you are saying, doing, or thinking. Now write a journal entry about your thoughts. Describe them in as much detail as possible.

Writing Practice

Read the Writing Practice feature on page 148 to students. Before students write their journal entries, you may want to model for them how to capture sensory details on a word web with arms for sights, sounds, smells, tastes, and touches. For example, for a career as a civil engineer who designs bridges, you might note such details as a standing on a bluff overlooking a river, taking soil samples and talking with geologists and local residents, smelling steel and newly poured concrete, and so on.

Think Positive

A positive attitude is one of the best educational tools there is. All students have classes in which they perform better. For example, perhaps math comes easily to you while writing is more difficult. A positive attitude about writing will give you confidence in your abilities. It will give you the extra energy you need as you work on writing better.

Conclusion

Your career plan includes the main points to talk about with others. Your plan should help you get the information you will need to make one or more of these decisions:

- Choose one career over another career
- Select to go to work or school or
- Choose one postsecondary school over another

Lesson 1 Review Write your answers to these questions on a sheet of paper.

1. Why is it important to share your plans for the future with your parents or guardians?

2. Why is it wise to consider two different careers when making plans for the future?

3. Suppose the two careers that interest you have very different values. What does this tell you?

Think Positive

Read the Think Positive feature on page 149 with students. Explain that negative self-talk (the voice in your head that says "I can't do it") is one powerful enemy of self-confidence. Ask students to monitor their thoughts for a period of time (an hour or two), note their negative thoughts, and rephrase them. For example, if they find themselves thinking "I shouldn't have done it that way. That was dumb." Students might try saying instead, "It would have been better if I had…." Students can also think of things they do well and rank these skills. Explain that by reflecting on their assets and positive qualities students can begin to feel better about themselves. In other words, positive self-talk builds a more positive self-image, which in turn affects behavior or performance.

Lesson 1 Review Answers

1. Reaching a career goal can be expensive, and parents and guardians will need to participate in plans to finance career training.

2. Possible answer: Since this is preliminary planning, there is no need to narrow down to one career. Also, two choices gives you more probability of finding the best one for you.

3. It tells you that you have more than just two strong values; it can help you better identify your values.

Chapter 5 Lesson 2

Overview In this lesson, students consider the importance to their future of completing high school and assess their basic skills and work experience.

Objectives

- To identify education as an investment in the future
- To evaluate basic skills in math, reading, and writing as a means to assess employability
- To consider part-time employment and postsecondary education as means to develop job skills
- To explore financial aid possibilities for postsecondary education

Student Pages 150–155

Teacher's Resource Library

Workbook Activity 28

Activity 28

Alternative Activity 28

Vocabulary

financial aid
investment

Write the vocabulary terms on the board. Read each definition and have students identify the matching term. Then ask students to expand on the definition by giving examples or explanations.

1 Warm-Up Activity

Ask students to name things or actions that illustrate ways of making an investment (*for example, buying a house or land, buying stocks, mutual funds, bonds, or CDs*). List these investments on the board and have students identify what the examples have in common. (*Investments are made in order to reap a benefit in the future, usually financial.*) Have students compare monetary investments to investing in an education. Ask students to explain how these actions are alike.

What are you going to do after high school? You need to decide how much education and training you will complete. Your parents or guardians can help you make this decision. Do you know what you want to do after high school? Now is the time to decide. The decisions you make now about your future can affect the rest of your life.

Why Is It Important to Finish High School?

About one-half of students who do not finish high school will not find work. Those who do find work usually do not have year-round, full-time jobs. Of the students who graduate from high school, about two-thirds will continue their training and education. On average, they will earn more money than those who do not continue their education.

High-school graduates are more likely to get jobs and be paid more than students who do not graduate.

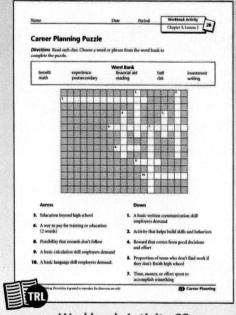

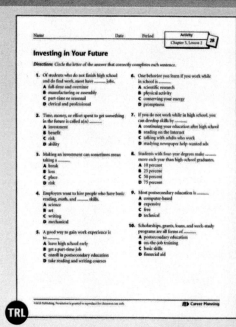

Workbook Activity 28

Activity 28

Investment
Time, effort, or money spent to get something in the future

Deciding to get more education is an **investment**. An investment is time, effort, or money you spend to get something in the future. Making an investment can mean taking a risk. Read the example below.

It is a hot summer day. You decide to buy some lemonade. You pay cash for the lemonade and then drink it. You pay for and receive the benefits of your purchase at the same time. You are very certain of the benefits of your purchase. You will get to enjoy a cool, refreshing drink. There is little risk involved in your decision.

Communication Connection

Talking to students at a variety of colleges is one of the best ways to learn more about education options. When you meet a college student, ask questions. Ask about degree programs and requirements. Ask about teachers and fellow students. You may learn more from one student's personal story than from several articles in college handbooks.

Now let's look at the decision you will be making. Should you get more education after high school? It might not be easy to answer that question. It is a much bigger decision than buying lemonade. You might not see the benefits of more education right away. The benefits come later. For example, people with more education make more money on average throughout their lifetimes. By deciding to continue your education, you make an investment in your future.

There are four questions you should consider when deciding whether to continue your education: 1) Do you have basic math, reading, and writing skills? 2) Do you have work experience? 3) How will you develop job skills? and 4) How many years of education do you want to complete?

Gender and Careers

For many years, some women had to choose between having children and having a career. If a woman was able to take a maternity leave, it was most likely unpaid. In addition, she lost seniority at work. Now, many companies have become more generous with parental leaves. Federal law now says that new parents must receive up to 12 weeks unpaid leave upon the birth or adoption of a child. This applies to both men and women. Unfortunately, many workers cannot afford several weeks of unpaid leave. More and more companies are granting paid parental leaves to both mothers and fathers. For example, one company gives up to 12 weeks paid parental leave to the primary caregiver in a family. It gives the other caregiver one week paid leave. In 2003, 12 percent of American companies offered paid parental leave.

Your Preferred Careers Chapter 5 **151**

---

2 Teaching the Lesson

Help students to understand that an investment in education is based on a foundation of skills in math, reading, and writing. Point out that getting these skills and work experience usually results in better jobs and higher pay.

You may want to have students explore both sides of the working student equation: The experience is invaluable, but some students fall behind in their schoolwork because of a demanding work schedule. Invite students to discuss the number of hours and types of work they feel are suitable for high school students.

3 Reinforce and Extend

GLOBAL CONNECTION

Whether and how many women work outside the home varies from country to country. In countries with a strong, developed economy, about 40 to 50 percent of the adult women are in the workforce. In poorer countries, far fewer women tend to work. (In Algeria, for example, 12 percent of the women work; in Pakistan, 3 percent do.) However, some of the poorest nations' statistics show many women as workers because they, like the men, are involved in subsistence farming (Ghana, 51 percent; Kenya, 46 percent) to live. Many women accept part-time work in order to meet the needs of their families. Ask students to locate statistics on women's share of part-time employment in various countries. (Suggest that they try the United Nations Statistics Division Web site at www.unstats.un.org/.) [Example statistics for 1998–2001, women's share of part-time employment: Mexico, 64 percent; France, 80 percent; Italy, 92 percent; United Kingdom, 80 percent; United States, 68 percent]

Gender and Careers

Explain to students that until the 1970s it was unusual for a wife and mother to pursue a career. Ask students why they think this was so. Have students read the Gender and Careers feature on page 151. Have them explain what a maternity leave is, and how this concept has expanded to parental leave at many companies.

Communication Connection

After students have read the Communication Connection feature on page 151, ask them to name a college that interests them. Have students write what they know about the college and why they are interested in it. Then have them write three questions they would ask students of this college.

Your Preferred Careers **151**

Body/Kinesthetic

List and discuss work situations in which workers must use math, reading, or writing skills (for example, making change, understanding instructions in a memo, or sending an e-mail message to all members of a department). Form small groups of students and have each group make up a scenario to illustrate the importance of these skills. Students can use their notes or scripts to role-play job situations.

Interpersonal/Group Learning

Have students work in small groups or pairs to prepare a survey to gather statistics about working high school students in your school. Students will need to work cooperatively to decide what questions to include, to design a form to capture data, to plan how and when to reach students, and so on. As different groups or partners share their ideas, you may want to have the class select the best features of each plan and conduct the survey. Help students summarize the data and interpret the results.

The Economy

Elicit from students what they already know about Social Security and Independent Retirement Accounts. Have them read The Economy feature on page 152. Create a diagram or other graphic organizer on the board or overhead projector to illustrate the problem in maintaining Social Security payments as the number of retirees grows very large and the number of workers paying into the system decreases. Ask interested students to read current articles about Social Security and report their findings. Stimulate a dialogue among students about how they think Social Security should be handled for the long term.

Do You Have Basic Math, Reading, and Writing Skills?

Employers want to hire people who have basic math, reading, and writing skills. They want workers who can think, solve problems, and communicate well. Employers are very good at identifying those who have poor basic skills in reading, writing, and mathematics. Having poor basic skills can keep you from being hired. People who have strong basic skills often earn higher salaries. Students who take math, science, reading, and writing courses will have more career choices. The career plan you will complete at the end of this chapter will help you identify your strengths. It can also show you the areas in which you need to improve your skills. You may need to take more classes to get the skills an occupation requires.

The Economy

When you set career goals, retirement is probably the last thing on your mind. The end of your career seems a long way off. But retirement is a reality that even the youngest workers must consider. When you work, the federal government withholds part of your paycheck for Social Security. Every American worker contributes to Social Security throughout his or her working life. When workers retire, they receive money back each month. However, Social Security payments alone do not provide a comfortable retirement. Also, a huge number of American workers will retire in the next 20 years. Some people doubt that all Americans will receive the Social Security funds they have counted on. Financial experts advise workers to create their own retirement accounts. Many companies have retirement plans in which workers invest a percentage of their salary. When they retire, workers receive benefits from the plan. Another option is an Individual Retirement Account, or IRA. People can contribute a certain amount of money to the account each year. An IRA offers tax advantages and a good way to invest money for retirement.

Do You Have Work Experience?

Do you have a job now? Working while you are still in school has several benefits. You can learn more skills. You may have more chances to learn about different careers. Working part time can help you build skills and behaviors that employers value. On the job, you learn to show respect to others. You also can show a willingness to learn new things. Employers also value people who can communicate well. They want to hire people who can follow directions and be on time. Working while in school also gives you a chance to learn about a specific industry. You can learn the skills needed for an occupation. You can practice these skills while working. You can see what other skills you need to learn.

There are even more benefits to working while in school. Teens who work while in high school continue to work as adults. They are less likely to be unemployed. If they become unemployed, they are able to find work more quickly than those with no high school work experience. Young adults who worked 20 hours a week in high school have higher yearly pay after they graduate. They earn 25 to 30 percent more than young adults who did not work in high school.

Get Involved

Have you ever considered teaching preschoolers? Three-, four-, and five-year-olds often love the attention of young people. Head Start is an organization that provides education for preschoolers from low-income families. It helps prepare children so that they do their best when they enter school. Head Start was started by the federal government in 1965. It has helped more than 15.3 million children. There are many volunteer opportunities with community Head Start organizations. High school and college students participate by helping provide educational play for the preschoolers. They also help get buildings ready for Head Start classes. Volunteering for Head Start gives students an opportunity to practice teaching while helping people.

IN THE ENVIRONMENT

During class discussion of student work experience, you may want to suggest that some students consider doing environmental volunteer work. They could learn about opportunities in an existing program or organize a recycling program for your neighborhood or school. Have students explore existing organizations or businesses in your community. Ask them to determine who will buy recycled materials, and whether it can be profitable for an organization to recycle.

Get Involved

Invite students who have experience in caring for young children to tell what they like about it. Have students read the Get Involved feature on page 153. Answer any questions students have about the Head Start program. (See the Background Information note below, or refer students to www.acf.hhs.gov/ for information.) Have interested students find out about local centers for Head Start and research volunteer opportunities there.

BACKGROUND INFORMATION

Head Start

The Head Start program is part of the federal Department of Health and Human Services. Its purpose is to help poor children meet their emotional, social, health, nutritional, and psychological needs so that they can enjoy success in school. In 2003, the program enrolled 909,608 children, paid 206,000 staff members, and attracted 1,372,000 volunteer workers. Since 1965, the Head Start program has served more than 22 million children.

Financial aid
Money available to students to help pay for postsecondary education

How Will You Develop Job Skills?

If you do not work while in high school, you need other ways to develop job skills. One way you can do this is by continuing your education after high school. This will help you to be ready to enter an occupation. Graduates of educational programs are better trained to immediately enter jobs than non-graduates. Most college graduates have more employment opportunities than those who do not graduate. You need to think about the occupations you want to pursue. Then decide how you will study and prepare for those occupations.

How Many Years of Education Do You Want to Complete?

If you decide to get more education after high school, how much should you get? Students who graduate from two-year degree programs earn 25 to 30 percent more each year than high school graduates. Students with four-year degrees make 75 percent more money each year than high school graduates. You can see that investing in more education can result in increased pay.

How Can You Pay for a Postsecondary Education?

Training and education beyond high school is a big investment. For many people, it is the biggest investment they make. You have seen the many benefits of continuing your education. But how will you pay for it? Postsecondary education is expensive. However, **financial aid** can help with the cost. Financial aid is money available to students to help pay for postsecondary education. It includes scholarships, grants, loans, and work-study programs. It is important to get information about school costs and financial aid. Share this information with your parents or guardians. This will help them plan financially for your education. If you are well-informed about costs and financial aid, you can make good decisions. The career plan you will complete on pages 156–157 will help you do this.

Lesson 2 Review Write your answers to these questions on a sheet of paper.

1. Explain why deciding to finish high school is important.

2. Why does the decision to get more education after high school involve risk?

3. Why do you think young adults who worked part-time in high school have more success in later jobs than those who did not?

Technology Note

You can find out a lot about colleges and other postsecondary schools on the Internet. Almost all colleges and schools have Web sites. They offer all kinds of information about courses of study, students, and teachers. Many also have e-mail addresses. You can e-mail people at the school and ask questions you have about the school.

AT HOME

After students have explored some resources for information about financial aid, ask them to talk with a parent or guardian about their educational goals. Students can show facts they have learned about the sources of scholarships, grants, loans, and work-study programs and ask for help in making plans to pay for higher education.

Lesson 2 Review Answers

1. Many people who drop out of school earn quite a bit less than those who graduate; many do not find any kind of work, or find only temporary work. High school dropouts have fewer opportunities for postsecondary training programs.

2. The benefits of the investment are not immediately apparent; the benefits depend on many variables.

3. Possible answer: People who work part-time in high school learn valuable job skills and responsibility. They have positive traits such as willingness to work hard.

Technology Note

Have students read the Technology Note on page 155. If possible, provide computer time for your class to locate Web sites for two or three colleges that interest them. Have students compose and send an e-mail with questions to a specific office (such as Admissions) at one school. Invite discussion of students' experience online. Ask students what worked and what did not.

Portfolio Activity

Your Career Plan

Before students begin their career plans, have them review the Self-Assessment Profile they completed at the end of Chapter 2. They should consider the career groups they selected at that time, but re-evaluate them based on what they learned in Chapters 4 and 5. This review will also help students to re-evaluate and confirm or revise their earlier choices of abilities and work values.

The CDMCareerZone Web site address is www.cdmcareerzone.com. An alternative site with information is http://www.bls.gov/foresee/site1/scout.html which gives online access to the *Occupational Outlook Handbook* via the Department of Labor Statistics.

Encourage students to elaborate on their responses to each part of the plan in a draft. For many, this will be the first time they have thought so concretely about their futures and the personal qualities and values that will help them achieve their dreams. They should have much to say or explore. On the other hand, they will need a legible, well-organized plan to keep and share with a parent or guardian. After they have written a first response, ask students to create a clean, neat, and well-organized version of their plan.

Portfolio Activity

Your Career/Education Plan

Complete each part of this career plan. Write your responses on a separate sheet of paper. Include this activity in your career portfolio.

Part A: Preferred Careers
After you identify two careers you want to explore further, write a brief description of what you would do in each. Also indicate whether each career is available in your community or within driving distance from your home. To do this, use resources such as the CDMCareerZone Web site mentioned in Chapter 3 or the list of careers included in the career clusters in Chapter 4.

Part B: School Subjects
Write down the school subjects required for each career. Have you studied the school subjects required for each of your chosen careers? Do you still need to take certain courses? Write down any courses you still need to take to prepare for each career.

Part C: Abilities
What abilities do you have? How do your skills relate to your two chosen careers? What skills must you develop in order to be prepared for your desired careers?

Part D: Values
What values can you fulfill in each of your chosen careers?

Part E: Employment Outlook and Wages
Will jobs be available in this field when you are ready to begin work? How much money will you be paid for doing the work?

156   *Chapter 5   Your Preferred Careers*

Name _____ **Date** _____ **Period** _____ | Portfolio Activity, Page 1 / Chapter 5 | 5

Your Career/Education Plan

Part A: Preferred Careers
Choose two careers you want to explore further. Write a brief description of each.

Career 1 Description: _____
Career 2 Description: _____

To learn more about the two careers, use the CDMCareerZone Web site and review Chapter 4. Find out whether each career is available in your community or within driving distance of your home.

Career 1: Yes/No   Career 2: Yes/No

Part B: School Subjects
Write down the school subjects required for each career.

Career 1: _____
Career 2: _____

Write down the school subjects/knowledge required for each career.

Career 1: _____
Career 2: _____

Part C: Abilities
Think about your abilities and skills. How can you use your skills in your chosen careers?

Career 1: _____
Career 2: _____

What skills should you develop to prepare for your desired careers?

Career 1: _____
Career 2: _____

Part D: Values
Think about the benefits you want to get from a job. What work-related values can you fulfill in each of your chosen careers?

Career 1: _____
Career 2: _____

©AGS Publishing. Permission is granted to reproduce for classroom use only.   ▶ Career Planning

---

Name _____ **Date** _____ **Period** _____ | Portfolio Activity, Page 2 / Chapter 5 | 5

Your Career/Education Plan, continued

Part E: Employment Outlook and Wages
What will the job outlook be for each career when you are ready to begin work? Choose one: excellent, good, fair, poor

Career 1: _____
Career 2: _____

How much money will you be paid in each career?

Career 1: _____   Career 2: _____

Part F: Plans After High School
What are your plans after finishing high school? (List plans other than going to college or postsecondary school.)

_____

Part G: Postsecondary Education
What schools offer programs for the careers you are interested in?

_____

How are these schools similar?

_____

How are they different?

_____

Think about your financial options. How could you pay for postsecondary education?

_____

How could you get more information about paying for postsecondary education?

_____

©AGS Publishing. Permission is granted to reproduce for classroom use only.   ▶ Career Planning

156   *Chapter 5*   **Portfolio Activity 5, Pages 1–2**

Part F: Plans After High School
What are your plans after finishing high school? (Other than going to college or other postsecondary school.)

Part G: Postsecondary Education
What schools offer the programs you are interested in? How are these schools similar? How are they different?

It is important to share and explain your career plan with a parent or guardian.

You may want to discuss Part F with students before they answer this question. Ask students to list long-term goals other than education. (They may suggest an entry level job, a long-term career, plans for marriage and a family, buying a home, and so on.) Suggest that students write the date when they hope to reach each goal they list.

As students complete their career plans, ask them to schedule a time to talk with a parent or guardian about their plan. Have students add their completed plans to their career portfolios.

Portfolio Activity Answers

Answers will vary.

Chapter 5 Review

Use the Chapter Review to prepare students for tests and to reteach content from the chapter.

Chapter 5 Mastery Test TRL

The Teacher's Resource Library includes two forms of the Chapter 1 Mastery Test. Each test addresses the chapter Goals for Learning. An optional third page of additional critical-thinking items is included for each test. The difficulty level of the two forms is equivalent.

Chapters 1– 5 Midterm Mastery Test TRL

The Teacher's Resource Library includes the Midterm Mastery Test. This test is pictured on page 325 of this Teacher's Edition. The Midterm Mastery Test assesses the major learning objectives for Chapters 1–5.

Review Answers
Vocabulary Review

1. investment 2. financial aid
3. postsecondary

Concept Review

4. B 5. C 6. A 7. D

Chapter 5   R E V I E W

> **Word Bank**
> financial aid
> investment
> postsecondary

Vocabulary Review

Choose the word or phrase from the Word Bank that best completes each sentence. Write the answer on your paper.

1. The time, effort, or money spent to get something in the future is a(n) _____.

2. Money available to students to help pay college costs is _____.

3. The time after high school is described as _____.

Concept Review

Choose the word or phrase that best completes each sentence. Write the letter of the answer on your paper.

4. Two-year college degree graduates earn about _____ more than high school graduates.
   - **A** 10 percent
   - **B** 30 percent
   - **C** 50 percent
   - **D** 5 percent

5. The best advice for a classmate considering a part-time job is that _____.
   - **A** it is a bad idea because it is too time-consuming
   - **B** it is a poor choice because it will not pay well
   - **C** it is a good way to develop valuable skills
   - **D** it is necessary in order to be employed later

6. An important piece of information to examine when choosing a career is _____.
   - **A** how many jobs are available right now
   - **B** whether more men or women work in it
   - **C** its history
   - **D** how much it pays

Chapter 5 Mastery Test A (Page 1)

Name _____ Date _____ Period _____ Mastery Test A, Page 1 / Chapter 5

Chapter 5 Mastery Test A

Part A Circle the letter of the answer that correctly completes each sentence.

1. The first step in a career plan is to choose careers that _____.
   A pay well   C interest you
   B are nearby   D train you

2. When you consider school subjects in the second step of career planning, you identify _____.
   A how you'll pay for your education
   B the courses you still need to take for your chosen careers
   C whether you like the courses you have taken so far
   D schools that can provide later education and training

3. Researching job outlooks for careers will tell you about _____.
   A values you will find fulfilling at work   C people who like the jobs
   B schools you should attend   D job openings and wages

4. When you finish high school, it is important that you have _____.
   A a definite plan for what you will do next   C a car so that you can commute if you need to
   B a full-time job lined up   D classmates who can guide your choices

5. Sharing your career plan with your parents or guardians will show them _____.
   A what your abilities are   C that you have been thinking about your future
   B that you do not need help to succeed   D what classes you have taken in school

Part B Match the decision-making steps in Column 1 with their descriptions in Column 2. Write the letter on the line.

Column 1	Column 2
_____ 6. Make Priorities	A First step in the decision-making process
_____ 7. Assess the Risks	B Second step in the decision-making process
_____ 8. Set Goals	C Third step in the decision-making process
_____ 9. Make a Plan	D Fourth step in the decision-making process
_____ 10. Explore the Options	E Fifth step in the decision-making process

©AGS Publishing. Permission is granted to reproduce for classroom use only.   Career Planning

Chapter 5 Mastery Test A (Page 2)

Name _____ Date _____ Period _____ Mastery Test A, Page 2 / Chapter 5

Chapter 5 Mastery Test A, continued

Part C Write the correct word or phrase from the Word Bank to complete each sentence.

Word Bank				
ability	financial aid	investment	postsecondary	skill

11. A(n) _____ is a competency that comes from training or practice.

12. Time, money, or effort that you spend to get something in the future is a(n) _____.

13. A(n) _____ is something a person does well.

14. Money available for students to help pay for education is called _____.

15. Education that takes place after high school is called _____ education.

Part D Write the answers to these questions. Use complete sentences.

16. What are two sources of information about training schools and colleges?

17. In what three areas do employers demand basic skills?

18. What are two things you can learn working part time that employers value?

19. If you do not work in high school, what is another way you can develop job skills?

20. How does the amount of education you have affect your wages?

©AGS Publishing. Permission is granted to reproduce for classroom use only.   Career Planning

Chapter 5 Mastery Test A (Page 3)

Name _____ Date _____ Period _____ Mastery Test A, Page 3 / Chapter 5

Chapter 5 Mastery Test A, continued

Part E Write your answer to each question. Use complete sentences. Support your answers with facts and examples from the book.

21. What do values have to do with making a career plan? Why is prioritizing an important part of this process? (2 points)

22. What are the benefits of working part-time while in high school? What might be a disadvantage? (2 points)

Part F Write a paragraph for each topic. Include a topic sentence, body, and conclusion. Support each answer with facts and examples from the textbook.

23. Why is finishing high school important to your career plan? (3 points)

24. Why should you make a detailed career plan? (3 points)

©AGS Publishing. Permission is granted to reproduce for classroom use only.   Career Planning

7. Choosing postsecondary education _____.

    A is something everyone should do

    B is not necessary for most careers

    C always pays off

    D is an investment that involves risk

Critical Thinking

Write the answer to each question on your paper.

  8. Why do you think a willingness to learn new things is a behavior that employers value?

  9. A friend does not take math courses because she says math is not necessary in her chosen career. Explain why this is a good decision or not.

10. A friend says he is not going to college because he cannot afford it. What would you tell the friend?

Test-Taking Tip

When studying for a test, review any previous tests or quizzes that cover the same information. Make sure you have the correct answers for any items you missed.

Critical Thinking

8. Possible answer: A job involves learning new skills at the beginning and often throughout the life of the job. A person who thinks he or she already knows everything about the job or who is close-minded about learning new things will not be a valuable employee. **9.** Possible answer: Math skills are among the basic skills that all employers look for. Even though a person may not think a job requires these skills, employers will often not hire people who do not have them. **10.** Possible answer: There are many kinds of financial aid, including scholarships, loans, and work study, to help students. Students should not let a lack of funds prevent them from checking into these options.

ALTERNATIVE ASSESSMENT

- Meet with each student briefly. Have the student explain the career plan he or she completed in the Portfolio Activity and tell how the plan helped clarify his or her goals for the future.

- Have each student write a paragraph or brief essay explaining the educational investment required to attain the career he or she has chosen. Ask students to include information about specific schools they might attend and how they might pay for costs of higher education.

Chapter 5 Mastery Test B, Pages 1–3

Chapter

6

Planning Guide

Opportunities in Your Community

	Student Pages	Vocabulary	Lesson Review	Critical-Thinking Questions	Chapter Review
			Student Text Lesson		
Lesson 1 Industries in Your Community	162–166	✔	✔	✔	✔
Lesson 2 Educational, Networking, and Internship Resources	167–170	✔	✔	✔	✔
Lesson 3 Visiting and Selecting a Postsecondary School	171–175		✔	✔	✔
Lesson 4 Living and Working with Others	176–181	✔	✔	✔	✔

Chapter Activities

Student Text
Chapter 6 Portfolio Activity

Teacher's Resource Library
Chapter 6 Chapter Outline
Chapter 6 Self-Study Guide
Chapter 6 Portfolio Activity

Assessment Options

Student Text
Chapter 6 Review

Teacher's Resource Library
Chapter 6 Mastery Tests A and B

Teacher's Edition
Chapter 6 Alternative Assessment

Student Text Features											Teaching Strategies					Learning Styles					Teacher's Resource Library				
Portfolio Activity	Writing Practice	Communication Connection	The Economy	Career Tip	Career Profile	On the Job	Gender and Careers	Think Positive	Technology Note	Get Involved	Background Information	Applications (Home, Community, Global, Environment)	Personal Journal	Online Connection	ELL/ESL Strategy	Visual/Spatial	Body/Kinesthetic	Interpersonal/Group Learning	Logical/Mathematical	Auditory/Verbal	Activities	Alternative Activities	Workbook Activities	Self-Study Guide	Chapter Outline
			166									164, 165		166	163	165		166		164	29	29	29	✔	✔
				169						170	169		170				169		168		30	30	30	✔	✔
	172					175			173		173	172		173	172	174			174		31	31	31	✔	✔
182		177			178		181	178				179	180		177		179		181	177	32	32	32	✔	✔

Alternative Activities

The Teacher's Resource Library (TRL) contains a set of lower-level worksheets called Alternative Activities. These worksheets cover the same content as the regular Activities but are written at a second-grade reading level.

Career Interest Inventory

The AGS Publishing Harrington-O'Shea Career Decision-Making System (CDM) may be used with this textbook. Students can use the CDM to explore their interests and identify careers. The CDM defines career areas that are indicated by students' response on the inventory.

Chapter at a Glance

Chapter 6: Opportunities in Your Community

pages 160–185

Lessons

Portfolio Activity

Conducting an Informational Interview
pages 182–183

Chapter Review

pages 184–185

Audio CD 🎧

Teacher's Resource Library TRL

Workbook Activities 29–32

Activities 29–32

Alternative Activities 29–32

Portfolio Activity 6

Chapter 6 Chapter Outline

Chapter 6 Self-Study Guide

Chapter 6 Mastery Tests A and B
(Answer Keys for the Teacher's Resource Library begin on page 328 of this Teacher's Edition.)

Chapter 6 Self-Study Guide

Chapter

Opportunities in Your Community

Going to college is a unique learning experience. Students learn subjects such as math and English that will help them in their careers. They also learn about other people and about themselves. They learn more about living in a community and their own responsibilities as citizens. What are some opportunities in postsecondary schools and your community after high school? In this chapter, you will find out.

Goals for Learning

- ◆ To recognize career opportunities in one's community
- ◆ To understand how networking can help in finding a job
- ◆ To learn how to select a postsecondary school or college
- ◆ To realize the importance of getting along with others
- ◆ To learn conflict-resolution skills

Introducing the Chapter

Have students look at the photo on page 160 in the Student Edition and tell what place they think it shows. Invite students to tell what they think the students are doing seated in a circle on the grass. Point out that college gives more flexibility but calls for more responsibility by students. Read the chapter title and have students mention several institutions in your community that offer a career opportunity. Ask a volunteer to read the introductory paragraph on page 161.

Have students read the Goals for Learning and ask about any terms they do not understand. Ask them to tell what they think will be involved in each goal by rephrasing it in their own words.

Career Tips

Ask volunteers to read the career tips that appear in the margins throughout the chapter. Then discuss them with the class.

Alternative Assessment

The Alternative Assessment box on page 185 of the Chapter Review includes activities using various learning styles to assess students' understanding of the Goals for Learning.

161

Name _____ Date _____ Period _____ | Chapter Outline, Page 1 / Chapter 6 | **6**

Opportunities in Your Community

Directions Fill in the outline below. Filling in the blanks will help you as you read and study Chapter 6.

I.   Lesson 1: Industries in Your Community (pp. 162–166)

  A. Core Services

    1. _____ are the 11 industries a community needs in order to function.

    2. A community needs industries in 11 of the 16 _____

  B. Industries in Your Community

    1. All communities have education and _____ services.

    2. Law enforcement officers are in _____ community.

    3. Knowing the industries in your community, tells you what types of

    _____ and _____ are available locally.

    4. You can find out where industries are located by searching the _____

    5. You can also find out by asking _____ or _____

II. Lesson 2: Educational, Networking, and Internship Resources (pp. 167–170)

  A. Networking

    1. Networking is talking to people you know to _____

    2. Networking is the most _____ of all ways to do a job search.

  B. Internships

    1. Some internships pay a _____ Others do not.

    2. An internship gives you an opportunity to do a _____ It is like a job _____

©AGS Publishing. Permission is granted to reproduce for classroom use only.   **Career Planning**

Name _____ Date _____ Period _____ | Chapter Outline, Page 2 / Chapter 6 | **6**

Opportunities in Your Community, continued

  C. How to Begin Networking

    1. Find a company that _____ people in a career that you would like to enter.

    2. Write or call a person at the company and ask for an _____

    3. Send a _____ after the interview.

III. Lesson 3: Visiting and Selecting a Postsecondary School (pp. 171–175)

  A. Choose a Career Direction and a School

    1. Decide what you want to do _____ after high school.

    2. Keep in mind your past and current _____

    3. Discuss your thoughts with school _____, parents, or guardians.

  B. Learn More About Schools

    1. Visit schools that vary in _____ and _____

    2. Learn about activities and _____ available to students.

    3. Ask about the special _____ of a school's program.

    4. Record your thoughts and reactions to _____ you visit.

IV. Lesson 4: Living and Working with Others (pp. 176–181)

  A. Living and Working with Others and Showing Respect

    1. No matter what job you choose, you will have some _____ with people.

    2. Show people _____ Treat them the way you want to be treated.

  B. Resolving Conflict and Authority Figures

    1. When someone makes you angry, try to _____

  C. Authority Figures

    1. Explain why you think a decision is unfair in a _____ way.

©AGS Publishing. Permission is granted to reproduce for classroom use only.   **Career Planning**

Chapter 6 Chapter Outline

Opportunities in Your Community **161**

Chapter 6 Lesson 1

Overview Students learn the industries needed in a community and the career opportunities they create. Students also locate industries on a map and consider examples of these industries in their community.

Objectives

- To identify the 11 core services necessary to a community and the careers associated with each
- To explore ways of learning the location of core services within a community

Student Pages 162–166

Teacher's Resource Library TRL

Workbook Activity 29

Activity 29

Alternative Activity 29

Vocabulary

core services

Write the vocabulary term on the board. Ask students to predict what it means based on the meanings of *core* and *services*. (*Possible response: the central or basic work that serves others*) Read the definition aloud and invite students to name services or occupations that they consider essential to a community.

1 Warm-Up Activity

Ask students to name industries or businesses in your community that are important to its economy. List them on the board as students mention them. Then have students suggest ways in which these industries offer opportunities to them.

> **Core services**
> The 11 industries a community needs in order to function

Your community can be an important resource as you plan your career. By learning about the economy in your community, you can find opportunities to learn about occupations. Think about the occupation you want to explore. Do you know anyone in your community who has that occupation? You may be able to talk to that person to get more information. What companies or businesses related to that occupation are in your community?

What Industries Does a Community Need?

A community needs industries in 11 of the 16 career clusters (covered in Chapter 4) to function. These 11 industries are referred to as **core services**. Read the 11 core services listed here. Sample careers in each area are provided.

Natural Resources

People need electric power in their homes. Farms and businesses also need power. Electric lines bring power where it is needed in a community. Cities and towns also need to treat drinking water and wastewater. Most communities employ power line, telephone, and cable repairers. Water treatment plant operators are also employed in most communities.

Architecture and Construction

Some areas have a lot of new construction. Other areas have none. Even if there is no new construction in your area, many workers provide the maintenance and repair necessary in every community. Workers who fix and maintain homes and buildings include roofers, electricians, carpenters, plumbers, and heating and air-conditioning mechanics. Roads also need to be repaired. Road-paving and surfacing operators do this job.

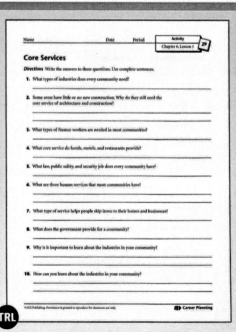

Workbook Activity 29

Activity 29

Education and Training Services

Schools are located in all communities or regions. Some communities have many schools. Smaller towns may have only one or two schools. Teachers and administrators work in schools.

Finance

Banks are needed in each community so people can manage their money. Most people must also pay taxes. Bank managers, tellers, accountants, and tax preparers are needed in each community.

Government and Public Administration

Government provides the structure for a community to exist. It keeps the community organized. Administrators, tax collectors, and highway maintenance workers are some examples of government workers.

Health Science

People need medical care close to where they live. Health science occupations include doctors, therapists, and nurses. These people provide necessary medical care at clinics, hospitals, or private offices.

Hospitality and Tourism

Many communities have hotels or motels and restaurants to serve visitors. Motel desk clerks, housekeepers, cooks, and food servers are employed in most communities. Some communities also have tourist information centers.

 ## Teaching the Lesson

Students have encountered the career clusters listed in this lesson in Chapter 4. If necessary, quickly review them by having students scan titles and heads in Lessons 2–17 of Chapter 4. Point out that other career groups may exist in your community (such as agriculture or science and technology), but those listed here are necessary in every community.

 ## Reinforce and Extend

ELL/ESL STRATEGY

Language Objective: *To use syntax as an aid to comprehension*

English syntax differs from that of many other languages. In their native language(s), ELL students may expect verbs to precede subjects, and adjectives to follow nouns. Review with students that in many English sentences, the subject (the who or what of the sentence) comes first, followed by the predicate (what the subject did or was), as in the text sentence *Most communities (S) / employ power line, telephone, and cable repairers (P)*. Then point out that for questions, the normal order changes. The subject appears later, the verb (the main word or phrase in the predicate), or a portion of it, may come first. Write the heading *What Industries Does a Community Need?* on the board. Underline the subject (*a community*) with one line and the verb (*does need*) with two lines. Select other sentences from the lesson, have students identify their subjects and verbs, and then turn them into questions and locate the subjects and verbs in the questions.

> *Cities and towns <u>need</u> to treat drinking water.*
>
> *Why <u>do cities and towns need</u> to treat drinking water?*

Human Services

Usually a community has one or more churches or places of worship. Communities also have barbershops and beauty salons. Other services provided in the Human Services cluster include funeral services, child care, and mental health care. Occupations related to human services include clergy members, hairdressers, barbers, and funeral directors. Child-care providers, social workers, and counselors also work in the community.

Law, Public Safety, and Security

Police, fire, and emergency medical services need to be near where people live. Law enforcement officers are in every community.

Marketing, Sales, and Service

Most communities have grocery and retail stores. Store managers and salespeople work in these stores. Some cities or towns might have small stores that are owned by someone who lives in the community.

Transportation, Distribution, and Logistics

People need to be able to get the things they need to their homes or businesses. People also need to be able to travel within their community. Some communities have airports, bus and train stations, and taxis. Occupations that help connect and serve communities include truck drivers, bus drivers, service station attendants, and mechanics.

Look at the map of Millberg on page 165. Use the key to locate industries in each of the 11 core services. Do you know the location of these services and industries in your community?

Millberg

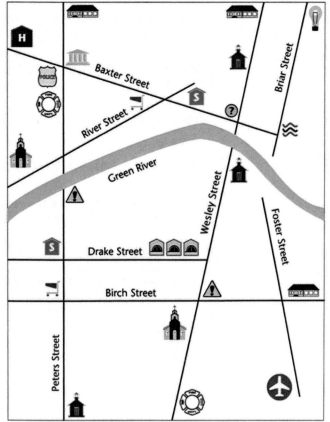

KEY

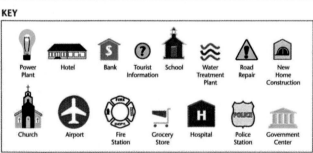

Power Plant	Hotel	Bank	Tourist Information	School	Water Treatment Plant	Road Repair	New Home Construction
Church	Airport	Fire Station	Grocery Store	Hospital	Police Station	Government Center

Many communities have a local organization of the U.S. Chamber of Commerce. This national institution was created to represent and promote the unified interests of U.S. business. Suggest that students visit the U.S. Chamber of Commerce Web site at www.uschamber.com. From there, they can click on the link "Locate a Chapter." Listings for state and local chambers list the local Web address at the end of each entry. The local chamber site will have a business directory students can access to get basic information about businesses in your community that belong to the organization.

The Economy

Ask students what effect it has on a community when a business closes or lays off workers. (*The business no longer pays taxes to the community. People who are not working cannot buy goods and services. The economy suffers.*) Have a volunteer read The Economy feature on page 166 aloud. Talk with students about your community. Ask them to tell whether they think its economy is healthy and growing or stagnant and shrinking. Have students give examples of local business activity to support their opinions.

Lesson 1 Review Answers

1. Core services are the 11 services that are necessary and central to the functions of a community.

2. Examples are churches, barbershops and beauty salons, funeral services, child care, and mental health care.

3. Answers will vary. Examples include names of banks, stores, police departments, churches, and transportation companies.

Knowing the industries in your community also tells you what type of work and careers are available locally. The yellow pages of the telephone directory can be very helpful in finding addresses and telephone numbers. You can also find out where industries are located by searching for them on the Internet. Another way you can find information is by asking police officers or mail carriers. They are familiar with the community and can help you locate businesses, schools, and other places.

Lesson 1 Review Write your answers to these questions on a sheet of paper.

1. What are core services?

2. What are some examples of human services found in every community?

3. Name two specific companies or organizations in your community that provide core services.

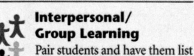

The Economy

The industries in your community can be an important resource as you seek an occupation. The stronger your community's economy, the better resource it is. What makes a community's economy strong? Money comes into a community when people there sell products or services to others. The following industries bring a lot of money into a community: farming, mining, forestry, fishing, manufacturing, tourism, and government. Many communities encourage new businesses such as banks that serve a large area. Amusement parks or large shopping centers would also bring in money. They would attract people from other cities and states. On the other hand, when people must go outside the community for services, money leaves the community. So if a community had no hospital or medical services, the community would lose money. Building a hospital in the community would improve its economy.

Interpersonal/ Group Learning

Pair students and have them list businesses and organizations in your community that they think offer them the best career opportunities. Remind students that career opportunities can include, but are not limited to, jobs and internships. Students can also learn from chosen businesses by interviewing workers there, studying company policies on hiring and workers, and so on. Bring several pairs together as a small group to discuss their choices. Remind students to give facts to support their choices.

Networking
The exchange of information or services among individuals, groups, or institutions

Internship
Doing work for an employer for a specified period of time to learn about an industry or occupation

You have now learned about the core workers in your community. These people can be a great resource as you plan your career. They can answer your questions about certain occupations. Meeting and talking with a person about his or her job experience can give you information you cannot get by doing research or reading a book.

What Is Networking?

Most people know very little about how to get a job. It can take months. A job search is more than filling out applications, mailing out résumés, and having interviews. One of the best ways to get a job is **networking.** Networking is talking to people you know to learn about possible job opportunities. Networking is the most productive of all ways to do a job search. Personal contact with someone you know can give you valuable information about a company. You can find out who to talk with at the company. You can also find out whether the company is hiring. Personal contacts can be parents, guardians, relatives, neighbors, friends, part-time employers, classmates, or church members. Building relationships with these people can help you find a job.

What Is an Internship?

Networking can help you find a job. It might also help you get an **internship.** An internship involves working for an employer for a specified period of time to learn about a certain industry or occupation. An internship provides an opportunity to develop specific job skills. Some internships pay a wage. Others do not. You can often complete an internship while you are still in school. Some schools offer credit for an internship.

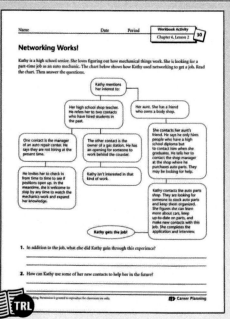

Workbook Activity 30

Activity 30

Lesson at a Glance

Chapter 6 Lesson 2

Overview This lesson explains networking and internship opportunities and gives guidelines for interviewing a contact at a local business.

Objectives

- To define networking and explain how it helps in a job search
- To understand the nature of an internship
- To list guidelines and prepare for a networking interview with a contact person

Student Pages 167–170

Teacher's Resource Library

Workbook Activity 30

Activity 30

Alternative Activity 30

Vocabulary

informational interview
internship
networking

Write the vocabulary terms on the board and read the text definition for each one. Ask students to draw a diagram that represents the concept of networking. Tell them that in this lesson, they will consider networking as an exchange of information about available jobs. Have them indicate where they fit into their diagrams.

1 Warm-Up Activity

Ask students to review some ways they have already gone about learning about careers or jobs in careers that interest them. If they do not mention talking with people in the field, explain that this is a method called networking. They will learn how to network as they read this lesson.

2 Teaching the Lesson

Emphasize to students that networking is more than talking to people. It involves relationship-building and mutual support.

In other words, a person needs to maintain a warm and respectful relationship with contacts, treat them as professionals, and establish ways he or she can be helpful to the contact. It is not too early for students to begin building a base of contact people in the area(s) that interest them.

If possible, acquire some descriptions of internship opportunities in your community or area to read to students. Have students compare and contrast their length, type of duties, and possible income.

The Portfolio Activity on pages 182–183 gives students a full range of questions appropriate to ask in the networking interview they plan in this lesson. You may refer them to those pages whenever you assign the interview activity—when teaching Lesson 2, or after students have completed the chapter.

 3 Reinforce and Extend

LEARNING STYLES

Logical/Mathematical
Develop a diagram to model why networking is an effective way of finding out about job opportunities. One possibility is shown:

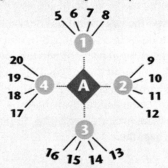

Have students develop a problem in which person A contacts four people to ask about a job. Suppose that each of those four gives information leading to four additional contacts. Have students calculate how many people person A will have talked to if this cycle continues for a third round. ($[4 \times 4] + 4 = 16 + 4 = 20$; $[16 \times 4] + 4 = 64 + 4 = 68$)

Have you ever gone to work with your parent or guardian for a day? If so, you probably got to see what he or she does on the job. An internship is different. It is more detailed than observing what a person does on the job. An internship gives you an opportunity to do a job. It is like a job tryout. In an internship, you might complete special projects. You might perform a variety of tasks from different jobs. Or, you might focus on a single occupation. For example, suppose your career goal was to be an accountant. You could get an internship doing accounting work. You would be supervised by an accountant. An internship offers a chance to learn about an occupation by experiencing it.

How Can I Begin Networking?

In Chapter 4 you identified the names, addresses, and telephone numbers of contact people in your community. Now is the time to use this information.

1. Identify a company or organization that employs people in a career that you would like to enter. Write down the address and phone number.

2. Identify a person within the company or organization in a career area of your choice. Write or call this person and ask for an **informational interview.** An informational interview is an opportunity to talk to someone at a business to gather information.

3. If there is nobody in your region in the career area you want to explore, try to identify someone in a related career. Suppose you want to be an engineer. You might interview a science teacher in physics or chemistry at your school. He or she would have knowledge related to engineering.

Career Tip

Be wary of job placement agencies that ask for money or charge a fee at the beginning. Often, these agencies get paid for placing someone at a job.

You can call someone you know in a business or company to set up an informational interview.

Here are some things to keep in mind as you interview someone about his or her work.

- Communicate clearly to the contact person that this is not a job interview.
- Set a time limit for the interview. Thirty minutes is a reasonable amount of time. Ask the person to answer some questions to help you in your decision making about the career area.
- Prepare for the interview. The more you know about the career you are discussing and your abilities, the better the interview will go.
- Keep a record of your interview dates. In your initial contact, mention that you are a student and give the name of your school. Tell the interviewee who suggested that you contact him or her. State that you have researched the career.
- Conclude by thanking the person for the interview. Ask for a business card or get the person's correct title and address to send a thank-you note.

Networking

The majority of jobs (some sources estimate from 70 percent to 80 percent) are filled by people who learned of them through word of mouth. Therefore, the larger a personal network one develops, the better his or her chances of finding out about jobs when they become available. To network successfully, remember to tell friends, colleagues, and business contacts specifics about what you are looking for. Be sure they know you are looking for help. Attend lots of professional meetings, civic, or social events and bring business cards. Send a thank-you note to every person who has given you time. Networking mistakes include calling people you don't know at home, putting people on hold, using someone's name without permission, and pressuring people to get a conversation with someone.

LEARNING STYLES

Body/Kinesthetic

Before students communicate with contact persons, have them practice good business telephone etiquette and try out what they are going to say on the phone. Post and discuss these rules:

1. Identify yourself clearly.
2. Be polite.
3. Ask if the person has time for you. If not, briefly state the purpose of the call and ask for an appointment to follow up later.
4. Take notes about important points during the conversation. Use them to recap at the end of the call and be sure you are both "on the same page."
5. Thank the person for his or her time.

Pair students and have them role-play the first phone conversation with the person each wants as a business contact.

Most students will not feel comfortable interviewing a professional for the first time. Suggest that they write a journal entry on their own paper expressing their concerns about the interview. One or two days later, have students revisit their journal entries and write a sentence telling one way they could make sure the imagined problem does not occur. After students have completed their interviews, have them write follow-up entries telling how they went.

Lesson 2 Review Answers

1. Meeting a person in your field is a way to get more information about the career than you could get from other places. In addition, the person can inform you of job openings.

2. The job might include helping with a variety of tasks, focusing on one project, and meeting a variety of other employees and observing their work.

3. The purpose of this kind of interview is to get as much information as possible. You do not want the person to think that you are really trying to get a job; the person would probably be less informative.

Get Involved

Ask volunteers to read the Get Involved feature on page 170 aloud. Invite students to share what they already know about the United Way organization in your community. Ask them to explain what skills the student volunteers for the Lubbock, Texas, United Way are getting. Have them pose problems they think the volunteers must solve and rewards they enjoy through their work. Have several interested students communicate with leaders of your local United Way to get more information about its services to the community. Have students report what they learn.

It is best to write down your questions before the interview. Having questions ahead of time may make you more relaxed. You will know what to ask. Many people enjoy talking about themselves, so the interview may be easier than you think. Remember that first impressions are powerful. Be sure to dress appropriately, be on time, and be polite. Practice asking and answering questions before an interview. You can find sample interview questions in the Portfolio Activity on pages 182–183 in this chapter.

Lesson 2 Review Write your answers to these questions on a sheet of paper.

1. Why is networking one of the best ways to get a job?

2. Suppose you had an internship at an advertising agency. Describe some ways you would probably spend your time.

3. Suppose you are interviewing someone about his or her job. Why should you inform the person that you do not expect this to be a job interview?

Get Involved

The United Way is a non-profit organization that exists in many communities. Here's how it works: individuals and companies contribute money to the United Way fund. The United Way distributes the money to many local organizations that help people. These organizations range from the Red Cross to local food banks. There are many volunteer opportunities for young people at local United Way organizations. For example, the Lubbock, Texas, United Way sponsors a program for young people. The students are in charge of distributing several thousand dollars. These high school students quickly learn about the many organizations that need money and volunteers. They also develop valuable management skills.

Lesson 3 — Visiting and Selecting a Postsecondary School

Knowing what you want to do after high school is a big challenge. Many high school students think they need to decide what they want to do for the rest of their lives. This is not true! In fact, most adults make six or seven job changes in their working lives. The world of work is continually changing. It doesn't make sense to decide now what job you will do for the rest of your life. However, you can identify what direction you want your career to take immediately following high school.

How Do I Choose My Career Direction?

To make this decision, you can use the information you learned about yourself in Chapter 2. For example, based upon your abilities, interests, and values, you can decide whether to pursue work immediately after high school graduation. Maybe you would prefer to enroll in postsecondary training. You might decide that you want to attend college. Once you are clear about your plans after high school, the next step is deciding where you want to work or study.

What Should I Consider When Choosing a School?

Deciding which school to attend is a hard decision. How can you sort through the options available to you? If you are planning to attend a college or university, then there are several things for you to consider. Think about the following questions:
- Is it important for you to stay close to home?
- What amount of tuition can you and your family afford?
- Does a school have the areas of study you are considering?
- Would you feel more comfortable in a large, medium, or small school?

Opportunities in Your Community Chapter 6 **171**

Lesson at a Glance

Chapter 6 Lesson 3

Overview In this lesson, students answer questions to help them decide what to do after high school and how to choose a postsecondary school.

Objectives

- To determine whether to work or study after high school
- To consider personal values, abilities, and interests to decide what kind of college is suitable
- To gather information about schools from catalogs, the Internet, and visits
- To evaluate impressions and facts about schools in order to make a choice

Student Pages 171–175

Teacher's Resource Library

Workbook Activity 31

Activity 31

Alternative Activity 31

1 Warm-Up Activity

Ask students to imagine themselves ten years from now. Where will they be? What will they be doing? What will they have to do to reach these goals? Have students read the lesson to get strategies for postsecondary plans.

2 Teaching the Lesson

Try to make college guides or Internet time on computers available to students as they complete this lesson. If your community has postgraduate institutions, you may want to provide information about them as examples.

Small group discussion may be useful for students as they consider the questions in the lesson. Some subjects may be difficult for them to assess because of their limited exposure. Experiences and perceptions of peers may help them think through and identify situations that are comfortable to them.

Workbook Activity 31   **Activity 31**   *Opportunities in Your Community* **171**

GLOBAL CONNECTION

Few countries have the extensive network of post-secondary schools found in the United States. Explain that only the United States has a national system of junior colleges offering students a two-year program for a degree or as a bridge to a four-year college. Have students select another country and research its university system to compare it with that of the United States. Questions they might answer include: *Who is eligible for admission? How do students pay for higher education? What percentage of high school graduates go to university?* Have students report their findings to the class.

ELL/ESL STRATEGY

Language Objective: *To discuss questions about schools and communities as a group*

Have ELL students practice oral interaction skills by sharing their impressions about community and school as well as their thoughts and questions about researching colleges. Place students in groups of four to six. Encourage them to use language they have learned (for example, *What I like about our school is...*) and to introduce new vocabulary (for example, *application deadlines, student-to-faculty ratio*) by modeling questions and rephrasing them to show meaning: *Why is student-to-faculty ratio important? This means why is it important to know the number of students per teacher in a college.*

As you think about these questions, keep in mind your past and current experiences. Your experiences can guide you in making plans about your future. To begin narrowing down school options, consider your current situation. For example, ask yourself how you feel in your current school. Do you like the size of your school? What are some of the things you wish were different about your school? What are some of the things that you really like about your school? You may attend a small high school and you feel comfortable there. A large state university might be a shock to you. Or, you might feel limited by your small school and wish you had more opportunities. In that case, you might consider a larger college.

Consider the same sort of questions about the community in which you live. What do you like about it? What do you wish was different? Think about your values. How might they influence your decisions? For example, suppose you value being close to family. How would you feel about going to a school several states away? Perhaps you value living in a city. It is important for you to consider these things as you make your plans. Using your values in this way will help you to make a good decision.

Your thoughts about these questions can help you plan for your future. If you are planning on attending college, then you need to decide what kind of college is right for you. Perhaps you know that a smaller college is right for you. Then you can cross large state universities off your list. If a college does not offer the courses you are interested in, you can stop researching that school.

Writing Practice

To better understand your attitudes about your current school, keep a journal. Write every day or so about what you like and what you wish were different. After a few weeks, reread your journal. What does it tell you about the sort of school you might prefer after high school? Use your journal entries to help you decide.

Writing Practice

Read the Writing Practice on page 172 to students. You may want to allow students five minutes of class time daily for a week to journal about their school likes and dislikes. Then have students reread their entries and highlight the positive comments they have made. You may want to have students make a table summarizing the positives and negatives about your school. Students can evaluate their tables to make a conclusion about the best size and type of postsecondary school for them.

If you still cannot decide, ask others for help. Discuss your thoughts about school options with school counselors, parents, or guardians. Share your thoughts and ask for their input. Even if they haven't attended college, they can help. They may be able to help you with your career plans.

How Can I Learn More About Schools?

You may find it helpful to visit several schools that vary in size and location. This strategy helps you to compare what you like about different schools. It also helps you to see if your ideas about what kind of a school you'd like are correct. As you gather information, keep in mind that schools have Web sites. Use the Internet to get information about schools you might be interested in. A school's Web site can give you information about programs or majors, application materials, application deadlines, and financial aid. You can also learn about activities and services available to students. For example, many schools have clubs, sports teams, and support services such as career counseling, tutoring, and academic advising.

Once you have gathered information about schools that interest you, identify specific schools to visit. Discuss your thoughts about the sort of school you might prefer with your parents or guardians. Try to identify at least three schools to visit. Talk with your school counselor about your choices.

Technology Note

You can use e-mail to communicate with college administrators. Many admissions offices provide names and e-mail addresses of people who can answer your questions. Take advantage of this quick and easy way to get information.

BACKGROUND INFORMATION

Choosing Colleges to Visit

To narrow your list of colleges or to get a look at schools too far away to visit, you can take a virtual tour or gather information from a college fair. On those campuses that students are able to visit, they should take a tour, but also do some of the following activities to get a sense of what the student community and student life is like: attend a class or classes, read the campus newspaper, eat at a typical cafeteria, and spend the night in a dorm if possible. During a visit, prospective students should also talk to enrolled students to ask questions that are on their minds. (Obviously, it is best to visit while school is in session, not during a vacation time.) These activities help students to see whether the school is a "good fit" for them.

Technology Note

After students read the Technology Note on page 173, model locating e-mail addresses for an admissions officer at a college in your community or state. Show students how to use links on Web page for the school to get this information.

ONLINE CONNECTION

The following resources are useful to students as they gather information about colleges to create their initial lists:

www.AnyCollege.net (a user-friendly search engine containing more than 5,400 U.S. colleges)

www.CampusDirt.com (first-hand information about campus life on more than 600 college campuses)

www.CampusTours.com (virtual tours, college Web cams, and so on)

Logical/Mathematical

To gather information to help them decide what colleges to visit, suggest that students use college catalogs, Web sites, and e-mail to get answers to the questions that are most important to them. They might make a table like the one shown below to capture information about schools and compare them:

	School 1	School 2
Specialty		
Distance from Home		
Safety		
Social Life		
Class Size		
Percent Receiving Financial Aid		
Number of Yearly Applications		
Number of Yearly Acceptances		
Graduation Rate/Time		
Job Placement for Grads		

After this, students need only focus on colleges that meet their criteria and are reasonably likely to accept them.

Visual/Spatial

Students who prefer expressing understanding of concepts visually might make a collage to show the traits and programs of a school that are important to them. For example, they might include pictures, drawings, colors, and symbols that characterize the type of campus they would like, suggest programs that interest them, communicate the mood of the ideal campus, and show how students are given help at that school.

What Should I Ask When I Visit a School?

When you have identified schools to visit, contact each school's admissions office. To help with your visit, admission offices offer tours and information sessions. Here are some questions to ask admissions office representatives:

- What is your student-to-faculty ratio (the number of students for each professor)?
- What assistance is provided to students who need help deciding what to study?
- What assistance is provided to graduating students who are looking for jobs?
- How many of your students get jobs after graduation?
- What is your school most known for?
- What percent of your students receive financial aid?
- What is the average financial aid package?
- What clubs, sports teams, and other activities are available?
- How many students apply and are accepted each year?
- How many of your classes are taught by graduate students?

Try to meet with a faculty member from the program(s) of study you are considering. Here are some questions you might ask:
- What are the special strengths of your program or major?
- What priority do faculty members place on teaching?
- Do students have the chance to meet with their advisors on a regular basis?

Think about other questions you might have about the faculty or the program. Try to get a good sense of how much support faculty members will offer you in your area of interest. Pay attention to how enthusiastic faculty members are about their work. When teachers enjoy what they do, they are more likely to provide a positive learning experience.

What Should I Do After Visiting Schools?

Keep a record of your thoughts and impressions of every school you visit. Pay attention to whether the people you met with were friendly, knowledgeable, and helpful to you during your visit. After you have completed your visits, discuss your experiences with your school counselor and your parents or guardians. How did your experiences compare with the preferences you identified before visiting? Review your thoughts about each school. What did you like and dislike? In what ways did each school meet or not meet your expectations? Based upon what you know now, what are your thoughts about the school you would prefer? Is your preferred school a realistic option? To which schools should you apply?

Take time to research and visit schools you think you would like to attend. The more information you have, the better decision you will make. If you base your decision upon your experiences, you will be happier with your choice.

Lesson 3 Review Write your answers to these questions on a sheet of paper.

1. What are three options people may choose after high school?

2. When choosing a college, you should consider what you like and dislike about your current school. Why is this useful?

3. What are two steps to take when you research a college?

On the Job

Are you overwhelmed by all of the paperwork involved in choosing a college or other school? You may be juggling college and test applications, financial aid applications, and other resources. Keeping organized is a valuable skill in any occupation. It can help you now as well. Spend time each day organizing paperwork into files. Keep material on your computer organized as well.

Lesson 3 Review Answers

1. They may go to work immediately, enroll in postsecondary training, or attend college.

2. It helps you understand what you would like to look for and avoid in a college environment.

3. Look for information on the Internet, and visit colleges to talk to administrators and faculty members.

On the Job

Place an assortment of school supplies, books, and papers on a table. Have students sort the material and explain why they would organize it in this way. Invite comments from students about why keeping supplies and papers organized is helpful. Have students read the On the Job feature on page 175. You may want to model organizing materials into file folders or an expandable file using labels.

Chapter 6 Lesson 4

Overview In this lesson, students learn reasons and methods for getting along with and respecting others, including authority figures, people with whom they have conflicts, and people from other cultures.

Objectives

- To understand the importance of showing respect to others
- To identify benefits of a positive attitude
- To list steps for resolving conflict with others
- To learn methods of communicating with people in authority

Student Pages 176–181

Teacher's Resource Library TRL

Workbook Activity 32

Activity 32

Alternative Activity 32

Vocabulary

attitude
authority

Write the vocabulary words on the board. Ask volunteers to name types of attitudes and demonstrate postures and gestures that reveal each attitude. Have students name someone who has authority over them. Ask them to give original definitions for each word. Then compare student definitions with those in the text.

1 Warm-Up Activity

Ask students to think about the way they interact with friends, strangers, teachers, and parents. How are the ways they communicate with each group of people different? How are they the same? Invite students to summarize what they consider the best way to treat coworkers and bosses. Have students read the lesson to learn ways of showing respect to and resolving conflicts with others.

Do you prefer to work with people? If you do, you probably enjoy talking with others. Or, would you rather work with things? Perhaps you are more comfortable working with machines and computers. You may have to answer questions like these when you are looking for a job. No matter what job you choose, you will have some contact with people. Learning how to work well with others is an important skill for all jobs. Many people think it is the most important skill for a successful career.

What Are Some Challenges of Living and Working with Others?

You might think that learning to live and work with others is simple. Many times, this is true. It is easy to interact with people you know or people who are similar to you. However, in your community and at your job, you will meet many different people. Some may have different backgrounds from yours. They may have different religions or cultural traditions, and may speak different languages.

Communication Connection

How do people in your community tend to behave toward one another? Do strangers speak to one another? Do you and your neighbors know one another? How might communications with others differ in cities, suburbs, and rural areas? How might they differ in another country?

You might find it challenging to interact with people who are different from you. Perhaps this is because you don't know about their culture. For example, in some cultures it is important to make eye contact with the person you are talking to. Eye contact lets that person know you are interested in what they are saying. It also makes them feel you are being truthful. Making eye contact is considered a basic communication rule. In another culture, however, it may be considered rude for a person to make eye contact, especially with an older person.

You also need to know how to talk to different people. For instance, you probably would not talk the same way to your school principal as you talk to your best friend. You change the way you communicate depending on who you are talking to. Likewise, it is important to develop communication skills for different living and work situations. Living and working with others can be pretty complicated.

How Can I Show Respect to Others?

Attitude
How someone thinks, feels, and acts

One thing you want to do in all of your interactions with others is show respect. When you show respect to others, you treat people like you would want to be treated. To show respect to others you need to listen to what they say. You can also learn about people who are different from you. The more you know about them, the more respect you will have for them. All of these things help build good communication.

When talking with someone, carefully listen to what the person is saying. For example, you might start thinking about your response while someone is still talking. This distracts you from really listening. The next time someone talks to you, practice listening to what he or she is saying. Focus only on understanding what he or she says. When he or she is finished talking, you will have time to form your response. You may even respond by summarizing what the other person said. This will confirm that you heard the person correctly. It will also communicate to the other person that you did really listen!

Everyone deserves respect. If you believe that everyone is worthy of respect, you make it a habit to treat them well. With this **attitude,** you show that you believe everyone matters. Helping people feel that they matter is a powerful communication tool. You can help people feel that they matter by taking time to learn about them. Learn what other people like and what their values are. You might be scared by what you do not know. But that doesn't mean you should avoid interacting with others who are different from you. There is little chance for good communication when there is no communication at all. Spend time learning about cultures and traditions that are different from your own. You will find that people who seem different might actually have a lot in common with you. You might also discover that it is fun learning about different cultures and traditions. Imagine how dull the world would be if everyone was exactly alike.

Communication Connection

Read and discuss the questions in the Communication Connection feature on page 176. Explore students' impressions of their community and ideas about community customs in other countries.

Teaching the Lesson

Having an attitude of respect toward others, being willing to listen to them carefully, and resolving conflicts with them are three invaluable skills. You may want to open a dialogue among students about respect and conflicts and have them explore such methods as peer mediation and negotiation to expand on the lesson.

Reinforce and Extend

LEARNING STYLES

Auditory/Verbal
Pair students and have them complete this listening exercise. One student tells his or her partner about an object that is important to him or her. The communication should describe the object, tell why it is important, and express how the person feels about it. When the speaker has finished, the listener responds by telling what he or she heard the speaker say. Students exchange roles and repeat the process. Have speakers assess how well their partners listened.

ELL/ESL STRATEGY

Language Objective: *To speak about traditions of a native culture*

As they work to master English, ELL students can educate other students about their native cultures and promote multicultural understanding. Ask ELL students to prepare a short talk or demonstration about unique traditions of their native cultures and accepted ways of communicating with older individuals, younger individuals, and authority figures. You may want to suggest that students make notes and use an English-proficient student as a consultant to answer any questions about vocabulary or syntax. Encourage these speakers to model the cultural norms they explain.

Think Positive

After students read the Think Positive feature on page 178, ask them to describe ways they have discovered to find humor in awkward or disappointing situations and overcome negative feelings.

Career Profile

Chef

Have students name and describe chefs they know about from television cooking shows or other venues. Invite them to tell what they think this work is like and what traits and skills are needed by a chef. Then have students read the Career Profile on page 178. Students who are especially interested in this career might study it further and follow up by demonstrating a technique or preparing a dish developed by a favorite chef.

Think Positive

Sometimes it takes courage to keep a positive attitude. You might think it is "cool" to be negative about the world and about your life. Try to remember that negativity does not make people happier or more productive. Keeping a sense of humor in the face of negative attitudes can make life more pleasant for everyone.

How Can My Attitude Affect My Job?

You have seen that showing respect toward those with whom you live and work is important. Other ways to live and work well with others include being honest, trustworthy, reliable, and having a positive attitude. Often employers state that these key traits are the main reasons why they hire someone. Likewise, employers may fire people who do not have these traits.

How Can My Friends Affect My Behavior?

In order to demonstrate positive behaviors, spend time with people who do the same. Your friends can affect your behavior. For example, you might say that you would never damage someone else's property. However, if you were in a group of friends who decided to paint graffiti, you might join them. Being part of the group makes it easier to do so. You may even feel pressure to go along with everyone else. Your friends can have a similar influence on you when it comes to using drugs and alcohol.

Career Profile

Chef

Have you ever helped prepare a big dinner for a dozen friends and family members? Then you have an idea of the excitement and challenges of being a chef. A chef spends his or her day testing recipes and planning menus. He or she is in charge of buying fresh meats and vegetables. Some chefs prepare most food themselves. Others manage a large team of workers.

Being a chef is a physically demanding job. Most chefs work nights and weekends, and their families must adjust to their unusual work schedule. Chefs work in a wide variety of places. These include formal restaurants, cafés, hotels, resorts, hospitals, corporations, and schools. Some chefs train at independent cooking schools. Others graduate from two-year or four-year college programs in hospitality or culinary arts.

Authority
The power to enforce rules

When your friends show negative behaviors or have a negative view toward life, you may begin to think more negatively. People who have a negative attitude are usually not as valued by their friends, teachers, and employers. Think about how you feel after you have interacted with someone who is very negative. How is that different from how you feel after you interact with someone who is very positive? Attitudes and behaviors can catch on. Try to demonstrate positive behaviors and attitudes rather than negative ones.

How Can I Resolve Conflict?

Even when you choose positive-thinking friends, conflicts can arise. Relationships are complicated. It can be easy to have your feelings hurt. It can be just as easy to hurt someone else's feelings. However, you can learn to handle conflict situations effectively. Conflict will occur in school and it will occur when you are at work. It is just part of life. The key to handling these situations is in what you do when a negative interaction happens.

The first response you might have to conflict is anger. This is normal. But acting on that anger may make the problem worse. When someone makes you angry, try to stay calm. Take a deep breath or count silently to 10. This will give you time to collect your thoughts before reacting. Let the other person know how you feel, but do not attack the other person. If you hurt another person's feelings, apologize. When people try to communicate well and show respect, the result is almost always positive.

How Should I Interact with Authority Figures?

So far, you have learned how to have good relationships with your friends. You must also communicate well with parents, teachers, and work supervisors. These people have roles of **authority** in your life. Knowing how to communicate effectively with people in authority is important. Some people find it is hard to accept advice and directions from others. They might react with anger when they are "told what to do." People in authority roles have the power to make decisions regarding rules and behavior. In fact, it is their job to do so.

Body/Kinesthetic

If your class has students who have been trained in student conflict resolution, you may want to have volunteers model methods of resolving conflict. Students can role-play individuals in conflict while mediators work to find out the nature of the problem (what it is about, what caused it), help them understand each other's point of view (what each believes is true), and try to work out a compromise (what it will take to satisfy each party).

AT HOME

Encourage students to evaluate their communication style in their interactions with parents or guardians. Explain that these authority figures usually make and enforce rules designed to benefit a young person in the long run. Students might list rules they feel are unfair and ask a parent or guardian to explain each rule's purpose. Remind students of the need to listen carefully with an open mind instead of thinking of how they want to respond while the other person is talking. If students feel unable to sustain a calm dialogue, they might write their response. Suggest that they first write down what they understand about the adult's purpose.

Express your opinion respectfully if you disagree with someone in authority.

You are expected to work and live by the rules. If you are not clear about a rule or decision, speak up. Respectfully ask the person in authority to explain why an action was taken. If you think a rule or decision is unfair, explain why you think so in a respectful way. As you have learned, it is important to respect everyone. It is possible to disagree with people and also show them respect.

Living and working with others is not always easy. You need to respect other people. Listen to them when they talk to you. If you have a disagreement with someone, stay calm. Let that person know how you feel, and do so respectfully. You will find it is easier to live and work with others if you treat them well.

Lesson 4 Review Write your answers to these questions on a sheet of paper.

1. Why is learning to work well with others an important job skill?

2. What are some ways to show respect when you are talking with someone?

3. Suppose a person in authority takes an action with which you disagree. Describe the best way to communicate with the person.

4. Think of a time when you had a disagreement with an authority figure in your life. Did you act respectfully? If not, how might you have responded differently to show your respect?

Gender and Careers

American women did not have equal rights in education for many years. Harvard, the first college in America, was founded in 1636. It admitted only men. Many people felt that women should focus on taking care of children and the home. In fact, many felt that women were unfit for both physical and mental exercise. But in 1833, Oberlin Collegiate Institute opened. It was the first college for both men and women in the United States. In 1837, Mary Lyon founded Mount Holyoke Female Seminary. This was one of the first colleges for women in the United States. Many women who graduated from Mount Holyoke became teachers. In 1910, only 2.7 percent of American women had completed four or more years of college. By 2000, this number had risen to 25.6 percent. In comparison, in 2000, 27.8 percent of men had completed four years of college.

Lesson 4 Review Answers

1. You will have some contact with people in all jobs. People have many differences that can make communication challenging.

2. Treat others as you would like to be treated; listen to people carefully; learn about other people and their values.

3. Question the person respectfully and explain why you disagree respectfully.

4. Answers will vary.

Gender and Careers

Have volunteers read the Gender and Careers feature on page 181 aloud. Have students who are interested research the history of Oberlin College or Mount Holyoke Female Seminary. You may want to suggest that they compile a list of famous graduates and their accomplishments.

LEARNING STYLES

Logical/Mathematical
Have students use the data in the Gender and Careers feature on page 181 to answer the following questions: *How long have males in the United States been able to attend college in America?* (since 1636, or ____ years) *How long have females in the United States been able to attend college?* (since 1833, or ____ years) *How many years from this date did it take until the percent of women in college rose to 2.7 percent?* (1910 − 1833 = 77 years) *How many years did it take for the rate to rise from 2.7 percent to 25.6 percent?* (2000 − 1910 = 90 years) Have students make a graph showing the dramatic increase in education for women and offer reasons why the number of women going to college grew so quickly in the twentieth century. (*Possible answer: Women had fewer children. It became acceptable socially for women to work.*)

Conducting an Informational Interview

This activity expands on the networking interview suggested on pages 167–170 of Lesson 2. You may want to have students use the Portfolio Activity framework and questions as they complete the networking interview, or wait until they have finished reading the chapter and combine the two sets of directions.

Suggest that students write each question for the interview on a separate index card. This will allow them space to jot down notes about the response to each question and keep the cards in order. Students might also number their cards to be sure they can keep them in the proper order.

If students want to use a tape recorder, explain that they must ask the interviewee's permission. They should also practice operating the tape recorder before the interview so that it does not become a distraction during the interview.

Portfolio Activity

Conducting an Informational Interview

Identify a company or organization that employs people in a career that you would like to enter. Now, identify a person within the company or organization in a career area of your choice. Contact this person and ask for an interview. If there is nobody in your region in the career area you want to explore, try to identify someone in a related career. For example, if you want to be a music director, you might interview a band or choir teacher at your school.

Introduce yourself to the person you are interviewing with a firm handshake.

Ask the following questions during the interview. Write down the interviewee's answers. Include this information in your Career Portfolio.

1. How did you get into this occupation?
2. What attracted you to this career/organization?
3. What is the way people usually begin in this career area?
4. What does the company expect you to do in your job?
5. What are your company's products, services offered, customers, and competitors?

182 *Chapter 6   Opportunities in Your Community*

Name _____ Date _____ Period _____ Portfolio Activity, Page 1
Chapter 6   6

Conducting an Informational Interview

Use this form to record the interviewee's answers during the interview.

1. How did you get into this occupation?
2. What attracted you to this career/organization?
3. How do people usually begin in this career area?
4. What are your job responsibilities?
5. What products and services does your company offer? Who are your customers? your competitors?
6. What essential abilities and skills do you need to do your job?
7. What preparation and training are required for your position?
8. What personal satisfaction do you get from your job?
9. What's it like to work here? How is the morale?
10. What personal traits are helpful to succeed in your position?

Name _____ Date _____ Period _____ Portfolio Activity, Page 2
Chapter 6   6

Conducting an Informational Interview, continued

11. Are there things that create dissatisfaction in this type of work? What are they?
12. Can you tell me anything else about the working conditions? For example, are there dress codes? Does this work require a lot of extra hours?
13. What is the beginning wage? Do you get yearly raises?
14. Who makes the decisions and how are they made in this company/organization?
15. Describe your typical work day.
16. Are there any opportunities to work part-time or during the summer?
17. Has the company experienced a lot of growth in the past few years?
18. Do you have any additional advice for me?
19. May I contact you again if I have other questions?
20. Is there anyone else you think I should talk with? Is it alright if I tell them that you suggested I contacted them?

6. What are the essential abilities and skills you need to do your job?

7. What is the preparation and training required for your position?

8. What personal satisfactions do you get from doing your job?

9. What is it like to work at this company? Do you need to work with many different people? Is there good morale in your company?

10. What personal traits are helpful to succeed in your position?

11. What creates dissatisfaction in this type of work?

12. Can you tell me about working conditions that I should be aware of? For example, what is the dress code? Does the job require extra work after hours?

13. What is the beginning wage? Do you get yearly raises?

14. Who makes the decisions and how are they made in this company/organization?

15. What is a typical day like working here?

16. Are there any opportunities to work part-time or during the summer?

17. Is this company/organization going to grow? Or, will this company get smaller in the future?

18. Do you have any advice for me?

19. Could I contact you again if I have other questions?

20. Could you suggest someone else I might talk with? Could I use your name as the person who suggested I contact him or her?

Conclude by thanking the person for the interview. Ask if he or she has a business card or at least be sure to get his or her correct title and address to send a thank-you note.

Point out to students that some questions may need to be adapted or tailored to the job of the particular interviewee. For example, in question 5, do not ask about products if the person offers a service. He or she may not have customers, but students, clients, or patients.

Point out that several questions, such as numbers 3, 16, 19, and 20, may provide leads for gaining experience as a part-time or volunteer worker with this business or institution or with a related one. You may want to suggest that students highlight these questions and be prepared to pursue opportunities that the interviewee mentions. If the interviewer is not in a position to work part-time with this business or institution, then he or she should respond graciously and clearly indicate interest for the future.

When students have completed their interviews, allow class time for them to share the outcomes and to write thank-you notes. You may also want to have them write a follow-up evaluation of their interview technique. They can summarize what they did well, what they could have done better, and what they would avoid doing next time.

Portfolio Activity Answers

1.–20. Answers will vary.

Chapter 6 Review

Use the Chapter Review to prepare students for tests and to reteach content from the chapter.

Chapter 6 Mastery Test

The Teacher's Resource Library includes two forms of the Chapter 1 Mastery Test. Each test addresses the chapter Goals for Learning. An optional third page of additional critical-thinking items is included for each test. The difficulty level of the two forms is equivalent.

Review Answers
Vocabulary Review

1. internship 2. attitude 3. core services 4. networking 5. authority 6. informational interview

Concept Review

7. C 8. D 9. B 10. D 11. D

Chapter 6 REVIEW

Word Bank
attitude
authority
core services
informational interview
internship
networking

Vocabulary Review

Choose the word or phrase from the Word Bank that best completes each sentence. Write the answer on your paper.

1. Working for an employer for a specified period of time to learn about an occupation is a(n) _____.

2. How someone thinks, feels, and acts is that person's _____.

3. The 11 industries a community needs in order to function are known as _____.

4. The exchange of information or services among individuals, groups, or institutions is _____.

5. The power to enforce rules is _____.

6. An opportunity to talk with someone at a business to get information is a(n) _____.

Concept Review

Choose the word or phrase that best completes each sentence or answers each question. Write the letter of the answer on your paper.

7. Which of the following is NOT a core service?
   - **A** transportation
   - **C** arts
   - **B** natural resources
   - **D** sales

8. The most productive way to do a job search is _____.
   - **A** filling out applications
   - **C** mailing out résumés
   - **B** scheduling interviews
   - **D** networking

9. Many people think the most important skill for a successful career is _____.
   - **A** word processing
   - **C** public speaking
   - **B** working well with others
   - **D** computer programming

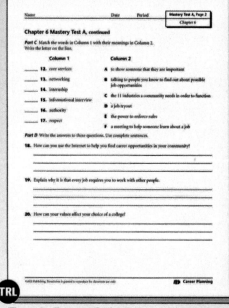

Chapter 6 Mastery Test A, Pages 1–3

10. To find out more information about a college, you could _____.

    A visit the campus   **C** ask a student at the college

    B check the college   **D** do all of these
        Web site

11. One thing people should do in all interactions with others is _____.

    A make eye contact   **C** accept advice

    B ignore conflicts   **D** show respect

Critical Thinking

Write the answer to each question on your paper.

12. A friend refuses to use networking to get a job. She wants to get hired based on her merits and not on whom she knows. Do you agree or disagree with her? Explain your thoughts.

13. Why is it important for a job seeker to know about his or her community's core services?

14. Describe some ways to be a good listener.

15. Deciding on a single career course in high school does not make sense in today's world. Explain why.

Test-Taking Tip

Do not wait until the night before a test to study. Plan your study time so that you can get a good night's sleep before a test.

Opportunities in Your Community   Chapter 6   **185**

Review Answers
Critical Thinking

12. Possible answer: You might tell the person that networking does not mean that you are using connections to get a job. It is an effective method for finding a job because it gets you in touch with people who can quickly let you know if there are hiring opportunities instead of wasting your time sending résumés to places where there are no opportunities.
13. Since you will be looking for a job in a specific community, it makes sense to know about the job opportunities that are there. 14. Focus carefully on what a person is saying instead of thinking about what you will ask or say next; consider summarizing what the person has said. 15. It does not make sense because you can change a lot after high school based on your postsecondary job and educational experiences. In addition, the world is always changing; jobs that are plentiful now may not be in 5 years.

ALTERNATIVE ASSESSMENT

- Have students list two businesses, organizations, or institutions in your community that offer part-time or volunteer opportunities in the career group that interests them and outline a plan for pursuing them

- Have students draw a diagram to illustrate how networking functions as a communication tool and use the drawing to explain why networking helps people find jobs

- Place students in small groups have them discuss, then summarize, the important steps in choosing a college that is right for them

- Ask students to write as many reasons as they can think of why it is important to get along with others

- Pair students and have partners write and perform a role-play to demonstrate effective and poor ways of resolving differences

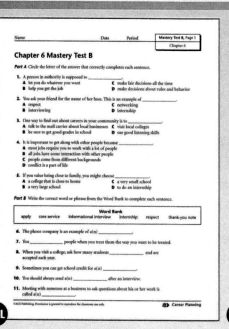

Chapter 6 Mastery Test B, Pages 1–3

7

Planning Guide

Job Training Readiness Skills

	Student Text Lesson				
	Student Pages	Vocabulary	Lesson Review	Critical-Thinking Questions	Chapter Review
Lesson 1 The Hiring Process	188–193	✔	✔	✔	✔
Lesson 2 Personal Goal Statement	194–199	✔	✔	✔	✔
Lesson 3 Writing a Résumé	200–210	✔	✔	✔	✔
Lesson 4 Getting References	211–213	✔	✔	✔	✔

Chapter Activities

Student Text
Chapter 7 Portfolio Activity

Teacher's Resource Library
Chapter 7 Chapter Outline
Chapter 7 Self-Study Guide
Chapter 7 Portfolio Activity

Assessment Options

Student Text
Chapter 7 Review

Teacher's Resource Library
Chapter 7 Mastery Tests A and B

Teacher's Edition
Chapter 7 Alternative Assessment

	Student Text Features											Teaching Strategies					Learning Styles					Teacher's Resource Library				
Portfolio Activity	Writing Practice	Communication Connection	The Economy	Career Tip	Career Profile	On the Job	Gender and Careers	Think Positive	Technology Note	Get Involved	Background Information	Applications (Home, Community, Global, Environment)	Personal Journal	Online Connection	ELL/ESL Strategy	Visual/Spatial	Body/Kinesthetic	Interpersonal/Group Learning	Logical/Mathematical	Auditory/Verbal	Activities	Alternative Activities	Workbook Activities	Self-Study Guide	Chapter Outline
		193				189		191			191	189, 190, 193	192		189		192		191	190	33	33	33	✔	✔
	195											196				198		197	196	199	34	34	34	✔	✔
				202	205		208		210		202, 205	201, 202, 208	204	203	201, 209	206	207	203	207, 209	204	35	35	35	✔	✔
214	212									213					212					212	36	36	36	✔	✔

Alternative Activities

The Teacher's Resource Library (TRL) contains a set of lower-level worksheets called Alternative Activities. These worksheets cover the same content as the regular Activities but are written at a second-grade reading level.

Career Interest Inventory

The AGS Publishing Harrington-O'Shea Career Decision-Making System (CDM) may be used with this textbook. Students can use the CDM to explore their interests and identify careers. The CDM defines career areas that are indicated by students' response on the inventory.

Chapter 7:
Job Training Readiness Skills
pages 186–217

Lessons

Portfolio Activity

Chapter Review
Audio CD 🎧

Teacher's Resource Library **TRL**

Workbook Activities 33–36

Activities 33–36

Alternative Activities 33–36

Portfolio Activity 7

Chapter 7 Chapter Outline

Chapter 7 Self-Study Guide

Chapter 7 Mastery Tests A and B
(Answer Keys for the Teacher's
Resource Library begin on page 328
of this Teacher's Edition.)

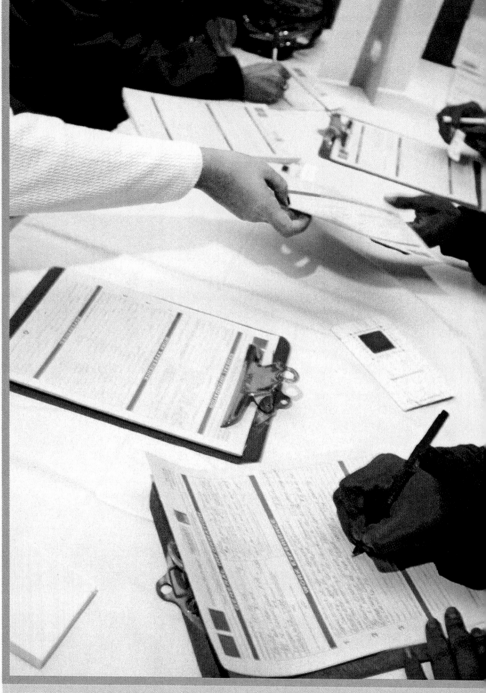

Chapter 7 Self-Study Guide

Chapter

7 Job Training Readiness Skills

Paperwork is a part of every job search. Whether it is filling out a job application, preparing a résumé, or taking a skills test, you will need to write. Good writing will go a long way toward helping you get the job you want. Making the best impression during the hiring process requires plenty of research and preparation. While your self-assessment has been helping you think about careers you might pursue, it has also been helping you organize the information you will want to include on an application and in your résumé. You want to use this information to get an employer's attention. In this chapter, you will learn more about the hiring process and steps you need to take to apply for and get a job.

Goals for Learning

◆ To understand the hiring process

◆ To prepare a personal goal statement

◆ To learn how to write an effective résumé

◆ To obtain references

187

Introducing the Chapter

Have students look at the photo on page 186 and describe what is happening in the picture. Discuss the kinds of paperwork that need to be done when a person applies for a job. Ask students to predict why writing skills are important for getting a job. Read the chapter title and ask a volunteer to define *readiness*. Have students consider whether each of them has the readiness skills to create a résumé and apply for a job. Read the introductory paragraph together.

Have students read the Goals for Learning and attempt to answer questions such as the following:
- What are the steps in the hiring process?
- What makes a résumé effective?
- What are job references?

Write down their responses and tell students they will revisit the questions after reading the chapter to see what new information they have learned.

Career Tips

Ask volunteers to read the career tips that appear in the margins throughout the chapter. Then discuss them with the class.

Alternative Assessment

The Alternative Assessment box on page 217 of the Chapter Review includes activities using various learning styles to assess students' understanding of the Goals for Learning.

Name _____ Date _____ Period _____ Chapter Outline, Page 1 — Chapter 7 [7]

Job Training Readiness Skills

Directions Fill in the outline below. Filling in the blanks will help you as you read and study Chapter 7.

I. **Lesson 1: The Hiring Process (pp. 188–193)**

A. **The Process of Hiring**
1. Getting a number of applicants for a position is called _____
2. Employers reject résumés that are _____ and disorganized.
3. In the _____ process, employers choose applicants.

B. **What Employers Ask During an Interview**
1. Employers will ask questions to find out if the applicant has the knowledge and _____ for the job.

C. **Other Expectations of Employers**
1. You may need to do some _____ about the job requirements to show your interest in the job.

D. **After the Interview**
1. Usually, the manager or _____ of the department with the job opening will call you if you get the job.

II. **Lesson 2: Personal Goal Statement (pp. 194–199)**

A. **Importance of a Personal Goal Statement**
1. A clear _____ is the first step for a job search.

B. **Contents of a Personal Goal Statement**
1. Start with your _____ and present situation.
2. Then you describe your _____
3. Include the _____ you have now, and the ones you still need.
4. Also include the _____ goals you should complete on the way to your career goal.

TRL ©AGS Publishing. Permission is granted to reproduce for classroom use only. ▶ Career Planning

---

Name _____ Date _____ Period _____ Chapter Outline, Page 2 — Chapter 7 [7]

Job Training Readiness Skills, continued

III. **Lesson 3: Writing a Résumé (pp. 200–210)**

A. **Starting to Prepare a Résumé**
1. Keep a record of _____ you have worked.
2. Use _____ to state your skills on your résumé.

B. **Different Types of Résumés**
1. The _____ résumé focuses on education and work history going backward in time.
2. The _____ résumé focuses on the job tasks or skills the applicant can perform.

C. **Information in a Résumé**
1. The career objective of a résumé states your career _____
2. In the _____ section, mention courses you've taken that relate to the job.
3. The work history section shows that you have the _____ required.
4. Extracurricular activities, rewards, or skills that make you stand out go in the _____ section of your résumé.
5. You need to write, rewrite, and edit your résumé until it is _____

D. **The Cover Letter**
1. The purpose of a cover letter is to _____ you to the employer.

IV. **Lesson 4: Getting References (pp. 211–213)**

A. **Why You Need References**
1. Employers may _____ references before or after an interview.

B. **People Who Can Be References**
1. If you are a good worker, an ideal reference is your _____

C. **Getting Good References**
1. Only use references who will speak _____ about you.

TRL ©AGS Publishing. Permission is granted to reproduce for classroom use only. ▶ Career Planning

Chapter 7 Chapter Outline

Job Training Readiness Skills 187

Lesson at a Glance

Chapter 7 Lesson 1

Overview The lesson outlines steps in the hiring process, lists resources employers use to recruit employees, and explores effective résumés. It also discusses employers' expectations of job applicants.

Objectives

- To list ways employers recruit new employees
- To understand how employers screen for qualified job applicants
- To identify employers' expectations of job applicants
- To explain reasons for not being chosen for a job

Student Pages 188–193

Teacher's Resource Library

Workbook Activity 33

Activity 33

Alternative Activity 33

Vocabulary

recruitment   screening
résumé   selection

Write the vocabulary words on the board. Have students look them up in the glossary to learn their meanings and pronunciations. Then ask students to write a sentence using each word in context.

1 Warm-Up Activity

Display and read aloud one or two job openings described in local newspaper ads. Ask students to describe the ideal job applicant for each job. What would this applicant put on a résumé to interest employers?

2 Teaching the Lesson

Point out to students that only during the selection phase of the hiring process will the job applicant get to speak face to face with the employer. This means that the applicant must make an impression on paper in order to even be considered. Stress the importance of creating a focused, error-free résumé and filling out application forms neatly, correctly, and completely.

Résumé

A summary of knowledge, abilities, and experience that shows how a person is qualified for a particular occupation

Recruitment

Getting a number of applications from which to choose new employees

Screening

Going through a number of applications to pick out the most suitable people for a job opening

Selection

Choosing a person for a job opening

In your everyday life, you may hear about or see advertisements for jobs that you would like to get. You might see a job advertised while you are at school or work. Or you might hear or see a job advertisement when you are spending time with your friends. You probably know that in order to get a job, you need to send a **résumé** to the employer who is advertising the job. But what happens after employers receive your résumé? How do they go about selecting the person they think is the best qualified for the job? After you send your résumé, you may be nervous. You might feel as if you are in the dark as you wait to hear from the employer. However, once you know a little more about the hiring process, you can relax and continue your job search with confidence.

What Is the Hiring Process?

Not all employers have the same process for hiring people. As a result, you may have different experiences with different employers. Generally, the size of the company is a factor. Larger companies usually have a human resources department. Workers in this department are involved in the different stages of the hiring process. In smaller companies, department managers may be responsible for taking care of the entire hiring process for their departments. As a result, even within the same company, employees may be hired in different ways. In spite of these differences, there are steps in the hiring process that most employers follow. **Recruitment, screening,** and **selection** are the three basic steps in the hiring process.

Recruitment

The hiring process starts when the manager of a department needs to fill a job opening. In large companies, department managers send written requests to the human resources department. These requests state the requirements for the job and how soon a new employee is needed. The human resources department checks to see if there are any applications on file that fit the job. If there aren't any or if there aren't enough, the human resources department advertises the job opening.

Workbook Activity 33

Name _____ Date _____ Period _____ | Workbook Activity Chapter 7, Lesson 1 | 33

Hiring Process Puzzle

Directions Read each clue. Choose a word from the Word Bank to complete the puzzle.

Word Bank
dependability
hiring
Internet
interview
networking
newspaper
recruitment
résumé
screening
selection

Across

2. Getting a number of applications from which to choose new employees
5. A company may use this computer-based "bulletin board" to advertise openings
8. Going through a number of applications to pick out the most suitable people for a job opening
9. A summary of a person's knowledge, abilities, and experience
10. A meeting at which an employer asks questions

Down

1. When employers narrow the field and choose the person for the job
3. The most effective way to find job opportunities
4. The process by which jobs are filled
6. A source of many ads for jobs that may be hard to get
7. An important personal quality sought by employers

Activity 33

Name _____ Date _____ Period _____ | Activity Chapter 7, Lesson 1 | 33

The Hiring Process

Directions Write the answers to these questions. Use complete sentences.

1. What role in the hiring process does a human resources department play?

2. In small companies, who is responsible for the entire hiring process?

3. What are two reasons companies post job openings on bulletin boards for their employees?

4. Why should you respond to a newspaper ad for a job immediately?

5. Why must your résumé look good and have no typing errors?

6. Why do some companies make no response at all to a résumé?

7. What is the purpose of most questions in a job interview?

8. If an employer calls you in for an interview, how could you learn more about the company?

9. How do you usually learn if you will be offered a job?

10. Why might you not be offered a job even though you are qualified? Give two reasons.

Have you ever considered the many kinds of equipment in a typical office? Most offices contain computers, printers, copiers, fax machines, postal machines, and even coffee makers. When you have a chance to learn to use any of these machines, take it. Your skill will pay off in your job search.

Some companies list all new job openings on a bulletin board or on a Web page that contains company career opportunities. This practice helps to build employee morale by offering career advancement within the company. Letting people know about the job opening so they can apply for it is called recruitment.

Advertising in the newspaper is a common method used by employers to recruit applicants. This is an excellent way for employers to advertise because they can get the information about their job openings to a lot of people at a relatively low cost. However, you should be aware of a few things when looking for job openings in the newspaper.

First, the need for employers to reach as many people as possible may be a sign that they are having trouble keeping employees. This doesn't mean you should not respond to newspaper advertisements, but you should be aware of problems the company may be having. For example, you should be prepared to ask questions about workplace conditions, wages, and other factors that could affect your decision to accept the job.

Second, because job openings advertised in the newspaper are seen by more job seekers, the competition is much greater. The number of people applying for a job may be very high. An employer may decide to look at only the first 100 applications they receive. So you need to respond immediately to newspaper advertisements. If you don't, your résumé may not even be seen.

Finally, newspaper advertisements represent only a small percentage of available jobs. Some authorities suggest only about 20 percent of available job openings are found in help-wanted advertisements. Many employers use other ways to recruit applicants. Here are some other places where you may see or hear about job openings.

- Job fairs
- Youth centers
- Employment offices
- Business windows
- Radio
- Television
- The Internet
- People you know who are working

On the Job

Have students read the On the Job feature on page 189. Ask volunteers to describe each type of office equipment listed and explain its function(s) in an office. Survey the class to see which machines students have used.

ELL/ESL STRATEGY

Language Objective: *To use headings and emphasized text as an aid in reading for meaning*

To help English language learners comprehend the text, have them first focus on headings and bulleted lists to understand key concepts in the lesson. Show them how to use the heads and subheads as anchors in an outline:

I. The Hiring Process
  A. What is it?
    1. _____
    2. _____
  B. Recruitment
    1. _____
    2. _____
    3. _____
  C. Screening
    1. _____
    2. _____
    3. _____
  D. Selection
    1. _____
    2. _____

As they read, students can fill in their outlines by writing in important supporting details from the text. If necessary, pair each ELL student with an English proficient partner to complete the outline.

IN THE COMMUNITY

Ask students to study a local newspaper, contact an employment office, and canvas likely local businesses to learn how local job opportunities are advertised. Students with access to the Internet can find Web sites that list available jobs in your area. Suggest that student try to locate local companies' Web pages of job listings. Have students report their findings to the class.

Finding job openings in the newspaper may be easy. There may be a lot of jobs listed. However, you should not focus your efforts on newspaper advertisements alone. Remember that networking, discussed in Chapter 6, is the most effective way to find a job.

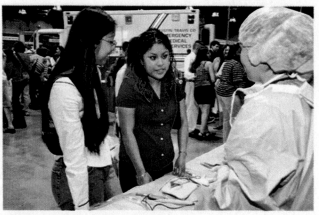

You can find out about job openings at job fairs.

No matter where you see or hear about a job advertisement, you must make sure you read it carefully. Look for clues that tell you what an employer really wants. An employer might expect applicants to have knowledge of a specific computer language, good communication skills, or a willingness to work flexible hours.

Screening

The next step in the hiring process is screening. When employers begin looking at the applications and résumés they have received, they are screening for a qualified applicant. The more résumés an employer receives, the longer time screening takes. To save time, employers may spend less than a minute reviewing each résumé. Employers expect résumés to be organized. They should have correct spelling, punctuation, and grammar. Employers quickly reject résumés that are sloppy and disorganized.

Employers also want to be able to tell quickly which applicants have the basic qualifications for the job. If your résumé highlights important information, you are more likely to be considered for the job. Employers receive so many applications for each job that they often don't have the time to respond to every applicant. Many employers respond only to those applicants who have been selected for an interview.

Selection

After employers narrow down the number of résumés, they begin looking more closely at the job applicants. They compare the qualifications of applicants. They contact applicants' employers to verify work history. Then, they choose the applicants they would like to interview. In the interview, employers can collect more information about an applicant. Then, they make their final selection for who will fill the job. Usually, the manager or person who will be supervising the new employee will be involved in the interview. That person will either do the interview alone or will be a member of the team that is doing the interview.

What Will Employers Ask During an Interview?

Employers usually ask questions to verify that the applicants have the knowledge, skills, and other requirements that are needed for the job. To get that kind of information, employers may ask applicants what they would do in certain situations. Besides knowledge and skills, employers will also try to find out which applicant has the qualities they are looking for. Here are some qualities that employers would expect job applicants to have.

- Dependability
- Leadership
- Creativity
- Positive attitude
- Willingness to learn new skills
- Passion for doing excellent work
- Ability to work with others

What Else Do Employers Expect from Applicants?

Employers will also expect applicants to be familiar with the job requirements. If you hear about the job from a friend, for example, it is important for you to find out specifics about the requirements you need to have. Some employers may even expect applicants to have some knowledge of the company. This means taking the time to do some "homework" that will show your interest in working there. You can learn what a typical work day is like at the company by talking to people who work there. You can also read brochures that the company uses to recruit applicants. The interview is the last opportunity you have to let the employer know that you are the best person for the job.

What Happens After the Interview?

After your interview is finished, you may be told how many other people are being interviewed for the position. You will also learn how long you will have to wait for the final decision. If the number of applicants is small and you did well in your interview, you may receive a call on the same day. Usually, the manager or supervisor of the department with the job opening decides who to hire. That person will call you if he or she wants to offer you the job.

If you don't get the job, the hiring manager may call you to tell you so. Or, the employer may send you a letter saying so. If your interview went well, you might not know why you did not get the job. Sometimes, the hiring manager may tell you the reasons they hired someone else. However, employers usually are not specific in their letters about the reason why applicants did not get the job. They may briefly state that they had many well-qualified people apply for the job.

Sometimes, you will not get offered a job, even if you are qualified. You may never know why you didn't get called for an interview or why your interview was not successful. Many factors in the hiring process are beyond your control. These factors include the reason why an employer advertised a specific job opening, the amount of time an employer has to screen applicants, and the interviewer's personal opinions about qualities necessary for the job. You may not be aware of any of these things when you apply for the job.

It can be discouraging when you don't get a job you thought was perfect for you. However, it is important for you to continue your job search. A well-planned job search will help you find suitable job openings in your career area.

Lesson 1 Review Write your answers to these questions on a sheet of paper.

1. How does the hiring process of larger companies differ from that of smaller companies?

2. What are two reasons that newspaper ads may not be the best way to find a job?

3. What are some reasons that you may not get a job for which you are qualified?

The Economy

City or suburbs? Not only individuals, but companies too, must make this decision. In the early 1900s, most large companies were located in big cities. In the 1950s and 1960s, many people moved out of cities into nearby suburbs. Soon more and more people had to commute into cities to work. Many companies moved to the suburbs too. This made them attractive to employees. Workers could live near their work. They could save time and money on commuting.

Today some companies that had moved to the suburbs are moving back to cities. They find that many creative people like living in cities more than in suburbs. For example, one company moved into a poor area of Baltimore. Many of the company's employees wanted to be near the city's cultural attractions. The company also hired some people from nearby neighborhoods. These workers appreciated the steady jobs with good wages. The company participated in community projects such as tutoring. Soon the neighborhood improved, and the company's profits increased. Moving to the city was a plus for everyone.

Lesson 1 Review Answers

1. Larger companies often have a human resources department that handles employment for the whole company, while in smaller companies department managers may take care of employment for their departments.

2. A company that is trying to reach a very wide audience may be having trouble keeping employees; and a very large number of people responds to newspaper ads, so competition is stiff.

3. Many factors in the hiring process are beyond an applicant's control, such as the amount of time an employer has to hire someone, the interviewer's personal opinions, and the large number of applicants.

The Economy

Invite students to give their impressions about jobs available in a city versus those available in the suburbs or rural areas. Discuss changes they have observed in a city in your state or area. Is there more economic growth in the city or in smaller communities? Have students read the Economy feature on page 193. Have students name some pros and cons about working in a city. Then have them do the same for jobs in the suburbs and in rural areas. Write their ideas in a chart on the board.

IN THE ENVIRONMENT

Initiate a discussion about the environmental issues of living and working in a city versus the suburbs. Factors that might be mentioned include air and water quality, noise level, and amount of artificial light. While large cities generally offer more opportunities than smaller cities and towns, they also tend to be more expensive, crowded, noisy, and polluted. Ask interested students to research statistics about population density, pollution, waste management, and other environmental quality concerns in your area.

Chapter 7 Lesson 2

Overview This lesson defines the personal goal statement and explains information included in each part of the statement. It also displays a sample personal goal statement.

Objectives

- To understand how a personal goal statement helps one identify steps to be taken to achieve the goal
- To list parts of a personal goal statement and identify parts related to lifestyle and personal values

Student Pages 194–199

Teacher's Resource Library

   Workbook Activity 34

   Activity 34

   Alternative Activity 34

Vocabulary

personal goal statement
personal resources

Write the vocabulary terms on the board and ask students to predict their meanings based on the meanings of the words in each phrase. Then read the definitions aloud. Have students skim the lesson to find clues about the kinds of information included in a personal goal statement and the types of qualities called personal resources.

 Warm-Up Activity

Ask students why it is important to know the steps to take in order to reach a goal, such as running in a 10K race or starting a rock band. (*Students may suggest that a person will never reach the goal if he or she does not proceed through the steps one by one.*) Point out that the list of steps gives direction and helps the person keep moving toward a goal. Explain that students will learn how to construct a personal goal statement in this lesson.

Personal goal statement

A description of a career goal along with the knowledge, abilities, skills, and personal values that are related to the goal

When you are going on a road trip, you need a road map. A road map guides you on your trip. It shows you how far away your destination is. It also shows the various routes you can take to get there. A map even shows places where you can stop along the way.

What Is a Personal Goal Statement?

A **personal goal statement** is similar to a road map. It helps you to reach the goal you have in mind. The goal may be to change a specific behavior, increase your grade point average, get a specific job, or gain admission to college. A personal goal statement also contains information that makes it easy for you to identify the various things you may need to learn or do in order to achieve the goals you have in mind.

Personal goal statements are useful in many parts of your life. In this lesson you will learn how to prepare a personal goal statement that will help you reach your career goal. A clear and focused personal goal statement is the first step for a successful job search.

A personal goal statement can be a guide, much like a road map.

So far, you have done self-assessment and career research activities. These activities helped you to identify the careers you would like to pursue. In selecting those careers, you collected some important information. You identified your favorite school subjects, your abilities, and your personal values. You also learned about the occupations and jobs that are available in the career that interests you. With the information about yourself and the careers you chose, you are ready to prepare your personal goal statement.

What Is Included in a Personal Goal Statement?

Your personal goal statement will include the following sections:
- Your name and present situation
- A description of your career goal or the job you would like to have
- The knowledge, abilities, skills, and personal values required for the career goal or job
- The knowledge, skills, abilities, and personal values you have
- The requirements you still need to get to achieve the career goal or get the job
- In-between or short-term goals to be achieved in order to reach your career goal

Name and Present Situation

In this section you may use your educational level, employment position, or volunteer experience to indicate your present situation. For example, you may describe your situation as middle school student, cashier at a store, high school student, or volunteer community organizer.

Writing Practice

Where you want to live is an important lifestyle decision. It affects your career goals. Write a comparison and contrast of city, suburban, and country living. Discuss the positive and negative features of each kind of living as you see them.

2 Teaching the Lesson

The personal goal statement builds upon the Portfolio Activities completed by students in Chapter 2 (Self-Assessment Profile) and Chapter 5 (Career Plan). You may wish to have students reread their copies of these Portfolio Activities and note any information that will be helpful in creating a personal goal statement about a career: abilities, skills, and values, for example.

Remind students that the *Occupational Outlook Handbook* (OOH) provides information about the knowledge, abilities, skills, and personal values required for many different careers.

The Portfolio Activity on pages 214–215 directs students in creating a personal goal statement. You may refer them to these pages whenever you feel they are ready to write their personal goal statements—when they complete Lesson 2 or after completing the chapter.

3 Reinforce and Extend

Writing Practice

Before they write, suggest that students create a three-column chart to organize pros and cons of city, suburban, and rural living:

	City	Suburbs	Country
Pros			
Cons			

You may want to have students share their conclusions in small groups. Remind them that what is positive for one person may be negative for another person.

Students may not have considered lifestyle decisions before. Suggest that they use the bulleted list of questions on page 196 to approach adults at home or relatives and friends with whom they can communicate easily. By matching answers with the careers of the adults, students can begin to deduce patterns that fit certain careers. For example, a person who places great value on helping others and less value on a high income might be happy working as the director of a local nonprofit volunteer organization.

LEARNING STYLES

Logical/Mathematical
Have students consider the implications of their answers to the lifestyle questions on page 196. For questions they rank as being very important, have students ask themselves, "How well does my chosen career goal match this value?" For example, if financial success is very important, does the career outlook seem promising and the earning capacity above average? If involvement in many activities is important, does the desired career demand attention to many different tasks? If students find their career goals do not help them meet important lifestyle goals, they may need to reconsider their choices.

Description of Your Career Goal or Job

This section contains the description of the goal you are focusing on. It may be to get a part-time job or to gain admission to a college. You may also write the description for a career goal that is further into the future, after you have finished college.

When you write the description of your goal, you want to make sure that the description of your goal is as complete as possible. There are two ways to make sure that this happens. First, try to be as specific as you can be about your goal. For example, if your goal is to become a nurse, in what area of nursing do you want to work? Do you want to be a nurse who takes care of babies, the elderly, or patients who just had an operation? Or, if you want to work as a salesperson, would you prefer to work in a sports, electronic, or general department store? When you make the description of your goal specific, it helps you to see more clearly the knowledge, abilities, and skills you already have. It also helps you identify the knowledge, skills, and abilities you need to reach your goal.

Lifestyle is the second point to consider when you want to make sure that the description of your goal is as complete as possible. Your lifestyle is the kind of life you live as a result of the personal values you have. Often, the jobs people have and the lifestyle they live are closely related. Here are some lifestyle questions to consider:

- How important to you is helping to make things better for others?
- How important to you is spending time with your family?
- Does involvement in a lot of different activities make your life more satisfying?
- Do you prefer to live in the city, suburbs, or a rural area?
- How important to you are financial success and fame?

When the description of your goal includes lifestyle information, you get a better chance to see how all the requirements of your goal may fit together in the best way for you.

Requirements for Your Career Goal or Job

You use this section to record the requirements needed for the job or career goal you described earlier. The requirements include the knowledge, abilities, skills, and lifestyle that are necessary for the career or job you identify as your goal. You may organize these requirements in your own way under various headings such as Knowledge, Abilities/Skills, and Lifestyle/Personal Values. The more you know about what your goal requires, the more confident you will be later when you are checking off the requirements you already have and getting an idea of how much learning you have ahead of you.

Your Personal Resources

Your **personal resources** are all the skills, abilities, knowledge, personal qualities, and values that you have learned and developed over the years. You already have much of the information for this section from the self-assessment activities you did in Chapter 2 of this textbook. Review the information you collected about your interests, abilities, school subjects, volunteer and work experience, and personal values. Add more information if you can.

Skills Needed

Compare the requirements of your career goal and your personal resources. What skills or experience do you still need to get? For example, suppose your career goal requires you to have computer skills. You don't have the skills required. You will need to get computer skills.

LEARNING STYLES

Interpersonal/ Group Learning

After students have reviewed their personal resources information from the Chapter 2 Self-Assessment Profile, have them list the specific skills and knowledge they need to acquire to meet their career goals. Students can form small groups based on similar needs. Have groups research opportunities at school or in the community that allow them to gain needed skills or knowledge. For example, at school, students might learn of extracurricular activities, committees, and volunteer opportunities. In the community, students might discover internship opportunities with a company or volunteer opportunities for a local chapter of a nonprofit organization or charity. Have each group write a summary report of the possibilities it discovers.

Visual/Spatial

Some students may have only a general idea of the type of field that attracts them, such as health care or sales. These students might list several possible careers within this field and design a graphic organizer to show steps they could take to reach each goal from their present situations. Students might also add drawings or clippings and photographs from magazines around their graphic organizers to represent the work-place, lifestyle, tools, and tasks that fit each career. Ask students to use their graphic organizers to explain how each career path differs and which is most appealing to them at this stage in their lives.

Steps to Reach Your Career Goal or Job

This section is useful for making a note of the in-between goal or goals that you need to fulfill before you achieve your main career goal. For example, to get the computer skills you need for a job you might take a computer class or read a book. Or, if you want a job at a department store, you might first need to get retail experience at a fast food or convenience store. Getting a job at a fast food or convenience store becomes an in-between goal.

If you have a long-term plan to get the job you want, that is excellent. However, it is okay if you have only an idea of the career you would like to pursue. You may have chosen a career in the social service area but you are not sure if you want to become a social worker, a counselor, or a psychologist. Your personal goal at this point may be to get a job in which you can learn about the social service field after you graduate from high school. You can write an effective personal goal statement for that goal.

As you get ready to prepare your personal goal statement, remember that your idea of where you want to end up in life may change. As circumstances change in your life, they may influence your personal goal. For example, you may plan on becoming a professional sports player. Later, you may realize that you would rather be a high school coach. Or you may plan on becoming an English teacher. Later, you discover that you would rather use your creativity to be a writer. You may even change careers completely. It is not unusual for someone to change careers several times. It is important to remember that your personal goal statement is an indication of where you want to be in the future. You can change it as your goals change. You can add to and reshape your personal goal statement as you move toward your goal in life.

Look at the example of a personal goal statement on page 199. It shows how you can arrange information in each section.

Personal Goal Statement

Name and Present Situation • Miko Tanaguchi • Student • Employed as a cashier at local convenience store *Description of Career Goal or Job* A part-time sales position in the clothing section of a department store within walking distance of my home or on bus route *Requirements for Career Goal or Job* Knowledge: • High school • Clothing/fashion • Dealing with cash, credit cards, and personal checks Abilities/Skills: • Dealing with the public • Good spoken and written communication • Measuring clothing for alteration Lifestyle/Personal Values: • Shift work • Weekend work • Well-groomed	*Personal Resources* Knowledge: • High school senior • Top of my class in English language arts • Cash registers, computer programming, Excel Abilities/Skills: • Experience dealing with the public • Good written and spoken communication skills Lifestyle/Personal Values: • Like variety in activities • Like talking to people • Like looking well-dressed • Honest • No car but can get a ride sometimes *Skills Needed* Abilities/Skills: • Measuring clothes for alteration • Credit cards and personal checks transactions *Steps to Reach Career Goal or Job* Not applicable

Lesson 2 Review Write your answers to these questions on a sheet of paper.

1. What is a personal goal statement?

2. Explain why your personal goal statement might include an in-between goal.

3. How does this statement relate to lifestyle and personal values?
   > I want a part-time position in a community center in which I can lead exercise programs. I prefer working with the elderly.

Lesson 2 Review Answers

1. A personal goal statement is a description of a career goal that includes knowledge, skills, abilities, and personal values.

2. You may have things to learn or training jobs to do before you have the skills or experience necessary for your ultimate job goal.

3. Part-time relates to the lifestyle value of weekend work. Exercise programs relates to the personal value of being healthy and fit. Working with the elderly relates to the personal value of helping others.

Lesson at a Glance

Chapter 7 Lesson 3

Overview In this lesson, students learn what to include in a résumé and different methods of organizing a résumé.

Objectives

- To identify information needed in a résumé
- To contrast different methods of organizing a résumé
- To list information needed in a résumé
- To explain what a cover letter is and what it contains

Student Pages 200–210

Teacher's Resource Library TRL

Workbook Activity 35

Activity 35

Alternative Activity 35

Vocabulary

action verb
chronological résumé
functional résumé

Have a volunteer look up *résumé* in a dictionary and explain the history of the word. (Résumé *is the past participle of the French verb* resumer, *which means "to summarize."*) Ask students to explain what the noun means in American usage. (*a document listing one's history and accomplishments in order to get a job*) Write the vocabulary terms on the board and read their meanings aloud. Have students explain how they think each term is related to writing a résumé.

 Warm-Up Activity

Print the sample résumés on pages 206 and 207, or distribute sample résumés from another source. Have students look at them and point out similarities and differences. Ask students to imagine they are employers. What information would they want to see on a job applicant's résumé? Have them read the lesson to find out what a résumé contains.

Action verb
A word that shows action

Writing a résumé is an important part of preparing to search for a job. Your résumé represents the skills, accomplishments, and qualifications that you want employers to know about you. The purpose of your résumé is to convince employers that you are the person they should hire. If your résumé gets you an interview, it means you were successful in preparing an effective résumé. You presented yourself as qualified for the job that you are seeking. In this lesson, you will learn how to prepare an effective résumé.

How Do I Start to Prepare a Résumé?

To prepare a good résumé, you need to do some planning. In Lesson 2, you wrote your personal goal statement. This included a description of the occupation or job you would like to have. You also identified the qualifications that the occupation or job requires. You will need to use this information as you write your résumé.

You will also need to gather information about your past employment, related experiences, awards, and accomplishments. You can mention these things in your résumé. Keep a record of places you have worked and the job titles you had. Note the exact dates you worked at each job. Keeping careful records will help you make sure that there are no mistakes in your résumé.

You may have made a list of your skills. Now you need to identify examples of places where you've used your skills. Stating the skills you used during employment is very effective on a résumé. Employers are interested in the skills you have used while on the job. What you say is important, but how you say it is just as important. In stating your skills, use language that highlights them. One way to do so is to use **action verbs**. Look at the list of common action verbs on page 201. Keep the list nearby as you write your résumé.

What Are the Different Types of Résumés?

There are many ways to present your qualifications in a résumé. However, most résumés can be grouped into three types: chronological, functional, and combination.

| Name | Date | Period | Workbook Activity Chapter 7, Lesson 3 **35** |

Organizing a Résumé

Directions The chart below shows information in a functional résumé. Use the items in the Answer Bank to complete the résumé. Write the correct items on the lines.

Answer Bank
- Administrative: operate cash registers and make accurate change
- Experience in food-service and restaurant industries
- 2002–2003: Crew member, Megaburger, Inc., Oak Park, Illinois
- Flexible, well organized, and reliable
- Graduated from Central High School, Oak Park, Illinois, 2004
- 2003–present: Host/cashier, Alice's Family Restaurant, Oak Park, Illinois
- Public contact: greet customers and serve them in a friendly, efficient way
- Professional attitude and excellent communications skills
- Restaurant organization: distribute seating appropriately, manage customers, wait staff, and cash register effectively
- Seeking a position as host at a fine-dining restaurant in the Chicago area

Emily A. Seeker
411 Career Street
Oak Park IL 60302

Career Objective
1.

Summary of Qualifications
2.
3.
4.

Relevant Skills and Experience
5.
6.
7.

Employment History
8.
9.

Education
10.

TRL

Workbook Activity 35

| Name | Date | Period | Activity Chapter 7, Lesson 3 **35** |

Writing a Résumé

Directions Match the words in Column 1 with the descriptions in Column 2. Write the letter on the line.

Column 1	Column 2
___ 1. action verbs	A These show participation outside of school that may interest an employer.
___ 2. career objective	B This section of a résumé shows the schools you attended.
___ 3. chronological	C This type of résumé combines the format of both chronological and functional résumés.
___ 4. combination	D This is often the result of an effectively written résumé.
___ 5. cover letter	E These need not appear on a résumé unless they apply directly to a job.
___ 6. disabilities	F This part of a résumé briefly states a career goal or position.
___ 7. editing	G Other activities, skills, and awards can be include in this section.
___ 8. education	H This one-page introduction is sent out with your résumé.
___ 9. extracurricular activities	I This type of résumé focuses on skills you acquired from your experiences.
___ 10. functional	J Use these when writing about your skills.
___ 11. interview	K This document is meant to convince an employer that you are the right person for the job.
___ 12. personal information	L This is the step of rewriting and checking your résumé until it is perfect.
___ 13. related information	M This type of résumé shows your experience with the most recent events first.
___ 14. résumé	N Your job experience is in this part of a résumé.
___ 15. work history	O This section of a résumé tells who you are and how to reach you.

TRL

Activity 35

The **chronological résumé** focuses on education and work or volunteer history. Your education and work or volunteer history are given in chronological order with the most recent dates listed first. Your education or work history can come first depending on which one relates better to the requirements of the job you are applying for. A sample chronological résumé is shown on page 206.

The **functional résumé** focuses on skills you acquired from various experiences. Instead of focusing on individual work experiences, you put the emphasis on particular skills in such areas as dealing with the public, supervision, communication, and leadership. A sample functional résumé is shown on page 207.

The combination résumé shows specific work experiences as well as areas of skills. It combines the format of a chronological and a functional résumé.

Each of these three résumés contains basically the same information. However, the information is organized or arranged differently. You want to arrange the information to get the attention of employers. The chronological résumé is the type of résumé that most employers are familiar with, so this lesson will focus on the chronological résumé.

Common Action Verbs		
Achieved	Encouraged	Invented
Applied	Enlarged	Investigated
Arranged	Equipped	Maintained
Awarded	Established	Recorded
Built	Estimated	Researched
Coached	Examined	Reviewed
Compared	Excelled	Revised
Composed	Expanded	Scheduled
Controlled	Formed	Secured
Convinced	Grouped	Selected
Created	Guided	Sold
Designed	Handled	Solved
Developed	Improved	Succeeded
Directed	Increased	Supported
Distributed	Installed	Taught
Earned	Introduced	Translated

GLOBAL CONNECTION

Some students may aspire to international work experience. Assign interested students the task of researching the job search experiences and hiring processes in various foreign countries. For example, students might answer questions such as *What sort of résumé should a job applicant submit in Japan? What cultural considerations should a worker take into account when seeking a job in Australia? What is the cost of living in Spain? What sort of paperwork must be completed and approved for a citizen of the United States to work in Europe? in Asia?*

2 Teaching the Lesson

If it is practical, arrange for several people who have recently been hired to visit the class and share how they designed successful résumés and what kinds of cover letters they wrote.

As they read the lesson, remind students they should look not only for the parts of a résumé, they should also pinpoint what makes each part effective.

 Reinforce and Extend

ELL/ESL STRATEGY

Language Objective: *To identify and practice using common action verbs*

Students who are not native speakers of English may find English grammar and syntax considerably different from that of their first language. Explain or review the role of verbs in English sentences. Demonstrate the role of action verbs in expressing what a subject does by modeling actions of common verbs such as *walk, sit, smile,* and *wave.* Have students choose action verbs from the list on page 201 and learn their meanings. Ask students to model the actions the words express, if possible, and have them write a sentence using each verb to inform an imaginary employer about their skills. Analyze student sentences with the group to point out subject-verb placement.

What Information Is Included in a Résumé?

A résumé should contain the following information:

- Personal information
- Career objective
- Education
- Work history
- Related information

Personal Information

This section tells employers who you are and how they can contact you. Personal information appears first in your résumé. It is the section of the résumé that includes your name, address, telephone number, and your e-mail address if you have one. It is important to respond promptly to messages from someone who is considering hiring you. Therefore, you must be sure that you can get your messages from the telephone number and the e-mail address you put on your résumé.

Although the purpose of your résumé is to introduce yourself and your qualifications as clearly as possible to employers, it is not necessary to put certain information on your résumé. For example, information about your age, height, weight, gender, race, religion, and any disabilities is not necessary.

Career Objective

This section briefly states your career goal. You can use information from the personal goal statement you wrote in Lesson 2 for this section. The purpose of your career objective is to let employers know quickly the type of job you want and the qualifications you have. Employers usually read the objective first. If it catches the employer's attention, he or she is very likely to read the rest of your résumé.

It is important to write your career objective according to the job you are applying for. However, the objective is not the place to be too specific. If you are too specific about the duties you wish to perform, and such a job does not exist in the company, you may not be considered for other jobs that you might be suitable for.

In most cases, you will be sending your résumé to an employer in response to a specific job opening. In those cases, your career objective must show the employer that you have the required qualifications for that specific job. Here is an example of a career objective for a specific job and one for a more general approach.

Specific:

Seeking a position in a high school teaching grades 11 and 12 math and computer science with responsibility for coordinating the computer lab.

General:

Seeking a position teaching English in a high school that can benefit from my experience in student leadership programs and community literacy.

Education

This section lists the education you are completing or have completed. In this section, you put the names of the schools you attended with the city and state where they are located. You also include what years you attended each school. If you are completing high school, list your expected graduation date. You do not need to include any other schools. If you have attended more than one high school, include all of them and the years you attended each one. Your major subject areas or courses that are relevant to the job are also important to include here. Other information related to your education includes honors and awards received for your performance in particular courses.

It is important to take the time to think of things related to your education that could make you stand out as the best person for the job. Suppose you had a part-time job during the year or semester. You worked to gain experience in you career field. While working, you maintained a GPA of 3.5. This information would be an excellent selling point to employers. It shows that you have the ability to balance work and study. It also shows you are committed to the career you want to pursue.

ONLINE CONNECTION

There are literally thousands of sites on the Internet that discuss how to create an effective résumé. Some offer templates for different types of résumés. Have students use a search engine and key phrases such as *résumé for first job* or *guidelines for writing résumés* to find sites that can assist them as they write their first résumés. You may also want to recommend these two sites: www.easyjob.net/ and www.readyaimhired.com/

Both have extensive guidelines, explanations, and examples. Easyjob also offers a number of résumé templates.

LEARNING STYLES

Interpersonal/ Group Learning

First-time job applicants are often stumped for items to include on a résumé. Remind students that they have acquired skills as students that employers value: communication skills, speaking a second language, organizational skills, leadership skills, critical thinking and problem-solving skills, capacity to work independently (and cooperatively with others), and so on. Have students work in small groups to brainstorm a list of their skills. Be sure students use strong action verbs and phrase the skills in language that will interest employers.

In a résumé there is no room for modesty. Students may not be comfortable describing themselves in the flattering way a résumé demands. Help students brainstorm a list of adjectives and adjective phrases that describe positive personal traits. Such a list might include words such as *adaptable, alert, assertive, energetic, exceptional, experienced, flexible, helpful, persistent, practical, punctual, reliable, resourceful*. Have students use the list as a starting point to develop their own résumé word banks. Ask students to write their lists in their personal journals, and then select their five strongest personal traits and write a paragraph for each one. The paragraphs should explain how the student exhibits this trait and why it is desirable in an employee.

LEARNING STYLES

Auditory/Verbal
Model for students how a résumé is developed. Ask them to choose a popular cartoon character or book character and invent a "job" for which this character will apply. Brainstorm with students to create lists of qualifications, skills, and experiences based on the character's exploits in film or print. Invent education and work history facts that fit the character. Emphasize use of action verbs to accentuate skills and experience. Show students how the information can be prioritized and sequenced in each section.

Work History/Experience
This section lists the jobs or work experience you have. If you have no work experience but a lot of volunteer experience that is relevant to the job you are applying for, include it here. The idea is to show that you have the skills that the job requires. The information in this section will be arranged with the latest dates first, just as you did with the information in the education section. List the names of the places you worked, including the city and state. Under each place of employment, include the position(s) or title(s) you held and awards and other accomplishments earned from your work.

Related Information
This section may include extracurricular activities, special skills, and awards outside of school and work. They should be relevant to the job. Mention accomplishments that reflect your energy, interests, successes, and other strong qualities you have. Some examples include involvement in 4-H organizations, obtaining cardiopulmonary resuscitation (CPR) certification, teaching a computer course to other teenagers or adults. Depending on the type of activities you list, this section of your résumé may have a heading such as Extracurricular Activities, Other Experiences, or Volunteer Experiences.

You can include job-related volunteer experience on your résumé.

Remember, you want to make your résumé stand out from others. When you have completed a draft of your résumé, here are some questions you should ask:

- Could someone reading my résumé easily understand what my skills are?
- Does my résumé specify what I can do to help the employer?
- Have I included only those items that are directly related to the specific job opening?
- Is the content of my résumé organized and attractive?
- Does my résumé give someone a desire to learn more about me?

Finally, you will write, rewrite, and edit until your résumé is perfect. It is a good idea to have someone else read your résumé. You may also want someone to read aloud your résumé so you can hear what it says. Keep your résumé up-to-date. As you grow by learning more skills and achieving more accomplishments, your résumé should grow with you. Its development should match a similar development in the personal goal statement you wrote in Lesson 2.

Career Profile

Personnel Specialist

Did you ever wonder who reads your résumé when you send it to a company? Or who interviews you for a job opening? If you apply to a fairly large company, chances are the person is a personnel specialist. Personnel specialists work in the human resources department of a company.

Some personnel specialists help hire new employees. They communicate with all the departments of their company to find out about job openings. Then they are responsible for advertising the job openings. Next they receive and review résumés. They may interview applicants or schedule interviews with department managers. Finally, they make job offers and help new employees learn the company ropes.

Other personnel specialists work with employee benefits. They inform company employees about their insurance and retirement programs. Still others work to train both new and veteran employees.

If you are organized and enjoy meeting people, you might enjoy working in human resources. Depending on the position, human resources work requires a high school diploma or a two-year, four-year, or even a graduate degree.

Career Profile

Personnel Specialist

Have a volunteer or volunteers read aloud the Career Profile on page 205. Have students work in pairs to create a graphic organizer showing the different functions of a personnel specialist. A possible diagram might look like this:

Hire new employees ➔ screen résumés
advertise job openings
interview applicants
make job offers
explain benefits

Employee education and training ➔ train employees
notify employees of educational opportunities

Visual/Spatial

Have students compare and contrast the formats and contents of the two types of résumés on pages 206 and 207. First, have students point out features and headings that are the same. (*name and personal information, career objective, and education sections*) Discuss formatting features that make the résumés easy to read. (*clear separations of sections, upper case for heads; bulleted lists, table format*) Then have students summarize differences. (*The functional résumé focuses on qualifications, skills, and experience. The chronological résumé gives more space and priority to education and extracurricular activities.*) Ask students to point out details of content that are different (*the functional résumé is much more detailed*) and explain in what circumstances each form is a better choice.

Leslie M. Student

1234 High School Street

Philadelphia, PA 19019

888-555-1234

`Personal Information`

CAREER OBJECTIVE   `Career Objective`

Seeking a position teaching English in a high school that can benefit from my experience with student leadership programs and community literacy.

EDUCATION   `Education`

July 2004	Earned Pennsylvania teaching certificate
June 2004	Graduated from Bingham Teachers' College in Philadelphia, PA, with majors in English Literature and United States History
June 1999	Graduated from Western High School in Johnstown, PA

EXPERIENCE   `Work History`

2003–2004	Volunteered as literacy tutor to non-reading adults in Philadelphia, PA
2000–2003	Worked summers at Western Community College in Johnstown, PA, as program coordinator of youth leadership development

EXTRACURRICULAR ACTIVITIES   `Related Information`

2003–2004	President, Society for Educators-in-Training
May 2001	Elected Education Department Representative to student government association
April 2000	Winner of Joe Ford Scholarship for Student Educators

---

Sample Functional Résumé

Diego Employee
98765 Working Avenue
San Diego, CA 92101
888-555-9876

`Personal Information`

CAREER OBJECTIVE `Career Objective`

Seeking a position as a hotel desk clerk.

SUMMARY OF QUALIFICATIONS

- 10 years experience in the hotel industry as a housekeeper and desk clerk
- Excellent communication skills
- Enjoy talking with and helping people
- Hard working, reliable, and organized

RELEVANT SKILLS AND EXPERIENCE `Related Information`

Customer Service
- Treated customers with respect
- Greeted customers with a smile
- Answered customer questions in a friendly way

Supervision
- Prepared work schedules for 12 employees
- Trained new clerks
- Trained new housekeepers

Administrative
- Answered telephones at front desk
- Organized time cards and payroll for 12 employees
- Handled credit card, check, and cash payments from customers

EMPLOYMENT HISTORY `Work History`

2000–present	Front Desk Clerk	Hotel La Bienvenida	San Diego, CA
1996–2000	Assistant Clerk	Comfort Hotel	Coronado, CA
1995–1996	Housekeeper	Comfort Hotel	Coronado, CA

EDUCATION `Education`

Hospitality and Tourism classes, 1996   Coronado Community College

LEARNING STYLES

Logical/Mathematical
Have students practice writing a résumé for a specific job (real or imaginary). Students may choose one of the formats illustrated on pages 206 and 207, locate a template online, or design their own format. Ask them to record information needed for each section of the résumé. They should write each item on an index card and write the heading of the section in which it should be included on the top line. Then cards can easily be sequenced before they are input. After students produce a rough draft, have them exchange résumés with a partner. Partners should each other's résumé and provide feedback about how it might be improved. Be sure students proofread their résumés carefully and correct any grammatical or typographical errors.

LEARNING STYLES

Body/Kinesthetic
Schedule class time on computers with word processing and/or desktop publishing software. Have students design a résumé format and create their own sample résumés. Students may need assistance manipulating software tools to place information on the page and create a professional-looking layout. Encourage students with graphic design experience to help inexperienced students learn to use software tools.

Gender and Careers

Ask students to list reasons why child care is important to working parents. Have students read the Gender and Careers feature on page 208. Discuss ways in which child-care centers had an impact on lifestyles and the economy. (*For example, women gained economic power because they were able to work; families earned more money and purchased more goods; men began to take a more active role in raising children.*) Have one group of students research companies in your region that offer child care to employees and a second group research the history of private child care in America. Groups should share their findings with the class.

GLOBAL CONNECTION

The child-care revolution in America led to a society in which the majority of mothers work. In some (usually poor) countries of the world, absence of child care, illiteracy, and a primitive economy still prevent most women from entering the workforce in meaningful numbers. Ask students to find statistics about numbers of women with children, women who work, and women who are educated in other countries. You may want to suggest that students gather statistics for an industrialized nation (such as Japan) and a less developed country (such as Guatemala).

Cover letter
A one-page letter that you send with your résumé to introduce yourself to employers

What Is a Cover Letter?

When you send your résumé to an employer, you should also send a **cover letter** with it. A cover letter introduces you to the employer. It should be written specifically for the job opening you are applying for. Its main purpose is to tell the employer briefly and clearly why you are qualified for the job. Here are some general guidelines for writing a good cover letter.

- Address the letter to the appropriate person. If you don't know that person's name, call the company and ask. If you are responding to an advertisement, address the cover letter to the person listed in it.
- State the job you are applying for.
- Say why you are interested in the position.
- Highlight your qualifications that are relevant to the job.
- Say that you will call to arrange an interview.

You may be able to submit your résumé and cover letter electronically. If you will be faxing your résumé and cover letter, make sure the copies are clear. Use a plain font and do not use extra formatting. If you are sending your résumé and cover letter by e-mail, you can send attachments. Some companies may also have a form for your résumé that you fill out online. Make sure you follow the instructions for such forms.

Gender and Careers

Child care has helped women become more active in the work force. Up until the 1960s, many women with children stayed at home. In the 1960s and 1970s, more mothers wanted or needed to work outside their homes. But who would care for their children? At first, many women had to depend on family, friends, and hired babysitters for child care. Soon, private child care centers began opening. They were bright and cheerful but often expensive. Women often spent much of their salaries on child care. They asked their companies to provide child care. Today, many large companies have on-site child care. Parents can bring their young children to their workplaces. Their children are nearby all day. Mothers and fathers can often spend lunchtime or playtime with their children during the day. The companies pay part of the child care expenses. Of course, not all companies can provide this service. Still, parents have more options than they had in the past.

Sample Cover Letter

July 28, 2004

Ms. Pat Brown
Brighton School District
456 Lee Road
Philadelphia, PA 19019

Dear Ms. Brown:

I am writing in response to your teacher recruitment brochure given out at Bingham Teachers' College. I am very interested in a position as an English teacher at a high school in your school district.

As my résumé shows, I am a certified English and History teacher. I am prepared to teach both English and History courses. I understand that your district is trying to promote community literacy. My experience as a literacy tutor could make me a valuable addition to your school district. Also, my involvement in student leadership development can help to combine students' activities and community literacy efforts.

I would appreciate it if you considered my application. You may reach me at 888-555-1234 to schedule an interview. I look forward to meeting with you.

Sincerely yours,

Leslie M. Student

Leslie M. Student

ELL/ESL STRATEGY

Language Objective: *To use standard business letter format in a cover letter*

The format that is appropriate to use in business correspondence can vary from country to country. Give ELL students background information about the parts of an American business letter:

- heading (or date)
- inside address
- salutation (title, last name, colon)
- body (single spaced, concise, clear)
- closing (avoid informality)
- signature (write above typed name; allow space)

Have students use sticky notes to label each part on the sample cover letter on page 209. Inform students about appropriate abbreviations in a business address and salutation and common salutations and closings. Have students make a chart listing these items for handy reference.

LEARNING STYLES

Logical/Mathematical Have students compare the cover letter by "Leslie M. Student" on page 209 with her résumé on page 206. Have them note information from the résumé that has been included in the cover letter. Discuss reasons why this repetition is necessary. (*The cover letter introduces the applicant and is thus the first opportunity to show that he or she is qualified for the job.*) A lackluster cover letter that fails to mention major qualifications might result in failure of an employer to read the résumé. Have students draw a conclusion about information that can be duplicated in résumé and cover letter. (*Possible response: In order to advertise the applicant, a cover letter should emphasize an applicant's most important qualifications even if it repeats information from the résumé.*)

Lesson 3 Review Answers

1. The main purpose of a résumé is to get the attention of employers so that they will interview you and hire you.

2. If a person doesn't have a lot of work experience, it will be more useful to show the skills he or she has.

3. A cover letter is written specifically for one job opening and introduces an applicant to an employer.

Technology Note

Ask a volunteer with fax experience to explain what a fax machine is and how it works. Read the Technology Note on page 210 to students. If possible, have students observe a fax being sent or received in the school office. Display faxed pages and point out the loss in quality and read-ability of the original that can occur in the process. Explain that an original résumé must be clear, clean, and dark in order to produce a legible and attractive copy on the receiving end of a fax.

Lesson 3 Review Write your answers to these questions on a sheet of paper.

1. What is the main purpose of a résumé?

2. Why might a person choose to write a functional résumé instead of a chronological résumé?

3. Why is it important to send a cover letter with a résumé?

Technology Note

You are probably an expert at using e-mail. But are you familiar with faxing? Using a fax machine is a good way to send important letters and documents. By dialing a telephone number, you can send pages that are received almost immediately. Many companies encourage job applicants to send résumés by fax. Find out if this is an option when you apply for a job. Sending a résumé by fax gets your application process off to a quick start.

Reference
Someone who can share your skills, personal qualities, and job qualifications with an employer

You want your résumé to give employers a good impression of yourself. When employers are considering hiring you, they want to make sure that the information in your résumé is correct. To get that information, they talk to people who know something about you. It is your responsibility to provide the names of those people to the employer. These people are your **references.**

Why Do You Need References?

It is important to have references who can speak positively about who you are and what you can do. Some employers may ask for a list of references with the application. These employers check your references before the interview. Other employers may ask for your references at the interview. The important thing is not to wait until the last moment to find people who will be good references for you.

Who Can Be References?

Your references can be former employers, teachers, coaches, sponsors of clubs that you are involved with, and other adults who know you well. Your employer is an ideal person to ask to be a reference. If you've been a good worker and are leaving your job on good terms, your employer is in the best position to speak about your job skills. However, certain laws permit previous employers to discuss only job-related issues with other employers who are asking about an applicant. Therefore, you will need to make sure you include other references who can speak on your behalf about other matters besides work-related things.

Teachers and guidance counselors can also be good references. Those who know you are dependable, cooperative, and hard working would be happy to help you. They can tell employers about your personal qualities. Coaches, sponsors of community clubs, and other adults who know you well could also give employers the information they are looking for about your personal qualities.

Job Training Readiness Skills Chapter 7 **211**

Lesson at a Glance

Chapter 7 Lesson 4

Overview In this lesson, students learn what references are, why good references are necessary, and how to get them.

Objectives

- To understand the importance of strong, positive references to getting a job
- To evaluate which people will give helpful references
- To explain how to get good references

Student Pages 211–213

Teacher's Resource Library TRL

Workbook Activity 36

Activity 36

Alternative Activity 36

Vocabulary

reference

Write the vocabulary word on the board. Provide a broad clue by using the word in a sentence. Have students write down the meaning they think the word has. Continue providing increasingly helpful clues, until all students can write a definition. Clue sentences might include:

1. Can you give me a good *reference*?
2. The interviewer asked me for my *references*.
3. I asked my former employer if he could give me a good *reference*.

Have students check their definitions against that given in the student text.

1 Warm-Up Activity

Ask students what factor or information they think would have the most influence on an employer's decision to hire an applicant. Have them explain why the recommendation of a prior supervisor or another person might carry great weight. (*Actions speak louder than words. A proven track record shows that the worker can perform, has good character, and so on.*) Have students read the lesson to learn strategies for getting good references.

Job Training Readiness Skills **211**

2 Teaching the Lesson

Stress to students the importance of finding adults who will give them positive references. A negative or lukewarm reference can be harmful in a job search.

Communication Connection

After students have read the Communication Connection on page 212, have them make a list of adults with whom they have worked or interacted directly over a period of months or years. (The list might include supervisors at a volunteer activity, organization leaders, teachers, coaches, family friends, or ministers, but NOT family members or relatives.) For each person on their list, ask students to write a description of what they did with the person. Students should then describe their behavior and attitude toward the adult during this period. Have students reread their notes and highlight names of people they believe would give them good references.

3 Reinforce and Extend

LEARNING STYLES

Auditory/Verbal

Pair students and have them practice asking for a reference. The student who plays the role of an adult employer or supervisor should find out from his or her partner what the person seeking a reference did for him or her in the past and how long they have known each other. Have partners role-play a conversation in which the applicant asks for a reference. After the role play, have the "adult" evaluate the applicant's communication style and suggest improvements. Then have students switch roles and repeat the activity.

Communication Connection

Adults who serve as references for you must respect you. They must know you can be a good employee. So it is important to communicate well with teachers, employers, and other adults. When you work with adults, be polite and friendly. Work hard and show interest in the work. Ask important questions. You will have many people to choose from for references.

It is not a good idea to include relatives as references. It is very unlikely that employers would call them to find out if you are suitable for a job. Employers expect relatives to say only positive things about you because they are related to you.

How Can You Get Good References?

When you have selected three or four people to give references on your behalf, the next step is to get permission from them to give their names to employers. Most people will agree to be a reference for you. However, you need a good reference. If a reference will not speak positively about you, it will not do you any good. You don't want a negative reference to keep you from getting a job.

Therefore, it is important to ask the people you have selected if they think they know you and your work well enough to give you a good reference. If you are honest, most people will be honest with you in return. If they say they are unable to give you a positive reference, thank them for their honesty and move onto the next person on your list. You can be sure that those who say "yes" will be good references. They can be even better references if you let them know what type of job you are applying for. They will have a better idea of how to present your abilities and qualities to fit the job opening.

When you have three or four people who have agreed to give you references, prepare a reference list. Type your list or prepare it on a computer. At the top of the sheet of paper, include your name and address and then the heading "References." List each person's name, title or occupation, the company where he or she works, address, daytime phone number, and e-mail address. If the advertisement for a job does not ask for a list of references with the application, it is still a good idea to have a copy with you at the interview.

ELL/ESL STRATEGY

Language Objective: *To learn vocabulary specific to the job application process*

Some of this chapter's vocabulary words have several more common meanings in addition to their meanings as career jargon (*reference, recruitment, screening, selection*). These terms may confuse students who are learning English. To give

them practice in using a dictionary and add depth to their English vocabulary, have students look up and write several different meanings for each word on a 4 x 6 index card. They should leave space after each definition and write a context sentence to go with each. (For example, a *reference* book; a *reference* to a letter; *references* for a research paper) As a group, have students tell the meanings of the terms as they are used in this chapter.

Lesson 4 Review Write your answers to these questions on a sheet of paper.

1. Why is it a good idea to have a list of references before you apply for a job?

2. In general, who are some people who might make good references? Who are some people who would not make good references?

Get Involved

Have you ever wanted to become a teacher? Or do you simply want to help others? Tutoring is a great way to get involved in your community. Many organizations such as Boys and Girls Clubs and Big Brothers/Big Sisters sponsor tutoring programs. Tutors may be matched with one or two young people who need help in reading or math. A tutor may lead a group of small children in educational games. Tutors may read to children or help them with computer skills. In fact, tutors do many of the same jobs a teacher does each day. Tutoring teaches valuable skills and helps others. It can become a valuable addition to your résumé.

Lesson 4 Review Answers

1. Making sure you have good references on hand takes time and effort. If you wait until the last minute, you will not have references available when an employer asks for them.

2. Good references would be former employers, teachers, guidance counselors, coaches, and sponsors of community clubs. Relatives would not be good references.

Get Involved

Ask a volunteer to explain what a tutor does. Survey the class to find out which students have experience tutoring others. Read the Get Involved feature on page 213 together. Have students brainstorm a list of skills they could teach to younger students. Remind students that these skills can be skills other than academic skills, such as reading or math. Students might also include athletic, computer, music, or dramatic skills, for example. Encourage students to explore the community resources through which they might offer their services as tutors.

Portfolio Activity

Personal Goal Statement

This activity calls for students to write their own personal goal statements. Students can use their completed Portfolio Activities from Chapters 2 and 5 as references. Have students review the illustration that appears on page 199 and plan the layout for their own personal goal statements. Students can write their responses on their own paper or on Portfolio Activity 7 in the TRL.

Ask students to write index cards with information for each section of the statement, placing one item of information on each card. This will give them flexibility in ordering cards within sections and moving them from section to section, if necessary.

Portfolio Activity

Personal Goal Statement

In Lesson 2 you learned the importance of a personal goal statement. You saw an example of a statement. Read through the main parts of a personal goal statement below. Then, answer the questions on page 215 on a sheet of paper. Add the activity to your career portfolio.

Name and Present Situation
- include your name
- include whether you are a student
- include the job or jobs you currently have

Description of Your Career Goal or Job
- describe your career goal
- describe the job you want to get

Requirements for Your Career Goal or Job
- include what knowledge is required
- include what abilities and skills are required
- include the lifestyle and personal values required

Personal Resources
- include what knowledge you have
- include what abilities and skills you have
- include your lifestyle and personal values

Skills Needed
- include abilities and skills you need to get

Steps to Reach Your Career Goal or Job
- if there are in-between goals you need to reach before you reach your main career goal, include them here

214   *Chapter 7   Job Training Readiness Skills*

Personal Goal Statement

1. Write your name and present job.

   Write whether you are a student, and if so, where.

2. Describe your career goal or job.

3. What knowledge does your career goal or job require?

4. What abilities and skills does your career goal or job require?

5. What knowledge do you have now that relates to your career goal or job?

6. What abilities and skills do you have now that relate to your career goal or job?

Personal Goal Statement, continued

7. How does your lifestyle relate to your career goal?

   What personal values do you have that can help you reach your career goal?

8. What knowledge do you need to gain to reach your career goal?

9. What abilities and skills do you need to gain to reach your career goal?

10. If you need to reach in-between or short-term goals before you reach your career goal, what steps do you need to take?
    a.
    b.
    c.
    d.
    e.

Portfolio Activity 7, Pages 1–2

214   *Chapter 7*

1. Write your name and present job. Also write whether you are a student.

2. Describe your career goal or job.

3. What knowledge does your career goal or job require?

4. What abilities and skills does your career goal or job require?

5. What knowledge do you have now that relates to your career goal or job?

6. What abilities and skills do you have now that relate to your career goal or job?

7. How does your lifestyle relate to your career goal? What personal values do you have that can help you reach your career goal?

8. What knowledge do you need to gain to reach your career goal?

9. What abilities and skills do you need to gain to reach your career goal?

10. If you need to reach in-between or short-term goals before you reach your career goal, what steps do you need to take?

In answering question 3, students need to supply educational requirements as well as the fields of knowledge used by an employee in this career. For example, an elementary school teacher must have a four-year college degree with a teaching certificate and thorough understanding of child development and psychology as well as basic understanding of all academic subjects taught.

Question 4 calls for students to think about the activities involved in the job and list the skills necessary to complete them. For example, an elementary school teacher deals with children all day and must be able to communicate effectively at a basic level, problem solve, master teaching methods and techniques, and so on.

Remind students the values in question here may be related to ethics, but should address broader concerns of a specific job, such as whether you value job security more than high achievement or value creativity more than high salary.

Portfolio Activity Answers

1.–10. Answers will vary.

Chapter 7 Review

Use the Chapter Review to prepare students for tests and to reteach content from the chapter.

Chapter 7 Mastery Test

The Teacher's Resource Library includes two forms of the Chapter 7 Mastery Test. Each test addresses the chapter Goals for Learning. An optional third page of additional critical-thinking items is included for each test. The difficulty level of the two forms is equivalent.

Review Answers
Vocabulary Review

1. reference 2. screening 3. personal goal statement 4. functional résumé 5. personal resources 6. résumé 7. recruitment 8. cover letter 9. chronological résumé 10. selection 11. action verb

Concept Review

12. C 13. D 14. B 15. B 16. C

Critical Thinking

17. Answers will vary. Possible answer: It is okay to have a general idea of your career path. As long as you know the kind of education and experience you need to get, you can have a productive start on the path to a goal. 18. It is your first introduction to a potential employer, and it must catch the employer's attention and interest. 19. Answers will vary. Possible answer: You might say that employment decisions are often made based on factors that are out of an applicant's control, so she should not take the decision personally. Since she had a good interview, she knows she has a useful skill that will help her get a job soon. 20. Answers will vary. Possible answer: It is not a good plan because by the time references are requested it will be too late to form the relationship necessary to have a guaranteed good reference.

Word Bank

action verb
chronological résumé
cover letter
functional résumé
personal goal statement
personal resources
recruitment
reference
résumé
screening
selection

Vocabulary Review

Choose the word or phrase from the Word Bank that best completes each sentence. Write the answer on your paper.

1. A person who can share your personal qualities and job qualifications with an employer is a(n) _____.
2. Going through a number of applications to pick out the most suitable people for a job opening is called _____.
3. A description of a career goal along with information related to the goal is called a(n) _____.
4. A résumé that focuses on job tasks or skills of an applicant is a(n) _____.
5. The knowledge, skills, abilities, and personal values a person can use to be successful are known as _____.
6. A summary of knowledge, abilities, and experience that shows how a person is qualified for a particular occupation is a(n) _____.
7. Getting a number of applications from which to choose new employees is known as _____.
8. A one-page letter sent with a résumé is a(n) _____.
9. A résumé that focuses on an applicant's education and work experience is a(n) _____.
10. Choosing a person for a job opening is called _____.
11. A word that shows action is a(n) _____.

Concept Review

Choose the word or phrase that best completes each sentence or answers each question. Write the letter of the answer on your paper.

12. Which is an important lifestyle question to consider in making a personal goal statement?
    A What career cluster do you like most?
    B What job do you want to get?
    C Do you want to live in a city, suburb, or country?
    D What is your in-between career goal?

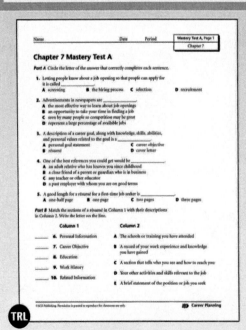

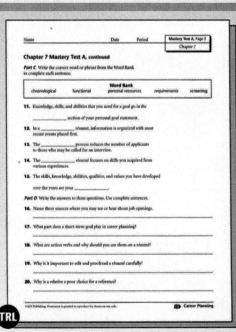

13. Which information is not needed on a résumé?

  A career goal   **C** last job

  B high school attended   **D** gender

14. An example of a good reference is _____.

  A your grandfather

  B your basketball coach

  C your best friend since first grade

  D your cousin

15. About how many of the available job openings are found in newspaper help-wanted ads?

  A 5 percent   **C** 60 percent

  B 20 percent   **D** 90 percent

16. The first step in the hiring process is _____.

  A a job interview   **C** recruitment

  B selection   **D** screening

Critical Thinking

Write the answer to each of the following questions.

17. Do you need to know your specific career goal before looking for your first job? Explain why or why not.

18. Why is it important to create a strong résumé?

19. A friend has an excellent job interview with a company. When the company does not hire her, she is upset. What might you say to help her feel better?

20. A friend is applying for jobs. He says he does not need to ask people to be his references yet. He will wait until he is called for an interview. Explain why you think this is a good plan or not.

Test-Taking Tip

Look over a test before you begin answering questions. See how many sections there are. Read the directions for each section.

ALTERNATIVE ASSESSMENT

- Give students sticky notes with the terms *screening, interview, recruitment,* and *selection* printed on them. Have students sequence these steps in the hiring process in order and explain what occurs in each step.

- Have students use the personal goal statements they prepared for the Portfolio Activity to explain what the statement is for and what it should contain.

- Copy and distribute a faulty résumé to students. Ask them to highlight its mistakes and flaws and explain how to correct them.

- Ask students to list two people they could ask for a reference. Have them write a paragraph explaining why they chose each person.

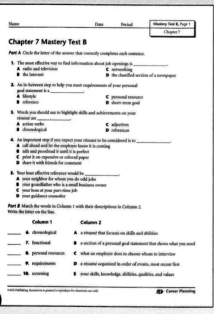

Chapter 7 Mastery Test B, Pages 1–3

Planning Guide

Communication Skills

		Student Pages	Vocabulary	Lesson Review	Critical-Thinking Questions	Chapter Review
Lesson 1	Interviewing Skills	220–225		✔	✔	✔
Lesson 2	The Interview	226–233		✔	✔	✔
Lesson 3	Self-Advocacy Skills	234–237	✔	✔	✔	✔

Chapter Activities

Student Text
Chapter 8 Portfolio Activity

Teacher's Resource Library
Chapter 8 Chapter Outline
Chapter 8 Self-Study Guide
Chapter 8 Portfolio Activity

Assessment Options

Student Text
Chapter 8 Review

Teacher's Resource Library
Chapter 8 Mastery Tests A and B

Teacher's Edition
Chapter 8 Alternative Assessment

			Student Text Features								Teaching Strategies					Learning Styles					Teacher's Resource Library				
Portfolio Activity	Writing Practice	Communication Connection	The Economy	Career Tip	Career Profile	On the Job	Gender and Careers	Think Positive	Technology Note	Get Involved	Background Information	Applications (Home, Community, Global, Environment)	Personal Journal	Online Connection	ELL/ESL Strategy	Visual/Spatial	Body/Kinesthetic	Interpersonal/Group Learning	Logical/Mathematical	Auditory/Verbal	Activities	Alternative Activities	Workbook Activities	Self-Study Guide	Chapter Outline
		220			221						224	221, 224			223	222	223		221, 222	225	37	37	37	✔	✔
	226		233	227				230	229		230, 231	229, 231	228	229	232	233	232		227, 228		38	38	38	✔	✔
238						235	235	236		237	239							237	236		39	39	39	✔	✔

Alternative Activities

The Teacher's Resource Library (TRL) contains a set of lower-level worksheets called Alternative Activities. These worksheets cover the same content as the regular Activities but are written at a second-grade reading level.

Career Interest Inventory

The AGS Publishing Harrington-O'Shea Career Decision-Making System (CDM) may be used with this textbook. Students can use the CDM to explore their interests and identify careers. The CDM defines career areas that are indicated by students' response on the inventory.

Chapter at a Glance

Chapter 8:
Communication Skills
pages 218–241

Lessons

Portfolio Activity

Chapter Review

Audio CD 🎧

Teacher's Resource Library **TRL**

Workbook Activities 37–39

Activities 37–39

Alternative Activities 37–39

Portfolio Activity 8

Chapter 8 Chapter Outline

Chapter 8 Self-Study Guide

Chapter 8 Mastery Tests A and B
(Answer Keys for the Teacher's
Resource Library begin on page 328
of this Teacher's Edition.)

Chapter 8 Self-Study Guide

Chapter

8 Communication Skills

When you speak with a possible employer, you want to give a specific message about yourself. You'll have a short amount of time to communicate your qualifications and the reasons you're right for the job. Simple, right? Not really. Like any other skill area, good communication requires practice and preparation. In this chapter, you will learn some techniques and tips for getting a strong, positive message across to an employer. A good interview could make the difference between being one more applicant in a crowd to being the stand-out applicant the interviewer remembers—and hires.

Goals for Learning
◆ To understand the purpose of an interview
◆ To prepare for an interview
◆ To learn the importance of self-advocacy

219

Introducing the Chapter

Have students look at the photo on page 218 in the Student Edition and tell what these young people might be dressed for. Discuss what type of clothing students think is appropriate to wear to an interview. Ask students to tell what impression is communicated by neat, clean, professional-looking clothing. Read the chapter title and have students name ways an applicant communicates with an interviewer. (*Students may mention tone of voice, type of questions, eye contact, posture, clothing, and attitude.*) Have volunteers read the introductory paragraph aloud.

Have students read the Goals for Learning and recall from Chapter 7 what the interviewer wants to learn from the applicant during an interview. (*the applicant's level of knowledge and skills necessary for the job; qualities such as dependability, leadership, creativity, positive attitude, and willingness to learn*) Tell students they will read the chapter to meet the three Goals for Learning.

Career Tips

Ask volunteers to read the career tips that appear in the margins throughout the chapter. Then discuss them with the class.

Alternative Assessment

The Alternative Assessment box on page 241 of the Chapter Review includes activities using various learning styles to assess students' understanding of the Goals for Learning.

Name _____ Date _____ Period _____ | Chapter Outline, Page 1 | Chapter 8 | 8

Communication Skills

Directions Fill in the outline below. Filling in the blanks will help you as you read and study Chapter 8.

I. **Lesson 1: Interviewing Skills (pp. 220–225)**

A. **How to Prepare for an Interview**

1. In an interview, be clear about why you are a good _____ for the job.

2. Share the _____, _____, _____ and values that connect you to the job.

B. **What the Interviewer Is Looking For**

1. The interviewer is looking for someone with the skills and experience needed for a _____ job.

2. You want to _____ the interviewer that you are the best fit for the job.

C. **First Question: Can You Do the Job?**

1. Tell about your skills in terms of _____.

2. To prepare, make a _____ of the skills required to do the job.

3. Then list your _____ related to those skills.

D. **Will You Do the Job?**

1. Connect your _____ to those needed for the job.

2. Answer the questions in clear, direct _____.

E. **Will You Fit Into the Job Situation?**

1. Be clear about how your _____ connect to the job.

2. What you say and how you say it are _____ important.

©AGS Publishing. Permission is granted to reproduce for classroom use only.   Career Planning

Name _____ Date _____ Period _____ | Chapter Outline, Page 2 | Chapter 8 | 8

Communication Skills, continued

II. **Lesson 2: The Interview (pp. 226–233)**

A. **Interview Dos and Don'ts**

1. Wear clothes that are _____ -looking.

2. Be _____ and treat people with _____.

3. Don't chew _____, tell _____, use _____, or talk _____ about others.

B. **After an Interview**

1. Write a _____ to the interviewer within 24 hours.

2. Write about additional _____ if you have thought of some.

C. **When You Don't Get a Job Offer**

1. Review your _____ experience to see how you can get better.

2. Call, write, or e-mail the interviewer and ask for _____.

III. **Lesson 3: Self-Advocacy Skills (pp. 234–237)**

A. **Self-Advocacy Skills Are Important**

1. It is very important to _____ for yourself.

B. **Using Self-Advocacy Skills**

1. You can use these skills in your life to _____ or _____ yourself.

2. You can use these skills to let your employer know how you are _____.

C. **Other Self-Advocacy Skills**

1. On the job, you may communicate _____ accomplishments.

2. There are _____ that let your employer know you are a good worker.

3. By changing your behaviors, you can help others to see you _____.

©AGS Publishing. Permission is granted to reproduce for classroom use only.   Career Planning

TRL   TRL

Chapter 8 Chapter Outline

Chapter 8 Lesson 1

Overview The lesson helps students prepare for an interview. It outlines ways to communicate what interviewers want to know: whether an applicant can and will do the job and whether he or she will fit into the job situation.

Objectives

■ To review skills, interests, and experience in terms of a specific job interview

■ To understand what an interviewer needs to know about you

■ To learn ways to communicate skills and personal qualities in an interview

Student Pages 220–225

Teacher's Resource Library TRL

Workbook Activity 37

Activity 37

Alternative Activity 37

1 Warm-Up Activity

Have volunteers pretend to be job applicants you are going to interview. Have them introduce themselves to you using the body language, gestures, and tone they think is appropriate. Discuss details that make a positive impression on someone you are meeting for the first time. Tell students that in this lesson, they will learn how to predict what an interviewer wants to learn about them and how to communicate that information effectively.

Communication Connection

Have a volunteer read aloud the Communication Connection feature on page 220. Invite students to demonstrate handshakes that are too weak or too aggressive for a job interview. Pair students and have them practice different styles of handshakes until they find one they think is the most appropriate.

Communication Connection

You may not think of hand shaking as a kind of communication. However, it is a form of body language that may have a big impact in a job interview. Always be ready to shake hands with your interviewer. Practice a handshake that is not weak but also not too hearty. With your handshake, offer a smile and a polite greeting.

Many people feel nervous or afraid before an interview. They imagine being put on the "hot seat" and being asked all sorts of questions that they will not be able to answer. Some people describe this as the "sweaty palms" experience. The good news is that you can be prepared for these situations. You might still be nervous, but you can avoid being surprised by the questions that come up. By preparing effectively for an interview, you will be able to handle any situation that arises.

How Can You Prepare For an Interview?

By doing the activities in the previous chapters of this book, you have already done much of the work that you need to do to prepare for an interview. Being effective in an interview is based on knowing yourself and having a clear sense about why you are a "good fit" for the position for which you are applying.

The interview is where you get to share important information about yourself and your goals. The information you share focuses on the skills, interests, experience, and values that connect you to the job. If you are interviewing for a job in carpentry, for example, you need to share the skills you have that relate to the work a carpenter does. Specifically, you need to tell the interviewer the things you have done in the past that demonstrate that you could do the job successfully.

What Is the Interviewer Looking For?

The interviewer is looking for someone who can do a specific job. The interviewer has identified the skills and experiences necessary for doing the job well. The interviewer also has an idea of the type of person needed in a particular work situation. When you have done a good job preparing for an interview, you have taken the time to do self-assessment (Chapter 2) and to research career options (Chapters 3 and 4). You have also learned how to connect information about yourself with appropriate careers. By doing these activities, you have become the expert about why you are an excellent fit for the job for which you are interviewing.

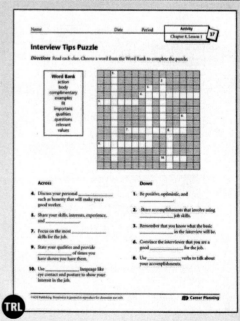

Workbook Activity 37   **Activity 37**

Then, all you need to do is to communicate to the interviewer what you know about yourself. Your job is to convince the interviewer that you are the best person for the job.

Many people are scared or nervous about interviews because they do not know the questions that will be asked ahead of time. This may be true. Even though you do not know the exact questions, keep in mind that most interviewers want to know the same things:

1. Can you do the job?
2. Will you do the job?
3. Will you fit into the job situation?

Almost all interview questions will relate to one of these three questions. While the words may be different, the information is the same.

Can You Do the Job?

This question asks you to identify the skills you have that connect with the job. To answer this question, think about how you can communicate your skills in terms of accomplishments. For example, consider the difference between a baseball player saying "I can catch, hit, and throw the ball" and "My batting average is .303 and I did not make any fielding errors last season." The first example simply communicates that the baseball player has the relevant skills.

Career Profile

Retail Merchandise Buyer

There are many job opportunities in retail sales. Sales clerks and sales managers work for small shops, large discount stores, and department stores. They sell everything from gift items to clothing to furniture. One interesting retail job opportunity is that of a buyer.

A buyer is responsible for purchasing goods from a wholesaler to sell in a retail store. First a buyer must be in touch with his or her customers. He or she must understand the prices, quality, and styles of goods that customers want. The buyer must also communicate with the store or shop management. The buyer needs to know the store's selling philosophy. Finally, a buyer must work with wholesale salespeople. These are the people from whom he or she buys goods.

A buyer may travel to large markets several times a year. For example, a clothing buyer for a department store may go to New York City twice a year for big fashion shows. A furniture buyer may go to home fashion shows several times a year.

Many retail buyers start their careers as sales assistants. This helps them understand customers and merchandise. A two-year or four-year college degree is needed for many retail buying positions.

---

2 Teaching the Lesson

Students will refer to their work values, personal skills, and abilities extensively as they think about how to present themselves positively in specific interview situations. Before they read this lesson, you may want to have students review Chapter 2 and refer to the self-assessment profiles they completed. Students may need to reconsider their earlier responses and update skills and experiences.

3 Reinforce and Extend

IN THE COMMUNITY

Students might try to find out when and where a job fair is to be held in your community or inquire about the near-term hiring plans for several local companies. The organizer of a job fair or a human resources employee of a company can be a good source of basic recommendations for first time interviewees, such as appropriate dress, frequently asked questions, and so on.

LEARNING STYLES

Logical/Mathematical
Point out that headings and subheadings in this chapter are questions. Have students read each section to find the answer to the heading question and write it on their own paper. Explain that they will use these notes for another activity when they finish reading the chapter.

Career Profile

Retail Merchandise Buyer

Ask students to describe the merchandise style at their favorite clothing store. Invite volunteers to tell how they think the merchandise is chosen. Explain that a retail merchandise buyer must make many decisions and be knowledgeable about current fashion trends. Have students read the Career Profile feature on page 221 to learn about this career. Interested students can find more details about it online or in the *Occupational Outlook Handbook*.

Logical/Mathematical

Be sure students understand the difference between a general statement of abilities and a specific statement about an accomplishment. List several skills or abilities on the board in general terms, for example:

- *I have good organizational skills.*
- *I get along well with others.*
- *I pay close attention to detail and am accurate.*

Have students work in small groups to write sentences that demonstrate these skills specifically. (For example, *I planned and organized the fund drive for new uniforms for the high school band.*) Explain that using statistics or numbers can paint a precise picture of abilities. (For example, *As treasurer for FBLA, I kept track of all expenses and income. The account was consistently balanced in the two years I held this office.*) Remind groups that experiences as students and volunteer workers illustrate skills as well as part-time jobs.

Visual/Spatial

If students have a hard time pinpointing skills required for specific jobs, suggest that they observe someone at work in the relevant job or create a drawing or collage representing the work this person does. For example, students might observe a school secretary's workplace and activities or create a collage about police work. Then ask students to use their visual impressions as a starting point to list the skills demonstrated.

The second example communicates the player's skills in terms of accomplishments. The first statement communicated only that the player had the skills. The question remains as to how well the player can catch, throw, and hit. The second statement communicated not only that the player has the skills but also a high skill level. Thus, the second statement would be a better way to convince the interviewer that the player can do the job well. In a similar way, you should try to communicate your skills by describing accomplishments that involve using relevant job skills.

How Can You Communicate Your Job Skills?

At first, communicating your skills in terms of accomplishments may seem like a difficult task. A good way to begin is by making a list of the skills required to do the job in which you are interested. For example, a secretary must be able to follow directions, have computer skills, communicate effectively, and be organized. A bank teller must be good with details, have basic math skills, be able to work with a computer, and be reliable. Choose two jobs that you are currently interested in. For each job, make a list of the relevant skills.

How Are Skills and Experiences Related?

After you have made a list of relevant skills you can list your experiences related to those skills. List the times you have demonstrated the skills. (You may find it helpful to review the information in Chapter 2, Lessons 1 and 2.) Describe these times in terms of accomplishments. Use action verbs to begin the descriptions. For example, "managed," "organized," "coached," "planned," and "filed." You can also work with a parent, teacher, or counselor to find ways to describe your skills in terms of what you have accomplished. Once you have done this, you can begin to practice how you will answer the question, "Can you do the job?" Your answers should be clear and to the point. You can practice stating these answers in a small group in class, with your counselor, with your parents or guardians, or with your teacher. Focus on the most important skills for the job in which you are interested.

Will You Do the Job?

To answer this question, focus on your interests. You must be able to communicate what it is about the job that you find interesting. This question gives you the chance to let the interviewer know you are excited about the job. (Referring back to the work you did in Chapter 2, Lessons 3 and 4 may be helpful.)

Identify the interests that connect most closely to those required for the job for which you are interviewing. Once you have connected your interests to those required for the job, begin transferring these connections into statements. For example, "I enjoy helping others and have done this in my role as a tutor to other students." You can practice your statements by rehearsing them with an interview partner. Your partner's task is to ask the question, "What about this job interests you?" Your task is to provide the answer in clear, direct statements.

Will You Fit into the Job Situation?

This is a very important question. You will have the chance to discuss your personal qualities, such as honesty and reliability that make you a good worker. Many people advance in their jobs because they are a good fit for their job situation.

Other people lose their jobs because they cannot fit in. Many times, this happens because people do not have positive attitudes and good social skills. For example, they are not reliable, they do not work hard, or they have trouble getting along with their coworkers.

Employers want to hire people who can work well as part of a team.

All students should practice answering likely interview questions. For students who are learning English, this step is crucial. List questions like the following and have students ask about them until they are confident they know what each means:

How much experience have you had in _____ (sales, teaching, etc.)?

What makes you a good candidate for this job?

How would you describe yourself as a worker?

What contribution could you make to our _____ (organization, company, corporation, etc.)?

Have ELL students work with English proficient partners to draft and revise a response to each question and practice delivering it.

LEARNING STYLES

Body/Kinesthetic
Point out to students that practicing how to communicate and being aware of body language are crucial in an interview. Nonverbal messages may speak louder than verbal responses. Have students discuss, then practice, ways of showing interest, enthusiasm, and positive energy through body language. Explain that they should have:

- erect, not slouching, posture
- a firm handshake
- natural hand gestures (not exaggerated)
- no fidgeting
- consistent eye contact (but not stare constantly at the interviewer)

Pair students and have them practice acting as interviewer and applicant to model appropriate body language.

Interview Tips

Studies suggest that "three Vs" control the way people evaluate each other: visual (appearance), vocal (voice), and verbal (what is said). The first minute or two of an interview give the hiring manager that all-important first impression. To make a positive impression:

- Make sure you look well-groomed and neat. Think of yourself as a book. Would others want to read more?

- Wear conservative, neutral clothes and accessories. This kind of "packaging" does not distract attention from the "product," but enhances it.

- Sit up straight and stand tall, with shoulders back and head held high, to project confidence.

- Smile and make eye contact to project an upbeat attitude and confidence.

- Make sure your hands are not hot and sweaty or cold and clammy. If they're cold, run hot water on the insides of your wrists. If they're hot, run cold water. To control sweating, use a deodorant gel.

- Speak with enthusiasm in a firm voice.

GLOBAL CONNECTION

Assign interested students the task of locating information on the Internet about job interviews in another country. They might e-mail individuals or search for informative articles to answer questions such as *How are interviews conducted in _____? What criteria are used to evaluate applicants?*

How Can You Connect Your Values with a Job?

Fitting in also includes being clear about your values and how your values connect with the job. (Remember, you learned about values in Chapter 2, Lesson 4.) It is important to note that although interviewers will very likely ask you direct questions about your skills, experiences, and interests, they might not ask you a direct question as to whether you will fit in. The interviewer will try to get clues by observing what you communicate through your body language and how you speak.

How Can You Show Interest in a Job?

Body language that demonstrates that you are interested in the job includes making good eye contact, maintaining good posture, having a firm handshake, dressing appropriately, and demonstrating that you have done some research about the employer and the job. Speaking with an appropriate level of enthusiasm is also important. If you speak too quietly, then you will communicate a lack of interest and energy. If you speak too loudly you will communicate insensitivity to others. Keep in mind that what you say and how you say it are equally important in the interview process.

Having a positive attitude is also important. Would you rather spend time with people who demonstrate positive behaviors and attitudes or negative ones? Most of us enjoy being around positive and optimistic people. Demonstrate in your interview that you are the sort of person with whom your prospective employer would want to spend time. Be positive, optimistic, and complimentary.

What Qualities Do Employers Want?

Although the answer to whether you will fit into any specific job situation requires you to know something about the particular job you are interviewing for, there are some factors that it is safe to assume are common across all job situations. For example, all employers want their employees to be honest, hard working, and reliable. Employers want people who will contribute to the work environment by displaying positive attitudes toward their jobs, their coworkers, and their supervisors.

How Can You Communicate These Qualities?

It is important for you to communicate that you have these qualities. You can do this by stating that you have them. You can also provide examples of times in your life when you have demonstrated them. For example, suppose you were involved in a group project at school. You could explain how you encouraged the group to take a positive approach to problem solving. Or, suppose you rarely miss a day of school and are always on time. This shows that you are dedicated and prompt. Sharing these qualities is important to demonstrate that you are a positive person and someone who works hard to fit in.

You can practice your responses to the question of how well you will fit in by making a list of all the qualities and values that you possess. Try to identify instances or experiences in which you demonstrated these qualities and values. Now turn those instances into statements. Practice stating the examples in ways that give the interviewer evidence that you will fit in. Practice your statements with peers, parents or guardians, your counselor, or your teacher.

Remember, even though you may be nervous about an interview, you know what the basic questions will be. The interviewer wants to know if you are the "right" person for the job. Your role in the interview is to convince the interviewer that you are the right person. You must connect your skills and experience to the job for which you are being interviewed. By preparing effectively for the interview, you will be ready to provide the answers. You can draw from your past and present experiences to convince the interviewer that you have the skills, interests, values, and experience necessary to perform the job well.

Lesson 1 Review Write your answers to these questions on a sheet of paper

1. What are the main things an interviewer wants to know when he or she interviews someone?

2. What is the best way to prepare to communicate your skills in an interview?

3. Besides skills and knowledge, what are the main things a person needs to fit into a job situation?

Lesson 1 Review Answers

1. An interviewer wants to know if you can do the job, if you will do the job, and if you can fit into the job situation.

2. Write down a list of skills required for the job and any skills you have that match.

3. A positive attitude and good social skills.

Lesson at a Glance

Chapter 8 Lesson 2

Overview This lesson poses likely interview questions and suggests how to answer them. It also lists interview dos and don'ts.

Objectives

- To plan answers for interview questions
- To identify specific dos and don'ts for interviewing
- To plan post-interview activities
- To get interview feedback

Student Pages 226–233

Teacher's Resource Library

Workbook Activity 38

Activity 38

Alternative Activity 38

 1 Warm-Up Activity

Ask volunteers to offer wording for questions they think they would be asked in an interview. List these questions on the board and discuss what the answers tell an interviewer (*for example, skill level, attitude, people skills*) As they read the lesson, students should analyze the questions to determine what the answers would reveal about them.

Writing Practice

Before students write their responses to the question in the Writing Practice on page 226, remind them that they want to present themselves in the best way when they answer interview questions. The discussion after question 8 on page 227 addresses this purpose further. Be sure students give examples to support their statements.

Lesson 2 The Interview

You have learned that you know much of what happens in an interview ahead of time. You have been preparing for interviews by completing many of the activities in this book. The interview is the time when you pull it all together and show that you are a good fit for a job. As you focus on the interview, remember that most interview questions will relate to the three basic questions discussed in the previous lesson. Here are some typical interview questions and suggestions for answering them.

1. **What experiences have you had that relate to this position?** This question requires you to discuss your relevant skills in terms of your accomplishments.

2. **What interests you about this job (or college or other postsecondary institution)?** This question requires you to discuss your relevant interests and activities and show how you have put your interests into action.

3. **What are your long-term goals?** This question requires you to discuss how your interests, skills, motivation, and values connect with goals that are a good fit for the job.

4. **In what kind of work environment are you most comfortable?** This question requires you to discuss how you fit in. This is the time to mention your positive qualities such as being reliable, hard working, and able to communicate well with others.

5. **What are your strengths?** This question gives you the chance to discuss your relevant skills in terms of your accomplishments.

Writing Practice

An interviewer might ask you, "How would your friends describe you?" Write an answer to this question. Give examples to support the descriptions.

Interview Checklist

Directions Write the answers to the questions. Use complete sentences.

List two things to do before an interview.

1.
2.

List six things to do or say during an interview.

3.
4.
5.
6.
7.
8.

List two things to do after an interview.

9.
10.

List five things not to do during an interview.

11.
12.
13.
14.
15.

Workbook Activity 38

Answering Interview Questions

Directions Match the interview questions in Column 1 with the suggested responses in Column 2. Write the letter on the line.

Column 1

1. What are your strengths?
2. How would you describe yourself?
3. What are your weaknesses?
4. What is most important to you in a job?
5. What two accomplishments have given you the most satisfaction?
6. What interests you about this job?
7. What do you think you could contribute to this organization?
8. What do you know about our organization?
9. What are your long-term goals?
10. How would your friends describe you?

Column 2

A Share what you have learned and say something positive and specific.

B Discuss your relevant skills in terms of your accomplishments.

C Discuss your interest in developing more skills related to the job.

D Discuss your relevant interests and activities and show how you put them into action.

E Discuss how it is important for you to use your skills. You also want to do work that connects with your interests and to make positive contributions.

F Use your summary statement of your accomplishments and personal qualities.

G Discuss your skills, interests, and qualities that will allow you to be a positive contributor.

H Discuss how your interests, skills, motivation, and values connect with goals that are a good fit for the job.

I Focus on the accomplishments that contain skills that connect with the job.

J Focus on the positive things that would be said.

Activity 38

Career Tip

Never exaggerate your skills or experience on your résumé. If you do get an interview or job offer, your employer will soon find out about any exaggerations.

6. **What are your weaknesses?** Be careful! An interview is not the time to discuss your shortcomings but rather to highlight your current skills. You can also mention the skills you would still like to learn and develop. This question provides you with the chance to discuss your interest in developing more skills related to the job.

7. **Describe a time when you have demonstrated the skills required for this job.** Show how you can connect your skills with the job.

8. **How would your friends describe you?** To answer this question, focus on the positive things your friends would say about you. For example, "My friends would describe me as honest, reliable, loyal, and hard working. They might also say that I try to see the positive in all situations."

9. **What do you think you could contribute to this organization?** This question provides the chance to talk about your skills, interests, and personal qualities that connect with the job. Remember you want to be a positive contributor to the environment and this is the time to let the interviewer know this.

10. **What two or three accomplishments have given you the greatest satisfaction in your life?** For this question, focus on the accomplishments that contain skills that connect with the job.

11. **What is most important to you in a job?** This question provides the opportunity to bring together your answers to all three questions in Lesson 1. Talk about how it is important for you to use your skills that connect with the job. Tell how the job you are interviewing for connects to your interests. Stress how it is important for you to be able to contribute positively to your work environment.

Communication Skills   Chapter 8   **227**

 Teaching the Lesson

The extensive list of interview questions is important, but to hold students' interest, you may wish to divide the class into small groups after they read and assign each group 4–5 of the questions to analyze. Suggest that they agree on a specific job opening and draft sample answers for the questions. When students read their answers to the class, they should be able to explain why they answered in the way they did. That is, they should know what effect the answer will have.

In the Portfolio Activity on pages 238–239, students are asked to write responses to 15 of the questions that appear in this lesson: 1–6, 9–11, 13–14, 16, 18, and 20–21.

 Reinforce and Extend

LEARNING STYLES

Logical/Mathematical
Remind students that the principal things an employer wants to know about an applicant are

- Can you do the job? (Do you have the skills?)
- Will you do the job? (Where do your interests lie?)
- Will you fit in? (What personal qualities do you have?)

As they read the interview questions on pages 226–230, have students decide which kind of information they will be supplying to the interviewer as they answer each question. Students might write each question on an index card and separate the cards into the three categories. (Note that a few questions touch on two or all three of the aspects.) Then as they draft answers to each question, students can approach one theme at a time: skills and experience, interests, and personal strengths.

Communication Skills   **227**

It takes thought and practice for a young interviewee to turn a negative question into an opportunity to show something positive about himself or herself. Have students respond to question 12 on their own paper. First, have them summarize what went wrong or could have gone better. Then have them focus on the parts that went right and tell how they learned from the experience. When students are satisfied with their responses, have them practice them aloud.

LEARNING STYLES

Logical/Mathematical
When an interviewer asks "Tell me about a time when..." or "Can you give me an example..," students should be ready to present an illustrative story about their past experience. An acronym can help them to stay focused on the important points they want the interviewer to know. (Explain that any story has a beginning, middle, and end, so there will be three parts to their answer.) For example, STAR could stand for Situation/Task – Action – Result. First, tell about a situation or a task you faced—the reason for taking action. What challenges did it present? Then, explain what action you took and why. Finally, tell about the positive results. Have students make up their own acronym to help them recall information in an interview. Have them teach others how to use the acronym.

12. **Describe a time when you failed to achieve a goal you had established for yourself.** Focus on a time when you achieved some of what you hoped to achieve but maybe not everything. Tell also what you learned from the experience. For example, "As a newspaper delivery person, I set the goal of having 100 percent of my customers satisfied with my work. I came very close to achieving this goal. But, a couple of customers became upset when I was not able to deliver the paper at the usual time. As a result, I decided to contact my customers personally when I knew that the paper would be late. All of my customers appreciated this approach. Several customers even noted that they had never had such good service."

13. **Why should I hire you?** Once again, this is a question that provides the chance to share your answers to all three questions in Lesson 1.

14. **What was your most rewarding experience in high school?** To answer this question, try to identify a time when you were able to demonstrate positive personal qualities and use skills that are relevant to the job. For example, if the ability to set and achieve goals is important for the job, then the following example would be appropriate: "I tried out for the tennis team in 10th grade and barely made the varsity team. I decided that I would have the goal of being one of the top three players by my senior year. I worked hard. By the time I was a senior I was ranked number two on the team."

15. **How do you feel about moving to take this job?** The answer to this question is one that you need to be clear about. If moving is important for this particular job and you don't want to move, then the job may not be a good one for you. If you wouldn't mind moving, then say so.

16. **Describe a time when you were faced with a major problem and tell me how you handled it.** Identify a major "problem" as a major "challenge" that you experienced. Successfully learning a new skill or dealing effectively with a challenging task in school sports or in the community are good possibilities for an answer.

17. **How do you work under pressure?** To answer this question, you should note that you handle pressure effectively. Say that you stay focused on the job, work well with others, and keep a positive attitude.

18. **What would you contribute to our work environment?** For questions like this, it is helpful to develop a one- or two-sentence summary about your relevant accomplishments and your personal qualities. Once you develop this summary, write it down. Then practice saying it out loud.

19. **What do you know about our organization?** This is the time for you to share what you have learned about this particular organization. Note that "nothing" is never a good answer. You need to prepare for the interview by taking the time to learn something about the organization. Check it out on the Internet and talk to people who may know something about it. Do your homework and be ready to say something positive and specific about the organization.

20. **Do you think your grades are a good indication of how you would perform on the job? Why or why not?** If your grades are good, then it makes sense that they provide a good indication of your abilities. If your grades are not so good, then you may want to focus on areas in which you have been more successful. Some very good workers are better performers on the job than they are in the classroom. It is okay to say this if that is the case for you.

21. **How would you describe yourself?** This is another opportunity to use your summary statement of your accomplishments and positive personal qualities.

Technology Note

Computers have not only changed life for workers in offices. They have changed the way almost every business operates. Retail businesses rely on scanners for customer payment and inventory. Airlines use computers to book flights, check in passengers—and fly the planes! Factories use lathes and other machines that are computer controlled. Find out about the newest technology used in your career area of interest. This knowledge could pay off in interviews.

IN THE ENVIRONMENT

 Stress can be a major factor in the work environment. Deadlines, pressure to achieve, noise levels, poor lighting, and long hours all are factors related to stress level. Explain that as part of their research before an interview, students should note the nature of the work environment in the job they are seeking. Besides being able to answer questions about working under pressure, applicants will then be able to show understanding of the stresses of the job and how to handle them.

ONLINE CONNECTION

 Students will find many Web sites with advice for people who are preparing to interview for jobs. Monster.com has a number of good articles about an array of subjects, from how to do your homework before an interview to how to avoid nonverbal communication faux pas. To access articles directly, go to http://interview.monster.com/articles/.

Technology Note

Ask students to name some ways that technology has changed the way grocery stores are run. What has changed in the past 50 years? (*Computers scan items for checkout and maintain accurate inventories. Faster, more efficient flights and trucking mean that products can come from farther away, increasing variety and freshness, and so on.*) After students have read the Technology Note on page 229, ask them to list new types of technology that have changed the work or the approach to work in an industry they hope to pursue.

Ask student athletes what strategies they use before a game to gain confidence and remain positive. Visualizing the kind of play and the positive outcome has been shown to lead to better performance and self-confidence. Inform students that they will also benefit from practice. A mock interview, in which an adult acts as the interviewer, can give invaluable feedback and insights. If possible, have students videotape the mock interview so they can observe and correct their mistakes in body language, attitude, and verbal responses.

BACKGROUND INFORMATION

Asking Your Own Questions

If an interviewer asks a candidate for questions, it provides an opportunity to show an applicant has researched the company and the specific job. Before an interview, the applicant needs to do some homework. Point out to students that they should study the Web site of the company with which they will interview, read the company's mission statement, and consider how the job fits into it. If possible, they should find biographical and corporate information about the interviewer and his or her company activities. Magazines, newspapers, trade journals, and research sources may have analyzed the company and published statistics about it. Armed with information such as this, the applicant can generate several questions that will show he or she has learned a lot about the company and the role he or she will play in it.

Think Positive

One way to think positive in a job interview is to imagine yourself in the interview beforehand. "See" yourself in the situation. Imagining that you do well will give you confidence.

22. **Do you have plans for continuing your education?** Your plans should indicate your interest in continuing to learn and develop new skills.

23. **What do you see yourself doing five years from now?** It may be important to have a five-year plan related to the job. You might note that in five years you will have learned more about the industry in which the job is located, developed more advanced skills related to the job, and gotten additional education related to the job. For example, if the job is in the food service industry, you might note that you hope to have the chance to take on more responsibility. You want to learn more about the food service industry. You might also note that you hope that the organization will think of you as one of its best employees.

24. **Do you have any questions for me?** "No" is not a good answer to this question. It suggests that you are not interested in the job. There are some questions you can prepare ahead of the interview. For example, you can ask the interviewer to describe the ideal candidate for this job. You can ask the interviewer to share his or her opinion about what the biggest challenges are in this job. You can ask what the opportunities are for advancement. With each of these questions, the interviewer's response will give you important information. Note how you welcome the sort of challenges the interviewer identifies. If the interviewer said something earlier in the interview that you think would be helpful to learn more about, this is the time to ask. By responding with a few questions regarding the job, you will communicate that you are interested in the job and motivated to do the work.

Doing well in an interview requires preparation, homework, and practice. Find an interview partner and practice asking and responding to each of these questions. If you do this, you will notice that the more you practice, the easier interviewing gets. If you find that you cannot give a good answer to any of these questions, ask your teacher, parent, guardian, or counselor for help.

What Are Some Interview Dos and Don'ts?

Once you have prepared for an interview, there are some basic things you should keep in mind before the interview.

It is important to dress properly for an interview.

DO

- Dress properly for the interview. Wear clean, neatly ironed, and professional-looking clothing.
- Arrive on time for your interview. To be sure that you will arrive on time, know where the interview will take place. If it is somewhere that you are not familiar with, go to the location the day before the interview. Be sure you know how to get there and how much time it will take. If there is likely to be heavy traffic, plan for extra time.
- Make sure that you are well groomed for the interview. Make sure you hair is neat. Make sure you are clean and presentable. Keep in mind that an interview is not a time to splash on perfume or cologne.
- Be polite. The interview begins the moment you make contact with anyone who works for the organization. On interview day, it begins the moment you walk in the door. Treat everyone with respect.
- Act as if you want the job. Be sure to say so toward the end of the interview. Remind the interviewer why you are a good fit for the position before you leave.
- Ask the interviewer when you can expect to hear about the job. Find out what the time line is for the employer to make a decision.

Have students check their closets at home for possible interview outfits. Stress that for most interviews, clothing should be conservative in style and color. Shades of blue and gray are good, and a dress shirt and slacks or a skirt with a jacket generally make a good impression. Females should avoid bare legs. Jeans and a T-shirt are never appropriate. Avoid the following:

- short skirts
- out-of-date suits
- leather jackets
- turtlenecks
- jewelry that jangles
- open-toed or backless shoes
- printed or trendy handbags

Students may want to discuss their choices with an adult at home or bring them in and ask for feedback from classmates.

BACKGROUND INFORMATION

Time and the Interview

Perhaps the worst mistake an applicant can make for an interview is being late. An excuse such as "I was stuck in bad traffic" won't correct the bad impression lateness makes. In addition, the interviewee should allow at least two hours for the interview. Some employers may want an applicant to spend more time in order to meet people, tour the workplace, or take screening tests. If the applicant has to excuse himself or herself for another commitment—even another interview—it leaves the impression that this interview is not important. Moreover, if an applicant feels rushed, his or her anxiety will affect interview performance.

DON'T
- Chew gum during an interview.
- Tell jokes or use inappropriate humor.
- Talk negatively about others or about previous employers.
- Use slang or improper language during an interview.
- Leave the interview without expressing your interest in the job.

What Should You Do After an Interview?

You have now learned what to do before and during an interview. The interview does not end, however, when you leave. You should write a thank-you note to the interviewer within 24 hours of the interview. Thank the interviewer for his or her time. Express your interest in the position. Restate how your skills and abilities qualify you for the position. If you thought of additional qualifications you have for the job, you can mention them in the note. The note should be brief and sincere.

What If You Do Not Get a Job Offer?

No matter how prepared you are for an interview, it is a fact of life that sometimes you will not get a job offer or be accepted into a school. This can be a difficult experience. When this occurs, there are several things that you can do. Review your interview experience. How well did you do? What could you do better in the next interview? The goal is to keep getting better at interviewing. Another thing you can do is call, write, or e-mail the interviewer. Express your thanks for having had the chance to interview. Also share your disappointment that it did not work out this time.

You can also ask what the interviewer thinks you could do to improve your chances in the future. Asking for feedback gives you the opportunity to find out what things you can do to get better. Thank the interviewer for his or her time. If an interview doesn't turn out how you expected, don't be discouraged. The more interviews you have, the better you will become at interviewing. Remember, everyone has had this experience. If you keep working at it, you will be successful!

Lesson 2 Review Write your answers to these questions on a sheet of paper.

1. In what ways is an interview a positive opportunity for the person being interviewed?

2. Why is it important to research an organization where you are interviewing?

3. An interviewer might ask a question such as, "What are your weaknesses?" Write an answer to this question.

The Economy

When the nation's economy is strong, many good jobs are available for people. Likewise, when the economy is poor, many people are unemployed. A time in American history when many people were unemployed was the Great Depression.

In 1929, the country had many economic problems. The stock market crashed. In other words, the value of most stocks fell or disappeared. Because people soon had little money to spend, businesses began to fail. Soon millions of Americans were unemployed.

Franklin Roosevelt became president in 1933. He started many programs to employ people. For example, he started the Works Progress Administration. This program employed people to build roads, bridges, and post offices. Roosevelt gave people confidence in the government and in the economy.

Roosevelt also signed the Social Security Act. Under this plan, money from each American's earnings was put into a special fund. When people retired, they received benefits. Although the Social Security program has some problems today, it has given key benefits to Americans for many years.

The Great Depression lasted for about 10 years. However, the government learned how to avoid similar problems in the future. Today there are many programs in place to prevent similar economic difficulties.

Lesson 2 Review Answers

1. It gives a person a chance to get to know his or her goal and values better, to get more interview experience, and to practice interview skills.

2. It is important to show that you are not merely looking for a job anywhere, and to show that you are not entirely ignorant of the organization and that you are interested in it.

3. Answers will vary. Students should write answers that do not describe weaknesses that will put employers off, such as laziness. Instead, they should describe a trait that has positive aspects, such as great curiosity or being concerned with details.

LEARNING STYLES

Visual/Spatial

Students who learn best through visual cues might be asked to draw cartoons that express important ideas about successful interviewing. Display students' work and encourage them to explain what concept(s) it illustrates.

The Economy

Display photos or read a short description or encyclopedia article showing the effects of the Great Depression on the American people. Invite students to share any stories they have heard from older family members about this period in American history. Have several volunteers read the Economy feature on page 233 aloud. Assign different small groups of students to research and report on different aspects of Social Security. For example, they might interview older Americans who remember its beginnings, read about problems the program has encountered today, or investigate plans for the future of Social Security. Students might debate the best course for the country to take so that people will continue to receive benefits in the future.

Chapter 8 Lesson 3

Overview In this lesson, students learn the meaning of self-advocacy and how to use self-advocacy skills to communicate their accomplishments.

Objectives

- To define self-advocacy
- To list reasons why self-advocacy skills are important
- To identify appropriate times for using self-advocacy skills
- To practice communicating accomplishments

Student Pages 234–237

Teacher's Resource Library **TRL**

Workbook Activity 39

Activity 39

Alternative Activity 39

Vocabulary

self-advocacy

Write *advocate* on the board and have students look it up in the dictionary. Ask a volunteer to explain what an advocate does. (*pleads the cause or supports the interests of someone, in general or in court*) Then write *self-advocacy* on the board and have students predict its meaning. Read the text definition aloud so that students can check their predictions.

1 Warm-Up Activity

Ask students to describe the actions that accompany modesty and bragging. What is their opinion of people who brag? Have students think of times when it is appropriate to tell others positive things about your skills and experiences.

 Lesson 3 Self-Advocacy Skills

Self-advocacy
Supporting, defending, or speaking up for yourself

You have learned that in interviews, you must explain the reasons you are the right person for a job. The interview is not the time to be shy. You should say positive things about yourself. This is not always easy. You might not feel it is polite to speak very positively about yourself. You might feel like you are bragging. But, in an interview, it is important to speak up for yourself. This skill is called **self-advocacy.** You may not have heard the term "self-advocacy" before. Advocacy means "to defend or support a person or a cause." In self-advocacy, the person you are supporting or defending is you!

Why Are Self-Advocacy Skills Important?

Using self-advocacy skills is very important in an interview. During an interview you are required to "speak up for yourself." Self-advocacy skills are also important for other parts of the job search process. When you write your résumé, you put your strengths into words on paper. When you write a cover letter for an application, you include a summary of your strengths and accomplishments. When you engage in networking, you must use self-advocacy skills effectively. Being able to state your skills, interests, experience, and values is an important self-advocacy skill. Supporting yourself in this way can be useful throughout the job search process. Self-advocacy can help achieve your goals in work and in life.

When you use self-advocacy skills, you communicate clearly and effectively who you are and what you can do. Remember that stating your accomplishments is important. Your accomplishments are proof that you have the skills a job requires. It is one thing to *say* that you have a skill. It is even better to *show* that you have the skill. You can practice your self-advocacy skills as you prepare for interviews. The more you practice standing up for yourself, the better you will be able to show that you can get the job done.

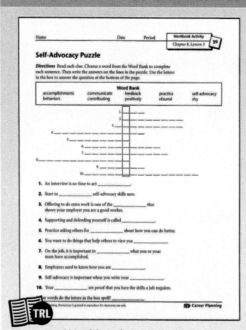

Workbook Activity 39

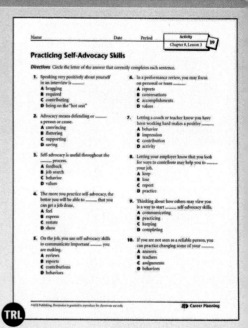

Activity 39

When Will You Need to Use Self-Advocacy Skills?

You can use self-advocacy skills in situations other than job interviews. There will be other times in your life when you will need to support or defend yourself. Once you have a job, you will need to let your employer know you are doing a good job. You need to communicate the important contributions you are making. You can do this in the same way you communicate your qualifications and accomplishments during your job search. Find opportunities to let your employer know how you are contributing. Times when you can do this include your regular performance reviews, update meetings, written reports, or informal conversations with your supervisor.

How Can You Communicate Your Accomplishments?

Sometimes, you will communicate your accomplishments in terms of what you personally have been able to achieve. For example, in a performance review your supervisor may ask you to explain the work you have been doing. You might say, "In the past three months, I have helped increase sales at our store by 25 percent. I have done this by changing the displays in the store and creating new signs in the store window." Other times, you might communicate your accomplishments in terms of what your work group or team has accomplished. This is especially important if you are a supervisor or manager. For example, you might say something like, "In the past three months, we have increased sales at our store by 25 percent. We did this by meeting together to identify ways that we could better market our products. We changed the displays in the store and created new signs for the store window to attract new customers. It has really been a team effort."

Gender and Careers

Before the 1970s, many more men than women had full-time careers. Women had traditionally put caring for children and homes above a business or other career. Of course, this situation has changed. Women work in many careers that used to be mainly pursued by men. All aspects of employment have changed as a result. Even job interviews are different today. In the past, an employer might ask a woman if she planned to get married. An interviewer might ask a woman if she planned to have children soon. Employers sometimes thought that a woman would only work until she had children. Today, questions like these cannot be asked in a job interview. If an interviewer does ask a question like this, politely refuse to answer.

Most young people are socialized to avoid bragging about their accomplishments and may feel that bragging in an interview reflects negatively on them. This lesson provides an opportunity for them to discuss and practice "selling themselves" by learning how to talk positively about their abilities and promote their best interests. Most student need to practice before they are comfortable with self-advocacy.

Point out to students that they should not exaggerate their skills and experiences. As students practice communicating their accomplishments, help them to choose language that is precise and accurate, rather than grandiose and overblown. If you are able to videotape student communications, they may be surprised to observe that self-advocacy does not come across as bragging.

3 **Reinforce and Extend**

On the Job

Ask a student to define the word *supervisor* and name some activities in which people supervise others. (*Students may name babysitting, tutoring, teaching, coaching, training a new employee.*) After students have read the On the Job feature on page 235, discuss with them the skills necessary to supervise others. (*A partial list might include good communication skills, social skills, responsibility, ability to motivate, and so on.*) If students have difficulty listing skills, have them describe the strategies they have observed in use by someone they consider to be a good supervisor.

Gender and Careers

Have students read the Gender and Careers feature on page 235. Poll them to learn how many have mothers, aunts, and grand-mothers with careers. Encourage students to ask their parents about female family members in the past who pursued careers in the 1970s or earlier. These personal histories can help students to appreciate how much the world of work has changed for women in recent decades.

Think Positive

Have a volunteer read the Think Positive feature on page 236 aloud. Ask each student to write a paragraph telling about ways he or she has contributed to a job, a team, or a group activity. As an alternative, a student could think of a way he or she would like to contribute and write a plan for doing so.

LEARNING STYLES

Logical/Mathematical

Check students' comprehension of the chapter material by having them convert the notes they have taken for each lesson (see the Logical/Mathematical activity, page 221) into a chapter outline. Review outline structure on the board and help students begin their outlines:

I. Interviewing Skills

  A. How to Prepare for an Interview

    1.

    2.

  B. What Interviewers Are Looking For

    1.

    2.

Think Positive

Self-advocacy is based on being positive. Do not think of self-advocacy as bragging or exaggerating your strengths. Employers sometimes need to be reminded of their employees' strengths. If you don't do this for yourself, who will?

Think about a time you have been in a class, on a team, or involved in some other group activity. Your teacher or coach may want to know whether you have completed your homework or practiced on your own. The only way someone would know this is if you told them. If your teacher asked who had completed the required assignment, you would want to be sure that he or she knew you had done so. You would also want your coach to know if you had been doing extra practice. Letting a teacher or coach know you have been working hard creates a positive impression of the kind of person you are. If you do not complete your homework on a regular basis, what kind of impression do you think this creates? Your teacher probably won't have a very good impression of you. You want to be sure that you are doing the things that will help you to be viewed positively by others. More importantly, you need to let them know what you are doing.

How Can You Let Employers Know You Are a Good Worker?

It is important as a worker that you learn to communicate to your employer that you work hard and do your best to contribute. You can communicate this by volunteering for additional assignments, completing your assignments on time, and doing a good job on them. You can also try to provide answers to problems that occur, and maintain a positive attitude. These behaviors are ways that you let your employer know that you are a good worker. They are self-advocacy skills. The best time to start practicing them is right now. To start, think about ways in which others may view you. Do you think they see you as the sort of person who works hard and tries her or his best? Do they view you as a person who is reliable and positive? If the answer to these questions is "yes," keep up the excellent work! If the answer to these questions is "maybe" or "no," you may need to change some of your behaviors.

How Can You Change Your Behaviors?

Some ways in which you might change your behaviors and begin practicing self-advocacy skills include:

- Get your assignments done on time. Do them well.
- Volunteer to help when there is the chance to do so.
- Ask your teachers, coaches, and advisors if there are ways you can help them.
- Do more than what is expected. Do extra work on some assignments. Put in extra practice time. Then, let your teacher or coach know that you are working hard to do your best.
- Ask your teachers, coaches, advisors, parents, or guardians for feedback about how you can do better.
- Be reliable, on time, and positive.
- Try to provide solutions to problems when they occur.
- Express your thanks to others when they help you.

By practicing these behaviors, you can help others to see you positively. You are advocating for a very important person—you!

Lesson 3 Review Write your answers to these questions on a sheet of paper.

1. What is self-advocacy?
2. Why is self-advocacy important in a job interview?
3. Explain how you can practice self-advocacy skills in a job.
4. Describe two ways that you can start practicing self-advocacy skills right now.

Get Involved

Volunteers can work with a huge number of organizations that help people. Perhaps you have had the chance to help people with a variety of needs. But have you ever thought about forming your own organization to help others? Each year, individuals see a need and start a group to fill it. For example, one young boy discovered that people were cold and homeless in his city. He took coats to these people that very day. Then he formed a group to keep helping these people. High school students have started groups that befriend the elderly. They have collected food and clothing for victims of hurricanes and tornadoes. Look around you. Discover how you can help those in need. This will show the kind of spirit that most employers are looking for.

Lesson 3 Review Answers

1. Self-advocacy is supporting, defending, or speaking up for yourself.
2. It is important because it can help you describing your accomplishments in positive terms.
3. Answers will vary. A person could ask his or her boss for feedback, or volunteer for extra jobs.
4. Answers will vary. A person could volunteer for assignments and help find solutions for problems.

Get Involved

After students have read the Get Involved feature on page 237, brainstorm with them a list of people in need of help in your community or state. Once students select several categories from the list, have them form small groups and discuss practical ways of helping those in need. Students may need to research existing networks of support, inquire about specific needs that are not met, and learn appropriate methods for assisting the group they have identified (e.g., the homeless, abused children, or foster children).

Interview Preparation

Students will prepare answers for a
number of the potential interview
questions they analyzed in Lesson 2:

Portfolio item no.	Lesson 2 item no.
1	1
2	2
3	3
4	4
5	5
6	6
7	21
8	9
9	10
10	11
11	13
12	14
13	16
14	18
15	20

Students can write their responses on their
own paper or on Portfolio Activity 8 in
the TRL. Students may need encouragement as they assess their strengths and
abilities. Growth in self-awareness benefits
by open and honest discussion with peers,
teachers, and family. You may want to suggest that students discuss with trusted,
familiar adults the skills and interests
those adults perceive them to have.

Interview Preparation

You have read about effective interview techniques. You have
read some common interview questions. Answering these
questions can help you prepare for an interview. Imagine you
have been called for an interview for a job. On your own paper,
write down the name of the job. Then answer the questions
below as you would answer them in a job interview. Add this
activity to your career portfolio.

1. What experiences have you had that relate to this position?

2. What interests you about this job?

3. What are your long-term goals?

4. In what kind of work environment are you most
comfortable?

5. What are your strengths?

6. What are your weaknesses?

7. How would you describe yourself?

8. What do you think you could contribute to this
organization?

9. What two accomplishments have given you the greatest
satisfaction in life?

10. What is most important to you in a job?

11. Why should I hire you?

12. What was your most rewarding experience in high school?

13. Describe a time you were faced with a major problem. How did you handle it?

14. What would you contribute to our work environment?

15. Do you think your grades are a good way to see how you would perform in this job? Why or why not?

You can practice answering common interview questions with a friend or classmate to prepare for job interviews.

In forming answers to these questions, students should keep in mind that even though many of the questions are focused on them, their answers need to show how they can make a valuable contribution to the employer.

BACKGROUND INFORMATION

Skills versus Personality

Students with little or no work experience may feel they cannot compete in an interview with experienced workers for an entry-level job. Actually, simply by making it to the interview stage, they have been evaluated as meeting the basic requirements for the job. In general, personality weighs much more heavily with the hiring manager than skills. Usually, it is easier to teach someone specific skills for a job than how to get along with others or how to make a good impression. Applicants should keep in mind that everything they do during the interview is evaluated—from neatness in filling out an application to being observant, to showing flexibility, and of course, appearance, voice, handshake, and body language.

Portfolio Activity Answers

1.–15. Answers will vary.

Chapter 8 Review

Use the Chapter Review to prepare students for tests and to reteach content from the chapter.

Chapter 8 Mastery Test

The Teacher's Resource Library includes two forms of the Chapter 8 Mastery Test. Each test addresses the chapter Goals for Learning. An optional third page of additional critical-thinking items is included for each test. The difficulty level of the two forms is equivalent.

Review Answers
Vocabulary Review

1. Self-advocacy is supporting, defending, or speaking up for yourself.

Concept Review

2. D 3. C 4. B 5. C

Critical Thinking

6. Answers will vary. Possible answer: The interview would give you valuable experience so you would practice your skills and know what to expect next time. 7. Answers will vary. Possible answer: The best action would probably be to ignore the rudeness and not let it affect your positive attitude. 8. Answers will vary. Possible answer: You could talk privately with the coach and describe several examples of times when you demonstrated team work, leadership, and skill. 9. Answers will vary. Possible answer: You might practice interviewing with a friend. Practice talking louder and responding fully. You might also tell the interviewer that you tend to be shy but discuss other positive traits you have. 10. Answers will vary. Possible answer: How large is the company? How long have you been in business? Who are some of your competitors?

Chapter 8 REVIEW

Vocabulary Review

Write the answer to this question on your paper.

1. What is self-advocacy?

Concept Review

Choose the word or phrase that best completes each sentence or answers each question. Write the letter of the answer on your paper.

2. Which question would most likely be asked in a job interview?

   A "How did you enjoy grade school?"

   B "Are you a good basketball player?"

   C "What is your favorite color?"

   D "What are your long-term goals?"

3. Which would be the most effective action verb to describe someone's accomplishments?

   A was   **C** invented

   B tried   **D** did

4. Which long-range goal would a successful job applicant most likely mention in an interview?

   A to make a lot of money

   B to become a sales manager

   C to have four children

   D to be able to retire young

5. Which is the best preparation for a job interview for an accounting firm?

   A reading a math book

   B buying a new outfit

   C practicing interviewing with a friend

   D researching the company president

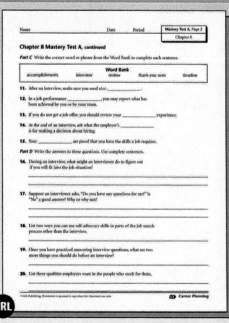

Critical Thinking

Write the answer to each question on your paper.

6. Explain how an interview might be a positive experience even if you do not get the job.

7. Suppose you walk into a workplace for a job interview and are treated rudely by the receptionist. Explain how you would react and why.

8. Suppose you feel you have not had a chance to shine on a school athletic team. How might you use self-advocacy to change this situation?

9. Suppose you are a quiet, shy person. For this reason, you feel that an interview does not show your best traits. What might you do to improve this situation the next time you have an interview?

10. What are three questions you could ask an interviewer who asks, "What would you like to know about our organization?"

Test-Taking Tip

Before you take a test, skim through the whole test to find out what is expected of you.

ALTERNATIVE ASSESSMENT

■ Have students write a three-paragraph essay explaining the purpose of an interview from the interviewer's point of view. In the writing, they should describe what the interviewer wants to learn about the applicant and give example questions that help him or her find out.

■ Ask each student to make a poster naming at least three things that should be done to prepare for an interview and at least six behaviors that should be remembered during the interview. Have students illustrate these concepts with appropriate photographs, symbols, or drawings.

■ Have students give an oral definition of self-advocacy and present a one-minute talk to demonstrate that they can advocate for themselves.

Chapter 8 Mastery Test B

Part A Circle the letter of the answer that correctly completes each sentence.

1. A good way to start thinking about your skills and interests is to _____.
 A write a résumé C get feedback
 B make lists D change some behaviors

2. After an interview, be sure you send a(n) _____.
 A e-mail C timeline
 B cover letter D thank-you letter

3. A good way to answer the interview question, "Do you have any questions for me?" is to _____.
 A ask what the opportunities are for advancement
 B restate that you are a good fit
 C say you have no questions
 D ask for feedback

4. An interviewer will observe your body language in order to get clues about _____.
 A how your skills relate to the job C whether you will fit into the job situation
 B what experiences you have had D how your interests connect to the job

5. The skill of speaking up for yourself is called _____.
 A performance review C self-advocacy
 B long-term goals D career research

Part B Match the words in Column 1 with the details in Column 2. Write the letter on the line.

Column 1	Column 2
_____ **6.** your weaknesses	A These are proof that you have the skills a job requires.
_____ **7.** your clothes	B You will use these in writing your résumé and in networking.
_____ **8.** your team	C Before your interview, you should be sure these are professional looking.
_____ **9.** your self-advocacy skills	D When an interviewer asks about these, you can discuss the skills you would like to develop.
_____ **10.** your accomplishments	E If you are a manager, you may be asked to report the accomplishments of this.

Chapter 8 Mastery Test B, continued

Part C Write the correct word from the Word Bank to complete each sentence.

Word Bank				
accomplishments	convince	practice	reliable	slang

11. All employers want their employees to be _____.

12. You should not use _____ during an interview.

13. You should use action verbs to describe your _____.

14. You want to _____ an interviewer that you are the best person for the job.

15. Doing well in an interview requires homework and _____.

Part D Write the answers to these questions. Use complete sentences.

16. List two kinds of body language that you want to remember during an interview.

17. What are two qualities that help people fit in and advance in their jobs?

18. Name three behaviors that let your employer know you are a good worker.

19. If you do not get a job offer, what are two things to think about or do?

20. What are two things to remember to do before you leave an interview?

TRL   **TRL**

Chapter 8 Mastery Test B, Pages 1–3

Chapter

9

Planning Guide

Life Outside of Work

		Student Text Lesson				
		Student Pages	Vocabulary	Lesson Review	Critical-Thinking Questions	Chapter Review
Lesson 1	Developing Hobbies and Interests	244–251	✔	✔	✔	✔
Lesson 2	Managing Time	252–257	✔	✔	✔	✔
Lesson 3	Making Healthy Lifestyle Choices	258–265	✔	✔	✔	✔
Lesson 4	Living Ethically	266–271	✔	✔	✔	✔

Chapter Activities

Student Text
Chapter 9 Portfolio Activity

Teacher's Resource Library
Chapter 9 Chapter Outline
Chapter 9 Self-Study Guide
Chapter 9 Portfolio Activity

Assessment Options

Student Text
Chapter 9 Review

Teacher's Resource Library
Chapter 9 Mastery Tests A and B

Teacher's Edition
Chapter 9 Alternative Assessment

Portfolio Activity	Writing Practice	Communication Connection	The Economy	Career Tip	Career Profile	On the Job	Gender and Careers	Think Positive	Technology Note	Get Involved	Background Information	Applications (Home, Community, Global, Environment)	Personal Journal	Online Connection	ELL/ESL Strategy	Visual/Spatial	Body/Kinesthetic	Interpersonal/Group Learning	Logical/Mathematical	Auditory/Verbal	Activities	Alternative Activities	Workbook Activities	Self-Study Guide	Chapter Outline
	247			247, 250	251						251	245, 247, 249	246	250	246	248	245		248	249	40	40	40	✔	✔
			254			256		253, 255				255			257			254	253	256	41	41	41	✔	✔
		263	262						261	265	259, 261	264		261	260	261	260, 262	263	264		42	42	42	✔	✔
272						269	271					268, 269			267				267, 270	270	43	43	43	✔	✔

Column group headers: **Student Text Features** | **Teaching Strategies** | **Learning Styles** | **Teacher's Resource Library**

Alternative Activities

The Teacher's Resource Library (TRL) contains a set of lower-level worksheets called Alternative Activities. These worksheets cover the same content as the regular Activities but are written at a second-grade reading level.

Career Interest Inventory

The AGS Publishing Harrington-O'Shea Career Decision-Making System (CDM) may be used with this textbook. Students can use the CDM to explore their interests and identify careers. The CDM defines career areas that are indicated by students' response on the inventory.

Name _____ Date _____ Period _____ **SELF-STUDY GUIDE**

Chapter 9: Life Outside of Work

| **Goals 9.1** To understand the importance of developing interests and hobbies outside of work |

Date Assignment Score

____ **1.** Read pages 243–251 ____
____ **2.** Complete the Lesson 1 Review on page 251. ____
____ **3.** Complete Workbook Activity 40. ____

Comments:

| **Goal 9.2** To learn time-management skills |

Date Assignment Score

____ **4.** Read pages 252–257 ____
____ **5.** Complete the Lesson 2 Review on page 257. ____
____ **6.** Complete Workbook Activity 41. ____

Comments:

| **Goal 9.3** To realize the impact of lifestyle choices on personal health and well-being |

Date Assignment Score

____ **7.** Read pages 258–265 ____
____ **8.** Complete the Lesson 3 Review on page 265. ____
____ **9.** Complete Workbook Activity 42. ____

Comments:

TRL ©AGS Publishing. Permission is granted to reproduce for classroom use only. **Career Planning**

Name _____ Date _____ Period _____ **SELF-STUDY GUIDE**

Chapter 9: Life Outside of Work, continued

| **Goal 9.4** To recognize the effects of ethical decisions |

Date Assignment Score

____ **10.** Read pages 266–271. ____
____ **11.** Complete the Lesson 4 Review on page 271. ____
____ **12.** Complete Workbook Activity 43. ____
____ **13.** Complete the Portfolio Activity on pages 272–273. ____
____ **14.** Complete the Chapter Review on pages 274–275. ____

Comments:

TRL ©AGS Publishing. Permission is granted to reproduce for classroom use only. **Career Planning**

Chapter

9 Life Outside of Work

You already know that people have to work in order to make a living. You may even have heard the saying that all work and no play makes a person dull. Failing to balance work and free time doesn't just make a person dull. It can lead to stress and other negative factors. It can damage a person's health and relationships. It is important to develop interests outside of work and make choices that will enhance your health and well-being. Striking the right balance will help you work smarter and feel better in every area of your life.

Goals for Learning

◆ To understand the importance of developing interests and hobbies outside of work

◆ To learn time-management skills

◆ To realize the impact of life choices on personal health and well-being

◆ To recognize the effects of ethical decisions

243

Introducing the Chapter

Have students look at the photo on page 242 and create a brief narrative about who these people are and what they are doing. Ask students what they think activities such as sports have to do with an adult lifestyle and the world of work. Read the chapter title and the introductory paragraph. Have students list some interests outside of work that adults they know are pursuing.

After students read the Goals for Learning, answer any questions they have about the vocabulary used there. Then ask students to read the chapter to meet these goals.

Career Tips

Ask volunteers to read the career tips that appear in the margins throughout the chapter. Then discuss them with the class.

Alternative Assessment

The Alternative Assessment box on page 275 of the Chapter Review includes activities using various learning styles to assess students' understanding of the Goals for Learning.

Name _____ **Date** ___ **Period** ___ | Chapter Outline, Page 1 / Chapter 9 | 9

Life Outside of Work

Directions Fill in the outline below. Filling in the blanks will help you as you read and study Chapter 9.

I. Lesson 1: Developing Hobbies and Interests (pp. 244–251)

  A. Work as an Obligation

    1. An activity done for enjoyment is called a _____

    2. An obligation is something you _____

  B. Hobbies and Interests

    1. Free time when you are not performing work is called _____

    2. Things that people want to learn more about are _____

  C. Reasons People Pursue Hobbies

    1. People have hobbies to keep fit, relieve stress, and _____

  D. Developing New Hobbies

    1. In school, to find activities that could become hobbies, look at the _____

    2. You can also look _____

  E. Connections Between Hobbies and Work

    1. Hobbies can help you develop _____ you can use in your career.

II. Lesson 2: Managing Time (pp. 252–257)

  A. How You Spend Time

    1. Activities that take more time than you want them to are _____

    2. You should do a personal time survey that covers _____

  B. Using Time Survey Results

    1. To make changes based on your personal time survey, make a _____

©AGS Publishing. Permission is granted to reproduce for classroom use only.   ➡ Career Planning

TRL

Name _____ **Date** ___ **Period** ___ | Chapter Outline, Page 2 / Chapter 9 | 9

Life Outside of Work, *continued*

III. Lesson 3: Making Healthy Lifestyle Choices (pp. 258–265)

  A. Nutrition, Diet, and Fitness

    1. Food contains about _____ nutrients your body needs.

    2. Regular exercise reduces the chance of _____

  B. Illness and Disease

    1. The signs of an illness are called _____

    2. _____ is the leading cause of death in the United States.

  C. STDs

    1. More than _____ diseases are transmitted sexually.

    2. The best way to protect yourself from STDs is to _____

  D. Preventing the Spread of Illness

    1. To prevent illness from spreading, _____ your hands often.

  E. Tobacco, Alcohol, and Drugs

    1. One of tobacco's damaging chemicals is _____

    2. An addiction to alcohol is called _____

    3. _____ are drugs that confuse the brain and nervous system.

IV. Lesson 4: Living Ethically (pp. 266–271)

  A. Ethical Living

    1. _____ are rules for behavior.

  B. Group Values and Universal Values

    1. Group values are _____ that a group considers important.

    2. Universal values are beliefs shared by most people around _____

  C. Guidelines for Making Ethical Decisions

    1. You should consider the _____, or _____ of a decision you make.

©AGS Publishing. Permission is granted to reproduce for classroom use only.   ➡ Career Planning

TRL

Chapter 9 Chapter Outline

Chapter 9 Lesson 1

Overview The lesson compares and contrasts the goals of work and hobbies and explores reasons for having hobbies.

Objectives

- To explore various hobbies and their functions that relate to work
- To suggest techniques for deciding on new hobbies to pursue
- To identify connections between hobbies and work

Student Pages 244–251

Teacher's Resource Library **TRL**

  Workbook Activity 40

  Activity 40

  Alternative Activity 40

Vocabulary

hobby
leisure time
obligation
stress

Write the word pairs *obligation/stress* and *hobby/leisure time* on the board. Have students look up the meaning of each term and explain how the pairs are related.

---

1 Warm-Up Activity

Poll students about their hobbies or those of others in their families. Begin a discussion about hobbies using questions like these:

- Why do you do this hobby?
- When do you do it?
- What effect does the activity have on you?

2 Teaching the Lesson

Students will be asked to pursue ideas for new hobbies in this lesson. You may want to alert them as they begin the lesson and ask them to check with hobby stores and local organizations for ideas.

> **Hobby**
> *An activity done for enjoyment*
>
> **Stress**
> *A state of physical or emotional pressure*
>
> **Obligation**
> *Something that is required or must be done*

Just as it is not too early to plan for your career, it is not too early to think about how you can develop your **hobbies** and interests. A hobby is an activity you do for enjoyment. Your job might help you fulfill some of your values. Hobbies and interests can also help you fulfill your values. You might think that hobbies and interests are not related to work at all. It may seem that an activity you do for fun is completely the opposite of an activity you do for pay. Some people might even have hobbies that give them a break from the **stress** of their jobs. Although that may be true in some cases, hobbies and interests have other connections with work. In this lesson you will learn about those connections. You will also discover some of the reasons people have hobbies and interests. Then, you will learn how you can find new hobbies to try.

How Is Work an Obligation?

You have learned that work is a specific activity that people do to earn a living. People work in order to provide for themselves and others. They work for wages. They need to be paid in order to fulfill their needs or to support a family. Work is an **obligation**. An obligation is something you have to do. If you want to earn a living, you must work. Another part of work is providing goods or services to others. For many people, providing for others is satisfying and enjoyable.

If you are in school, you are doing work when you study and complete assignments. Of course, you do not get paid for doing this kind of work. However, you get an education that prepares you for work later in life. Schoolwork is also an obligation. If you want to get an education, you must do schoolwork. Besides the work you do for school classes, you might also do other learning activities. If you want to be a musician, you might take music lessons. Practicing your musical instrument would be an obligation. You must practice if you want to develop the required level of knowledge and skill you need.

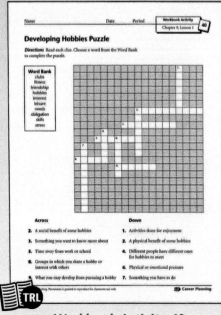

What Are Hobbies?

Leisure time
Free time away from work or school

Hobbies are activities that people choose to do. They are not obligations. For example, you may decide to learn how to ski because you enjoy the activity. Hobbies also give you the chance to learn new skills. Because hobbies are fun, they can help you reduce stress in your life. Notice how you feel after participating in a hobby. You will probably feel more relaxed, happier, and calmer. The free time that you have when you are not performing work is called **leisure time.** The activities people do in their free time can range from playing sports to researching an interesting subject at the library. The list below includes some of the many different activities that people consider their hobbies.

Bicycling	Fishing	Photography
Boating	Gardening	Playing a musical instrument
Collecting coins	Going to sporting events	Rock climbing
Dancing	Hiking	Reading
Developing Web sites	Listening to music	Volunteering
Dining at restaurants	Painting	Writing poetry

How Are Hobbies and Interests Related?

You have learned that interests are things that people want to learn more about. For example, you might be interested in learning about rare coins. However, you do not collect coins. You just want to read about and learn more about them. In this case, your interest is rare coins. Your hobby is reading or learning about the coins. For the rest of this lesson, the word *hobbies* will be used to include interests as well.

This lesson offers an opportunity for students to develop the comprehension skill of comparing and contrasting. Students will learn how work and hobbies are alike and different. Students can use a Venn diagram or a T-chart to show how hobbies can provide a welcome contrast to work or a means of developing skills for work.

 Reinforce and Extend

LEARNING STYLES

 Body/Kinesthetic
Students may find that their time surveys show that much of their leisure time is taken up by sedentary pastimes such as watching TV or playing video games. Have each student choose two or more activities from the list on page 245 and find out enough about it to demonstrate the activities it involves. For example, gardening involves digging, hoeing, fertilizing, weeding, planting, harvesting, and carrying assorted materials. Have students draw conclusions about why it is a good idea to have at least one active hobby.

AT HOME

Ask students to interview an adult who has a hobby. They can ask the person to explain the hobby, demonstrate what it involves, and tell about how his or her interest in it has evolved over time. Be sure students find out if and how the hobby helps the person to relieve stress.

Ask students to think of their favorite leisure activity. They can write details about how it makes them feel, what they enjoy about it, and so on. Then have students write a paragraph on their own paper explaining what this activity means to them.

ELL/ESL STRATEGY

Language Objective: *To read text to find transitional phrases and relationship words*

Students who are learning English can improve their comprehension of texts by learning the meanings of transitional words and phrases that show the relationships between sentences or ideas. Prepare a chart with words and phrases such as the following:

Relationship	Transitions
cause/effect	*as a result, because, if, therefore*
compare/ contrast	*however, on the other hand, unlike, like*
example	*for example, for instance*
time	*after, before, finally, next, meanwhile, then*
place	*above, beside, next to, below*
importance	*mainly, primarily, more importantly*

Have students learn the words and then look for examples in the text. (*For example* and *on the other hand* appear on page 246. *If, for example, on the other hand,* and *however* appear on page 247.)

Why Do People Pursue Hobbies?

People have different reasons for pursuing and developing their hobbies. Some people might really enjoy the things they do at work. So they transfer those skills to activities during their leisure time. Other people develop hobbies to do something different from their jobs. For example, suppose a person has a competitive job that has a lot of interaction with other people. He or she may turn to practicing yoga or sketching landscapes as a hobby. On the other hand, a person in a solitary, routine job may feel the need to participate in a competitive team sport as a hobby.

Think about your hobbies. What reasons do you have for doing these activities? If you said the reason for doing at least one of your hobbies is to keep physically fit, you are like a lot of other people. Next to keeping fit, relieving stress is another reason people develop hobbies. Almost everyone experiences stress at some time. Stress is physical or emotional pressure. It is built up tension that comes from trying to balance the demands of school, work, family, and friends. You most likely have experienced stress at some point. You might have felt stress when studying for final exams. Another time you may have experienced stress is when waiting to hear whether you made the team for a sport. Learning and getting used to the tasks that you have to perform in a new job might be stressful. When you are feeling stress, you may have headaches, back pain, and sore muscles. You might also have trouble sleeping. One way to relieve this stress is to do something you enjoy like jogging or reading.

Hobbies can help you develop new skills.

Many people relieve stress by doing physical activity. For example, a hard-played game of basketball can be useful for releasing pent-up emotions. On the other hand, playing a competitive game might create more tension rather than relieve it. If this happens to you, you might consider other activities. Some of these non-competitive activities might be aerobics or weight lifting. Becoming aware of the activities that relieve or contribute to tension in your life will help you choose your hobbies.

Another reason people develop hobbies is to meet new people. For many people, belonging to a group is very important. You can meet new people by joining various clubs and organizations. Some of these clubs are devoted to arts and crafts, drama, and reading. Other clubs involve indoor and outdoor sports. There are also groups that do work for a cause, like taking care of the environment. By joining a club, you can spend time with friends doing something you enjoy. You also have the opportunity to make new friends. If you are shy and have a hard time meeting new people, pursuing a hobby that involves other people is a good way to make friends.

What Are Some Other Reasons to Develop Hobbies?

You have just read about three important reasons for having hobbies: keeping fit, relieving stress, and being socially involved with other people. These are not the only reasons you may have for your hobbies, however. Another reason might be to develop your skills in sports or a musical instrument. Hobbies can also provide you the opportunity to be recognized or rewarded for an ability you have.

Writing Practice

Take some time to write your hobbies on a sheet of paper so you can be sure that you have thought of all of them. Then write the reasons you do these activities. Check with your peers to see what their reasons are.

Writing Practice

Give students several minutes to list their hobbies. If they have difficulty thinking of activities that "qualify" as hobbies in their minds, you might have them discuss their leisure activities in small groups. Students may want to set up a chart listing hobbies in one column and their reasons for participating in another.

IN THE ENVIRONMENT

Many outdoor activities provide good exercise but may harm the environment if participants do not educate themselves about the activity's impact. For example, camping, hiking, SCUBA diving, fishing, and mountain biking can create problems for wildlife and even damage habitats. Ask students with an interest in such hobbies to research and report on environmental dos and don'ts for participants.

Visual/Spatial

As students look for additional hobbies to pursue, they can help one another. Have each student make a poster or set up a display advertising his or her favorite hobby. Suggest that students include information and graphics or materials to persuade others to try the hobby. For example, a display about skiing could show pictures of equipment and people skiing in beautiful places. It might also include a video that demonstrates techniques. A stamp-collecting poster could show rare stamps and their value as well as information about the hobby.

LEARNING STYLES

Logical/Mathematical

Reproduce the chart from page 248 on the board. Ask students to list other needs a hobby can fulfill. (They might suggest the following: to improve self-confidence, to learn strategy, to sharpen thinking skills, and so on.) Write these in the first column. Then have students suggest other types of hobbies to list on the right. Have them tell you which skills to check for each hobby they list.

What are some of your hobbies? What needs do they fulfill? Let's look at an example of a hobby that might fulfill all the needs you have learned about. Basketball is a leisure activity that can have many purposes. Playing basketball can help you stay fit. It can also help you relieve stress. Basketball is a team sport, so it provides the chance to meet new people. Playing basketball will also help you develop skills like coordination, strategy, and working with others. Many sports besides basketball can fulfill these needs.

Some people prefer hobbies that are not physical activities. Playing a board game like chess, for example, will not help you stay in shape. However, it may be a way for you to relieve stress because it provides a break from your everyday life. You might also get better at thinking, planning, and making strategies as you play.

No matter what hobbies you pursue, think about how they meet your needs. People choose different leisure activities because they have different needs. You might find that physical activity is a good way for you to relieve stress. Or, you might find that reading is a better way to do so. Thinking about your needs will help you choose hobbies. To help you think about the needs your hobbies fulfill, look at this chart of hobbies and the needs they might fulfill.

Need Fulfilled	Hobby		
	Team Sports	Board Games	Reading or Other Quiet Activities
Stay in Shape	✓		
Relieve Stress	✓	✓	✓
Meet New People	✓	✓	
Improve Skills	✓	✓	✓
Get Recognition for Ability	✓	✓	

How Can You Decide What New Hobbies to Pursue?

If the hobbies you have now are not helping you to fulfill your needs, you can find and develop new hobbies. This is a good time for you to explore leisure activities. You may have tried a hobby earlier in your life and didn't like it. Now, you might find it interesting. You might be physically stronger now or have greater coordination and concentration. These changes might make it easier for you to take part in physical activities. This is the time to develop interests and learn skills from leisure activities. These skills can help you throughout your life.

To start finding new hobbies, look at the classes you are taking in school. The activities you enjoy in your schoolwork can lead you to develop a hobby that uses those same activities. Here are some examples of activities from various school subjects.

Subject	Activities or Interests
Art	drawing, painting, sculpture, graphic design, photography
Science and Technology	electronics, computer programming, astronomy
Music and Theater	dance, drama, singing, instruments
English	fiction writing, poetry, public speaking
Family/Consumer Science	cooking, sewing, managing a budget
Shop	automotive, metal work, wood work
Physical Education	sports, exercise

LEARNING STYLES

Auditory/Verbal
Have interested students investigate school or local organizations that focus on environmental protection. Students can post or report information they locate. If no such organizations exist, students can research online to find an environmental organization for teens and find out how to establish a local chapter.

IN THE COMMUNITY

After students have compiled a list of hobbies they would like to pursue, have them check local community agencies and organizations to find out which activities are offered. In addition, they can check retail establishments for supplies and classes. (For example, a fabric store or discount store may sell crafts and offer classes from time to time.) If a hobby on their list is not offered, local agencies might be able to suggest an alternative related activity or refer the students to a Web site or other organization. Using the information they have gathered, students can compile a directory of local hobby resources.

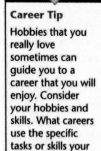

Career Tip

Hobbies that you really love sometimes can guide you to a career that you will enjoy. Consider your hobbies and skills. What careers use the specific tasks or skills your hobby uses? You may be able to turn what you do in your free time into a career.

Another way you can find new hobbies is by looking at the clubs and teams that your school has. Many of these clubs or teams expand on class activities. Here are some examples: computer club, poetry club, and business club. Other clubs may not be based directly on classroom activities. Groups might meet to discuss ways to protect the environment or to do community service projects. Another way to find hobbies to try is by going to local community agencies such as the YMCA/YWCA or a community center. These places might offer activities like indoor and outdoor sports, and leadership, environmental, arts, gardening, and computer clubs.

What Are the Connections Between Hobbies and Work?

Hobbies can also help you develop skills you can use in your career. One of the greatest benefits of a hobby is when it turns into a career. For example, you might begin to learn playing the piano for fun. You take lessons and practice regularly. Perhaps you become good enough to be a piano teacher. Similarly, you might start playing basketball after school with your friends. Then you try out for and make the school team. You might go on to play at college or as a professional. Or, you might become a basketball coach.

Your hobby may not turn out to be exactly what you do for work later in life, however. Just because you like an activity as a hobby does not mean that you will want to do it as a career. Even if you become very good at your hobby, some jobs are very difficult to get. For example, very few people end up being professional basketball players. You might enjoy basketball and also have strong business skills. You might enjoy working in a management position for a basketball team. Perhaps you have artistic ability. Then, you might become an illustrator for a sports magazine. For most careers, you use skills from more than one hobby. For example, an illustrator for a sports magazine combines the hobbies of sports and art.

Pursuing your hobbies and developing new ones can help you learn new skills and meet new people. You can also stay physically fit and find good ways to relieve stress. Taking part in leisure activities that you enjoy can also help develop skills you can use in your career.

Lesson 1 Review Write your answers to these questions on a sheet of paper.

1. How are hobbies and interests different from work?

2. What are some reasons for pursuing hobbies?

3. How can hobbies be directly related to your career? How are they indirectly related?

Career Profile

Personal Trainer

Some career paths combine hobbies and health with earning a paycheck. Professional trainers often begin with a personal interest in health and wellness. They develop this personal interest through education and practice. Personal trainers work in a variety of settings: health clubs, medical and chiropractic practices, rehabilitation centers and hospitals, and community centers. They might also work for a sports team or club. They work with a wide range of clients. But the goal is always similar: to help a client get stronger and healthier. Personal trainers provide information about safe exercise programs, develop training plans, monitor progress, and provide feedback to people.

Personal trainers generally have to be certified. They need to demonstrate an understanding of how exercise and diet affects the body. Trainers who work with athletes, people with diabetes, or individuals learning to use an artificial limb also spend time learning about the special needs of their clients. In addition, personal trainers have to pay close attention to their own health and fitness. Helping people achieve their health goals can be rewarding and meaningful work for a person with a passion for personal wellness.

Life Outside of Work   *Chapter 9*   **251**

1. Work is an obligation, or something that you have to do. Hobbies and interests are activities that you choose to do.

2. Hobbies can be a way to relieve stress, meet people, stay physically fit, or have some quiet time to yourself.

3. Hobbies can be directly related to your field by building specific skills or by providing practice. Hobbies can be indirectly beneficial to your work by developing skills such as communication, teamwork, and problem solving; by relieving stress so that you can do your work better; and by building a network.

Career Profile

Personal Trainer

Ask students what they think the job of a personal trainer is about. Then have several volunteers read the Career Profile on page 251 aloud. Students may be familiar with the career of an athletic trainer. If there is an athletic trainer at your school, invite him or her to speak to your students and explain how his or her job is like that of a personal trainer and how it differs. Students who are interested in learning more can enter the key words *personal trainer career* in a search engine to locate more information online.

BACKGROUND INFORMATION

Personal Trainer
The job of personal fitness trainer involves being an educator, a coach, an advisor, and even a friend to clients. The trainer generally meets with clients about an hour at a time, taking them through workouts to help them reach goals. Aside from working for individuals, personal trainers are also often hired by health clubs, universities, spas, resorts, and cruise ships. Corporate fitness is growing in popularity, so companies may also hire personal trainers to oversee workplace wellness programs. Personal trainers can take certification programs through organizations such as the National Strength and Conditioning Association and the American College of Sports Medicine.

Chapter 9 Lesson 2

Overview This lesson defines *time management* and helps students analyze their use of time by completing a personal time survey.

Objectives

- To explain what time management is and demonstrate techniques for time management
- To analyze a personal time survey and complete one
- To set up a time-management schedule and implement it

Student Pages 252–257

Teacher's Resource Library **TRL**

Workbook Activity 41

Activity 41

Alternative Activity 41

Vocabulary

time management

Explain to students that this lesson is all about how to manage time well. Start a word web on the board with the term *time management* in the center circle. As they read, have students add details related to time management in circles around this one. At the end of the lesson, ask students to use the word web as a source to write a paragraph defining time management.

---

 1 Warm-Up Activity

Ask students to think of activities they do each day that they think are important and other activities they think are a waste of time. Record students' ideas on a chart.

Daily Activities

Important	Waste of Time

Ask students to explain how they decided on the placement of each activity. Save the chart for reference during the lesson.

Lesson **2** Managing Time

Time management
The best use of your time to achieve your goals

Think Positive

Searching for a job can be frustrating and exhausting. During this stressful time, it is very important to eat right, exercise regularly, and get plenty of sleep. These steps will help you keep stress under control.

This lesson is about managing your time. **Time management** is how you use your time to complete your activities and achieve your goals. It involves deciding what activities you want to participate in and how much time you want to give to each of them. Time management also involves discovering what activities are taking up more time than you want them to. You can call these activities "time wasters."

This lesson will help you understand time management and practice time management skills. It will guide you through a survey of how you spend your time. Then you will make some decisions about the time you spend on those activities. The decisions can help you subtract time from some activities, add time to others, or even get rid of "time wasters." These time management skills will be useful throughout your life. It is important to start developing them now.

How Do You Spend Your Time?

It is important to have a clear idea of how you spend your time. What activities are you involved in? How much time do you spend on them? One way to answer these questions is to do a personal time survey. Make a list of the activities you participate in each day. Use the chart on page 253 for activity suggestions. Then determine how much time you spend on each activity. Finally, total the hours to find out how much time you spend doing the activities.

You should do your personal time survey for at least a week. There are 168 hours in a week. (24 hours × 7 days = 168 hours) Estimate the amount of time you spend on each activity each day. Then multiply that time by seven to get the total for a week. You will need to multiply your time spent in school by five instead of seven. You are in school only five days each week. Make sure that your total hours do not add up to more than 168.

Here is an example of a completed personal time survey.

Activity	Hours Per Day	Hours Per Week
1. Number of hours for sleep	8 × 7 =	56
2. Number of hours for meals	1½ × 7 =	10½
3. Number of hours for homework	1½ × 7 =	10½
4. Number of hours for chores, errands, etc.	½ × 7 =	3½
5. Number of hours for scheduled activities (clubs, church, family events, etc.)	1 × 7 =	7
6. Number of hours for sports	1 × 7 =	7
7. Number of hours traveling to and from activities	1 × 7 =	7
8. Number of hours spent with friends	½ × 7 =	3½
9. Number of hours on the phone	½ × 7 =	3½
10. Number of hours watching TV	1½ × 7 =	10½
11. Number of hours on the computer	½ × 7 =	3½
12. Number of hours at school	6½ × 5 =	32½
Total	24	155

Notice that the total of 155 hours is less than 168. This is because the number of hours in school is counted for only five days. Now that you have completed your personal time survey, look at the total for each item and compare them. Make a note of anything you find interesting or had not realized about the way you spend your time. Are you spending too much time preparing for school? Not enough time sleeping? How much time is spent on the phone compared to socializing in person? Answering these questions is part of balancing your time between work and leisure.

Ask students how they feel on a day when they have not slept well the night before, have skipped meals, or have not moved around much. Point out that rest, nutrition, and exercise are keys to wellness and feeling good. Have a volunteer read the Think Positive feature on page 252 aloud.

2 Teaching the Lesson

Be sure students understand that their estimates of hours spent on each category of activity must lead to a total of 24 hours or less in a day. You may want to have students keep a record for several days of their activities and the amount of clock time spent (for example, 3:30–4:30, soccer practice; 4:30–5:30 with friends, etc.). Then they can find an average for each category.

You may wish to have students complete the Portfolio Activity on pages 272 and 273 after they read this lesson. The activity is a survey about hobbies, but the final question calls for students to make a plan to fit in adequate time for hobbies (covered in Lesson 1). Students can reference the personal time survey done in this lesson in order to complete the Portfolio Activity.

3 Reinforce and Extend

LEARNING STYLES

Logical/Mathematical
Review the skills of averaging and estimating with students. Work through sample problems like these:

- Homework: Monday—40 min.; Tuesday—1 hr. 10 min.; Wednesday—15 min.; Thursday—35 min. (40 + 70 + 15 + 35 = 160; 160 ÷ 4 = 40 min.)

- Scheduled activities: tai chi class, 1 hr., MWF; church, 1.5 hr., T & Sun; piano lesson, 1 hr., Th; visit Grandma, 2 hr., Sat. (3 + 3 + 1 + 2 = 9; 9 ÷ 7 = 1.3 hr.)

Have students write out their calculations for the amounts of time they put on their personal time surveys.

LEARNING STYLES

Interpersonal/ Group Learning

Students who are overcommitted may have difficulty perceiving reasonable ways of cutting back on activities. Set up small groups of students and have them review and discuss each other's schedules and time survey results. In discussion, students may be able to prioritize activities as obligations (cannot be cut) and choices (optional). Students can then evaluate activities in the second group to assess what benefits come from them.

Remember that networking is a very effective way to find a job. Developing interests that bring you into contact with a variety of people is a great way to develop a relationship that will lead to a good job.

How Can You Use Your Time Survey Results?

Your personal time survey has given you a better picture of how you spend your time. Now you can think about how you might want to change the amount of time you spend on your activities. Are you spending too much time on one activity or too little on another? Are there any time wasters? As you subtract or add time to the activities, just remember to keep the total for the week at or less than 168 hours.

Once you have made changes to your personal time survey, you can make a schedule. A schedule will help you remember the things you have to do and how much time you want to spend doing them. A good way to start is to make a simple "To Do" list. Include activities you have to do for the week, when they need to be done, and the amount of time they will take. The activities should be things you have committed yourself to doing, such as homework, practice for a sports team, and family functions. This schedule will ensure that you have time to complete your most important activities.

If you have a lot of activities to fit into your week, you may need to create a more detailed schedule. Making time for all of your activities and obligations can be a lot to handle. You need a well-organized plan to manage your time. This kind of plan involves making a schedule for the week. For each day, write the activities that you must do. These would be the same activities you wrote in your "To Do" list. Also include the activities you would like to do.

Think Positive

A proverb says, "The journey of a thousand miles begins with one step." Thinking about your career and all the coming changes may feel overwhelming. Instead of focusing on this enormous task, think about the small steps. This will help you see your progress day by day. Instead of being overwhelmed, you will be encouraged and challenged with each new step.

Making a schedule can help you manage your time effectively.

You will need to take some time to set up your time-management schedule. It may take effort and persistence to make it work. If the first attempt with your time-management plan does not work, go over the plan again and make changes as necessary. For example, make sure that you are setting aside enough time to complete the activities you have on your plan. You should also make sure that you are not spending more time on activities than you have planned. You may have set aside one hour for leisure reading, for example. When the hour is up, you may need to stop reading and move on to the next activity.

Learning how to make and use a time-management plan will help you complete work. It will also help you use your leisure time wisely. If you follow your plan, you may have more time to include other valuable activities you would like to do.

After students read the Think Positive feature on page 255, have them write out three small steps they are currently taking to move toward a career.

At Home

As students attempt to enforce their time management plans, they may need to use a timer to keep track of time while they complete an activity. For example, if they have planned 30 minutes for the activity, they can set the timer for 30 minutes. If this is not enough time, they will know they have to adjust their schedule by increasing the time allowed for that activity and decreasing the time for another activity.

Students can apply the time-management principles mentioned here for completing work projects in order to improve their ability to complete schoolwork. After students have read the On the Job feature, have them create a "To Do" list of homework assignments, upcoming tests, and projects and prioritize it. Students' lists can have subdivisions for weekly tasks and a main calendar for the month.

LEARNING STYLES

Auditory/Verbal

After students have implemented a time management schedule and used it for a week, open the class to discussion. Ask volunteers to read the bulleted tips on page 256 aloud, and have students describe experiences that illustrate these aspects of time management. What worked for them and what didn't? Invite students to offer additional tips they would give to a person who is trying to schedule his or her time better.

On the Job

Time management is as important on the job as it is in life outside of work. To accomplish all of your work tasks, work on prioritizing your to-do list. If you aren't sure when something is due or what is most important, ask a supervisor. This will ensure that what needs to get done first gets attention.

Here are some hints to help you make your time-management plan work well.

- Put aside some time to prepare your schedule, preferably on a weekend.
- Schedule the most important activities first. Important activities might include homework, family functions, and research projects for school.
- Allow time to get from one activity to the next one. For example, if your last class of the day finishes at 3:00 P.M., don't schedule the next event for 3:00 P.M.
- Allow some non-scheduled time. If you fall behind in your schedule, this time will allow you to catch up. If you stay on schedule, this non-scheduled time can be free time to fill however you like.
- Consider the times of the day when you work best. Some people work best right after school. Others work best early in the morning.

Recognize the difference between activities that require the best of your mental and physical abilities and those that don't. You need to place these activities at suitable times in your schedule. Some household chores such as vacuuming the carpet or washing the car demand little of your ability or skill. Other chores can be tiring, leaving you with little energy to focus on other activities. Do not participate in activities that are not on your schedule. For example, if watching TV is not on your schedule for a particular day, don't give in to the temptation.

You can get an idea of how to arrange your time by studying the sample schedule on page 257.

Time Schedule

SATURDAY

9:00–9:30 A.M.	Breakfast
10:00–12:00 P.M.	Work on science project
12:00–1:00 P.M.	Lunch
1:30–3:30 P.M.	Work on friend's car
4:00–6:00 P.M.	Soccer practice
6:30–7:30 P.M.	Dinner
7:30–8:00 P.M.	Household chores
8:00–9:30 P.M.	Socialize with friends

SUNDAY

9:00–9:30 A.M.	Breakfast
10:00–11:00 A.M.	Finalize science project with classmate
11:30–1:30 P.M.	Family function and lunch
2:00–4:00 P.M.	Soccer game
4:30–5:30 P.M.	Mow lawn
6:00–8:00 P.M.	Go to see a movie with friends
8:30–9:30 P.M.	Prepare schedule for week

Lesson 2 Review Write your answers to these questions on a sheet of paper.

1. What are some benefits of good time management?

2. How is a "To Do" list different from a schedule? How are they related?

3. Why is it important to leave non-scheduled time in your schedule?

Lesson 2 Review Answers

1. Good time management helps to relieve stress by ensuring that important things get done and that time is not being wasted.

2. A "To Do" list describes tasks that need to be accomplished, while a schedule allots specific times for working on those tasks. Making a "To Do" list is a good start for creating a schedule because it shows what needs to be done and helps you prioritize the tasks to make sure more gets done.

3. Non-scheduled time provides a buffer so when certain activities take longer than expected, you are not stressed out about falling behind on other tasks. Non-scheduled time can also be a "bonus," because if you get done on time or early, extra time can be used to relax or do something you enjoy.

Lesson at a Glance

Chapter 9 Lesson 3

Overview This lesson discusses the role of diet, fitness, and illness prevention in a healthy life. It discusses the harmful effects of STDs, tobacco, alcohol, and other drugs.

Objectives

- To explain how diet and fitness contribute to health
- To understand the symptoms and effects of common diseases
- To identify STDs and learn how to prevent them
- To understand the effects of harmful drugs such as tobacco and alcohol

Student Pages 258–265

Teacher's Resource Library

Workbook Activity 42

Activity 42

Alternative Activity 42

Vocabulary

addictive
alcoholism
diabetes
diet
drug
nicotine
nutrient
physical fitness
sexually transmitted disease
symptom

Write the vocabulary terms on the board. Have students look up their meanings and use them as clues to make a cross-word puzzle. Provide graph paper for students to create their puzzles. Students can exchange puzzles and complete them.

> **Diet**
> *The food that you regularly eat and drink*
>
> **Nutrient**
> *A substance in food that your body needs to work properly*

Part of having a successful career is living a healthy lifestyle. Your career choices can be limited by not making healthy choices. Many employers require their workers to be in good physical shape. Employers also want employees who make good decisions about drugs and alcohol. Being unhealthy can affect your job performance. The information presented in this lesson focuses on making healthy choices.

Nutrition and Fitness

Food is fuel for your body. Food provides the energy your body needs to work properly. Deciding what food to eat is important. Good food choices help you stay healthy. Poor food choices can lead to poor health. Eating too much or not enough food also can cause problems.

Why Is Diet Important to Your Health?

Your **diet** is the food that you eat and drink. Your diet affects the way you look, feel, and perform. A healthy diet helps you look your best. It makes your hair shine and helps keep your skin clear. It gives you energy to do things you need or want to do. Eating healthy also contributes to your emotional health. It gives you energy to think clearly and to deal with stress.

Scientists have discovered that food contains about 50 substances that your body needs to work and grow properly. These substances are called **nutrients.** Foods vary in the nutrients they provide. For example, green beans have more nutrients than sugar. A healthy diet includes foods that are good sources of nutrients. If your diet does not include enough nutrients, you might experience headaches, stomachaches, tiredness, or depression. A lack of nutrients can lead to health problems.

To make sure you eat foods with the right amount of nutrients, you can plan your diet. The U.S. government publishes guidelines for a healthy diet. You can use these and other resources to make sure you are eating healthy.

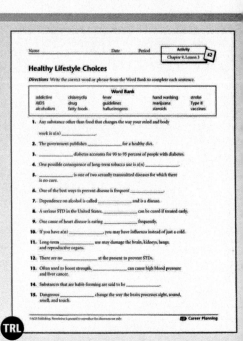

Workbook Activity 42   **Activity 42**

Physical fitness

The body's ability to meet the demands of everyday living

Symptom

A physical sign or indication that you have an illness

Why Is Fitness Important to Your Health?

Along with having a healthy diet, it is important to get physical exercise. Exercise keeps your body fit. **Physical fitness** is your body's ability to meet the demands of daily living. That means having enough energy to do all the things you want to do. Physical fitness is a key part of your overall good health. It affects your emotional, social, and physical well-being. Exercising regularly to be physically fit is another way you can take care of yourself.

To exercise means to move the larger muscles of your body, such as those in your arms and legs. Regular exercise can help build a strong heart and lungs. It helps build strong, firm muscles. It improves your body's ability to move in ways you want it to move, such as by twisting and turning. Exercise gives you more energy so you can do more without becoming tired. Active people sleep better, feel better, and are less depressed than people who are not active.

Exercise can reduce the chance for illness. For example, regular exercise reduces the risk of heart disease. Regular exercise can also shorten the time it takes to get well if you become sick. Not getting enough exercise can cause serious health problems. According to a government report, the lack of physical activity contributes to 400,000 preventable deaths (17% of total deaths) a year in the United States. You can keep yourself healthy by doing 30 to 60 minutes of physical activity a day.

Recognizing and Preventing Illness

Our bodies need food, plenty of fluids, exercise, and rest to stay healthy. However, there are times when the body does not work properly and an illness occurs. Being able to recognize the signs, or **symptoms,** of an illness will help you know when and how to get treatment.

1 Warm-Up Activity

Have students name things they consider to be a threat to their health and well-being. Jot these down on the board, choose several that are discussed in the lesson, and ask volunteers to explain why these things are harmful. Leave the list on the board if possible, so that students can add to it as they complete the lesson.

2 Teaching the Lesson

Discuss nutritional requirements and guidelines with students. You may want to have students keep a food diary as they complete this lesson and check it against the government's nutritional recommendations and guidelines.

If possible, invite a nutritionist and/or a health professional to speak to students about healthy lifestyles.

BACKGROUND INFORMATION

Diet and Obesity

Research shows a growing percentage of Americans (including children) are obese. The trend is attributed to an increase in the number of calories consumed and to the kinds of foods consumed. From 1985 to 2000, average daily calories consumed in the United States increased 12 percent (about 300 calories). Much of that increase was due to an increase in consumption of refined grains, fat, and sugar. In general, American diets are low in nutritious whole grains, fruits, and vegetables. By contrast, research has shown that people who eat more servings of fruit and vegetables daily have a lower body mass index (BMI). (This is a measure of body fat related to size.) In addition, the diseases that result from obesity are taking a growing share of health-care dollars. Young people should be educated to include plenty of fruits, vegetables, and whole grains in their diets and to limit their consumption of fat and refined sugar and flour.

LEARNING STYLES

Body/Kinesthetic

A personal testimony about feeling stronger, more agile, and more upbeat can persuade teens to choose a more active lifestyle. Have students with an active hobby prepare a demonstration for the class to show the kinds of exercise it involves. Encourage demonstrators to include specific information about the muscle groups that are strengthened, energy that is gained, and other benefits they have realized from the exercise. If possible, allow presenters to teach key movements to other students.

ELL/ESL STRATEGY

Language Objective: *To prepare a presentation*

Ask students to choose one of the common diseases or STDs discussed on pages 260 and 261 and learn more about it. Suggest specific questions students should answer as they read about the disease, such as

What are the symptoms?
What are the causes of the disease?
What results from having the disease?
How can the disease be prevented?

Students who are learning English can be assigned an English-proficient aide, on whom they can call for assistance if they have difficulty with reading materials. Review with students the technique of skimming a text for key words in the questions they want to answer. Have students take notes as they read. Then group those who chose the same disease and ask them to prepare a brief presentation about the disease.

Diabetes

A disease in which the body is not able to use sugar from food

What Diseases Are Considered Common?

The most common disease in the United States is the cold. A cold usually lasts from several days to more than a week. Symptoms include sneezing, cough, stuffy or runny nose, fever, headache, and sore throat. These symptoms differ throughout the time that you have the cold. They may also differ from person to person and from cold to cold. The flu, or influenza, has some of the same symptoms as a cold. Flu symptoms are usually more severe. Symptoms include fever, headache, sore throat, and coughing. Aching muscles, chills, nausea, vomiting, and diarrhea are some other flu symptoms. These symptoms also differ throughout the illness and from person to person.

In addition to the cold and flu, other common diseases include heart disease, cancer, and **diabetes.** Heart disease is the leading cause of death in the United States. You can protect yourself from heart disease, high blood pressure, high cholesterol, heart attack, and stroke by eating a healthy diet and getting enough exercise. Cancer is the second leading cause of death in the United States. Cancer is an abnormal and harmful growth of cells in the body. There are more than 100 types of cancer. Cancer symptoms can vary. Often, people will feel pain or discomfort in the area where the cancer is growing. Sometimes, a person will not feel well but not have specific symptoms. Unusual weight loss and poor appetite may occur as a result of cancer. The most important factor for cancer survival is finding the cancer early. Here are some warning signs of cancer.

Change in bowel or bladder habits

A sore that will not heal

Unusual bleeding or discharge

Thickening or lump in the breast or elsewhere

Indigestion or difficulty swallowing

Obvious change in wart or mole

Nagging cough or hoarseness

Another common disease is diabetes. Diabetes is a disease in which the body cannot use sugar and other food for energy. Type I and Type II are the two most common types of diabetes. Type I diabetes usually starts during childhood. Symptoms include frequent urination, extreme thirst and hunger, rapid weight loss, and tiredness. About 5 to 10 percent of people with diabetes have Type I diabetes.

Type II diabetes is the most common form of diabetes. It usually occurs in adults over age 40. Type II diabetes is milder than Type I. People who are inactive or overweight are at risk for getting Type II diabetes. Type II diabetes can often be controlled and prevented through weight loss and exercise. Symptoms include blurry vision, slow-healing sores, tiredness, and tingling in the hands or feet. Type II diabetes accounts for 90 to 95 percent of people with diabetes.

What Are STDs?

Sexually transmitted diseases, or STDs, are spread through sexual activity. In the United States, one in four people under age 21 has an STD. More than 20 diseases are transmitted sexually. Some of the most common and serious STDs are AIDS, gonorrhea, chlamydia, syphilis, and genital herpes. Except for genital herpes and AIDS, most sexually transmitted diseases can be cured when they are treated early. For diseases without cures, medical treatment can make people more comfortable. There are no vaccines to prevent sexually transmitted diseases. The best way to protect yourself from STDs is to refrain from sexual activity.

Technology Note

Keeping track of nutrition and exercise has never been as easy as it is today. Inexpensive electronic logs can help you keep track of eating patterns and daily activity. You can also go online to find "personal health assistants" and many other resources about developing healthy habits. Take advantage of these resources to help you make healthy choices.

LEARNING STYLES

Visual/Spatial

Ask students who learn more easily from visual cues to create a collage or a poster summarizing important steps to take to prevent a disease such as the flu or heart disease. Encourage students to be creative and include pictures as well as words to make their points. Have students organize the information logically and then use their collages or posters to teach others about disease prevention.

BACKGROUND INFORMATION

STDs

An estimated 65 million people in the United States have an incurable STD. Some 15 million new cases of STDs occur each year. The most common STD in America is genital herpes, with more than 45 million individuals having contracted this lifelong (but relatively harmless) virus. Two-thirds of all STDs occur in people 25 years of age or younger. One in four new STD infections occurs in teenagers. Hepatitis B, a more recent addition to the list of STDs, is 100 times more infectious than HIV.

ONLINE CONNECTION

Students can get information on a variety of health-related topics at the Department of Health and Human Services Web site. Information on eating right, exercise and fitness, and smoking and drinking can be found at: http://www.hhs.gov/safety/index.shtml.

Technology Note

After students have read the Technology Note on page 261, have them go online to locate a personal health assistant site. Students can work in pairs to enter data. Be available to assist or answer questions they may have.

Body/Kinesthetic

Have a small group of students work together to make up brief skits demonstrating dos and don'ts for preventing the spread of disease. Students may wish to create humorous skits but should end with a serious message.

The Economy

Invite volunteers to think about how the American epidemic of obesity affects the economy. Read the feature on page 262 aloud together, and have students summarize these effects. (*increased government spending, higher insurance rates, lost time at work, lower productivity, greater percentage of income spent on health care*) Discuss the seriousness of the growing obesity rate in America. You may wish to have students form groups and discuss strategies that could be implemented to turn this trend around. Have students present their top five ideas to the class.

How Can You Prevent the Spread of Illness?

Drug
Any substance, other than food, that changes the way your mind and body work

People cannot prevent all illnesses from happening to them. However, many diseases can be prevented. Diseases such as the cold and flu are spread from person to person. Germs that cause disease are passed from person to person. Other diseases are caused by a person's behaviors. For example, consider a person who eats many fatty foods, avoids exercise, and smokes cigarettes. The person's behaviors may cause high blood pressure or trigger a heart attack. Another way disease is spread is through the environment. For example, small children who eat chips of lead-based paint can get lead poisoning. Nonsmokers who breathe other people's cigarette smoke may get lung diseases, including cancer. Here are some things you can do to prevent illnesses from spreading.

- Avoid physical contact with a sick person
- Cover your mouth when coughing
- Wash your hands often
- Avoid second-hand smoke
- Protect yourself from STDs

Mood-Modifying Substances

Another part of having a healthy lifestyle is avoiding harmful **drugs.** Drugs like tobacco and alcohol have damaging physical and mental effects.

The Economy

Being overweight or obese can impair both physical and financial health. A study by the Medical Expenditure Panel Survey estimated that individuals, insurance companies, and government programs spent more than $51 billion in 1998 for illnesses directly related to being overweight and obese. The amount does not seem to be declining. As a result, health insurance costs have increased. People have to spend more of their own money for health care.

Other research has shown a direct impact on productivity in the workplace as well. Obese people have a significantly greater likelihood of developing illnesses. This means they are also much more likely to miss time at work. Between higher medical costs and reduced productivity, the overall cost of obesity has created both a healthcare crisis in this country as well as an economic dilemma.

How Does Tobacco Affect People?

Nicotine

A chemical in tobacco to which people become addicted

Addictive

Habit forming

Alcoholism

A disease in which a person is dependent on alcohol

Every time a person smokes, he or she breathes in about 2,000 harmful chemicals. One of the most damaging chemicals is **nicotine.** Nicotine is **addictive,** or habit forming. Nicotine is found in cigarettes, cigars, pipe tobacco, and chewing tobacco. It speeds up the heart rate and increases blood pressure. Long-term tobacco use can lead to a heart attack, stroke, or cancer. In fact, smoking is responsible for 87 percent of lung cancer deaths. Smoking can also cause other breathing diseases. Cigarette smoke also can harm nonsmokers. Studies prove that healthy nonsmokers can get breathing diseases and cancers by inhaling smoke from burning cigarettes. Because of the harm second-hand smoke causes, laws forbid smoking in many public places. In addition, many workplaces are smoke free.

How Does Alcohol Affect the Body?

People can become physically and psychologically addicted to the alcohol found in wine, beer, and hard liquor. People drink alcohol to feel more self-confident, to relax, or to escape uncomfortable emotions. In realty, alcohol doesn't help and instead often hinders people. Alcohol has a damaging effect on every major system in the body. Alcohol is not digested but absorbed directly from the stomach into the bloodstream and carried throughout the body. When people drink alcohol, their judgment, vision, reaction time, and muscle control are affected. The amount of alcohol in their blood begins to rise. Short-term effects of alcohol include slurred speech, dizziness, flushed skin, stumbling, and dulled senses and memory. Physical and mental dependence on alcohol or lack of control over drinking is called **alcoholism.** Alcoholism is classified as a disease.

Communication Connection

Many people who use drugs and alcohol believe these substances will help them feel relaxed around others. In reality, people who use drugs often say and do things they regret later. Instead of using substances to relieve your anxiety, try a more healthy way to deal with stress. For example, you can practice interviewing with a friend. Try to make it a fun activity. This will help you get used to asking and answering questions in a friendly setting. You can prepare for job interviews without any negative side effects.

Life Outside of Work   Chapter 9   **263**

Interpersonal/Group Learning

Place students in small groups and have them research either tobacco or alcohol as drugs. The purpose of each group will be to persuade peers to avoid tobacco or alcohol. Have groups decide what tasks need to be done for their presentation (such as research, script writing, graphic design, or props and sets creation). Then assign tasks so that every member is involved in both preparation and presentation.

Communication Connection

Have students read the Communication Connection on page 263. Prompt students to list effects of alcohol and drugs. List these on the board. Categorize them as myths or facts. Then have students brainstorm a list of alternative strategies for relieving stress and anxiety.

What Other Affects Can Alcohol Use Have?

Alcohol use can also affect driving ability. About half of all teenagers who are involved in traffic accidents have been drinking alcohol. The penalties for drunken driving vary from state to state. Some penalties include spending the night in jail or having your driver's license suspended. Even if you do not drink alcohol, drunken driving can affect you. Some people accept rides from others who have been drinking alcohol. Turning down such an offer ensures your safety and protects you from injuries that could affect you for a lifetime.

What Are Some Other Harmful Drugs?

Besides tobacco and alcohol, other drugs can have harmful effects on a person's mind and body. These drugs include marijuana, inhalants, steroids, heroin, pain-killers, and hallucinogens. Many of these drugs are addictive. Marijuana affects each person differently. Long-term use of marijuana damages the brain, kidneys, liver, lungs, and reproductive organs. Inhalants are chemicals that people purposely breathe in. They include gasoline fumes, paint thinner, lighter fluid, glue, hair spray, and nail polish remover. Inhalants can harm the mind and body by slowing down the brain and nervous system. Steroids are often used illegally to boost muscle size and strength. These drugs can cause high blood pressure, heart and kidney disease, and liver cancer. Heroin is a drug that is used to relieve pain. It is illegal in the United States. Heroin is addictive and deadly. Other pain-killing drugs that are not illegal are still dangerous if not used properly. They can produce physical and mental dependence quickly. Hallucinogens are drugs that confuse the brain and nervous system. They change the way the brain processes sight, sound, smell, and touch information. A person may feel, hear, or see things that are not there. This might cause people to injure others or themselves. Hallucinogens increase the heart rate and blood pressure. Hallucinogens can cause permanent brain damage.

Making healthy lifestyle choices is not always easy. You may end up making a decision based on what others are doing instead of making a decision that is good for you. Even if you make a poor decision at an early age, long-term success is possible. However, it may be more difficult to achieve. People who abuse drugs or alcohol will likely have fewer chances for success in a career and in relationships with others. They may need to work harder to overcome some obstacles before they can reach their goals. Making healthy decisions now will help you reach your goals for the future.

Lesson 3 Review Write your answers to these questions on a sheet of paper.

1. How can an unhealthy diet and lack of exercise affect your work life?

2. A common saying is that "prevention is the best cure." Explain how that is true in relation to such diseases as Type II diabetes, heart disease, and sexually transmitted diseases.

3. What are some common effects of drug and alcohol use?

Get Involved

If there is something you enjoy doing, it is very likely that there are local organizations that can put your interests and talents to work. Do you like to play basketball? Volunteer your time helping coach an after-school program. Do you like computers? Find an organization that repairs old computers and gives them to not-for-profit organizations. Do you enjoy painting? Help work on a home with Habitat for Humanity. You don't have to use "job" skills to be of service. Anything that you like to spend your time on can benefit other people. Contact a local community center, library, YMCA, or park district office to find out about volunteer opportunities in your area.

Lesson 3 Review Answers

1. If you do not eat right and get enough exercise, you may be more tired, less able to focus, and grumpier at work. It can also lead to you being sick more often, which could mean missed days and less productivity.

2. Type II diabetes, heart disease, and sexually transmitted diseases are usually preventable diseases. Healthy lifestyle decisions that prevent these diseases are cheaper and easier to implement than treatment for the diseases themselves.

3. Drug and alcohol use impairs judgment and often has damaging effects on the heart, brain, and other vital organs. It can also affect mood and cause problems in relationships.

Get Involved

Read the Get Involved feature on page 265 to students. Then have students brainstorm a list of local organizations and centers that might need volunteer help. Assign each student or pair of students an organization and ask them to write e-mails or letters or to call appropriate individuals at the organizations to find out about these opportunities. For each place, students should learn what kinds of tasks need to be performed, what guidelines (for example, training or screening) must be met, and what age restrictions, if any, apply. You might also want to have volunteers from the community send an e-mail or speak to the class about the rewards of their experiences.

Lesson at a Glance

Chapter 9 Lesson 4

Overview This lesson looks at ethical behavior and explores the differences between personal, group, and universal values. It also has students think about conflicting values.

Objectives

- To understand the dilemma of making ethical decisions when values conflict
- To define group values and universal values
- To explain a strategy for making ethical decisions

Student Pages 266–271

Teacher's Resource Library

Workbook Activity 43

Activity 43

Alternative Activity 43

Vocabulary

dilemma
ethics
group values
universal values

Have students look up the vocabulary terms in the glossary. Use questions such as the following to open discussion of the terms' meanings:

- Why does every group develop its own values?
- What is one ethical dilemma you can think of?
- What are some ways group values might differ from personal values?

Have students write sentences using the terms.

1 Warm-Up Activity

Have students think about their personal values. Ask them to write down some values they hold that conform to society's expected rules of behavior. Then have them make a second list of values that might conflict with society's expectations.

Ethics
Rules for behavior

Dilemma
A situation that requires a choice between two or more values

Your ability to get and keep a job can be affected by the things you consider important in life. This lesson is about what some employers consider most important when hiring someone. For example, employers will want to know if you are a responsible person. They will want to know if you are dependable and respectful. Employers evaluate a good employee as someone who values time and can be counted on. This lesson shows how you can develop these behaviors.

What Does It Mean to Live Ethically?

Ethics are rules for behavior. Living ethically means making choices or doing things that follow these rules. Ethics are similar to but not the same as values. Values are what you think is important or good. For example, you may think that making a lot of money is important. Someone else may value having more leisure time and may be willing to work for less money. Neither choice is right or wrong. Each choice is based on what a person values.

Both ethics and values guide your behavior. For example, suppose you see a friend cheating on a test in school. Should you report the friend to your teacher? The right, or ethical, decision would be to tell the teacher. You may also value hard work. Suppose that you studied hard for the test. You report your friend to the teacher because you value hard work. Suppose you need to decide whether to spend time with your family or go out with your friends one evening. You value both your family and your friends. You need to choose between two values. A situation in which you must choose between two or more values is called a **dilemma**. Many times, the decisions you face are difficult. Think about your experiences. What are some times you have had to make decisions based on ethics or values?

Workbook Activity 43

Ethics Scramble

Directions Read each clue. Unscramble the answer to the clue. Write the letters in the boxes. To find the last answer, copy the letters in the numbered boxes to boxes at the bottom with the same number.

1. A situation that requires a choice between two or more values:
   MADLEIM

2. Type of values that members of a specific set of people consider to be important:
   GORPU

3. Type of values that people in many societies all over the world consider important:
   REIVUNLAS

4. An opinion people have of you:
   NUDM/JGET

5. The outcomes of choices you make:
   SOENUECENSQC

6. Rules for behavior
   CSEHIT

7. What you must use to tell you what is the right thing to do:
   NCNEICOESC

8. You may face this if you make a choice that goes against people's values:
   CIRCTMISI

9. Being this is a quality valued in almost all groups:
   SORWYTHUTRT

10. Choices for which you will use your values:

Activity 43

Living Ethically

Directions Circle the letter of the answer that correctly completes each sentence.

1. The rules that groups have for what is right and wrong are called _____.
   A standards
   B characteristics
   C ideals
   D ethics

2. A dilemma occurs when you _____.
   A don't know right from wrong
   B are persuaded to do something you should not do
   C must choose between two or more values
   D have a clear sense of what to do

3. The beliefs that a specific group of people considers to be important are its _____.
   A universal values
   B group values
   C conditions
   D traditions

4. _____ are beliefs that most people in many societies all over the world consider important.
   A Universal values
   B Job requirements
   C Governments
   D Principles

5. Personal values may affect others when they _____ group values.
   A agree with
   B clash with
   C are less important than
   D give in to

6. Criticism for disregarding universal values is _____ criticism for disregarding personal and group values.
   A stronger than
   B less than
   C the same as
   D rarer than

7. When faced with a hard decision, ask _____.
   A "How could I have avoided this problem?"
   B "What will do me the most good?"
   C "What is the right thing to do?"
   D "Who can tell me what to do?"

8. To "put yourself in another's shoes" is to _____.
   A try to stay far away from a person
   B imagine how you would feel in the other person's situation
   C try to see how you can gain from the situation
   D avoid looking at a problem directly

9. Consequences and benefits of your decisions should relate to _____.
   A the success of your future career
   B only your immediate family
   C what will make it easiest for you
   D all the people who might be affected

10. Living ethically is not always easy because _____.
    A it is difficult to have a conscience
    B your choices do not affect others
    C choices are often between two or more values
    D there are few things that are really wrong

Workbook Activity 43   **Activity 43**

You have learned that values are beliefs that people consider to be very important. If you believe that being at home for the family's evening meal is very important, then that is one of your values. Everybody has values. They are what help to determine how people act or behave. Remember that personal values are different from work values. Work values are the things you want to get out of your job. Personal values are the beliefs that are important to you but may not be considered important by others, even your friends. For example, personal values may include the importance of family, socializing with friends, maintaining friendships, and having time for yourself.

What Are Group Values?

Another kind of values are **group values.** Group values are the beliefs that a group of people considers to be important. These groups may include your family, neighborhood friends, or the members of the sports team to which you belong. Some of the values that groups may consider to be important are loyalty to the group, sticking to group decisions, or some other belief that sets them apart from others. There may even be a group at your school that places a lot of importance on getting good grades. They may meet regularly to encourage each other in that goal. Employers may be more likely to hire someone who shares the group values of the company.

Suppose you have a busy evening planned. You have to review for a test that you need to score well on tomorrow, watch a video with your friends, and then go to bed early. However, on the evening you arranged to get together, you realize that reviewing for the test is taking longer than you thought it would. What do you do? Do you cancel the invitation to see the video and spend the evening studying instead? Or do you have your friends over anyway and give up the opportunity to prepare better for the test and get the amount of sleep you want?

2 Teaching the Lesson

If students have difficulty verbalizing values that define a system of ethics, have them name several people they believe have good character. Ask students to list actions of these people that illustrate their character. Discuss what values these actions reveal.

3 Reinforce and Extend

LEARNING STYLES

Logical/Mathematical
Have students write a paragraph telling how their values compare with the values of their friends. How are they alike? How are they different? (If students are unsure about friends' values, have them recall actions that give clues.) Suggest that students use a graphic organizer such as a Venn diagram or a T-chart to collect and organize details and examples before they write.

ELL/ESL STRATEGY

Language Objective: *To become familiar with vocabulary related to ethics*

Give students learning English more exposure to the meaning of ethics and the values that society expects. Have students learn and model the meanings of terms such as *responsible, dependable, respectful, loyal, brave, hard-working, trustworthy, compassionate, honest,* and *fair.* You might give one or two terms to each student and make him or her responsible for teaching their meaning to the others. Suggest that they use definitions, examples, visuals, and role playing or skits to help others understand and remember these qualities. Following the presentations, have all students write a sentence using each term in an appropriate context.

IN THE COMMUNITY

Discuss with students the activities and examples that taught them their values when they were younger. Have students brainstorm a list of activities they could use to help children learn ethics. List these on the board and circle the ones that students agree are most useful. Have students choose one activity and write a plan telling how they would interact with children and what values they would be teaching.

GLOBAL CONNECTION

Universal values are held by people in all cultures. Discuss the universal values listed in the text and have students list any others they can think of. Have students collect news stories, photographs, and information gathered online and use it along with a map of the world to create a bulletin board display about shared human values.

Universal values
The beliefs that most people in many societies all over the world consider important

Keeping a promise or sticking to a plan made by the group may be an important value to you. Getting good grades may also be important. Then you may view your dilemma as making a decision between personal success and loyalty or commitment to a group decision.

What Are Universal Values?

Universal values are the beliefs that most people in many societies all over the world consider important. They include being trustworthy, truthful, fair, and kind or helpful to others. Following these values means you act in a way that causes people to trust you with their secrets, money, and other property.

Let's look more closely at the idea of living ethically. You have learned about personal and group values. Generally, your personal values affect other people only when they clash with group values. For example, suppose you have to decide whether to study for a test or spend the time watching a video instead. This decision does not affect others. However, choosing between watching the video with friends and spending the time studying for the test is different. If you choose to spend the time studying, your choice of personal success instead of group loyalty may not sit well with your group of friends.

However, their judgment may not affect you very much. Their judgment may not affect you because there may be other groups that judge your action differently. For example, if your parents or guardians hear about your decision, they may think very highly of you. You may be living up to a value that they consider important. Because you earned the respect of your parents or guardians, what your friends think doesn't bother you as much.

Because most members of many groups consider universal values to be important, criticism for disregarding universal values is stronger than criticism concerning personal and group values. The choice of preparing for the test instead of watching a video with a group of friends shows how personal success may be more important than group loyalty in some situations. However, honesty may be always more important than personal success. Therefore, friends and teachers very likely will not think highly of anyone cheating on a test to get the highest grade in the class.

What Are Some Guidelines for Making Ethical Decisions?

Living ethically is not always easy. Some people might say that it is never easy. Living ethically can be very difficult because of the dilemmas involved. But with practice, you can learn to make ethical decisions more easily. When you are faced with a difficult decision, you can ask yourself these three questions:

1. **What is the right thing to do?**

   Do what your conscience tells you is the right thing to do. This guideline says that there are some values most people share. These will include the universal values you read about in the earlier sections of this lesson.

2. **Would I like anyone to do to me what I am going to do to this person?**

   Do to others what you would like others to do to you. This guideline calls on you to imagine yourself as the person who will benefit or suffer from the action you are about to take. Some people refer to it as putting yourself in the other person's shoes. How you imagine yourself feeling in the other person's situation should determine the action you take.

3. **Would my action result in what is good for the greatest number of people?**

   Think of how the consequences of your action will affect the greatest number of people in the best way. With this guideline, you consider the outcome or results of your actions. Your decision will be based on what will create the greatest benefit for the greatest number of people. The consequences and benefits that you think about should not relate to you alone, but to all the people who might be affected.

List career categories or industries on the board that represent students' interests. Ask students to think of a situation in each category in which they might face an ethical dilemma. (For example, in medicine, a doctor might have to decide whether to keep a patient alive on life support machines. A politician might have to decide whether to compromise about a strongly held value in order to get a bill passed.) Then have students read the On the Job feature on page 269.

At Home

Have students share the three questions on page 269 with an adult whose opinions they respect and explain the questions' purpose. Students can talk with the person about how he or she makes difficult decisions and which of these three questions is most important to making the decision. Suggest that students record the conversation, if possible. Invite students to share their impressions and conclusions after their interviews.

LEARNING STYLES

Logical/Mathematical

Provide a scenario such as the following and have students use the three guideline questions on page 269 to determine what ethical decision they would make:

You and a friend find a wallet in the mall parking lot. Your friend goes through it to find the owner's name. It contains $130 in addition to credit cards and personal information. She takes $20 out, saying that the person would want to give a reward, and then turns in the wallet to the police. What would you do?

Have students work in small groups to discuss what is right and wrong with the friend's actions and which of their values are in conflict as they decide whether to report the friend for taking money. Encourage groups to think of their own scenarios and repeat the process.

LEARNING STYLES

Auditory/Verbal

Have students review the chapter and write quiz questions covering key vocabulary and concepts. Students can write each question on a separate index card and add the answer on the back of the card. Divide the class into teams and have teams answer questions from the cards to determine the winner. A player who gives the wrong answer sits down. The team with the last person standing wins.

You may find it easiest to try to answer these three questions in order when you are trying to make a decision. Call on your sense of right and wrong to decide what is the right thing to do. If there is no clear answer, or if taking two actions seem right, the next step is to check to see what values are in conflict. Identify the values involved and decide which is more important to you. If you find that the values are equally important, then think of the person who will be affected by your action. Put yourself in the person's position and ask yourself if you would like anyone to do to you what you are going to do to the person. This question will give you an answer that is either yes or no. If the answer does not make the decision clear for you, think of how the consequences may affect other people. Try to determine to the best of your knowledge how your action might result in what is best for the greatest number of people.

Each dilemma you face is different. The place, the people, and other details involved will vary. As a result, going through every step to reach a decision in each situation may not be necessary. Also, you may go through this sequence of steps without arriving at a very clear decision to act on. In living ethically, the important thing is often to make every effort to find the best ethical decision according to the situation you are dealing with.

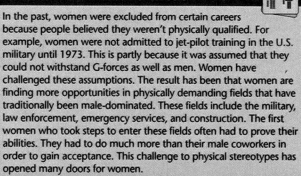

Gender and Careers

In the past, women were excluded from certain careers because people believed they weren't physically qualified. For example, women were not admitted to jet-pilot training in the U.S. military until 1973. This is partly because it was assumed that they could not withstand G-forces as well as men. Women have challenged these assumptions. The result has been that women are finding more opportunities in physically demanding fields that have traditionally been male-dominated. These fields include the military, law enforcement, emergency services, and construction. The first women who took steps to enter these fields often had to prove their abilities. They had to do much more than their male coworkers in order to gain acceptance. This challenge to physical stereotypes has opened many doors for women.

Lesson 4 Review Write your answers to these questions on a sheet of paper.

1. Give three examples each of personal values, group values, and universal values.

2. Is it possible for personal, group, and universal values to overlap? Explain.

3. What are some guidelines for making ethical decisions?

Lesson 4 Review Answers

1. Answers will vary. Possible personal values include being on time, working hard, being healthy and physically fit, getting good grades, respecting older people, and being the best at something. Possible group values include being loyal to the group, spending time with people, working as a team, being in agreement, and achieving a particular goal. Possible universal values include telling the truth, considering the needs and feelings of others, and taking responsibility for your actions.

2. It is possible for these different levels of values to overlap. Presumably a universal value is one that most groups and individuals will hold as well. An individual probably would not belong to a group if he or she did not hold similar values with other members of the group.

3. Listen to your conscience. Consider who will be affected by your decision and how they will feel. Consider what will bring the greatest good to the greatest number of people. After taking these things into consideration, you have to weigh your values and consider which are most important and appropriate to the situation.

Gender and Careers

Ask students what the term *G-force* means. If no one knows, explain that it is the force of gravity or acceleration on the body. During take-off of spacecraft or extremely fast planes such as fighter jets, these forces can be very strong. Have students read the Gender and Careers feature on page 271. Discuss what stereotypes or generalizations might have led to the earlier assumption that women could not meet the physical demands of certain jobs. (Students may offer statements such as *Women are weak. Women are too emotional. Women are illogical.*)

Your Hobbies

Students will take a general survey about their hobbies and then answer specific questions in order to assess whether their hobbies meet social, physical, and stress-relieving needs adequately, and whether the amount of time they spend on hobbies is well balanced.

Use the introductory paragraph to have students review the ways in which hobbies benefit their lives. Reproduce the survey form on page 272 or have students use Portfolio Activity 9 on the TRL to respond to the questions. Then have them evaluate the overall response. How many *no* answers did they mark? Point out that if they lack positives in their responses, they need to think about trying out new hobbies.

Your Hobbies

You have learned in this chapter that how you live your life *outside* of work and school has a big impact on how well you do *in* work and school. People develop hobbies and interests for different reasons. Consider the benefits of hobbies in your life. Think about how you would answer each question in the form below. Then, on your own paper, answer the questions on page 273. Use complete sentences. Add the activity to your portfolio.

Which column best represents your answer to each question?

Questions About Your Hobbies	Yes	Somewhat	No
Do you have a variety of hobbies?			
Do you participate in your hobby activities regularly?			
Do you feel that you spend the right amount of time on your hobbies?			
Are most of your hobbies active (requiring physical activity) rather than passive (TV, video games)?			
Do your hobbies help to relieve your stress?			
Do your hobbies involve socializing with other people?			
Do your hobbies involve skills and knowledge that you use at school or work?			

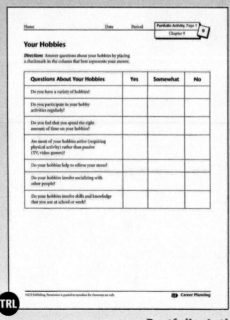

Portfolio Activity 9, Pages 1–2

1. Name one activity you do for each of these reasons: to relieve stress, to be competitive, to meet other people, to stay physically fit, to practice or develop a skill, and to be quiet or reflective.

2. Which of the needs noted in question 1 (stress relief, competition, social outlets, physical fitness, skill development, and quiet time) do you consider most important in your life? Which do you consider least important? Why?

3. Consider the activities you identified in question 1. Do any of these activities meet more than one need? Which ones?

4. Which of the activities do you enjoy the most? How often do you do that activity?

5. Write a brief plan for how you can ensure that you fit in a healthy amount of time to pursue hobbies and interests. If a need that you consider important is not being met, is there a new hobby you would like to try that could meet that need?

Your hobbies can help you stay physically fit.

Have students answer the questions on page 273 on their own paper or on Portfolio Activity 9 on the TRL.

Remind students that they should make their answers complete sentences so that they will make sense without having to refer to the questions. For example, *I do yoga to relieve stress* gives complete information. If they just write *yoga*, they won't know why when they look back at their papers later.

Point out that question 1 requires students to write six sentences. These are important, since they form the basis for answering questions 2 through 4.

Have students refer to their personal time surveys as they answer question 5. Reviewing their actual use of time will allow them to assess if and how it can be adjusted to include a new hobby or more time for existing hobbies.

Portfolio Activity Answers

1.–5. Answers will vary.

Chapter 9 Review

Use the Chapter Review to prepare students for tests and to reteach content from the chapter.

Chapter 9 Mastery Test 🔴

The Teacher's Resource Library includes two forms of the Chapter 9 Mastery Test. Each test addresses the chapter Goals for Learning. An optional third page of additional critical-thinking items is included for each test. The difficulty level of the two forms is equivalent.

Review Answers
Vocabulary Review

1. leisure time 2. physical fitness 3. drug 4. time management 5. group values 6. nicotine 7. diet 8. hobby 9. ethics 10. universal values 11. nutrient 12. stress 13. alcoholism 14. dilemma 15. obligation 16. sexually transmitted disease 17. symptom 18. addictive 19. diabetes

Concept Review

20. A 21. B 22. B 23. D

Critical Thinking

24. Physical fitness varies from person to person. The definition of physical fitness is the body's ability to meet the daily demands of living. People have different demands, depending on their careers, hobbies, location, age, and so on. Someone with a really demanding job is going to need to be physically stronger than someone who works at a desk job. What those two individuals eat to be healthy and the kinds of exercise they do will not be the same. 25. Answers will vary. Students should be able to identify a specific area to focus on. For example, if a student recognizes that he or she is not eating well, that student may describe some improvement that could be made by eating better, such as improved energy and alertness.

Chapter 9 REVIEW

Chapter 9 REVIEW

Word Bank

addictive
alcoholism
diabetes
diet
dilemma
drug
ethics
group values
hobby
leisure time
nicotine
nutrient
obligation
physical fitness
sexually transmitted disease
stress
symptom
time management
universal values

Vocabulary Review

Choose the word or phrase from the Word Bank that best completes each sentence. Write the answer on your paper.

1. Free time away from work or school is also called _____.
2. The body's ability to meet the demands of living is _____.
3. A(n) _____ changes the way your mind or body works.
4. Using your time well to achieve your goals is known as _____.
5. Beliefs important to a specific group are called _____.
6. One addictive chemical found in tobacco is _____.
7. Your _____ is the food that you regularly eat and drink.
8. A(n) _____ is an activity done for enjoyment.
9. The rules for behavior in a society are _____.
10. Beliefs considered important by most societies in the world are _____.
11. A substance found in food and that your body needs to work properly is a(n) _____.
12. A state of physical or emotional pressure is _____.
13. A disease in which a person is dependent on alcohol is _____.
14. If you are in a situation where you must choose between two values, you are facing a(n) _____.
15. An activity that is required is a(n) _____.
16. Any disease spread through sexual activity is called a(n) _____.
17. A high fever is a(n) _____, or physical sign, of an illness.
18. If a substance is _____, it is habit forming.
19. When the body is not able to use sugar from food, a disease called _____ may be to blame.

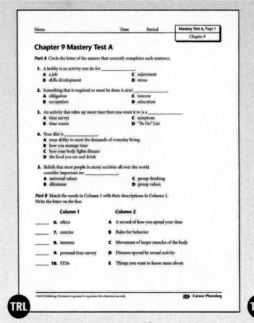

Concept Review

Choose the word or phrase that best completes each sentence.
Write the letter of the answer on your paper.

20. People pursue hobbies for all of these reasons EXCEPT _____.
A to fulfill an obligation   C to stay physically fit
B to relieve stress   D to meet people

21. A good schedule will include _____.
A no non-scheduled time
B time to get from one activity to the next
C only the most important activities
D time-wasting activities

22. People who use drugs or alcohol when they are young _____.
A usually do not become addicted
B risk their health, their future, and the safety of others
C are hurting only themselves
D are better at decision making

23. Ethical decisions are made in all of these ways EXCEPT _____.
A thinking about how other people will be affected
B considering what is best for the most people
C following your conscience
D doing what feels good to you at the moment

Critical Thinking

Write the answer to each question on your paper.

24. Is physical fitness and a healthy lifestyle the same for everyone? Explain. Give examples to support your answer.

25. Think about the four areas discussed in the chapter: hobbies, time, health, and ethics. What is one area you want to work on? How will improvements in that area help you pursue your career goals?

Test-Taking Tip
Be sure you understand what a test question is asking. Read it twice if necessary.

ALTERNATIVE ASSESSMENT

■ Have students make a poster illustrating their hobbies and explaining what they gain from each hobby: health benefits, social and mental benefits, and possible work benefits.

■ Ask each student to write several tips to help a person who is trying to make and implement a time-management schedule. Have students think about their experience in making a schedule in Lesson 2 and include ideas that worked for them or warnings about problems they experienced and how to avoid them.

■ Challenge students to create a graphic organizer, such as a circle graph, to represent the relative importance of nutrition, physical fitness, illness prevention, and drug avoidance to their lifelong health. For each of these areas, students should be able to give rules and explain the advantages of following them.

■ Have students write an essay explaining their personal system of ethics and telling how personal, group, and universal values play a role in it. Ask students to include examples of ethical decisions they have made to support their statements.

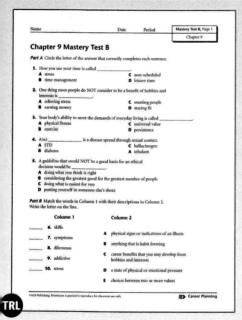

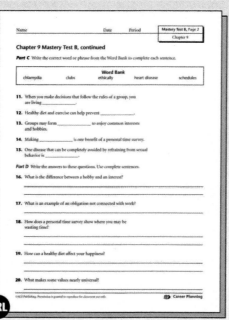

Chapter 9 Mastery Test B, Pages 1–3

Chapter

10

Planning Guide

Looking Ahead

	Student Text Lesson				
	Student Pages	Vocabulary	Lesson Review	Critical-Thinking Questions	Chapter Review
Lesson 1 Getting and Responding to Feedback	278–283		✔	✔	✔
Lesson 2 Developing Your Career Action Plan	284–287		✔	✔	✔

Chapter Activities

Student Text
Chapter 10 Portfolio Activity

Teacher's Resource Library
Chapter 10 Chapter Outline
Chapter 10 Self-Study Guide
Chapter 10 Portfolio Activity

Assessment Options

Student Text
Chapter 10 Review

Teacher's Resource Library
Chapter 10 Mastery Tests A and B
Chapters 1–10 Final Mastery Test

Teacher's Edition
Chapter 10 Alternative Assessment

	Student Text Features											Teaching Strategies					Learning Styles					Teacher's Resource Library				
Portfolio Activity	Writing Practice	Communication Connection	The Economy	Career Tip	Career Profile	On the Job	Gender and Careers	Think Positive	Technology Note	Get Involved	Background Information	Applications (Home, Community, Global, Environment)	Personal Journal	Online Connection	ELL/ESL Strategy	Visual/Spatial	Body/Kinesthetic	Interpersonal/Group Learning	Logical/Mathematical	Auditory/Verbal	Activities	Alternative Activities	Workbook Activities	Self-Study Guide	Chapter Outline
	281	278		281	282	279					282	282			280	281	280	283		279	44	44	44	✔	✔
288			284	284			285	285	287	286		285, 286	288	285					287, 289		45	45	45	✔	✔

Alternative Activities

The Teacher's Resource Library (TRL) contains a set of lower-level worksheets called Alternative Activities. These worksheets cover the same content as the regular Activities but are written at a second-grade reading level.

Career Interest Inventory

The AGS Publishing Harrington-O'Shea Career Decision-Making System (CDM) may be used with this textbook. Students can use the CDM to explore their interests and identify careers. The CDM defines career areas that are indicated by students' response on the inventory.

Chapter 10:
Looking Ahead
pages 276–291

Lessons

1. **Getting and Responding to Feedback**
   pages 278–283

2. **Developing Your Career Action Plan**
   pages 284–287

Portfolio Activity

Career Action Plan
pages 288–289

Chapter Review

pages 290–291

Audio CD 🎧

Teacher's Resource Library **TRL**

Workbook Activities 44–45

Activities 44–45

Alternative Activities 44–45

Portfolio Activity 10

Chapter 10 Chapter Outline

Chapter 10 Self-Study Guide

Chapter 10 Mastery Tests A and B

Chapters 1–10 Final Mastery Test

(Answer Keys for the Teacher's Resource Library begin on page 328 of this Teacher's Edition.)

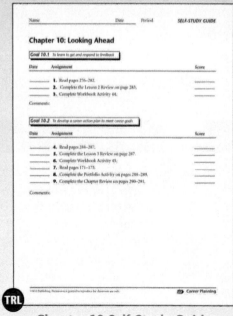

Chapter 10 Self-Study Guide

Chapter

10 Looking Ahead

Throughout this book you have identified your strengths and skills. You have set career goals and learned more about your options. These are the first steps down a lifelong road. As you take this journey, you will continue to learn, grow, and change. Your experiences and choices along the way may take you down paths you never dreamed of. You can make the most of the trip by knowing yourself, responding to feedback, and making good decisions about your life and your career. Good decisions are true to who you are. They match your talents, strengths, and values. As you read this chapter, you will learn to adapt your career goals and map out the path to achieving them.

Goals for Learning

◆ To learn to get and respond to feedback
◆ To develop a career action plan to meet career goals

277

Introducing the Chapter

Have students look at the photo on page 276 in the student edition and describe what it shows. Ask them how the walkway could represent their outlook on the future. Invite students to list steps they have taken that have built a framework to launch them on their career path.

Have students read the introductory paragraph to consider what skills and attitudes will be important to them as they travel through life. Invite volunteers to predict what *feedback* is.

Have students read the Goals for Learning and write two questions about feedback and about a career action plan that they will answer as they read the chapter.

Career Tips

Ask volunteers to read the career tips that appear in the margins throughout the chapter. Then discuss them with the class.

Alternative Assessment

The Alternative Assessment box on page 291 of the Chapter Review includes activities using various learning styles to assess students' understanding of the Goals for Learning.

Chapter 10 Chapter Outline

Looking Ahead 277

Lesson at a Glance

Chapter 10 Lesson 1

Overview In this lesson, students review some steps in career planning and consider how to seek and use feedback about their career planning steps to advance their plan.

Objectives

- To review the role of self-assessment and information gathering in career development
- To identify kinds of feedback and ways of evaluating its relationship with career planning
- To understand ways to respond to feedback to adjust behaviors or goals

Student Pages 278–283

Teacher's Resource Library **TRL**

Workbook Activity 44

Activity 44

Alternative Activity 44

1 Warm-Up Activity

Ask a volunteer to role-play a scene with you in which you play a coach and he or she plays an athlete. First, give the athlete praise for an accomplishment. Then give criticism about a skill that is weak and needs improvement. Have the student respond naturally, and then explain the immediate effect of this feedback. Discuss with the class different ways for a student to accept and use feedback of this sort.

Communication Connection

Ask students to explain what criticism is and tell how they feel about it. For example, what reaction do they have when a teacher points out mistakes in their work? How do they respond when they receive a grade that is lower than they expected? Read the Communication Connection on page 278 aloud. Have volunteers suggest self-talk statements a person could use to help him or her turn criticism into an opportunity for improving or for meeting a goal.

Communication Connection

Feedback can be a very helpful tool. The key: Be open to it. No one wants to give feedback to someone who doesn't listen or who takes criticism badly. So listen politely and try to see the other person's point of view when you receive feedback, whether it is positive or negative.

You have now learned a lot about work and which work options you want to consider. If you practice the skills that you have learned in this book, you will manage your career well, now and in your future. This lesson will review some of the key steps in career planning. It will also show you how to respond to feedback from others.

Work, Careers, and Self-Assessment

Remember that you first learned about the nature of work and what a career is. Then, you practiced self-assessment to understand your abilities, interests, and values. Understanding yourself is the most important part of your career development. You can use the information you have learned about yourself to guide your career decisions. If you do this, you will be on your way to putting an effective career plan into action.

Using Self-Assessment

The information that you learn about yourself is useful as you consider which occupations you would like to explore. In Chapter 3, you learned how to use self-information to make career decisions. When you follow the five decision-making steps, you pull together information about yourself and occupations. As you learn about different occupations, you should also use what you have learned about yourself. This will help you understand which career clusters will contain the occupations that you should investigate further.

For example, suppose you enjoy social studies and get good grades in your social studies classes. You also enjoy helping others and have good communication skills. Considering these things, occupations in Education and Training as well as Human Services are likely good matches for you. You can explore these career clusters to learn more about them.

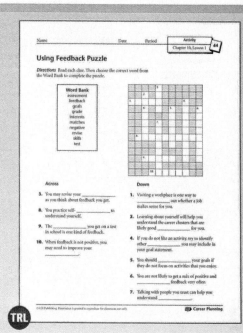

Workbook Activity 44

Activity 44

Perhaps you are good in science. You enjoy researching and reading about health. You also value helping others, especially when they are sick or hurt. Occupations within the Health Science cluster are good choices for you to explore. By focusing on occupations within career clusters that make sense for you, you take part in effective career planning and exploration.

Gathering Additional Information

Besides exploring careers you have interest in, you can gather additional information about the options you are exploring. For instance, you can learn about jobs by networking or visiting a workplace. You can also learn about possible careers by visiting postsecondary schools or colleges. As you gather more information, you are taking an important step—you are "testing out" whether certain actions make sense for you. For example, you might decide whether attending a college to study business administration is a good choice for you. You make these decisions based on what you know about yourself and the options you are exploring.

Taking Action

Throughout this book, you have been asked to take action. You have gathered information about yourself and about occupations. You have made a career plan. You have written your resume and collected references. Taking action in these ways helps you to manage your career effectively. When you take action, you learn things about yourself and about career options. You receive feedback about the career planning you have done so far. Another important step in your career planning is using feedback effectively.

2 Teaching the Lesson

This lesson reviews briefly the steps students took in Chapters 2 through 7. You may want to have students consult the table of contents or skim the headings in the earlier chapters before reading.

On the Job

If possible, acquire and display an employee evaluation form from one or more local employers. Discuss traits and performance objectives on which the employee is evaluated. Have students tell what they think the evaluation does for the employer and for the employee. Then have students read the On the Job feature on page 279.

3 Reinforce and Extend

LEARNING STYLES

Auditory/Verbal
Assign each subsection of Lesson 1 to a pair of students. Make each pair responsible for paraphrasing/summarizing the important ideas of this section for the class. If the section refers to concepts taught in an earlier chapter, have partners review these concepts. For sections on pages 280 and 281, partners should create and build on a definition for *feedback*.

Receiving Feedback

You receive feedback at all stages in your career planning. When you take a test in school, your grade gives you feedback about your performance in a subject area. When you try out for a school sports team, you receive feedback about your skills in that sport. When you apply for a job, you receive feedback about your job skills and about how prepared you were for the job interview. When you apply to attend a postsecondary school, you receive feedback about your education and career preparation. As you make plans and set goals, you are receiving different kinds of feedback along the way.

Listening to feedback from others can help you set and reach your career goals.

Using Feedback

How can you use the feedback you receive? It can sometimes be a challenge to sort through the feedback you receive. Sometimes you might get different feedback from different people. For example, you may be trying to get a short story published in a magazine. You will likely get different responses from each magazine you send your story to. Getting a mix of positive and negative feedback might not be very helpful to you. Examples like this are not very common, however. Most of the feedback you receive from teachers, employers, parents, guardians, coaches, and school counselors is very useful. This is especially true when the feedback you receive from several sources is the same. For example, you might think you are not very good at drawing. Your art teacher and your parents think that you are good at drawing, however. In this case, you are receiving important feedback that you may be a better artist than you think you are.

How Feedback Affects Your Goals

It is risky if you do not pay attention to the feedback you receive. It can be helpful to talk with someone you trust, such as a school counselor or parent. These people can help you understand feedback and to make decisions about your career and educational planning. As you think about feedback you receive from your teachers, coaches, advisors, school counselors, parents, guardians, and employers, think about your personal goal statement. (You made a personal goal statement in Chapter 7, Lesson 2.) Does the feedback fit your goals? Does the feedback suggest you are on the right path or does it suggest that you should revise your goals? If your feedback matches the direction you need to take to reach a goal, that is great! If the feedback does not match or is not so positive, don't be discouraged. This does not always mean that you need to change your plans. You may just need to strengthen your skills in a particular area. For example, suppose you are not getting good grades in a math class. You want to improve your grades because math is a class you need to do well in for your career goals. Talking with a counselor, teacher, parent, or guardian can help you answer questions like these:

- Are you working as hard as you can?
- Are you using good study skills?
- Could some extra help from a tutor help you improve your skills?

It is important to think about whether you are doing what you need to do in order to achieve your goals. If you think you are doing everything you can, then it may be the right time to discuss whether you need to change your goals.

Writing Practice

Consider a time recently when you have received feedback. Was it positive or negative? How did it make you feel? What action did you take or do you plan to take? What would have made the feedback more constructive or helpful? Write a journal entry describing the feedback and your response to it.

LEARNING STYLES

Visual/Spatial

Ask students with strong visual/spatial learning skills to create a drawing or diagram that illustrates the concept of feedback as a communication loop. Students may also represent different kinds of feedback—for example, verbal, grades, awards, applause, and so on. Ask each artist to explain his or her drawing and tell about the areas or goals relevant to the feedback represented.

Writing Practice

Before students write their journal entries, you may want to model for them an example of feedback and how you might respond to it. (For example, your art instructor might have critiqued your latest painting and pointed out ways you could improve it.) Point out to students that if you think only about the negative aspect, you might decide to drop the class and give up painting. However, if you decide to take the instructor's advice and work on your weak points, you can make the painting better and improve your skills. Suggest that students jot down their answers to the questions in the feature before they write their entries.

Encourage students to talk with a trusted adult at home about their goals. If they are thinking of changing a goal, they can use the adult as a sounding board to resolve such issues as:

- why the goal was important
- why it no longer seems important
- what negatives are involved in the activity
- what positives are involved in the activity
- what changes should be made so that positives outweigh negatives

Career Profile

Financial Advisor

Have students read the Career Profile on page 282. Explain that financial advisors study a client's finances and financial goals in order to develop a comprehensive plan. The advisor's recommendations are based on the client's goals, feelings about risk, and need for a return on investment.

BACKGROUND INFORMATION

Financial Advisor

Make the following data available to students who are interested in pursuing this career:

- An individual must have good mathematical, computer, analytical, and problem-solving skills to be a good financial advisor.

- The career requires good communication skills. A financial advisor presents complex financial concepts in simple, easily understood language.

- Certification (the certified financial planner credential) is obtained from the Certified Financial Planner Board of Standards. To receive it, the advisor must pass an exam, complete education requirements, have experience, and follow a code of ethics.

- In 2002, median annual earnings of personal financial advisors were $56,680.

Revising Your Goals

You may also decide to revise your goals if they do not focus on activities that you enjoy. You are not likely to achieve your goals in the long run if you don't enjoy the activities you need to do along the way. If you try an activity and find that you do not enjoy it, think about why that is. What is it that you do not like about the activity? To figure this out, you can talk with a teacher, school counselor, parent, or guardian. In your discussion, be sure that it is the activity itself that you do not like. For example, it is possible to like playing basketball but not like the basketball coach. When this occurs, it often makes sense to continue with the activity. If you decide that you really do not like the activity, then discuss what you have learned about yourself from your participation in the activity. Try to identify other interests that may be important to include in your revised goal statement.

Career Profile

Financial Advisor

Most people have some idea of how to make money. However, they might not be certain how to invest their money to provide more financial gain. Personal financial advisors provide analysis and guidance to individuals to help them with their investment decisions. They gather financial information, analyze it, and make recommendations to their clients.

Personal financial advisors are also called *financial planners*. They use their knowledge of investments, tax laws, and insurance to recommend financial options to their clients. Some of the issues that planners address are retirement and estate planning, funding for college, and general investment options. An advisor develops a financial plan that identifies problem areas, makes recommendations for improvement, and selects appropriate investments for the client.

Because investment by businesses and individuals is expected to continue to increase, this field is seeing employment growth that is faster than the average. Good candidates must have excellent math skills and good business knowledge, and most employers require a college degree.

Lesson 1 Review Write your answers to these questions on a sheet of paper.

1. What are some sources of feedback that you can consider?

2. Is feedback always true? Explain.

3. What is a possible result of ignoring feedback?

Lesson 1 Review Answers

1. Some sources of feedback include test results and grades; comments by teachers, counselors, coaches, and parents/guardians; awards; and the outcomes of job applications, college applications, and interviews.

2. Feedback is often a person's opinion and therefore may not be true. However, the feedback of people who know you well, even though it may be an opinion, can be very valuable.

3. Ignoring feedback can lead you down a career path that will be very difficult and not enjoyable for you or may cause you to overlook a good career option.

LEARNING STYLES

Interpersonal/Group Learning

Put students into small discussion groups. Have them use the Lesson 1 Review questions to begin a discussion about feedback and the way it has affected their ideas about the future. Encourage students to establish criteria they can use for evaluating feedback and deciding whether it is true and should be heeded. (For example, they might ask themselves, *What is this person's motive for giving me this feedback? Is this person in a good position to understand and evaluate my performance?*)

Lesson at a Glance

Chapter 10 Lesson 2

Overview In this lesson, students learn about the career action plan.

Objectives

- To understand that a career action plan maps out concrete steps to achieve a goal
- To list ways a career action plan may need to be revised
- To recognize the need to stay flexible in career planning

Student Pages 284–287

Teacher's Resource Library TRL

Workbook Activity 45

Activity 45

Alternative Activity 45

 1 Warm-Up Activity

Ask students to tell the difference between having a goal and achieving a goal. (*Possible response: Having a goal simply means you have decided what you want. To achieve a goal, a person has to have a plan and carry it out.*)

 2 Teaching the Lesson

In the Portfolio Activity for Chapter 7 (pages 214–215), students wrote a personal goal statement. It included a question about steps needed to reach the short-term and long-term goals involved. Have students use this activity as a starting point when they begin their career action plan.

Explain to students that they will create their career action plans in the Portfolio Activity for Chapter 10, on pages 288–289.

Career Tip

One common question interviewers ask is "What is a mistake you have made and what did you learn from it?" The interviewer wants to know that you are flexible and willing to learn and grow. Be prepared with an exact answer that shows you aren't afraid of change.

A career action plan is related to your personal goal statement. But it is not the same thing. Your personal goal statement identifies where you would like to go in your career. Your career action plan describes how you can get from where you are in your career to where you would like to go. In other words, your career action plan is a description of how you plan to achieve your goal. Here is a simple example:

Goal Statement: "I would like to visit Orlando, Florida."

Action Plan: "In order for me to visit Orlando, I need to save enough money for an airplane ticket to Florida. I will need to make travel plans and hotel reservations. I will need to get directions to Orlando once I am in Florida."

Your goal statement is your destination and your career action plan is your road map for getting there.

The Economy

When a region is heavily dependent on one industry or type of workforce, the local economy can be affected. Many communities that are hit hard by unemployment because of declines in a local industry see a desperate cycle begin. As people are less able to afford goods and services because of job loss and decreased wages, local business owners have to increase prices to maintain profits. Spending more on basic needs, people are less able to save. They have more debt. The effect on communities when this cycle continues can make economic recovery difficult.

It is for this reason that researchers are now looking at ways to improve economic opportunities at the community level. If there were more job opportunities locally, a community might be less hurt by a weak national economy. Providing low-cost loans and tax incentives to small business owners can increase the availability of local jobs. It can also encourage local spending. The hope is that it will create economic advantages and opportunities that improve the overall health of the economy.

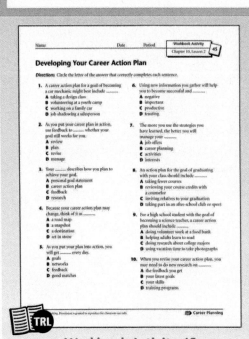

Workbook Activity 45

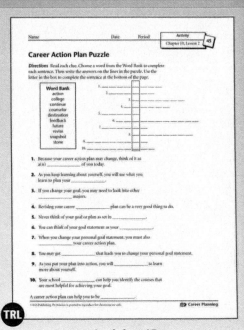

Activity 45

Revising Your Career Action Plan

When the feedback you receive leads you to revise your personal goal statement, then you will also need to revise your career action plan. For example, suppose that you cannot save enough money to go to Orlando. You would need to identify another place to visit. You would not follow the same plans you had for your trip to Orlando. You would need to identify a new destination that is less expensive. Revising your travel plans would probably require you to do additional research. The same is true when you revise your career action plan. You may need to do new research on specific occupations, college majors, or other training programs that relate to your new goal. You may need to get new experiences in new activities. For example, if you revised your personal goal statement related to your choice of college major from English to engineering, you may find out that you need to take additional science and math courses. You would then probably talk to your school counselor about which courses would be most helpful to you in achieving your new goal.

Gender and Careers

Both women and men can face the problem of sexual harassment in the workplace. Sexual harassment is defined as any unwelcome sexual advances, requests for sexual favors, and other verbal abuse or physical contact of a sexual nature. All sexual harassment is considered a form of gender discrimination that violates the Civil Rights Act of 1964. It is important that people who feel they have been victims of sexual harassment be vocal about their experiences. If someone is making you uncomfortable, you need to tell the offender and/or your supervisor. Use any employee complaint system your company has in place. If the problem continues, the U.S. Equal Employment Opportunity Commission can investigate. Your refusal to give in to sexual pressure in the workplace *cannot* be used as grounds for dismissal. It is up to you to stand up for your rights.

ONLINE CONNECTION

For facts about sexual harassment and how to file a charge, students can visit www.eeoc.gov/facts/fs-sex.html or www.eeoc.gov/facts/howtofil.html.

Ask volunteers to read aloud the Economy feature on page 284. Discuss examples of regions or communities that have experienced a depressed economy because of a slump in a main industry. (*For example, the steel towns of Pennsylvania which languished as competition from foreign steelmakers led to the closing of many giant U.S. steel manufacturers, and the Carolinas once led the nation in textile production but now face competition from foreign markets.*)

GLOBAL CONNECTION

Low cost loans have been used in some countries to boost the economy at a local level. For example, an international organization loans a small amount of money to women, who use it to establish a cottage industry. This is a business operated out of one's home, such as sewing or crafts. This practice has shown that women are able to succeed financially in places where they have been given few opportunities. Ask interested students to find Internet or magazine articles about this practice and report their findings.

3   Reinforce and Extend

Think Positive

Have students read the Think Positive feature on page 285. Ask them to write a paragraph or give a brief talk telling about a disappointment or setback in their career planning. Instruct them to include at least one positive outcome of this setback.

Gender and Careers

After students have read the Gender and Careers feature on page 285, explain that the Civil Rights Act of 1964 put in place the code establishing an employee's right to be free from sexual harassment. Sexual harassment by definition "affects an individual's employment, unreasonably interferes with an individual's work performance, or creates an intimidating, hostile, or offensive work environment."

Get Involved

Have students read the Get Involved feature on page 286. Ask them to reflect on the actions and services they have benefited from and jot down the ones that are most important to them. You might have students make a word web for each, listing several actions they might take to help others in the way they were helped.

IN THE ENVIRONMENT

 Point out to students that organizations which work to protect the environment benefit us all by keeping air and water clean, minimizing global warming, and ensuring a proper ecological balance in the world. Encourage interested students to locate several such organizations online and report ways citizens can help them.

IN THE COMMUNITY

 Encourage students to put the ideas they recorded on their word webs for the Get Involved feature into action. They can write letters or e-mails or make phone calls to local organizations that serve those in need and welcome volunteers. Examples include the Salvation Army, American Cancer Society, United Way, Big Brothers and Big Sisters, and the auxiliary of a local hospital.

Revising a personal goal statement and career action plan is not a negative thing. In fact, it can be a very good sign of the ways in which you are learning more about yourself and the world of work!

Putting Your Plan Into Action

As you put your plan into action, remember to use the feedback you get to review whether your personal goal statement still works for you. As you plan for your future, you will continue to network. You will also seek out opportunities to learn more about your goal. Never consider your goal to be "written in stone." Rather, consider your goal statement and career action plan a "snapshot" of how things stand today in your life. Because you will receive feedback every day, your plan may be different tomorrow, next week, next month, or next year. You will continue to learn more about yourself and about the workplace. Using the new information you receive as you plan your future will help you to become productive and successful. The more you use the strategies in this book, the more skilled you will become at managing your career planning.

Get Involved

You might have heard the phrase "pay it forward." This is an idea that many not-for-profit organizations count on. The idea is that when you have personally benefited from the service of someone, you turn around and do something to help someone else. Gus Samuel, Jr., a high school student in Greenville, S.C., did just that. After benefiting from the work of the Salvation Army Boys and Girls Club of Greenville, he turned around and became a volunteer there. He served for four years as a junior staff member, coach, recreation aide, and mentor. His decision to "pay it forward" helped other kids grow and learn as he had. You can do the same. Think of people and organizations that have made a difference to you and your family. Remember that people have taken time to invest in your life and your future. Then pay that involvement forward. You can make a difference, too.

286   *Chapter 10   Looking Ahead*

Lesson 2 Review Write your answers to these questions on a sheet of paper.

1. How is a career action plan different from a career goal statement?

2. How might a career action plan for a goal of becoming a nurse practitioner be different from a career action plan for becoming an interior designer?

3. Why is it important that you never consider a career action plan as "set in stone"?

Technology Note

Many career fields require certification, or proof of your qualifications through testing and other methods. This certification, if it is not done directly through a government agency, is usually offered through a national or international professional organization. If you need to prepare for certification, this step should be part of your career action plan. Do research to find out certification requirements. This will give you clues about subjects to pursue and skills that you may have overlooked.

Many professional organizations provide online study tools, discussion groups, and testing for certification. Contact an organization that includes professionals in your chosen field. Find out about certification requirements and programs that may be available online.

Lesson 2 Review Answers

1. A career goal statement is a general idea of the final "destination," while a career action plan is a list of specific actions to take to get there.

2. A person who wants to become a nurse practitioner will probably want to take more science and health classes and might focus on activities where he or she will learn skills needed in a health-care environment. A person who wants to become an interior designer will probably need to pursue classes in art and design and might focus on activities related to art and architecture.

3. A career action plan needs to change to suit your career goals, which are flexible. When you receive feedback or simply discover new interests that lead you down different paths, these tools need to be adapted to help you accomplish new goals.

LEARNING STYLES

Logical/Mathematical
As they complete Lesson 2 Review questions 1 and 2, have students use a Venn diagram or a T-chart to collect and organize information comparing and contrasting 1) a career action plan and a career goal statement and 2) a career action plan for a nurse practitioner and one for an interior designer. Encourage students to list ways the paired concepts are similar as well. This will give them a better grasp of what a career action plan entails.

Technology Note

Have students read the Technology Note on page 287. Then do an Internet search to learn about any certification requirements that apply to their chosen career. After students report their findings, have them work cooperatively to create a booklet of online resources for career certification.

Students will create a career action plan by answering these questions. Previous Portfolio Activities (pp. 156–157 and 214–215) have asked students to pinpoint a career interest and state a career goal. This final activity expands on the earlier ones, requiring students to include a list of specific subjects they need to study, specific abilities they need to develop, and specific steps they must take for the short-term and the long-term. Refer students to the *Occupational Outlook Handbook*. The OOH provides in-depth information about numerous careers which students can use to develop their plans.

Some students may have difficulty distinguishing the types of actions they should take now versus those that must be completed later to advance their career plans. You may want to brainstorm with students a list of things they can be doing to prepare themselves for a career. As students suggest actions, place them in one of two columns:

Do Now	Do Within 5 Years

PERSONAL JOURNAL

Explain to students that if they practice picturing themselves succeeding in their chosen careers in the future, it can help them stay motivated and improve their chances of reaching their goals. Have students visualize themselves as adults ten years from now. What are they doing? Where do they live? Who are their friends? What kind of home and lifestyle do they have? Ask students to write a paragraph or two on their own paper describing the person they have become and answering these questions.

Career Action Plan

You have learned in this chapter that getting feedback and using it to revise your career goals is an important part of finding a career and making a living. You use these goals to create a career action plan, or specific steps for getting where you want to be in your career. Write answers to each question to develop a career action plan based on your current career goal statement. Then add the activity to your career portfolio. Use the format on page 289 as a way to organize your answers.

1. Summarize your current career goals.

2. What skills and abilities do you need to have to pursue that career?

3. What classes or activities are you involved in now to develop those abilities?

4. What classes or activities will you need to be involved in during and after high school to develop those abilities?

5. What subjects will you need to learn more about in a post-secondary setting?

6. What are some specific steps you need to take in the coming year to pursue this career?

7. What are some specific steps you need to take in the next five years to pursue this career?

Name _____ Date ____ Period ____   Portfolio Activity Chapter 10 10

Developing a Career Action Plan

Directions Write one or more sentences to answer each question from the Portfolio Activity on pages 288–289. Add this activity to your career portfolio.

1. **My Current Career Goals**
   Goal 1: _____
   Goal 2: _____

2. **Skills Needed**
   _____
   _____

   Abilities Needed
   _____

3. **Current Classes and Activities**
   _____

4. **Classes and Activities Needed**
   _____

5. **Postsecondary Subjects**
   _____

6. **This Year's Steps**
   Step 1: _____
   Step 2: _____
   Step 3: _____

7. **Future Steps**
   Step 1: _____
   Step 2: _____
   Step 3: _____

TRL

Portfolio Activity 10

My Career Action Plan

1. **My Current Career Goals**

   Goal 1:_____

   Goal 2:_____

2. **Skills Needed**

   _____

   _____

   Abilities Needed

   _____

   _____

3. **Current Classes and Activities**

   _____

   _____

4. **Classes and Activities Needed**

   _____

   _____

5. **Postsecondary Subjects**

   _____

   _____

6. **This Year's Steps**

   Step 1:_____

   Step 2:_____

   Step 3:_____

7. **Future Steps**

   Step 1:_____

   Step 2:_____

   Step 3:_____

LEARNING STYLES

Logical/Mathematical
Students' career action plans will be most useful if they are logically organized, neat, and visually appealing. Ask students to design a form into which they can place the information they gather as they answer the questions on page 288. For example, students might create a form with sections for question 1, questions 2–4, questions 5–6, and questions 7–8. A possible format is shown:

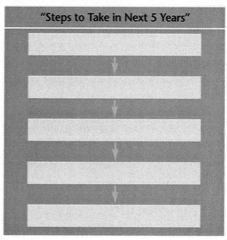

Career Goals

Skills/ Abilities Needed	Current Classes/ Activities to develop skills	Postsecondary Classes/ Activities to develop skills

Subjects Needed in High School	Subjects Needed in Postsecondary Training

"Steps to Take Now"

"Steps to Take in Next 5 Years"

Chapter 10 Review

Use the Chapter Review to prepare students for tests and to reteach content from the chapter.

Chapter 10 Mastery Test TRL

The Teacher's Resource Library includes two forms of the Chapter 10 Mastery Test. Each test addresses the chapter Goals for Learning. An optional third page of additional critical-thinking items is included for each test. The difficulty level of the two forms is equivalent.

Chapters 1–10 Final Mastery Test TRL

The Teacher's Resource Library includes the Final Mastery Test. This test is pictured on pages 326–327 of this Teacher's Edition. The Final Mastery Test assesses the major learning objectives of this text, with emphasis on Chapters 6–10.

Review Answers
Concept Review

1. B 2. A 3. B 4. D 5. C

Review Answers
Critical Thinking

6. Answers will vary. Possible answer: Getting and responding to feedback is a skill because it is something most people have to learn how to do. It is sometimes difficult to receive negative feedback and use it to make positive changes, so people probably have to practice and try different ways of sorting out and applying feedback. 7. Answers will vary. Possible answer: You might want to find out if your friend has gotten other feedback to indicate that engineering might not be the right career path. What exactly were the judges' comments? Remind your friend that not winning in one science fair is probably not the best indicator of her future abilities. 8. Answers will vary. Possible answer: Your attitude about a particular activity may have less to do with your interests and abilities than with the leadership, the setting, and other factors.

Concept Review

Choose the word or phrase that best answers each question or completes each sentence. Write the letter of the answer on your paper.

1. Feedback is _____.
   A always positive and constructive
   B information you receive about how you are doing at something
   C information about college admissions and financial aid
   D rarely useful

2. If you are receiving feedback that consistently and over a long period of time suggests that you aren't really on the right track, you should _____.
   A look at your career goal and use the feedback to revise it
   B have a discussion with your parents and teachers to get them to change their views
   C ignore the feedback and keep going down the same path
   D assume that everyone is out to get you

3. A career action plan should _____.
   A be vague so that you won't be disappointed
   B change as your career goals change
   C be "set in stone" to be effective
   D take into account many possible scenarios

4. A career action plan includes all of the following EXCEPT _____.
   A abilities and skills you will need to develop
   B school subjects or degree programs you will need to pursue
   C school or community activities that will help to prepare you
   D names of companies you expect to work for

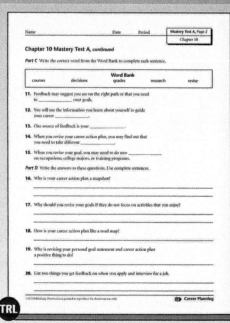

5. Career goal statements and career action plans can be considered "snapshots" because they _____.

A never change

B are good reminders of what your dreams are when you are young

C tell who you are and what your dreams are at a particular point in time

D are done on a whim and without much thought

Critical Thinking

Write the answer to each question on your paper.

6. How can getting and responding to feedback be considered a skill?

7. You have a friend who wants to be an engineer. She enters a project in the school science fair but does not win. Now she is considering changing her career goal. What is some advice you can give her about dealing with this kind of feedback?

8. Why is it important to evaluate why your attitude about a particular activity has changed before you change your career plans?

9. Imagine you are an author whose novel was turned down repeatedly before becoming a bestseller. What kinds of encouragement or motivation might have contributed to your persistence?

10. How specific do you think a career action plan should be? Explain.

Test-Taking Tip

To answer a multiple-choice question, read every choice before you answer the question. Cross out the choices you know are wrong. Then choose the best answer from the remaining choices.

9. Answers will vary. Possible answer: You may have had friends and teachers who told you they enjoyed the story. It is also possible that the publishers gave you specific feedback to help you rewrite parts of the story, or that you recognized that different people often like different kinds of writing. **10.** Answers will vary. Possible answer: A career action plan should be specific enough to serve as a good guide for making decisions related to your career, but still flexible or "open" enough to allow for variations.

ALTERNATIVE ASSESSMENT

- Prepare index cards with different feedback scenarios on them, such as getting a poor grade in a class, selling a painting, or failing to make the first string of the basketball team. Have students draw a card and explain what this feedback communicates to them and how they would respond to it to get the greatest benefit.

- Have each student present and defend his or her career action plan, completed in the Portfolio Activity. Specifically, ask the student to explain why he or she included those particular steps to be completed this year and others to be completed over the next five years.

Chapter 10 Mastery Test B, Pages 1–3

Appendix: Definitions of Occupational Titles

A

accountant studies financial information, keeps track of money spent and money earned, and prepares financial reports for a business or organization (Ch. 1–2, 4, 6)

actor/actress Performs in plays, television shows, radio shows, videos, or movies to entertain, inform, or instruct (Ch. 2, 4)

administrative assistant provides support to workers by doing research, writing reports, writing letters and e-mails, scheduling meetings, and other clerical tasks (Ch. 2, 4) *See also* executive secretary (Ch. 2)

administration services manager plans and directs recordkeeping, mail delivery, telephone, and other office support services; may also be in charge of building operations planning and maintenance (Ch. 4) *See also* office manager (Ch. 2, 4)

advertising and promotion representative sells advertising such as graphic art, advertising space in publications, custom made signs, or television and radio advertising time; gets retailers to display items in their stores (Ch. 4)

advertising manager plans and directs advertising for products; oversees creation of posters, coupons, or give-away materials (Ch. 2)

agricultural inspector makes sure food products; equipment; and food production, fishing, and logging operations meet laws and standards for health, quality, and safety (Ch. 2)

aircraft structure assembler puts together a section of aircraft such as the tail, wing, or fuselage; installs functional equipment such as landing gear, doors, and floorboards (Ch. 4)

airplane pilot flies aircraft to transport passengers and cargo; must have Federal Air Transport rating and certification (Ch. 2, 4)

air traffic controller monitors air traffic near an airport, keeps track of flight movement between locations, makes sure commercial airline flights follow government and safety rules (Ch. 2)

animal caretaker feeds, waters, herds, brands, weighs, or provides other care for animals on farms, ranches, or other facilities (Ch. 2, 4)

animal scientist researches the genetics, nutrition, reproduction, growth, and development of animals (Ch. 4)

announcer talks on radio, television, or in front of an audience; may conduct interviews, read news, or introduce music (Ch. 4) *See also* radio/TV announcer (Ch. 2)

anthropologist studies the beginnings and behavior of humans and cultures (Ch. 4)

architect plans and designs homes, office buildings, theaters, factories, and other structures (Ch. 1–2, 4)

architectural drafter creates drawings of building designs and plans based on plans from an architect (Ch. 4)

art director designs and creates art for products such as books, magazines, newspapers, packaging, television and Internet ads, etc.; is in charge of workers who work on these products (Ch. 2)

artist creates art by drawing, painting, taking photographs, or sculpting (Ch. 2)

art teacher teaches art classes about painting, drawing, photography, sculpture, and design (Ch. 2)

athletic trainer helps athletes stay physically fit, avoid being hurt, and recover from injuries (Ch. 2, 4) *See also* personal trainer (Ch. 9)

auditor studies financial records and prepares reports about the financial status of a business or organization; makes sure a business or organization is following rules and regulations related to accounting (Ch. 2)

auto mechanic repairs cars, trucks, buses, and other vehicles (Ch. 2)

automotive master mechanic repairs any part on cars, trucks, buses, and other vehicles; often specializes in the transmission system (Ch. 2)

auto salesperson sells cars, trucks, buses, and other vehicles (Ch. 2)

auto technician repairs only one system or part of a vehicle, such as brakes, steering, or alternator (Ch. 2)

B

baker, manufacturing bakes products such as breads and pastries in large amounts to be sold at grocery stores and other retailers (Ch. 4)

bank manager oversees activities of tellers, loan officers, and other workers at a bank; may also be responsible for bank policies and rules, managing the budget, and hiring bank employees (Ch. 2, 6)

bank teller handles the exchange of money with customers at a bank (Ch. 2) *See also* teller (Ch. 2, 6)

barber cuts, trims, shampoos, styles hair; trims beards and gives shaves (Ch. 6)

bill collector finds and notifies customers of late bills, receives payments from customers, and keeps records of customer accounts (Ch. 4)

biologist studies plant and animal life (Ch. 2, 4)

boilermaker builds, maintains, and repairs steam boilers; inspects and repairs safety valves and control systems of boilers (Ch. 4)

bookkeeping clerk keeps track of data to maintain financial records for a business or organization; may also verify other workers' calculations for accuracy (Ch. 2)

brickmason and blockmason lays brick, tile, concrete block, glass block, and other block; binds block with mortar to build or repair walls and other structures (Ch. 4)

brokerage clerk writes orders for stock purchases and sales; figures taxes; keeps records of stock transactions and prices (Ch. 4)

building inspector makes sure buildings are structurally sound and are built according to safety codes and regulations (Ch. 4)

bus driver drives a city, charter, private, or school bus; may enforce safety rules, help riders get on and off the bus, or collect bus fares (Ch. 2, 6)

business executive oversees operation of a business; supervises and oversees employees; handles budget, sales, and other financial plans (Ch. 2)

buyer purchases equipment, supplies, or services needed to operate a business or organization; or purchases farm products to resell (Ch. 2, 4) *See also* purchasing agent (Ch. 4), retail merchandise buyer (Ch. 8)

C

cabinetmaker cuts and puts together wooden parts for wood products; sets up and operates power saws and other woodworking tools (Ch. 4) *See also* carpenter (Ch. 2, 4, 6)

camera operator uses a camera and darkroom equipment to take and develop pictures to be printed; uses a television, video, or movie camera to capture images for television news, advertisements, or film (Ch. 4)

cargo and freight agent plans and oversees movement of cargo and freight on plans, trains, trucks, and ships; takes customer orders; calculates shipping charges and taxes (Ch. 4)

carpenter cuts and puts together wooden parts for wood products; sets up and operates power saws and other woodworking tools (Ch. 2, 4, 6) *See also* cabinetmaker (Ch. 2)

cartoonist creates cartoon art by drawing, painting, sculpting, or other technique (Ch. 2, 4)

cashier handles exchange of money with customers at businesses or organizations other than banks (Ch. 2–4)

cement mason finishes or patches poured concrete floors, sidewalks, roads, or curbs (Ch. 4)

chef prepares and directs the preparation of food; may plan menus, order supplies, and keep records (Ch. 4, 6)

chemical engineer designs equipment for chemical plants; creates ways to manufacture chemicals and products such gasoline, plastics, cement, and paper (Ch. 4)

chemist conducts studies and chemical experiments to help develop new products or knowledge (Ch. 2, 4)

child care provider dresses, feeds, bathes, and supervises children at schools, homes, or child care centers (Ch. 6) *See also* child care worker (Ch. 2, 4)

child care worker dresses, feeds, bathes, and supervises children at schools, homes, or child care centers (Ch. 2, 4) *See also* child care provider (Ch. 6)

chiropractor helps patients with back pain by adjusting the spine (Ch. 2, 4)

choral director directs performances of a choir; selects music to perform; conducts practice sessions with singers (Ch. 2)

choreographer creates and teaches dances; may also direct performances on stage (Ch. 2)

civil drafter makes drawings and maps for projects such as highways, bridges, pipelines, and water control systems (Ch. 4)

civil engineer plans, designs, and oversees construction and maintenance of buildings, roads, airports, bridges, dams, pipelines, power plants, and water and sewage systems (Ch. 4)

clergy lead religious worship and ceremonies; provide support and guidance to members (Ch. 2, 4, 6)

clinical psychologist diagnoses and treats mental and emotional disorders; observes, interviews, and tests patients (Ch. 2, 4)

coach teaches people individual or team sports, including techniques and rules (Ch. 2)

college administrator plans and oversees teaching, student life, research, and other educational services and activities at postsecondary institutions, including universities, colleges, and junior and community colleges (Ch. 2) *See also* educational administrator (Ch. 2), school administrator (Ch. 2, 4, 6)

college professor teaches classes at a college or postsecondary school (Ch. 2) *See also* postsecondary teacher (Ch. 4)

columnist writes stories or opinion pieces for newspapers, news magazines, or Web sites (Ch. 4)

comedian tells jokes in front of an audience; writes and performs material for comedy shows (Ch. 2)

commercial designer designs and create products such as cars, appliances, and toys (Ch. 2, 4)

composer writes music for an instrument, singer, instrumental group, or choral group (Ch. 2, 4)

computer hardware engineer studies, tests, and designs computers or computer equipment; may oversee the manufacturing and installation of computers or computer equipment (Ch. 4)

computer operator use computer and electronic equipment to keep records of data; may enter commands, set computer controls, and track error messages (Ch. 2)

computer programmer writes programs using various computer languages that tell a computer what to do; may write programs for Web sites (Ch. 2, 4)

computer scientist studies, tests, and designs computers, computer equipment, or computer software (Ch. 2)

computer service technician helps computer users with technical problems, answer users' questions regarding use of computer hardware and software (Ch. 2) *See also* computer support specialist (Ch. 2, 4)

computer software engineer studies, designs, develops, and tests computer software and programs; may design and study databases (Ch 2, 4)

computer support specialist helps computer users with technical problems, answer users' questions regarding use of computer hardware and software (Ch. 2, 4) *See also* computer service technician (Ch. 2)

computer systems analyst studies and solves problems related to computer systems and software; finds ways to use computer systems better (Ch. 2, 4)

computer systems manager oversees the study of computer systems and software to solve problems and find ways to use computer systems better (Ch. 4)

conductor directs performances of a instrumental group or choir and conducts practice sessions with musicians (Ch. 2)

construction equipment operator operates machines used in construction such as excavators, dump trucks, crushers, boring machines, and cranes (Ch. 2, 4)

construction laborer provides physical labor for the construction of buildings, roads, and other projects; may operate tools, clean up building sites, and transport construction materials (Ch. 4)

construction manager plans and oversees the construction and maintenance of buildings and other structures (Ch. 2)

continuous mining machine operator operates machines that remove coal, metal, ores, rock, stone from the earth and load it for transport in a continuous operation (Ch. 4)

contractor arranges for an individual or business to perform work involved with building houses, roads, or other structures (Ch. 4)

cook prepares food in restaurants, fast-food restaurants, schools, hospitals, or cafeterias; may order supplies, plan menus, and keep records (Ch. 2, 6)

copywriter writes advertising copy that will promote a product or service in newspapers, magazines, Web sites, television, or radio (Ch. 4)

corporate trainer trains and educates workers at businesses or organizations (Ch. 4) *See also* training and development specialist (Ch. 4)

corrections officer guards prisoners in jails or other correctional institutions (Ch. 4)

counseling psychologist interviews and observes patients to help them with personal, social, educational, or work-related problems (Ch. 4)

counselor helps people with their problems by talking with them (Ch. 2, 6) *See also* educational counselor (Ch. 2), school counselor (Ch. 2, 4), vocational counselor (Ch. 2)

court reporter takes word-for-word reports of speeches, meetings, conversations, and other legal proceedings (Ch. 2)

credit analyst studies financial data of people or businesses to find out how risky it would be to lend them money (Ch. 4)

customer service representative handles questions and complaints from customers, usually by answering phones at a business or organization; may place customer orders (Ch. 2, 4)

customs inspector makes sure goods and merchandise arriving in or leaving from another country or state does not violate customs laws and regulations (Ch. 2) *See also* immigrations and customs inspector (Ch. 4)

D

dancer performs dances; may also sing or act (Ch. 2, 4)

data entry keyer operates a keyboard or other data entry device to verify data and prepare materials for printing (Ch. 2)

database administrator oversees, tests, and coordinates changes to computer databases (Ch. 2, 4)

Career Planning Appendix **295**

dental assistant helps dentist, sets up equipment, and keeps records (Ch. 2)

dental hygienist cleans teeth and looks for signs of oral disease; may teach patients about oral hygiene, take X-rays, or administer fluoride treatments (Ch. 2)

dentist diagnoses and treats oral diseases and injuries (Ch. 2, 4)

derrick operator, oil and gas sets ups derrick equipment and operate pumps to circulate mud through a drill hole (Ch. 4)

desktop publisher prepares documents using computer software to produce material for publication (Ch. 4) *See also* desktop publishing specialist (Ch. 2)

desktop publishing specialist prepares documents using computer software to produce material for publication (Ch. 2) *See also* desktop publisher (Ch. 4)

detective investigates crimes to find criminals, prevent further crime, and solve cases (Ch. 4) *See also* police detective (Ch. 2)

diagnostic medical sonographer takes X-rays of patients to determine broken bones or other internal injuries (Ch. 2)

dietician plans food and nutritional programs to keep people healthy, supervises food service programs, gives nutritional advice, and conducts nutritional research (Ch. 2, 4)

dispatcher schedules and sends construction, repair, and installation workers or equipment to a site (Ch. 4) *See also* police dispatcher (Ch. 2)

doctor diagnoses, treats, and helps prevent diseases and injuries; may specialize in one of various medical fields (Ch. 6) *See also* physician (Ch. 2, 4)

drafter prepares detailed drawings of buildings, structures, or machinery based on an architect's or engineer's plans (Ch. 2) *See also* mechanical drafter (Ch. 2)

drama teacher teaches courses in drama and acting (Ch. 2)

drywall installer applies plasterboard or other wallboard to ceilings and walls inside of buildings (Ch. 4)

E

economist studies economic problems dealing with the production and distribution of good and services; conducts research and prepares economic reports (Ch. 2, 4)

editor performs editorial duties such as laying out, indexing, and revising content of written materials to prepare them for publication (Ch. 2)

educational administrator plans and oversees teaching, student life, research, and other educational services and activities at elementary, secondary, or postsecondary schools (Ch. 2) *See also* college administrator (Ch. 2), school administrator (Ch. 2, 4, 6)

educational counselor helps individuals with education and career planning (Ch. 2) *See also* counselor (Ch. 2, 6), school counselor (Ch. 2, 4), vocational counselor (Ch. 2)

electrical engineer designs, develops, and tests electrical equipment (Ch. 2, 4)

electrician installs, maintains, and repairs electrical wiring and equipment according to proper codes (Ch. 2, 4, 6)

electronic assembler puts together electronic equipment, such as computers and electric motors (Ch. 4)

electronic equipment installer and repairer installs and repairs communications, sound, security, or navigation equipment in motor vehicles, home entertainment, and other electronic products (Ch. 2)

electronics repairer repairs communications, sound, security, or navigation equipment in motor vehicles, home entertainment, and other electronic products (Ch. 2)

elementary school teacher teaches students basic academic and social skills in public or private schools at the elementary level (Ch. 2, 4)

elevator installer puts together and installs repair electric or hydraulic elevators and escalators (Ch. 4)

emergency medical technician (EMT) provides emergency medical care by assessing injuries, freeing trapped individuals, and transporting patients to medical facilities (Ch. 2, 4)

engineer designs and plans activities and projects in architectural, civil, electrical, mechanical, or other engineering fields (Ch. 2)

engraver engraves designs or lettering onto objects (Ch. 2)

environmental scientist studies sources of pollutants and hazards that affect the air, food, soil, and water (Ch. 4)

executive secretary provides support to workers by doing research, writing reports, writing letters and e-mails, scheduling meetings, and other clerical tasks (Ch. 2, 4) *See also* administrative assistant (Ch. 2, 4)

explosive worker and blaster places and set off explosives to tear down structures or to remove rock or other materials (Ch. 4)

F

faller cuts down trees using axes and chainsaws and controls the direction in which trees fall when they are cut down (Ch. 4)

farmer owns and operates a farm that produces crops and/or livestock; plants, cultivates, harvests, and markets crops and livestock; maintains and operates farm machinery (Ch. 2)

farm and ranch manager oversees the activities of farm or ranch workers engaged in crop or livestock production for farm or ranch owners (Ch. 2, 3)

farmworkers, farm and ranch animals feed, water, herd, brand, weigh, and provide other care for animals on farms or ranches (Ch. 4)

fashion designer designs clothing and accessories (Ch. 2)

FBI agent government worker who investigates crimes, gathers evidence, and interviews witnesses to capture criminals (Ch. 2, 4)

film and video editor edits movie soundtracks, film, and video (Ch. 4)

finance manager oversees the financial activities of workers in a bank, brokerage firm, insurance agency, or credit department (Ch. 4)

financial advisor counsels individuals or businesses on ways to best spend, save, or invest their money; helps individuals plan for retirement (Ch. 10) *See also* financial planner (Ch. 2)

financial analyst studies information regarding how a business or organization investments its money (Ch. 2, 4)

financial planner counsels individuals or businesses on ways to best spend, save, or invest their money; helps individuals plan for retirement (Ch. 2) *See also* financial advisor (Ch. 10)

firefighter responds to emergency calls of fires; puts out fires; may conduct investigations to determine causes of fires and explosions (Ch. 2, 4)

fisher catches fish or other aquatic animals by using nets, fishing rods, traps, or other equipment (Ch. 2)

flight attendant greets passengers, verifies tickets, explains safety equipment, and serves food or beverages to airline passengers during flight (Ch. 2)

floral designer cuts and arranges flowers and other plants (Ch. 2, 4)

food preparation worker prepares food, but does not cook; may prepare cold foods, slice meat, or brew coffee (Ch. 2)

food server serves food to restaurant customers, or to customers in hotels, hospital rooms, or cars (Ch. 6)

food service manager plans and oversees workers in a business or organization that serves food and beverages (Ch. 2, 4)

food services manager *See* food service manager (Ch. 2, 4)

forest and conservation worker transports tree seedlings, fights insects and pests, inspects soil, and plants trees to develop, maintain, and protect forests (Ch. 2, 4)

forester manages forested lands for economic, recreational, and conservation purposes; keeps track of number and types of trees, conserves wildlife habitats, and makes plans to plant new trees (Ch. 2, 4)

funeral director arranges and directs funeral services such as transportation and embalming of the body, interviewing family members, finding religious officials, and providing transportation for mourners (Ch. 6)

G

geologist studies the earth's crust, rocks, minerals, and fossils (Ch. 4)

glazier installs glass for windows, skylights, store fronts, display cases, interior walls, ceilings, and tabletops (Ch. 4)

government administrator plans, directs, and coordinates activities related to the operation of a government department or office (Ch. 4, 6)

graphic designer designs or creates graphics for product packaging, displays, or logos (Ch. 2, 4)

H

hairdresser, hairstylist, and cosmetologist shampoos, cuts, colors, and styles hair; massages and treats scalp; applies makeup; provides nail and skin care (Ch. 4, 6)

hair stylist shampoos, cuts, colors, and styles hair (Ch. 2)

heating and air-conditioning mechanic installs, maintains, and repairs heating and air-conditioning systems (Ch. 2, 6)

helper, construction and trades helps construction workers by performing duties such as holding materials or tools and cleaning the work area and equipment (Ch. 4)

highway maintenance worker keeps highways and roads in safe condition by patching broken pavement, repairing guard rails and signs, and clearing brush or plowing snow from road (Ch. 2, 6)

home health aide bathes, dresses, and cares for elderly, injured, or disabled people in their homes or in care centers (Ch. 2)

hotel/motel clerk registers guests, hands out room keys, answers phones, takes messages, takes reservations, and collects payments at a hotel or motel front desk (Ch. 2–4, 6)

hotel/motel manager oversees the activities of workers at a hotel or motel; directs and coordinates record keeping and billing, as well as housekeeping and maintenance activities (Ch. 2) *See also* lodging manager (Ch. 4)

housekeeper makes beds, cleans rooms, vacuums, and performs other cleaning duties in homes or other businesses such as hotels and hospitals (Ch. 6) *See also* maid/housekeeper (Ch. 4, 6)

human resources assistant keeps records of employee addresses, paychecks, and attendance; updates employee files and gives information to other human resources workers (Ch. 2, 4)

I

immigration and customs inspector makes sure people, goods, or merchandise arriving in or leaving from another country or state does not violate immigration and customs laws and regulations (Ch. 4) *See also* customs inspector (Ch. 2)

industrial designer designs, models, creates, and tests new products or finds ways to improve old products (Ch. 2)

information systems manager plans and oversees workers who are involved in data processing, information and computer systems analysis, and computer programming (Ch. 2)

insulation worker installs insulation materials in structures such as homes, offices, and other buildings; applies insulation materials to pipes, ducts and other temperature-control systems (Ch. 4)

insurance agent sells life, automobile, homeowner's, and other kinds of insurance (Ch. 2) *See also* insurance sales agent (Ch. 4)

insurance claim and policy processing clerk gets information from people filing or otherwise involved in insurance claims; takes applications for and keeps records of insurance policies (Ch. 4)

insurance claims adjuster determines how much an insurance company will pay to a claimant by investigating losses and damages and interviewing witnesses and claimants (Ch. 2)

insurance sales agent sells life, automobile, homeowner's, and other kinds of insurance (Ch. 4) *See also* insurance agent (Ch. 2)

insurance underwriter determines whether an insurance company will cover an applicant and how much risk is involved in doing so (Ch. 4)

interior designer plans and designs the decoration and layout of rooms inside homes or businesses (Ch. 2–4)

interpreter translates one language to another in writing, words, or sign language (Ch. 4) *See also* translator (Ch. 2, 4)

J

janitor cleans floors, rugs, walls, and windows of buildings; may also remove garbage, clean snow from sidewalks, and keep track of needed repairs (Ch. 1)

jeweler designs, creates, cleans, and repairs various pieces of jewelry (Ch. 4)

judge oversees cases in a court of law, advises participants, sentences defendants; may also issue licenses for marriages (Ch. 2)

L

landscaper plans, designs, and completes projects to beautify land at homes, parks, or businesses (Ch. 2)

landscaping and groundskeeping worker lays sod; mows, trims, plants, and waters grass; installs trees, shrubbery, sprinklers, rock, and retaining walls (Ch. 2, 4)

law enforcement officer enforces laws, directs and monitors traffic, controls crowds, provides security, arrests criminals, and responds to emergencies (Ch. 6) *See also* police officer (Ch. 2, 4)

lawyer represents, manages, and advises clients in legal cases or transactions (Ch. 2, 4)

legal assistant helps lawyers by doing legal research and preparing documents (Ch. 2) *See also* paralegal (Ch. 2, 4)

legal secretary prepares legal documents, writes letters, takes messages, and assists with legal research (Ch. 4)

librarian selects books for libraries and provides library services such as cataloguing and circulating books and other library materials; may conduct research and set up computer databases to manage library information (Ch. 4)

licensed nurse practitioner provides care for patients in hospitals, health care centers, private and group homes, and other institutions; gives medication, prepares equipment, and assists doctors; license required (Ch. 2) *See also* licensed practical nurse (Ch. 4), nurse (Ch. 2, 6), nurse practitioner (Ch. 2), registered nurse (Ch. 4)

licensed practical nurse provides care for patients in hospitals, health care centers, private and group homes, and other institutions; gives medication, prepares equipment, and assists doctors; license required (Ch. 4) *See also* licensed nurse practitioner (Ch. 2), nurse (Ch. 2, 6), nurse practitioner (Ch. 2), registered nurse (Ch. 4)

loan officer determines whether a bank, credit union, or other financial institution should give a loan to a customer, advises customers on loan accounts (Ch. 4)

locomotive engineer drives passenger or freight trains according to railroad signals, rules, and regulations (Ch. 4)

lodging manager oversees the activities of workers at a hotel, motel or other lodging facility or department; directs and coordinates record keeping and billing, as well as housekeeping and maintenance activities (Ch. 4) *See also* hotel/motel manager (Ch. 2)

log grader and scaler inspects and measures logs to determine their volume and market value (Ch. 4)

logger cuts down trees using axes and chainsaws and controls the direction in which trees fall when they are cut down (Ch. 4) *See also* faller (Ch. 4)

M

machine operator sets up and operates various machines used to manufacture, produce, or assemble products (Ch. 2)

machinist sets up and operates various machines to make parts and tools; may also make parts to build, maintain, or repair machines (Ch. 4)

maid/housekeeper makes beds, cleans rooms, vacuums, and performs other cleaning duties in homes or other businesses such as hotels and hospitals (Ch. 4, 6) *See also* housekeeper (Ch. 6)

mail carrier sorts and delivers mail (Ch. 4)

management analyst studies organizations to see how they operate and recommends ways to simply or improve work procedures (Ch. 4)

manufacturer's representative sells products from the manufacturer to a business or individual; acts as a product expert for the manufacturer (Ch. 4) *See also* wholesale sales representative (Ch. 4)

manufacturing optician produce lenses and frames for glasses according to prescription; may grind lenses and set them in frame (Ch. 4)

marketing manager studies the market to see what products or services are in demand, studies competitor offerings, sets prices, and oversees the development of new products and services (Ch. 2, 4)

mathematician studies mathematics and does mathematical research to solve problems related to business, science, management, and other fields (Ch. 2, 4)

mechanic tests, repairs, and maintains mechanical equipment such as automobiles, aircraft, farm equipment, engines, and industrial machinery (Ch. 4, 6)

mechanical drafter prepares detailed drawings of machinery based on an engineer's plans (Ch. 2) *See also* drafter (Ch. 2)

mechanical engineer plans and designs tools, engines, and machines; oversees the installation, maintenance, and repair of mechanical equipment and systems (Ch. 2, 4)

mechanical inspector inspects and tests motors, vehicles, and other machines and mechanical systems to make sure they are in good working order (Ch. 4)

medical and clinical laboratory technician does regular medical laboratory tests to diagnose and treat diseases (Ch. 4) *See also* medical lab technician (Ch. 2)

medical and clinical laboratory technologist does complicated medical laboratory tests to diagnose and treat diseases; may supervise and train medical and clinical laboratory technicians (Ch. 4)

medical and health services manager plans and oversees health service activities and employees at hospitals, clinics, health care centers, and other health care organizations (Ch. 2, 4)

medical assistant schedules appointments, maintains records, tracks billing; takes vital signs and medical histories, draws blood, administers medications under the direction of a doctor (Ch. 2, 4)

medical lab technician does regular medical laboratory tests to diagnose and treat diseases (Ch. 2) *See also* medical and clinical laboratory technician (Ch. 4)

medical records and health information technician gathers and maintains medical records; processes and maintains patient information (Ch. 4) *See also* medical records technician (Ch. 2)

medical records technician gathers and maintains medical records (Ch. 2) *See also* medical records and health information technician (Ch. 4)

medical technician does regular medical laboratory tests to diagnose and treat diseases (Ch. 2) *See also* medical and clinical laboratory technician (Ch. 4), medical lab technician (Ch. 2)

medical transcriptionist uses medical terminology to compile and maintain medical records, charts, reports, and letters (Ch. 4)

meeting and convention planner plans and oversees arrangements and travel for group meetings and conventions (Ch. 4)

mental health counselor talks with people about addiction, substance abuse, family problems, stress management, self-esteem and other mental health issues (Ch. 4)

metal-refining furnace operator operates gas, oil, coal, electric, or oxygen furnaces that melt and refine metal (Ch. 4)

military office member of the Armed Forces who supervises and manages other military personnel (Ch. 4)

mining and geological engineer locates coal and ores to be extracted, makes geological maps, finds ways to extract deposits, and supervises mining workers (Ch. 4)

mobile heavy equipment mechanic inspects and repairs mechanical equipment such as cranes, bulldozers, and conveyors used in construction, logging, and mining (Ch. 4)

model wears clothing for display at fashion shows, stores, or for photographers; may pose for paintings, sculptures or other kinds of art (Ch. 2)

molding and casting worker mixes materials, puts together mold parts, and fills and stacks molds to create a variety of products (Ch. 4)

music arranger writes musical notes and arranges musical parts for music to be performed by an individual or group (Ch. 2)

musician plays a musical instrument or instruments in a solo performance or as a member of a musical group (Ch. 2, 4)

music teacher teaches music classes such as note-reading, performance, music theory, or individual singing or instrumental lessons (Ch. 2)

N

network systems and data communications analyst designs and tests network systems or groups of computers working together; recommends ways to use hardware and software better; finds ways for computer systems to work together with telephone and other communications systems (Ch. 4)

new accounts clerk helps customers open new bank accounts by explaining bank services and preparing application forms (Ch. 4)

novelist writes original books for publication (Ch. 2, 4)

nurse provides care for patients in hospitals, health care centers, private and group homes, and other institutions; gives medication, prepares equipment, and assists doctors (Ch. 2, 6) *See also* licensed nurse practitioner (Ch. 2), licensed practical nurse (Ch. 4), nurse practitioner (Ch. 2)

nurse practitioner provides care for patients in hospitals, health care centers, private and group homes, and other institutions; gives medication, prepares equipment, and assists doctors (Ch. 2) *See also* licensed nurse practitioner (Ch. 2), licensed practical nurse (Ch. 4), nurse (Ch. 2, 6)

O

oceanographer studies ocean and sea life (Ch. 1)

office clerk performs clerical duties such as answering phones, keeping records, typing, taking messages, operating office machines, and filing (Ch. 4)

office manager plans and directs recordkeeping, mail delivery, telephone, and other office support services; May also be in charge of building operations planning and maintenance (Ch. 2, 4) *See also* administration services manager (Ch. 4)

operations research analyst studies see how an organization operates by looking at management, use of time, costs, and logistics; uses mathematical models to suggest solutions for a business or organization; may develop software and products to collect and study data and model solutions (Ch. 2, 4)

optometrist examines the eyes, treats eye and visual system diseases, prescribes glasses or contact lenses (Ch. 2, 4)

P

painter paints original artwork using watercolors, oils, acrylics, tempera, or other kinds of paint (Ch. 2, 4)

painter, construction and maintenance paints surfaces such of walls, buildings, bridges, and equipment; may remove old paint and mix new paint (Ch. 4)

painting, coating, and decorating worker applies paint or decoration to products such as furniture, glass, dishes, pottery, jewelry, toys, and books (Ch. 4)

paralegal helps lawyers by doing legal research and preparing (Ch. 2, 4) *See also* legal assistant (Ch. 2)

park ranger patrols national, state, or local parks to ensure visitors are following rules; provides maintenance for parks; may plan or conduct informational programs about the history and natural features of a park (Ch. 1)

paving, surfacing, and tamping equipment operator operates equipment used to build and maintain roads, parking lots, and other surfaces (Ch. 4) *See also* road paving and surfacing operator (Ch. 4)

payroll clerk keeps track of hours worked and pay rates for employees; may prepare paychecks (Ch. 2)

personal and home care aide helps the elderly or disabled with daily tasks at the person's home; may make beds, wash clothes, wash dishes, and prepare meals (Ch. 4)

personal trainer helps people stay physically fit, avoid being hurt, and recover from injuries; may suggest exercise and nutritional programs (Ch. 9) *See also* athletic trainer (Ch. 2, 4)

personnel recruiter searches for applicants for job opportunities at a business or organization; may interview and screen applicants (Ch. 4)

personnel specialist finds, interviews, and screens job applicants for a business or organization (Ch. 7)

petroleum engineer studies the drilling of oil and gas, and finds ways to improve drilling processes and tools; oversees drilling operations (Ch. 4)

pharmacist prepares and gives out medications according to prescriptions from medical professionals (Ch. 2, 4)

pharmacy technician measures, mixes, counts, and labels medications according to directions from a pharmacist (Ch. 4)

photographer takes photographs of various subjects for artwork, advertising, magazines, newspapers, Web sites, or scientific purposes (Ch. 2, 4) *See also* professional photographer (Ch. 2)

photographic developer produces prints of images by putting film into chemical and water baths (Ch. 2)

photographic processing machine operator uses machines to develop film and produce print of images (Ch. 4)

physical therapist helps patients recover from disease or injury by creating programs to help with movement, pain relief, and strength (Ch. 2, 4)

physician diagnoses, treats, and helps prevent diseases and injuries; may specialize in one of various medical fields (Ch. 2, 4) *See also* doctor (Ch. 6)

physicist studies matter and energy, including mechanics, heat, light, sound, electricity, magnetism, and atomic energy (Ch. 2)

pipefitter puts together and installs pipes and pipe systems for air-conditioning, heating, water, and other systems (Ch. 4)

plant scientist studies plants, including how to produce crops and control pests (Ch. 4)

plasterer applies plaster, cement, or stucco to building interiors or exteriors (Ch. 4)

playwright writes original plays or dramas to be performed on stage (Ch. 2)

plumber puts together, installs, and repairs pipes and fixtures for heating, water, and drainage systems (Ch. 4, 6)

poet writes original poems to be published or performed (Ch. 2)

police chief oversees the activities of workers of a police force, including detectives, officers, and dispatchers (Ch. 4)

police detective investigates crimes to find criminals, prevent further crime, and solve cases (Ch. 2) *See also* detective (Ch. 4)

police dispatcher operates radio, telephone, and computer equipment to receive reports of crimes or emergencies; relays information to proper officials (Ch. 2) *See also* dispatcher (Ch. 4)

police officer enforces laws, directs and monitors traffic, controls crowds, provides security, arrests criminals, and responds to emergencies (Ch. 2, 4) *See also* law enforcement officer (Ch. 6)

post office clerk receives letter and packages, sells stamps and postcards, examines mail for proper postage (Ch. 4) *See also* postal service clerk (Ch. 2)

postal service clerk receives letter and packages, sells stamps and postcards, examines mail for proper postage (Ch. 2) *See also* post office clerk (Ch. 4)

postsecondary teacher teaches classes at a college or postsecondary school (Ch. 2) *See also* postsecondary teacher (Ch. 4), college professor (Ch. 2)

preschool teacher teaches young children social skills and school readiness skills at a preschool, child care center, or other facility; certification required in certain states (Ch. 2, 4)

printing press machine operator runs printing machines that print on paper, plastic, cloth, or other materials (Ch. 4)

private investigator gathers information for a customer; determines whether people or businesses have been breaking laws (Ch. 2)

producer plans and oversees activities involved in making a radio, television, or stage show, or a movie; may choose scripts, oversee writing and directing, and arrange ways to pay for the production (Ch. 2) *See also* radio/TV/movie producer (Ch. 2, 4), television news producer (Ch. 5)

product assembler puts together parts of a product or products (Ch. 2)

professional photographer takes photographs of people, events, and other subjects to be sold to customers or media outlets (Ch. 2) *See also* photographer (Ch. 2, 4)

property or real estate manager plans and oversees the sale or leasing of various properties including businesses, apartments, and homes (Ch. 2)

psychiatric aide helps patients who are mentally or emotionally impaired, under supervision of nursing or medical professionals (Ch. 2)

psychiatrist examines and treats patients with disorders of the mind (Ch. 2)

public relations specialist helps people or organizations create a positive public image; may write publicity material, prepare displays, and give speeches (Ch. 4)

pump operator controls or operates gas, oil, water, and other pumps (Ch. 4)

purchasing agent purchases equipment, supplies, or services needed to operate a business or organization; or purchases farm products to resell (Ch. 4) *See also* buyer (Ch. 2, 4), retail merchandise buyer (Ch. 8)

R

radio/TV announcer interviews guests, reads news, acts as host or hostess, announces music on radio or television (Ch. 2) *See also* announcer (Ch. 4)

radio/TV/movie producer plans and oversees activities involved in making a radio or television show, or a movie; may choose scripts, oversee writing and directing, and arrange ways to pay for the production (Ch. 2, 4) *See also* producer (Ch. 2), television news producer (Ch. 5)

radio/TV program assistant assists a program director with tasks involved in preparing radio or television schedules and shows (Ch. 2)

radio/TV program director plans and oversees workers involved in preparing radio or television schedules and shows (Ch. 4)

railroad conductor oversees passenger and freight train workers and coordinates railroad activities such as train makeup, yard switching, and scheduling (Ch. 4)

real estate appraiser inspects property or land to determine how much it is worth (Ch. 2)

real estate agent represents a customer who is buying or selling property; creates property listings, interviews customers, and prepares real estate documents (Ch. 2) *See also* real estate sales agent (Ch. 4)

real estate sales agent represents a customer who is selling property; creates property listings, interviews customers, and prepares real estate documents (Ch. 4) *See also* real estate agent (Ch. 2)

receptionist answers phone calls to a business from the public and from customers; gives information about the business or organization including department or office locations, phone numbers, and employees (Ch. 2, 4)

recreation leader plans and oversees activities such as arts and crafts, sports, games, music, trips, and hobbies for groups in public or private organizations; considers individual members' needs and interests when planning activities (Ch. 2)

recreational worker conducts activities such as arts and crafts, sports, games, music, trips, and hobbies with groups in public or private organizations (Ch. 2, 4)

registered nurse helps determine patients' health needs and problems; maintains medical records; cares for ill, injured or disabled patients; licensing or registration required (Ch. 4) *See also* licensed nurse practitioner (Ch. 2), licensed practical nurse (Ch. 4)

reporter gathers facts for news stories; writes news stories for newspapers, magazines, Web sites, radio, or television (Ch. 2, 4)

reservation and transportation ticket agent makes airline, bus, railroad, and ship reservations for passengers; sells tickets; may check luggage and give passengers directions (Ch. 4)

restaurant host/hostess welcomes and seats customers at a restaurant; may provide menus and take beverage orders (Ch. 4)

restaurant manager supervises employees who prepare and serve food at a restaurant; oversees business activities such as ordering food and supplies, setting prices, planning menus, and paying bills (Ch. 2)

retail merchandise buyer purchases equipment, supplies, or services needed to operate a business or organization; or purchases farm products to resell (Ch. 8) *See also* buyer (Ch. 2, 4), purchasing agent (Ch. 4)

retail salesperson sells products or merchandise in a furniture, appliance, clothing, or other retail store (Ch. 2, 4) *See also* retail sales worker (Ch. 2) salesperson (Ch. 2, 6)

retail sales worker sells products or merchandise in a furniture, appliance, clothing, or other retail store (Ch. 2) *See also* retail salesperson (Ch. 2, 4) salesperson (Ch. 2, 6)

road paving and surfacing operator operates equipment used to build and maintain roads, parking lots, and other surfaces (Ch. 4) *See also* road paving and surfacing operator (Ch. 4)

roofer covers roofs with shingles, slate, asphalt, aluminum, wood, and other roofing materials (Ch. 4, 6)

rotary drill operator, small oil and gas sets up and operates mining and extraction drills (Ch. 4)

roustabout, oil and gas puts together or repairs equipment used in oil and gas mining and extraction (Ch. 4)

S

sailor performs various duties aboard a ship such as navigating, standing watch, measuring water depth, and working with rigging (Ch. 4)

sales agent: securities and commodities buys and sells bond or stock certificates; develops financial plans for businesses and organizations (Ch. 4)

sales manager oversees sales workers; may be in charge of purchasing, budgeting, and accounting (Ch. 2, 4)

salesperson sells products or services for retail or wholesale stores, or as an individual (Ch. 2, 6) *See also* retail salesperson (Ch. 2, 4) retail sales worker (Ch. 2)

school administrator plans and oversees teaching, student life, research, and other educational services and activities at elementary, secondary, or postsecondary schools (Ch. 2, 4, 6) *See also* college administrator (Ch. 2), educational administrator (Ch. 2)

school counselor helps individuals with education and career planning (Ch. 2, 4) *See also* counselor (Ch. 2, 6), educational counselor (Ch. 2), vocational counselor (Ch. 2)

school psychologist studies ways people learn and teach in schools; uses psychology to solve educational problems related to learning and teaching (Ch. 4)

science teacher teaches science courses such as biology, chemistry, and physics (Ch. 4)

script editor prepares and makes changes to scripts of movies, plays, or radio and television programs for performance (Ch. 4)

secondary school teacher teaches students in secondary public or private schools; may teach one or more subjects such as English, mathematics, or science (Ch. 2, 4)

secretary writes letters, schedules appointments, organized files, gives information to callers, and performs other clerical duties (Ch. 2, 4)

security guard watches a building, buildings, or other area to prevent trespassing, violence, or crime (Ch. 2, 4)

service station attendant pumps fuel, changes oil, replaces tires, and provides other service for automobiles and other vehicles (Ch. 6)

Career Planning Appendix **305**

sheet metal worker makes, puts together, and installs products and equipment made from sheet metal such as ducts, pipes, and furnace casings (Ch. 4)

sheriff enforces laws in rural areas or towns and responds to emergencies; may guard courthouses and provide escorts (Ch. 2)

ship and boat captain is in charge of all operations on a ship or boat in an ocean, bay, lake, river, or coastal waters (Ch. 4)

ship's engineer oversees the operation and maintenance of a ship's boilers, electrical and refrigeration equipment, and deck machinery (Ch. 4)

shipping, receiving, and traffic clerk keeps records of shipments coming in and leaving a business and arranges for the transportation of products (Ch. 4)

short order cook cooks and prepares foods that need only a short amount of preparation time; may take customer orders (Ch. 4)

singer performs vocal music as an individual or part of a group (Ch. 2, 4)

ski instructor teaches people to ski at a resort, ski school, or other recreational area (Ch. 1)

sketch artist creates drawings of people involved in legal cases or suspects in criminal cases (Ch. 2)

social and human services assistant helps psychologists or social workers provide services to clients; may develop, organize, and conduct programs to resolve substance abuse, relationship, or other problems (Ch. 4)

social worker provides services to clients to help them solve substance abuse, relationship, or other social problems (Ch. 2, 4, 6)

sociologist studies human society and behavior, including group behavior (Ch. 2)

special education teacher teaches students who have educational, emotional, mental, or physical needs (Ch. 2, 4)

speech-language pathologist diagnoses and treats people who have speech, language, voice, and fluency disorders (Ch. 4)

stage director plans and oversees movement of people and props on stage in a play, television show, or movie (Ch. 2)

stationary engineer runs and maintains industrial engines and mechanical equipment such as steam engines, generators, motors, and steam boilers (Ch. 4)

statistician studies and develops mathematical theories to gather and summarize numbers and data (Ch. 4)

store manager supervises employees at a retail store; oversees business activities such as ordering products and supplies, setting prices, arranging store displays, and paying bills (Ch. 2, 6)

structural iron and steel worker builds structures out of iron or steel such as buildings, building framework, and metal storage tanks (Ch. 4)

structural metal fabricator makes and puts together metal framework for machinery, ovens, tanks, and metal parts for buildings and bridges (Ch. 4)

surgeon performs medical surgery to treat diseases and injuries (Ch. 2)

surveyor measures land boundaries; collects data to create maps of land for mining, construction, and other purposes (Ch. 2, 4)

T

tax collector collects taxes from people or businesses in accordance with laws and regulations (Ch. 6)

tax preparer gets tax returns ready to send to people or businesses (Ch. 2, 6)

taxi driver transports passengers in automobiles or vans and collects fares from passengers (Ch. 2, 4)

teacher teaches students in a variety of settings from child care centers to colleges; may teach basic social and academic skills or higher educational courses such as mathematics, science, and social studies (Ch. 1–2, 6)

teacher assistant helps teachers instruct students and provide educational programs and services to students and parents; may prepare and grade assignments and talk with parents about students (Ch. 4)

technical illustrator creates technical drawings and diagrams for owner guides, operating and maintenance manuals, and repair instructions (Ch. 2)

technical writer writes materials for technical manuals such as owner guides, operating and maintenance manuals, and repair instructions (Ch. 2, 4)

telecommunications line installer strings telephone, television, and fiber optic cables for communication and television programming (Ch. 4)

telephone, power line, and cable repairer finds problems with and repairs telephone lines, power lines, and cable lines (Ch. 6)

television news producer plans and oversees activities involved in making television news program; may select news stories, oversee writing and directing, and arrange ways to pay for the production (Ch. 5) *See also* producer (Ch. 2), radio/TV/movie producer (Ch. 2, 4)

teller handles the exchange of money with customers; keeps records of money for a financial institution such as a bank or credit union (Ch. 2, 6) *See also* bank teller (Ch. 2)

therapist provides treatment of physical or emotional problems, diseases, or disorders (Ch. 6)

tile and marble setter installs wood, marble, and other hard tiles to walls, floors, ceilings, and roofs (Ch. 4)

tool and die maker creates and puts together parts to fix dies, cutting tools, jigs, and other hand tools used by machinists (Ch. 4)

tour guide takes people or groups of people to various tourist attractions and places of interest; provides background or historical information to tourists and visitors (Ch. 4)

tractor-trailer truck driver drives tractor-trailer trucks to transport products, livestock, mail, or other materials from one location to another (Ch. 4)

training and development specialist trains and educates workers at businesses or organizations (Ch. 4) *See also* corporate trainer (Ch. 4)

translator translates one language to another in writing, words, or sign language (Ch. 2, 4) *See also* interpreter (Ch. 4)

transportation attendant takes tickets, greets passengers, answers questions, and provides other services to make passengers aboard ships, buses, and trains feel safe and comfortable (Ch. 4)

travel agent organizes trips and vacations; sells transportation and lodging to customers (Ch. 2, 4)

truck driver drives trucks to transport products, livestock, mail, or other materials from one location to another (Ch. 2, 6)

truck driver, light or delivery services drives trucks or vans with a gross vehicle weight under 26,000 tons to deliver products or packages (Ch. 4)

V

veterinarian diagnoses and treats diseases or injuries in animals (Ch. 2, 5)

veterinarian technologist and technician cares for animals and assists veterinarian in treatment of animal diseases or injuries; may administer medications to animals and conduct laboratory tests (Ch. 4)

vocational counselor helps individuals with education and career planning (Ch. 2) *See also* counselor (Ch. 2, 6), educational counselor (Ch. 2), school counselor (Ch. 2, 4)

vocational education teacher teaches students vocational and occupational subjects such as woodworking, auto mechanics, and metal working (Ch. 4) *See also* vocational teacher (Ch. 2)

vocational teacher teaches students vocational and occupational subjects such as woodworking, auto mechanics, and metal working (Ch. 2) *See also* vocational education teacher (Ch. 4)

W

waiter/waitress takes customer orders and serves food and beverages at a bar, restaurant, cafeteria, or other dining establishment (Ch. 2, 4)

water treatment plant operator oversees the controls for a system that treats or transports water or liquid waste (Ch. 6)

Web site developer creates Web sites for individuals, businesses, or organizations by using computer programming languages or software (Ch. 2)

welders, production put together metal parts on a production line using welding equipment (Ch. 4)

well and core drill operator operates machines that drill wells or take rock samples from the earth (Ch. 4)

wholesale sales representative sells products and materials to businesses or people; acts as the wholesaler's or manufacturer's expert on material sold (Ch. 4) *See also* manufacturer's representative (Ch. 4)

word processor/typist uses a computer or typewriter to prepare final copies letters, reports, forms, and other written materials (Ch. 2, 4)

Z

zookeeper cares for and trains animals in zoos; may also supervise zoo workers and oversee activities such as accounting, marketing, and zoo management (Ch. 1)

Glossary

A

ability (ə bil′ ə tē) a talent; something a person is able to do well (p. 24)

achievement (ə chēv′ mənt) something you earn based on performance or something you do with success (p. 23)

action verb (ak shən vėrb) a word that shows action (p. 200)

addictive (ə dik′ tiv) habit forming (p. 262)

agriculture (ag′ rə kul chər) farming; producing crops and raising livestock (p. 80)

alcoholism (al′ kə hȯ liz əm) a disease in which a person is dependent on alcohol (p. 263)

apprenticeship (ə pren′ tis ship) on-the-job training to learn the skills required for a job (p. 78)

architecture (är′ kə tek chər) planning and designing buildings or other structures (p. 92)

assemble (ə sem′ bəl) to put together (p. 85)

attitude (at′ ə tüd) how someone thinks, feels, and acts (p. 177)

authority (ə thȯr′ ə tē) the power to enforce rules (p. 179)

automation (ȯ tə mā′ shən) the use of machines to do jobs that used to be done by people (p. 87)

B

business cycle (biz′ nis sī′ kəl) the pattern of ups and downs in production and need, supply and demand, in the economy (p. 11)

C

career (kə rir′) a job path one prepares for and follows for a lifetime (p. 7)

career group (kə rir′ grüp) occupations with related abilities, interests, and education requirements (p. 32)

chronological résumé (kron ə loj′ ə kəl rez ə mā′) a résumé that focuses on the history of an applicant's education and work experience (p. 201)

clergy (klėr′ jē) people who do religious work, such as priests, rabbis, ministers, nuns, or pastors (p. 113)

commodity (kə mod′ ə tē) something that is bought or sold (p. 123)

competency (kom′ pə tən sē) being able to do something well (p. 20)

construction (kən struk′ shən) the act of building (p. 92)

core services (kôr ser′ vis iz) the 11 industries a community needs in order to function (p. 162)

corrections (kə rek′ shənz) field that involves the treatment and rehabilitation of prisoners in jails (p. 119)

cover letter (kuv′ər let′ ər) a one-page letter that you send with your résumé to introduce yourself to employers (p. 208)

D

database (dā′ tə bās) stored information (p. 102)

decision (di sizh′ ən) a choice to take action (p. 64)

developer (di vel′ ə pər) person who plans for putting up buildings on open land (p. 93)

diabetes (dī ə bē′ tēz) a disease in which the body is not able to use sugar from food (p. 260)

a	hat	e	let	ī	ice	ȯ	order	u̇	put	sh	she	ə	{ a in about
ā	age	ē	equal	o	hot	oi	oil	ü	rule	th	thin		e in taken
ä	far	ėr	term	ō	open	ou	out	ch	child	ŦH	then		i in pencil
â	care	i	it	ȯ	saw	u	cup	ng	long	zh	measure		o in lemon
													u in circus

diet (dī′ ət) the food that you regularly eat and drink (p. 258)

dilemma (də lem′ ə) a situation that requires a choice between two or more values (p. 266)

distribute (dis trib′ yüt) to move or give out goods and products to buyers or customers (p. 88)

drug (drug) any substance, other than food, that changes the way your mind and body work (p. 262)

E

economy (i kon′ ə mē) state of business of an area or country, including how resources are used for goods and services (p. 11)

engineering (en jə nir′ ing) the science of planning and building machines, tools, and transportation systems (p. 98)

ethics (eth′ iks) rules for behavior (p. 266)

extraction (ek strak′ shən) the pumping of oil and natural gas from underground (p. 82)

F

finance (fī′ nans) management of money (p. 123)

financial aid (fī nan′ shəl ād) money available to students to help pay for postsecondary education (p. 154)

freight (frāt) goods or products transported by truck, train, boat, or airplane (p. 88)

functional résumé (fungk′ shə nəl rez ə mā′) a résumé that focuses on the job tasks or skills that the applicant can perform (p. 201)

G

goal (gōl) a plan, an intention, or aim; something that a person want to get or reach (p. 64)

group values (grüp val′ yüz) the beliefs that a specific group of people considers to be important (p. 267)

H

hobby (hob′ ē) an activity done for enjoyment (p. 244)

hospitality (hos pə tal′ ə tē) taking care of guests or customers (p. 116)

I

industry (in′ də strē) a large-scale business or service area that provides a product or service (p. 76)

information technology (in fər mā′ shən tek nol′ ə jē) the way information is stored and used in a computer or computer system (p. 102)

informational interview (in fər mā′ shən əl in′ tər vjü) an opportunity to talk with someone at a business to gather information (p. 168)

interest (in′ tər ist) something you like, want to know more about, or want to see or do (p. 32)

interest rate (in′ tər ist rāt) a percentage of money charged for borrowing money (p. 11)

internship (in′ tėrn ship) doing work for an employer for a specified period of time to learn about an industry or occupation (p. 167)

investment (in vest′ mənt) time, effort, or money spent to get something in the future (p. 151)

J

job (job) a specific activity done for pay; employment (p. 3)

job security (job si kyůr′ ə tē) an understanding that workers will not lose their jobs (p. 11)

L

leisure time (lē′ zhər tīm) free time away from work or school (p. 245)

logistics (lō jis′ tiks) planning and operations involved in moving people and products (p. 88)

a	hat	e	let	ɪ	ice	ô	order	ů	put	sh	she	ə	a in about
ā	age	ē	equal	o	hot	oi	oil	ü	rule	th	thin		e in taken
ä	far	ėr	term	ō	open	ou	out	ch	child	ᴛʜ	then		i in pencil
â	care	i	it	ò	saw	u	cup	ng	long	zh	measure		o in lemon
													u in circus

M

manufacturing (man yə fak′ chə ring) turning raw material into products people use every day (p. 85)

manufacturing plant (man yə fak′ chə ring plant) a group of buildings where manufacturing happens (p. 85)

mining (mī′ ning) removing minerals from the earth (p. 82)

motivation (mō tə vā shən) an inner drive or encouragement from others for a person to act on or seek a goal (p. 68)

N

natural resources (nach′ ər əl rē′ sôr səz) minerals and other things found in nature (p. 80)

network (net′ wėrk) a group of computers linked together (p. 102)

networking (net′ wėr king) the exchange of information or services among individuals, groups, or institutions (p. 167)

nicotine (nik′ ə tēn) a chemical in tobacco to which people become addicted (p. 262)

nutrient (nü′ trē ənt) a substance in food that your body needs to work properly (p. 258)

O

obligation (ob lə gā′ shən) something that is required or must be done (p. 244)

occupation (ok yə pā′ shən) a group of similar or related jobs or job skills (p. 4)

offshore outsourcing (ôf′ shôr out′ sôr sing) giving jobs to workers in countries outside the United States (p. 87)

option (op′ shən) a choice (p. 66)

P

personal goal statement (pėr′ sə nəl gōl stāt′ mənt) a description of a career goal along with the knowledge, abilities, skills, and personal values that are related to the goal (p. 194)

personal resources (pėr′ sə nəl rē′ sôr səz) the knowledge, skills, abilities, and personal values a person can use to be successful (p. 197)

physical fitness (fiz′ ə kəl fit′ nis) the body's ability to meet the demands of everyday living (p. 259)

portfolio (pôrt fō′ lē ō) a collection of evidence of planning, skills, competencies, achievements, letters of recommendation, résumés, references, jobs held, activities performed, and writing samples (p. 49)

postsecondary (pōst′ sek ən der ē) after high school (p. 148)

prestige (pre stēzh′) how important or valuable people believe something is (p. 5)

priority (prī ôr′ ə tē) something that is more important than something else (p. 65)

probability (prob ə bil′ ə tē) the likelihood that an event will happen (p. 66)

production worker (prə duk′ shən wėr kər) person who manufactures products (p. 85)

psychological (sī kə loj′ ə kəl) having to do with the mind or brain (p. 112)

psychologist (sī kol′ ə jist) someone who studies the mind and human behavior (p. 112)

R

recruitment (ri krüt′ mənt) getting a number of applications from which to choose new employees (p. 188)

reference (ref′ ər əns) someone who can share your skills, personal qualities, and job qualifications with an employer (p. 211)

a	hat	e	let	ī	ice	ô	order	u̇	put	sh	she	ə	a in about
ā	age	ē	equal	o	hot	oi	oil	ü	rule	th	thin		e in taken
ä	far	ėr	term	ō	open	ou	out	ch	child	ᵺ	then		i in pencil
â	care	i	it	ȯ	saw	u	cup	ng	long	zh	measure		o in lemon
													u in circus

résumé (rez ə mā´) a summary of knowledge, abilities, and experience that shows how a person is qualified for a particular occupation (p. 188)

risk (risk) a chance of danger or loss (p. 40)

S

screening (skrē´ ning) going through a number of applications to pick out the most suitable people for a job opening (p. 188)

selection (si lek´ shən) choosing a person for a job opening (p. 188)

self-advocacy (self ad´ və kə sē) supporting, defending, or speaking up for yourself (p. 234)

self-assessment (self ə ses´ mənt) finding out your strengths and weaknesses (p. 20)

self-confidence (self kon´ fə dəns) feeling good about oneself (p. 24)

sexually transmitted disease (sek´ shü ə lē tranz mit´ təd də zēz´) any disease that is spread through sexual activity (p. 261)

skill (skil) something you can do that comes from training or practice (p. 20)

software (sóft´ wâr) program that tells a computer what to do (p. 104)

stereotype (ster´ ē ə tīp) general belief about a person or group of people that is not necessarily true (p. 6)

stress (stress) a state of physical or emotional pressure (p. 244)

symptom (simp´ təm) a physical sign or indication that you have an illness (p. 259)

T

technology (tek nol´ ə jē) the use of science to create new products or make old ones better (p. 98)

time management (tīm man´ ij mənt) the best use of your time to achieve your goals (p. 252)

tourism (tùr´ iz əm) business of providing services to visitors and travelers (p. 116)

U

unemployed (un em ploid´) to be without a job (p. 12)

universal values (yü nə vėr´ səl val´ yüz) the beliefs that most people in many societies all over the world consider important (p. 268)

V

value (val´ yü) what is important to a person (p. 38)

W

wage (wāj) a set amount of money earned per hour of work (p. 56)

wage equity (wāj ek´ wə tē) men and women earn the same amount of money for doing the same job (p. 57)

work (wėrk) what people do or how they spend their time to earn a living (p. 2)

workplace (wėrk plās) where work is done (p. 8)

work value (wėrk val´ yü) something people want to get our of a job or that brings them job satisfaction (p. 39)

a	hat	e	let	ī	ice	ò	order	ù	put	sh	she	ə	a	in about
ā	age	ē	equal	o	hot	oi	oil	ü	rule	th	thin		e	in taken
ä	far	ėr	term	ō	open	ou	out	ch	child	ᵀH	then		i	in pencil
â	care	i	it	ó	saw	u	cup	ng	long	zh	measure		o	in lemon
													u	in circus

Index

J

Job, 3, 7, 16, 75. *See also* Career; Occupations; Work
  defined, 3
  fairs, 189
  openings, 58, 84, 87, 90, 94, 97, 101, 103, 105, 109, 111, 115, 117, 122, 125, 129, 133, 136, 188–90
  readiness skills, 152, 154, 187–217
  requirements, 190, 192, 195, 197, 204, 227
Job market, 1, 56–57, 77–78, 84, 87, 90, 94, 97, 101, 105, 109, 111, 115, 117, 122, 125, 129, 133, 136
Job security, 11, 16, 39, 95–96, 98–100, 110–15, 119–21, 123–24, 130–32
  defined, 11
Judgments, 83, 90, 268

K

Knowledge, 195–97, 272

L

Language ability, 26, 92–93, 95–96, 98–100, 102–4, 110–16, 119–21, 123–24, 126–28, 130–32. *See also* Education and training careers; Human Services careers; Literary careers
Law careers, 48, 69, 119–22
  community industry, 164
  outlook, 122
  sample occupations, 35, 122
  workers, 119
  workplace, 119
Law enforcement, 119–21
Leadership ability, 26, 33, 39, 88–90, 95–96, 98–100, 102–4, 106–8, 110–15, 119–21, 123–24, 126–28, 130–32, 191. *See also* Business management careers; Health science careers; Law careers
Legal system, 119

Leisure time, 38, 245–51, 274
  defined, 245
  money for, 3
  using time wisely, 255–57
Life and physical science, 99
Lifestyle, 196–97, 199, 216
  choices surrounding, 243, 258–65
  happiness with, 4, 266–71
  work effect on, 3
Listening skills, 130–32, 177, 180, 278
Literary careers, 106–9
  outlook, 109
  sample occupations, 35, 106
  workers, 106, 109
  workplace, 106
Living wage, 59
Loans, 154
Logistics defined, 88

M

Management positions, 76. *See also* Business management careers
Management skills, 35, 170
Manners, 170, 176–81, 231
Manual ability, 27, 36, 80–83, 85, 88–90, 92–93, 95–96, 98–100, 106–8, 116, 119–21, 130–32. *See also* Construction careers; Transportation careers
Manufacturing, 85, 140
  defined, 85
Manufacturing careers, 85–87
  outlook, 87
  sample occupations, 86
  workers, 86
  workplace, 85
Manufacturing plant defined, 85
Marijuana, 264
Marketing careers, 126–29
  community industry, 164
  outlook, 129
  sample occupations, 128
  workers, 126
  workplace, 126

Q

Qualifications, 190–91, 202–3, 208, 235
Qualities. *See* Hard-working; Honesty; Reliability
Questions, asking, 23, 26
Quiet time, 273

R

Reactions, 26
Recruitment, 188–90, 216
    defined, 188
References, 49, 187, 211–13, 216–17, 279
    defined, 211
Reliability, 178, 223–25, 227, 236
Relocation, 228
Research, 7, 56–63, 145, 184, 233
Residence, place of, 3. *See also* Relocation
Resources, 55, 216
Respect, 153, 177–78, 180–81, 185, 231
Résumés, 49, 167, 187, 189–91, 216–17, 279, 281
    defined, 188
    kinds of, 200–1
    information to include on, 202–5, 234
    organizing, 205
    writing, 200–10
Retirement, 152
Risk, 40, 52, 80–83, 88–90, 92–93, 116, 119–21
    assessing, 64, 66–68, 71
    defined, 40

S

Salaries, 39. *See also* Wages
    gender and, 44, 57
Sales careers, 126–29, 221
    community industry, 164
    outlook, 129
    sample occupations, 36, 128
    workers, 127–28
    workplace, 126
Satisfaction, 38
Schedules, 17, 256–57, 275

Science careers, 3, 7, 9, 41, 98–101
    outlook, 101
    sample occupations, 36, 100
    workers, 99
    workplace, 99
Scholarships, 154
School, 3, 20
    counselors, 173, 175, 280–82
    grades, 23, 64, 203, 229, 239, 280–81
    references or feedback from, 211–13, 280–82
    resources, 62–63
    subjects, 20–22, 31, 42–51, 78–79, 146, 156, 195, 197
Scientific ability and interests, 29, 34, 53, 85–86, 88–90, 92–93, 95–96, 98–100, 102–4, 112–15, 119–21, 130–32. *See also* Architecture careers; Health science careers; Science careers
Screening, 188, 190–91, 216
    defined, 188
Seasonal unemployment, 13
Security careers, 119–22, 270
    community industry, 164
    outlook, 122
    sample occupations, 122
    workers, 120–21
    workplace, 120
Selection, 188, 191, 216
    defined, 188
Self-advocacy, 219, 269
    defined, 234
    skills, 234–37
Self-assessment, 19, 52
    defined, 20
    profile, 42–51
    using, 278–79
Self-confidence, 24, 31, 52
    defined, 24
Self-employment, 76
September 11th (2001), 12
Service careers, 126–29
    community industry, 164
    outlook, 129
    sample occupations, 128
    workers, 128
    workplace, 126
Sexual harassment, 285

Career Planning Index **321**

Photo Credits

Midterm Mastery Test

Midterm Mastery Test

Part A Circle the letter of the answer that correctly completes each sentence.

1. A job path you prepare for carefully and may follow for a lifetime is a(n) _____.
   A outlook
   B occupation
   C work stereotype
   D career

2. The _____ is the state of business of an area or country, including resources used for goods and services.
   A economy
   B industry
   C employment
   D workplace

3. When you have developed _____ in something, you are able to do it well.
   A interest
   B assessment
   C competency
   D value

4. Something you have earned based on your performance is an _____.
   A occupation
   B achievement
   C ability
   D option

5. The *Occupational Outlook Handbook*, published by the U.S. Department of Labor, organizes information in groups of related _____.
   A salaries
   B occupations
   C regions
   D sciences

6. You _____ when you put your goals in order of importance.
   A make priorities
   B explore options
   C assess risks
   D make plans

7. The U.S. government collects information about 1,100 occupations and groups them into similar areas called _____.
   A job outlooks
   B industry analysis
   C career clusters
   D work studies

8. As you complete your career plan, the final step is to _____.
   A share it with parents or guardians
   B choose a career that interests you
   C learn which career pays the best
   D make sure the job is near where you live

9. People with _____ ability are skilled in the use of their hands.
   A scientific
   B mathematical/numerical
   C manual
   D technical/mechanical

10. About _____ of students who do not finish high school will not find work of any kind.
    A one-tenth
    B one-quarter
    C three-quarters
    D one-half

Midterm Mastery Test, continued

Part B Write the correct word or phrase from the Word Bank to complete each sentence.

Word Bank			
ability	basic skills	equity	motivation	production worker
agriculture	business cycle	goal	occupation	risk
automation	career planning	hospitality	probability	workplace culture

11. Employers are very good at identifying those who do not have _____ in reading, writing, and mathematics.

12. A group of related jobs or job skills is called a(n) _____.

13. If you worked at a hotel or travel agency, you would be part of the _____ industry.

14. Something a person can do well is called a(n) _____.

15. When you set a(n) _____, you decide on something you want to get or reach.

16. A(n) _____ is someone who manufactures items in a plant or factory.

17. The practice of paying equal money for equal work is called wage _____.

18. The _____ is the pattern of ups and downs in production and need, or supply and demand, in the economy.

19. Forestry is a part of the _____ career cluster.

20. A person's _____ is what drives him or her to act or to seek to accomplish something.

21. When you identify occupations that interest you, you have taken the first step in _____.

22. An event's _____ is the likelihood that it will happen.

23. A company's rules and ways of dressing, behaving, and interacting are its _____.

24. The use of machines to perform jobs once done by humans is called _____.

25. A(n) _____ is the chance of danger or loss in any activity.

Midterm Mastery Test, continued

Part C Match the words in Column 1 with the details in Column 2. Write the letter on the line.

	Column 1		Column 2
_____	26. work	A	a choice
_____	27. stereotype	B	a wish or plan to be reached in the more distant future
_____	28. long-term goal	C	turning material into products people use every day
_____	29. skill	D	a set amount of money earned per hour of work
_____	30. value	E	something that is important to a person
_____	31. self-confidence	F	taking place after high school
_____	32. option	G	what people do or how they spend time to earn a living
_____	33. priority	H	something you can do that comes from training or practice
_____	34. wage	I	giving jobs to workers in other countries
_____	35. outsourcing	J	a large-scale business or service area that provides a product or service
_____	36. information technology	K	a general belief about a person or group that is not necessarily true
_____	37. manufacturing	L	the way information is stored and used in a computer system
_____	38. industry	M	something that is more important than something else
_____	39. investment	N	time, effort, or money spent to get something in the future
_____	40. postsecondary	O	feeling good about oneself

Midterm Mastery Test, continued

Part D Write the answers to these questions. Use complete sentences.

41. What are some reasons, besides money, that people work? (2 points)
    _____
    _____

42. In terms of career planning, what is self-assessment? (2 points)
    _____
    _____
    _____

43. List the five steps in the decision-making process. (2 points)
    _____
    _____

Part E Write the answers to these questions. Use complete sentences. Use examples and facts to support your answer.

44. What might be the result if you took a job that paid well, but whose work values or working conditions did not match your ideas? Give several examples. (2 points)
    _____
    _____
    _____
    _____

45. If somebody offered you a full-time job, buy you had to quit high school to do it, would you take the job? Why or why not? (2 points)
    _____
    _____
    _____
    _____
    _____

Final Mastery Test

Final Mastery Test

Part A Circle the letter of the answer that correctly completes each sentence.

1. In terms of careers, work is _____.
   A something that is required or that you have to do
   B a group of similar or related jobs and skills
   C what people do or how they spend their time to earn a living
   D a job path one prepares for and follows for a lifetime

2. A community's core services are _____.
   A its water and sewage treatment plants
   B its educational institutions
   C the military business of an area
   D the industries a community needs in order to function

3. The three steps of the hiring process are _____.
   A recruitment, screening, and selection
   B interest, assessment, and application
   C advertising, interviewing, and offering
   D education, training, and internship

4. During an interview, you can show interest in a job by _____.
   A telling about any other jobs you have had
   B interrupting the interviewer to ask questions
   C saying nothing unless you are specifically asked
   D having positive body language and a good attitude

5. Prestige is _____.
   A a way to impress the person conducting an interview
   B how important people think something is
   C useful in developing skills
   D an obligation to help others

6. Feedback from others is important because _____.
   A people giving feedback control your future
   B feedback is positive and encouraging
   C it can help you decide whether you are on the right path
   D it tells you how well others know you

7. The process of self-assessment is one of _____.
   A learning to do what you don't want to do
   B finding your strengths and weaknesses
   C getting a job that pays well
   D working to achieve a goal

8. When you think about possible outcomes in the decision-making process, you _____.
   A assess risks
   B make priorities
   C make a plan
   D set goals

9. The knowledge, skills, abilities, and personal values a person can use to be successful are his or her _____.
   A goals
   B achievements
   C personal resources
   D career plans

10. To begin assessing your skills, look at the school subjects you _____.
   A have struggled with the most
   B think are the best for college prep
   C have not yet taken
   D enjoy the most

Career Planning

Final Mastery Test Page 1

Final Mastery Test, continued

11. During an interview, one way to communicate that you can do the job is to _____.
   A promise to arrive on time and ready for work each day
   B use action verbs that describe your skills and specific experiences
   C criticize other candidates for the job when possible
   D tell your potential employer to study your résumé

12. One of the best ways to find out about job opportunities is _____.
   A a local newspaper
   B an Internet job search or a company Web site
   C networking
   D sending out cover letters

13. The type of résumé that focuses on skills you acquired from various experiences is called a(n) _____.
   A chronological résumé
   B functional résumé
   C expertise résumé
   D combination résumé

14. The _____ is the pattern of ups and down in production and need, supply and demand, in the economy.
   A workplace
   B business cycle
   C unemployment rate
   D interest rate

15. Your _____ describes how you can get from where you are to where you would like to go in your career.
   A résumé
   B personal goal statement
   C self-assessment
   D career action plan

16. After doing a personal time survey, it makes sense to _____.
   A make a schedule
   B arrange an interview
   C reduce the amount of time you sleep
   D develop your hobbies

17. An example of a human service found in a community would be _____.
   A a taxi service
   B an emergency medical center
   C a child-care center
   D a grocery store

18. The job of cabinetmaker would be in the _____ career cluster.
   A Agriculture, Food, and Natural Resources
   B Manufacturing
   C Architecture and Construction
   D Marketing, Sales, and Service

19. Scholarships, loans, grants, and work-study programs are all forms of _____.
   A postsecondary education
   B internships
   C personal resources
   D financial aid

20. You should discuss _____ with an interviewer who asks, "What are your strengths?"
   A the reasons you need to work
   B your physical fitness and health
   C your accomplishments in skills related to the job
   D how you became aware of the position

Career Planning

Final Mastery Test Page 2

Final Mastery Test, continued

Part B Write the correct word from the Word Bank to complete each sentence.

Word Bank				
action verbs	cover letter	nicotine	priority	self-advocacy
apprenticeship	finance	option	reference	skill
chronological	group values	physical fitness	revise	stereotype

21. A(n) _____ can share your job qualifications with an employer.

22. A harmful chemical in tobacco to which people become addicted is _____.

23. You show _____ when you support, defend, or speak up for yourself in a job interview.

24. A(n) _____ is doing work for an employer for a specified period of time in order to learn about the job.

25. You may have to _____ your career plan if it does not match up with feedback you get and the experiences you have.

26. Any choice you have is a(n) _____.

27. In a(n) _____ résumé, the most recent events are listed first.

28. You should use _____ in your résumé to link your experience to relevant skills.

29. A bank is an example of a core service in _____.

30. You can develop a(n) _____ with training or practice.

31. Your _____ is a one-page introduction of you to a possible employer.

32. A(n) _____ is more important than something else.

33. A(n) _____ is a general belief about a person or group of people that is not necessarily true.

34. The body's ability to meet the demands of everyday living is its _____.

35. Beliefs that a specific group of people consider to be important are _____.

Career Planning

Final Mastery Test Page 3

Final Mastery Test, continued

Part C Match the words in Column 1 with the details in Column 2. Write the letter on the line.

	Column 1		Column 2
_____	36. action plan	A	personal beliefs that can change with experience
_____	37. attitude	B	part of the hiring process
_____	38. CareerZone	C	this should be sent to an interviewer after an interview
_____	39. discouraged	D	time, effort, or money spent to get something in the future
_____	40. ethics	E	rules for behavior
_____	41. feedback	F	taking place after high school
_____	42. industry	G	review your interview experience if you do not get this
_____	43. investment	H	a source of career information
_____	44. job offer	I	the best use of your time to achieve your goals
_____	45. motivation	J	large-scale business that provides a product or service
_____	46. occupation	K	a summary that shows a person is qualified for a job
_____	47. personal goal statement	L	an inner drive to act on or seek a goal
_____	48. postsecondary	M	a group of similar or related jobs or job skills
_____	49. résumé	N	how you plan to achieve a personal goal
_____	50. screening	O	what not to be if you get feedback that does not match your goals
_____	51. stress	P	beliefs important to most societies in the world
_____	52. thank-you note	Q	responses that you get from situations and people, which you use to achieve goals or revise plans
_____	53. time management	R	a description of your career goal along with your related knowledge, skills, and values
_____	54. universal values	S	how someone thinks, feels, and acts
_____	55. values	T	physical or emotional pressure

Career Planning

Final Mastery Test Page 4

Final Mastery Test

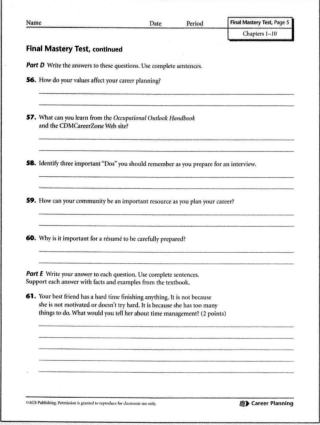

Final Mastery Test Page 5

Final Mastery Test, continued

Part D Write the answers to these questions. Use complete sentences.

56. How do your values affect your career planning?

57. What can you learn from the *Occupational Outlook Handbook* and the CDMCareerZone Web site?

58. Identify three important "Dos" you should remember as you prepare for an interview.

59. How can your community be an important resource as you plan your career?

60. Why is it important for a résumé to be carefully prepared?

Part E Write your answer to each question. Use complete sentences. Support each answer with facts and examples from the textbook.

61. Your best friend has a hard time finishing anything. It is not because she is not motivated or doesn't try hard. It is because she has too many things to do. What would you tell her about time management? (2 points)

Final Mastery Test Page 6

Final Mastery Test, continued

62. Suppose that it has been your plan since you were small to be a scientist. However, math is hard for you, and you have trouble memorizing things well. Your guidance counselor and friends would like to see you do something with your ability to draw. Your art teacher knows of an internship with a graphic arts company. What should you do with this feedback? (2 points)

Part F Write a paragraph for each topic. Include a topic sentence, body, and conclusion. Support each answer with facts and examples from the textbook.

63. Ramone is a basketball player. He is a very good player and spends every spare moment practicing. In fact, he neglects his schoolwork sometimes in favor of playing. His only thought about career planning is that he intends to play professional basketball someday. What would you tell Ramone? (3 points)

64. Compare and contrast a résumé and an interview. Tell how they are alike and how they are different. (3 points)

The lists below show how items from the Midterm and Final correlate to the chapters in the student edition.

Midterm Mastery Test

Chapter 1	1, 2, 12, 18, 23, 26, 27, 28, 41
Chapter 2	3, 4, 9, 14, 17, 25, 29, 30, 31, 42
Chapter 3	5, 6, 15, 20, 22, 32, 33, 34, 43
Chapter 4	7, 13, 16, 19, 24, 35, 36, 37, 38
Chapter 5	8, 10, 11, 21, 39, 40

Critical Thinking Themes and Issues

Values and Compensation   44

Finishing High School   45

Final Mastery Test

Chapter 1	1, 5, 14, 33, 46
Chapter 2	7, 10, 30, 55, 56
Chapter 3	8, 26, 32, 38, 45
Chapter 4	18, 42, 57
Chapter 5	19, 43, 48
Chapter 6	2, 12, 17, 24, 29, 37, 59
Chapter 7	3, 9, 13, 21, 27, 28, 31, 47, 49, 50, 60
Chapter 8	4, 11, 20, 23, 39, 44, 52, 58
Chapter 9	16, 22, 34, 35, 40, 51, 53, 54
Chapter 10	6, 15, 25, 36, 39, 41

Critical Thinking Themes and Issues

Time Management   61

Feedback   62

Career Planning   63

Résumé and Interview   64

Teacher's Resource Library Answer Key

Activities

Activity 1—Thinking About Work
1. H **2.** O **3.** A **4.** F **5.** N **6.** C **7.** L **8.** J **9.** G **10.** I **11.** K **12.** D **13.** M **14.** B **15.** E

Activity 2—Work and the Economy Puzzle
1. security **2.** seasonal **3.** percentage **4.** economy **5.** carpenters **6.** replaced **7.** borrow **8.** cycle **9.** affect **10.** demand
Answer to acrostic puzzle: unemployed

Activity 3—Subject Area Strengths
1. C **2.** A **3.** B **4.** D **5.** C **6.** B **7.** A **8.** B **9.** D **10.** C

Activity 4—Choosing a Career
1–3. teller, cashier, secretary **4–6.** music arranger, musician, singer **7–9.** carpenter, landscaper, firefighter **10–12.** lawyer, psychiatrist, construction manager **13–15.** home health aide, social worker, recreational worker

Activity 5—All About People's Interests
1. Sample response: A person who cannot play football might like to watch the game each week, following the players and their statistics. A person who does not have artistic abilities might still enjoy looking at and collecting art. **2.** One way to find out your interests is by choosing an interest area that is most important to you. The other way is to use career groups. **3.** People with scientific interests are curious and creative. They study a lot. They like thinking about ideas. **4.** A nurse, teacher, and counselor all have social interests. **5.** Accept any three of the following: auto or airplane mechanic, carpenter, cook, electrician, farmer, and truck driver. **6.** The occupations in a career group are for people with similar abilities, interests, and education levels. **7.** Accept any three of the following jobs: editor, novelist, playwright, poet, reporter, technical writer, and translator. **8.** All of these jobs belong to the Skilled Crafts career group. **9.** You can ask a teacher or counselor what those workers do. Or, you can look it up in the school's career center. **10.** You can find out about jobs that use your interests.

Activity 6—Values Crossword Puzzle

Activity 7—Create a Self-Assessment Profile
1–2. English, art **3–5.** manual, leadership, language **6–8.** crafts, the arts, social **9.** Art career group **10.** Entertainment career group **11–12.** physical activity, creativity

Activity 8—Researching Careers
1. C **2.** B **3.** A **4.** B **5.** D **6.** C **7.** C **8.** A **9.** B **10.** D

Activity 9—Making Career Decisions
1. C **2.** D **3.** A **4.** E **5.** B **6.** E **7.** B **8.** C **9.** A **10.** D

Activity 10—Facts About Career Clusters
1. 1,100 **2.** 97 **3.** 9.2 **4.** 12.9 **5.** 15 **6.** 13.1 **7.** 4 **8.** 1 **9.** 2 **10.** 33,125

Activity 11—Agriculture, Food, and Natural Resources
1. C **2.** B **3.** A **4.** C **5.** A **6.** D **7.** C **8.** D **9.** B **10.** A

Activity 12—Manufacturing Matching
1. I **2.** H **3.** N **4.** A **5.** M **6.** B **7.** C **8.** F **9.** O **10.** E **11.** D **12.** G **13.** K **14.** J **15.** L

Activity 13—Transportation Distribution, and Logistics Occupations
1. A **2.** B **3.** D **4.** B **5.** C **6.** A **7.** D **8.** C **9.** D **10.** B

Activity 14—Building a Bridge
1. 3 **2.** 1 **3.** 2 **4.** 4 **5.** 6 **6.** 5 **7.** 7 **8.** 8 **9.** 10 **10.** 9

Activity 15—Health Science Careers
1. B **2.** A **3.** C **4.** A **5.** D **6.** B **7.** D **8.** C **9.** C **10.** D

Activity 16—Identify the Field
1. S **2.** E **3.** M **4.** E **5.** M **6.** S **7.** E **8.** S **9.** M **10.** E **11.** E **12.** M **13.** M **14.** S **15.** E

Activity 17—Careers in Information Technology
1. home **2.** computers **3.** eyestrain **4.** database **5.** network **6.** technical writer **7.** help-desk technician **8.** Internet **9.** Web editor **10.** software **11.** programmer **12.** scientific **13.** systems analyst **14.** increase **15.** education

Activity 18—Literary, Arts, Music, and Entertainment Jobs
1. Literary workers often work in offices and newsrooms. They may also work from their own homes. **2.** Three examples of jobs in the literary field are (accept any three of the following): news writers, authors, technical writers, script writers, editors, copywriters, translators, columnists, film and video editors, interpreters, novelists, reporters, and script editors. **3.** Literary workers need to be able to express ideas clearly. They need to use correct grammar and to be sure to get the correct facts. **4.** Arts workers often work in studios, design firms, or their own homes. **5.** People in the arts need to understand color. They need to pay attention to detail, size, and proportion. They also need to have good eye-hand coordination. **6.** Music workers often work in theaters, recording studios, and concert arenas. Composers may work in their homes. **7.** Two examples of jobs in the music field are (accept any two of the following): dancer, choreographer, singer, musician, and composer. **8.** Music workers should be able to read music. Dancers should be strong and move gracefully. They all need to practice a lot.

9. Entertainment workers usually work on TV or movie sets, in radio studios, and on stages. **10.** Entertainers need to appear comfortable in front of large crowds. They also need to be good at making conversation. Performers need to have nice-sounding voices and pronounce words clearly.

Activity 19—Education and Training Jobs
1. school **2.** help students choose classes **3.** businesses **4.** provide programs for workers and managers **5.** school library **6.** buy materials for school library **7.** preschool **8.** teach young children **9.** school **10.** manage teachers and school staff

Activity 20—Human Services Careers
1. care **2.** memory **3.** occupations **4.** personal **5.** preschool **6.** medical **7.** relief **8.** advice **9.** human **10.** clergy
Answer to acrostic puzzle: counseling

Activity 21—Hospitality and Tourism
1. Hospitality means taking care of and giving good service to guests, visitors, or customers. **2.** They want to be treated nicely and to feel comfortable. **3.** Restaurant occupations are (accept any three of the following): chef, food services manager, food service worker, host/hostess, short order cook, or waiter/waitress. **4.** Hotel occupations are (accept any three of the following): hotel and motel clerk, reservation agent, housekeeper, groundskeeper, bellhop, or lodging manager. **5.** Transportation jobs related to tourism are (accept any three of the following): train driver, bus driver, cab driver, reservation and transportation ticket agent, tour guide, or travel agent. **6.** Tourist locations are (accept any three of the following): beaches, natural beauty spots, historical places, cultural places, or places like Las Vegas, Nevada. **7.** People want to take vacations and be entertained. **8.** Hospitality and tourism workers work in (accept any four of the following): hotels, motels, national parks, cruise ships, resorts, amusement parks, restaurants, or travel agencies. **9.** More people are using the computer to make travel plans on their own. **10.** Workers in hospitality and tourism will make up 11.4 percent of the workforce by 2012.

Activity 22—Working in Law, Public Safety, and Security
1. O **2.** F **3.** I **4.** H **5.** K **6.** M **7.** L **8.** A **9.** E **10.** N **11.** B **12.** D **13.** G **14.** C **15.** J

Activity 23—The Finance Industry
1. C **2.** D **3.** A **4.** B **5.** C **6.** D **7.** A **8.** B **9.** D **10.** B

Activity 24—Jobs in Marketing, Sales, and Service
1. buyers **2.** marketing **3.** training **4.** cashiers **5.** increase **6.** travel **7.** college degree **8.** workforce **9.** specialty **10.** products or services

Activity 25—Working in the Business World
1. C **2.** A **3.** A **4.** C **5.** A **6.** B **7.** A **8.** A **9.** D **10.** C

Activity 26—Working in Government and Public Administration
1. Government workers are employed in many different places, including offices, courthouses, national parks, and military bases. The workplace is different according to the job. **2.** There are government jobs like jobs in other industries in (accept any four of the following): hospitals, airports, schools, parks, tourism agencies, power plants, highways, courthouses, and research libraries.

3. The interest areas are: business, office operations, social, the arts, scientific, and crafts. **4.** Enlisted personnel make up 85 percent of workers in the military. **5.** There are governments in every city and town, county and state, across the country. **6.** Military officers are leaders, managers, and supervisors. **7.** Enlisted personnel are involved in combat, transportation, construction, and healthcare. **8.** Wages in this cluster are the same as wages for similar jobs in other clusters. **9.** Along with wages, military personnel receive free housing, food, healthcare, and clothing. **10.** The outlook depends on the industry a worker is in. Most government occupations are expected to grow.

Activity 27—Career Planning and Decision Making
1. K **2.** J **3.** C **4.** A **5.** O **6.** I **7.** N **8.** F **9.** G **10.** E **11.** L **12.** D **13.** M **14.** B **15.** H

Activity 28—Investing in Your Future
1. C **2.** A **3.** D **4.** C **5.** B **6.** D **7.** A **8.** D **9.** B **10.** D

Activity 29—Core Services
1. All communities must have 11 of the 16 career clusters to function. These are called core services. **2.** Homes and other buildings still need to be repaired. Roads and bridges also need to be repaired. **3.** Most communities need bank managers, tellers, accountants, and tax preparers. **4.** Hotels, motels, and restaurants provide the core service of hospitality and tourism. **5.** Every community has law enforcement officers. **6.** Answer should include three of the following: churches or places of worship, barbershops, beauty salons, funeral homes, child care centers, or mental health care centers. **7.** Transportation, distribution, and logistics services help them ship items. **8.** Government provides the structure for a community to exist. **9.** If I know about the industries in my community, I can find out what types of careers are available locally. **10.** I can learn about the industries in my community by looking in the yellow pages, searching on the Internet, or asking police officers or mail carriers.

Activity 30—Education, Networking, and Internships
1. applications **2.** résumés **3.** networking **4.** contacts **5.** internship **6.** tryout **7.** credit **8.** career **9.** interview **10.** job **11.** limit **12.** reasonable **13.** questions **14.** impressions **15.** thank-you

Activity 31—Choosing a Postsecondary School
1. C **2.** A **3.** D **4.** C **5.** B **6.** A **7.** A **8.** B **9.** D **10.** B

Activity 32—Living and Working with Others
1. cultures **2.** authority **3.** attitudes **4.** listen **5.** values **6.** respect **7.** conflict **8.** disagree **9.** employers **10.** skill
Answer to acrostic puzzle: challenges

Activity 33—The Hiring Process
1. The human resources department handles the different stages of the hiring process. **2.** In smaller companies the department manager handles the hiring process. **3.** Posting jobs within the company (accept two of the following): helps employees advance, improves morale, and generates a pool of people who already know the company. **4.** Newspaper ads generate so many responses that only the ones submitted early are likely to be considered. **5.** Employers quickly reject sloppy and disorganized résumés. **6.** There could be so many applicants that it would take too much employee time to respond to all of them. **7.** Most questions help the employer find out whether a person has the knowledge, skills, and abilities to perform the job well.

8. You could read brochures about the company, study its advertising, talk to other employees, and ask questions during interviews. **9.** Usually the manager or supervisor of the department with the job opening calls the person selected for a job. **10.** There are many factors beyond your control, including (accept two of the following): the number of applicants, the time required to fill the job, the personality of the hiring manager, and the quality of a résumé or job interview.

Activity 34—Personal Goal Statement
1. B **2.** A **3.** D **4.** C **5.** B **6.** C **7.** C **8.** D **9.** C **10.** A

Activity 35—Writing a Résumé
1. J **2.** F **3.** M **4.** C **5.** H **6.** E **7.** L **8.** B **9.** A **10.** I **11.** D **12.** O **13.** G **14.** K. **15.** N

Activity 36—Getting References
1. C **2.** D **3.** B **4.** A **5.** D **6.** C **7.** B **8.** A **9.** C **10.** B

Activity 37—Interview Tips Puzzle

```
        ¹C
        O              ²R
        M         ³Q   E
        P       ⁴Q U A L I T I E S
     ⁵V A L U E S   E     A
        I           S     V
        M           T        ⁶F
        E           A        I
        N    ⁷I M P O R T ⁸A N T
        T           N     C
     ⁹E X A M P L E S     T
        R                 I
        Y             ¹⁰B O D Y
                          N
```

Activity 38—Answering Interview Questions
1. B **2.** F **3.** C **4.** E **5.** I **6.** D **7.** G **8.** A **9.** H **10.** J

Activity 39—Practicing Self-Advocacy Skills
1. B **2.** C **3.** B **4.** D **5.** C **6.** C **7.** B **8.** A **9.** B **10.** D

Activity 40—Developing Hobbies and Interests
1. B **2.** D **3.** A **4.** C **5.** C **6.** B **7.** C **8.** A **9.** D. **10.** B

Activity 41—Managing Time
1. Time management is making the best use of your time to get things accomplished. You decide what activities you want to participate in and how much time you want to give to each of them. **2.** A personal time survey is a guide to how you spend your time. **3.** Non-scheduled time lets you catch up if you fall behind schedule, or have free time if you have no other use for it. **4.** You should schedule activities that need your best effort at times when you are likely to be at your best. **5.** You may want to do things longer than they are scheduled for or do things that are not on your schedule.

Activity 42—Healthy Lifestyle Choices
1. drug **2.** guidelines **3.** Type II **4.** stroke **5.** AIDS **6.** hand washing **7.** alcoholism **8.** chlamydia **9.** fatty foods **10.** fever **11.** marijuana **12.** vaccines **13.** steroids **14.** addictive **15.** hallucinogens

Activity 43—Living Ethically
1. D **2.** C **3.** B **4.** A **5.** B **6.** A **7.** C **8.** B **9.** D **10.** C

Activity 44—Using Feedback Puzzle

```
              ¹T
        ²M    E
   ³G O A L S          ⁴I
        ⁴T  T    ⁵R N     ⁶N
        C        E  T     E
        H  ⁷F    V  E     G
        E   E    I  R     A
     ⁸A S S E S S M  E N T
            D    E  S     I
            B    T        V
        ⁹G R A D E S      E
            C
        ¹⁰S K I L L S
```

Activity 45—Career Action Plan Puzzle
1. snapshot **2.** future **3.** college **4.** action **5.** stone **6.** destination **7.** revise **8.** feedback **9.** continue **10.** counselor
Answer to acrostic puzzle: successful

Alternative Activities

Alternative Activity 1—Thinking About Work
1. D **2.** L **3.** B **4.** E **5.** A **6.** C **7.** I **8.** G **9.** J **10.** F **11.** H **12.** K

Alternative Activity 2—Work and the Economy Puzzle
1. training **2.** security **3.** unemployed **4.** cycle **5.** rates **6.** economy **7.** seasonal **8.** demand
Answer to acrostic puzzle: replaced

Alternative Activity 3—Subject Area Strengths
1. D **2.** B **3.** B **4.** C **5.** B **6.** A **7.** D **8.** C

Alternative Activity 4—Choosing a Career
1–3. carpenter, landscaper, forest and conservation worker **4–6.** music arranger, musician, singer **7–9.** police dispatcher, travel agent, tax preparer **10–12.** home health aide, social worker, psychiatric aide

Alternative Activity 5—All About People's Interests
1. One way to find out your interests is by choosing an interest area that is most important to you. The other way is to use career groups. **2.** Sample response: I cannot play football but I like to watch the game each week. I follow the players and their statistics. **3.** People with scientific interests are curious and creative. They study a lot. They like thinking about ideas. **4.** Accept any three of the following: animal caretaker, auto mechanic, construction equipment operator, cook, electrician, farmer, and truck driver. **5.** The jobs in a career group are for people with similar abilities, interests, and education levels. **6.** All of these jobs belong to the Skilled Crafts career group. **7.** You can ask a teacher or counselor what those workers do. Or, you can look it up in the school's career center. **8.** You can find out about jobs that use your interests.

Alternative Activity 6—Values Crossword Puzzle

		¹L	²E	I	S	U	³R	E		
			X				I			
			⁴P	L	A	N	S			
			E				K			⁵F
	⁶V		R							A
⁷V	A	R	I	E	T	Y				M
	L		E							I
	U		N							L
	E		⁸C	O	M	M	U	N	I	T	Y
			E							

Alternative Activity 7—Create a Self-Assessment Profile

1–2. English, art **3–5.** manual, leadership, language **6–8.** crafts, the arts, social **9.** Art career group **10.** Entertainment career group **11–12.** physical activity, creativity

Alternative Activity 8—Researching Careers

1. B **2.** C **3.** D **4.** C **5.** C **6.** A **7.** B **8.** D

Alternative Activity 9—Making Career Decisions

1. B **2.** A **3.** C **4.** B **5.** E **6.** D **7.** A **8.** E

Alternative Activity 10—Facts about Career Clusters

1. 16 **2.** 1,100 **3.** 97 **4.** 9.2 **5.** 13.1 **6.** 4 **7.** 1 **8.** 2

Alternative Activity 11—Agriculture, Food, and Natural Resources

1. D **2.** A **3.** C **4.** A **5.** D **6.** C **7.** B. **8.** A

Alternative Activity 12—Manufacturing Matching

1. E **2.** H **3.** D **4.** L **5.** C **6.** F **7.** K **8.** A **9.** G **10.** I **11.** B **12.** J

Alternative Activity 13—Transportation, Distribution, and Logistics Occupations

1. B **2.** D **3.** B **4.** C **5.** A **6.** D **7.** D **8.** B

Alternative Activity 14—Building a Bridge

1. 2 **2.** 1 **3.** 4 **4.** 3 **5.** 7 **6.** 5 **7.** 6 **8.** 8

Alternative Activity 15—Health Science Careers

1. C **2.** B **3.** A **4.** D **5.** B **6.** C **7.** B **8.** D

Alternative Activity 16—Identify the Workers

1. M **2.** S **3.** S **4.** E **5.** E **6.** S **7.** M **8.** E **9.** E **10.** M **11.** S **12.** E

Alternative Activity 17—Careers in Information Technology

1. information **2.** writers **3.** help-desk technician **4.** network **5.** Web editor **6.** increase **7.** software **8.** programmer **9.** scientific **10.** systems analyst **11.** Internet **12.** education

Alternative Activity 18—Literary, Arts, Music, and Entertainment Jobs

1. Arts workers often work in studios, design firms, or their own homes. **2.** Two jobs in the arts field are (accept any two of the following): cartoonist, painter, photographer, designer, illustrator, sculptor, commercial designer, floral designer, graphic designer, interior designer, industrial designer, camera operator, and multi media artists and editors. **3.** Music workers often work in theaters, studios, and concert arenas. Composers may work in their homes. **4.** Two examples of jobs in the music field are (accept any two of the following): dancer, choreographer, singer, musician, and composer. **5.** Two examples of jobs in the literary field are (accept any three of the following):): news writers, authors, technical writers, script writers, editors, copywriters, translators, columnists, film and video editors, interpreters, novelists, reporters, and script editors. **6.** Literary workers need to be able to express ideas clearly. They need to use correct grammar and to be sure to get the correct facts. **7.** Two entertainment jobs are (accept any two of the following): producer, actor/actress, announcer, director, program director, talk show host, disc jockey, comedian, and circus performer. **8.** Entertainers need to appear comfortable in front of large crowds. They also need to be good at making conversation. Performers need to have nice-sounding voices and pronounce words clearly.

Alternative Activity 19—Education and Training Jobs

1. high school **2.** teach older students **3.** any school **4.** help students choose classes **5.** school library **6.** buy materials for school library **7.** preschool **8.** teach young children **9.** any school **10.** manage teachers and school staff **11.** college or university **12.** teach college students

Alternative Activity 20—Human Services Careers

1. preschool **2.** clergy **3.** personal **4.** private **5.** relief **6.** advice **7.** mental **8.** social
Answer to acrostic puzzle: services

Alternative Activity 21—Hospitality and Tourism

1. Two hotel occupations are (accept any two of the following): hotel and motel clerk, reservation agent, housekeeper, groundskeeper, bellhop, or lodging manager. **2.** Two types of transportation work related to tourism are (accept any two of the following): train driver, bus driver, cab driver, reservation and transportation ticket agent, tour guide, or travel agent. **3.** Three tourist locations are (accept any three of the following): beaches, natural beauty spots, historical places, cultural places, or places like Las Vegas, Nevada. **4.** Hospitality means taking care of and giving good service to guests, visitors, and customers. **5.** Three restaurant occupations are (accept any three of the following): chef, food services manager, food service worker, host/hostess, short order cook, or waiter/waitress. **6.** Three places workers in hospitality and tourism work are (accept any three of the following): hotels, motels, national parks, cruise ships, resorts, amusement parks, restaurants, or travel agencies. **7.** More people are using the computer to make travel plans on their own. **8.** Jobs that will grow are (accept any three of the following): food preparation, food serving, meeting planners, convention planners, and hotel or motel desk clerks.

Alternative Activity 22—Working in Law, Public Safety, and Security

1. L **2.** F **3.** B **4.** I **5.** K **6.** G **7.** E **8.** A **9.** H **10.** D **11.** J **12.** C

Alternative Activity 23—The Finance Industry
1. C 2. A 3. C 4. D 5. B 6. C 7. D 8. A

Alternative Activity 24—Jobs in Marketing, Sales, and Service
1. entry level 2. training 3. buyers 4. cashiers 5. increase 6. travel 7. workforce 8. advertising

Alternative Activity 25—Working in the Business World
1. C 2. C 3. C 4. B 5. A 6. C 7. D 8. A

Alternative Activity 26—Working in Government and Public Administration
1. There are governments in every city, county, and state across the country. 2. The interest areas are business, office operations, social, the arts, scientific, and crafts. 3. Government workers are employed in many different places, including offices, national parks, and military bases. The workplace is different according to the job. 4. There are government jobs like jobs in other industries in (accept any four of the following): hospitals, airports, schools, parks, tourism agencies, power plants, highways, courthouses, and research libraries. 5. The outlook depends on the industry a worker is in. Most government occupations are expected to grow.

Alternative Activity 27—Career Planning and Decision Making
1. G 2. A 3. L 4. C 5. K 6. F 7. I 8. E 9. J 10. B 11. D. 12. H

Alternative Activity 28—Investing in Your Future
1. D 2. B 3. A 4. C 5. B 6. A 7. C 8. D

Alternative Activity 29—Core Services
1. Core services are the 11 industries a community needs to function. 2. Some occupations in the core service of hospitality and tourism are motel desk clerks, cooks, food servers, and housekeepers. 3. Most communities need bank managers, tellers, accountants, and tax preparers. 4. Every community has law enforcement officers. 5. Answer should include three of the following: churches or places of worship, barbershops, beauty salons, funeral homes, child care centers, or mental health care centers. 6. Transportation, distribution, and logistics services help them ship items. 7. If I know about the industries in my community, I can find out what types of careers are available locally. 8. I can learn about the industries in my community by looking in the yellow pages, searching on the Internet, or asking police officers or mail carriers.

Alternative Activity 30—Education, Networking, and Internships
1. search 2. networking 3. internship 4. tryout 5. credit 6. contacts 7. career 8. interview 9. job 10. limit 11. questions 12. thank-you

Alternative Activity 31—Choosing a Postsecondary School
1. B 2. D 3. C 4. B 5. D 6. A 7. B 8. C

Alternative Activity 32—Living and Working with Others
1. authority 2. interact 3. attacking 4. listen 5. treated 6. cultures 7. disagree 8. employers
Answer to acrostic puzzle: attitude

Alternative Activity 33—The Hiring Process
1. Large companies may handle the hiring process differently from smaller companies. 2. A résumé is a summary of a person's knowledge, ability, and experience that shows how that person is qualified for a job. 3. Newspaper ads bring in many responses, so only the first ones received are likely to be considered. 4. Employers quickly reject sloppy and disorganized résumés. 5. There could be so many people applying that it takes too much time to respond to all of them. 6. Most questions help the employer find out whether a person has the knowledge, skills, and abilities to perform the job well. 7. Usually the manager or supervisor of the department with the job opening calls the person selected for a job. 8. There are many factors beyond your control, including (accept two of the following): the number of applicants, the time required to fill the job, the personality of the hiring manager, and the quality of a résumé or job interview.

Alternative Activity 34—Personal Goal Statement
1. B 2. D 3. C 4. B 5. C 6. C 7. D 8. A

Alternative Activity 35—Writing a Résumé
1. F 2. K 3. J 4. B 5. H 6. C 7. I 8. A 9. G 10. L 11. E 12. D

Alternative Activity 36—Getting References
1. B 2. B 3. D 4. A 5. D 6. B 7. C 8. C

Alternative Activity 37—Interview Tips Puzzle

			(1)A		(2)Q			
			C		U			
			T		E			(3)F
			I		S			I
(4)I	M	P	O	R	T	A	N	T
			N		I			
				(5)B	O	D	Y	
	(6)P				N			
(7)H	O	N	E	S	T	Y		
	S							
	I							
	T							
	I							
	(8)V	A	L	U	E	S		
	E							

Alternative Activity 38—Answering Interview Questions
1. A 2. G 3. F 4. B 5. D 6. E 7. H 8. C

Alternative Activity 39—Practicing Self-Advocacy Skills
1. C 2. B 3. B 4. C 5. B 6. A 7. D 8. C

Alternative Activity 40—Developing Hobbies and Interests
1. A 2. C 3. B 4. C 5. D 6. B 7. A 8. B

Alternative Activity 41—Managing Time

1. A personal time survey is a guide to how you spend your time. 2. Use your personal time survey to help you make a schedule. 3. Time management is making the best use of your time to get things accomplished. 4. Non-scheduled time lets you catch up if you fall behind schedule, or have free time if you have no other use for it. 5. A "time waster" is an activity that takes up more time than you want it to. 6. You may want to do things longer than they are scheduled for or do things that are not on your schedule.

Alternative Activity 42—Healthy Lifestyle Choices

1. fatty foods 2. stroke 3. Type II 4. AIDS 5. hand washing 6. alcoholism 7. drug 8. fever 9. marijuana 10. vaccines 11. steroids 12. addictive

Alternative Activity 43—Living Ethically

1. D 2. B 3. C 4. A 5. C 6. B 7. D 8. C

Alternative Activity 44—Using Feedback Puzzle

```
. . . F . . . . . . .
. T E S T . . . . . .
. . E . . . . . . . .
G R A D E S . . . . .
. . B . . . . . G . .
R O A D M A P . O . .
. C . . . O . . A . .
. K . . . S . . L . .
. . . S K I L L S . .
. . . . . T . . . . .
. . . . . I . . . . .
. . . . . V . . . . .
. M A T C H E S . . .
```

Alternative Activity 45—Career Action Plan Puzzle

1. stone 2. training 3. map 4. personal 5. destination 6. how 7. good 8. action

Answer to acrostic puzzle: snapshot

Workbook Activities

Workbook Activity 1—The Work You Choose

1. fun 2. occupation 3. paid 4. all 5. career 6. money 7. stereotypes 8. reasons 9. work 10. enjoy

Workbook Activity 2—The Workplace and the Economy

1. D 2. C 3. B 4. C 5. B 6. C 7. B 8. D 9. A 10. C

Workbook Activity 3—Finding Your Strengths

1. self-assessment 2. knowledge 3. plans 4. subjects 5. skills 6. Business 7. Computers 8. Science 9. achievements 10. earned 11. competency 12. grades 13. compare 14. feedback 15. jobs

Workbook Activity 4—Describe the Abilities

1. I 2. A 3. D 4. C 5. J 6. E 7. B 8. G 9. F 10. H 11. manual 12. organizational 13. clerical 14. visual (spatial) 15. artistic

Workbook Activity 5—Your Interests

1. conductor 2. career groups 3. counselor 4. education 5. physicist 6. career center 7. technical 8. interest 9. social worker 10. bank manager

Answer to acrostic puzzle: occupation

Workbook Activity 6—Name the Value

1. S 2. M 3. P 4. H 5. M 6. O 7. M 8. S 9. H 10. M 11. O 12. S 13. H 14. P 15. O

Workbook Activity 7—Completing a Self-Assessment Profile

1. I would write the names of classes I liked and did well in. 2. These would all be written in the list of abilities. 3. Answers may vary but students should understand that their values are important part of them and will affect the types of job choices they will make. 4. You write a Career Group in the First Choice box. 5. Work means how people spend their time to make a living. 6. A Self-Assessment Profile will help you get where you want to go. 7. Sample response: The profile helps you to see what is important to you, what you enjoy, and what you are good at. This can help you choose a job you are more likely to enjoy. 8. A portfolio is a collection of items to use when exploring career choices and developing a career plan. 9. Accept any of these answers: achievements, letters of recommendation, resumes, references, jobs held, activities performed, and writing samples. 10. An early step in creating a portfolio is to include the Self-Assessment Profile.

Workbook Activity 8—Using a CDMCareerZone Web Page

1. This screen shows part of the page for Counter and Rental Clerks. 2. There are 11 sections of description from which to choose. 3. The typical job tasks in this occupation are (accept any two of the following): receive orders, describe options, compute cost, accept payment. 4. To find out about earnings for these workers, one would click the "Wages" section of the screen. 5. To see if this occupation is growing, one would click on "Job Outlook."

Workbook Activity 9—Career Decisions Puzzle

```
. . . . . P L A N . . . . .
. G . . . R . . . . . . . .
M O T I V A T I O N . . . .
. A . . . B . . D . . . . .
. L . . V A L U E S . . N .
. . . . O B . . C . . . E .
. . . P R I O R I T Y . G .
. . . T L . . . S . . . A .
. . . I I . . . I . . . T .
. . . O T . P O S I T I V E
. . . N Y . . . N . . . V .
. . . S . . . . S . . . E .
```

Workbook Activity 10—Exploring Occupations in the Future

1. F 2. J 3. C 4. B 5. G 6. I 7. H 8. E 9. A 10. D

Workbook Activity 11—Education and Training Key
1. Entry Level **2.** On-the-job training **3.** Apprenticeship **4.** Technical/Vocational Training **5.** College **6.** a few days to two months **7.** two to six months **8.** six months to five years **9.** one to four years **10.** four-year degree or more

Workbook Activity 12—Manufacturing Puzzle

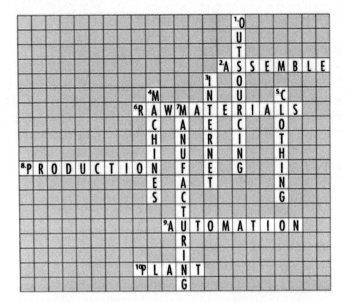

Workbook Activity 13—Describing Transportation
1. The transportation industry deals with the use of roads, waterways, and rail and air systems. **2.** Transportation distributes materials and products. Another purpose is to help people get where they need to go. **3.** Freight truck drivers are usually paid by the number of miles they drive. **4.** Dispatchers keep track of where trucks are and let drivers know of bad weather or road conditions. **5.** Three common railroad occupations are locomotive engineer, brake operator, and conductor (or laborer). **6.** Most seamen or deckhands learn on the job. **7.** The Federal Aviation Administration licenses pilots. **8.** Transportation workers usually have (accept any three of the following): physical strength, the ability to handle emergencies, good eye-hand coordination, and the ability to make good judgments. **9.** Employment of drivers is expected to increase by 15 to 20 percent. **10.** By 2012, about 9.3 percent of all workers will be employed in transportation, distribution, or logistics occupations.

Workbook Activity 14—Name the Architecture or Construction Job
1. developer **2.** inspector **3.** contractor **4.** architect **5–6.** plumber, electrician **7.** steelworker **8–9.** cabinetmaker, plasterer **10.** surveyor

Workbook Activity 15—How Much Education Is Needed?
1. pharmacy technician **2–4.** medical and clinical laboratory technician, medical records and health information technician, licensed practical nurse **5–10.** athletic trainer, dentist, social worker, pharmacist, dietician, speech-language pathologist

Workbook Activity 16—Science, Technology, Engineering, and Mathematics
1. Technology is the use of science to create new products or make old ones better. **2.** The four main engineering fields are electrical, civil, mechanical, and industrial. **3.** Industrial engineers help companies make the best use of their people, machines, and raw materials. They also make sure workers stay safe. **4.** Life scientists work in fields related to biology, food and agriculture, forestry, and the environment. **5.** Physical science includes nuclear energy and aerospace. **6.** Possible answer: Scientists have to keep good records of their research. **7.** Mathematics workers need reasoning and computer skills. **8.** An architectural drafter needs technical or vocational training. **9.** Mining, nuclear, and petroleum engineering jobs are expected to decrease by 2012. Jobs for mathematicians are also expected to decrease. **10.** The average salary for a worker with an advanced degree is $65,500 a year.

Workbook Activity 17—Information Technology Jobs
1. I **2.** P **3.** N **4.** N **5.** T **6.** P **7.** I **8.** T **9.** N **10.** T **11.** P **12.** T **13.** I **14.** I **15.** N

Workbook Activity 18—The Arts Crossword

Workbook Activity 19—Careers in Education and Training
1. G **2.** A **3.** E **4.** I **5.** B **6.** J **7.** F **8.** C **9.** H **10.** D

Workbook Activity 20—Jobs in Human Services
1. A **2.** D **3.** C **4.** C **5.** B **6.** A **7.** B **8.** C **9.** B **10.** A

Workbook Activity 21—Jobs in Hospitality and Tourism
1. C **2.** B **3.** D **4.** A **5.** C **6.** B **7.** A **8.** D **9.** B **10.** B

Workbook Activity 22—Law, Public Safety, and Security Puzzle

Crossword answers:
1. LEGAL
2. EMERGENCY (down)
3. DISPATCH (down)
4. WAGES
5. SAFETY (down)
6. PARALEGAL
7. SECURITY
8. PRISON (down)
9. FEDERAL — FERS (down)
10. OUTLOOK

Workbook Activity 23—Working in the Finance Industry

1. J 2. E 3. F 4. G 5. N 6. A 7. H 8. K 9. L 10. D 11. M 12. C 13. I
14. B 15. O

Workbook Activity 24—Marketing, Sales, and Service

1. F 2. G 3. I 4. B 5. J 6. D 7. E 8. A 9. H 10. C

Workbook Activity 25—Business Occupations

1. leadership 2. managers 3. college degree 4. services 5. management
6. technology 7. travel 8. job growth 9. operations 10. support

Workbook Activity 26—Government and Public Administration Puzzle

1. organized 2. county 3. visit 4. decisions 5. military 6. communicate
7. Homeland 8. elderly 9. housing 10. postal
Answer to acrostic puzzle: government

Workbook Activity 27—Exploring Careers Scramble

1. preference 2. school subjects 3. abilities 4. values 5. sharing
6. financial aid 7. postsecondary 8. basic skills 9. investment
10. career planning

Workbook Activity 28—Career Planning Puzzle

Crossword answers:
1. WRITING (down)
2. EXPERIENCE (down)
3. POSTSECONDARY
4. BENEFITS (down)
5. HALF (down)
6. FINANCIAL AID
7. INVESTMENT (down)
8. RISK
9. MATH
10. READING

Workbook Activity 29—Industries in Your Community

Crossword answers:
1. PLUMBERS
2. MECHANICIAN (down)
3. RESOURCE (down)
4. FINANCE
5. THEFT (down)
6. CORE
7. BARBERS
8. REPAIRS (down)
9. TRAINING
10. VISITORS — VISITORS / VILLS (down)

Workbook Activity 30—Networking Works!

1. Kathy learned more about careers in her field. She also got some interviewing practice and met more contact people. 2. Sample answer: Kathy can use her new contacts to help her get a different job in the future. She can also develop friendships with people in her profession. This can help her learn more about what is going on in the field of auto mechanics.

Workbook Activity 31—Visiting Postsecondary Schools

1–2. Is it important to stay close to home? Do you like the adventure of being on your own? 3–5. What amount of tuition can you and your family afford? What percent of students receive financial aid? What is the average financial aid package? 6–7. Do you like the size of your high school? Do you wish your high school was larger and offered more opportunities? 8–9. What clubs, sports teams, and other activities are available? What sports is the school most known for?
10. How many students apply and are accepted each year?

Workbook Activity 32—People Skills

1. Be sure to focus on what the person is saying. Do not think about how you will respond to them. Wait until they are finished talking. Then take time to form your response. **2.** Showing respect to other people means treating them the way that you want to be treated. It means listening to what they say. **3.** You can become better at working with people who are very different by taking the time to learn about them. Find out about their cultures and traditions. Ask them what they like and don't like. Try to understand their values. **4.** Employers value the qualities of honesty, reliability, trustworthiness, and a positive attitude. **5.** You should respond to conflict by trying to stay calm. Try to communicate well and show respect. If you hurt someone else's feelings, apologize for your words or actions. If they hurt you, calmly tell the person how you feel.

Workbook Activity 33—Hiring Process Puzzle

```
            ¹S
²R E C R U I T M E ⁿN T   E       ⁴H
            N         L       I
    ⁵I N T E R ⁶N E T   E       R
            E   T         C       I
            W   W     ⁷D   T       N
            ⁸S C R E E N I N G       G
            P   K     P   O
            A   I     E   N
            P   N     N
        ⁹R E S U M E   G     D
            R           A
                        B
                    ¹⁰I N T E R V I E W
                        L
                        I
                        T
                        Y
```

Workbook Activity 34—Personal Goal Statement Scramble

1. description **2.** name **3.** knowledge **4.** lifestyle **5.** specific **6.** requirements **7.** resources **8.** skills **9.** short-term **10.** personal goal

Workbook Activity 35—Organizing a Résumé

1. Seeking a position as host at a fine-dining restaurant in the Chicago area **2–4.** Experience in food-service and restaurant industry; Flexible, well organized, and reliable; Professional attitude and excellent communications skills **5–7.** Administrative: operate cash registers and make accurate change; Public contact: greet customers and serve them in a friendly, efficient way; Restaurant organization: distribute seating appropriately, manage customers, wait staff, and cash register effectively **8.** 2003–present: Host/cashier, Alice's Family Restaurant, Oak Park, Illinois **9.** 2002–2003: Crew member, Megaburger, Inc., Oak Park, Illinois **10.** Graduated from Central High School, Oak Park, Illinois, 2004

Workbook Activity 36—Getting References

1–7. Answers will vary.

Workbook Activity 37—Interviewing Skills

1. The main types of important information I will share are my skills, interests, experience, and values that connect to the job. **2.** Researching career options will let me connect information about myself to the position. **3.** Information about my personal qualities and about my values helps an interviewer find out whether I will fit into the job. **4.** The three basic questions are: Can you do the job? Will you do the job? Will you fit into the job situation? **5.** Stating skills in terms of accomplishments is a good way to convince the interviewer that I can perform the skills required for the job well. **6.** A good way to describe accomplishments is to begin the descriptions with action verbs. **7.** I will need to communicate that I find the job interesting. I can do this by connecting my interests to those required for the job. **8.** An interviewer will observe my body language and how I say what I say. **9.** All employers want their employees to be honest, hardworking, and reliable and to have a positive attitude. **10.** My role in an interview is to convince the interviewer that I am the right person for the job. By preparing I will be ready to provide answers to the questions asked.

Workbook Activity 38—Interview Checklist

1–2. Accept any two of the following: dress properly, know how to get there, be well groomed. **3–8.** Accept any six of the following: arrive on time, be polite and respectful, act as if you want the job, say you want the job toward the end, remind the interviewer why you are a good fit before you leave, ask when you can expect to hear about the job. **9–10.** Accept any two of the following: send a thank-you note, review your interview experience and ask for feedback if you don't get a job offer. **11–15.** Accept any five of the following: chew gum, tell jokes, use inappropriate humor, talk negatively about others or about previous employers, use slang or improper language, leave without expressing your interest in the job.

Workbook Activity 39—Self-Advocacy Puzzle

1. shy **2.** practice **3.** behaviors **4.** self-advocacy **5.** feedback **6.** positively **7.** communicate **8.** contributing **9.** résumé **10.** accomplishments
Answer to acrostic puzzle: speaking up

Workbook Activity 40—Developing Hobbies Puzzle

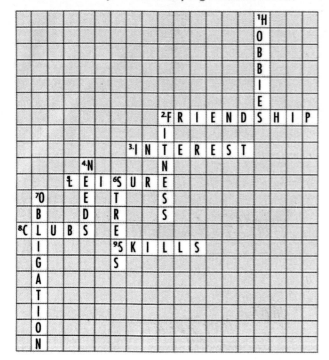

Workbook Activity 41—Time Management Puzzle

1. compare **2.** wasters **3.** weekend **4.** activities **5.** recognize
6. survey **7.** important **8.** schedule **9.** persistence **10.** time
Answer to acrostic puzzle: management

Workbook Activity 42—Healthy Lifestyle Choices

1. C **2.** H **3.** K **4.** O **5.** A **6.** B **7.** J **8.** M **9.** E **10.** L **11.** F **12.** I **13.** D
14. N **15.** G

Workbook Activity 43—Ethics Scramble

1. dilemma **2.** group **3.** universal **4.** judgment **5.** consequences
6. ethics **7.** conscience **8.** criticism **9.** trustworthy **10.** decisions

Workbook Activity 44—Responding to Feedback

1. I **2.** G **3.** K **4.** B **5.** M **6.** J **7.** D **8.** L **9.** O **10.** N **11.** E **12.** H **13.** C
14. F **15.** A

Workbook Activity 45—Developing Your Career Action Plan

1. C **2.** A **3.** B **4.** B **5.** C **6.** C **7.** B **8.** B **9.** C **10.** D

Portfolio Activities

Completed activities will vary for each student. Portfolio Activities
can be added to students' career portfolios. Check completed activities
to see that students have followed directions, completed the steps,
filled in all charts and blanks, provided reasonable answers, and
written legibly.

Chapter Outlines

Chapter 1
I.
  A.
    1. time, living
    2. examples
    3. job
    4. life
    5. occupation
    6. enjoy
  B.
    1. not
    2. help
    3. build
    4. express
    5. prestige
    6. meaning
  C.
    1. stereotype
    2. work
    3. career

II.
  A.
    1. workplace
    2. formal
    3. informal
  B.
    1. economy
    2. understanding
    3. interest rates
    4. more, more
    5. business cycle
  C.
    1. events
    2. products
    3. business cycle
    4. positive
    5. unemployed
  D.
    1. technology
    2. change in seasons

Chapter 2
I.
  A.
    1. skills
    2. to do something well
  B.
    1. skills, school
  C.
    1. achievement
    2. grades
    3. comparing

II.
  A.
    1. strengths
    2. feeling good about oneself
  B.
    1. requires
    2. information

III.
  A.
    1. interests
    2. career
  B.
    1. occupations
  C.
    1. abilities, interest, education requirements
    2. occupation

IV.
  A.
    1. important to a person
    2. experience
  B.
    1. work value
  C.
    1. career
    2. plans

V.
  A.
    1. career path
    2. map
  B.
    1. career, plan

Chapter 3
I.
  A.
    1. skills, knowledge
    2. wage equity
  B.
    1. job description
    2. occupational brief
    3. drop-down menu
  C.
    1. related occupations
    2. index
  D.
    1. catalogs
    2. career information
    3. shadow

II.
  A.
    1. Career
    2. five
  B.
    1. decision-making
    2. realistic goals
  C.
    1. priority
    2. values
  D.
    1. choices
    2. goal
  E.
    1. negative outcome
    2. probability
    3. risky
    4. motivation
  F.
    1. write down
    2. motivated

Chapter 4
I.
  A.
    1. clusters
  B.
    1. grow
    2. education

II.
  A.
    1. food production
  B.
    1. mining, extraction
  C.
    1. less (or more slowly)

III.
  A.
    1. assembled
  B.
    1. machines
    2. physical activities
  C.
    1. 8.5

IV.
  A.
    1. companies, warehouses, distribution centers
  B.
    1. crafts
  C.
    1. increase

V.
  A.
    1. job site
  B.
    1. on the job
  C.
    1. 15

VI.
  A.
    1. Doctors, nurses
  B.
    1. helping others
  C.
    1. increase

VII.
  A.
    1. industrial
  B.
    1. computer
  C.
    1. symbols
  D.
    1. education

VIII.
  A.
    1. computer
  B.
    1. database
  C.
    1. help
  D.
    1. Web sites
  E.
    1. software
  F.
    1. growing

IX.
  A.
    1. writing
  B.
    1. design
  C.
    1. Composers
  D.
    1. directors
  E.
    1. creativity
    2. very small

X.
- **A.**
  1. schools, businesses
- **B.**
  1. their minds, people
- **C.**
  1. largest growing

XI.
- **A.**
  1. 1.3 million
- **B.**
  1. non-medical
- **C.**
  1. social workers
- **D.**
  1. home care aides
- **E.**
  1. 3.3

XII.
- **A.**
  1. many different places
  2. good service
- **B.**
  1. 20 percent

XIII.
- **A.**
  1. elected officials
- **B.**
  1. police officers
- **C.**
  1. emergency medical technician
- **D.**
  1. job growth

XIV.
- **A.**
  1. financial institutions
  2. salespeople, financial analysts
- **B.**
  1. real estate

XV.
- **A.**
  1. consumers
  2. personal contact
- **B.**
  1. challenges
  2. cashiers, retail salespersons
  3. customer complaints
- **C.**
  1. retail salespeople, cashiers

XVI.
- **A.**
  1. office buildings
- **B.**
  1. benefits
- **C.**
  1. organized
- **D.**
  1. secretaries, data entry workers

XVII.
- **A.**
  1. different types of jobs
  2. 2.5 million
- **B.**
  1. postal workers

Chapter 5
I.
- **A.**
  1. careers of interest to you
  2. what you need to learn in school
  3. abilities
  4. values
  5. job outlook
  6. high school
  7. sharing your plan
- **B.**
  1. occupations
  2. school subjects
  3. skills
  4. values
  5. job outlook, wages
  6. plan
  7. postsecondary

II.
- **A.**
  1. one-half
  2. investment
- **B.**
  1. poor basic skills
  2. higher salaries
- **C.**
  1. skills, behaviors
  2. 25 to 30
- **D.**
  1. continuing education
- **E.**
  1. 25 to 30
  2. four-year
- **F.**
  1. postsecondary education
  2. scholarships, grants, loans, work-study programs

Chapter 6
I.
- **A.**
  1. Core services
  2. career clusters
- **B.**
  1. training
  2. every
  3. work, careers
  4. Internet
  5. police officers, mail carriers

II.
- **A.**
  1. learn about possible job opportunities
  2. productive
- **B.**
  1. wage
  2. job, tryout
- **C.**
  1. employs
  2. informational interview
  3. thank-you note

III.
- **A.**
  1. immediately
  2. experiences
  3. counselors
- **B.**
  1. size, location
  2. services
  3. strengths
  4. every school

IV.
- **A.**
  1. contact
  2. respect
- **B.**
  1. stay calm
- **C.**
  1. respectful

Chapter 7
I.
- **A.**
  1. recruitment
  2. sloppy
  3. selection
- **B.**
  1. skills
- **C.**
  1. homework
- **D.**
  1. supervisor

II.
- **A.**
  1. personal goal statement
- **B.**
  1. name
  2. career goal
  3. knowledge, skills, and abilities
  4. short-term (or in-between)

III.
- **A.**
  1. places
  2. action verbs
- **B.**
  1. chronological
  2. functional
- **C.**
  1. goal
  2. education
  3. skills
  4. related information
  5. perfect
- **D.**
  1. introduce

IV.
- **A.**
  1. check
- **B.**
  1. employer
- **C.**
  1. positively

Chapter 8
I.
- **A.**
  1. fit
  2. skills, interests, experience
- **B.**
  1. specific
  2. convince
- **C.**
  1. accomplishments
  2. list
  3. experiences
- **D.**
  1. interests
  2. statements
- **E.**
  1. values
  2. equally

II.
- **A.**
  1. professional
  2. polite, respect
  3. gum, jokes, slang, negatively

- **B.**
  1. thank-you note
  2. qualifications
- **D.**
  1. interview
  2. feedback

III.
- **A.**
  1. speak up
- **B.**
  1. support, defend
  2. contributing
- **C.**
  1. personal
  2. behaviors
  3. positively

Chapter 9
I.
- **A.**
  1. hobby
  2. have to do
- **B.**
  1. leisure time
  2. interests
- **C.**
  1. meet new people
- **D.**
  1. classes you are taking
  2. clubs and teams that your school has
- **E.**
  1. skills

II.
- **A.**
  1. "time wasters"
  2. at least a week
- **B.**
  1. To Do List

III.
- **A.**
  1. 50
  2. illness
- **B.**
  1. symptoms
  2. Heart disease
- **C.**
  1. 20
  2. refrain from sexual activity
- **D.**
  1. wash
- **E.**
  1. nicotine
  2. alcoholism
  3. Hallucinogens

IV.
- **A.**
  1. Ethics
- **B.**
  1. beliefs
  2. the world
- **C.**
  1. outcome, results

Chapter 10
I.
- **A.**
  1. yourself
- **B.**
  1. yourself, occupations
- **C.**
  1. information
  2. decisions
- **D.**
  1. plan, résumé, references
  2. manage
- **E.**
  1. all, planning
  2. plans, goals
- **F.**
  1. challenge
  2. useful
- **G.**
  1. risky, attention
  2. trust
  3. changing
- **H.**
  1. activities
  2. interests, statement

II.
- **A.**
  1. personal goal statement
  2. career action plan
- **B.**
  1. goal statement, career action plan
  2. negative
- **C.**
  1. feedback, review
  2. snapshot
  3. successful

Chapter Mastery Tests

Chapter 1 Mastery Test A

Part A: **1.** D **2.** C **3.** A **4.** D **5.** C

Part B: **6.** C **7.** A **8.** E **9.** D **10.** B

Part C: **11.** meaning **12.** stereotype **13.** workplace **14.** unemployment **15.** school

Part D: **16.** You should not believe the ways jobs are shown on TV and in the movies because the images of what jobs are like are not usually true. They are based on work stereotypes. **17.** When interest rates are low, more people can buy homes. So, the need to build houses increases. More houses are built. More jobs are created building houses. **18.** If you choose an occupation you enjoy, you will be happier in your life. Adults spend a lot of time working, and they want their work to have meaning. **19.** Three reasons people work are (accept any three): to make money, to help others, to work with their hands, to express themselves creatively, and to gain prestige. **20.** Workers wear uniforms, salute officers, follow a set schedule, and follow rules as they do their work. The rules are strongly enforced.

Part E: **21.** Answers will vary. Students should support their answers with at least some of these ideas: The kind of people that workers are should not be stereotyped (doctors are not all rich, smart, cool-headed, and hard working; nurses are not only—or all—kind, caring, and patient.) Both men and women should be shown in all jobs (doctor, nurse, ambulance driver, surgeon, and so on). **22.** Answers will vary. Students should support their answers with at least some of these facts: When the business cycle is not positive, there are fewer work opportunities. When people are out of work, they have less money to spend, so there is less demand for products and services. That means there will be fewer jobs. People also spend less money in a downturn because interest rates are high. Again, that means there is less demand. In a long downturn, the number of people unemployed may be greater than in other times.

Part F: **23.** Answers will vary. Students' paragraphs should identify a job and use some of these supporting details: going to school to prepare for the job; having money and time for fun activities and outside interests; living in a certain location; dressing for work; having interesting co-workers; being in a comfortable workplace. **24.** Answers will vary. Students' paragraphs should identify which job they chose and use some of these supporting details: A job that is considered important or that is highly valued has appeal and/or benefits. An informal or formal workplace has appeal and/or benefits.

Chapter 1 Mastery Test B

Part A: **1.** C **2.** C **3.** B **4.** B **5.** C

Part B: **6.** D **7.** C **8.** A **9.** E **10.** B

Part C: **11.** education **12.** stereotypes **13.** slows **14.** full-time **15.** business cycle

Part D: **16.** Knowing the kind of workplace I like will help me find a job where I will be comfortable. Also, it will help me ask questions and use what I find out in job interviews. **17.** Some jobs, including ones in home building, are more affected by the business cycle than others. **18.** Believing work stereotypes might stop me from looking into a career I would enjoy. **19.** When there are more new jobs, fewer people are unemployed. **20.** I may need to think about how many years of school I will need to prepare for the job.

Part E: **21.** Answers will vary. Students should support their answers with at least some of these ideas: The grocery clerk may need to change his work schedule. If the clerk works fewer hours, he may have less money for things he wants and needs. Working and going to school may give him less free time. He may have added expenses because of school and he will need to figure out how to pay for those. **22.** Answers will vary. Students should explain whether an informal workplace has appeal and/or benefits.

Part F: **23.** Answers will vary. Students' paragraphs should use some of these supporting details: When the business cycle is not positive, interest rates rise, people spend less money, and there are fewer work opportunities. The longer it takes to find a job, the harder it can be to find one. This may depend in part on the type of work involved. Some types of work are more affected by the business cycle than others. **24.** Answers will vary. Students should support their answers with at least some of these ideas: Work stereotypes are general beliefs that many people have. Stereotypes are not necessarily true. Work stereotypes can be about the work that people do and about the group of people who do them. People may draw conclusions about jobs based on what they see on TV and in the movies. They may find that the jobs are not what they appear to be on TV shows and in the movies.

Chapter 2 Mastery Test A

Part A: **1.** D **2.** A **3.** C **4.** C **5.** B

Part B: **6.** self-assessment **7.** competency **8.** self-confidence **9.** interests **10.** skill

Part C: **11.** B **12.** G **13.** F **14.** D **15.** A **16.** C **17.** E

Part D: **18.** Accept any three of the following for clerical: bookkeeping clerk, cashier, court reporter, data entry keyer, hotel/motel clerk, medical records technician, police dispatcher, postal service clerk, receptionist, secretary, teller, word processor; accept any three of the following for manual: animal caretaker, bus driver, carpenter, construction laborer, firefighter, food preparation worker, forest and conservation worker, highway maintenance worker, landscaper, machine operator, painter, product assembler, truck driver; accept any three of the following for sales: auto salesperson, buyer, financial planner, insurance agent, real estate agent, retail sales worker, travel agent. **19.** Looking at your favorite school subjects will help you to figure out what your interests are. It also may help you figure out your skills and competencies. **20.** Answers may vary, but students should realize that values can change as a result of life experiences.

Part E: **21.** Answers will vary. Sample values include: good salary, job security, leadership, prestige, or work with your mind.

22. Answers will vary, but students should identify these steps from the text: Identify your subject area strengths. Determine your abilities, interests, and values. Examine different careers that relate to those abilities, interests, and values. Figure out what schooling or training you still need for your desired career.

Part F: **23.** Answers will vary but students should demonstrate understanding that different abilities are used in different types of jobs. For example, artistic abilities can be used in manual jobs, such as construction; in entertainment jobs, such as a stage director or actress; in literary jobs, such as poet and playwright. **24.** Answers will vary but students should include several of these reasons from the text: Some people do not have the work value of good salary so they might not like the job. Some people do not enjoy school and would not want to continue on to college. Some people cannot afford the cost of a higher education.

Chapter 2 Mastery Test B

Part A: **1.** C **2.** B **3.** C **4.** A **5.** D

Part B: **6.** ability **7.** risk **8.** values **9.** experience **10.** prestige

Part C: **11.** E **12.** C **13.** A **14.** G **15.** B **16.** F **17.** D

Part D: **18.** Answers will vary but students should explain that self-assessment can help them to plan for the future, apply for a job or college, and so on. **19.** A person with the work value of job security will want to keep the same job for a long time. **20.** Answers will vary, but students should list jobs that are appropriate for their interests.

Part E: **21.** Answers will vary but students should explain that educational requirements are the amount of training or schooling that is needed for a job. They affect people's career choices because a person has to decide whether or not they can meet that requirement. **22.** Answers will vary but students should include some of these facts from the text: People look at their abilities to decide what types of jobs they can do now. They use their abilities to decide what types of careers they can pursue after getting an education or special training.

Part F: **23.** Answers will vary. Sample values include: good salary, job security, leadership, prestige, or work with your mind. **24.** Answers will vary but students should clearly point out the importance of doing a self-assessment. They should include some of these facts from the text: A self-assessment will help them know more about themselves. They will identify their subject area strengths. They will determine their abilities, interests, and values. They can use the self-assessment to help them make future career and education plans. They can use their self-assessment to help them apply for a job or for college.

Chapter 3 Mastery Test A

Part A: **1.** C **2.** A **3.** B **4.** A **5.** D

Part B: **6.** D **7.** B **8.** E **9.** C **10.** A

Part C: **11.** values **12.** positive outcome **13.** risks **14.** decisions **15.** plan

Part D: **16.** Wage equity is men and women being paid the same amount for doing the same job. **17.** The index in the *Occupational Outlook Handbook* (OOH) directs you to the exact page for an occupation. **18.** This section tells you what schooling or training you will need for an occupation. **19.** Realistic goals are easier to attain and will suit your ability or personality. **20.** Shadowing could teach you what the actual day-to-day life of a given occupation is like.

Part E: **21.** Answers will vary. Students should support their answers with some of these ideas or examples: Knowing what an occupation requires allows you to set more realistic goals. You can assess more accurately whether an occupation matches your abilities, interests, and values. Knowing the requirements of an occupation also allows you to make a more useful plan. **22.** Answers will vary. Students should support their answers with some of these ideas or examples that reveal them: A negative outcome to an event teaches you that a goal was unrealistic. A negative outcome may teach you to plan more carefully or thoroughly. A negative outcome may turn you toward the best possible career for you. A negative outcome may motivate you to try harder.

Part F: **23.** Answers will vary. Students' paragraphs should include at least some of these ideas: Values reveal what people prefer, and what people prefer determines their priorities. The order of priorities shapes planning, or even lack of planning, therefore the choices that get made. If values are ignored in planning, the plan may fail or the attainment of goals may be unsatisfying because it does not match what really matters to a person.

24. Answers will vary. Students' paragraphs should include at least some of these ideas: People sometimes make poor decisions because they do not follow a decision-making process, have unrealistic goals, make plans that do not match their values, or fail to follow through on their plans.

Chapter 3 Mastery Test B

Part A: **1.** A **2.** C **3.** C **4.** B **5.** B

Part B: **6.** D **7.** B **8.** E **9.** A **10.** C

Part C: **11.** goal **12.** probability **13.** motivation **14.** priority **15.** options

Part D: **16.** Writing your plan helps you keep track of your movement toward your goal and helps motivate you.

17. CDMCareerZone is a Web site with occupational information that may be accessed via the Internet from home or from a library. **18.** Three groups of related occupations in the OOH are (accept any three of the following): management, business, and financial; professional; service; sales; office and administrative support; farming, fishing, and forestry; construction trades; installation, maintenance, and repair; production; transportation and material moving; Armed Forces. **19.** You assess risks by judging the probability of a positive or negative outcome. **20.** School resources for career planning included guidance counselors, catalogs from many schools and organizations, computer programs and videos, and books.

Part E: **21.** Answers will vary. Students should support their answers with some of these ideas or examples: When you research information about occupations, you will know what an employer expects you to do on a job. You will know what skills and knowledge you need for an occupation. You can plan for college or other schooling or training based on what you need to know. **22.** Answers will vary. Student should support their answer with at least some of these ideas or examples: Friends and family know you well enough to help you determine whether your goals are realistic. They may also have real-world experience to help you assess risks and make attainable plans. They may also be a source of ideas and information about careers, or may help you to make contact with other people who are a source.

Part F: **23.** Answers will vary. Students' paragraphs should include at least some of these ideas, supported by examples: Motivation often determines whether a person will think carefully or follow through with any step of the decision-making process. A highly motivated person will work harder to find information, assess risks, and overcome obstacles. Highly motivated people often move toward those values that most satisfy them. Motivation can also come from people you respect, who help steer you in the right direction. **24.** Answers will vary. Students' paragraphs should include at least some of these ideas or examples: A person's work values usually determine whether he or she is right for a job. People usually know if a career is right for them by whether they find the work satisfying, important, or consistent with their needs and values, including their interests as well as the amount of money earned. A career also must match a person's knowledge, skills, abilities, and education. If it does not, it is unlikely that the person will succeed in a chosen field.

Chapter 4 Mastery Test A

Part A: **1.** D **2.** B **3.** A **4.** A **5.** C

Part B: **6.** B **7.** E **8.** A **9.** D **10.** C

Part C: **11.** education **12.** human services **13.** hospitality **14.** corrections **15.** finance

Part D: **16.** Most people in the Marketing, Sales, and Service cluster work as cashiers and retail salespersons. **17.** Accountants keep track of money for a business. **18.** The four types of governments are federal, state, county, and city. **19.** The Department of Education groups occupations with similar preparation, similar skills, and similar workplaces into clusters. **20.** An industry is a large-scale business or service area that provides a product or service.

Part E: **21.** Answers will vary. Students should support their answers with some of these ideas or examples: The job outlook tells you whether there will be many or few opportunities in a given field. Areas with much expected growth may offer good opportunities. Areas with little projected growth will require people to prepare better or perhaps choose another career. **22.** Answers will vary. Students should support their answers with at least some of these facts: Although there are few job openings in the arts fields, those jobs have a huge impact because they create what we see on television and in movies, what we read in newspapers and magazines, and what we hear on the radio.

Part F: **23.** Answers will vary. Students' paragraphs should include at least some of these ideas: Personal qualities of being well organized, well trained, hard working, and eager to learn will help in any field or occupation. Honesty, reliability, and getting along with others are also very valuable qualities. **24.** Answers will vary. Sample answer: Job areas grow or shrink in response to demands from people. For example, the health science field is growing because there are more people who need these services. Growth in manufacturing is slow because outsourcing, automation, and new technologies have changed both the way and the location of products that are manufactured. **25.** Answers will vary.

Chapter 4 Mastery Test B

Part A: **1.** C **2.** B **3.** A **4.** D **5.** A
Part B: **6.** C **7.** B **8.** A **9.** E **10.** D
Part C: **11.** developers **12.** health science **13.** information technology **14.** engineering **15.** arts
Part D: **16.** Career clusters are groups of related occupations. **17.** An associate's degree usually requires two years of study at a college or vocational school. A bachelor's degree usually requires four years or more of study at a college. **18.** Agriculture deals with plants, animals, and the production of food. Natural resources deals with the mining of resources from the earth. **19.** Offshore outsourcing is the moving of jobs to countries where wages are lower. It is one reason for the small growth expected for manufacturing jobs in the United States. **20.** The purpose of transportation is to distribute materials, products, and people to places they need to be.

Part E: **21.** Answers will vary. Students should support their answers with some of these ideas or examples: Knowing areas of interest for an occupation in a cluster can help you decide whether it is a good fit for you. For example, people in sales often like to work with other people and enjoy challenges. If you enjoyed these things, sales could be for you; if not, you might consider another career. **22.** Answers will vary. Student should support their answer with at least some of these ideas or examples: A person who is interested in a career that is not expected to have much growth needs to work even harder to prepare, or to consider another area. Because there will be fewer job openings, people will compete fiercely for those that do exist. If one is determined to go into an area where competition is stiff, one should be realistic about what it will take to succeed.

Part F: **23.** Answers will vary. Students' paragraphs should include at least some of these ideas, supported by examples: Knowing what education and training will be required for various occupations in a career cluster allows students to make realistic choices and to plan their paths to their careers. For example, most colleges require certain courses to be taken in high school, so a high school student can plan which ones to take. Or, if a student is not going into a field that requires college, that person can seek other training. **24.** Answers will vary. Students' paragraphs should include at least some of these ideas or examples: Most students will agree that honesty should be an important trait in the Arts, Audio-Video Technology, and Entertainment cluster. This cluster provides news and information to the rest of the country. **25.** Answers will vary.

Chapter 5 Mastery Test A

Part A: **1.** C **2.** B **3.** D **4.** A **5.** C
Part B: **6.** B **7.** D **8.** A **9.** E **10.** C
Part C: **11.** skill **12.** investment **13.** ability **14.** financial aid **15.** postsecondary
Part D: **16.** Guidance counselors and school career centers are good sources for information about postsecondary information. **17.** Employers demand good basic skills in reading, writing, and mathematics. **18.** Employers value workers who can (accept two of the following): follow directions, be on time, show respect to others, and communicate well. **19.** If you do not work in high school, you can develop job skills through education or training after high school. **20.** The more education one has, the more money one usually earns.

Part E: **21.** Answers will vary. Students should support their answers with some of these ideas or examples: Fulfilling work values can bring you job satisfaction. By deciding which values are most important to you, you can match careers that speak to those values. **22.** Answers will vary. Students should support their answers with some of these ideas or examples: Working part-time during high school allows one to build skills and behaviors that employers want. Workers learn promptness, respect for others, and job skills. They also learn more about an industry and get a better idea of what skills would be useful. A possible disadvantage is that there is less time to study for school subjects.

Part F: **23.** Answers will vary. Students' paragraphs should include at least some of these ideas: Students who do not finish high school do not do as well in the job market as those who do finish high school. Only about half find work. Those who finish high school earn much more money than those who do not. In addition, many postsecondary programs will not accept a person who has not finished high school, so failing to finish can be a lifelong roadblock. Study skills learned in high school are also similar to those needed in postsecondary education. **24.** Answers will vary. Students' paragraphs should include at least some of these ideas: A detailed career plan makes it possible to know what one should do to have a satisfying and rewarding career. Most occupations require specific things of employees, and having a career plan allows you to decide what interests you, learn about the career, and prepare for it. You also learn more about yourself and your values and abilities. With this knowledge and a plan, a person can make better career choices.

Chapter 5 Mastery Test B

Part A: 1. B 2. A 3. B 4. D 5. C

Part B: 6. C 7. A 8. D 9. E 10. B

Part C: 11. set goals 12. exploring options 13. make priorities 14. assess risk 15. make a plan

Part D: 16. The first step in career planning is to choose careers that interest you. 17. You should identify what courses you still need to take for your chosen careers. 18. When researching careers, one will learn whether there will be jobs available and what they pay. 19. You should prepare a definite plan for what you will do after you finish high school. 20. Parents or guardians should know your plans so that they know you are thinking of your future and can help you with your plan.

Part E: 21. Answers will vary. Students should support their answers with some of these ideas or examples: You should consider more than one specific occupation in case an occupation that interests you does not work out. If you have planned for more than one occupation, you can change your direction and know what to do next if one goal does not work for you. 22. Answers will vary. Students should support their answer with at least some of these ideas or examples: People who finish high school make more money than those who do not. Only about half of those who quit find work. High school graduates almost always earn more money than those who did not finish. Finishing high school also provides chances to learn about and enter further training or education.

Part F: 23. Answers will vary. Students' paragraphs should include at least some of these ideas, supported by examples: Working part-time while in high school offers valuable experience as well as extra cash. Workers learn behaviors such as promptness, respect, and effort that employers will always seek. They also learn about specific occupations and skills within an industry. They will learn about the industry in which they work. People who held jobs in high school tend to make more money even later in life than those who did not. A possible disadvantage is that there would less time to study school subjects, which might affect one's grades. 24. Answers will vary. Students' paragraphs should include at least some of these ideas or examples: The guidance counselor should advise Maggie to find out if her work values match with the career of social work. If they do not, then Maggie may want to reconsider her career choice or look for a related career that matches these values. Another option is for Maggie to re-evaluate her work values.

Chapter 6 Mastery Test A

Part A: 1. C 2. B 3. D 4. C 5. A

Part B: 6. career 7. admissions offices 8. attitude 9. tuition 10. interact 11. financial aid

Part C: 12. C 13. B 14. D 15. F 16. E 17. A

Part D: 18. Sample answer: I can use the Internet to help me find career opportunities in my community by looking at the Web sites of local companies. I can also go to my town's Web site. 19. All jobs require you to work with people because the boss is a person. Even if you are the boss, then you have to work with customers or your employees. 20. Values can affect the college a person chooses because he or she might value being close to home, or an inexpensive education, or living in a city. Then the person would choose a college that helped keep his or her values.

Part E: 21. Answers will vary. Students should support their answer with at least some of these facts: Use personal contacts to find someone who has a job in a career that interests them. Call the personal contact to set up an informational interview. Be sure to explain that it is not a job interview. Prepare questions ahead of time for the interview. 22. Answers will vary. Students should support their answer with at least some of these facts: Hotels, motels, and restaurants serve visitors in a community. They provide a core service. Serving visitors means that the businesses in a community can sell products and services to outsiders. It also means that the people in the community have access to the services.

Part F: 23. Answers will vary. Students' paragraphs should include at least some of these ideas: Conflict resolution should be respectful, with both peers and authority figures. We don't act the same way with our peers and people in authority over us. It is important to respectfully tell the person in authority why you think a rule is unfair or explain how you were misunderstood. When resolving a conflict with peers, do not act if you are angry. Stay calm. 24. Answers will vary. Students' paragraphs should include many of these steps as described in the text: Decide whether or not you want a large or small school. Decide if you want a school close to home or far away. With your family, decide on the cost the family can afford. Decide on an area of study and choose a school that offers those classes. Visit several schools. Ask questions about the schools. Talk with parents, guardians, and counselors about your feelings.

Chapter 6 Mastery Test B

Part A: 1. D 2. C 3. A 4. B 5. A

Part B: 6. core service 7. respect 8. apply 9. internship 10. thank-you note 11. informational interview

Part C: 12. C 13. A 14. D 15. F 16. B 17. E

Part D: 18. Sample answer: I will make sure to tell the person that I am not looking for a job. I just want to learn more about the career and the company. I'll set a beginning and ending time, such as from 2:00 P.M. to 2:30 P.M. 19. Some businesses that provide the core service of hospitality and tourism are hotels, motels, and restaurants. 20. I only need to decide what direction I want my career to take immediately after high school.

Part E: 21. Answers will vary. Students should include at least some of these reasons from the text in their answers: Visiting a school will give them a chance to meet faculty and see how they feel about the school. It will help them learn more about the school—how big or small it feels. They can take a tour. And they can ask someone in the admissions office questions about the school. The more informed they are, the better their decision will be. 22. Answers will vary. Students should include at least some of these facts from the text in their answers: When you treat other people the way you want to be treated, you show them respect. Do this when resolving conflict. Remember to remain calm. Speak respectfully. Listen to the other person. Explain your feelings.

Part F: 23. Answers will vary. Students' paragraphs should include at least some of these facts and questions from the text: An informational interview is not a job interview. Its purpose is to help the student learn more about a career or career field. Some possible questions include: What are your job responsibilities? What is a typical work day like?

24. Answers will vary. Students' paragraphs should include three of the core services described in the chapter. These are: natural resources; finance; health science; education and training services; law, public safety, and security; architecture and construction; government and public administration; hospitality and tourism; marketing, sales, and service; transportation, distribution, and logistics; and human services. Students should explain what makes the service so critical to a community.

Chapter 7 Mastery Test A

Part A: **1.** D **2.** C **3.** A **4.** D **5.** B

Part B: **6.** C **7.** E **8.** A **9.** B **10.** D

Part C: **11.** requirements **12.** chronological **13.** screening **14.** functional **15.** personal resources

Part D: **16.** Places you may see or hear about job openings include (accept any three of the following): newspapers, job fairs, youth centers, employment offices, business windows, radio, television, and the Internet. **17.** Achieving a short-term goal can fulfill requirements on your career path. This will help you achieve your long-term goal. **18.** Action verbs are words that show action. They highlight your achievements on a résumé. **19.** Employers quickly eliminate sloppy and error-filled résumés from the screening process. **20.** Employers expect that relatives will say only good things about you because they want you to succeed.

Part E: **21.** Answers will vary. Students should support their answers with some of these ideas or examples: It is all right to feel discouraged if you are not selected for a job. You may never know why you weren't chosen. The manager may have had someone else in mind, there may have been too many applicants, there may have been too little time to look carefully, or the manager's opinions may differ from yours about what is required. You should look at this experience as a learning process, and get ready for the next time. **22.** Answers will vary. Students should support their answers with some of these ideas or examples: It's important to include these lifestyle values in a personal goal statement because the goals you set should be based on these values. Usually someone's job and their lifestyle are closely related. For example, if you value time with your family, you should consider a career that allows you to do that. If you don't take your lifestyle choices into consideration, you may find that you are unhappy even if you get the job you want.

Part F: **23.** Answers will vary. Students' paragraphs should include at least some of these ideas: Personal goal statements could be used to reach almost any personal goal. The same information applies to almost any accomplishment. If you were trying to do a better job with homework, for example, you would need to define "better" as a first step. Then you would decide what the requirements would be to satisfy that description, what you are doing now, and what steps you need to meet the goal. **24.** Answers will vary. Students' paragraphs should include at least some of these ideas: The purpose of an interview is to get an idea of whether a person has the ability to do the job. Much of a job involves dealing with people or with a new experience, change, or unexpected developments. An interviewer would like to know how you will deal with these things, and you can point to how you've handled similar problems in the past.

Chapter 7 Mastery Test B

Part A: **1.** C **2.** D **3.** A **4.** B **5.** B

Part B: **6.** D **7.** A **8.** E **9.** B **10.** C

Part C: **11.** work history **12.** personal information **13.** career objective **14.** related information **15.** education

Part D: **16.** There are often too many applicants to respond to everyone who applies. **17.** Newspapers draw many applicants and the job may be filled before you can apply. **18.** A personal goal statement is description of your career goal, along with the knowledge, abilities, skills, and personal values related to that goal.

19. You should ask a person who will be honest, who knows your ability and skills, and who will speak positively about you.

20. Employers do not have time to carefully read every résumé that comes in and may spend only a minute looking at yours. It must make a very good first impression.

Part E: **21.** Answers will vary. Students should support their answers with some of these ideas or examples: A personal goal statement identifies exactly what you want, where you are, and what you need to do to get where you want to go. The description section helps you to decide exactly what it is you seek. The personal resources section helps you identify what you already have in place, and the requirements section helps you understand exactly what you need. By thinking about these things specifically, you can compare what you have in place with what you do not. Then you identify steps to take to supply what you need. **22.** Answers will vary. Students should support their answer with at least some of these ideas or examples: First, you can demonstrate these qualities in the interviewer's first impression of you. Your attitude, appearance, and confidence should show these qualities. Next, as you respond specifically to questions, you can connect to experiences you have in which you demonstrated these qualities. You can also invite the interviewer to contact your references who will verify that you have these qualities.

Part F: **23.** Answers will vary. Students' paragraphs should include at least some of these ideas, supported by examples: Your lifestyle shapes your personal resources. If you lead a life that values solitude and study, you will be naturally drawn to behaviors, hobbies, occupations, and careers that include those qualities. As a consequence, you will get better at those skills and abilities and they will become part of your personal resources. If you have a lifestyle with lots of human contact, you will learn how to deal with people and will find "people skills" among your gifts. Even material goods shape what you are comfortable with. If you are comfortable with certain things now, you will probably want to continue at that level of comfort or better.

24. Answers will vary. Students' paragraphs should include at least some of these ideas or examples: First, you should try not to be too discouraged. There are lots of people out there looking for jobs, and perhaps these weren't for you. There are many things in the selection process that are beyond your control, and many people search for the right job for a long time. Next, you should look hard at your interview skills. You should practice to improve your performance. Next, look hard at your résumé. Is it really an accurate representation of who you are and what you've done? You may need to change your résumé to reflect the real you. Finally, maybe you need to look again at your personal goal statement. Is it realistic and specific in each of its sections? Try to learn from the experience of your job search, and move on. Don't give up.

Chapter 8 Mastery Test A

Part A: **1.** B **2.** C **3.** A **4.** D **5.** C

Part B: **6.** C **7.** A **8.** E **9.** B **10.** D

Part C: **11.** thank-you note **12.** review **13.** interview **14.** timeline **15.** accomplishments

Part D: **16.** An interviewer is likely to look for clues by observing your body language and how you say what you say. **17.** "No" is not a good answer because it suggests you are not interested in the job. **18.** Two parts of the job process in which you can use self-advocacy skills are (accept any two): the résumé, the cover letter, and net-working. **19.** Two things you should do before an interview are (accept any two of the following): plan how you will dress properly, make sure you will be well groomed, and know where you are going and how long it will take to get there. **20.** Employers want the people who work for them to be honest, reliable, and hard working. (Accept any other reasonable answers.)

Part E: **21.** Answers will vary. Students should support their answers with details about how they practice self-advocacy skills (accept any three): letting others know you are doing a good job and working hard; letting others know you are making a contribution; communicating your accomplishments; volunteering for extra assignments and doing a good job on them; trying to provide solutions to problems that occur; maintaining a positive attitude; volunteering to help; doing more than is expected; asking for feedback; being reliable and on time; expressing thanks when others help you. **22.** Answers will vary. Students should support their answers with details about an accomplishment of a group or team they have been a part of and the skills that connect to that accomplishment.

Part F: **23.** Answers will vary. Students' paragraphs should include these ideas: They are excited about the job; they should include clear, direct statements about ways their interests connect to those required for the job. **24.** Answers will vary. Students' paragraphs should support their answer with details about some of these ideas: Knowing about the organization lets the interviewer know that you cared enough about the job to find out more about it. During the interview, students can have questions prepared to ask the interviewer; try to get clues by observing what the interviewer communicates through body language, manner of speaking, and attitude; and observe the workplace to see whether you would be comfortable there. Questions to ask might be about: the ideal candidate for the job, the biggest challenges in the job, opportunities for advancement, or something the interviewer said earlier in the interview.

Chapter 8 Mastery Test B

Part A: **1.** B **2.** D **3.** A **4.** C **5.** C

Part B: **6.** D **7.** C **8.** E **9.** B **10.** A

Part C: **11.** reliable **12.** slang **13.** accomplishments **14.** convince **15.** practice

Part D: **16.** Two kinds of body language to remember during an interview are (accept any two of the following): making good eye contact, having good posture, having a firm handshake, and dressing appropriately. **17.** Two qualities that help people fit in and advance in their jobs are (accept any two of the following): positive attitudes, good social skills, honesty, being reliable, and being a good worker. **18.** Three behaviors that are ways to let an employer know you are a good worker are (accept any three of the following): volunteering for additional assignments, completing assignments on time, doing a good job on assignments, trying to provide answers to problems that occur, and maintaining a positive attitude.

19. Two things to think about or do after not getting a job offer are (accept any two of the following): review your interview experience; remember that you will be better at interviewing next time; call, write, or e-mail the interviewer, express your thanks for the chance to interview and your disappointment that it did not work out; ask the interviewer for feedback about what you could to improve your chances in the future; remember not to be discouraged. **20.** Two things to do before leaving an interview are (accept any two of the following): say that you want the job, remind the interviewer that you are a good fit, find out about the timeline for making a decision, and ask when you can expect to hear about the job.

Part E: **21.** Answers will vary. Students' questions should be about at least two of these ideas: the ideal candidate for the job; the biggest challenges in the job; opportunities for advancement; something the interviewer said earlier in the interview that the student wants to learn more about. **22.** Answers will vary. Students should support their answers with two clear, direct statements, each of which communicates one of their interests in terms of how it connects to those required for the job and how the student has put the interest into action.

Part F: **23.** Answers will vary. Students' paragraphs should support their answers with details that show awareness of these ideas: show how they have worked as part of a team; provide clear, direct statements about accomplishments; state accomplishments in terms of skills that connect to those required for the job; focus on the most important skills. **24.** Answers will vary. Students should support their answers with details that show awareness of these ideas: speaking up for oneself is important; statements should be clear and direct; statements of their personal qualities should connect to those related to agreements on curfew, such as being reliable and honest, being on time, handling well the work and responsibilities that are expected of the student, being helpful, volunteering to help or do extra work, checking in as agreed.

Chapter 9 Mastery Test A

Part A: **1.** C **2.** A **3.** B **4.** D **5.** A

Part B: **6.** B **7.** C **8.** E **9.** A **10.** D

Part C: **11.** skills **12.** symptoms **13.** dilemma **14.** addictive **15.** stress

Part D: **16.** Time management is how you use your time to complete your activities. **17.** Three main benefits of hobbies and interests are keeping fit, relieving stress, and being socially involved with people. **18.** Being physically fit affects your emotional, social, and physical well-being and reduces the chance for illness. **19.** The best way to protect yourself from sexually transmitted diseases is to refrain from sexual activity. **20.** Your conscience is your sense of right and wrong, based on personal, group, and universal values in which you believe.

Part E: **21.** Answers will vary. Students should support their answers with some of these ideas: Alcoholism is a disease because the effects of alcohol are physical, and one of its effects is addiction. Although people may choose to drink at first, if they keep choosing to do so, they might become physically dependent. They cannot overcome the addiction by themselves at that point. The physical damage that alcohol does to the body also brings about other diseases, such as heart disease, liver problems, and cancer.

22. Answers will vary. Students should support their answers with some of these ideas or examples: Universal values and group values may clash because they may not be the same, or different values may compete. For example, if you think loyalty is good, and honesty is also good, but someone in your group did something wrong, you might have to choose between lying and being loyal or telling the truth and being disloyal.

Part F: **23.** Answers will vary. Students' paragraphs should include at least some of these ideas: This friend may not fully realize the amount of time being spent on video games, or may not realize that extra time spent on them reduces his ability to do other things. You might ask him to keep a log of how much time he spends in a week playing video games, as well as a log of time spent on homework. He could also estimate how much time he needs to do his homework each day. Then he could make a plan to cut some of his video game time. **24.** Answers will vary. Students' paragraphs should include at least some of these ideas: The friend needs to realize the health consequences of cigarette smoking. Though some effects may not be immediate, nicotine addiction does not take long to develop, and then she will not be able to quit easily. If she cannot quit smoking easily, she may not quit at all, and will experience the harmful effects on her health. In addition, secondhand smoke harms those around her, and she is being inconsiderate of others.

Chapter 9 Mastery Test B

Part A: **1.** B **2.** B **3.** A **4.** A **5.** C
Part B: **6.** C. **7.** A **8.** E **9.** B **10.** D
Part C: **11.** ethically **12.** heart disease **13.** clubs **14.** schedules **15.** chlamydia
Part D: **16.** A hobby is an activity that you perform, while an interest is something you want to know about but that you may or may not participate in. **17.** An obligation is anything you must do, so obligations to care for family members, practice a musical instrument, or obey the law are just as real as work you have to do. **18.** By listing exactly how much time you spend on each activity, you can easily see where extra time is going. **19.** A healthy diet improves your appearance and protects your health, so you feel better and you feel better about yourself. **20.** Universal values are ones that benefit people and help them get along, no matter where they live or what their culture.
Part E: **21.** Answers will vary. Students should support their answers with some of these ideas or examples: A schedule may be hard to keep because a person cannot predict all the things that may interrupt it. It may also be hard to keep because it did not take into account all the commitments that must be kept. It may also have simply underestimated the time it takes to do some things. It may also be that a person has not yet developed the self-discipline necessary to follow the schedule. **22.** Answers will vary. Students should support their answer with at least some of these ideas or examples: Tobacco use harms non-smokers physically. Secondhand smoke is dangerous to people and pollutes the air. Smokers also harm non-smokers by harming themselves. Those who lose a loved one to heart disease or cancer are harmed for life. Smokers also raise medical costs for everyone because the cost of their illnesses raises the overall price of medical care.

Part F: **23.** Answers will vary. Students' paragraphs should include at least some of these ideas, supported by examples: This problem is difficult because it places group and universal values in direct conflict. The first guideline says to do what is right, but it may be hard to know whether harming your friend by telling or letting him or her cheat is more right. The second guideline says to put yourself in another's place. Although the friend would not like to be reported, the rest of the students would not like to be cheated either. The third guideline says to consider the greatest good for the greatest number of people. What are the consequences of putting a stop to the cheating? Here, not letting the cheater succeed clearly benefits more people, including the cheater, whether he or she knows it. Finally, the universal values of fairness and honesty should take precedence over the loyalty to a friend. Do you really want a close friend who is dishonest? Most students will conclude that although it may be painful, the cheater should be stopped. **24.** Answers will vary. Students' paragraphs should include at least some of these ideas or examples: Though there is much information available on the harm of tobacco, lack of exercise, and poor diet, there are also many influences pushing the other way. Most of these are in media such as television, movies, and magazines that suggest it's "cool" or attractive to smoke or drink. Food sellers try to sell as much as they can, and they try to make their products look appetizing. There are also many forms of popular entertainment such as television and video games that make it seem more fun to sit around than to do something active. The main reason, of course, is that whether food or drink, smoking, entertainment, or transportation, someone is trying to sell something, and will advertise the product in any way possible to make it seem worthwhile, whether or not it poses risks to health.

Chapter 10 Mastery Test A

Part A: **1.** B **2.** C **3.** B **4.** C **5.** A
Part B: **6.** E **7.** B **8.** C **9.** A **10.** D
Part C: **11.** revise **12.** decisions **13.** grades **14.** courses **15.** research
Part D: **16.** My career action plan is like a snapshot because it is a picture of how things stand today in my life. As I learn more about myself and about the workplace, and as I get feedback, my plan may be different. **17.** I am not likely to achieve my goals in the long run if I don't enjoy the activities I need to do along the way. **18.** My career action plan is like a road map because it tells how I plan to get where I am going. It tells how I plan to achieve my goal.
19. Revising my personal goal statement and my career action plan reflects the ways in which I have been learning more about myself and about the world of work. **20.** When I apply and interview for a job, I get feedback on my job skills and about how prepared I was for the interview.
Part E: **21.** Answers will vary. Students should support their answers with these ideas: Gathering more information lets you test out whether certain actions make sense for you. You will make decisions based on what you learn about yourself and about the options you are exploring. **22.** Answers will vary. Students should support their answers with at least one example of feedback related to the career. The feedback may be positive, negative, or both. The relationship of the feedback to the goal should be clear.

Part F: **23.** Answers will vary. Students' paragraphs should support their answers with details about some of these ideas: allowing oneself to be discouraged by negative feedback; using negative feedback as an opportunity to learn more about oneself; discussing feedback with a trusted person; using feedback to plan or take action. **24.** Answers will vary. Students' paragraphs should support their answers with details that demonstrate an awareness of some of these ideas: The distinction between not liking the activity itself and not liking some aspect of the activity might change under different circumstances. There is wisdom in revising one's goals if an activity related to the goal turns out not to be enjoyable. Students should describe at least one thing they learned about themselves from taking part in the activity.

Chapter 10 Mastery Test B
Part A: **1.** D **2.** D **3.** C **4.** C **5.** B
Part B: **6.** C **7.** D **8.** E **9.** A **10.** B
Part C: **11.** common **12.** positive **13.** feedback **14.** understand **15.** personal goal statement
Part D: **16.** Getting the same positive feedback from two sources suggests that I may be better at track than I think I am. **17.** Roles adults play in my life that make them people who might have good feedback for me are (accept three responses such as the following): teacher, parent, counselor, advisor, guardian, employer. **18.** If I am doing everything I can, the best thing to do may be to discuss with someone I trust whether I need to change my goals. **19.** Things I may need to do new research on are (accept two responses such as the following): specific occupations, college majors, training programs. **20.** I have not wasted my time. Taking part in the activity gives me an opportunity to learn from the experience. As a result, I am able to revise my goals to focus on activities I do enjoy.
Part E: **21.** Answers will vary. Students' paragraphs should support their answers with details that show awareness of these ideas: the importance of figuring out what it is about an activity that one does not like; the distinction between not liking the activity itself and not liking some aspect of the activity that might change under different circumstances; the wisdom in continuing with an activity when it is possible that the student likes the activity but does not like some aspect of his or her experience that could change; the importance of talking with a trusted person when making a career decision. **22.** Answers will vary. Students should support their answers with details about some of these ideas: paying attention to the feedback; not being discouraged by negative feedback; using negative feedback as an opportunity to learn more about oneself; discussing feedback with a trusted person; not assuming that negative feedback means you need to change your plans; using the feedback to decide if you can do more to strengthen your skills in a particular area; if you are doing all you can, discussing whether you need to change your goals.
Part F: **23.** Answers will vary. Students' paragraphs should support their answers with details that show awareness of some of these ideas: Getting a mix of positive and negative feedback may not have been very helpful and may have been challenging to sort out. Receiving the same feedback from several sources was likely to have been very useful. Students may have discussed the feedback with one or more trusted people. If the feedback was positive, students may have decided that they were on the right path. If the feedback was not so positive, students may have evaluated whether they just needed to strengthen some skills or it was appropriate to change

their plans. **24.** Answers will vary. Students' paragraphs should support their answers with details about three opportunities for learning more about their career goal, such as these: networking, visiting a workplace, visiting postsecondary schools or colleges, trying related activities, getting and using feedback, talking with school counselors and other trusted people.

Scoring Rubric for Short-Response Items in Part E of Chapter Mastery Tests
2 points— The student demonstrates a solid understanding of the content by providing:
- a complete set of accurate facts that support the answer
- a clearly stated answer to the question

1 point— The student demonstrates a partial understanding of the content by providing *one* of the following:
- a complete set of accurate facts that support the answer
- a clearly stated answer to the question

0 points— The student fails to demonstrate understanding of the content by doing *one* of the following:
- includes no facts or incorrect facts, and fails to provide a clearly stated answer
- provides no answer at all

Scoring Rubric for Essay Items in Part F of Chapter Mastery Tests
3 points— The student demonstrates a solid understanding of the content by providing:
- a complete set of accurate facts that support the answer
- a clearly stated answer to the essay's primary question
- a standard essay response (topic sentence, body, conclusion)

2 points— The student demonstrates a good understanding of the content by providing *two* of the following:
- a complete set of accurate facts that support the answer
- a clearly stated answer to the essay's primary question
- a standard essay response (topic sentence, body, conclusion)

1 point— The student demonstrates a partial understanding of the content by providing *one* of the following:
- a complete set of accurate facts that support the answer
- a clearly stated answer to the essay's primary question
- a standard essay response (topic sentence, body, conclusion)

0 points— The student fails to demonstrate understanding of the content by doing *one* of the following:
- includes no facts or incorrect facts, fails to answer the essay's primary question, and fails to include a standard essay response (topic sentence, body, conclusion)
- provides no answer at all

Midterm Mastery Test

Part A: **1.** D **2.** A **3.** C **4.** B **5.** B **6.** A **7.** C **8.** A **9.** C **10.** D

Part B: **11.** basic skills **12.** occupation **13.** hospitality **14.** ability **15.** goal **16.** production worker **17.** equity **18.** business cycle **19.** agriculture **20.** motivation **21.** career planning **22.** probability **23.** workplace culture **24.** automation **25.** risk

Part C: **26.** G **27.** K **28.** B **29.** H **30.** E **31.** O **32.** A **33.** M **34.** D **35.** I **36.** L **37.** C **38.** J **39.** N **40.** F

Part D: **41.** Besides working for money, people like to use skills they enjoy, to express themselves creatively, to help people, and to find challenges. People may like the prestige they get from some careers, or they make like the chances for travel or self-improvement. They may also value time spent with co-workers, the chance to please parents and family, or performing a service for other people or for their country. **42.** Self-assessment is questioning or evaluating your own interests, abilities, skills, and values. Self-assessment provides knowledge about oneself that can be used to choose a career. **43.** The five steps of the decision-making process are to set a goal, make priorities, explore options, assess risks, and make a plan.

Part E: **44.** Answers will vary, but should include some of the following ideas and concepts: If your job did not match your sense of values, prestige, or working conditions, you would likely be unhappy in that job, and might do poorly at it. A satisfying career will match your entire sense of self, not just pay you well. **45.** Answers will vary, but should include some of the following ideas and concepts: It is a bad idea to quit high school because doing so blocks you from getting most good jobs. Quitting high school also limits your chances of further training or education. Though the idea of a full-time job at the present may sound good, most such jobs are low-paying and will not provide enough money as time goes on. In addition, there are not as many jobs available to non-graduates, and the few who get them are usually unable to keep them for long.

Final Mastery Test

Part A: **1.** C **2.** D **3.** A **4.** D **5.** B **6.** C **7.** B **8.** A **9.** C **10.** D **11.** B **12.** C **13.** B **14.** B **15.** D **16.** A **17.** C **18.** B **19.** D **20.** C

Part B: **21.** reference **22.** nicotine **23.** self-advocacy **24.** apprenticeship **25.** revise **26.** option **27.** chronological **28.** action verbs **29.** finance **30.** skill **31.** cover letter **32.** priority **33.** stereotype **34.** physical fitness **35.** group values

Part C: **36.** N **37.** S **38.** H **39.** O **40.** E **41.** Q **42.** J **43.** D **44.** G **45.** L **46.** M **47.** R **48.** F **49.** K **50.** B **51.** T **52.** C **53.** I **54.** P **55.** A

Part D: **56.** Your values may determine your interests in specific career areas. They also may influence whether a career is acceptable to you in terms of wages, prestige, interests, working conditions, and purpose. Knowing your values helps you make choices well suited to you.

57. The *Occupational Outlook Handbook* and CDMCareerZone Web site provide descriptions of many occupations. They include the knowledge, skills, and education needed for many jobs, as well as their wages, job outlook, and location of job openings. **58.** Answers will vary. Accept any three of the following: Dress properly, wear clean clothing, make sure you are well groomed, arrive on time for your interview, be polite to everyone, act as if you want the job, and ask politely when you can expect to hear about the job. **59.** Your local community has many resources such as core services and educational and social institutions that you are familiar with. You can use your personal connections to learn about local businesses, for possible internships or job opportunities. **60.** Employers use a résumé as a quick part of the screening process. They may take less than a minute with each one. A résumé that is sloppy, disorganized, incomplete, confusing, or full of errors will be rejected.

Part E: **61.** Answers will vary, but should include some of the following ideas: You should advise your friend to write down all of her activities for one week. She should determine whether she has allowed herself non-scheduled time, engages in "time wasters", or has under-estimated the amount of time a task requires. She should decide which activities are important her her by following the five steps of the decision-making process, with special attention to making priorities. **62.** Answers will vary, but should include some of the following ideas: You need to pay attention to feedback from many sources. Feedback from several sources suggests that your original goal may not be right for you. It may mean that you may have to study harder in those areas that qualify you for the sciences. It may also mean that you have to revise your plan. It does not necessarily mean, however, that you have to give up on science as a career field. Perhaps you can research careers in the sciences that use some of the talents your feedback suggests, such as medical illustration, or graphic arts for science texts. You could look into an internship and see whether you might want to shift your career plan in a new direction.

Part F: **63.** Answers will vary. Students should include some of the following ideas: Ramone's career plan is not very realistic. First, Ramone needs to understand that the job market for professional basketball players is very small. Second, he needs to understand that if he neglects his schoolwork, he may not get into college or even graduate from high school. Third, even if against great odds, Ramone did make it to the professional ranks, athletic careers are very short, and he will need to do something for the rest of his life. Ramone can keep his dream and also have a back-up plan for a career in case he can't reach his goal or gets injured along the way. The path Ramone is on now offers great risk and little chance of long-term success. **64.** Answers will vary. Students should include some of the following ideas: A résumé is a summary of the knowledge, abilities, and experiences that shows how a person is qualified for a particular occupation. An interview is a face-to-face meeting of the applicant and the person doing the hiring. Résumés and interviews are similar in that both are part of the job application process. They are different in that the résumé is written and the interview is a personal meeting.

Teacher Questionnaire

Attention Teachers! As publishers of *Career Planning,* we would like your help in making this textbook more valuable to you. Please take a few minutes to fill out this survey. Your feedback will help us to better serve you and your students.

1. What is your position and major area of responsibility? _____
_____
_____

2. Briefly describe your setting:

____ regular education ____ special education ____ adult basic education

____ community college ____ university ____ other _____

3. The enrollment in your classroom includes students with the following (check all that apply):

____ at-risk for failure ____ low reading ability ____ behavior problems

____ learning disabilities ____ ESL ____ other _____

4. Grade level of your students: _____

5. Racial/ethnic groups represented in your classes (check all that apply):

____ African-American ____ Asian ____ Caucasian ____ Hispanic

____ American Indian ____ Other

6. School Location:

____ urban ____ suburban ____ rural ____ other _____

7. What reaction did your students have to the materials? (Include comments about the cover design, lesson format, illustrations, etc.)

_____
_____
_____

8. What features in the student text helped your students the most?

_____
_____
_____

9. What features in the student text helped your students the least? Please include suggestions for changing these to make the text more relevant.

_____

_____

10. How did you use the Teacher's Edition and support materials, and what features did you find to be the most helpful?

_____

_____

11. What activity from the program did your students benefit from the most? Please briefly explain.

_____

_____

_____

12. Optional: Share an activity that you used to teach the materials in your classroom that enhanced the learning and motivation of your students.

_____

_____

_____

Several activities will be selected to be included in future editions. Please include your name, address, and phone number so we may contact you for permission and possible payment to use the material.

Thank you!

▼ fold in thirds and tape shut at the top ▼

- -

Name: _____
School: _____
Address: _____
City/State/ZIP: _____
Phone: _____

NO POSTAGE
NECESSARY
IF MAILED
IN THE
UNITED STATES

BUSINESS REPLY MAIL

FIRST-CLASS MAIL PERMIT NO.12 CIRCLE PINES MN

POSTAGE WILL BE PAID BY ADDRESSEE

AGS Publishing ATTN: Marketing Support
4201 WOODLAND ROAD
PO BOX 99
CIRCLE PINES MN 55014-9911